D1355974

A Companion to Anglo-Saxon Literature

Blackwell Companions to Literature and Culture

This series offers comprehensive, newly written surveys of key periods and movements and certain major authors in English literary culture and history. Extensive volumes provide new perspectives and positions on contexts and on canonical and post-canonical texts, orientating the beginning student in new fields of study and providing the experienced undergraduate and new graduate with current and new directions, as pioneered and developed by leading scholars in the field.

A COMPANION TO

ANGLO-SAXON
LITERATURE

EDITED BY **PHILLIP PULSIANO**
AND **ELAINE TREHARNE**

Copyright © Blackwell Publishers Ltd 2001
Editorial matter, selection and arrangement copyright © Phillip Pulsiano and Elaine Treharne 2001

First published 2001

2 4 6 8 10 9 7 5 3 1

Blackwell Publishers Ltd
108 Cowley Road
Oxford OX4 1JF
UK

Blackwell Publishers Inc.
350 Main Street
Malden, Massachusetts 02148
USA

British Library Cataloguing in Publication Data
A CIP catalogue record for this book is available from the British Library

Library of Congress Cataloging-in-Publication Data

A companion to Anglo-Saxon literature / edited by Phillip Pulsiano and Elaine Treharne.
p.   cm. – (Blackwell companions to literature and culture; 11)
Includes bibliographical references and index.
ISBN 0-631-20904-2 (acid-free paper)
1. English literature – Old English, ca. 450–1100 – History and criticism – Handbooks, manuals, etc.   2. Great Britain – History – Anglo-Saxon period, 449–1066 – Handbooks, manuals, etc.   3. England – Civilization – To 1066 – Handbooks, manuals, etc.   I. Pulsiano, Phillip, 1955–
II. Treharne, Elaine M.   III. Series.
PR173 .C66 2001
829.09 – dc21
2001025924

ISBN 0631 209042 (hbk)
Typeset in 11 on 13 pt Garamond 3
by Best-set Typesetter Ltd., Hong Kong
Printed in Great Britain by T.J. International, Padstow, Cornwall

This book is printed on acid-free paper

In memory of
PHILLIP PULSIANO
heahþungen wer

Contents

Contributors

Robert E. Bjork is Professor of English and Director of the Arizona Center for Medieval and Renaissance Studies at Arizona State University. His book publications include (with Daniel G. Calder, Patrick K. Ford and Daniel F. Melia) *Sources and Analogues of Old English Poetry II: The Major Germanic and Celtic Texts in Translation, The Old English Verse Saints' Lives: A Study in Direct Discourse and the Iconography of Style, Cynewulf: Basic Readings* and (with John D. Niles) *A Beowulf Handbook*. He is currently working on the Scandinavian involvement in Anglo-Saxon studies and is General Editor of the forthcoming *Oxford Dictionary of the Middle Ages*.

Rolf Bremmer is Senior Lecturer in Old and Middle English at the University of Leiden. He is the author of *A Bibliographical Guide to Old Frisian Studies* and has (co-)edited *A Companion to Old English Poetry, Approaches to Old Frisian Philology, Franciscus Junius F. F. and his Circle* and *Rome and the North: The Reception of Gregory the Great in Medieval North-Western Europe*. He is currently completing *An Introduction to Old Frisian*.

Michelle P. Brown is Curator of Illuminated Manuscripts at the British Library. She is a Fellow of the Society of Antiquaries of London, a Fellow of the Courtauld Institute, and a Visiting Research Fellow of the School of Advanced Studies of the University of London. Her areas of special interest range across the field of medieval book production, with a particular focus upon the illumination and palaeography of Anglo-Saxon and Celtic manuscripts. Her publications include *The Book of Cerne, Prayer, Power and Patronage in Ninth-century England, Anglo-Saxon Manuscripts, A Guide to Western Historical Scripts from Antiquity to 1600, Understanding Illuminated Manuscripts* and the Jarrow Lecture 2000.

Patrick W. Conner is the Eberly Centennial Professor in English at West Virginia University and Director of the West Virginia University Press. He is author of *Anglo-*

Saxon Exeter: A Tenth-century Cultural History and editor of *The Abingdon Chronicle, AD 956–1066 (MS C, with Reference to Bede)* in *The Anglo-Saxon Chronicle: A Collaborative Edition* (Cambridge). His work examines cultural and historical problems in the light of palaeographical and codicological issues.

Allen Frantzen is Professor of English and Faculty Scholar at Loyola University Chicago, where he also directs the Loyola Community Literacy Center. He has published extensively on Old English literature and culture. His most recent book is *Before the Closet: Same-Sex Love from 'Beowulf' to 'Angels in America'*.

Timothy Graham is Assistant Director of the Medieval Institute, Western Michigan University. He is the author of articles on the early Anglo-Saxonists Robert Talbot, Matthew Parker, John Joscelyn, William L'Isle and Abraham Wheelock, and is the editor of *The Recovery of Old English: Anglo-Saxon Studies in the Sixteenth and Seventeenth Centuries*. He is currently working with Raymond Clemens on *An Introduction to Manuscript Studies*. He is a Fellow of the Royal Historical Society.

J. R. Hall is Professor of English at the University of Mississippi. He has published extensively on Old English poetry, particularly on *Exodus* and *Genesis B*; on Anglo-Saxonism; and on the reception and use of Old English texts by nineteenth-century scholars. He is currently continuing his research on the Thorkelin transcripts of *Beowulf*, and is contributing a number of articles on Latin authors to the *Sources of Anglo-Saxon Literary Culture* project.

Thomas Hall is Associate Professor in the Department of English at the University of Illinois at Chicago. He is editor of *Via Crucis: Essays on Early Medieval Sources and Ideas in Memory of J. E. Cross*. His articles on Old English and Old Norse literature and medieval sermon studies have appeared in numerous journals. He is presently editing the 'C' volume of *Sources of Anglo-Saxon Literary Culture* and has in progress several studies of Anglo-Saxon sermon manuscripts.

Joyce Hill is Professor of Old and Middle English Language and Literature at the University of Leeds and a former Director of the Centre for Medieval Studies. She is the editor of *Old English Minor Heroic Poems* and the co-editor of, among other publications, *The Community, the Family and the Saint: Patterns of Power in Early Medieval Europe*. She is the author of an extensive number of articles, many of which concern Ælfric, his sources, and the cultural and intellectual contexts of his work, and she is Chair of the *Fontes Anglo-Saxonici* database project. She is one of the editors of the *Review of English Studies* and is a Fellow of the Royal Society of Arts.

Stephanie Hollis is a Professor in the Department of English at the University of Auckland. She is the author of numerous books and articles, including *Anglo-Saxon*

Women and the Church and, with Michael Wright, *Old English Prose of Secular Learning*. She is currently working on aspects of medieval literature and medievalism.

Carole Hough is a Lecturer in the Department of English Language at the University of Glasgow. She has published extensively on Anglo-Saxon law and other topics in a wide variety of journals and books, and is currently preparing a new edition of the early Kentish law-codes. She is editor of *Nomina* and co-editor of the forthcoming memorial volume for Christine E. Fell. She is a Fellow of the Society of Antiquaries of London.

Nicholas Howe is Professor of English and Director of the Center for Medieval and Renaissance Studies at the Ohio State University. He is author of *The Old English Catalogue Poems* and *Migration and Mythmaking in Anglo-Saxon England*. He edited Irving Howe's *A Critic's Notebook* and the second edition of the Norton Critical Edition of *Beowulf*, and co-edited *Words and Works: Essays in Honour of Fred C. Robinson*.

Susan Irvine is Senior Lecturer in English at University College London. She is the editor of *Old English Homilies from MS Bodley 343*, co-author (with Bruce Mitchell) of *Beowulf Repunctuated*, and author of articles on Old English prose and on *The Dream of the Rood*. She is currently working on an edition of the Peterborough manuscript of the *Anglo-Saxon Chronicle*.

Patrizia Lendinara is Professor of Germanic Philology at the University of Palermo and Dean of her Faculty. She has published widely on Old English language and literature, and on Old Frisian, Gothic and medieval Latin literature. Her present research work focuses on Germanic glosses, both in Latin and in the vernacular, dating from the Anglo-Saxon period. Her works on glosses have been recently republished as the Variorum volume *Anglo-Saxon Glosses and Glossaries*. She is co-editor of *Schede Medievali* and is president of the Associazione Italiana di Filologia.

Roy M. Liuzza is Associate Professor of English at Tulane University. He is the editor of *The Old English Version of the Gospels* and recently published a translation of *Beowulf*. He is the author of numerous articles on Old English poetry and prose, and is currently editing a volume on the Junius manuscript, and writing a book on Anglo-Saxon prognostics.

Hugh Magennis is Professor of Old English Literature at Queen's University Belfast. He is the author of numerous articles and books on Old English literature, including *The Legend of the Seven Sleepers*, *The Old English Lives of St Margaret* (with Mary Clayton) and *Images of Community in Old English Literature*. He is currently working on Old English prose saints' lives and on aspects of the language of Old English poetry.

Joseph P. McGowan is Associate Professor of English at the University of San Diego, and editor of the sermons of Augustine of Ancona and (with Vincent McCarren) of the *Medulla grammatice*. He is currently working on the prose texts of the *Beowulf*-manuscript.

Phillip Pulsiano was Professor of English at Villanova University in Pennsylvania. He was the author of an extensive range of articles on Old and Middle English poetry and prose, and co-editor (with Kirsten Wolf and Paul Acker) of *Medieval Scandinavia: An Encyclopedia* and (with Elaine Treharne) of *Anglo-Saxon Manuscripts and their Heritage*. He had many specialist interests, including Old English glosses and Latin female saints' lives, but his particular research project concerned the Anglo-Saxon Psalters. At the time of his death in August 2000, he was nearing completion of an edition of all the extant Psalter manuscripts that will be published by Toronto University Press.

Fred C. Robinson is the Douglas Tracy Smith Professor Emeritus of English at Yale University. His specialities are Old English language and literature and English philology of all periods. His most recent book is an edition (with Bruce Mitchell) of *Beowulf*. He is a Fellow of the American Academy of Arts and Sciences and of the Medieval Academy of America, Corresponding Fellow of the British Academy, and Foreign Member of the Finnish Academy of Arts and Sciences.

Hans Sauer is Professor of the History of English and Medieval English Literature at LM University, Munich. He is the author of a number of monographs, including an edition and translation of *The Owl and the Nightingale* and *Nominal Komposita im Frühmittelenglischen*. His current research centres on medieval English plant names, and word-formation and lexicography. In addition, the editing of Old and Middle English texts forms a major research interest.

Donald G. Scragg is Professor of Anglo-Saxon Studies at the University of Manchester, and Director of the Manchester Centre for Anglo-Saxon Studies. He has edited the *Battle of Maldon* and the *Vercelli Homilies*, and co-edited collections of essays on *Maldon*, on the editing of Old English, and on the literary appropriation of the Anglo-Saxons. He is currently working on an introductory grammar of Old English, on prose hagiography and on eleventh-century language.

Mary Swan is Director of Studies of the Centre for Medieval Studies, University of Leeds. She is the co-editor (with Elaine Treharne) of *Rewriting Old English in the Twelfth Century*, and a founder, along with Elaine Treharne and Jonathan Wilcox, of the Research Group on Post-Conquest Old English Manuscripts. She is currently researching the transmission of Old English texts in the post-conquest period, and women and Old English prose.

Elaine Treharne is Reader in Medieval Literature at the University of Leicester. She has recently published *The Old English Life of St Nicholas with the Old English Life of St Giles* and *Old and Middle English: An Anthology*, and has co-edited (with Phillip Pulsiano) *Anglo-Saxon Manuscripts and their Heritage* and (with Mary Swan) *Rewriting*

Old English in the Twelfth Century. She is currently writing a book entitled *The Use of English, 1000–1200*. She is Chair of the English Association.

Jonathan Wilcox is an Associate Professor of English at the University of Iowa and editor of the *Old English Newsletter*. He is the author of *Ælfric's Prefaces*, editor of the essay collection *Humour in Anglo-Saxon Literature*, and author of numerous essays, mostly dealing with Old English homiletic literature, manuscript studies, and the interpretation of gesture and tone in Anglo-Saxon literature.

Charles D. Wright is Associate Professor of English at the University of Illinois at Urbana-Champaign, and is author of *The Irish Tradition in Old English Literature* and of various essays on Old English poetry and prose and Hiberno-Latin literature.

Preface

Professor Phillip Pulsiano died in August 2000 at the age of forty-four just as this volume was heading towards completion. He worked tremendously hard in the planning and careful preparation of the numerous contributions, and in the creation of his own, substantial chapters. He had edited and worked through much of the book, giving each detail his undivided attention. As with everything that Phill did, he tackled this book with energy and enthusiasm, commitment and meticulousness; and, despite his illness, he worked to bring the volume, and his other projects, to fruition with more dedication than most scholars could muster in perfect circumstances. This book is one of many testimonies to Phill's scholarship, as well as evincing his desire to bring Anglo-Saxon studies to a wider audience. Indeed, the *Companion* will be of substantial importance for all academics and students in the field of early medieval studies, and Anglo-Saxon studies in particular. Each of the contributors is an outstanding scholar in their respective field, and the perspectives and debates they offer are timely, representing contemporary research and writing at its best.

Phillip Pulsiano would be justly proud of this volume, and it is dedicated to him with great affection by all of the contributors. Any errors or slips (which Phill would never have tolerated) belong to the co-editor, and should not be permitted to detract from a collective endeavour that goes some way to honouring the work of Phillip Pulsiano.

Elaine Treharne
University of Leicester
October 2000

Acknowledgements

This volume is an immensely valuable contribution to the ongoing debates in the field of Anglo-Saxon studies. It is the first book to address, within a single remit, the subject from a wide range of perspectives, including the topics of analysing the corpus of Old English and Anglo-Latin texts; of manuscript production; the post-Conquest continuation of Old English; the later antiquarian activities of scholars of early medieval English writings; and the state and status of the subject in the new millennium.

Both editors should wish to thank the contributors for their splendid individual essays, and for their assistance in bringing this volume to completion. Their patience with their colleagues who submitted well after the deadline, and the commitment of all the scholars involved in the volume, is testimony to the importance attached to the project. Special words of appreciation and thanks are owed to Professor Joseph McGowan for his long-standing friendship to Phillip Pulsiano, and his willingness to assist throughout the production process, in addition to writing and checking substantial chapters. Professor Jill Frederick has always been a source of great support and friendship to both editors. Professors Nick Doane, Andrew Prescott, Carl Berkhout and Pat Conner have constantly offered assistance, encouragement and innumerable words of wisdom.

The Librarians of the British Library, the Parker Library, Trinity College, Cambridge, the Bodleian Library and the many other major manuscript libraries have helped the contributing scholars in countless ways: thank you. Blackwell Publishers have, as always, been a wonderful press to work with. Thanks are due to Andrew McNeillie for suggesting the project, and to Ally Dunnett, Angela Cohen, Fiona Sewell and Lisa Eaton for seeing the book through publication.

Elaine Treharne thanks Professor Greg Walker, Paula Warrington and her colleagues at Leicester; and, of course, more than words could say, Andy, Jonathan and the Lady Isabel. Most of all, Phillip Pulsiano would wish to thank his wife Professor Kirsten Wolf, and their daughter, Anne, for their constant inspiration, love and support.

Abbreviations

BL	London, British Library
CCSL	Corpus Christianorum, Series Latina
Corpus	Cambridge, Corpus Christi College (manuscript)
CSASE	Cambridge Studies in Anglo-Saxon England
CUL	Cambridge University Library
ed(s)	editor(s)
EETS	Early English Text Society
e.s.	extra series
HE	Bede, *Historia ecclesiastica gentis Anglorum*. Eds and trans B. Colgrave and R. A. B. Mynors, *Bede's Ecclesiastical History of the English People*. Oxford Medieval Texts. Oxford. 1969.
Ker, *Catalogue*	N. R. Ker, *Catalogue of Manuscripts Containing Anglo-Saxon*. Oxford. 1957. Repr. with suppl. 1990.
n.s.	new series
OE	Old English
o.s.	original series
PL	Patrologia latina
s.s.	supplementary series
s.viii/ix	eighth, ninth century, etc. (date of manuscript)
s.viii^1/s.viii^2	first half of the eighth century; second half of the eighth century, etc.
s.x^{ex}	end of the tenth century, etc.
s.x^{in}	beginning of the tenth century, etc.
s.x$^{4/4}$	fourth quarter of the tenth century, etc.
s.xi^2	second half of the eleventh century, etc.
7	Old English abbreviation for *and*

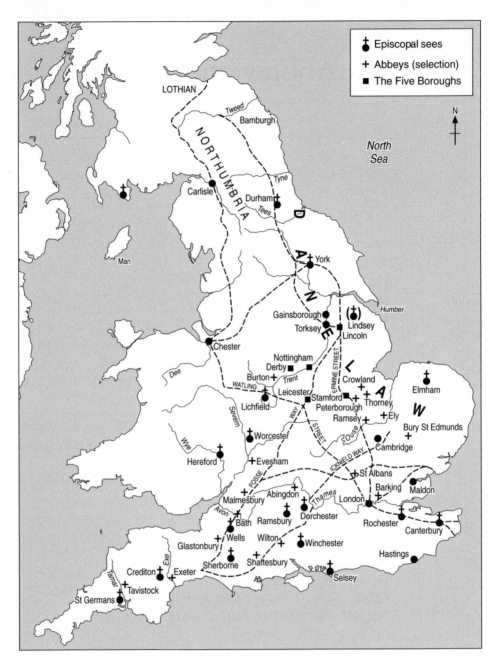

Map 1 Late Anglo-Saxon England

PART I
Contexts and Perspectives

1

An Introduction to the Corpus of Anglo-Saxon Vernacular Literature

Elaine Treharne and Phillip Pulsiano

In terms of extant manuscript numbers, the more significant body of prose writings that survives from Anglo-Saxon England is Anglo-Latin. Along with the arrival of Christianity in southern England at the very end of the sixth century came the need for religious preaching and teaching texts, and in the earlier centuries of the period, these texts were copied, it seems exclusively, in Latin. Thus authors such as Bede, Aldhelm and Alcuin flourished, and their writings were, partially, to form the basis for the emergence of a literary corpus within England in the earlier medieval period. Although English writings may have been transmitted in this early period (Cædmon's *Hymn*, for example, survives in the eighth-century copies of Bede's *Ecclesiastical History*) it is towards the end of the ninth century that Old English, alongside Latin, emerged as an important medium for the written word, and there has subsequently been no hiatus in the development of English as a literary form. As far as prose texts in Old English are concerned, 90 per cent of the surviving corpus of vernacular literature up to *c.*1170 is comprised of prose. Poetry forms only 10 per cent of extant literary works: some thirty thousand lines or so in total. There are over two hundred manuscripts in which substantial amounts of Old English appear (Ker, *Catalogue*), but this range of material can be supplemented by manuscripts in which the vernacular appears as individual glosses and notes, as scratched glosses, or as marginal phrases within a predominantly Latin manuscript.

The prose that was produced by Anglo-Saxon scribes and authors can be categorized generically and chronologically. The former classification system would yield religious prose, subdivided, for example, into the Biblical, homiletic, hagiographic, patristic translation, pastoral and liturgical; glossographical; medical; educational; prognosticatory; legal; historical; travel narrative; and romance. These subdivisions can be further broken down into types of specific prose texts; for example, anonymous homilies and hagiographies as opposed to those where the author of the work is known (Lees 1999: 22–7). Known authors of prose in the Anglo-Saxon period are relatively rare; yet the larger proportion of what survives is attributable to them: to King Alfred and his circle of scholars (in the 890s and 900s); to Æthelwold, bishop of Winchester (writing in the 960s to 980s); to Ælfric (writing in the 990s and 1000s), in particular; to Wulfstan (writing *c.*995–1020); and to Byrhtferth of Ramsey (writing 990–1020). Ælfric, for example, was responsible for writing over one hundred and fifty texts in English, an achievement that marks him out as the most prolific prose writer of the Anglo-Saxon period.

The other categories of prose can be subdivided further also. The educational prose, for example, can be classified into the colloquy, debate literature, encyclopaedic and prognosticatory collections, and so forth. Generic classification, while useful, must also be recognized as creating its own false distinctions, for many prose works do not fall neatly into a particular genre; the same, incidentally, is true of the poetry that survives. Thus, for example, some of the texts in Ælfric's *Catholic Homilies* series are actually saints' lives (Hill 1996); some of the patristic translations, principally Latin works translated into Old English during the reign of King Alfred, and at his instigation, also incorporate original composition. This is the case with Alfred's *Preface* to his translation of Gregory's *Pastoral Care*, or his numerous additions and adaptations to the translation of Boethius' *Consolation of Philosophy* (Greenfield and Calder 1986: 38–67).

A chronological classification of the prose texts surviving from the Anglo-Saxon period can be, and often is, simplified by the division of the works into those of the Alfredian era, and those of the Benedictine Reform period and later. Among the former works are the translations mentioned above, and the earliest manuscript of *The Anglo-Saxon Chronicle* (Cambridge, Corpus Christi College 173, known as the 'Parker Chronicle' or 'A' version). In addition, the Old English version of Bede's *Ecclesiastical History*, the translation of Gregory's *Dialogues*, Augustine's *Soliloquies*, the Old English version of Orosius' *Historiarum adversum paganos*, and other prose works are attributed to this period, and, in particular, to the work of Alfred and his group of scholars. Subsequent prose works include the English version of the *Benedictine Rule*; the English translations of the New Testament Gospels and some Old Testament books (Marsden 1995); and Old English versions of the Psalter. The two best-known individual Old English writers were contemporaries in the late tenth and early eleventh century: Ælfric, abbot of Eynsham, who wrote two series of *Catholic Homilies* (Godden 1979; Clemoes 1997), additional homilies (Pope 1968), a series entitled the *Lives of Saints* (Skeat 1966), a *Grammar*, a *Colloquy*, a translation of Bede's *De temporibus anni*, part of the *Hexateuch*, and a number of pastoral letters; and Wulfstan, bishop of Worcester and archbishop of York, who composed numerous homilies and legal writings. These important writers are intellectual second-generation products of the Benedictine Reform, inspired both by the monastic renaissance in the tenth century and by the confidence provided by the established tradition of writing and teaching in the vernacular. Other prose collections of the tenth century preceded the work of Ælfric and Wulfstan. Among the most important are the Vercelli and Blickling collections of homiletic and hagiographic texts (Scragg 1992; Morris 1967), which share the obvious emphasis on edification through the medium of Old English, but do not always share the orthodox approach of Ælfric and his peers. Substantial apocryphal texts are extant both in these two anonymous collections and in other manuscripts. It may seem curious nowadays that apocryphal and non-orthodox texts such as *The Gospel of Nicodemus*, which relates the story of Christ's harrowing of hell, or *The Apocalypse of St Thomas*, which narrates the signs and events heralding the imminent end of the world, were sometimes copied alongside texts of a more authoritative nature, including those written by Ælfric. Cambridge, Corpus Christi College 303, for example, is a good case in point; a twelfth-century manuscript containing more than sixty Ælfrician texts, this English manuscript also includes *The Gospel of Nicodemus*, adaptations of Vercelli Homilies, and other anonymous hagiographic and homiletic texts. While Ælfric was determined that his collections of *Catholic Homilies* remain intact, thereby preserving the authority and orthodoxy of his works, within a decade or so his texts were copied with apocryphal or non-orthodox material (see Hill's chapter in this volume). This issue – of the authority and orthodoxy of texts – seems not to have concerned a good many manuscript compilers in the period, who, pragmatically, gathered their materials from a range of sources in order to satisfy their respective audiences' needs. Indeed, determining the nature of collections of texts, and the intended use of the manuscripts, has become an area of great interest to scholars in the last few decades.

In the case of the collection of homiletic and poetic texts in Vercelli, Biblioteca Capitolaire cxvii (the Vercelli Book), it is difficult to ascertain the reasons behind the compilation (see, for example, Ó Carragáin 1981). Dated to the middle of the second half of the tenth century, the manuscript, possibly copied at St Augustine's Canterbury (Scragg 1992), contains twenty-three prose homilies and six poetic texts. The homilies themselves appear to have few detectable thematic links other than the, perhaps obvious, penitential and eschatological emphases. How, or indeed whether, these homilies might be unified thematically with the accompanying poetic texts (*Andreas, Fates of the Apostles, The Dream of the Rood* and *Elene* among them) is an interesting question, but one which perhaps did not vex the compiler of the manuscript as much as it vexes current scholars.

Other works such as the prose texts in London, British Library, Cotton Vitellius A. xv (the *Beowulf*-manuscript), might represent a thematically linked collection with the emphasis on the monstrous (Orchard 1995). The texts, *Marvels of the East, The Letter of Alexander to Aristotle* and *The Life of St Christopher*, all dwell, to an extent, on the relation of the fantastic or monstrous. As *Beowulf* and *Judith* poetically narrate the encounters of the heroes with the grotesque Grendel and his mother, and Holofernes, respectively, it is possible to deduce this textual facet of the monstrous as providing unity of subject matter throughout this manuscript, and this focus of scholarly interpretation in this area has yielded interesting results. These efforts by modern critics to discover thematic unification within Anglo-Saxon manuscripts is, though, perhaps the obvious outcome of a desire to obtain neat and tidy results from research on individual texts or codices; the ultimate aim, then, is to understand and contextualize the contemporary cultural significance of the English texts produced. Some texts, however, deny such a comfortable thematization. The romance *Apollonius of Tyre*, copied in the mid-eleventh century, is a useful example (see further Scragg's chapter in this volume). Adapted from a Latin source, itself possibly derived from the Greek legend of Apollonius, the text occurs in Cambridge, Corpus Christi College 201. This manuscript, in its present form, contains an extensive collection of homiletic, confessional and legal materials. Within this codicological context, the romance of *Apollonius* becomes something of an anomaly, and one must wonder what prompted the manuscript compiler to include this particular text. In what manner was *Apollonius* interpreted within its contemporary Anglo-Saxon milieu? One scholar, Patrick Wormald (1999: 208–9), using analogous monastic evidence, has recently proposed that the text's edifying nature, as well as its entertainment value, would have made it ideal for inclusion in a manuscript constituting 'a Wulfstanian primer of Christian standards' (208). While this is a perceptive interpretation, one might still wonder why a text with such explicit romantic overtones would be considered appropriate reading material within a monastic setting.

The majority of texts so far mentioned are those that might arguably be termed 'literary'. Other prose texts that survive would be difficult to classify as literary, except in the sense that they are 'lettered' or committed to a written format. Among these, for example, would be the numerous works that testify to the administration of government, both ecclesiastical and secular, in Anglo-Saxon England. Some of the most important extant manuscripts from the period are those that contain legal documentation: law-codes and ecclesiastical regulations, in both Latin and Old English (Wormald 1999; see Hough's chapter in this volume). The law-codes range in date from the seventh century to the twelfth. While some of the codes, usually labelled according to the specific reign under which they were written (the Laws of Ine, Alfred, Æthelræd and Cnut, for example), are clearly adapted from earlier examples, they each provide an indication of the types of crimes committed and the ways in which these might have been dealt with. They also illustrate the co-operation of church and state in the maintenance of social order, and evince the hierarchies implicit within the organization of Anglo-Saxon society throughout the centuries. In addition to these legal manuscripts is the substantial body of individual charters, writs and wills that bears witness to land ownership and transfer, and the acquisition and bequest of personal possessions and estates. These, together with the legislative materials, are important for the light that they throw upon the historical, social and cultural contexts of institutional bodies, and indeed some of the wealthier and more aristocratic individuals in England at this time.

Also contributing significantly to our understanding of the society and culture of the Anglo-Saxons are the extant manuscripts containing medical and magical texts (see Hollis' chapter in this volume). Two manuscripts copied from Latin sources are the *Herbarium* and the *Medicina de quadrupedibus*, the latter text following the former in the same manuscript; each provides a series of different antidotes for a variety of illnesses, physical disorders and injuries, the *Herbarium* using plants as curative, the

Quadrupedibus using animal products. Other medical and superstitious cures appear in the *Lacnunga* (which incorporates charms as well as more useful remedies) and Bald's *Leechbook*, the third part of which forms a magico-medical addition to the first two parts. Each of these texts, together with the later medical work known as the *Peri Didaxeon*, provides an interesting insight into the beliefs and illnesses of the Anglo-Saxons, and the ways in which physicians and those with some medical knowledge attempted to combat serious physical and psychological illnesses, and some more trivial ailments or irritations.

Attempting to combat the inexplicability of some aspects of life falls to some of the more prognosticatory prose that survives from the period, in both Latin and Old English. Prognostications attempt to pre-empt particular bad fates or unfortunate outcomes, by warning, among other things, of the probable occurrence of events on specific days or in specific periods. Prognostications survive, for example, in the mid-eleventh-century manuscript London, British Library, Cotton Tiberius A. iii, amidst a host of homiletic, hagiographic, liturgical and pastoral materials. The prognosticatory texts, arguably akin to modern-day horoscopes and star-signs, were clearly regarded as integral to a monastic manuscript such as Tiberius A. iii. Similarly, London, British Library, Cotton Vespasian D. xiv (Warner 1917), a handbook useful for those teaching and preaching to less well-educated laypersons or monks, incorporates homilies, saints' lives, teaching texts and basic catechetical materials, and prognosticatory texts. The inclusion of the last once more demonstrates the encyclopaedic and quotidian nature of these texts; their possible adoption as part of the pastoral duties of the monastic priest working amongst the laity, or the parish priest himself, illustrates their utility and authority within a Christian context.

The prognostications illustrate a real concern with the passing of time, with the days of the week, or the seasons. If, for example, New Year's Day falls on a Thursday (Warner 1917: 66), then it is prophesied that a good winter, a windy Lent, a good summer and good harvest will follow that year; if New Year's Day is on a Saturday, not only will it be a dreadful winter and a windy Lent, but then all the crops will spoil, sheep will die, and the same fate will befall old men. It seems obvious that, to a society that depended almost entirely on agricultural success to survive, weather forecasting in this (from a modern perspective, superstitious) manner formed an important part of the body of learning. Time also played a major role in other texts composed and copied during the period, such as Ælfric's late tenth-century *De temporibus anni*, which draws on Bede's scientific works calculating the movement of the sun and moon, and the ways in which these assist in ascertaining the passage of time. Byrhtferth's early eleventh-century *Enchiridion* (Baker and Lapidge 1995), a Latin and English commentary on his own Latin *Computus* (for calculating Easter and the major movable feasts in the church year), and numerous additional computistical works that allowed the Anglo-Saxons to determine the dates of major Christian festivals are other texts crucial to the smooth running of the sequences of the church. Although this type of prose might barely be considered literary, certainly in the modern sense of that description, each work nevertheless assists the scholar in providing a more accurate historical and cultural context for the Anglo-Saxon author and his or her audience.

Four major codices contain the bulk of the surviving poetry:

1   The 'Exeter Book', Exeter, Cathedral Library 3501 (dated to the second half of the tenth century), containing the following in the order in which they appear in the manuscript (standard titles given; users of Muir's 1994 edition should note that he retitles certain poems): *Christ I* (or *Advent Lyrics*), *Christ II* (or *Ascension*), *Christ III*, *Guthlac A*, *Guthlac B*, *Azarius*, *The Phoenix*, *Juliana*, *The Wanderer*, *The Gifts of Men*, *Precepts*, *The Seafarer*, *Vainglory*, *Widsith*, *Fortunes of Men*, *Maxims I*, *Order of the World*, *The Rhyming Poem*, *The Panther*, *The Whale*, *The Partridge*, *Soul and Body II*, *Deor*, *Wulf and Eadwacer*, *Riddles* 1–59 (1–57 in Williamson 1977), *The Wife's Lament*, *Judgement Day I*, *Resignation* (sometimes divided into *Resignation A* and *Resignation B*), *Descent into Hell*, *Almsgiving*, *Pharoah*, *Lord's Prayer I*, *Homiletic Fragment II*, *Riddle* 30b (28b in Williamson), *Riddle* 60 (58 in Williamson), *The Husband's Message*, *The Ruin*, *Riddles* 61–95 (59–91 in Williamson). The entire codex is edited by Krapp and Dobbie 1936, and by Muir 1994.
2   The 'Vercelli Book', Vercelli, Biblioteca Capitolaire CXVII (dated to the second half of the tenth century), containing a combination of poetic and prose texts. The poetic texts are: *Andreas*, *The Fates of the Apostles*, *Soul and Body I*, *Homiletic Fragment I*, *The Dream of the Rood*, *Elene* (all edited by Krapp 1932).
3   The 'Junius Codex', Oxford, Bodleian Library, Junius 11 (sc 5123), containing *Genesis A* and *B*, *Exodus*, *Daniel* (all tenth–eleventh century); *Christ and Satan* (first half of the eleventh century) (all edited by Krapp 1931).
4   The '*Beowulf* Codex', London, British Library, Cotton Vitellius A. xv, containing both prose and poetic works. The poetic texts are: *Beowulf*, *Judith* (the manuscript is dated to *c*.1000; edited by Krapp 1953).

In addition to the codices, numerous poetic texts are found in other manuscripts: *The Finnsburh Fragment* (lost, but printed in Hickes' *Thesaurus* 1705), *Waldere* (Copenhagen, Kongelige Bibliotek, N. K. S. 167b (4°), fragmentary), *The Battle of Maldon* (burnt; originally London, British Library, Cotton Otho A. xii; partially preserved in a transcript by David Casley before 1731), *Durham* (Cambridge, University Library Ff. 1. 27; a burnt text originally from London, British Library, Cotton Vitellius D. xx, printed in Hickes' *Thesaurus* 1705; see also Fry 1992), *The Rune Poem* (burnt; originally London, British Library, Cotton Otho B. x, but printed in Hickes' *Thesaurus* 1705), *Solomon and Saturn* (two fragmentary texts contained in Cambridge, Corpus Christi College 41 and 422), *The Menologium* and *Maxims II* (both in London, British Library, Cotton Tiberius B. i, the C-text of the *Anglo-Saxon Chronicle*), *A Proverb* (Vienna, Nationalbibliothek 751), *Judgement Day II*, *An Exhortation to Christian Living*, *A Summons to Prayer*, *The Lord's Prayer II*, *Gloria I* (all contained in Cambridge, Corpus Christi College 201), the *Benedictine Office* (see Dobbie 1942: lxxvi–vii for distribution of poetic renderings of the psalm verses), the *Creed*, *The Lord's Prayer III*, and another copy of *Gloria I* (all in Oxford, Bodleian Library, Junius 121), *The Kentish Hymn* and *Psalm 50* (London, British Library, Cotton Vespasian D. vi), *Gloria II* (London, British Library, Cotton Titus D. xxvii), *A Prayer* (London, British Library, Cotton Julius A. ii, and London, Lambeth Palace 427), *Thureth* (London, British Library, Cotton Claudius A. iii), *Aldhelm* (Cambridge, Corpus Christi College 326), *Seasons for Fasting* (preserved in a transcript by Laurence Nowell (*c.*1510/20–*c.*1571), London British Library, Additional 43703), *The Leiden Riddle* (Leiden, Bibliotheek der Rijksuniversiteit, Voss. Q. 106; in the West Saxon version as *Riddle* 35 of the Exeter Book). To these can be added the poems found in the *Anglo-Saxon Chronicle*: *The Battle of Brunanburh*, *The Capture of the Five Boroughs*, *The Coronation of Edgar*, *The Death of Alfred*, *The Death of Edward*, *The Death of Edgar*. One of the most important poems, *Cædmon's Hymn*, is preserved in over twenty manuscripts, and *Bede's Death Song* is preserved as part of the *Epistola Cuthberti de obitu Bedæ* in thirty-five manuscripts. There are a number of Latin-English proverbs, the metrical prefaces to King Alfred's *Pastoral Care* and Wærferth's translation of Gregory's *Dialogues*, a metrical epilogue in a copy of Bede's *Historia ecclesiastica* (Cambridge, Corpus Christi College 41), and the *Metres of Boethius* (London, British Library, Cotton Otho A. vi). Runic verse inscriptions are found on the Ruthwell Cross and the Bewcastle Cross, and on the Franks Casket. Finally, some twelve charms from various manuscripts can be said to be written in verse.

The literature that survives, and that has been briefly touched upon in this rapid survey, is analysed more thoroughly and in far greater detail in the chapters that follow. Its chief characteristics are its immense diversity and interest; its intellectual and social importance; and the relative neglect of the prose in comparison with the poetry of the period. A volume such as this is designed to inform and stimulate, and it may be that the engagement with Anglo-Saxon literature prompted by this and other, similar critical works will be sufficient to inspire much-needed and very welcome further research on the part of the individual reader.

REFERENCES

Primary sources

Baker, P. and M. Lapidge, eds 1995. *Byrhtferth of Ramsey: Enchiridion*. EETS, s.s. 15. Oxford.

Clemoes, Peter, ed. 1997. *Ælfric's Catholic Homilies: The First Series*. EETS, s.s. 17. Oxford.

Dobbie, Elliott Van Kirk, ed. 1942. *The Anglo-Saxon Minor Poems*. Anglo-Saxon Poetic Records 6. New York and London.

Godden, Malcolm, ed. 1979. *Ælfric's Catholic Homilies: The Second Series*. EETS, s.s. 5. Oxford.

Hickes, George 1703–5. *Linguarum vett. septentrionalium thesaurus grammatico-criticus et archaeologicus*. Oxford.

Krapp, George Philip, ed. 1931. *The Junius Manuscript*. Anglo-Saxon Poetic Records 1. New York and London.

——, ed. 1932. *The Vercelli Book*. Anglo-Saxon Poetic Records 2. New York and London.

——, ed. 1953. *Beowulf and Judith*. Anglo-Saxon Poetic Records 4. New York and London.

——, and Elliott Van Kirk Dobbie, eds 1936. *The Exeter Book*. Anglo-Saxon Poetic Records 3. New York and London.

Morris, R., ed. 1967. *The Blickling Homilies*. EETS, o.s. 58, 63, 73. London, 1874–80. Repr. 1 vol., London.

Muir, Bernard James, ed. 1994. *The Exeter Anthol-*

ogy of Old English Poetry: An Edition of Exeter Dean and Chapter MS 3501. 2 vols. Exeter.

Pope, John C., ed. 1967–8. *Homilies of Ælfric: A Supplementary Collection*. EETS, o.s. 259–60. London.

Scragg, D. G., ed. 1992. *The Vercelli Homilies and Related Texts*. EETS, o.s. 300. London.

Skeat, Walter W., ed. and trans. 1966. *Ælfric's Lives of Saints*. EETS, o.s. 76, 82, 94, 114. London, 1881–1900. Repr. 2 vols. London.

Warner, R. D. N., ed. 1917. *Early English Homilies from the Twelfth-century MS Vespasian D. xiv*. EETS, o.s. 152. London. Repr. 1971.

Williamson, Craig, ed. 1977. *The Old English Riddles of the Exeter Book*. Chapel Hill, NC.

Secondary sources

Fry, Donald K. 1992. 'A Newly Discovered Version of the Old English Poem "Durham"'. *Old English and New: Studies in Language and Linguistics in Honor of Frederic G. Cassidy*, pp. 83–96. Eds J. H. Hall, N. Doane and D. Ringler. New York and London.

Greenfield, Stanley B. and Daniel G. Calder 1986. *A New Critical History of Old English Literature*. With a survey of the Anglo-Latin background by Michael Lapidge. New York and London.

Hill, J. 1996. 'The Dissemination of Ælfric's *Lives of Saints*: A Preliminary Survey'. *Holy Men and Holy Women: Old English Prose Saints' Lives and their Contexts*, pp. 235–59. Ed. Paul E. Szarmach. Albany, NY.

Lees, Clare A. 1999. *Tradition and Belief: Religious Writing in Late Anglo-Saxon England*. Medieval Cultures 19. Minneapolis.

Marsden, Richard 1995. *The Text of the Old Testament in Anglo-Saxon England*. CSASE 15. Cambridge.

Ó Carragáin, É. 1981. 'How Did the Vercelli Collector Interpret *The Dream of the Rood*?'. *Occasional Papers in Linguistics and Language Learning* 8: 63–104.

Orchard, A. 1995. *Pride and Prodigies: Studies in the Monsters of the Beowulf-Manuscript*. Cambridge.

Wormald, Patrick 1999. *The Making of English Law: King Alfred to the Twelfth Century*. 1: *Legislation and its Limits*. Oxford.

2

An Introduction to the Corpus of Anglo-Latin Literature

Joseph P. McGowan

The 1980s and 1990s saw the emergence of medieval Latin studies as a branch of medieval studies proper. No longer confined simply to the role of quarry for sources and analogues of vernacular literatures, nor under the constraint of the 'classical fallacy' (Rigg 1992: 3–4), the study of medieval Latin, if still subsidiary to the study of vernacular literature, is accorded a more serious role now in the *literary* history of the European Middle Ages. The establishment of the *Journal of Medieval Latin* (1991–) attests to this shift in thinking about the language in which the preponderance of medieval documents survives. The separation of medieval Latin into national literatures can be problematic, not least because the distinctions would often be false – Jerome, Ambrose, Augustine, Gregory wrote for and were read throughout Christendom, where Latin was the ecclesiastical language, and early Christian Latin poets such as Prudentius could expect an international audience. None the less it is possible to speak of *Anglo-Latin* in at least two major divisions, pre- and post-Conquest. The latter is more difficult to define as a period (Rigg 1992: 6), though A. G. Rigg has given us the masterly *A History of Anglo-Latin Literature, 1066–1422* (Rigg 1992). Pre-Conquest Anglo-Latin has no complete historical outline to date (Bolton 1967), though the work of Michael Lapidge has helped define the corpus and brought much of it to print for the first time (Lapidge 1972, etc.).

Despite the hesitation in speaking of 'national' Latin literatures in the early medieval period, especially when concerning scribes and scholars who may not have all had Latin as their native tongue (Mantello and Rigg 1996: 71–6) and who, as in the case of Anglo-Saxon England, hailed from a homeland which produced a national literature in its vernacular (Conte 1994: 725–6), contemporary scholars of the early medieval period regularly speak of Hiberno-Latin, Cambro-Latin, Anglo-Latin (Rigg 1992: 6) – and there are very good reasons for seeing the writings in Latin in England *c.*AD 500–1100 as part of a continuous, coherent, distinct literature.

Before the Saxons: British Latin, British Christianity

'Anglo-Latin' as a term denotes the use of the Latin language in Anglo-Saxon England following the *adventus Saxonum* of approximately the middle of the fifth century or slightly earlier. Latin had been present in the British Isles in some form for a period comparable in length to that of the Anglo-Saxon period from Hengest and Horsa (AD 449) to the end of the reign of Alfred (AD 899). The island first known in Celtic or pre-Celtic form as Albion was within the ken of the classical world by the third century BC. Caesar himself reached the largest of the British Isles first in 55–54 BC. By AD 43, during the reign of Claudius, the province Britannia was beginning to take shape. A rebellion led by the late Prasutagus' queen Boudicca (of the Iceni, in East Anglia) in AD 60–1 signalled the beginning of the end for the Celtic client-kings in southern Britain, while the conquests of the governor Agricola pushed Roman control towards Scotland. This historical raw material of Roman Britain is relevant to the description at hand since it found its way into later Anglo-Latin chronicles, histories (or *res gestae*), sermons – even if not so efflorescently as in Elizabethan times.

What writings we have in Latin from pre-Christian Roman Britain consist largely of letters connected with Roman imperial administration, inscriptions (Lapidge and Sharpe 1985: 71–3; Jackson 1953) and graffiti from Romano-British sites, including a number of soliders' grafitti from border posts. The fort of Vindolanda by Hadrian's Wall proved an important source of Romano-British Latin with the discovery in the 1970s and 1980s of letters written either with stylus or with pen and ink on wooden boards in cursive script (Bowman 1983; Bowman and Thomas 1984); 400 further letters were discovered in 1993. The leaf tablets in general date to around AD 90–120 and provide much-needed material for the examination of 'British Latin' (Jackson 1953; Gratwick 1982). There is actually much of interest to our later period of concern in Romano-British use of Latin, but little of it is on firm ground – particularly concerning to what extent British Latin may have differed from varieties spoken in Gaul (much less the Mediterranean zone) and the fate of Latin loans of this period into the Celtic languages of Britain and thence, in some cases, into early Old English (Wollmann 1990).

Of concern from this period too is the coming of Christianity to Roman Britain. The syncretic Romano-British culture cultivated gods Celtic and Roman; Christianity was well established by the early fourth century. So too was the Latin language. The period 43 AD–*c*.430 AD saw the Romanization of Celtic peoples, the establishment of Romano-British elites speaking Latin, and the coming of Christianity to the British Isles. A process of contact and assimilation occurred *c*.AD 430–597, with the coming of Germanic peoples to a collapsing Roman province – though this era is perhaps less understood than the former. Christianity and Latin, the language of its transmission and expression in the British Isles, would provide the link between late Roman Britain and early Anglo-Saxon England.

Christianity was perhaps in Roman Britain by the end of the second century. We know at any rate of British representatives at the Councils of Arles (314) and Nicaea (325). British missionaries figure prominently in ecclesiastical history and pseudo-history (Ninian in Scotland, Patrick in Ireland), and a British martyr of the Diocletian persecution is commemorated in the placename St Albans (Roman Verulamium; Bede, *HE* I.7 recounts an epitome of Alban's *vita*).

The emperor who made Christianity the official state religion of the Roman Empire spent part of his youth in Britain; Constantine the Great's father Constantius had fought to recover Gaul and Britain in AD 293–6 from the usurping Carausius (who had worked to curb Saxon pirates in the English channel; Bede, *HE* I.6, describes Carausius as *genere quidem infimus, sed consilio et manu promtus*, 'a man of mean birth, but able and energetic'). When Constantius died at York (Eburacum) 25 July 306, Constantine was declared a senior Augustus by his father's troops (Galerius made him a junior Caesar). At the end of the Romano-British period, Germanus of Auxerre visited Britain in 429 and 447 in part to combat Pelagianism. If the details are not well known, there is at least in place a general framework for speaking of British Christianity – Pelagianism felt then to be a peculiar development of the Church in Britain.

Born in Britain, Pelagius provides a name and corpus (Lapidge and Sharpe 1985: 3–8; Sharpe 1997: 415–16) to Christianity in early Britain. This corpus is hard to delineate with any certainty as Pelagius' views were declared heretical and he was banished from Rome in 418 (having arrived there *c.*380; where he died is not certain, though the date is believed to be before 429). Extant are roughly a dozen of his letters (Rees 1991) and a number of Biblical commentaries (Rees 1991); attributed also to him, with varying certainty, are a number of treatises on the Christian life, on chastity, on riches, on faith, and a number of fragments on free will. A treatise on the potential of man to avoid sinning (*De possibilitate non peccandi*) alludes to the doctrinal direction in Pelagius that led to his eventual condemnation. Pelagius evidenced the sort of education possible in the Britain of his day and came into contact (though not with positive results) with the leading lights of the age (Jerome and Augustine).

Other British Latin from this period is scanty until we come to St Patrick (see Lapidge and Sharpe 1985: 315ff). As to the quality of British Latinity we have reference in the *Life of St Catoc the Elder* to an Italian teacher in Britain offering instruction in the language *more Romano*. We have as testimony as well the oeuvre of St Patrick (*c.*AD 373–463): his *Confessio* ('Confession') and *Epistola ad Coroticum* ('Letter to Coroticus'; Bieler 1952; Howlett 1994). The 'Apostle of the Irish' was not the first to bring the Latin language to Ireland, or the first to bring Christianity, but was the first to give us in Latin from the British Isles a full, reflective spiritual autobiography. Though his Latin has been judged 'barbarous' heretofore, and he himself cast aspersion on his learning – establishing a rhetorical pattern to be followed by Gildas and many another – a more recent estimate is more favourable (Howlett 1994). The moral tone and prose style of Gildas bring us into the age of the Germanic invasions.

Adventus Saxonum: The Coming of the Saxons

The establishment of forts along the *litus Saxonicum* or 'Saxon Shore' by the Romans in the third and fourth centuries gives some indication of continual contact – if consisting of little more than piracy and raiding – between Britain and Germanic tribes from the continent. The fort at Pevensey may indicate more intense contact in the 330s and later. To the following century can be dated the *adventus Saxonum* or 'Coming of the Saxons', who settled mainly in the south and east of Britain at first. Trouble from across the northern border of Roman Britain had already taxed the imperial resources in this corner of the empire; Britons, Bede tells us in his *Historia ecclesiastica gentis Anglorum* ('Ecclesiastical History of the English People'), were under the duress of raids from Picts (*Picti*) and 'impudent Irish bandits' (*inpudentes grassatores Hiberni*; *HE* I.14). Moreover, and more importantly from Bede's perspective, the Britons had grown unmindful of God's providence and 'abandoned Christ's light yoke', putting themselves under all kinds of wickedness (*ebrietati animositati litigio contentioni inuidiae ceterisque huiusmodi facinoribus sua colla, abiecto leui iugo Christi, subdentes*; I.14). Though there seem already to have been Saxon settlements in the south and east, King Vortigern of the Britons invited in Saxon mercenaries and opened the door to further Saxon settlements. The collapse of Roman Britain, to an extent already under way, ensued. How gradually this occurred historians may debate, but for Bede the working of God's providence was paramount. The *adventus Saxonum* became a centrepiece of Latin historical writing in Britain, with Gildas, Bede and the *Anglo-Saxon Chronicle* chief among those treating of it. The Bede passages cited above exhibit the uses and strategies offered by using the Fall of Britain (the title of Gildas' work, *De excidio Britanniae*). The 'fall' in Bede's rhetorical scheme can be seen in the exchange of 'yokes': by syntactic parallelism, the Britons had thrown off (*abiecto*) Christ's easy yoke (Matthew 11:30) and placed their necks under all types of vice, which are given in catalogue style. Bede's account of the *adventus* itself employs language concerning origins (*stirps, origo, gens*) and genealogy (not a necessarily Biblical device but certainly echoing scripture: *filii Uictgilsi, cuius pater . . . cuius pater . . . cuius pater . . . de cuius stirpe*) and adumbrating nation-building or 'peopling' (Vortigern asking the Saxons to defend Britain as if a fatherland: *quasi pro patria pugnatura*). What follows (*HE* I.15) is one of Bede's most famous passages: an enumeration of the Germanic peoples settling Britain, the Angles, Saxons and Jutes. Bede is writing in Anglo-Latin, participating in a tradition already well established by the time he completed his *Ecclesiastical History* in 731. It is a tradition discontinuous with the Romano-British Latin of some half-millennium in duration, and stems from the reintroduction of Christianity to Britain.

Celtic Latin and Anglo-Latin

Until the correspondence associated with the mission dispatched by Pope Gregory I to Britain in 597, we have little else besides inscriptions from the period of the *adven-*

tus to the conversion of the English. There are some regnal lists written down later (Dumville 1976, 1977), and the *Tribal Hidage* for Mercia. Texts that can be said to constitute Anglo-Latin await the seventh century. But we do have writings from the British Isles in Latin from this period before the seventh century, from writers British, Welsh and Irish. Pelagius and Patrick have been mentioned already. Gildas, author of the *De excidio Britanniae*, may be added near the start of long traditions of writing in Latin in Britain, Wales, Scotland and Ireland. Hiberno-Latin, for one, is older than Anglo-Latin and along with Cambro-Latin influenced Anglo-Saxon education and Latinity.

Gildas is important also as a bridge between British Latin at the time of Pelagius (early fifth century) and the sixth century and between British Latin of the sixth century and Anglo-Latin of the seventh and eighth centuries. By the end of the fifth century Irish monastic houses had been founded in western Britain following Irish raids on Scotland, Wales, the Isle of Man, and northern and western Britain. Ireland had Christian communities at least from AD 431 (the time of Palladius' mission *ad Scottos in Christum credentes*, 'to the Irish believing in Christ') and, like Roman Britain, exhibited the influence of Gallic Latinity and church practices. By the sixth century influence flowed both ways and Irish and British writers give us some sense of the level of Latinity in the British Isles at the time. In a letter to Pope Gregory I the Great *c*.AD 600, the Irish writer Columbanus notes that a *Uennianus auctor* (often believed to be St Finnian of Clonard; the name form, Uinniau/Vinniau or Findbarr, varying by source, is discussed in detail in Dumville 1984, who argues that the name is British, possibly of a bishop) had written to Gildas and received a reply *elegantissime*.

Born in the year of the battle of Mount Badon (AD 500), Gildas apparently received traditional Roman educational training under a *grammaticus* then a *rhetor* (Lapidge 1984); the correctness of his Latin has often been noted (in contrast with, say, that of Pelagius). Though Gildas cites the Bible more often than any other text, his prose is more complex in style than the Vulgate (Kerlouégan 1968); he exhibits also the influence of Jerome and Vergil, and possibly Orosius and Cicero. His text gives us a rare and controversial (in terms of the scholarly debate over its historical value) look at the end of Roman Britain and displays in its 110 chapters the author's rhetorical polish and force. The *De excidio Britanniae* is also in some ways a forerunner of Bede's *Historia ecclesiastica*, lamenting then current abuses in civil and ecclesiastic power and considering proper ecclesiastic authority. Gildas' vocabulary, often seen as esoteric with its learned words (even if not derived from glossaries as sometimes supposed; Lapidge 1984: 37–9), technical terms, neologies and Graecisms, exhibits characteristics one finds later with the *Hisperica famina* and Aldhelm. And a number of terms from Gildas made their way into glossaries, there for use by later writers in Britain.

The century following Gildas is crucial to the start of Anglo-Latin; it is in the seventh century that we can speak of 'Anglo-Latin literature' (while we can first speak of 'Hiberno-Latin literature' in the fifth). It is also the age of Aldhelm (*c*.640–709), perhaps indeed Anglo-Saxon England's first man of letters (Lapidge 1979). Aldhelm, like other Anglo-Latin and Celtic Latin authors of the late seventh to eighth centuries, was influenced by the 'hisperic' style – the use of vocabulary cultivated for its arcane and learned quality (Herren 1981). The trait has been seen as pompous, bombastic and reflecting an interest in the encyclopaedic, under the influence of a Solinus or Isidore of Seville (Herren 1974; Winterbottom 1976a). The *Hisperica famina* are a collection of poems, the work of 'faminators' (Late Latin *famen*, 'speech, word') known for the exotic 'hisperic' style, on a variety of subjects in a variety of forms (the line of the A-recension has been described as 'assonantal prose'; Herren 1974). The A-text contains a cluster of poems, the preface to which introduces us to groups of students (one a group of newcomers who are queried *Quos edocetis fastos? / Cuique adheretis rhetori?*, 'What texts do you recite / and what rhetor do you adhere to?'; Herren 1974: 64–5) from whose perspective a number of the poems are told. The preface and second section (*De duodecim uitiis ausonicae palathi*, 'On the twelve faults of Ausonian diction') proceed with the band of students (as they seem to be, still under a *rhetor*) and their scholarly 'faminating'; their concern is with the *hispericum . . . sceptrum* (l. 54) or *his-pericum . . . tollum* (l. 109), both referring to diction, eloquence in the style *hispericus* (that is, *hespericus*, western, of Italy, and in contrast to that which is *scottigenus*, 'from Ireland'). Other pieces consider matters cosmological (*lex diei*, the rule or order of the day, ll. 133–357; *De caelo*, 'On the sky', ll. 358–80; *de mari*, 'On the sea', ll. 381–425; *de uento*, 'On the wind', ll. 477–96) and mundane (the last section heroically protrays a boar hunt, ll. 571–612; others return to students' concerns such as verse on the wax writing tablet, *De tabula*, ll. 531–46). Other manuscripts contain the two *loricae* in the collection (the hendecasyllabic *Lorica of Laidcenn* and *Leiden lorica*), the *Rubisca* (in double rhythmic adonics and abecedarian quatrains, it is a poem in praise and for the protection of a little red bird), the *Altus prosator* ('Lofty Creator'), and the 'St Omer Hymn' (*Adelphus adelpha meter*, 'Brother, sister, mother', varying between octosyllabic and heptasyllabic lines).

Much debate has centred on the provenance of the collection's verses; while English or Irish or Breton origins (Herren 1987) have been advanced for the *Rubisca*, much of the collection is still believed to be of Irish origin, on the basis of similarities metrical, stanzaic, grammatical, phonological and lexical. Hiberno-Latin verse of the seventh century seems its nearest kin. None the less, poems like the two *loricae* enjoyed English manuscript transmission and, more important for the subsequent history of Anglo-Latin, were frequently imitated and glossed in the vernacular (whether in Irish, Breton or English). A number of connections are of interest: the *Hisperica famina* style influenced Aldhelm and later Anglo-Latin authors; the manuscript transmission and glossarial histories evidence the exchange and mutual influence of Celtic and Anglo-Latin writers; the colloquy style seen in the A-text proved enormously popular in the educational programme of Anglo-Saxon England; poems such as the *loricae* influenced vernacular productions that began to appear in the next century (for Old English); a number of the poems employ the catalogue style so pervasive in Anglo-Latin and especially Old English literature (Howe 1985) – the anatomical catalogues of the *loricae* have many analogues, including Alcuin's *Confessio pura* (an Old English adaptation of which appears in BL, Cotton Tiberius A. iii); and the diction of the collection was raided for glossaries (such as the bilingual Latin–Old English compilations now known as the Épinal-Erfurt and Harley Glossaries) and evidenced a common concern – useful knowledge and learned terms (whether from Latin, Greek or in some cases Hebrew) for its transmission.

The Celtic Latin traditions (Pelagius, Faustus, Patrick, Columbanus, Cummian, Virgilius Maro Grammaticus, Brigid's hagiographer Cogitosus, Adomnán, Moucan, Asser, Gildas' biographer Caradog of Llancarfan, and many others) can be seen in the crucial seventh century as a catalyst for Anglo-Latin. Their origins are earlier (Pelagius, Patrick) and their subsequent developments sometimes parallel, at other times divergent. But the contact seen in the early period continued through to the Conquest and beyond (writers from Wales or Cornwall made careers under English monarchs: Geoffrey of Monmouth, Gerald of Wales). For instance, a Mercian prayer-book of s. viii² (BL, MS Royal 2. A. xx) contains the Cambro-Latin *Orationes Moucani*, a series of nine prayers with an intricate rhyme scheme and series of cursus rhythms (of the sort familiar from the *Rhetorica ad Herennium*: planus, tardus, velox, medius, trispondiacus, dispondeus dactylicus); the manuscript is written in Anglo-Saxon majuscule and minuscule and contains Mercian glosses among the other prayers (Ker, *Catalogue*: item 248). The late sixth to eighth centuries are a crucible for Anglo-Latin, and the Celtic connections await a fuller, dispassionate study. In the late sixth century another source of influence came to England's eastern shore; its impact and that of the school developed at Canterbury later in the seventh century would be enormous for England, and for the continent soon after. And the monastic and educational centre in Kent would remain England's chief ecclesiastic locus to this day.

The Augustinian Mission and Theodore, Hadrian, the School at Canterbury

Pope Gregory I the Great's fateful decision to send Augustine (prior at St Andrew's, Rome) to the shores of Kent in 596 – whatever its impetus: the young enslaved Angles whom Gregory is said to have compared rather to *angeli*, or the influence of Columbanus, founder of Bobbio – can arguably be seen as a moment of the making of England, at least intellectually, as much as was the reign of Alfred politically. Augustine arrived in Kent in 597 and Aethelbert, king of Kent, whose Frankish wife Bertha was Christian (arriving with her bishop Liudhard), converted. Augustine had been consecrated bishop that year in Gaul, and his pallium arrived from Rome in 601. He now consecrated other bishops: Mellitus (bishop of London), Justus (bishop of Rochester). Three important sees now existed: Canterbury and Rochester (in the kingdom of Kent) and London (in the kingdom of the East Saxons); by the late seventh century York would emerge as a major ecclesiastical centre. Bede's *Ecclesiastical History* (completed in 731) chronicles the conversions, reversions to paganism, martyrdoms and wonder-working of Britain's Christianization. Cedda, student of the Irishman

Aidan of Iona (later bishop of Lindisfarne), had been sent to the East Saxons in 653. Bede's Northumbria had been evangelized by Paulinus in 625, the court converted in 627, and a period of relapse followed King Edwin's death in 632. The differing practices between Celtic regions and Anglo-Saxon (such as the calculation of the date of Easter – and which reflected continuing political animosity) notwithstanding, Britain was largely Christian by the time of the Synod of Whitby in 664.

Some sense of the Augustinian mission can be gained from Gregory's *Responsiones ad interrogationes Augustini*. Of particular note are the books Gregory donated to the mission: a two-volume Bible, two psalters, two copies of the Gospels, a New Testament commentary, and two hagiographic volumes. These are natural choices for a new Christian establishment, foundation volumes of the type with which Canterbury would become synonymous. One need only glance through Helmut Gneuss' 'Preliminary List of Manuscripts Written or Owned in England up to 1100' (Gneuss 1981) to see how important Canterbury (Christ Church and St Augustine's Abbey; Brooks 1984 is the fullest history of this centre) would be to Biblical production, study and manuscript-making in general. Manuscripts from Canterbury cover the range of types of texts the Catholic church brought to England: Bibles, psalters, hymnals, martyrologies, hagiographies, computus, calendars, commentaries, glossaries, rules, homiliaries, sacramentaries, pontificals, benedictionals, penitentials, canons, monastic annals and *libri vitae*, and sequences.

Canterbury is also to be intimately linked with educational books and the school and educational programme of Theodore and Hadrian. Theodore of Tarsus, in the eastern province of Cilicia, was born in 602 into the Byzantine world; his native city was occupied by the Persians while he was a boy and he may have pursued his education at Antioch, and perhaps also Edessa, gaining some familiarity with Syriac in addition to his native Greek (Bischoff and Lapidge 1994: 5–40). After the Arab conquest of Syria Theodore may have spent time in Constantinople (Bischoff and Lapidge 1994: 41–64); at any rate, by the 660s he was living at Rome when the Anglo-Saxon Wigheard arrived seeking consecration as archbishop of Canterbury. He died of the plague the year he arrived, 667, and Pope Vitalian appointed Theodore to assume the late Wigheard's duties, consecrating him to the see of Canterbury 26 March 668. Among those travelling with Theodore to England were two particularly important companions: Benedict Biscop, an Anglo-Saxon from a noble Northumbrian family living in Rome, who would be appointed abbot of Sts Peter and Paul in Canterbury and would found monasteries in Northumbria at Wearmouth in 674 and Jarrow in 682 – Bede tells us (*Historia abbatum* ch. 15; Plummer 1896: I, 379–80) of the books he brought to Northumbria from Rome (including an illustrated Apocalypse) and in an autobiographical note (*HE* V.25) relates how at 7 years of age he, Bede, was handed over to Biscop to begin his studies and life at his monastery; the other was Hadrian, an African monk (*natione Afir*) and native Greek-speaker probably from Libya Cyrenaica (Bischoff and Lapidge 1994: 82–92). Bede describes Hadrian as Theodore's constant companion, and he was Biscop's successor at Sts Peter and Paul, Canterbury.

Theodore, Hadrian and Biscop arrived in England on a Sunday, 27 May 669, with Biscop acting as interpreter on the way from Rome. Bede tells us, as do the products of the Canterbury school, that Theodore and Hadrian were highly skilled also in Latin, the language of western Christendom; in fact Theodore was well versed in its secular and ecclesiastical learning: *seculari simul et ecclesiastica philosophia praeditum virum, et hoc in utraque lingua, Graeca scilicet et Latina* (*Historia abbatum* ch. 3; Plummer 1896: I, 366). Theodore made a tour of this new region, the correct observance of articles of faith being his foremost concern (the observance of Easter after the Synod of Whitby in 664 was in accord with Roman practice; Wilfrid had represented the Roman side at the synod against the Celtic observance). But for the history of Anglo-Latin the greatest contribution is the school at Canterbury, founded by Augustine and developed by Theodore and Hadrian. Recent research (Bischoff and Lapidge 1994; Brooks 1984) has begun to show just how dramatic were the developments occasioned by the two eastern monks. Theodore may well be the influence behind the eighth-century vogue in octosyllabic verse; compare his address in rhymed octosyllabic couplets *Te nunc, sancte speculator* ('You now, holy bishop'; Lapidge 1995) to Hæddi, bishop of Winchester (676–705), perhaps the earliest specimen of Latin verse from Anglo-Saxon England. And he guided the course of study in the Canterbury school as its *magister*. Their school for a time allowed the study of Greek a place in southern England and was so known for its scholarship that even Irish monks were drawn to be instructed by Theodore. Theodore and Hadrian brought with them a number of books in Latin *and* Greek, though the story of Theodore reading from his *vademecum* Homer is legend (Bischoff and Lapidge 1994: 240–2). Unfortunately, none of the manuscripts brought by these monks appears to have survived; Michael Lapidge has worked to reconstruct a book list for Theodore and Hadrian and surmises that it can be said to have included the Septuagint and Greek New Testament, a booklet of Greek prayers, certain Greek fathers such as Basil, John Chrysostom and Procopius (deducible from their Canterbury Biblical commentaries), as well as writings of the Latin fathers Augustine and Jerome (Bischoff and Lapidge 1994: 241–2). Knowledge of Greek in Anglo-Saxon England may have been at its height with the school of Theodore and Hadrian; Bede perhaps could read Greek, so too the Breton monk Israel the Grammarian at Athelstan's court. And Graecisms survive in the glossary traditions and assorted minor texts and marginalia of Anglo-Saxon manuscript miscellanies (compare Oxford, St John's College MS 17; Ker, *Catalogue*: item 360).

The centrepiece of the school was scriptural study, and the Biblical commentaries now being identified with the Canterbury school (Bischoff and Lapidge 1994) were of tremendous influence, influence still awaiting fuller explication. The Biblical commentaries from the Canterbury school published by Bischoff and Lapidge are important not only to the history of Biblical studies in England (for their influence extended with Anglo-Saxon missions to the continent in the next century), but to the often underappreciated history of language education and glossography. Theodore, Bede records, took an interest in the English language, and the Biblical commentaries and the massive glossarial activity they generated (often eventually independent of the

commentaries) had a significant impact on pre-Carolingian and Carolingian scholarship on the continent, reaching centres such as Eichstatt, Reichenau and St Gall. St
Gall in particular preserves codices bearing the stamp of Canterbury school scholarship (such as Stiftsbibliothek MSS 9, 283, 295, 299). The Greek-speaking Theodore
and Hadrian are no doubt responsible (along with sources such as the *Hermeneumata
pseudodositheana* and other Graeco-Latin glossaries) for many of the Latinized Graecisms one finds in Anglo-Saxon and Anglo-Saxon-influenced continental glossaries.
These compilations, some class-books no doubt while others seem to be scholarly
reference works and proto-encyclopaedias, are crucial pieces of evidence, along with
stylistic and metrical analysis, in determining the level of Latinity in early medieval
Europe. In Anglo-Saxon England, the glossaries drew from local sources such as
Gildas, the *Hisperica famina*, and the Canterbury commentaries and related glossaries
(the 'Leiden-group' and related Milan biblical glossaries; Bischoff and Lapidge 1994).
Names of animals from Leviticus, terms for weights and measures in Greek and
Latin, bird names, fish names, shoe types – these and many more word or semantic
classes, often grouped in a-b-alphabetic order, formed a register of what words
gave readers pause, were considered useful, or reflected reading habits in schools and
scriptoria.

If there were no successors equal to Theodore in the following generations, the
Canterbury school influence none the less persisted. Tatwine's *aenigmata* and grammar
(the *Ars Tatwini*) benefited from the library and academic atmosphere Theodore built
up (as Bede was nurtured by the library Benedict Biscop helped build at
Wearmouth–Jarrow). Another composer of *aenigmata*, and the most famous student
of the school, would bring to fruition in native soil by native hands the work of
Theodore and Hadrian. Aldhelm too enjoyed a vocabulary of arcana, drew on the Canterbury library and glossaries, and accrued perhaps the richest glossarial appendix
bestowed upon a medieval English author. And in a number of respects Anglo-Latin
can be said to begin in earnest with Aldhelm.

Aldhelm, Man of Letters

Aldhelm (*c.*640–709; Sharpe 1997: 46) may very well be rightly seen as the pre-
eminent man of letters from Anglo-Saxon England; Bede (673–735) too is worthy of
such acclaim (Brown 1987). But any such ranking blurs important distinctions in
their styles of Latin composition and their interests. Perhaps it is not too reducibly
formulaic to say that Bede, with his wide-ranging interests and prolific output, is
more the scientist and exegete to Aldhelm's belletrist. Aldhelm's influence and reputation as a poet are certainly the greater (Orchard 1994). Aldhelm's fame, his poetic
diction, metrical craftsmanship (including the octosyllabic verse so many Anglo-Latin
poets imitated), and knowledge of earlier poets, classical and Christian, set him apart
and essentially without peer. His influence extends down through to the tenth century
– a span of three centuries.

Aldhelm was probably born in Wessex, though throughout his career he seems to have had close relations with the royal houses of Wessex and Northumbria (dedicating works to Kings Ine of Wessex and Aldfrith of Northumbria). He became abbot of the Irish foundation Malmesbury, and his two biographers also shared association with this monastery: Faricius of Arezzo (*Vita Aldhelmi*) and William of Malmesbury (*Gesta Pontificum Anglorum*). Aldhelm studied under an Irish teacher, although scholars are uncertain of his name (William of Malmesbury records that it was Maíldub/Maeldubh; cf. Herren 1998), at Malmesbury in a Wessex still populated by many Britons, and as a young priest (aged 30 or so) studied for some two years at the school of Theodore and Hadrian at Canterbury, where he seems to have studied some Greek in addition to Latin (compare the *vocabula graeca* list, much of it grammatical and metrical terminology, in Ehwald 1919: 752–3) and became their most illustrious alumnus (Aldhelm's *Ep.* ii, addressed to Hadrian, discusses briefly academic life there; Ehwald 1919: 478–9). He became abbot at Malmesbury *c.*675, and bishop of Sherborne 705–9.

Though the greatest poet of his age, Aldhelm was not alone in the seventh century. There is his near-contemporary Wilfrid, the son of a Northumbrian thane (634 to 12 October 709), who sparred with Theodore and spent much of his time in Northumbria (approximately 669–92); he was at the court of Aldfrith until his falling out with the monarch and expulsion in 692. His companion north was a younger monk named Æddi, known by the Latinized form Eddius Stephanus and identified with Stephen of Ripon (Sharpe 1997: 106, 634), who composed the *Vita Wilfridi c.*710–20, which was heavily influenced by the anonymous *Vita sancti Cuthberti*. The cult of Cuthbert (*c.*634–87) was already growing in Northumbria and the anonymous life must have been composed by *c.*710. That and a number of other Latin writings from Northumbria are generally portrayed as belonging to an 'Age of Bede' and will be considered along with the writings of Bede.

If Michael Lapidge's hypothesis and emendations are correct, we may have an example of anonymous octosyllabic verse from late seventh-century Anglo-Latin: four stanzas survive of a fragmentary abecedarian debate poem on divorce in *membra disiecta* (three bifolia) from a ninth-century manuscript containing B- and C-text *Hisperica famina* poems (with Old Breton glosses; Lapidge 1985a: 1–3). The Echternach provenance may help in identifying the poem as Anglo-Latin rather than Hiberno-Latin (as one might reasonably expect based on style, metre and *Hisperica famina* connection), as this was an Anglo-Saxon foundation (established 697/8 by Willibrord of Northumbria). The matter of the poem may also mirror contemporary events in seventh-century England (the possibility of a marriage's dissolution if one of the partners wished to enter monastic life; perhaps paralleled by Aldfrith's former queen Cuthburg, who founded the monastery at Wimborne) and the views of Theodore on divorce transmitted in the *Iudicia* (Theodore's answers to questions posed by 'Eoda'; Bischoff and Lapidge 1994: 150–1).

Such concerns were in a way at the core of Aldhelm's literary work; he wrote a prose treatise in sixty chapters in praise of virginity (with Sedulius' *Carmen paschale* as model and Prudentius' *Psychomachia* influencing his portrayal of the vices) dedicated to abbess Hildelith and the nuns at Barking abbey (he bids them farewell in his concluding congeries: *Valete, o flores ecclesiae, sorores monasticae, alumnae scolasticae, Christi margaritae, paradisi gemmae et caelestis patriae participes!*). At the beginning of chapter 60 Aldhelm promised to deliver a poetic paraphrase in hexameters of the prosa; this is an example of the medieval fashion of the *geminus stylus*, 'twinned style', found in the classroom: prose paraphrases of Vergil's hexametric epic or poetic paraphrases of a dialogue of Plato. The *carmen* Aldhelm too dedicated to the nuns at Barking (among whose number for a time was Aldfrith's former queen Cuthburg); the *carmen* begins with an intricate 38-line acrostic (incipit: *Metrica tirones nunc promant carmina castos*, 'Let these metrical songs now herald the chaste young soldiers') and telestich, with the first and last letter of each line spelling out the first line of the *praefatio* (descending with the initial letters, in retrograde order with the final letters). It is an example of versification showmanship (such acrostics were popular particularly in the early medieval period, such as the *In honorem sanctae crucis* ['In honour of the Holy Cross'] of Hrabanus Maurus; Hagen published some fantastic examples in the *carminum acrostichicorum repraesentatio* in his *Carmina medii aevi*; Hagen 1877: 215–22) and, like Aldhelm's diction, probably helped draw out the more dismissive tone of appraisal his work received from earlier scholars.

As has been the case with Theodore, more recent research has shown a greater appreciation for Aldhelm's style and oeuvre (Howlett 1997). The great influence and continuity of Aldhelmian 'hermeneutic' diction has been noted (Lapidge 1975a; Marenbon 1979) and among Anglo-Latin poets only Aldhelm has received a full-length study (Orchard 1994; this study also serves as a sort of *conspectus metrorum* to Aldhelm's verse). Aldhelm's metrical dexterity was put to practical use in his *Epistola ad Acircium*, his letter to King Aldfrith of Northumbria, known also under the title *De metris et enigmatibus ac pedum regulis*. Aldfrith was Aldhelm's godson, who, like his godfather, had studied under the Irish. Chapters 1–10 concern types of metre, with chapter 10 framed in a dialogue between *discipulus* and *magister*. Aldhelm's knowledge of classical and Christian Latin predecessors and scansion is impressive (Orchard 1992), his recall of specific hexameters equally so (Orchard 1994: 126–224). The *de metris* is interspersed with quotations of Arator, Audax, Cyprianus Gallus, Ennius, Juvenal, Juvencus, Lucan, Paulinus Nola, Persius, Phocas, Prosper *epigrammatus*, Sedulius, Venantius Fortunatus, Vergil, and poets collected in and circulated under the *Anthologia latina* (Sisebutus, Symphosius). Aldhelm's debt to Symphosius, the great composer of *aenigmata* whose verse circulated in the *Anthologia latina*, is apparent in the second section of the *epistola*: his 100 *aenigmata* (Ehwald 1919: 97–149; Glorie 1968a). These verse riddles, prefaced by an acrostic spelling out vertically *Aldhelmus cecinit millenis versibus odas* ('Aldhelm sang these odes in a thousand verses'), would be especially influential upon subsequent Anglo-Latin poets (Boniface and Tatwine) and Old English versifiers (a number of the Exeter Book riddles derive from Aldhelm's century of *aenigmata*).

The latter connection is particularly worth stressing: Anglo-Latin and Old English literature were not self-contained fields of activity; even if we have no solid evidence that Aldhelm did indeed compose also in Old English (as Bede reports), the manuscripts bear out such interactions. And Aldhelm's *aenigmata* are among the most heavily glossed texts from Anglo-Saxon England (his *De virginitate*, prosa and carmen, perhaps accrued the most glossarial activity, which glossing occurred on the continent too and in Old High German). Aldhelm's *aenigmata* clearly have Symphosius as their model; Symphosius' riddles often circulated in the collection of poems (or perhaps more rightly, the groups of *fasciculi*) from Latin North Africa known as the *Anthologia latina*. Symphosius' collection is a century, and many of his subjects recur in Aldhelm's hundred riddles. Aldhelm appears to have known good portions of the collection fairly well (Ogilvy 1967; McGowan forthcoming). He cites poems from the Anthology almost a score of times (at least nineteen have been identified, more are likely); Alcuin, by contrast, only thrice. Aldhelm's *aenigma* 86 ('Aries') parallels the distich *Aries sidus et animal* ('Aries, constellation and animal'; *Anthologia latina* 738b; Riese 1894) and employs a similar pun on *littera*. Aldhelm's range of reading, inculcated at the school of Canterbury, appears as eclectic as it was broad.

The third section of the *Epistola ad Acircium*, the *De pedum regulis*, comprising chapters 112–42, considers, again in dialogue form (*Da exemplaria verborum ionico minori subdita!*, 'Give examples of words set in ionic minor'; cap. 132), types of metrical feet (pyrrhic, spondee, iamb, trochee, tribrach, molossus, anapest, dactyl, amphibrach, amphimacer, etc.) and rhetorical figures and *partes orationum* (much of which is from Donatus). The work is in part derivative, but also exhaustive, and bears the stamp of Canterbury's educational concern (Bede, Tatwine and Ælfric, among others, would pen similar treatises on the trivial subjects of grammar, rhetoric and logic).

Besides the massive hexametric *Carmen De Virginitate* and hundred *aenigmata*, Aldhelm penned the *Carmina ecclesiastica*, three dedicated to particular churches – basilica of Peter and Paul in Rome, basilica of Mary Ever Virgin, and Bugga's church of St Mary in Wessex – and twelve to altars of the Apostles (Ehwald 1919: 3–32). The *Carmina rhythmica* (Ehwald 1919: 519–37) included among Aldhelm's oeuvre are five poems in Aldhelmian octosyllabic rhyming couplets; the first of them, in 100 couplets, may be by Aldhelm himself (Ehwald 1919: 524–8; Howlett 1997), the other four penned by Æthelwald (Aethilwaldus; his letter to Aldhelm is printed in Ehwald 1919: 495–7), one of Aldhelm's students and perhaps also to be identified with the Aediluualdus (Aedeluald) who was bishop of Lindisfarne 721–40 and penned an acrostic verse (reading vertically with initial letters: *Aedeluald episcopus*) found in the Book of Cerne (Sharpe 1997: 30; Howlett 1997: 128–35). Aldhelm may also very well be the author of an epitaph on Theodore; Bede (*HE* V.8) quotes eight of its thirty-four heroic verses (the first couplet: *Hic sacer in tumba pausat cum corpore praesul / Quem nunc Theodorum lingua Pelasga uocat*, 'Here lies a holy bishop's mortal frame; / In Grecian tongue is Theodore his name'). Besides the appositeness of having Aldhelm as author of Theodore's epitaph, or the rare chance of gleaning Aldhelm's elegiac verse possibly afforded by such an identification, the parallels in diction, word placement and style (e.g. Aldhelm's characteristic avoidance of elision) argue well for his authorship (Orchard 1994: 277–80). Aldhelmian authorship might also be attached to the famous *Liber monstrorum* (Porsia 1976); Michael Lapidge has argued (Lapidge 1982a) for a Wessex origin, possibly Aldhelm or someone of the Aldhelmian school, for this compendium with connections to *Beowulf* (Hygelac appears at I.2: *De Hyglaco Getorum rege*) and 'marvels' texts that circulated in Anglo-Saxon England such as the *Epistola Alexandri ad Aristotelem* ('Alexander's Letter to Aristotle') and *De mirabilibus Orientis* ('The Wonders of the East').

We have also some of Aldhelm's letters, including ten to various correspondents (Hadrian, Æthelwald, Wihtfrith, Cellanus, Wilfrid, Leutherius and others) and three sent to Aldhelm (from Æthelwald, Cellanus and an unnamed Irishman). Of particular interest is his letter to Heahfrith (Howlett 1997: 105–24 arranges the letter *per cola et commata* and marks the cursus rhythm). In it Aldhelm strives to impress upon Heahfrith, who had returned from six years of study in Ireland, the quality of an English education, the learning of Theodore, Hadrian and the Canterbury school in contrast to the 'jangling' of Irish rhythmical heptasyllabic verse, the influence of Virgilius Maro Grammaticus, and the alleged bombast of Irish diction (Howlett 1994). One senses an implied competition between Irish and English scholars for students:

> But I, wretched little man, meditating upon these matters as I wrote, was forthwith troubled and trembled with a twofold anxiety. Why, I ask, is Ireland, whither assemble the thronging students by the fleetload, exalted with a sort of ineffable privilege, as if here in the fertile soil of Britain, teachers who are citizens of Greece and Rome cannot be found, who are able to unlock and unravel the murky mysteries of the heavenly library to the scholars who are eager to study them? Although the aforesaid opulent and verdant country of Ireland is adorned, so to speak, with a browsing crowd of scholars, just as the hinges of heaven are decorated with stellar flashings of twinkling stars, yet nonetheless, Britain, although situated in almost the outer limit of the western world, possesses, for example, the luculent likeness, as it were, of the flaming sun and the moon, that is, Theodore, who discharges the duties of the pontificate and was from the very beginnings of his apprenticeship mature in the flower of the arts of learning, and his colleague of the same sodality, Hadrian, equally endowed with ineffably pure urbanity. (Lapidge and Herren 1979: 163; see Ehwald 1919: 492–3 for Latin)

The rhetorical aplomb (and, not unfairly, bombast) of the Latin is matched by the technical mastery Aldhelm displayed in his verse. One senses here too not just a concern for Heahfrith or the reputation of the English schools, but the headiness of a writer cognizant of his powers and an alumnus proud of his alma mater.

Bede and Northumbria

The Venerable Bede occasioned not only the most prolific corpus to survive from an Anglo-Latin author, but a period of cultural florescence in Northumbria (not to survive its progenitor by long), perhaps the greatest fame of an English writer in the Anglo-Saxon period, and certainly the most extensive manuscript legacy (over 1,500 manuscripts; Laistner and King 1943). There was Bede and the Age of Bede. Bede is most famous for his work of history or, more properly, ecclesiastical history, the *Historia ecclesiastica gentis Anglorum* (Wallace-Hadrill 1988: xviii–xix). Historians of Anglo-Saxon England have been indebted to Bede's *Historia ecclesiastica*, the fullest single record of the age. And succeeding ecclesiastical historians have likewise benefited from Bede's model. But Bede's corpus of writings included much more; he is principally known as historian and exegete, but was also a 'man of letters' – educator, metrist, encyclopedist, chronologist, hagiographer and, most of all, monk. Bede describes his joy at spending his life at Wearmouth–Jarrow; he was taken in there as a boy of 7, under first Benedict Biscop then Ceolfrith (the anonymous Northumbrian 'Life of Ceolfrith' provides important details of life in the monastery in the late seventh–early eighth century), and expired there 25 May 735.

Bede benefited from the library-building of founder Biscop and abbot Ceolfrith (and the monetary support of Aldfrith's father Ecgfrith), who did for the Northumbrian double centre (Monkwearmouth and, just to its north, Jarrow) what Theodore and Hadrian had done for Canterbury in Kent. And he read widely, knowing perhaps seventy-five authors or more (Brown 1987). The range of his writings is encyclopaedic – he is in some ways the Isidore of the British Isles – and though he never left his monastery, his teaching and treatises spread throughout western Christendom, becoming particularly pre-eminent on the continent following Northumbrian and other Anglo-Saxon missionaries in the eighth century.

The *Historia ecclesiastica* follows in a tradition of ecclesiastical history already familiar from Eusebius, Orosius and Gregory of Tours. Bede's *Historia ecclesiastica*, while cognizant of political alliances and intellectual endeavours that linked Anglo-Saxon England to Franks and others on the continent, is a local story. It is the history of the Roman church – and as such was seen as part of universal history, of salvation history – in the British Isles. The *HE* often reads like Adomnán's *Vita Columbae* ('Life of St Columba'; Anderson and Anderson 1961; Sharpe 1995); amidst episodes of major ecclesiastical import (conversions, journeys to Rome, the Synod at Whitby), exempla of the wonder-working providence of God ring through the five books. Miracles, wonders, divine acts of grace abound: the conversion and passion of Alban *subito diuina gratia respectus* ('divine grace suddenly shone upon him'; I.7); Germanus of Auxerre on his way to combat Pelagianism in Britain calmed a storm in the passage, among other wonders (I.17); Pope Gregory warns Augustine on his mission to England not to glory overmuch in his miracle-working there: 'And whatever power of working miracles you have received or shall receive, consider that these gifts have been conferred not on you, but on those for whose salvation they have been granted you' (I.31); Augustine heals a blind man before British bishops at *Augustinaes ac* ('Augustine's oak', on the border between the kingdoms of the Hwiccas and West Saxons) as a sign of God in favour of the Roman observance of Easter (II.2); King Edwin's vision of a stranger and conversion by Paulinus (II.12, which contains the famous *passer* 'sparrow' episode); the healings attributed to King Oswald's cross (III.2); how the field in which the Mercians cut down Oswald likewise healed many (III.9); Oswald's relics are efficacious in Ireland too (III.13); miracles attributed to Aidan, bishop of Lindisfarne (III.15–17);

Fursa's visions and saintly incorruptibility (III.19); miracles at Barking (IV.7–10); the virginal and incorruptible Æthelthryth (St Audrey; IV.19); the fetters on the thegn Imma are loosed by his brother's singing of masses (IV.22); and, amidst still more, perhaps the most famous wonder-working tale in the *HE* – if only for its appeal to those interested in vernacular literature – the story of Cædmon (IV.24). These are not the episodes of greatest appeal to historians, but indicative rather of Bede's purpose. For Bede was, besides a chronicler of church history (or just the history of a monastery; his *Historia abbatum* gives us biographies of the abbots Benedict Biscop, Ceolfrid, Eosterwine, Sigfrid and Hwætbert of Wearmouth–Jarrow), also a hagiographer.

Bede, like Aldhelm, practised the *geminus stylus* with his prose and metrical Lives of Cuthbert, the monk and later bishop of Lindisfarne about whom a celebrated cult grew. Bede drew on the anonymous Northumbrian *Vita sancti Cuthberti*, with the prosa following the anonymous life more closely than the hexametric version. Bede also paraphrased Paulinus of Nola's *Vita et passio Sancti Felicis* ('Life and Passion of St Felix') and said he corrected a translation from Greek of the 'Life of Anastasius' (*HE* V.24: Bede's bibliographical and autobiographical note). Bede's poetic work, besides the metrical 'Life of St Cuthbert', includes a lost *Liber epigrammatum* (extracts of which were recorded by Milred of Worcester; Lapidge 1975a); a hymn on St Æthelthryth (Audrey; *HE* IV.20); hymns in iambic dimeter collected in a *Liber hymnorum* (Fraipont 1955); and a poem in dactylic hexameter on the Day of Judgement (*De die iudicii*; it was paraphrased in Old English, entitled either *Be domes dæge* or 'Judgement Day II'). Bede's biographer Cuthbert (of Wearmouth–Jarrow; *Epistola Cuthberti de obitu Bedae*) reports that Bede was competent also in Old English verse; as with Aldhelm, the suggestion is tantalizing but no solid evidence suggests any surviving Old English verse is from their hands.

Bede was a remarkably prolific writer of prose treatises exegetical and didactic (CCSL has issued a number of volumes to date of his *Opera exegetica* and *Opera didascalica*). Bede saw himself in particular as a student of scripture, as someone whose whole preparation was aimed at divine study; among the products of this lifelong study are his commentary to the Catholic epistles (*In Epistolas VII Catholicas*), explanation of the Acts of the Apostles (*Expositio Actuum Apostolorum*), with a second book of retractions (*Retractatio in Actus Apostolorum*; influenced by Augustine's *Retractationes*), and an interesting brief text glossing literally and figuratively placenames from the Acts (*Nomina regionum atque locorum de Actibus Apostolorum*); two copies of this last text are housed in St Gall's Stiftsbibliothek (MS 259 of the late eighth century, MS 260 of the second half of the ninth), a library replete with Bedan texts that testify to the rapid spread of his influence and that of the Anglo-Saxon missionaries of the eighth century. St Gall would also be an important centre in Carolingian Biblical exegesis and in the development of Old High German vernacular writings. In particular, the monastic library of St Gall houses a number of Biblical glossaries and commentaries (by the likes of Hrabanus Maurus, a student of Alcuin, and Walahfrid Strabo). Bede's *Nomina* is often terse in glossary style (*Attalia: ciuitas Pamphiliae maritima*; *Cnidus: insula contra Asiam*; *Lycia: prouincia Asiae*; *Thessalonica: ciuitas Macedoniae*); at other times it reminds one of the *Etymologiae* of Isidore of Seville. Other works of Bede's exegetical oeuvre may be briefly listed: a collection or *collectaneum* of Augustine's observations on the Pauline epistles (*Collectio ex opusculis Sancti Augustini in epistulas Pauli apostoli*); an explanation of the Apocalypse (*Explanatio Apocalypsis*); commentaries to the Gospels of Luke and Mark (*In Lucae evangelium expositio, In Marci evangelium expositio*); the first eight questions (forming an *Opusculum de VIII quaestionibus*, on such matters as the magi and the star they followed [Matthew 2, 1–12] or David's apparent curse upon the mountains of Gilboa [2 Samuel 1, 19–27] of the *Aliquot quaestionum liber* ('A book of some questions'; PL 93)) appear to be Bedan; commentarial works on the temple of Solomon and tabernacle (*De templo, De tabernaculo*; Hurst 1969); an epitome of Admonán's *De locis sanctis* ('On the Holy Places'; Fraipont 1965); Old Testament commentaries on Genesis, 1 Samuel, Ezra and Nehemiah, Tobit, Proverbs, the Song of Songs and Habakkuk (Hurst 1969); excerpts from Jerome on the prophets; thirty questions on Kings (*In Regum librum XXX quaestiones*); and other works of dubious authenticity or now believed spurious (Sharpe 1997: 70–6).

The list gives credence to Bede's assertion that this was his life's work; his correspondence (Plummer 1896; letters to Albinus, Ecgbert, Helmwald, Plegwin, Wictred and others) and *Historia ecclesiastica* (which is a rather diverse work, with insertions of letters, hymns, reconstructed discourse and a chronicle) also share in his divine work. So too do his technical and didactic works; they are a means to an end, whether the correct reading of scripture or the correct fixing of dates (Bede's concern over the Easter controversy in the *Historia ecclesiastica* can be wearying). Thus Bede wrote treatises concerned with basic and more advanced education, such as those on correct orthography (*De orthographia*, Jones 1975a), metrical composition (*De arte metrica*, CCSL Jones 1975a), rhetorical figures (*De schematibus et tropis*, Jones 1975a), basic knowledge of the physical world (*De natura rerum*, Jones 1975a), and the measure of time, particularly in fixing the paschal cycle, in two works with his *chronica maiora* and *minora* (*De temporum ratione*, Jones 1975b, which includes his famous *De mensibus Anglorum* ['On the months of the English'] at *c*.xv; *De temporibus*, Jones 1980).

Bede's programme of learning did for Northumbria, however briefly, what the Canterbury school did for Kent and Southumbria in general. Bede ushered in what has come to be called the Age of Bede. Literary activity concurrent and subsequent to Bede's has survived: anonymous lives of Cuthbert (*Vita sancti Cuthberti*, composed *c*.699–705 and used by Bede), Gregory (*Vita sancti Gregorii*, composed at Whitby *c*.680–704) and abbot Ceolfrid (*Vita sancti Ceolfridi*, composed at Wearmouth–Jarrow after 716); Cuthbert's *Epistola de obitu Bedae*; an epistle of Acca of Hexham, prefacing Bede's commentary to Luke; one letter by Ælfflæd, abbess of Whitby and sister of Aldfrith, survives in the corpus of Boniface's correspondence (one of the richest sources of named Anglo-Latin writers; Sharpe 1997: 25); a letter and poem from Ceolfrid of Jarrow; and Eddius Stephanus' life of Wilfrid. Wilfrid's life was nearly as unstable as Bede's was anchored. The *vita* by Eddius, or Stephen of Ripon, is one of firsthand experience; Eddius accompanied Wilfrid on a journey to Rome. In sixty-eight chapters Eddius chronicles the life events, ecclesiastic and political struggles, and miracles of Wilfrid. Educated at Lindisfarne, Wilfrid became an active participant in the Easter controversy, sparring with Bishop Colman of Lindisfarne (*c.*10) while representing the Roman position at the synod held at abbess Hilda's Whitby. He was bishop of Ripon at the time of Theodore's arrival and assumed the see at York when Chad (Ceadda) was ruled to have been installed improperly. Wilfrid's relations with Theodore were not always good; Theodore removed him from the see at York in 677 and confiscated his property. Wilfrid travelled to Rome to appeal to the pope; negotiation resulted in his restoration to York, though the division of his diocese of York effected by Theodore (into three smaller dioceses: Deira, Bernicia and Lindsey) remained. Theodore, now full of days, ill and prescient of his own passing ('For I know that after this year the end of my life draws near, in accordance with the revelation of the Lord'; *Vita Wilfridi* ch. 43, Colgrave 1927), called Wilfrid and Erconwald to London and confessed his wronging Wilfrid. Though Eddius' Latinity is not esteemed as highly as Bede's (Colgrave 1927), his 'Life of Wilfrid', however partisan, is another important document of Northumbrian activity in the late seventh and early eighth centuries.

The Missions to the Continent

The upsurge in Latin writing emanating from Northumbria in this period was accompanied, though not matched, by writers from Mercia and Southumbria. But the monastic and cultural burst in Northumbria (church-building and ornamentation, manuscript production and illumination – the Codex Amiatinus, earliest complete copy of the Bible, is a Jarrow product) made Anglo-Saxon England worthy of note only a little over a century after it was a recently converted backwater of Christendom. In the eighth century, Northumbrians and other Anglo-Saxons travelled to the continent to convert unconverted peoples and found monastic houses as the Irish had started to do in the seventh. The student of Anglo-Latin texts has the privilege of having Wilhelm Levison's *England and the Continent in the Eighth Century* (Levison 1946), a study whose details and conclusions have been updated (particularly since the early 1980s) but whose main narrative remains magisterial.

By the early seventh century the Irish had active monastic schools, with particular achievement in grammar (Law 1982) and Biblical exegesis (Bischoff 1972); later in the century, particularly with the career of Columbanus, that scholarship was exported to the continent. Irish houses were founded in France, the Low Countries, Germany, Switzerland and northern Italy, among them Auxerre, Bobbio (where Columbanus expired in 615), Fiesole, St Gall, Laon, Luxeuil (for which Columbanus formulated a Rule which lasted until replaced by Benedict's *Regula*), Péronne (where Fursa was laid to rest *c.*650) Reichenau, Trier and Würzburg. And even before that these *peregrini* exerted their influence over northern England, founding Iona and Lindisfarne (the names of the abbots of Lindisfarne evidence the transition from founding Irish to the Northumbrians trained under them: Aidan acceding in 635, Finan in 651,

Colman in 661, Tuda in 664, Eata in 678, Cuthbert in 685). The English joined in the enterprise of conversion and house-founding, among them Boniface (in Old English, Wynfreth or Winfrid; later bishop of Mainz), Willibald (bishop of Eichstatt), Willibrord (archbishop of the Frisian church at Utrecht), and, at the pinnacle of Anglo-Saxon influence on the continent, Alcuin of York as advisor to Charlemagne and director of his school at Aachen.

Even during the early days of Anglo-Saxon England contact with the continent appears never to have been severed. Æthelbert of Kent married the Frankish Bertha, which, besides aiding in the Christianization of Kent, entailed political alliances with Merovingians; the slave trade brought Anglo-Saxons to Gaul and elsewhere (e.g. Rome, where Pope Gregory I beheld the *Angli/angeli*; *Historia ecclesiastica* II.1); trade flourished with merchants from Gaul, Frisia, Saxony and elsewhere; and the Christianization of Anglo-Saxon England led to a stream of visitors to and from Rome on pilgrimage, or papal or ecclesiastic business. Books in particular flowed along the latter routes; in the eighth century English missionaries and their books came back to the continent.

Though Wilfrid had made a beginning at coverting the Frisians after being deposed from his see at York 678–9 (Eddius, *Vita Wilfridi* chs 26–8), Willibrord took up the mission towards the beginning of the eighth century. Born in 658 in Deira, Northumbria, and educated at Ripon and for twelve years in Ireland, Willibrord was sent with his companions to Frisia in 690. After successful efforts at converting the Frisians, the Merovingian Emperor Pippin sent Willibrord to Rome, where he was consecrated as archbishop to the Frisians. He had his see at Utrecht and his monastery at Echternach (an important centre for manuscripts, located in what is now Luxembourg). We have a calendar said to belong to Willibrord (Wilson 1918) as well as Alcuin's *opus geminatum*, the *Vita sancti Willibrordi* in prose (Levison 1919–20) and verse (Dümmler 1966). Better attested through surviving Latin writings is fellow missionary Boniface, who had resided with Willibrord in Frisia for a time. Born in Wessex (probably Devon) *c.*672/3, he entered the monastery at Exeter and then continued his education at the monastery at Nursling (where he was elected abbot in 717; Levison 1946: 70–1). After an abortive attempt at missionary activity in Frisia in 716, he returned in 718 and spent the rest of his life there and in Germany. Boniface's German mission saw the organization of the church in that region and his accession to the see at Mainz (to remain an important see in the German church). On his return to Frisia in 753 he continued the conversion of the Frisians. In his second year of this mission he was martyred at Dokkum along with fifty-three companions (Levison 1946). His remains were transferred to Fulda, one of the monasteries he had founded. His literary remains consist of his correspondence (Tangl 1955), drawn together by an anonymous collector after his death; an *Ars grammatica* and *Ars metrica* (Gebauer and Löfstedt 1980); and poems (Dümmler 1966; James 1914).

In addition to giving us a sense of the workings of Anglo-Saxon missions and relations among religious houses and rulers (and among the religious themselves), Boniface's letters are an onomastic storehouse (Levison 1946: 280–90). Of the ninety-five or so named Anglo-Latin writers of the Anglo-Saxon period in Richard Sharpe's *Handlist of the Latin Writers of Great Britain and Ireland before 1540* (Sharpe 1997), approximately a score are correspondents with Boniface or his assistant Lul (who succeeded him to the see at Mainz): Ælfflæd, abbess of Whitby; Ælfwald, king of the East Angles; Æthelberht, king of Kent; Æthelberht, archbishop of York; Alchred, king of Northumbria; abbot Aldhun; Botwine, abbot of Ripon; Bregowine, archbishop of Canterbury; Bugga; Cuthbert, abbot of Wearmouth–Jarrow and author of the *Epistola de obitu Baedae*; Cyneheard, bishop of Winchester; abbess Eangyth; abbot Eanwulf; Eardwulf, bishop of Rochester; Ecgburg, princess of the Hwicce; Leofgyth, nun of Wilton; Sigewald; Tica, abbot of Glastonbury; Torhthelm, bishop of Leicester; Wigbert; and Wihtberht, priest of Glastonbury. Boniface's Latin writings exhibit a style more like that of Aldhelm of Wessex rather than Northumbrians such as Bede and Alcuin; like many another writer of the period he employed acrostics, such as that restored to his poem to Nithard, *Nithardus vive felix* (James 1914; Howlett 1997), or the magnificent example to accompany the prefatory letter to Sigeberht in the *Ars grammatica* (Gebauer and Löfstedt 1980: 4–5). The *Ars grammatica*, or *Ars Bonifatii*, circulated among houses in the Anglo-Saxon mission areas and gives a sense of which late antique–early medieval grammarians were known and taught in Anglo-Saxon schools. The *Ars Bonifatii* primarily concerns accidence at a rudimentary level (*de nomine, de pronomine, de verbo, de adverbio, de participio, de coniunctione, de praepositione, de interiectione*). His *Praefatio ad Sigibertum* offers a list of learned predecessors: Priscian and Donatus, Probus and Audax, Velleius Longus and Romanus, Flavinianus and Eutyches, Victorinus and Phocas, Asporius (*Ars Asporii*) and Pompeius (Gebauer and Löfstedt 1980: 10).

Boniface drew on the major grammarians taught in Anglo-Saxon schools, Priscian and Donatus, as well as Isidore of Seville, Hiberno-Latin grammatical treatises (Virgilius Maro, perhaps also the *Ars Asperi*), Charisius, Audax, Phocas, Diomedes and Aldhelm – and he knew of others, as his prefatory letter suggests (Law 1979). Boniface's grammatical treatise came together with that of Tatwine, archbishop of Canterbury 731–4, in a Lorsch manuscript (Vatican, Pal. lat. 1746, s. viii [Tatwine]–ix [Boniface]; Gebauer and Löfstedt 1980; Law 1979). Lorsch was in the Anglo-Saxon missionary sphere of influence and Tatwine's treatise, perhaps composed at the monastery library at Breedon, may have travelled there via Canterbury in the hands of Anglo-Saxon missionaries, thence to Charlemagne's court. Like Boniface, Tatwine of Mercia, in his *Ars de partibus orationis*, drew on major sources such as Priscian's *Institutiones* and Donatus' *Ars maior* and *Ars minor* as well as others (Law 1979); Tatwine too was a composer of *aenigmata*. Boniface composed a cycle of twenty *aenigmata* on the theme of the virtues and vices (ten to each: *De virtutibus et vitiis*) with acrostic tags (aenig. 1, *De ueritate: VERITAS AIT*; aenig. 2, *De fide catholica: FIDES CATHOLICA*; aenig. 3, *De spe: SPES FATVR*; Glorie 1968a: 273–343). Tatwine composed a cycle of forty: *Sub deno quater haec diuerse enigmata torquens / Stamine metrorum exstructor conserta retexit* ('With various twists the author will weave a texture / Of forty enigmas by means of a metrical thread'; Glorie 1968a: 165–208); Tatwine's four decades were filled out to the century of *aenigmata* that the models Aldhelm and Symphosius offered by Eusebius, or Hwætberht, abbot of Wearmouth–Jarrow (but see Lapidge 1986b on the attribution of the riddles to a Southumbrian Eusebius). The sixty riddles of Eusebius cover some of the same subjects as those of Tatwine, but with more from the natural or mythological world, some of the sort familiar to readers of texts such as the *Liber monstrorum* or *De mirabilibus Orientis*: XLI *De chelidro serpente* (the Hydra); XLII *De dracone* (dragon); XLIII *De tigri bestia* (tiger); XLIV *De panthera* (panther); XLV *De cameleone* (camelopard); XLIX *De anfibina sepente* (two-headed serpent); LII *De cymera* (chimaera); LIII *De yppopotamo pisce* (hippopotamus). The eighth-century vogue for *aenigmata* in Anglo-Latin is rounded out by the dozen Lorsch riddles in Aldhelmian style (Dümmler 1966).

The activity of Anglo-Saxons on the continent produced new monastic foundations, with their scriptoria and schools, and saints and martyrs. Early Anglo-Saxon glossaries, such as the Leiden (*olim* St Gall) and Épinal-Erfurt glossaries, provide evidence of educational activity and reading habits. They give evidence too of the influence of the school at Canterbury and of the international character of some of the continental centres. St Gall, for one, houses evidence of glossarial activity in the eighth and ninth centuries in Old Irish, Old English and Old High German. Willibald wrote a life of Boniface (*Vita sancti Bonifatii*) sometime before 768, probably at Mainz (Levison 1905; Lapidge 1986b). The Anglo-Saxon nun Hygeburh of Heidenheim wrote lives of the brother missionaries Willibald (later bishop of Eichstatt, not the biographer of Boniface) and Wynnebald. Felix of Crowland wrote the highly influential *Vita sancti Guthlaci*, one of the works of Anglo-Latin to last through imitations well into the post-Conquest period. It spawned a virtual Old English *opus geminatum*: a prose Old English translation and a verse Old English adaptation of Guthlac's life. Felix's 'Life of Guthlac' bears the imprint of Aldhelmian style and was composed in the first half of the eighth century at the request of King Ælfwald of East Anglia (a letter of his is preserved in the collection of Boniface's correspondence; Ep. 81). Felix had a number of hagiographic models, such as Bede's prose life of Cuthbert (Colgrave 1940) and Evagrius' translation of the *Vita sancti Antonii* by Athanasius. Hagiography, like *aenigmata*, acrostics, works in the *geminus stilus* and bilingual glossaries (Latin lemmata with Old English interpretations), is a hallmark of Anglo-Latin to 800. It would remain one its most vital genres until the Conquest. The 'twinned' *Vita sancti Willibrordi* of Alcuin, in prose first and then hexameters, testifies still further to the vitality of the genre; Alcuin's 'Life of Willibrord' is also tribute to the Anglo-Saxon missionary work in Germany and Frisia. His place at Charlemagne's court owed much to such predecessors.

Alcuin and Charlemagne

Born at or near York *c*.735, Alcuin was educated at the school of York with its great library; we know little of his family, other than that he was related to Willibrord of the Anglo-Saxon mission in Frisia. He went by pen-names or soubriquets, among them Albinus (acquired before his continental journeys) and Flaccus (his poetic name at Charlemagne's court). York had developed as an educational centre under arch-bishops Ecgbert (732–66), one of Bede's pupils (and addressee of Bede's last letter; possibly also the author of a penitential, Frantzen 1983a), and Ælberht (767–78). The latter's death Alcuin lamented in his *Versus de patribus, regibus et sanctis Euboricensis eccle-siae* (Godman 1984). Ælberht in particular Alcuin praises for his library-building efforts and dedicated teaching; upon Ælberht's elevation to the see at York in 767, Alcuin took over as master at the school of York (Dümmler 1966: 160). Alcuin's edu-cation at York, see of Deira, is further and late proof of the Northumbrian flowering in Latin letters and ecclesiastical development. Things would soon change. On his way to retrieve the pallium for Ælberht's successor Eanbald, Alcuin met Charlemagne at Parma 781/2; he was invited to run the palace school at Aachen, a post he accepted, leaving York not to return to England but for two visits (786, 790–3 – during the latter he served as an emissary of Charlemagne to Offa; Lapidge 1986b). Alcuin would write the majority of his works on the continent and leave behind the library at York he loved (though some its volumes apparently came with him to the continent), ending his career as the abbot at Tours (where he died, 19 May 804, and where Old English was apparently written: Lowe 1972: 342–4). But he became the 'architect of the "Carolingian Renaissance"' (Lapidge 1986b: 23) as Charlemagne's advisor. During Alcuin's lifetime the fate of first Northumbria, then the rest of Anglo-Saxon England, would be altered by the Viking raid on Lindisfarne in 793.

Though Alcuin is better remembered as a poet (at least more recently; Scott 1964), the scope of his writings is quite broad. The manuscript tradition of his surviving works is not as well investigated as that of Bede, but one need only consult the cata-logues of continental libraries to get a glimpse of how widespread his influence was (for example, that of the Bibliotheca Apostolica Vaticana). Alcuin's role in Carolin-gian Biblical exegesis is becoming better understood; he penned commentaries to Ecclesiastes, the genealogy of Christ in Matthew (*In genealogiam Christi*), the Gospel of John, and the Pauline epistles Ephesians (later used by Hrabanus Maurus for his own commentary), Titus, Philemon and Hebrews (Sharpe 1997: 36–46), as well as exegetical treatises on Genesis (*Quaestiones in Genesim*, of which there are fifty manu-script copies; PL 100: 515–66), the Psalms (*Expositio in Psalmos poenitentiales* and *Expo-sitio in Psalmos graduales*; PL 100: 569–96, 619–38), and the Song of Songs (*Compendium in Cantica canticorum*; PL 100: 642–64). He was also an active expounder of dogma, treating matters trinitarian and soteriological (*De fide sanctae et indiuiduae trinitatis*; PL 101: 11–58; *De trinitate ad Fredegisum quaestiones XXX*; PL 101: 57–64). He was, like Bede (at least on the matter of the date of Easter and orthodox chronol-ogy), a controversialist; his target was the heresy of Adoptionism in Visigothic and Muslim Spain, against which he wrote the *Aduersus Elipanum* (PL 101: 231–300; Eli-pandus was metropolitan of Muslim-controlled Toledo) and *Contra haeresim Felicis* (Blumenshine 1980; Bishop Felix of Urgel had defended Spanish teaching on Christ's *adoptio* of human nature). His letter to Beatus of Liébana in Asturias (Levison 1946:

314–23), Spanish abbot, author and defender against Adoptionism, also takes up the cause against Felix, who, in claiming Christ to be the adoptive son of God, 'step by step always sank to new depths' (Levison 1946: 319). Here in this letter Alcuin the churchman recapitulates arguments from the *Contra Felicem* and *Adversus Elipandum*, while Alcuin the rhetor deploys tricolon (*primo . . . secundo . . . tertio*) and antitheses (*unam . . . alteram . . . unam . . . alteram*) and Alcuin the poet concludes the letter with verse (*Incolomem Christi faciat te gratia semper*, 'Let Christ's grace ever make you safe and sound'; Levison 1946: 322; Rivera 1941).

The sacrament of confession held a particular concern for Alcuin; we have his *Confessio pura*, with its catalogue of body parts reminiscent of hisperic poems, and the treatises *De confessione peccatorum* (PL 101: 649–56) and *De uirtutibus et uitiis ad Widonem comitem* (PL 101: 613–38; also translated into Old English). Although what works precisely emanated from Alcuin's magisterial duties at Aachen's palace school have not been determined, we have sufficient evidence of his concern for education: a series of *disputationes* serving as rhetorical exemplars (*Disputatio de rhetorica et de uirtutibus*, PL 101: 919–46, Halm 1863: 525–50; *Disputatio Pippini cum Albino*, PL 101: 975–80), and trivial curricular texts such as the *Orthographia*, the *Dialogus Franconis et Saxonis de octo partibus orationis* (PL 101: 849–902; cf. Law 1994), and his edition of Priscian's *Institutiones grammaticae*.

Alcuin bequeathed the most extensive correspondence in Latin from the Anglo-Saxon period: over 270 letters survive (Chase 1975). A good many letters served to preface his numerous treatises, and a number of them included verses, such as those to monks going by the hypocorisms Dodo and Cuculus ('Cuckoo') or that concluding a letter to archbishop Æthelhard (Chase 1975).

Alcuin's letter to Bishop Speratus in December 796 expresses his growing worry at the state of affairs political and ecclesiastic in England. He recommends to Speratus Pope Gregory's *Pastoral Care* (*Cura pastoralis*), a work modestly described as a *libellus* in a letter that begins with effusions of modesty and self-deprecation then pro forma. Anglo-Latin writers, and Anglo-Saxon clerics in general, had a particular regard for Gregory the Great, natural enough in light of his role in the conversion. His letters were sought after and circulated in England, and the *Pastoral Care* was taken up as a handbook for ecclesiatical management. The *Pastoral Care* was one of the works included in King Alfred's translation programme; he seems to have made the translation himself (*c.*890) and his famous preface (Sweet 1871) expresses some of the same concerns Alcuin had a century earlier. Alcuin's letter to Speratus contains perhaps his most quoted phrase, *Quid Hinieldus cum Christo* ('What has Ingeld to do with Christ?'), an important reaffirmation of an opinion seen before and to be seen again in Anglo-Latin authors – a wariness of, if not at times contempt (moral in nature rather than aesthetic) for, the appeal of vernacular literature:

> Verba Dei legantur in sacerdotali conuiuio ibi decet lectorem audiri non citharistam sermones patrum non carmina gentilium. Quid Hinieldus cum Christo? Angusta est domus utrosque tenere non potuit.

The words of God are to be read at the priestly meal for there it is fitting to hear the reader not the harper, the sermons of the fathers not the songs of the folk. What has Ingeld to do with Christ? Narrow is the house – it cannot hold both.

Given the modern preoccupation (entirely warranted in Departments of English) with the vernacular literature of medieval England, Alcuin's statement is inconvenient for many critics whose opinion of what letters to value runs starkly contrary to Alcuin's, whose regard for Virgil, for one, has been described as ambiguous (Wieland 1992). Explaining it away is not at all necessary. Aldhelm, Bede, Boniface and many another Anglo-Latin author expressed similar sentiments – they were, after all, all of them churchmen. And the church in England was often in difficult straits (hence Alfred's concern a century later). Alcuin's letter is chiastically arranged to set off the vernacular songs with their 'antidote' in Gregory's *Pastoral Care* (Howlett 1997: 210). A series of antitheses shows Alcuin the teacher and rhetor at work: *decet lectorem audiri: non citharistam, sermones patrum: non carmina gentilium*. The choice is laid out with *Quid Hinieldus cum Christo?*, the constraint in a line with the terse gnomic style of the Vulgate: *Angusta est domus utrosque tenere non poterit*. The sentiment is similar to that expressed by St Augustine, who laments in his *Confessiones* the allure of the *dulcissimum spectaculum vanitatis* ('sweetest spectacle of vanity'; I.xiii) held out by Dido and Aeneas or the Trojan War, and asks *nonne ecce illa omnia fumus et ventus?* ('were not indeed all such things but smoke and wind?'; I.xvii). It is also a sentiment not a little disingenuous. Like Augustine, Aldhelm, Bede and Alcuin all press secular learning into the service of the church; and all, to judge for one by their allusions to and quotations of classical authors, never became immune to that sweetest spectacle of vanity. One sees in Alcuin the versifier one of the great Christian Latin poets who instructs as well as delights, and delights in his craft.

Alcuin's poetic corpus was assembled for the Monumenta Germaniae Historica edition (Dümmler 1966; Strecker 1923) from a variety of manuscript groups; Dümmler prints 124 verses, including the *Versus de patribus regibus et sanctis Euboricensis ecclesiae* (in 1,657 hexametric lines; Dümmler 1966: 169–206) and verse life of St Willibrord (Dümmler 1966: 207–20). Much of Alcuin's verse is occasional and concerns a 'circle' of friends and students, as well a series of poems to Emperor Charlemagne (carmina XLV, LXVIII explaining the books of the Bible, LXXIII, LXXVII). He wrote elaborate acrostics, which were imitated by his student Josephus Scottus; among them is the spectacular *De sancta cruce*, the acrostic lines of which form the figure of a diamond within a cross spelling out a sort of poem-within-the-poem.

Alcuin's poetic career spanned roughly 782–804, that is, his life after leaving York. His thoughts remained with his homeland; he produced, for instance, several poems on the sack of Lindisfarne (carmina XI–XIII). We have too a number of poems dealing with monastic life: the *praecepta vivendi* (carmen LXII), verses about libraries and refectories (C, CV), even the dormitory and latrine (XCVI). One of his most memorable verses is the *O mea cella*, one attributed to one of several of Alcuin's students rather than the master himself until recently (Godman 1985). The poem concerns in particular the loss of a monastic dwelling (surrounded by rivers and a little wood in bloom: *Silvula florigeris semper onusta comis* / . . . *Flumina te cingunt florentibus undique ripis*), in an extended sense the passing of a way of life – probably the life of Alcuin and his circle at Aachen. The poem opens up to a meditation on mutability, a genre well represented in the vernacular with the *lif is læne* ('life is fleeting') topos. Nothing lasts forever, nothing is really unchanging (*Nil manet aeternum, nihil immutabile vere est*): a sentiment expressed so well and often in Old English verse, the lines look back to Horace – it was not merely heady prepossession that led Alcuin to adopt the pseudonym Flaccus at Charlemagne's court.

Perhaps it is a curiosity of Anglo-Latin verse that one of its greatest practitioners spent his career at a foreign court. Life at court naturally enough serves as the subject of others of his verses. Charlemagne is addressed with his pseudonym David, and Alcuin's pupil and sometime rival poet Angilbert with 'Homerus'. Alcuin drew around himself an admiring circle of students and fellow poets, a number of whom are mentioned or addressed in his verses and would compose verse of their own (Frithugils, Moduin of Autun, Josephus Scottus, Angilbert, Dodo, Oswulf, Hrabanus Maurus, and possibly too Ædiluulf). Additionally, Alcuin was a hagiographer, as that was part of the function of his great poem on the church at York. Besides the 'Life of St Willibrord' *carmen* and *prosa* already mentioned, Alcuin penned a life of St Vaast and a poem on his church as well as a 'Life of St Richarius' (St Riquier).

Alcuin's output was all the more remarkable in that it preceded a relatively dormant period in Anglo-Latin. Early in the ninth century evidence of activity is provided by the Book of Cerne (Cambridge, University Library MS L1.1.10), a manuscript collection made for private devotion in Mercia *c.*820–40 (Brown 1996). An acrostic poem (fol. 21) is addressed to an *Aedeluald episcopus*, who may be Æthilwald, bishop of Lindisfarne (*c.*731–7/40); the manuscript also contains three prayers (the first to God the Father, the second to Christ, the third to the Virgin Mary) by the eighth-century monk Alchfrith (the *Orationes Alchfrithi*; Howlett 1997; Brown 1996). Also from the early ninth century is the *De abbatibus* of Ædiluulf of Northumbria (Campbell 1967). His poem, in 819 hexameters with some irregularities (Campbell 1967: xli–xliv), was dedicated to Ecgberht, bishop of Lindisfarne. As one would expect from its Northumbrian provenance, it was influenced by Bede's 'Life of Cuthbert' and Alcuin's poem on the bishops, kings and saints of York. Although Ædiluulf knew Aldhelm's verse (the *Carmen ecclesiastica* in particular), his diction is plainer than Aldhelm's 'hermeneutic' style. Ædiluulf also knew of the *Miracula Nynie episcopi* ('Miracles of St Nynia'), a metrical work produced in York by one of Alcuin's students (and sent to Alcuin for his perusal, as mentioned in one of his letters; Dümmler 1966: 431). The *De abbatibus* is part monastic chronicle, part miracle-book; internal evidence suggests it describes an unnamed Northumbrian monastery near Lindisfarne, in an area of Irish influence (Campbell 1967; Howlett 1997, who suggests Bywell). Ædiluulf gives us interesting portraits of the Irishman Ultan (a scribe so skilled that no writer living could be his equal, *ut nullus possit se aequare modernus* / *scriptor*; Campbell 1967) and Cwicwine, a monk skilled at iron-working: 'His hammer under wise guidance crashed on to the iron placed under it in different positions on the anvil, while the forge roared' (Campbell 1967: 24–5). Although Ædiluulf drew upon durable topoi in the literature of Anglo-Saxon England, we have little evidence of Anglo-Latin activity between his *floruit* (*c.*803–21) and the reform programme begun by King Alfred (871–99). Alfred lamented in the preface to his Old English version of Pope Gregory the Great's *Cura pastoralis* the decline in learning in England, Southumbria in particular. Viking raids and ecclesiastical disorganization had taken their toll. The flow of books to the continent in the eighth century that spurred on the Anglo-Saxon missions and new continental centres needed to be reversed in the ninth. It became a programme that had royal support from a king of the English.

The Age of Alfred

There is some debate whether King Alfred's lament for the decline in learning during the ninth century is to be taken literally or not. There is some evidence, from liturgical manuscripts and charters (Morrish 1988), of continued Anglo-Latin activity, albeit of less intensity and grammaticality. Viking forces entered Southumbria by 835 and the middle of the century was a time of constant skirmishing and warfare; Alfred's references to the burning of libraries by the Vikings seem borne out by the relatively small number of manuscripts surviving for the period; de luxe manuscripts seem to survive better, special efforts being made to save them from raids. Many manuscripts too seem to have been spirited away to the continent, to be returned later themselves or as copies. Scribal activity in presentation scripts such as uncial and half-uncial declines, though the early part of the century witnessed the production of illuminated large-format volumes. Few examples of more mundane manuscripts, such as classbooks, survive. Little Anglo-Latin literature can be dated to the period: perhaps one poem on St Swithun (d. 862) and a letter from Bishop Ecgred of Lindisfarne to Archbishop Wulfsige of York. Perhaps more telling are the infelicities and inferior Latinity of charters produced in the period. The picture on the continent is different, especially in Anglo-Saxon-influenced centres. The copying and assembly of *glossae collectae* continued (the Erfurt glossary was copied early in the late eighth to early ninth century at Cologne; Pheifer 1974), evidencing the survival of the teaching programme of Theodore and Hadrian *c.*670–710. At any rate, it remained for Alfred to enact systematic change.

Since the kingdom of Mercia fared somewhat better during ninth-century Viking raids than others, Alfred was able to draw on scholars from that region for his project of reconstruction – among them Plegmund (elevated to archbishop of Canterbury in 890) and Werferth (bishop of Worcester, translator of Gregory's *Dialogues*). With the fortunes of the English turning under Alfred's leadership, a need for a sense of origin and common destiny may have sparked the compilation of the Old English and Latin *Anglo-Saxon Chronicle*, the core of which may date to the 890s. The Welshman Asser, from St David's, composed the *De rebus gestis Ælfredi regis* (or *Vita Ælfredi regis*), the first biography of an Anglo-Saxon king (Keynes and Lapidge 1983). Asser had been elevated to the see of Aldhelm's Sherborne *c.*892–900; he seems to have imbibed Aldhelm's 'hermeneutic' or hisperic diction too. The work bears the imprint of Einhard's *Vita Karoli Magni*; the choice of model is apposite, as Alfred embarked on a similar programme of cultural renovation to that directed by Alcuin at Aachen. Alfred left a will datable to 888 or somewhat earlier (Harmer 1952: no. 11); it is one of only two wills of kings to survive (the other of Eadred, d. 955) among the fifty or so wills to survive from the Anglo-Saxon period.

Alfred's legacy of cultural revitalization extended through the reigns of Edward (899–924) and Æthelstan (924–39), his son and grandson. Writers and books from the continent came to Wessex and what could be called – after 927 – the 'Kingdom of the English'. By the late 890s the standard of Latinity had improved and insular Latin texts – such as Bede's *De temporum ratione*, Felix's *Vita sancti Guthlaci*, and the *Historia Brittonum* – were once again copied. Foreign-born scholars produced works in England, sometimes at court; three acrostics are believed to have been penned by John the Old Saxon, abbot of Athelney, including the *Archalis clamare* addressed to Æthelstan (Lapidge 1980c). The Frankish Fredegaud of Brioude (Frithegod of Canterbury) compiled the *Breviloquium uitae beati Wilfridi* at the request of Oda, archbishop of Canterbury (d. 959), following the removal of St Wilfrid's remains from Ripon (described as a *furtum sacrum*, 'sacred theft'), which had been burned down in the troubles involving Eric Bloodaxe. The hexametrical *Breviloquium*, and Oda's prose preface (which too may be by Frithegod), are influenced by the hermeneutic style (Lapidge 1975a; Campbell 1950). The involvement of talented foreigners in England would be evident as well in the next phase of revitalization, datable to the abbacy of St Dunstan (940–57), ushered in with the Benedictine Reform.

The Benedictine Reform

Alfred had sought to remedy the situation in which he claimed there to be no one south of the Humber sufficiently fluent in Latin. He had made a start with the recruitment of learned men and books, and provided for the founding of a monastery at Athelney and a convent at Shaftesbury. Much in the way of ecclesiastic reform was still needed and would come with the broad-ranging movement known as the Benedictine Reform. The movement in England was led by four Englishmen with experience on the continent: St Dunstan of Glastonbury, Æthelwold, bishop of Winchester, Oswald, bishop of Worcester, and Oda of Canterbury.

Oda came from an Anglo-Danish family of the Danelaw and had spent time at the monastery at Fleury (possibly receiving the tonsure there); he is said to have been fluent in Latin and Greek (Lapidge 1975a). Besides his prose *praefatio* to Frithegod's *Breviloquium* in 'hermeneutic' style (so popular in late Anglo-Latin), Oda concerned himself with ecclesiastical order and authored the *Constitutiones* (942–6), consisting of canons of ecclesiastic law (Whitelock et al. 1981; Gretsch 1999). Oda's nephew

Oswald, bishop of Worcester (961–92) and York (971–92), came to his uncle's residence at Canterbury and was instructed by Frithegod, though we have no surviving writings from him. Dunstan came from a wealthy Wessex family and was educated at Glastonbury; he was in residence at the court of Æthelstan, returning to Glastonbury sometime shortly after the king's death in 939. At Glastonbury Dunstan was joined by Æthelwold and the two studied together *c.*939–54 (Gretsch 1999); the *Vita Sancti Æthelwoldi* by Wulfstan of Winchester (fl. 1000) records as pleasant Æthelwold's tutelage under Dunstan.

Dunstan is said to have introduced the Rule of St Benedict while abbot at Glastonbury (Lapidge 1992). The two monks also brought new attention to fellow Wessex author Aldhelm and helped promote the *Regula Sancti Benedicti* in England. Dunstan's hand left its glosses and annotations to several manuscripts, including the famous 'St Dunstan's Classbook' (Oxford, Bodleian Library Auct. F.4.32). Dunstan left to us some poetry, including a complex acrostic verse *O Pater omnipotens* and three distichs on the organ, bell and ewer he received from Malmesbury abbey (Lapidge 1980a). Dunstan may very well have a biographer from his own household; the *Vita Sancti Dunstani*, which gives a stranger picture of Dunstan than Wulfstan's above, has been attributed to a late tenth-century author simply going by the initial B. Michael Lapidge has recently argued that B may have been a Byrhthelm, an associate who could have provided some of the vivid and seemingly first-hand details in the life.

Dunstan and Æthelwold both drew widespread admiration; about Dunstan grew a cult of veneration and lives by B, Adelard of Ghent (the early eleventh-century *Epistola de vita Sancti Dunstani*), William of Malmesbury, Osbern of Canterbury (*Vita et miracula Sancti Dunstani*) and Eadmer of Canterbury (Ramsay et al. 1992). Wulfstan of Winchester's *Vita Sancti Æthelwoldi* (abbreviated by Ælfric of Eynsham *c.*1004–6; Lapidge and Winterbottom 1991: 70–80) began the cult of Æthelwold; the future saint's mother is said to have had a vision while carrying him of a banner floating on high that lowered to cover her before wafting away once more, and of an eagle *quae uolando cuncta Wentanae ciuitatis aedificia auratis pennarum remigiis obumbrauit* ('in its flight it shaded all the buildings of Winchester with the gilded wings that carried it along'; Lapidge and Winterbottom 1991: 4–5). The subsequent wonders and signs of holiness in Wulfstan's Life of Æthelwold take us back to the 'Life of Wilfrid', the Lives of Cuthbert and Adomnán's 'Life of St Columba'.

His practical achievements in the English Benedictine Reform are worthy of equal praise. Æthelwold assembled the *Regularis concordia*, a 'monastic consuetudinary drafted . . . *c.*973 to establish uniformity in liturgical practice in the English reformed monasteries' (Gretsch 1999: 14), the *prohemium* to which gives play to the 'hermeneutic' style popular in the tenth century (Lapidge 1988c). The *Benedictional of Æthelwold* (London, British Library, Additional 49598), written in Caroline minuscule *c.*971–84, is a de luxe production recording the iconographic and liturgical style characteristic of Æthelwold's Winchester. Æthelwold was known as a great teacher; his students, such as Ælfric of Eynsham and Wulfstan of Winchester (precentor at the Old Minster), speak warmly of him. And his educational programme at Winchester rivalled, perhaps even surpassed, that of Theodore and Hadrian at Canterbury. The study of Aldhelm was given particular prominence in his school; some of the batches of glosses in the densely glossed Brussels 1650 manuscript of the prose *De virginitate* may derive from the school (Gretsch 1999: 148ff). Æthelwold was also a proficient Old English stylist. To him belong the Old English version of the *Regula Sancti Benedicti* commissioned by King Edgar and Queen Ælfthryth, an extensive corpus of Aldhelm glosses (such as those to the prose *De virginitate* in Brussels, Bibliothèque Royale 1650; Goossens 1974), and the Royal Psalter gloss (London, BL, Royal 2.B.v; Gretsch 1999). Æthelwold was on familiar terms with Edgar (Wulfstan, cap. 25), and perhaps had been the king's teacher at Abingdon, as suggested by Byrhtferth of Ramsey in his *Vita Sancti Oswaldi* (Lapidge and Winterbottom 1991: xlv). Æthelwold had been abbot at Abingdon *c*.954–63, which house produced an Anglo-Latin copy of the Benedictine rule *c*.1000 (Cambridge, Corpus Christi College 57; Gretsch 1999; Chamberlin 1982); Abingdon was also the centre for the cult of St Eustace in England, and it may have been there that a hexametrical version of the *Vita Sancti Eustachii* was made (Lapidge 1988c).

Liturgical reforms under Dunstan, Oswald and Æthelwold also brought to England (sometime in the period 940–70) the so-called 'New Hymnal', extant in England in Winchester and Canterbury recensions (Wieland 1982). The collection contains hymns by Ambrose, Prudentius, Sedulius, Venantius Fortunatus, Bede (Hymn 63, *Hymnum canamus domino*), Paul the Deacon, Alcuin (possibly Hymns 3–4), and Alcuin's student Hrabanus Maurus (Wieland 1982). A new age of productivity was ushered in at Winchester, which became a centre for Anglo-Latin and Old English literary activity (indeed, Winchester became the dialectal base for standard late Old English; Gneuss 1972). And the work of students of Æthelwold and his generation would represent the last stages of Anglo-Latin of the Anglo-Saxon age.

Late Anglo-Latin

Two of Æthelwold's students were remarkably prolific: Wulfstan in Latin, Ælfric in Latin and Old English. Wulfstan of Winchester wrote the longest and most metrically complex of Anglo-Latin works, the *Narratio metrica de Sancto Swithuno* in 3,300 hexameters *c*.992–4 (Campbell 1950; Lapidge and Winterbottom 1991: xxii for date). He also wrote hymns (*Aula superna poli, Aurea lux patriae*, and *Auxilium Domine qui te*) for Sts. Swithun and Birinus (both associated with the Old Minster, Winchester; Dronke et al. 1982), as well as the *Breviloquium de omnibus sanctis* in 716 hexameters framed by two acrostics (*VVLFSTANVS* and *NVNC ET IN AEVVM DEO GRATIAS AMEN*; Dolbeau 1988). Wulfstan, as precentor at Winchester, was instrumental in promoting the cult of St Æthelwold, composing, in addition to the *Vita Sancti Æthelwoldi episcopi* cited above (Lapidge and Winterbottom 1991), hymns, prayers and tropes required in the cult of this saint (Lapidge and Winterbottom 1991: xxv–xxvii; Sharpe 1997: 824–5; Frere 1894). As the man in charge of choral services at

Winchester and a renowned performer and composer (Gretsch 1999: 199), it comes as no suprise that a work on music is attributed to Wulfstan, the *De tonorum harmonia*; it survives only as quotations in the *Breviloquium super musicam* (Lapidge and Winterbottom 1991: xvi–xvii).

In his epitome of Wulfstan's *Vita Sancti Æthelwoldi*, Ælfric mentions himself as *Ælfricus abbas, Wintoniensis alumnus* and implies a contrast in styles with Wulfstan: the former more 'hermeneutic', himself briefer and 'rustic' or unsophisticated (*meatim sed et rustica*; Winterbottom 1972). Ælfric is less the belletrist and more the schoolman, as his pedagogical works show. After instruction in Æthelwold's school he assumed teaching duties at Cerne abbey; he became the first abbot of restored Eynsham in 1005. The bulk of his writings (two series of forty of *Sermones Catholici* and the *Lives of the Saints*) was in Old English. His *Grammar* and *Glossary* offer in Old English an introduction to the Latin language; his *Colloquy* offered practical assistance to the novice reader and writer of Latin. The *Colloquy* was imitated by others, including his student Ælfric Bata, who wrote the *Colloquia* and *Colloquia difficiliora*.

While at Cerne, Ælfric also made a translation into Old English of Bede's *De temporibus anni* (Henel 1942); one manuscript preserves the rubric *Incipiunt pauca de temporibus Bedae presbiteri* ('Here begin a few things concerning the times of Bede') and Ælfric notes his desire to make known the sense of Bede's treatise: *Ic wolde eac gif ic dorste gadrian sum gehwæde andgit of ðære bec þe BEDA se snotera lareow gesette · 7 gegaderode of manegra wisra lareowa bocum be ðæs geares ymbrenum · fram anginne middaneardes* ('I wished also if I might to gather some scant understanding of this book which Bede the wiser teacher composed, and I collected from the books of many wise teachers concerning the cycles of the year from the beginning of the world'; Henel 1942). It is significant that we have a churchman of this age whose primary output is in the vernacular; his *Grammar* (Zupitza 1880) is the first such guide to learning Latin in a European vernacular. His Latin style is also a break from the 'hermeneutic' style laden with Graecisms and arcana Æthelwold employed. As a grammarian, Ælfric seemed especially concerned with vocabulary (Law 1987); the concern of his *Glossary* is mirrored by the prodigious glossarial activity of late Anglo-Saxon scribes (one need only scan Ker's *Catalogue* to get a sense of how many of the 500 or so manuscripts containing Old English do so in the form of glosses). Ælfric's *Grammar* would remain a core text into the twelfth century and, as with his Old English *Lives of the Saints*, Ælfric left behind draft work of his endeavours: the unpublished *Excerptiones de Prisciano* show Ælfric selecting and abridging Priscian's standard *Institutiones grammaticae* (Law 1987). As a product of the Benedictine revival, Ælfric's concern for the monasteries extended to rules and customs; on these matters we have his *Epistola de ecclesiastica consuetudine* (often Anglicized as 'Letter to the Monks of Eynsham'; Jones 1998) and correspondence (Fehr 1914).

Associated also with Æthelwold's Winchester was the Frankish scholar Lantfred, who spent some time in residence at the Old Minster and penned the *Translatio et miracula Sancti Swithuni* (Bibliotheca hagiographica latina 7944–6) after the translation of the saint's relics to the Old Minster 15 July 971. Lantfred may have come to

Winchester, possibly from Fleury, at Æthelwold's request (Æthelwold had requested during his time at Abingdon and Winchester the assistance of monks from continental centres such as Corbie, Fleury and Ghent); the *Regularis concordia* shows the influence of Fleury practice. At any rate, Lantfred returned to Fleury after his Winchester stay. His writings include instances of Latinized French; he may be the author of three poems from Cambridge, University Library MS Kk.5.34 (Lapidge 1993a: 225–77, 484–6; cf. Orchard 1994: 68–9). The *Altercatio magistri et discipuli* consists of a dialogue in 125 hexameters between the teacher and student and a *responsio discipuli* in adonics (dactylic dimeter acatalectic, i.e. two dactylic feet, either – — or – –, not undergoing catalexis: the suppression of one or more syllables or positions in a line, usually in the final foot). The third poem is the *Carmen de libero arbitrio* ('Song on Free Will') in elegiac couplets (a line of dactylic hexameter paired with one in dactylic pentameter). The poem contains a number of Graecisms: *myrmica* ('ant'), *paradigma*, *sicophanta*, *hydromello* ('mead') and others; its vocabulary (in particular, terms of invective, ll. 14–18) may also display knowledge of Horace's *Sermones* ('Satires'; Lapidge 1993: 248–51).

As Lantfred may have come to Winchester at Æthelwold's invitation from Fleury, Abbo of Fleury came to Ramsey at the request of Bishops Dunstan and Oswald. Abbo stayed for two years (985–7) instructing students in matters metrical (his *Quaestiones grammaticales* may date to 985 × 987; Baker and Lapidge 1995) and computistical (for which studies he was well known; Sharpe 1997: 1–4). The Ramsey Abbo came to would have been a new establishment (founded *c.*966), in what was then fenlands, just north of Cambridge; it was considered a wealthy abbey by the time of the Domesday survey a little over a century later (Baker and Lapidge 1995: xv). For his students at Ramsey Abbo composed the *Passio Sancti Eadmundi*, chronicling the life of the martyred King Edmund of East Anglia (d. 869), the prologue to which is addressed to Dunstan (Winterbottom 1972). Abbo is said to have addressed a number of acrostics to Dunstan as well, some of which were quoted in Byrhtferth's *Vita Sancti Oswaldi* (Sharpe 1997: 1; Gwara 1992). Besides writing the two works for his students (his literary output in England), Abbo brought books with him to Ramsey, including his computus and Macrobius' Commentary to Cicero's *Somnium Scipionis* (Reynolds 1983: 229; Baker and Lapidge 1995: xxi–xxii).

Abbo's teaching at Ramsey covered the quadrivial subjects of arithmetic, music, geometry and astronomy, and his student Byrhtferth became the foremost scientific writer in pre-Conquest Anglo-Latin. Like Bede, he wrote treatises computistical, chronological and hagiographical. His style was less the classically influenced Latin of Bede and more the hermeneutic style of Aldhelm. No wonder then at the connections between 'glossary words' and Byrhtferth's diction; Byrhtferth collected glosses and supporting quotations to Bede's *De natura rerum* and *De temporum ratione* (Gorman 1996), and may be responsible for other glosses (Lapidge 1998). Byrhtferth wrote a *Vita Sancti Oswaldi* 997 × 1002, honouring the bishop of Worcester who had founded Ramsey during the Benedictine Reform (Baker and Lapidge 1995: xxix), and a *Vita Sancti Ecgwini*, written for the monks of Evesham to celebrate their monastery's founder St Ecgwine (d. 717; Lapidge 1979). Byrhtferth has been shown to have been behind the early sections of the *Historia regum* attributed to Symeon of Durham (Lapidge 1981a; Baker and Lapidge 1995: xxx–xxxi). His computus survives in one of the most fascinating manuscripts from Anglo-Saxon England: Oxford, St John's College MS 17 (Wallis 1985, 1996). Byrhtferth assembled in his computus or *Epilogus*, or computistical commonplace book (Lapidge 1986b: 30), his own knowledge of calendrical calculation (under the tutelage of Abbo and from his computus), with that of Bede and Helperic (*De computo ecclesiastico*). Included in this commonplace book is the *Anthologia latina* verse *Bis sena mensum uertigine uoluitur annus* ('The year turns on the axis of twice-six months'; Riese 1894: no. 680; Baker and Lapidge 1995: 46–7), contained in two ninth-century St Gall Bede manuscripts with Anglo-Saxon connections (Stiftsbibliothek MSS 250 and 251; McGowan forthcoming).

The major work in Byrhtferth's canon is his *Manual* or *Enchiridion* (Baker and Lapidge 1995), composed approximately 1010–12 (Baker and Lapidge 1995: xxviii). Byrhtferth's work is in large part pedagogical, and follows in Latin and Old English, with some sections marked with the rubric *þus on Englisc*. Included in the work is a version of the popular *sex aetates mundi* (Tristram); Byrhtferth explains that such things as the 'Six Ages of the World' are from ancient authorities and are well understood by monks nourished by the *alma mater* of the Catholic church (Baker and Lapidge 1995: 232). A similar concern for the ages of man led the Dorset ealdorman Æthelweard to translate the *Anglo-Saxon Chronicle* from creation to 975 into Latin (Æthelweard's *Chronica*; Sharpe 1997: 31). Æthelweard was also a patron of Ælfric of Eynsham. Time had its own genre in Anglo-Latin: the making of calendars (Wormald 1934) and metrical calendars, such as that composed at Ramsey in the 990s. Unbeknownst to these writers at the turn of the millennium, a new age was soon to come. It would particularly change the church hierarchy in England.

Eleventh-century Anglo-Latin remains the least investigated; as with other periods, hagiography remained an important genre. British Library, MS Cotton Vitellius E.xii, preserves the royal acclamations (the *Laudes regiae*) for Queen Mathilda's coronation at Westminster Abbey, 11 May 1068, by Ealdred, archbishop of York. Ealdred had revived the centre at York and was a leading figure of his day; he had also crowned Harold Godwinson and William the Conqueror. The author of the *Laudes regiae* may have come from Ealdred's household – namely, the Flemish Benedictine Folchard of Saint-Bertin (Lapidge 1983). Ealdred had requested Folchard to write a life of John of Beverley (*Vita Sancti Iohannis Beuerlacensis*), whose cult Ealdred was promoting. Folchard also wrote lives of Saints Bertin and Botulph and of Edward the Confessor (Sharpe 1997: 116–17). Goscelin, a fellow Flemish monk from Saint-Bertin, became precentor at St Augustine's, Canterbury, and wrote lives of a variety of saints from or associated with early England: Hildelith; Mildred; Edith; Æthelburga; the early bishops Laurence, Mellitus, Justus and Deusdedit; Milburg; archbishop Theodore; Werburg; Erkenwald; and others (Sharpe 1997). The *Encomium Emmae Reginae* may have been written in England by an anonymous Flemish monk, probably from the centre at Saint-Omer, Flanders (Campbell 1998). The sole witness, British Library,

Additional 33241, was written and illustrated towards the middle or last quarter of the eleventh century; for a time it was at St Augustine's, Canterbury (Campbell 1998: xli–xlvi). Emma (Ælfgifu Imma) had been queen twice, as wife of Æthelred the Unready (1002–16) and then of Cnut (1017–35), and had commissioned the work, perhaps while in exile in Flanders 1037–40 (Campbell 1998: xix). It is an important account of the Danish invasion of the early eleventh century and the turmoil during and after the reign of Cnut to approximately 1042, as well, of course, as a work in praise of Queen Emma.

The Fate of Anglo-Latin

The Anglo-Latin that had recorded the process of conversion of the English, served its liturgical needs, and put into writing deeds, charters, laws, manumissions, wills and episcopal letters, before the vernacular began also to assume those duties, was not to survive the Norman Conquest long. Forms of continuity to be sure may be found. Lives of Anglo-Saxon saints continued to be redacted and composed after the Conquest (for example, a life of St Ecgwine by Dominic of Evesham; Sharpe 1997: 99–100), and this genre was particularly productive during the critical eleventh century (Lapidge 1986b). Some of the great Anglo-Latin authors of the Anglo-Saxon period were still studied – Bede notably – while others, like Aldhelm, sank into obscurity. Latin remained the primary language of church and official state records. Its epistolary literature still thrived. But the changeover in church hierarchy from Anglo-Saxon to Norman altered for good the ecclesiastical centres and their schools.

The use of Latin in Anglo-Saxon England was essential to its intellectual development. The far better-known and better-studied vernacular literature of Anglo-Saxon England is only part of the picture (and constitutes a smaller surviving corpus). Vital to an understanding of the literary activity 500–1100 is the Anglo-Latin corpus: the authors we know of proficient in Latin and English make this clear. Latin was certainly altered by having been used in Anglo-Saxon England. The *Dictionary of Medieval Latin from British Sources* (Latham et al. 1975–) and its *Revised Latin Word-list from British and Irish Sources* (Latham 1965) evidence how vocabulary in particular developed in Britain. Bilingual glossaries (such as the Leiden group, Corpus, Épinal-Erfurt and Harley) preserve traces of educational habits, texts read and types of knowledge sought. And, for a time, Anglo-Latin extended its orbit beyond the British Isles, those versed in it travelling the paths of earlier Irish *peregrini* to found new houses and instruct their pupils. Anglo-Latin authors brought fame to Britain abroad that the vernacular literature of the time could not, one becoming among the most-read authors of early medieval Europe, another the architect of the Carolingian Renaissance. In a manuscript of Bede's *De arte metrica* now housed in Biblioteca Apostolica Vaticana (Ottobon. Lat. 1354, s. xi–xii), an anonymous acrostic on this *famulus Christi* gives modest witness to this achievement:

Largifluis libris praefatus fulsit in orbe,
Ex quis ornatus foecunda britannia splendet. (Kendall 1975: 71)

The aforesaid [Bede] shone the world over with his abundant writings,
Adorned by whom bountiful Britain glows.

References

References given here also apply to chapter 17.

Primary sources

Allott, Stephen, tr. 1974. *Alcuin of York, his Life and Letters*. York.

Anderson, A. O. and M. O. Anderson, eds 1961. *Adomnan's Life of Columba*. Edinburgh. 2nd edn, Oxford, 1991.

Baker, Peter S. and Michael Lapidge, eds and trans. 1995. *Byrhtferth of Ramsey: Enchiridion*. EETS, s.s. 15. Oxford.

Bieler, Ludwig, ed. 1952. *Libri Epistolarum Sancti Patricii Episcopi*. 2 vols. Dublin.

Bierbaumer, Peter 1975–9. *Der botanische Wortschatz des Altenglischen*. 3 vols. Bern.

Bischoff, Bernhard and Michael Lapidge, eds 1994. *Biblical Commentaries from the Canterbury School of Theodore and Hadrian*. CSASE 10. Cambridge.

Blumenshine, Gary B., ed. 1980. Alcuin. *Liber Alcuini contra haeresim Felicis*. Vatican City.

Bowman, Alan K. 1983. *The Roman Writing Tablets from Vindolanda*. London.

——and J. David Thomas 1984. *Vindolanda: The Latin Writing-Tablets*. London.

Campbell, Alistair, ed. 1950. *Frithegodi monachi Breuiloquium vitae beati Wilfredi et Wulfstani Cantoris Narratio metrica de sancto Swithuno*. Zurich.

——, ed. 1962. *Æthelweard. Chronica*. Edinburgh.

——, ed. 1967. *Æthelwulf. De abbatibus*. Oxford.

——, ed. 1973. *Charters of Rochester*. Anglo-Saxon Charters I. London.

——, ed. 1998. *Encomium Emmae Reginae*. Suppl. intro. Simon Keynes. Cambridge.

Chamberlin, John 1982. *The Rule of St Benedict: The Abingdon Copy*. Toronto Medieval Latin Texts 13. Toronto.

Chase, Colin 1975. *Two Alcuin Letter-Books*. Toronto Medieval Latin Texts 5. Toronto.

Colgrave, Bertram, ed. 1927. *The Life of Bishop Wilfrid by Eddius Stephanus*. Cambridge.

——, ed. 1940. *Two Lives of Saint Cuthbert: A Life by an Anonymous Monk of Lindisfarne and Bede's Prose Life*. Cambridge.

——, ed. 1956. *Felix's Life of Saint Guthlac*. Cambridge.

——1968. *The Earliest Life of Gregory the Great by an Anonymous Monk of Whitby*. Lawrence, KS.

——and R. A. B. Mynors, eds 1969. *Bede's Ecclesiastical History of the English People*. Oxford Medieval Texts. Oxford.

Corrêa, Alicia, ed. 1992. *The Durham Collectar*. Henry Bradshaw Society 107. London.

de Bruyn, Theodore 1998. *Pelagius's Commentary on St Paul's Epistle to the Romans*. Oxford.

De Marco, Maria, ed. 1968. *Tatuini opera omnia*. CCSL 133. Turnhout.

Dewick, E. S. and W. H. Frere, eds 1921. *The Leofric Collectar II*. Henry Bradshaw Society 56. London.

Dobbie, Elliott Van Kirk 1937. *The Manuscripts of Cædmon's Hymn and Bede's Death Song, with a Critical Text of the Epistola Cuthberti de obitu Bedae*. New York.

Dolbeau, F. 1988. 'Le *Breuiloquium de omnibus sanctis*: un poème inconnu de Wulfstan, chantre de Winchester'. *Analecta Bollandiana* cvi: 35–98.

Dümmler, Ernst, ed. 1966. Alcuin. *Carmina*. Monumenta Germaniae Historica, Poetae Latini Aevi Carolini 1. Berlin.

Dumville, David N. 1976. 'The Anglian Collection of Royal Genealogies and Regnal Lists'. *Anglo-Saxon England* 5: 23–50.

Ehwald, Rudolf, ed. 1919. *Aldhelmi Opera*. Monumenta Germaniae Historica, Auctorum Antiquissimorum XV. Berlin.

Fehr, Bernhard, ed. 1914. *Die Hirtenbriefe Ælfrics*. Bibliothek der angelsächsischen Prosa 9.

Hamburg. Repr. intro. Peter Clencoes. Darmstadt, 1966.

Fraipont, J., ed. 1955–80. *Bedae Venerabilis Opera*. CCSL 118A, 119, 119A, 120, 122, 123A, 123B, 123C. Turnhout.

Frere, W. H., ed. 1894. *The Winchester Troper*. Henry Bradshaw Society 8. London.

Garmonsway, G. N., ed. 1947. *Ælfric's Colloquy*. 2nd edn, London, 1965.

Gebauer, George John and Bengt Löfstedt, eds 1980. Boniface. *Ars grammatica. Ars metrica*. CCSL 133B. Turnhout.

Glorie, Fr., ed. 1968. *Collectiones aenigmatum Merovingicae aetatis*. CCSL 133. Turnhout.

Godman, Peter, ed. 1984. Alcuin. *Versus de patribus regibus et sanctis Eboracensis ecclesiae*. Oxford.

——1985. *Poetry of the Carolingian Renaissance*. Norman, OK.

Goolden, Peter, ed. 1958. *The Old English Apollonius of Tyre*. Oxford.

Goossens, Louis, ed. 1974. *The Old English Glosses of MS Brussels Royal Library 1650 (Aldhelm's De laudibus virginitatis)*. Verhandelingen van de Koninklijke Academie voor Wetenschapen, Letteren en Schone Kunsten van België, Klasse der Letteren 74. Brussels.

Günzel, Beate, ed. 1993. *Ælfwine's Prayerbook. (London, British Library, Cotton Titus D. xxvi + xxvii.)* Henry Bradshaw Society 108. London.

Gwara, Scott 1992. 'Three Acrostic Poems by Abbo of Fleury'. *Journal of Medieval Latin* 2: 203–35.

——1996. *Latin Colloquies from Pre-Conquest Britain*. Toronto Medieval Latin Texts 22. Toronto.

Hagen, Herman 1877. *Carmina medii aevi maximam partem inedita. Ex bibliothecis Helveticis collecta*. Bern.

Halm, Karl 1863. *Rhetores latini minores*. Leipzig.

Harmer, Florence E. 1952. *Anglo-Saxon Writs*. Manchester.

Henel, Heinrich, ed. 1942. *Ælfric's De Temporibus Anni*. EETS, o.s. 213. London.

Herren, Michael, ed. 1974–87. *The Hisperica Famina I: The A-Text. II: Related Poems*. Pontifical Institute of Mediaeval Studies, Studies and Texts 31 and 85. Toronto.

Hughes, Anselm, ed. 1958–60. *The Portiforium of Saint Wulstan*. 2 vols. Henry Bradshaw Society 89–90. London.

Hurst, D., ed. 1969–83. Bede. *Opera Exegetica*. CCSL 119–21. Turnhout.

James, M. R. 1914. 'St Boniface's Poem to Nithardus'. *English Historical Review*: 94.

Jones, C. W., ed. 1975a. Bede. *De orthographia. De natura rerum*. CCSL 123A. Turnhout.

——, ed. 1975b. Bede. *De temporum ratione*. CCSL 123B. Turnhout.

——, ed. 1980. Bede. *De temporibus*. CCSL 123C. Turnhout.

Jones, Christopher A., ed. 1998. *Ælfric's Letter to the Monks of Eynsham*. CSASE 24. Cambridge.

Keil, Heinrich, ed. 1855–80. *Grammatici latini*. 7 vols. Leipzig.

Kendall, Calvin B., ed. 1975. Bede. *De arte metrica. De schematibus et tropis*. CCSL 123A. Turnhout.

Keynes, Simon 1996. *The Liber Vitae of the New Minster and Hyde Abbey Winchester: British Library Stowe 944*. EEMF 26. Copenhagen.

——and Michael Lapidge 1983. *Alfred the Great: Asser's Life of King Alfred and Other Contemporary Sources*. Harmondsworth.

Kuypers, A. B., ed. 1902. *The Prayer Book of Aedeluald the Bishop Commonly called the Book of Cerne*. Cambridge.

Lapidge, Michael 1975a. 'Some Remnants of Bede's Lost *Liber epigrammatum*'. *English Historical Review* 90: 798–820.

——, ed. 1991. *Anglo-Saxon Litanies of the Saints*. Henry Bradshaw Society 106. London.

——and Michael Winterbottom, eds 1991. *Wulfstan of Winchester. Life of St Æthelwold*. Oxford Medieval Texts. Oxford.

Latham, R. E. 1965. *Revised Medieval Latin Word-List from British and Irish Sources*. London. Repr. 1989.

Law, Vivien 1987. 'Anglo-Saxon England: Ælfric's *Excerptiones de arte grammatica anglice*'. *Histoire, épistémologie, langage* 9: 47–71.

Levison, Wilhelm, ed. 1905. *Vita Bonifatii Auctore Willibaldo*. Monumenta Germaniae Historica. Leipzig.

——, ed. 1919–20. Alcuin. *Vita Willibrordi. Passiones Vitaeque Sanctorum Aevi Merovingici*, pp. 113–41. Eds B. Krusch and W. Levison. Monumenta Germaniae Historica, Scriptores rerum. Merovingicanum 7. Hanover.

Marsden, Richard 1995. *The Text of the Old Testament in Anglo-Saxon England*. CSASE 15. Cambridge.

O'Meara, John J., ed. 1949. Gerald of Wales. *Topographia Hiberniae*. Dublin.

Orchard, Andy 1995. *Pride and Prodigies: Studies in the Monsters of the Beowulf-Manuscript*. Cambridge.

Pheifer, J. D. 1974. *Old English Glosses in the Épinal-Erfurt Glossary*. Oxford.

Plummer, Charles, ed. 1896. *Venerabilis Baedae opera historica*. 2 vols. Oxford. Repr. 1966.

Porsia, Franco, ed. 1976. *Liber monstrorum*. Bari.

Pulsiano, Phillip, ed. 2001. *Old English Glossed Psalters: Pss 1–50*. Toronto.

Rees, B. R. 1991. *The Letters of Pelagius and his Followers*. Woodbridge.

Riese, Alexander, ed. 1894–1906. *Anthologia Latina*. 2 vols. Leipzig.

Roberts, Jane, ed. 1979. *The Guthlac Poems of the Exeter Book*. Oxford.

Schmeling, Gareth, ed. 1988. *Historia Apollonii regis Tyri*. Leipzig.

Sharpe, Richard 1995. *Adomnán's Life of St Columba*. Harmondsworth.

Stevenson, W. H. 1959. *Asser's Life of King Alfred together with the Annals of Saint Neots Erroneously Ascribed to Asser*. Oxford, 1904. Repr. ed. Dorothy Whitelock, 1959.

Strecker, Karl, ed. 1923. Alcuin. *Carmina rhythmica*. Monumenta Germaniae Historica, Poetae Latini Aevi Carolini 4.3.

Sweet, Henry, ed. 1871. *King Alfred's West-Saxon Version of Gregory's Pastoral Care*. EETS, o.s. 45, 50. London.

Talbot, C. H., trans. 1954. *The Anglo-Saxon Missionaries to Germany*. London.

Tangl, Michael, ed. 1955. *Die Briefe des Heiligen Bonifatius und Lullus*. Monumenta Germaniae Historica, Epistolae Selectae 1. Berlin.

Tristram, Hildegard L. C. 1985. *Sex aetates mundi: die Weltzeitalter bei den Angelsachsen und den Iren*. Heidelberg.

Whitelock, Dorothy, ed. 1955. *English Historical Documents I: 500–1042*. London. 2nd edn, 1979.

——, M. Brett and C. N. L. Brooke, eds 1981. *Councils and Synods with other Documents Relating to the English Church*. 2 vols. Oxford.

Wieland, Gernot, ed. 1982. *The Canterbury Hymnal*. Toronto Medieval Latin Texts 12. Toronto.

Wilson, H. A., ed. 1918. *The Calendar of St Willibrord*. Henry Bradshaw Society 55. London.

Winterbottom, Michael, ed. 1972. *Three Lives of English Saints*. Toronto Medieval Latin Texts 1. Toronto.

——ed. and trans. 1978. *Gildas: The Ruin of Britain and Other Works*. London.

Wormald, Francis 1934. *English Kalendars before A.D. 1100*. Henry Bradshaw Society 72. London.

Zupitza, Julius, ed. 1880. *Ælfrics Grammatik und Glossar*. Sammlung englischer Denkmäler. Berlin.

Secondary sources

Backhouse, Janet 1997. *The Illuminated Page: Ten Centuries of Manuscript Painting in the British Library*. London.

Bischoff, Bernhard 1972. 'Die Bibliothek im Dienste der Schule'. *Mittelalterliche Studien* Band III, pp. 213–33. Stuttgart, 1981.

Brooks, Nicholas 1984. *The Early History of the Church of Canterbury: Christ Church from 597 to 1066*. Studies in the Early History of Britain. Leicester.

Brown, George Hardin 1987. *Bede the Venerable*. Boston.

Brown, Michelle P. 1994. *Understanding Illuminated Manuscripts: A Guide to the Technical Terms*. Malibu, CA.

——1996. *The Book of Cerne: Prayer, Patronage, and Power in Ninth-Century England*. London.

Bruce-Mitford, Rupert 1967. *The Art of the Codex Amiatinus*. Jarrow Lecture. Jarrow.

Campbell, Alistair 1959. *Old English Grammar*. Oxford.

Cary, George 1956. *The Medieval Alexander*. Ed. D. J. A. Ross. Cambridge.

Conte, Gian Biagio 1994. *Latin Literature: A History*. Baltimore.

Deshman, Robert 1995. *The Benedictional of Æthelwold*. Princeton, NJ.

Dolbeau, François 1982. 'La tradition textuelle du poème d'Alcuin sur York'. *Mittellateinisches Jahrbuch* 17: 26–30.

Dronke, Peter, Michael Lapidge and P. Stotz 1982. 'Die unveröffentlichen Gedichte der Cambridger Liederhandschrift'. *Mittellateinisches Jahrbuch* xvii: 59–65.

Dumville, David N. 1977. 'Kingship, Genealogies and Regnal Lists'. *Early Medieval Kingship*, pp.

72–104. Eds P. H. Sawyer and I. N. Wood. Leeds.

——1984. 'Gildas and Uinniau'. *Gildas: New Approaches*, pp. 207–14. Eds Michael Lapidge and David Dumville. Woodbridge.

——1992. *Liturgy and the Ecclesiastical History of Late Anglo-Saxon England*. Woodbridge.

Frantzen, Allen J. 1983a. *The Literature of Penance in Anglo-Saxon England*. New Brunswick, NJ.

——1983b. 'The Tradition of Penitentials in Anglo-Saxon England'. *Anglo-Saxon England* 11: 23–56.

Gneuss, Helmut 1972. 'The Origin of Standard Old English and Æthelwold's School at Winchester'. *Anglo-Saxon England* 1: 63–83.

——1981. 'A Preliminary List of Manuscripts Written or Owned in England up to 1100'. *Anglo-Saxon England* 9: 1–60.

Gorman, M. M. 1996. 'The "Byrhtferth Glosses" on Bede's *De temporum ratione*'. *Anglo-Saxon England* 25: 209–33.

Gratwick, A. S. 1982. 'Latinitas Britannica: Was British Latin Archaic?' *Latin and the Vernacular Languages in Early Medieval Britain*, pp. 1–79. Ed. Nicholas Brooks. Leicester.

Gretsch, Mechthild 1999. *The Intellectual Foundations of the English Benedictine Reform*. CSASE 25. Cambridge.

Herren, Michael W. 1974. 'Hisperic Latin – "Luxuriant Culture-Fungus of Decay"'. *Traditio* 30: 411–19.

——1998. 'Scholarly Contacts between the Irish and the Southern English in the Seventh Century'. *Peritia* 12: 24–53.

Howe, Nicholas 1985. *The Old English Catalogue Poems*. Copenhagen.

Howlett, David R. 1994. 'Aldhelm and Irish Learning'. *Archivum Latinitatis Medii Aevi (Bulletin du Cange)* 52: 37–75.

——1997. *British Books in Biblical Style*. Dublin.

Jackson, Kenneth Hurlstone 1953. *Language and History in Early Britain: A Chronological Survey of the Brittonic Languages First to Twelfth Century* AD. Edinburgh.

——1968. 'Le Latin du De excidis Britanniae de Gildas'. *Christianity in Britain, 300–700*, pp. 151–76. Eds M. W. Barley and R. P. C. Hanson. Leicester.

Keynes, Simon 1985. 'King Æthelstan's Books'. *Learning and Literature in Anglo-Saxon England.*

Studies Presented to Peter Clemoes on the Occasion of his Sixty-fifth Birthday, pp. 143–201. Eds Michael Lapidge and Helmut Gneuss. Cambridge.

Lapidge, Michael 1972. 'Three Latin Poems from Æthelwold's School at Winchester'. *Anglo-Saxon England* 1: 85–137.

——1975b. 'The Hermeneutic Style in Tenth-century Anglo-Latin Literature'. *Anglo-Saxon England* 4: 67–111.

——1979. 'Aldhelm's Latin Poetry and Old English Verse'. *Comparative Literature* 31: 249–314.

——1980a. 'St Dunstan's Latin Poetry'. *Anglia* 98: 101–6.

——1980b. 'Some Latin Poems as Evidence for the Reign of Athelstan'. *Anglo-Saxon England* 9: 61–98.

——1981. 'Byrhtferth of Ramsey and the Early Sections of the *Historia Regum* Attributed to Symeon of Durham'. *Anglo-Saxon England* 10: 97–122.

——1982a. '"Beowulf", Aldhelm, the "Liber Monstrorum" and Wessex'. *Studi Medievali* 23: 151–92.

——1982b. 'The Study of Latin Texts in Late Anglo-Saxon England (1): The Evidence of Latin Glosses'. *Latin and the Vernacular Languages in Early Medieval Britain*, pp. 99–140. Ed. Nicholas Brooks. Leicester.

——1983. 'Ealdred of York and MS. Cotton Vitellius E. xii'. *Yorkshire Archaeological Journal* 55: 11–25.

——1984. 'Gildas's Education and the Latin Culture of Sub-Roman Britain'. *Gildas: New Approaches*, pp. 27–50. Eds Michael Lapidge and David Dumville. Studies in Celtic History 5. Woodbridge.

——1985. 'A Seventh-century Insular Latin Debate Poem on Divorce'. *Cambridge Medieval Celtic Studies* 10: 1–23.

——1986. 'The Anglo-Latin Background'. *A New Critical History of Old English Literature*, pp. 5–37. Eds Stanley B. Greenfield and Daniel G. Calder. New York.

——1988. 'Æthelwold as Scholar and Teacher'. *Bishop Æthelwold: His Career and Influence*, pp. 89–117. Ed. Barbara Yorke. Woodbridge.

——1992. 'B. and the *Vita S. Dunstani*'. *St Dunstan: His Life, Times and Cult*, pp. 247–59.

Eds Nigel Ramsay, Margaret Sparks and Tim Tatton-Brown. Woodbridge.

——1993. *Anglo-Latin Literature, 900–1066.* London.

——1995. 'Theodore and Anglo-Latin Octosyllabic Verse'. *Archbishop Theodore: Commemorative Studies on his Life and Influence*, pp. 260–280. Ed. Michael Lapidge. Cambridge.

——1998. 'Byrhtferth at Work'. *Words and Works: Studies in Medieval English Language and Literature in Honour of Fred C. Robinson*, pp. 25–43. Eds Peter S. Baker and Nicholas Howe. Toronto.

——and Richard Sharpe 1985. *A Bibliography of Celtic–Latin Literature 400–1200.* Dublin.

Law, Vivien 1979. 'The Transmission of the *ars Bonifacii* and the *ars Tatuini*'. *Revue d'Histoire des Textes* 9: 281–8.

——1982. *The Insular Latin Grammarians.* Studies in Celtic History 3. Woodbridge.

Lendinara, Patrizia 1996. 'L'attività glossatoria del periodo anglosassone'. *Les manuscrits des lexiques et glossaires de l'antiquité tardive à la fin du moyen âge*, pp. 615–55. Ed. Jacqueline Hamesse. Louvain-la-neuve.

Levison, Wilhelm. 1946. *England and the Continent in the Eighth Century.* Oxford.

Lowe, E. A. 1934–66. *Codices Latini Antiquiores.* 11 vols. Oxford. 2nd edn, 1934–72. 12 vols.

Mantello, F. A. C. and A. G. Rigg, eds 1996. *Medieval Latin: An Introduction and Bibliographical Guide.* Washington, DC.

Marenbon, J. 1979. 'Les sources du vocabulaire d'Aldhelm'. *Archivum Latinitatis Medii Aevi (Bulletin du Cange)* 41: 75–90.

McGowan, Joseph 1990. 'Apolloniana'. *Archiv für das Studium der neueren Sprachen und Literaturen* 227:130–8.

——forthcoming. 'Anthologia Latina'. *Sources of Anglo-Saxon Literary Culture.*

McGurk, Patrick 1956. 'The Irish Pocket Gospel Book'. *Sacris erudiri* 8: 250–69.

Meyer, Kuno 1913. *Learning in Ireland in the Fifth Century and the Transmission of Letters: A Lecture Delivered before the School of Irish Learning in Dublin on September 18th, 1912.* Dublin.

Morrish, Jennifer 1988. 'Dated and Datable Manuscripts Copied in England during the Ninth Century: A Preliminary List'. *Mediaeval Studies* 50: 512–38.

Ó Cróinín, Dáibhí 1983. 'The Irish Provenance of Bede's Computus'. *Peritia* 2: 229–47.

——1995. *Early Medieval Ireland.* London.

Ogilvy, J. D. A. 1967. *Books Known to the English 597–1066.* Cambridge, MA.

Orchard, Andy 1992. 'After Aldhelm: The Teaching and Transmission of the Anglo-Latin Hexameter'. *Journal of Medieval Latin* 2: 1–43.

——1994. *The Poetic Art of Aldhelm.* Cambridge Studies in Anglo-Saxon England 8. Cambridge.

Perry, Ben Edwin 1967. *The Ancient Romances: A Literary-Historical Account of their Origins.* Berkeley, CA.

Pfaff, Richard W. ed. 1995. *The Liturgical Books of Anglo-Saxon England.* Old English Newsletter Subsidia 23. Kalamazoo, MI.

Prescott, Andrew 1987. 'The Structure of English Pre-Conquest Benedictionals'. *British Library Journal* 13: 118–58.

——1988. 'The Text of the Benedictional of St Æthelwold'. *Bishop Æthelwold: His Career and Influence*, pp. 119–47. Ed. Barbara Yorke. Woodbridge.

——Pulsiano, Phillip 1999. 'Blessed Bodies: The Vitae of Anglo-Saxon Female Saints'. *Parergon* 16: 1–42.

Ramsay, N., M. Sparks and T. Tatton-Brown, eds 1992. *St Dunstan: His Life, Time and Cult.* Woodbridge.

Reynolds, L. D., ed. 1983. *Texts and Transmission: A Survey of the Latin Classics.* Oxford.

Rigg, A. G. 1992. *A History of Anglo-Latin Literature, 1066–1422.* Cambridge.

Rollason, D. W. 1989. *Saints and Relics in Anglo-Saxon England.* Oxford.

Scott, Peter Dale 1964. 'Alcuin as a Poet: Rhetoric and Belief in his Latin Verse'. *University of Toronto Quarterly* 33: 233–57.

Sharpe, Richard 1997. *A Handlist of the Latin Writers of Great Britain and Ireland before 1540.* Turnhout.

Stevenson, Jane 1989. 'The Beginnings of Literacy in Ireland'. *Proceedings of the Royal Irish Academy* 89C: 127–65.

Wallace-Hadrill, J. M. 1988. *Bede's Ecclesiastical History of the English People: A Historical Commentary.* Oxford Medieval Texts. Oxford.

Wallis, Faith 1985. 'MS Oxford, St John's College 17: A Medieval Manuscript in its Contexts'. PhD dissertation, University of Toronto.

——1996. 'Chronology and Systems of Dating'.

Medieval Latin: An Introduction and Bibliographic Guide, pp. 383–7. Eds F. A. C. Mantello and A. G. Rigg. Washington, DC.

Whitbread, Leslie 1974. 'The Liber Monstrorum and Beowulf'. *Medieval Studies* 36: 434–71.

Winterbottom, Michael 1967. 'On the *Hisperica Famina*'. *Celtica* 8: 127–39.

——1972. 'Three Lives of St Ethelwold'. *Medium Ævum* 41: 191–201.

——1976. Review of Herren 1974. *Medium Ævum* 45: 105–9.

Wollmann, Alfred 1990. *Untersuchungen zu den frühen lateinischen Lehnwörtern im Altenglischen: Phonologie und Datierung*. Munich.

3
Transmission of Literature and Learning: Anglo-Saxon Scribal Culture

Jonathan Wilcox

A colophon to the great Irish epic, *The Táin*, contained in the twelfth-century book of Leinster, nicely exemplifies the tension between a scribe and the work which he has transmitted:

> I who have copied down this story, or more accurately fantasy, do not credit the details of the story, or fantasy. Some things in it are devilish lies, and some poetical figments; some seem possible and others not; some are for the enjoyment of idiots. (Kinsella 1970: 283)

While Anglo-Saxon scribes have not recorded any such clear-cut critiques of the nature of fiction, they do occasionally critique the works they reproduce, as in the responses to Ælfric's writings described below. Such rejoinders are only the most explicit way that scribes intrude in the process of transmission. Everything that survives of Anglo-Saxon literature, after all, along with the vast bulk of what can be known of Anglo-Saxon culture, was once selected for copying by Anglo-Saxon scribes. Understanding that process of transmission is crucial to understanding the nature and the limitations of the literature so transmitted.

In the vast majority of cases, for reasons explored below, Anglo-Saxon scribes were monks or other ecclesiasts working in a regulated Christian culture. Their domination of the chain of transmission explains why it is so difficult to know much about Anglo-Saxon paganism or popular superstitions, or about Anglo-Saxon women or the daily life of common people, or about sex and romantic love, humour and frivolous entertainment, children and domestic life. Some insight into these various fields is possible, but the surviving record is heavily weighted towards Christian learning and details of monastic culture, or towards the affairs of people of high status.

The written record is in such ways highly selective, although it is also extensive. Some 421 manuscripts and fragments containing Old English are catalogued by N. R. Ker, while Helmut Gneuss' preliminary list of books in Latin or English from the Anglo-Saxon period comprises some 947 items (Gneuss 1981). A partly contemporary neighbouring people provides an instructive contrast: the Picts in Scotland had no tradition of scribal transmission, and the record of their culture that can be built up from archaeology, from placename evidence, from external comments and from the extensive corpus of stone carving is inevitably far less developed than for Anglo-Saxon England (see Henderson 1967; Sutherland 1994).

In this chapter I will approach Anglo-Saxon scribal culture from two directions. First I will consider theoretically the framework within which written transmission must have occurred: the likely schooling of readers and writers, the place where writing and copying went on and the evidence for libraries. I will then turn to the evidence of the texts that survive, centring on the transmission of Old English poetry, which mostly survives in unique copies, and considering the problems such scanty transmission presents for editing, interpreting or understanding the literature. Finally, I will turn to where the record is less scant – namely, religious prose – and take the dissemination of Ælfric's *Catholic Homilies* as a case study for the detailed picture that can be built up where multiple manuscript witnesses survive. Before launching into a consideration of manuscript culture, I will first briefly consider what must have been the normal form of transmission throughout Anglo-Saxon England – the one that leaves no trace.

Oral Transmission

Anglo-Saxon England was overwhelmingly an oral culture. The vast majority of transmission would have been by word of mouth. Wisdom about the sowing and harvesting of crops, or about manufacturing and using tools, or about a myriad other aspects of daily life would all have been passed orally. Such transactions were too quotidian and low-status to merit written record and so all are lost, but for occasional exceptional survivals, such as an account of estates' management from the viewpoint of the reeve (*Gerefa*; Liebermann 1903–16: 1.453–5) or various Anglo-Saxon prognostics and charms, some in Latin and some in Old English, which may have been recorded through monks' interest in cultivating their own fields (see Hollis 1997).

Songs and stories would have been told by peasants in the fields and by those gathered at the hearth over their meals. Again, there is no record of such events except in the most exceptional circumstances. For example, when the secular peasants who work at the fields of a monastery gather in the evening and sing songs accompanied by the harp, their party merits parchment and ink because one of their unfestive brethren who leaves the gathering in embarrassment is later inspired with the first Christian poetry – with the result that the story is recorded in Bede's account of the poet Cædmon (*HE* IV.24). Or, at a more bookish level, when a high-status child is so enamoured of Old English poetry and of the illuminated initials in a book of verse that he memorizes the entire collection, we learn of his exploit because he goes on to become Anglo-Saxon England's most notable king, Alfred, and the subject of Asser's biography (Stevenson 1904: ch. 23; Keynes and Lapidge 1983: 75). Some sense of the rich oral transmission of stories and poetry can be glimpsed through the historical fiction of another neighbouring culture, the Old Norse family sagas, written in the twelfth to fourteenth centuries but often portraying a world contemporary with Anglo-Saxon England (see Kristjánsson 1988). With rare exceptions, though, Old English literature lacks even such fictional accounts of oral transmission.

Stories and songs, learning and information, then, would have been transmitted pervasively but irrecoverably among families and communities as an oral act. Most schooling of children would have taken place in this informal context. Some schooling, though, was more formal and in those cases it is possible to recover a sense of the foundations for the transmission of learning.

Schools

Details of schooling will have varied through the Anglo-Saxon period, but classroom instruction would always have been closely associated with the church. The success of at least some schooling from the seventh and eighth centuries can be inferred from the accomplishments of the great Anglo-Latin writers whose works dominated the intellectual tradition of the period, namely Aldhelm, Bede and Alcuin. Little is known about the details of individual schools, although recent scholarship has illuminated the high standards of Theodore and Hadrian at Canterbury from the time of Theodore's arrival in 669 (see Lapidge 1986, 1995; Bischoff and Lapidge 1994).

Such school education was in decline by the ninth century, due in part to Viking attacks, which must have dismantled the infrastructure for learning. By the end of the ninth century King Alfred could make his famously dismissive assessment of the nature of education in England in the Preface to his translation of Gregory's *Cura pastoralis*. In this document, in addition to lamenting the decline of learning, Alfred lays out a programme of educational reform which implies increased attention to schooling with special emphasis on secular education. He proposes that

> eall sio gioguð ðe nu is on Angelcynne friora monna, ðara ðe ða speda hæbben ðæt hie ðæm befeolan mægen, sien to liornunga oðfæste, ða hwile ðe hie to nanre oðerre note ne mægen, oð ðone first ðe hie wel cunnen Englisc gewrit arædan. (Sweet 1871: 7)

> all the free-born young men now in England who have the means to apply themselves to it, may be set to learning (as long as they are not useful for some other employment) until the time that they can read English writings properly. (Keynes and Lapidge 1983: 126)

The multiple qualifications limit the range of this schooling programme, first to free-born males only, then to young men of means only, then to young men of means who are not being used elsewhere only. For all this qualification, though, the spirit of the proposal is clearly to boost literacy in English among secular people, a policy which goes hand in hand with the king's new emphasis on translation into the vernacular, outlined in the same document.

Asser reports that Alfred established a court school (chs 75, 102), but the clearest place to receive schooling was within the institution of the church. This is implicit even in Alfred's *Preface*, manuscripts of which were sent to his bishops. It is even more true in the tenth- and eleventh-century flourishing of monastic and cathedral schools which were associated with monastic reform. It is from the monastic schools of this later period that most detailed evidence for educational practice survives. At the end of the tenth century, for example, Ælfric composed a Latin grammar that was the first effectively designed to introduce the language to non-native speakers (ed. Zupitza 1880; see Law 1987). He also composed a colloquy in Latin for practice in Latin vocabulary by young monks (Garmonsway 1978), and his example was followed by one of his students, known as Ælfric Bata, who produced a more extensive and more colourful set of colloquies, which give some of the practicalities of schooling. On the one hand, the classroom sounds a somewhat brutal place, as the students take for granted a beating from the master for not perfecting their lessons. On the other hand, the imaginary and imaginative aspect of the colloquies suggests a playful community of young scholars: conversations allow students to imagine themselves in the act of fellowship through a heavy drinking session or through besting their teachers in competitive insults (Gwara and Porter 1997: 98–107, 136–55). Such exchanges presumably give no literal sense of daily life in the classroom, but they do suggest the employment of such pedagogical techniques as humour and role-playing, as well as effective language-acquisition strategies, in an interesting classroom environment (see Porter 1994).

The successes of this educational environment are hinted at by some incidental clues, such as the rise of a normalized lexis for writing in the later Old English period, known as Winchester standard, indirectly reflecting the dominance of the Winchester school established by Bishop Æthelwold (see Gneuss 1972; Hofstetter 1987); or by the range of surviving manuscripts with glosses that are indicative of classroom activity (see Wieland 1985); or, indeed, by the range of writings and concerns of such intellectuals as Ælfric, Byrhtnoth, Wulfstan of York and Wulfstan the Cantor. Monasteries and cathedrals would, then, have provided the schooling that permitted texts to be read and written. After Alfred's time, such schooling may have provided literacy skills in the vernacular for nobles, while basic literacy in Latin would have been necessary for all priests and monks (see Wormald 1977; Kelly 1990).

Scriptoria and Libraries

Monasteries and cathedrals also provided the scriptoria where books were transmitted in the most literal way and the libraries where learning would have accumulated. Some limited written transmission may have gone on away from ecclesiastical institutions. Meetings of the King's Council, the *Witan*, led to legislation and charters which were presumably drafted by scribes attending the meetings. Although those scribes may have been monks borrowed from monasteries, there is some evidence from the time of Alfred on of a central royal chancery (see Keynes 1980, 1990). Still, the vast majority of books both in Latin and in the vernacular were copied at monastic or cathedral scriptoria and resided in the libraries of those institutions.

Reference survives to early libraries of note, but very few surviving books can be identified from those collections. Bede comments on the library at his home monastery of Monkwearmouth–Jarrow, assembled in part by Benedict Biscop, and this library must have been considerable since it provided what he needed for his own scholarly career (*HE* V.24). Similarly Aldhelm must have drawn on a vast library, while Alcuin comments on the library at York in his poem on that city (Goodman 1982). By the time of the monastic reform, each of the major monasteries would have had a library, with those at the institutions in Winchester and Canterbury being particularly significant. It is from this later period that much of the Latin and almost all the Old English books survive. Alfred's policy encouraged the production of books in the vernacular, and the strong educational tradition of the monastic reform allowed copying to thrive. Of the 421 manuscripts containing Old English catalogued by Ker, only twenty-seven date from the middle of the tenth century or earlier; the other 394 all date from the second half of the tenth century or later (Ker, *Catalogue*: xv, 574–9). The vast majority of the writing that survives from Anglo-Saxon England, then, was recorded and preserved in the milieu of reformed monasticism. Not all manuscripts were copied specifically in reformed houses: many of the leading cathedrals continued with communities that were not reformed, often following their own regulated life, such as the Expanded Rule of Chrodegang (Napier 1916), while those monasteries that were reformed continued to play a major pastoral and educational role for their surrounding communities. It is this broad ecclesiastical milieu that should be considered the primary filter for the recording of Old English written culture.

The important reformed monasteries were predominantly male houses, which might lead to the assumption that only men partook in the process of textual transmission. However, even if male scribes predominated, female houses and their scriptoria presumably played a role. In the seventh and eighth century, Aldhelm dedicated his prose treatise *De virginitate* to Abbess Hildelith and the nuns of Barking Abbey (Ehwald 1919: 228–9). Bede provides ample evidence for the importance of Abbess Hild at Whitby, from whose monastery the miracle of Cædmon's Christian poetics was disseminated (*HE* IV.23–4). Boniface, in his mission to convert heathen Germany, writes to various women correspondents in England, sometimes asking them for books, and occasionally receiving verses from them. In one interesting letter from 735 (Rau 1968: 114), he writes to Eadburga, abbess of Minster-in-Thanet, thanking her 'who has brought light and consolation to an exile in Germany by sending him gifts of spiritual books'. He explicitly asks her to make for him a particularly high-status book, 'by copying out for me in gold the epistles of my lord St Peter, that a reverence and love of the holy scriptures may be impressed on the minds of the heathens to whom I preach' (Fell 1986: 112–13). In making this request, he thinks to provide her with the necessary gold but takes for granted the house's ability to do the writing. In the earlier period, then, women were demonstrably both authors and scribes (see Fell 1986; Hollis 1992).

The evidence for female participation in the later textual community is less clear. Various female houses continued to be important, such as Barking Abbey, while Shaftesbury Abbey and Nunnaminster, Winchester, were founded under King Alfred. These presumably entered into the textual community of the time and had scriptoria for the dissemination of manuscripts. Specific manuscripts from Anglo-Saxon England have not been clearly identified as written in women's houses, but the existence of such is likely. Ker lists the Gospel-book Oxford, Bodleian Library, Bodley 155 (s. x/xi) as belonging to Barking; the psalter in Salisbury, Cathedral Library 150 (s. x^{ex}) as possibly from Shaftesbury; and the prayer-book Oxford, Bodleian Library, Harley 2965 (s. viii) and possibly the prayer-book London, British Library, Cotton Galba A. xiv + Cotton Nero A. ii, fols 3–13 (s. xi^{in}) as belonging to Nunnaminster (Ker 1964: 6, 202, 1987: 62). The example of Hildegard of Bingen, writing a century later and on the continent, provides well-attested evidence for a woman scribe and illuminator, including a remarkable series of self-portraits (see Flanagan 1989). The female forms in a fragmentary translation of the *Regularis concordia* in Cambridge, Corpus Christi College 201 (s. xi^{in}), show this text was intended for a female house, perhaps Nunnaminster (Hill 1991: 310–11). Written transmission may have been the preserve of ecclesiastical institutions, but this would have included both male and female religious houses.

Transmission of Old English Poetry

In view of the religious framework for all book copying, the survival of secular literature is always anomalous. *Beowulf* itself includes numerous descriptions of the performance of poetry, and these illustrate why there is no manuscript record of such events. When the warriors of Heorot travel to the mere in celebration of Beowulf's killing of Grendel, for example, a thane of the king,

> guma gilphlæden   gidda gemyndig
> se ðe ealfela   ealdgesegena
> worn gemunde,
>> (lines 868–70a; Mitchell and
>> Robinson 1998: 77)

a man loaded with stories, mindful of songs, he who remembered a multitude of ancient legends,

recites the 'sið Beowulfes' ('the experience of Beowulf') along with the exploits of Sigemund. Later, in Heorot, the *scop* tells the story of Finnesburh. These are the imaginative performance contexts of a non-book-centred culture. The function and ideology of secular poets in this world are captured in two poems about exemplary poets: *Widsith*, with its account of the fame-dispensing potential of its widely travelled eponymous hero, and *Deor*, with its lament for the displaced *scop* (see, *inter alia*, Hill 1983).

The real-life equivalents of these functional performances have overwhelmingly been lost, removing any record of a mass of poetry and story-telling that cannot now be even guessed at. Occasionally such literature survived, through such chances as getting written into a book of monsters, or into an edifying poetic miscellany given to a new cathedral, or into a pious book of readings taken on a journey to Rome and left in an Italian cathedral city just beyond the Alps, or into an illustrated collection of Biblical verse – to speculate about survival of, respectively, the *Beowulf*-manuscript, the Exeter Book, the Vercelli Book and the Junius manuscript. These four manuscripts account for the vast majority of surviving Old English poetry, most of it Christian in content, but sometimes hearkening back to traditional secular poetry.

Where poetry does survive, it is not marked as verse in the manuscripts but is written out in the same manner as prose across the page. Just like Old English prose, it lacks the norms of word division and standardized punctuation familiar from a print culture. In addition, there are often ambiguities about where a particular work begins or ends. None of the poetry is titled in the manuscripts: all the titles and most of the familiar layout of Old English verse is editorial.

The vast bulk of what Old English poetry was written down survives in a single copy. Sometimes, indeed, even the single copy does not survive. *The Battle of Maldon* is known only from an early modern transcript by David Casley, since the manuscript, London, British Library, Cotton Otho A. xii, was burnt in the Ashburnham House fire of 1731, while *The Finnesburh Fragment* comes to us from the edition published by George Hickes in 1705, transcribed from a presumably fragmentary manuscript that has never been found (see Scragg 1981, 1991; Hill 1983).

In a very few cases, Old English poems survive in multiple copies and thereby preserve significant evidence for their transmission. The most straightforward case of demonstrating a lengthy and complex transmission process is probably *The Dream of the Rood* (Swanton 1970). Part of this poem about the cross's experience of the crucifixion – significantly, the part voiced by the cross itself – is found carved in runes on the borders of the thinner faces of the Ruthwell Cross, a large stone monument named for the town, now in south-west Scotland, where it survives. The monument is datable on historical and art historical evidence to probably the middle of the eighth century, when the central part of the poem would have joined the rest of the stone cross's iconography in dramatizing the fundamentals of the Christian message (see MacLean 1992). Some two centuries later, the full text of *The Dream of the Rood* as we know it was written into the Vercelli Book, the religious miscellany on parchment, perhaps written at Canterbury in the late tenth century (see Scragg 1973), which would be abandoned sometime later in the town of Vercelli. It is conceivable that the poet of the Vercelli Book version saw the poetic utterance upon the cross and used this as the kernel for his longer poem, but more likely that the creator of the cross abstracted out the most pertinent part of the poem for his programme. In either event, the same work was known by two transmitters of verse working in different media at opposite ends of the Anglo-Saxon world across a couple of centuries. The texts of the Ruthwell Cross and the Vercelli Book versions of *The Dream of the Rood* are strikingly different in details of wording, but some of the differences may result from the exceptional adaptation of the Ruthwell version to the cross. The intervening transmission cannot now be recaptured, but the case demonstrates that some poems, at least, had a long and complicated transmission history now lost to us.

Other poems which survive in multiple manuscripts also illustrate the fluidity of poetry in transmission. A few others survive in two versions, notably the poem *Soul and Body* in the Exeter Book and the Vercelli Book; the poem *Azarias* in the Exeter Book, which is a part of *Daniel* in the Junius manuscript; a part of *Solomon and Saturn* in both Cambridge, Corpus Christi College 422 and 41; and two Old English riddles, Riddles 30 and 35, described further below. A few other short poems survive in multiple copies, most notably *Bede's Death Song*, a five-line reflection on judgement, ostensibly composed by Bede as he faced his mortality, recorded in thirty-five manuscripts of the *Epistola Cuthberti de obitu Bedae*, and *Cædmon's Hymn*, which survives in twenty-one manuscripts in association with Bede's *Historia ecclesiastica* (Smith 1933; facsimiles in Robinson and Stanley 1991). A few of the *Chronicle* poems also survive in multiple texts. Scholarly consideration of these has raised important questions about the nature of Old English textuality.

Riddle 35, a translation of Aldhelm's riddle *De lorica*, is a brief poem which can well illustrate issues of transmission. It survives in two manuscripts, one now at Leiden University, the other at Exeter Cathedral. Leiden, Rijksuniversiteit, Vossianus Lat. 4° 106, fol. 25v, preserves what looks like the earlier version of the riddle. This manuscript primarily contains the Latin riddles of Symphosius and of Aldhelm, written by two scribes in Caroline minuscule of the earlier ninth century from western France. The Old English riddle is added to the final leaf of the manuscript, where part of its text is now illegible through damage. There is controversy over the date of its copying. Malcolm Parkes suggests that the riddle is added by a distinct third scribe, working at Fleury in the tenth century (1972: 215–16), whereas Johan Gerritsen considers the riddle to have been written by the second scribe and therefore copied in the early ninth century (Gerritsen 1969, 1984). Both scholars consider the scribe to have been unfamiliar with Old English, as is suggested by copying errors and by an inaccurate division of words. Such an uncomprehending scribe may have retained significantly earlier language forms whenever he wrote out the text. The language of the riddle is analysed by A. H. Smith, who concludes it 'may belong to the middle or second half of the eighth century' from Northumbria (1933: 37). I cite the riddle below from the edition of Dobbie 1942, which was based heavily on Smith 1933, who read the manuscript with the help of earlier transcriptions and of ultra-violet light, but I also incorporate the most convincing observations of Parkes 1972 and Gerritsen 1984. Punctuation, word division, versification and expansion of abbreviations are all editorial. Italics indicate letters now entirely illegible but with space to have been present; square brackets indicate emendations:

> Mec se ueta uong   uundrum freorig
> ob his innaðae   aerist candæ.
> [Ni] uuat ic mec biuorthæ   uullan fliusum,
> herum ðerh hehcraeft   hygiðonc*um* [min].
>
> 5   Uundnae me ni biað ueflæ,   ni ic uarp hafæ,
> ni ðerih ðrea*t*un giðrae*c*   ðret me hlimmith,
> ne me hrutendu   hrisil scelfath,
> ne mec ouana   aam sceal cnyssa.
> Uyrmas mec ni auefun   uyrdi craeftum,
> 10   ða ði goelu godueb   geatum fraetuath.
> Uil mec hu*e*htrae suae ðeh   uidæ ofaer eorðu
> hatan mith hęliðum   hyhtlic giuæ*de*;
> ni anoegun ic me   aerigfaerae egsan brogum,
> ðeh ði num*en* siæ   niudlicae ob cocrum.

> The moist cold plain wondrously
> bore me first from its womb.
> I know myself in [my] thoughts [not] to be made
> from fleeces of wool, from hairs, with great skill.
> Wefts are not wound for me, nor do I have a warp,
> nor does the thread resound for me through the tumult of crowds,
> nor does the whirring shuttle shake for me,
> nor must the weaver's reed beat me anywhere.
> Worms, which ornament golden precious cloth with adornments,
> do not weave me through their allotted skills.
> Nevertheless, people over the earth will widely
> call me among heroes a joyful garment;
> nor do I fear a flight of arrows with fearful terror,
> although they may be eagerly drawn from quivers.

The riddle occurs also in the context of other riddles in Exeter, Cathedral Library 3501, the Exeter Book, written at an unknown centre at the end of the tenth century and donated to Exeter Cathedral library by Bishop Leofric in the third quarter of the eleventh century. (For further details on the Exeter Book, see Conner 1993, whose argument that the book was copied at Exeter is not universally accepted; see also, e.g., Hill 1988.) The text of the Exeter Book version, which presents no palaeographical problems, is cited from the edition of Krapp and Dobbie (1936: 198), who provide editorial layout and make two emendations (*am* in line 8 emended from an ungrammatical plural *amas*, and likewise *gewæde* in line 14 from *gewædu*):

> Mec se wæta wong,   wundrum freorig,
> of his innaþe   ærist cende.

Ne wat ic mec beworhtne   wulle flysum,
hærum þurh heahcræft,   hygeþoncum min.
5   Wundene me ne beoð wefle,   ne ic wearp hafu,
ne þurh þreata geþræcu   þræd me ne hlimmeð,
ne æt me hrutende   hrisil scriþeð,
ne mec ohwonan sceal   am cnyssan.
Wyrmas mec ne awæfan   wyrda cræftum,
10   þa þe geolo godwebb   geatwum frætwað.
Wile mec mon hwæþre seþeah   wide ofer eorþan
hatan for hæleþum   hyhtlic gewæde.
Saga soðcwidum,   searoþoncum gleaw,
wordum wisfæst,   hwæt þis gewæde sy.

The moist cold plain wondrously
bore me from its womb.
I know myself in my thoughts not to be made
from fleeces of wool, from hairs, with great skill.
Wefts are not wound for me, nor do I have a warp,
nor does the thread resound for me through the tumult of crowds,
nor does the whirring shuttle stalk in me,
nor must the weaver's reed beat me anywhere.
Worms, which ornament golden precious cloth with adornments,
do not weave me through their allotted skills.
Nevertheless, people over the earth will widely
call me before heroes a joyful garment.
Say in true speech, one wise in cunning thoughts,
learned in words, what this garment may be.

As is immediately apparent, there are major differences of orthography, phonology and morphology between the two versions. Somewhere in the course of transmission, copyists felt free to update the language of the poem. There are straightforward mistakes in each version. The omission of any marker of negation from line 3 of the Leiden version makes nonsense of the clues, provided by the speaking object, while the plural at line 8a of the Exeter version is straightforwardly ungrammatical. Other changes in substance are more trivial: the additional negative in line 6b in the Exeter Book makes little difference to sense or rhythm; the *æt* in the Exeter Book at line 7a changes little but may be needlessly specific; the transposed word order at line 8a makes for different metrical forms, both of which are acceptable (Sievers' A-type in Leiden, C-type in Exeter); the *mon* in Exeter line 11a adds a perhaps redundant unstressed syllable; and the different prepositions at line 12a (*mith/for*) give alternative readings, either of which is acceptable.

There is one notable difference in content between the two versions, namely, the final two lines. Here it is useful to compare the surviving source for this riddle, Aldhelm's *De lorica* (Ehwald 1919). Each line of the Latin source riddle is reflected in two lines of Old English verse. This makes it possible to decide on the priority of the two endings: the final two lines of the Leiden riddle translate the final line of Aldhelm's riddle, where the further clue is provided that the garment is immune to a flight of arrows. In transmission to the Exeter Book, this final paradox was omitted (because it is redundant? anticlimactic? gives too much away? – or by accident?) and replaced with two taunting lines made up of concluding formulas common from other riddles.

Because of the survival of two versions of Riddle 35, it is possible to make some inferences that would not be possible if, as is more typical, only the Exeter Book copy survived. The dialect of the Leiden text, eighth-century Northumbrian, may not provide evidence about the origin of the riddle since this copy, too, may have an extensive lost history of transmission. At the least, though, it shows that a single poem circulated across at least two centuries, and found its way from Northumbria to the continent, where it became associated with the Latin riddles of Aldhelm, and also into the series of riddles copied into the Exeter Book. The version in the Exeter Book shows how little dialectal information was retained in transmission, since it gives almost no clues to the poem's antiquity or earlier provenance. On the other hand, most of the content of the poem, as opposed to its language, is preserved quite well through this process of transmission, except for the obvious copying errors and the complete alteration of two lines out of fourteen. The alteration, though, is only detectable due to the survival of the second version and the source. For the vast majority of poems, those that survive in only one manuscript without close identifiable sources, it is impossible to recover the degree of change in transmission, but reasonable to assume it may be just as much.

The ramifications of these facts of transmission have been pondered extensively in Anglo-Saxon scholarship, in their implications both for language study and for questions of editing and interpreting the literature. The traditional chronology and dating of most Old English poems, in the absence of any external clues to date, depended upon analysing archaic linguistic features that were seen to be retained in the surviving copies. The loss of evidence for antiquity in the case of the Exeter Book version of Riddle 35 hints that such a process is perilous, and the case against such linguistic tests was made in full in a book-length study by Ashley Crandell Amos (1980). The dating of *Beowulf*, in particular, has proved an exceptionally lively focus for scholarly contention. An older consensus around the probability of an original dated between about 650 and 800 was exploded by a collection of essays on the subject (Chase 1981), and by Kevin Kiernan's meticulous attention to the *Beowulf*-manuscript, which leads him to posit a date of composition contemporary with the surviving manuscript, namely *c.*1000 (Kiernan 1981). R. D. Fulk has gone some way to re-establishing the credibility of certain metrical tests as dating criteria (1992), but consensus on the dating of *Beowulf* has remained elusive (see Liuzza 1995).

If consciousness of transmission has problematized the dating of Old English poetry, it has done yet more to spark discussion about the nature of editorial practice. In 1946, Kenneth Sisam examined the three longer poems that survive in two manuscripts, posing the question 'Was the poetry accurately transmitted?' He answered the question generally in the negative and called for a more critical editorial practice, more willing to emend in aspiring to recreate a perfect authorial original (Sisam 1953). More recently, Michael Lapidge has made a similar call in comparing Old English with classical editing practice, while also acutely demonstrating the various challenges peculiar to the Anglo-Saxon tradition (Lapidge 1991). Douglas Moffat, in examining the changes introduced by scribes, points to the possibility that surviving texts are 'composite products of two, or very likely more, minds which were not necessarily working toward the same end' and therefore becomes pessimistic about the possibility for 'conventional literary analysis' (Moffat 1992: 826–7). Three recent volumes have been devoted to debate over the best way of editing Old English texts (Frank 1993; Scragg and Szarmach 1994; Keefer and O'Keeffe 1998). The theoretical conundrum between recreating a projected ideal original version and staying as close as possible to the fallen but recoverable manuscript witness may be resolved in large part by the advent of new technologies, where a range of different information and types of edition can be made available to the reader.

Discussion of editing practices has gone hand in hand with a developing sense of the nature of Anglo-Saxon texts, in particular of how the recorded tradition constitutes a transition between oral performance and the sense of a fixed text later reified by the practice of printing. Thus, Katherine O'Brien O'Keeffe's study of the variants in text, punctuation and *mise en page* of the versions of *Cædmon's Hymn* suggests a more nuanced model of the complexities of poetic transmission from the Old English period. She sees the poem as occupying an intermediate state between the fluid transmission of oral literature and the fixed text of a literate textual tradition:

> When we examine the variations in the five tenth- and eleventh-century records of the West Saxon version, we see in the despair of the textual editor palpable evidence of a fluid transmission of the *Hymn* somewhere between the formula-defined process which is an oral poem and the graph-bound object which is a text. We see a reading activity reflected in these scribal variants which is formula-dependent, in that the variants observe metrical and alliterative constraints, and which is context-defined, in that the variants produced arise within a field of possibilities generated within a context of expectations. (O'Keeffe 1990: 40)

The most striking aspect of poetic transmission that O'Keeffe's model accounts for is that surviving versions contain variants which cannot all be authorial, but which are all credible in terms of poetic metre and poetic sense, just like the last two lines of Riddle 35. In the case of *Cædmon's Hymn* such fluidity of layout ironically plays a role even into the modern period: Kevin Kiernan shows how the layout of the poem in the popular US reader the *Norton Anthology* encourages a reading of all the a-verses followed by all the b-verses, inadvertently continuing the process of rearranging variation within the poem (Kiernan 1990).

One more example of a poem in two versions from the riddles can usefully be cited. The double text of Riddle 30 is especially striking since, in this case, both copies are preserved in the Exeter Book alone. R. M. Liuzza (1988) examines the differences here in detail and shows how the two versions have many variations which, while minor in themselves, create strikingly different stylistic effects. This can be illustrated from the final sentence of the riddle, which is generally solved as *beam*, the Old English word for 'tree' or 'wood' or 'cross':

> þonne ic mec onhæbbe,   ond hi onhingaþ to me,
> monige mid miltse,   þær ic monnum sceal
> ycan upcyme eadignesse.
> > (Riddle 30a: 7–9; Krapp and Dobbie
> > 1936: 195–6, without emendation)

> While I raise myself up, and they bend down (?) to me,
> many with mercy, then I shall increase
> the growth of blessedness for people.

> þonne ic mec onhæbbe,   hi onhnigað to me,
> modge miltsum,   swa ic mongum sceal
> ycan upcyme eadignesse.
> > (Riddle 30b: 7–9; Krapp and
> > Dobbie 1936: 225)

> When I raise myself up, they bend down to me,
> the proud ones humbly; thus I shall increase
> the growth of blessedness for many.

The differences here are slight, yet the altered rhetorical effect is considerable. In Riddle 30b, a central paradox of the proud ones humbled matches the physical antithesis of the cross rising up while the people bend down. Riddle 30a has lost the interesting central paradox and, perhaps as a result, has also lost the parallel antithesis, since the verb for bending down has been replaced with a nonsensical form, emended away by the editors (line 7b). Liuzza points to the significance of such cumulative small variations: 'For this reason it is proper to think of the scribe as an "editor"; in a very real sense the scribe is the shaper, not merely the transmitter, of Old English poetry' (1988: 14). A. N. Doane turns again to Riddle 30 to make the case still more strongly, dismissing the idea of an author or any expectation of a vernacular fixed text and seeing instead a scribal respect for the visual layout of the exemplar, yet broad freedom to recreate the precise words of the text (Doane 1998). As Ursula Schaefer demonstrates, written poems need to achieve a performative voice for themselves that recreates in written form the expectations from oral poetry (1991; cf. also Pasternack 1995).

Scribal transmission and its ramification, the unstable text, can be seen as either a bane or a boon. A recent turn in Old English criticism has been towards a celebration of the discrete but recoverable performance moments offered by manuscripts – Old English literature in its most immediate context, in Fred C. Robinson's felicitous phrase (Robinson 1980). This has been reflected in the recent publication of a collection completing the availability of Old English poetry in manuscript facsimile (Robinson and Stanley 1991) and, at a more ambitious level, in a project to make all Anglo-Saxon manuscripts cheaply available in microfiche facsimile (Pulsiano and Doane 1994–). In the remaining space of this chapter, I will celebrate the facts of transmission rather than bemoan them by considering what they can show in a case where the record is impressively extensive, namely the works of Ælfric.

Transmission of Religious Prose

Homiletic collections of the reform period and after are dominated by the works of Ælfric, monk and mass-priest of Cerne Abbas from before 989 to 1005, and abbot of Eynsham from 1005 until his death. The circulation of Ælfric's works contrasts completely with that of the poetry. Where the poetry is mostly anonymous (and well-nigh contextless even when a name is attached), Ælfric has not only a name, but also intentions recorded in his prefaces. Where the poetry survives (generally) in a single copy only, Ælfric's works were copied repeatedly and disseminated widely. Studying that dissemination shows how officially sanctioned learning in the faith circulated among the people. It also reveals that Ælfric's sense of his work as an authorized and fixed text was not compatible with the practice of early medieval vernacular textual transmission.

Ælfric's first publication was a sequence of forty sermons for Sundays and saints' days through the year, known as the First Series of *Catholic Homilies*, probably first distributed around 989, followed a few years later with a second series of forty. Both collections circulated in huge numbers: thirty-four manuscripts or fragments of the First Series survive, dating from the time of Ælfric's composition to the thirteenth century, while the work's editor infers the existence of a further fifty lost manuscripts (Clemoes 1997: 134–68). This wealth of material allows for a remarkably precise analysis of the text, pinpointing, for example, Ælfric's changing stylistic practices. One small instance of this is his treatment of the appropriate case to follow the preposition *þurh*, 'through', where he first used a dative but later switched his usage to the accusative case. Clemoes detects some 134 instances in which Ælfric altered the case of the relevant phrases, and shows that such alterations characterize early phases of distribution of the text. Drawing on such evidence as this, Clemoes is able to build up a detailed picture of dissemination, showing that the manuscripts fall into six distinct phases of revision (Clemoes 1997: 64–134).

Such detailed evidence allows the reconstruction of a whole system of distribution. For *Catholic Homilies I* alone, Clemoes postulates the production of some twenty-one separate manuscripts in Ælfric's own scriptorium, which suggests that the monastery at Cerne Abbas must have developed a small cottage industry producing and copying manuscripts of Ælfric's works. Two such manuscripts survive: London, British Library, Royal 7 C. xii, which preserves the author's autograph corrections, and, most probably, Cambridge, University Library, Gg. 3. 28. Pattern manuscripts were then sent out for national release centring on distribution through Canterbury, to which each new phase of revision was sent and where, 'typically, the material was modified in details of its wording, reorganized in conjunction with items not by Ælfric, and given massive circulation, in which we can see a reflection of the "official" status accorded Ælfric's work' (Clemoes 1997: 162–3). Ælfric's homilies, then, were adopted as something of a national pastoral programme for the eleventh century, thus giving them a national status parallel to the Carolingian adoption of the homiliary of Paul the Deacon (see Clayton 1985). As a result, they have a distribution matched by no other work in Old English and have some claim to be the knowledge in Anglo-Saxon England considered 'most necessary for all people to know', in King Alfred's terminology of a century before.

In his prefaces, Ælfric explicitly addresses his scribes, exhorting them to keep his text stable:

> Nu bydde ic and halsige on Godes naman, gif hwa þas boc awritan wylle, þæt he hi geornlice gerihte be ðære bysene, þy læs ðe we ðurh gymelease writeras geleahtrode beon. Mycel yfel deð se ðe leas writ, buton he hit gerihte, swylce he gebringe þa soðan lare to leasum gedwylde; forði sceal gehwa gerihtlæcan þæt þæt he ær to woge gebigde, gif he on Godes dome unscyldig beon wile. (Preface to *Catholic Homilies I*; Wilcox 1994: Preface 1b, lines 86–91; cf. also Preface 2b.15–20, 2f.5–9, 3b.26–9, 4.115–18, 5b.32–4, 8c.31–3)

> Now I pray and implore in God's name, if anyone wants to copy this book, that he correct it carefully against the exemplar, lest we be reproached through careless copyists. He does much ill who writes a false thing, unless he correct it, as he may bring true doctrine to false error; therefore each must put right whatever he turned to crookedness, if he wants to be blameless at God's judgement.

Ælfric here lays a considerable responsibility at the hand of the scribe: the difference between 'þa soðan lare' and characteristically Ælfrician evil in 'leasum gedwylde'. While Ælfric is aware that his works will be used differently in different contexts – in the case of the First Series of *Catholic Homilies*, for example, he recognizes that his secular patron, Æthelweard, ealdorman of the western provinces, is going to want his own distinct copy (see Preface 1b.92–4) and, at a more extreme level, he realizes that his work on Judith will play to a range of different audiences (see Clayton 1994) – he specifically asks that his own work be kept distinct from that of others (Preface 1a.28–35), with the suggestion that writing authorized by his name will carry a certain guarantee of 'true doctrine'. Yet his desire to keep his works integrated and distinct was frustrated repeatedly in their circulation, as can be seen from the manuscript contexts in which they survive and, most spectacularly, in those cases where the scribes answer back against their author.

A relatively benign example is preserved in a colophon in Cambridge, Corpus Christi College 178. This manuscript comprises, in essence, twenty-four homilies by

Ælfric arranged in two groups, the first consisting of twelve items for any occasion, and the second of twelve homilies for specific occasions in the church year. Ælfric's authorship is spelled out in a Latin note at the head of the second group, and an English colophon between the two groups explains the arrangement and continues:

> Đa twa 7 twentig spell synd be fullan gesette swa swa hi æt fruman wæron on þære ealdan .æ. bysne. ac twa spel of þisum. an be þam heafodleahtrum. 7 oðer be þam wiglungum synd geeacnode. of oðrum spellum. (Clemoes 1997: 38)

> Twenty-two of the homilies are set down completely as they were originally in the old exemplar, but two of the homilies from among these [the twenty-four total], one concerning the deadly sins, and another concerning witchcraft, are augmented from other sources.

It is, indeed, the case that the relevant two sermons, Skeat 16 and 17, are augmented with material mostly drawn from other homilies by Ælfric (the first printed in full by Morris 1868: 296–304, the second augmentation edited by Pope 1967–8: 786–98). Such augmentation and rearrangement are not unusual; what is unusual here is that the scribe has so clearly spelled out the alteration, alerting the reader to his role as compiler.

Other scribal comments counter Ælfric's intentions less politely. Ælfric is explicit that there should be no preaching on the Thursday, Friday and Saturday of Easter week, which he calls *swigdagum*, 'silent days', in notes at the relevant point in both series of *Catholic Homilies* (see Hill 1985). Ælfric's desire is not respected in consolidated collections, such as Oxford, Bodleian Library, Bodley 340 (from Canterbury or Rochester at the beginning of the eleventh century), which includes anonymous homilies for each of these days. Ælfric's restrictive note is included in Cambridge, Corpus Christi College 178, p. 229, but has received a later marginal note, cryptically signed by Coleman (perhaps the late-eleventh-century Worcester-based biographer of St Wulfstan): 'Ac þis ne þynceð no us well gesæd' ('But this does not seem to us at all well said'), followed by an explanation of the need to preach (Ker 1949; Hill 1985: 121). A similar note is included in Oxford, Bodleian Library, Hatton 114, fol. 86r, from Worcester, perhaps also by Coleman: 'Đis nis no well gesæd' (Ker 1990: 395; 'This is not at all well said').

An even sharper rejoinder greets Ælfric's reluctance to discuss Mary's birth. Ælfric inserts a note into the second series of *Catholic Homilies* at the relevant point explicitly declining to discuss Mary's birth for fear of falling into 'ænigum gedwylde' ('any error'; Wilcox 1994: Preface 2d; see Clayton 1986). This receives the marginal addition in Oxford, Bodleian Library, Bodley 342 (a companion to Bodley 340): 'ne geberaþ ðys naht þærto, buton for ydelnysse' (Ker 1990: 395: 'it is not for that reason at all, but rather through laziness'). Both note and marginal comment are copied into a derivative manuscript, Cambridge, Corpus Christi College 303, of the first half of the twelfth century (Ker 1990: 63).

Ælfric's own desire for his works, then – that they stand as a distinctive repository of reliable vernacular learning – was frustrated even as those works were adopted for the official programme of pastoral care in late Anglo-Saxon England, since gaps he deliberately left were filled in as necessary. When written in the vernacular, even doctrinal work with the explicit authority of a named author was subject to revision and adaptation in transmission. Occasionally, whole homilies by Ælfric were rewritten and adapted (see, e.g., Swan 1997), but his learned exegetical style was generally not suitable for such wholesale adaptation. Archbishop Wulfstan's general moral exhortations, on the other hand, were ideally suited for this purpose, and his works were gutted and reused in more or less identifiable form extensively (see Jost 1950; Wilcox 1992). Where anonymous homilies survive in multiple copies, they, too, partake in *mouvance* to such an extent that separate copies are effectively new performances. I have shown elsewhere how this sometimes allows for insight into a contemporary sense of prose style, since alterations to a single homily which have little effect on the overall message seem instead to be motivated by a concern with and delight in particular prose rhythms (Wilcox 1997).

Conclusion

Beyond the world of Anglo-Saxon scribes, two further stages mark the transmission of Anglo-Saxon written culture to our time. First the manuscripts had to survive and get gathered into their modern repositories. The work of antiquaries of the sixteenth to eighteenth centuries is told by Timothy Graham elsewhere in this volume, but it is worth drawing attention here to the way the whole process provided an additional filter upon what would survive. Particular attention was devoted to religious works that would serve the polemical ends of the church reformers of the Elizabethan period (see Berkhout and Gatch 1982; Frantzen 1990). A work seen as less useful, such as the poem *Beowulf*, languished untended in the British Museum until it captured the imagination of a Danish scholar at the very end of the eighteenth century (Kiernan 1986).

Finally, works from Anglo-Saxon England need to be edited and distributed, glossed and annotated, translated and discussed in the modern period. This process has imposed yet a different filter in which vernacular poetry hearkening back to Germanic values is highly valued, and religious literature and works in Latin are relatively neglected. The latest move of significance for transmission is the renewed attention to manuscripts, combined with the potential of the new technologies for new methods of circulating both texts and contexts.

In mapping out the field of study for the discipline of the history of the book, Robert Darnton describes a general life cycle that printed books pass through – 'a communications circuit that runs from the author to the publisher . . . , the printer, the shipper, the bookseller, and the reader' – and sees the book historian's role as a concern with 'each phase of this process and the process as a whole' (Darnton 1990:

111). As Darnton recognizes, manuscript circulation involves a different but somewhat analogous life cycle. In Anglo-Saxon England, this cycle often began with a traditional voice exceptionally caught in writing, more rarely with a recognizable author. The work passed to scribes, who copied books in a recognizable ecclesiastical milieu and who left their mark as selectors and adaptors of what they copied. The resulting manuscript books circulated and were recopied mostly in ecclesiastical circles, where their movements can sometimes be followed. Such manuscripts served as prompts for readers, ecclesiastical or secular, most often reciting out loud to a listening audience. Every stage of this life cycle of Anglo-Saxon books is hard to recapture but, through successfully passing through successive filters and through a certain amount of blind good luck, an array of manuscripts and texts does survive from the England of a millennium or so ago. With careful attention, such books can still speak to listeners who would hear, 'niþum to nytte' ('with profit for the people'), as the speaking book of Riddle 26 puts it (line 27a; Krapp and Dobbie 1936: 194).

REFERENCES

Primary sources

Clemoes, Peter, ed. 1997. *Ælfric's Catholic Homilies: The First Series.* EETS, s.s. 17. Oxford.

Dobbie, Elliott Van Kirk, ed. 1942. *The Anglo-Saxon Minor Poems.* Anglo-Saxon Poetic Records 6. New York and London.

Ehwald, Rudolfus, ed. 1919. *Aldhelmi Opera.* Monumenta Germaniae Historica, Auctorum Antiquissimorum, 15. Berlin.

Garmonsway, G. N., ed. 1978. *Ælfric's Colloquy.* London, 1939. Rev. edn. Exeter.

Goodman, Peter, ed. 1982. *Alcuin: The Bishops, Kings and Saints of York.* Oxford.

Gwara, Scott, ed., and David W. Porter, trans. 1997. *Anglo-Saxon Conversations: The Colloquies of Ælfric Bata.* Woodbridge.

Hill, Joyce, ed. 1983. *Old English Minor Heroic Poems.* Durham and St Andrews Medieval Texts 4. Durham.

Keynes, Simon and Michael Lapidge, trans. 1983. *Alfred the Great: Asser's 'Life of King Alfred' and Other Contemporary Sources.* Harmondsworth.

Kinsella, Thomas, trans. 1970. *The Táin.* Dublin, 1969. Repr. Oxford.

Krapp, George Philip and Elliott Van Kirk Dobbie, eds 1936. *The Exeter Book.* Anglo-Saxon Poetic Records 3. New York and London.

Liebermann, F., ed. 1903–16. *Die Gesetze der Angelsachsen.* Halle.

Mitchell, Bruce and Fred C. Robinson, eds 1998. *Beowulf: An Edition with Relevant Shorter Texts.* Oxford.

Morris, Richard, ed. 1868. *Old English Homilies . . . of the Twelfth and Thirteenth Centuries.* Early English Text Society, o.s. 29, 34. London.

Napier, A. S., ed. 1916. *The Old English Version of the Enlarged Rule of Chrodegang.* Early English Text Society, o.s. 150. London.

Pope, John C., ed. 1967–8. *The Homilies of Ælfric: A Supplementary Collection.* Early English Text Society, o.s. 259–60. London.

Pulsiano, Phillip and A. N. Doane, eds 1994–. *Anglo-Saxon Manuscripts in Microfiche Facsimile.* Binghamton (vols 1–6), Tempe (vols 7–).

Rau, Reinhold, ed. 1968. *Bonifatii Epistulae, Willibaldi Vita Bonifatii.* Darmstadt.

Robinson, Fred C. and E. G. Stanley, eds 1991. *Old English Verse Texts from Many Sources: A Comprehensive Collection.* Early English Manuscripts in Facsimile, 23. Copenhagen.

Scragg, D. G., ed. 1981. *The Battle of Maldon.* Manchester.

Skeat, Walter W., ed. and trans. 1966. *Ælfric's Lives of Saints.* Early English Text Society, o.s. 76, 82, 94, 114. London, 1881–1900. Repr. 2 vols. London.

Smith, A. H., ed. 1933. *Three Northumbrian Poems.* London.

Stevenson, W. H., ed. 1904. *Asser's Life of King Alfred.* Oxford.

Swanton, Michael, ed. 1970. *The Dream of the Rood.* Manchester.

Sweet, Henry, ed. 1871. *King Alfred's West-Saxon Version of Gregory's Pastoral Care.* Early English Text Society, o.s. 45, 50. London.

Wilcox, Jonathan, ed. 1994. *Ælfric's Prefaces.* Durham Medieval Texts 9. Durham.

Zupitza, Julius, ed. 1880. *Ælfrics Grammatik und Glossar.* Sammlung englischer Denkmäler. Berlin.

Secondary sources

Amos, Ashley Crandell 1980. *Linguistic Means of Determining the Dates of Old English Literary Texts.* Cambridge, MA.

Berkhout, Carl T. and Milton McC. Gatch, eds 1982. *Anglo-Saxon Scholarship: The First Three Centuries.* Boston.

Bischoff, Bernhard and Michael Lapidge, eds 1994. *Biblical Commentaries from the Canterbury School of Theodore and Hadrian.* CSASE 10. Cambridge.

Chase, Colin, ed. 1981. *The Dating of Beowulf.* Toronto Old English Series 6. Toronto.

Clayton, Mary 1985. 'Homiliaries and Preaching in Anglo-Saxon England'. *Peritia* 4: 207–42.

——1986. 'Ælfric and the Nativity of the Blessed Virgin Mary'. *Anglia* 104: 286–315.

——1994. 'Ælfric's *Judith*: Manipulative or Manipulated?'. *Anglo-Saxon England* 23: 215–27.

Conner, Patrick W. 1993. *Anglo-Saxon Exeter: A Tenth-Century Cultural History.* Studies in Anglo-Saxon History 4. Woodbridge.

Darnton, Robert 1990. *The Kiss of Lamourette: Reflections in Cultural History.* New York.

Doane, A. N. 1998. 'Spacing, Placing and Effacing: Scribal Textuality and Exeter Riddle 30a/b'. *New Approaches to Editing Old English Verse*, pp. 45–65. Eds Sarah Larratt Keefer and Katherine O'Brien O'Keeffe. Cambridge.

Fell, Christine with Cecily Clark and Elizabeth Williams 1986. *Women in Anglo-Saxon England and the Impact of 1066.* London, 1984. Oxford.

Flanagan, Sabina 1989. *Hildegard of Bingen: A Visionary Life.* London.

Frank, Roberta, ed. 1993. *The Politics of Editing Medieval Texts.* New York.

Frantzen, Allen J. 1990. *Desire for Origins: New Language, Old English, and Teaching the Tradition.* New Brunswick, NJ, and London.

Fulk, R. D. 1992. *A History of Old English Meter.* Philadelphia.

Gerritsen, Johan 1969. 'The Text of the Leiden Riddle'. *English Studies* 50: 429–44.

——1984. 'Leiden Revisited: Further Thoughts on the Text of the Leiden Riddle'. *Medieval Studies Conference Aachen 1983*, pp. 51–9. Eds Wolf-Deitrich Bald and Horst Weinstock. Bamberger Beiträge zur englischen Sprachwissenschaft 15. Frankfurt.

Gneuss, Helmut 1972. "The Origin of Standard Old English and Æthelwold's School at Winchester'. *Anglo-Saxon England* 1: 63–83.

——1981. 'A Preliminary List of Manuscripts Written or Owned in England up to 1100'. *Anglo-Saxon England* 9: 1–60.

Henderson, Isabel 1967. *The Picts.* London.

Hickes, George 1703–5. *Linguarum vett. septentrionalium thesaurus grammatico-criticus et archæologicus . . . catalogus.* Oxford. Facsimile repr. Menston, 1970.

Hill, Joyce 1985. 'Ælfric's "Silent Days"'. *Leeds Studies in English* n.s. 16: 118–31.

——1988. 'The Exeter Book and Lambeth Palace Library MS 149: The Monasterium of Sancta Maria'. *American Notes and Queries* n.s. 1: 4–9.

——1991. 'The "Regularis Concordia" and its Latin and Old English Reflexes'. *Revue Bénédictine* 101: 299–315.

Hofstetter, Walter 1987. *Winchester und der spätaltenglische Sprachgebrauch.* Munich.

Hollis, Stephanie 1992. *Anglo-Saxon Women and the Church: Sharing a Common Fate.* Woodbridge.

——1997. 'Old English "Cattle-Theft Charms": Manuscript Contexts and Social Uses'. *Anglia* 115: 139–64.

Jost, Karl 1950. *Wulfstanstudien.* Swiss Studies in English 23. Berne.

Keefer, Sarah Laratt and Katherine O'Brien O'Keeffe, eds 1998. *New Approaches to Editing Old English Verse.* Cambridge.

Kelly, Susan 1990. "Anglo-Saxon Lay Society and the Written Word'. *The Uses of Literacy in Early*

Mediaeval Europe, pp. 36–62. Ed. Rosamond McKitterick. Cambridge.

Ker, N. R. 1949. 'Old English Notes Signed "Coleman"'. *Medium Ævum* 18: 29–31.

—— 1964. *Medieval Libraries of Great Britain: A List of Surviving Books*. 2nd edn. Royal Historical Society Guides and Handbooks 3. London.

—— 1987. *Medieval Libraries of Great Britain: A List of Surviving Books. Supplement to the Second Edition*. Eds Andrew G. Watson. Royal Historical Society Guides and Handbooks 15. London.

Keynes, Simon 1980. *The Diplomas of King Æthelred 'The Unready' 978–1016: A Study in their Use as Historical Evidence*. Cambridge.

—— 1990. 'Royal Government and the Written Word in Late Anglo-Saxon England'. *The Uses of Literacy in Early Mediaeval Europe*, pp. 258–96. Ed. Rosamond McKitterick. Cambridge.

Kiernan, Kevin S. 1981. *Beowulf and the Beowulf Manuscript*. Ann Arbor, MI.

—— 1986. *The Thorkelin Transcripts of Beowulf*. Anglistica 25. Copenhagen.

—— 1990. 'Reading Cædmon's "Hymn" with Someone Else's Glosses'. *Representations* 32: 157–74.

Kristjánsson, Jónas 1988. *Eddas and Sagas: Iceland's Medieval Literature*. Trans. Peter Foote. Reykjavik.

Lapidge, Michael 1986. 'The School of Theodore and Hadrian'. *Anglo-Saxon England* 15: 45–72.

—— 1991. 'Textual Criticism and the Literature of Anglo-Saxon England'. *Bulletin of the John Rylands University Library of Manchester* 73: 17–45.

——, ed. 1995. *Archbishop Theodore: Commemorative Studies on his Life and Influence*. Cambridge Studies in Anglo-Saxon England 11. Cambridge.

Law, Vivien 1987. 'Anglo-Saxon England: Ælfric's *Excerptiones de arte grammatica anglice*'. *Historia Épistémologie Langage* 9: 47–71.

Liuzza, Roy Michael 1988. 'The Texts of the Old English *Riddle 30*'. *Journal of English and Germanic Philology* 87: 1–15.

—— 1995. 'On the Dating of *Beowulf*'. *Beowulf: Basic Readings*, pp. 281–302. Ed. Peter S. Baker. Basic Readings in Anglo-Saxon England 1. New York.

MacLean, Douglas 1992. 'The Date of the Ruthwell Cross'. *The Ruthwell Cross*, pp. 49–70. Ed.

Brendan Cassidy. Index of Christian Art, Occasional Papers 1. Princeton, NJ.

Moffat, Douglas 1992. 'Anglo-Saxon Scribes and Old English Verse'. *Speculum* 67: 805–27.

O'Keeffe, Katherine O'Brien 1990. *Visible Song: Transitional Literacy in Old English Verse*. CSASE 4. Cambridge.

Parkes, M. B. 1972. 'The Manuscript of the Leiden Riddle'. *Anglo-Saxon England* 1: 207–17 + pl.

Pasternack, Carol Braun 1995. *The Textuality of Old English Poetry*. Cambridge Studies in Anglo-Saxon England 13. Cambridge.

Porter, David W. 1994. 'The Latin Syllabus in Anglo-Saxon Monastic Schools'. *Neophilologus* 78: 463–82.

Robinson, Fred C. 1980. 'Old English Literature in its Most Immediate Context'. *Old English Literature in Context: Ten Essays*, pp. 11–29. Ed. John D. Niles. Cambridge.

Schaefer, Ursula 1991. 'Hearing from Books: The Rise of Fictionality in Old English Poetry'. *Vox Intexta: Orality and Textuality in the Middle Ages*, pp. 117–36. Eds A. N. Doane and Carol B. Pasternack. Madison.

Scragg, D. G. 1973. 'The Compilation of the Vercelli Book.' *Anglo-Saxon England* 2: 189–207.

——, ed. 1991. *The Battle of Maldon, AD 991*. Oxford.

—— and Paul E. Szarmach, eds 1994. *The Editing of Old English: Papers from the 1990 Manchester Conference*. Cambridge.

Sisam, Kenneth 1953. 'The Authority of Old English Poetical Manuscripts'. *Review of English Studies* 22 (1946): 257–68. Repr. *Studies in the History of Old English Literature*, pp. 29–44. Oxford.

Sutherland, Elizabeth 1994. *In Search of the Picts: A Celtic Dark Age Nation*. London.

Swan, Mary 1997. 'Old English Made New: One Catholic Homily and its Reuses'. *Leeds Studies in English* n.s. 28: 1–18.

Wieland, Gernot R. 1985. 'The Glossed Manuscript: Classbook or Library Book?'. *Anglo-Saxon England* 14: 153–73.

Wilcox, Jonathan 1992. 'The Dissemination of Wulfstan's Homilies: The Wulfstan Tradition in Eleventh-century Vernacular Preaching'. *England in the Eleventh Century*, pp. 199–217.

Ed. Carola Hicks. Harlaxton Medieval Studies 2. Stamford.

——1997. 'Variant Texts of an Old English Homily: Vercelli X and Stylistic Readers'. *The Preservation and Transmission of Anglo-Saxon Culture*, pp. 335–51. Eds Paul E. Szarmach and Joel T. Rosenthal. Studies in Medieval Culture 40. Kalamazoo.

Wormald, Patrick 1977. 'The Uses of Literacy in Anglo-Saxon England and its Neighbours'. *Transactions of the Royal Historical Society* 5th ser. 27: 95–114.

4

Authorship and Anonymity

Mary Swan

Constructions

Mec feonda sum   feore besnyþede,
woruldstrenga binom;   wætte siþþan,
dyfde on wætre;   dyde eft þonan,
sette on sunnan,   þær ic swyþe beleas
herum þam þe ic hæfde.   Heard mec siþþan
snað seaxses ecg   sindrum begrunden,
fingras feoldan,   and mec fugles wyn
geond[sprengde] speddropum,   spyrede geneahhe
ofer brunne brerd,   beamtelge swealg,
streames dæle,   stop eft on mec,
siþade sweartlast.   Mec siþþan wrah
hæleð hleobordum,   hyde deþenede,
gierede mec mid golde;   for þon me gliwedon
wrætlic weorc smiþa   wire bifongen.
Nu þa gereno   and se reada telg
and þa wuldorgesteald   wide mæren
dryhtfolca Helm,   nales dol wite.
Gif min bearn wera   brucan willað,
hy beoð þy gesundran   and þy sigefæstran,
heortum þy hwætran   and þy hygebliþran,
ferþe þy frodran;   habbaþ freonda þy ma,
swæsra and gesibbra,   soþra and godra,
tilra and getreowra,   þa hyra tyr and ead
estum ycað,   and hy arstafum,
lissum bilecgað,   and hi lufan fæþmum
fæste clyppað.   Frige hwæt ic hatte
niþum to nytte.   Nama min is mære,
hæleþum gifre,   and halig sylf.

(Riddle 26; Whitelock 1967: 171–2)

A certain enemy deprived me of life, took my worldly strength; then wet me, dipped me in water; took me out of it again, set me in the sun, where afterwards I lost the hairs I had. Next the hard knife's edge cut me, polished off impurities, fingers folded, and the bird's joy sprinkled over me with useful drops, often made a track over the dark rim, swallowed wood-dye, a share of the stream, advanced again on me, journeyed leaving a black track. Afterwards the hero covered me with protective boards, wrapped me in skin, adorned me with gold; truly the splendid works of the smith adorned me, encompassed with wire. Now the adornments and the red dye and the glorious possessions far and wide make famous the protector of nations, not at all foolish blame. If children of men will make use of me, they will by that be safer and more victorious, bolder in their hearts and more glad in spirit, wiser in heart; they will have more friends, dearer and closer, truer and better, more virtuous and faithful, who will increase in them glory and prosperity, and surround them with affection in honour, and hold them fast in the embrace of love. Find out what I am called for humans to use. My name is famous, useful to heroes, and itself holy.

This poem was written down in the second half of the tenth century in Exeter, Cathedral Library 3501, commonly known as the Exeter Book. The manuscript contains a mixture of religious and secular Old English poetry: long poems on Christian themes; shorter, elegiac poems narrated by first-person personae; poems relating Germanic heroic traditions; poems on moral precepts; 'wisdom' poetry; and a collection of riddles. The riddles are notably lively and in most cases markedly secular in their contents, and the manuscript does not list their solutions, so readers from the tenth century to the present day have been at liberty to engage and re-engage with them and to ponder their meaning. Riddle 26, whose text is presented above, is one of the more sedate examples, and its solution is usually accepted as something like 'a beautifully prepared and ornamented manuscript of the Bible, or of another Christian text'. As is the case with most surviving Old English poetry, and much of the prose, we do not know the name of the person who composed it, or the name of the scribe who wrote it down. This frequent absence of identifiable authors is one of the most striking elements of Anglo-Saxon textual culture. In some cases, the author of a text may have been known to its Anglo-Saxon readership, but has been lost in the process of transmission. In the great majority of cases, however, texts from Anglo-Saxon England which survive today with no authorial attribution will also have been 'anonymous' when they were first read or heard. We might find it hard to imagine today that authors could compose texts and allow them to be circulated without marking them as their creation, and our desire to discover the context of production of Anglo-Saxon texts is often frustrated when we do not know who wrote them. Not knowing who wrote a text, or the status, occupation or gender of its author, or often where or precisely when it was written, hinders our attempts to read texts in their geographical, social and political contexts.

Modern scholars' feelings of frustration when confronted by an anonymous Anglo-Saxon text are revealing of assumptions about how texts mean, and about the information we should bring to bear when reading them. The problem here, of course, is with modern concepts and assumptions which have the effect of making Anglo-Saxon literature seem strange and evasive. Some of the key questions posed by twentieth-century critical theorists including Roland Barthes, Michel Foucault and Julia Kristeva help to problematize the central issues connected with nineteenth- and twentieth-century concepts of authorship, including the concept of identity, the relationship of the author and the reader, and the relationship of authors to the culture which creates and defines them (Foucault 1977; Barthes 1986; Kristeva 1986; Pasternack 1997; Szarmach 1997: 144–5, n. 12). In his influential essay 'The Death of the Author', first published in 1968, Barthes describes the characteristics of the desire to define an author and thereby understand a work of literature: 'the *author* is a modern character, no doubt produced by our society as it emerged from the Middle Ages . . . the image of literature to be found in contemporary culture is tyrannically centred on the author, his person, his history, his tastes, his passions' (Barthes 1986: 49–50). This modern 'image of literature' has resulted over the last two hundred years or so in much Anglo-Saxon literary production being ignored and pushed to the margins of the canon of English Literature simply because, as it has no identifiable author, we cannot validate it as worthy of study.

In 1969, Foucault published the essay 'What Is an Author?', in which he shows how the identification of an author allows us to establish textual groupings and the relationship among them. Foucault defines the 'author-function' as 'not formed spontaneously through the simple attribution of a discourse to an individual' but as the result of

> a complex operation whose purpose is to construct the rational entity we call an author. Undoubtedly, this construction is assigned a 'realistic' dimension as we speak of an individual's 'profundity' or 'creative' power, his intentions or the original inspiration manifested in writing. Nevertheless, these aspects of an individual, which we designate as an author (or which comprise an individual as an author), are projections, in terms always more or less psychological, of our way of handling texts: in the comparisons we make, the traits we extract as pertinent, the continuities we assign, or the exclusions we practise. (Foucault 1977: 123)

This definition of the 'author-function' offers an explanation for the difficulties experienced by many modern readers when they are confronted with an anonymous Anglo-Saxon text: we cannot 'construct' an individual author for it, and therefore cannot use what we define as significant about that author's personality to interpret the text. This makes it harder for a modern reader to value an anonymous Anglo-Saxon text in the ways modern texts are usually given value, as what we cannot know about an anonymous text inhibits the possibility of seeing it as an act of 'creation' and 'originality'.

The fact that it is possible for people to write texts and not to put their names to them has profound implications for the nature of Anglo-Saxon textual culture and for the applicability of our concepts of authorship, textuality, creativity and originality. Some recent work has identified groups of anonymous Anglo-Saxon texts as the work of a single author (Wilcox 1991; Scragg 1992, 1999), but even when an individual's literary output can be identified in this way, when that individual did not leave a name which can be used to fix him or her in terms of time, place and affiliations, that individual cannot be embodied as an author in the modern sense of the word.

Critical theory in the last three decades of the twentieth century, then, has been concerned with issues of authorship, identity and textuality, and this has given us a substantial modern critical vocabulary for discussing these things. In so far as we can tell from the surviving evidence, Anglo-Saxon culture was far less inclined to theorize about these issues. No body of critical, theoretical texts on the concept of authorship survives from Anglo-Saxon England. Because of this, the most satisfactory way for us to try to gain access to Anglo-Saxon attitudes to authorship and related concepts is by analysing the implications of surviving texts which touch on them, even if they do not explicitly discuss them. In order to analyse Anglo-Saxon texts, we need first to give some attention to what textuality might have meant in Anglo-Saxon England.

Textuality

Riddle 26 is a useful example of Anglo-Saxon attitudes to authorship and textuality. It is especially useful for forcing modern readers, through its concentration on the mechanics of manuscript production, to focus on the physical aspect of a text and the physical process of its writing (see O'Keeffe 1994; Szarmach 1997: 131). These are elements of authorship which we tend not to take into account: for modern readers, writing, or 'authorship', is primarily conceived of as an intellectual activity, whether or not it is regarded as creative in a literary sense. This is of course partly true of writing/authorship in Anglo-Saxon England, too, but the physical process of writing, its technology, tools and possibilities, was the focus of considerable attention in Anglo-Saxon England. This is doubtless partly because of the practical difficulties involved and the high degree of skill needed to produce the writing material, control the pen and ink and form the letters. The highly specialized training undergone by scribes is highlighted by the fact that even when prolific Anglo-Saxon authors such as Ælfric and Wulfstan annotate manuscripts of their own work, the script they use is not of scribal quality. Surviving texts have left us with a substantial number of Old English words associated with writing as a skilled physical process, or *cræft*: words for the stages of preparing writing material; for the implements used for writing; and for the different aspects of the process of copying a text, including making mistakes and correcting them (Roberts and Kay 1995: sect. 9). The fact that these materials and processes can be represented enigmatically and playfully in Riddle 26 is an indication that they are central to the lives of the intended audience for the riddle, and that an Anglo-Saxon audience can stand at a critical, perhaps even analytical, distance from them.

Questions of terminology are at the heart of the discussion in this chapter. Many of the concepts under discussion – including the very terms 'authorship' and 'anonymity' – may seem familiar and uncomplicated to us, but as we begin to look closely at how they operate in Anglo-Saxon culture it will become clear that modern definitions and categories do not always fit those of the early Middle Ages. We must therefore be alert to any lack of correspondence between modern definitions and Anglo-Saxon attitudes, and use our analysis of these differences to ask different questions of Anglo-Saxon texts from those we are accustomed to asking of modern ones.

The fundamental difference between early medieval and modern textuality is that we now live in a print culture, whereas the early Middle Ages was a manuscript culture. This difference might seem at first to be purely technological and physical, but it has profound implications for attitudes towards texts and textuality. Generally speaking, in a print culture, textual fixity is possible and common: multiple identical copies of a single text are easily produced and disseminated. A printed edition of a modern text is usually taken by its producers and consumers to be authorially endorsed, 'ideal' and unchangeable. A printed text is a record of a finalized act of creation. The way in which texts are most commonly received in a print culture is through private, solitary, silent reading. Because texts are relatively easily available, modern readers do not usually have to rely on memorizing their contents. Partly because such textual stability is possible in a print culture, and partly because individuality is such a highly prized concept nowadays, originality and invention are greatly valued, and derivativeness and the act of copying are downgraded. For the modern reader, therefore, some of the most characteristic features of Anglo-Saxon textual culture – the regard for authority, the textual chains established as material is transmitted from one version to another – might make us disinclined to award Anglo-Saxon texts the status of 'literature' and Anglo-Saxon writers the status of 'authors'.

Clearly, then, things are very different in a manuscript culture. No manuscript copy of a text is exactly like any other. When multiple manuscript copies of a single text survive, each one will differ from the others in ways ranging from tiny variations in the layout on the page to enormous differences in quality of production and detail of contents. This sort of textual fluidity is articulated in intellectual as well as physical terms. Three examples will demonstrate this: first, manuscript culture, on the whole, values texts which proclaim themselves as descending from other texts: authors go to some lengths to describe the sources they have used and the authors they have translated or adapted; second, in many cases we do not know the author of a text or of a particular version of it; and third, readers of manuscripts often marked them as they used them, and sometimes wrote their own alterations and comments into them to produce a manuscript text made up of layers of reception and response.

Asking what constitutes a text in a manuscript culture provokes further questions about the status of the following: multiple, variant copies of a single 'source' text where the scribe of each one has decided to make changes to the substance; a copy of a text where the scribe has reproduced the words faithfully enough, but has altered

the spelling to make it fit a new region or date; a copy where the scribe has accidentally made errors or introduced changes; two versions of a text, one copied from a
manuscript source, and the other copied from memory; an Old English text which is
created as the running gloss to an earlier Latin text, such as the gloss to the Lindisfarne Gospels. Which of these might we count as a text? Even where we are only considering a single author, we are confronted with the difficulty of establishing what
constitutes a text where an author is in the habit of issuing a text and then revising
it and issuing a reworked version. Ælfric, who worked in the late tenth and early
eleventh centuries (see the chapters by Wilcox and Hill in this volume), spent a considerable proportion of his career doing just this. By 994 he had issued the two series
of preaching texts known as the *Catholic Homilies*. In writing these homilies, Ælfric
drew extensively on Latin source materials. After completing and issuing this first
version of the *Catholic Homilies*, Ælfric repeatedly revised and rearranged them
(Clemoes 1959; Godden 1979); the surviving manuscript copies of homilies from
these series have been analysed by editors as representing different recensions of the
texts and of the *Catholic Homilies* as a work. By contrast with a printed text, then, a
single manuscript copy of a text could be said to resemble a snapshot of one moment
in a textual evolution which began before the manuscript copy was made, and which
will continue beyond it.

Writing

Considering the implications of textuality in Anglo-Saxon culture entails paying
attention also to other important concepts, such as writing. Textual and archaeological data can give us some information about where writing was carried out and by
whom. From texts themselves we know that most writing was done in monastic scriptoria, and it is now generally accepted that by the tenth century some was the product
of royal chanceries (Chaplais 1985; Keynes 1990; see Ker, *Catalogue*, for an account
of what is known of the origins of surviving Old English manuscripts). Most of the
named authors of texts in Old English and Anglo-Latin are male ecclesiastics, but
references to nuns reading and writing survive, for example in Boniface's letter to
Eadburg, abbess of Minster-in-Thanet, written in 735–6, in which he requests that
her colleagues produce a manuscript for him to use (Brown 1991: 25). Archaeological evidence implies that a scriptorium existed in at least two Anglo-Saxon double
male and female religious houses – Whitby in Yorkshire and Barking in Essex – in
the late seventh to eighth centuries and in the eighth and ninth centuries respectively,
and manuscript evidence points to women owning books (see Brown 1991: 40, 41).
Wealthy laypeople are also recorded as commissioning and reading books: Ælfric
states that he composed the *Lives of Saints* at the request of his patrons Æthelweard
and Æthelmær, for their personal use, and King Alfred is reported to have owned,
commissioned and written books as part of his campaign of personal and national educational development.

Tradition and Composition

As mentioned above, writing is often defined as a physical activity in Anglo-Saxon England. The intellectual act of creation and composition is often portrayed in Anglo-Saxon texts in the context of one particular genre: the oral performance of poetry. In his *Historia ecclesiastica*, written in 731, Bede recounts how Cædmon, a cowherd at Whitby Abbey, was cured of his inability to sing poetry in public by a vision which led to his composing verses in Old English on the Creation (Sweet 1970: 45–50; Shelley-Price 1990: 248–51). Bede stresses the performative aspect of Cædmon's composition in several ways: Cædmon initially has to leave feasts to avoid being asked to recite poetry; his miraculous composition of verses is at the request of the figure in his vision; and he repeats the verses he has made at the command of the abbess the next morning. The poetry Cædmon composes which Bede quotes (in Latin in the original version of the *Historia*, and translated into Old English in later manuscripts) is a catena of formulaic epithets in praise of God, all of which are echoed in much other religious poetry. The heroic poem *Beowulf*, which survives in a manuscript written in the late tenth or early eleventh century, figures scenes of public composition and recitation of poetry as central to the idealized life of the warrior community. These performances in *Beowulf* are carried out by a professional poet, or *scop*, who 'hwilum sang/hador on Heorote' ('at times sang clearly in Heorot [the warriors' hall]', lines 496–7; Wrenn 1973: 117), and who recounts old tales of heroic exploits. These examples stress the deeply conservative and derivative nature of early medieval literary culture, and the value placed on tradition above 'originality'. Early medieval authors are particularly proud of their inheritance, and uninhibited about naming it.

Authority

Authority is clearly an extremely important concept for Anglo-Saxon textual culture, and in fact it seems a more precise label for the system operating than does anything we might define as authorship. Even where an Anglo-Saxon writer seems to provide a self-definition as an individual author, it would be misleading to assume that the modern concept applies. The information that Ælfric records about himself in his works – his teacher, his affiliations and his opinions on other texts – is not so much an assertion of his authorial identity as it is an invocation of the authority which these connections and judgements give to his work (Hill 1994: 179).

In some cases, Anglo-Saxon writers are keen to assert the validity of their texts by proving that they come from a recognized and valued source. It might seem ironic, or simply contradictory, that in a culture where authors often do not name themselves they are sometimes keen to name the authors of their source texts. In fact, in doing this they are interested not in the authorial identity of the individuals named, but rather in the status of those individuals as authoritative sources which set up a chain

of affiliation and validation for the text which names them. As Joyce Hill notes with
regard to Bede's citing of sources, 'it is a means of identifying the authoritativeness
of what is said by identifying the authority; a commitment to derivation rather than
originality, to intertextuality rather than independence' (Hill 1998: 2). Ælfric's practice is another good example of this. In the Latin Preface to the First Series of *Catholic
Homilies*, he provides a list of his source authors, including patristic writers, Bede (who
is treated as an honorary patristic writer) and two Frankish compilers of patristic
homiletic texts, Smaragdus and Haymo (see Hill 1992):

> Hos namque auctores in hac explanatione sumus secuti, videlicet Augustinum
> [Y]pponiensem, Hieronimum, Bedam, Gregorium, Smaragdum, et aliquando
> [Hæg]monem, horum denique auctoritas ab omnibus catholicis libentissime suscipitur.
> (Wilcox 1994: 107)

> For, indeed, we have followed these authors in this exposition: namely, Augustine of
> Hippo, Jerome, Bede, Gregory, Smaragdus, and sometimes Haymo, for the authority of
> these is most willingly acknowledged by all the orthodox. (Wilcox 1994: 127)

Ælfric also names the source authors he has used at particular points in individual
texts, and in making this sort of acknowledgement he is following the practice of his
own sources, including Bede, Smaragdus and another Carolingian compiler, Paul the
Deacon (see Hill 1998). The citation of authorities in this way, then, is not a uniquely
Anglo-Saxon practice, but is rather inherited by Anglo-Saxon writers from their own
authoritative sources.

The modern reader might, however, see the very fact of textual transmission in a
manuscript culture as infringing upon the integrity of the text and blurring the
authority of its composer. If a scribe deliberately alters a text in copying it, for
example, is that text's author still the person who wrote the earlier version, or is the
scribe an author too? What is the authorial status of a person who joins together
excerpts from a range of earlier texts to make a new, composite one – a common activity in Anglo-Saxon England – or of a person who translates a Latin text into Old
English, and in doing so makes changes to its wording and sense? Modern scholars
still often wish to assert the distinctions implied by our use of the terms 'author',
'compiler' and 'scribe', but the more we examine Anglo-Saxon textual culture, the
more these distinctions look like the product of a desire to impose an ordered hierarchy on a complex and flexible process.

The flexibility and fluidity of Anglo-Saxon manuscript culture were not
always unproblematic even for its participants. A well-known example of authorial
anxiety is that of Ælfric's repeated pleas for his works to be copied accurately and
for their integrity to be preserved. In the final prayer of the *Catholic Homilies*, he
requests:

> Gif hwa ma awendan wille. ðonne bidde ic hine for godes lufon þæt he gesette his boc
> onsundron. fram ðam twam bocum ðe we awend habbað. (Godden 1979: 345, lines 7–9)

If anyone wants to write more, then I ask him for the love of God that he set his book apart from the two books which we have written.

And in the Preface to the *Lives of Saints* he asks that

gif hwa þas boc awritan wille . . . he hi wel gerihte be þære bysne and þær namare betwux ne sette þonne we awendon. (Skeat 1966: 1.6, lines 74–6)

if anyone wishes to copy out this book . . . he write it properly according to the exemplar and does not set down any more amongst it than we have written.

This might look to the modern reader like the assertion of an authorial identity and indeed ego. In fact, however, like Ælfric's naming of his teachers and sources, it is more likely to be an attempt on his part to preserve the orthodoxy of his writings and to keep their identity distinct from other texts and traditions which he knew to be circulating: an assertion of doctrinal rather than authorial identity. Whatever Ælfric's motives were in trying to ensure the uncorrupted transmission of his work, the force of manuscript culture rendered his efforts vain. Almost as soon as he issued the *Catholic Homilies*, scribes began copying them into manuscripts with other texts, some of which he would have strongly disapproved, and taking excerpts from them to weld with parts of other texts into composite homilies. These reuses of Ælfric's homilies are almost always transmitted without any note of his name as author. Authorial identity in a manuscript culture, then, is essentially unstable and usually unfixable. Moreover, it is not given the sort of value which it attracts in a print culture: an Anglo-Saxon author is most likely to have a self-image as somebody who inherits source materials, reworks them and issues them so that they can be passed on to new readers and new writers who will in turn rework them. Asserting one's name as an author in Anglo-Saxon England, then, must have seemed to be an irrelevant activity unless one wished to preserve the integrity of one's work. As Ælfric's attempts show, even this wish is ultimately unrealizable.

As mentioned above, articulating theories about writing, authorship and authority was not a common occupation in Anglo-Saxon England. Despite this, Anglo-Saxonists have in recent years found ways of using modern critical theories to expose some of the assumptions inherent in Anglo-Saxon scholarship and the ways in which these assumptions deprive us of major evidence for early medieval mind-sets. For example, it has been shown that nineteenth- and twentieth-century assumptions and value-judgements about authorship and anonymity produced a canon of Old English prose which privileges texts by named authors over anonymous ones, and lumps together the very diverse body of anonymous homiletic texts in a way which obscures the very different ecclesiastical traditions and styles they represent (Lees 1991). This structuring of the canon of Old English prose according to the nineteenth- and twentieth-century valuing of identified authors and 'original' works over the anonymous and derivative (or, as the Anglo-Saxons might say, the authorized or validated) text also led to the neglect by editors and critics of the many surviving multiple copies of prose homiletic texts. Such multiple and variant copies have only recently begun to receive scholarly attention, and the very valuable evidence they provide for attitudes towards authorship and textuality and for textual transmission and composition in Anglo-Saxon England is only now being thoroughly analysed.

One of the most useful schools of modern textual theory for Anglo-Saxon studies is that known as reception theory, which is concerned with the dynamics of the construction of textual meaning (Jauss 1982; Holub 1984). The model which it proposes is that of meaning being generated not at the moment of authorial creation, but rather in the interaction between an original, written text and its reader. For the study of Anglo-Saxon literary culture, this model can be modified to include memorized 'original' texts and audiences who hear texts as well as readers who read them. For the Anglo-Saxonist, reception theory can provide another useful way of articulating what is signified by transmission and reception, and thus of reconceptualizing authorship and anonymity (Frantzen 1990; Swan 1998).

Critical scrutiny has also been applied in recent years to the process of editing texts from Anglo-Saxon England. The act of editing has been defined as an interpretative process which is heavily dependent on the value the editor, or the culture in which the editor operates, ascribes to authorship, textual integrity and originality. In his discussion of reception theory, Allen Frantzen states that '[t]exts seen as events relate writing to rewriting, which includes both editing and reading' (Frantzen 1990: 128), and shows how the concept of the 'eventful' text may be used to describe the rewriting of an Anglo-Saxon text by its early medieval readers and annotators, and also by its modern editors. The assumptions modern scholars and readers make about authorship, and the problems they have with anonymity, have been highlighted recently in a vigorous debate about the proper ways to edit an Old English or Anglo-Latin text. Scholars are currently engaged in an evaluation of different schools of editorial politics and practice, whose two extreme positions are fundamentally opposed to each other. At one extreme are editors who seek to present an 'ideal' text and are willing to alter the text recorded in a manuscript, or to blend readings from more than one manuscript version, to achieve a version nearer to what they imagine to be the authorial, or correct, version. By contrast, the other extreme school of editing is keen to respect manuscript witnesses to a text, and to reproduce them precisely in an edition, even when this entails reproducing evident scribal mistakes and leaving gaps where a manuscript is faulty or damaged (see Scragg and Szarmach 1994). The current debate on editing Anglo-Saxon texts is also essentially a debate about the power of the author and the power of the reader.

If we consider the role of the reader (or, more accurately for a manuscript culture with low literacy levels, of the audience) as well as that of the author, it is possible to construct a critical model which comes closer to representing some of the interchange inherent in Anglo-Saxon literary culture. This interchange is particularly marked in manuscripts which have been written on by their readers or owners. Two interesting examples of this are provided by gospel manuscripts; the first is striking for its bilingual nature and the second for the entertaining insight it provides into the value of a manuscript text. The first is the mid-eighth-century Bible manuscript known as the Codex Aureus (Stockholm, Kungl. Biblioteket, A. 135). This manuscript was written in Kent, and its main text is all in Latin. In the top margin of fol. 11, a note was added in Old English in the ninth century to record that the manuscript was bought back from a Viking army by Ealdorman Alfred and his wife Werburh. Another mid-eighth-century gospel manuscript, Lichfield, Cathedral Library, s.n., known as the Lichfield or Chad Gospels, also has a main text in Latin, and was probably written in Northumbria, or in Ireland or another Celtic centre. On p. 218 of this manuscript, alongside and below a full-page illustration of St Luke, an early-ninth-century reader from Wales has recorded in Latin that somebody named Gelhi swapped the manuscript for his best horse, and gave it to the altar of St Teilo.

Marginal annotations such as this are of great value as evidence in our attempts to understand what constitutes authorship in Anglo-Saxon England, and how reception of and response to texts makes new texts out of old and authors out of readers. Like glosses, marginal annotations show that the layers of a manuscript text are part of an evolutionary process, and that the authority of writing can lie as much in the reader-who-writes as in the composer of the original text. Ælfric's compositions furnish us with a striking example of this from the latest stages of the use of Old English and of the transmission of Anglo-Saxon texts after the Norman Conquest (for further discussion of post-Conquest Old English see Treharne's chapter in this volume). When Ælfric gets to the point in the *Catholic Homilies* where he might be expected to provide homilies for preaching on the three days before Easter – Maundy Thursday, Good Friday and Holy Saturday – he instead writes a note stating that these are *swigdagas* ('silent days'), and that the church forbids preaching on them. If this were all the surviving evidence, we might assume that his view was widely shared, but in two of the surviving eleventh-century manuscript copies of the *Catholic Homilies*, Cambridge, Corpus Christi College 178, and Oxford, Bodleian Library, Hatton 114, a reader has written a critical note in the margin. In CCCC 178 the note is a rather lengthy explanation of why it is in fact important to preach on these three days. This note is signed *cplfmbn*, which is thought to refer to Coleman, a monk and author who was at Worcester in the late 1080s. In Hatton 114, an unsigned note in the margin at the same point of the *Catholic Homilies* is believed to be by Coleman too. In this manuscript Coleman simply registers a brief protest against Ælfric's stance: 'Ðis nis no wel gesæd' ('This is not at all well said') (Ker 1949; Hill 1985; see also Wilcox's chapter in this volume). Coleman's actions as a reader of these manuscripts, then, highlight some of the most important features of Anglo-Saxon authorship and some of its most important differences from the modern concept. In these examples, Coleman is both anonymous and named, and he is always a sort of author not admitted by the modern definition of the term. His outspoken and very visible example of reader response shows that this particular reader had an opinion, a voice and a pen and no hesitation about changing a text and its authority.

REFERENCES

Primary sources

Clemoes, Peter, ed. 1997. *Ælfric's Catholic Homilies: The First Series. Text.* Early English Text Society, s.s. 17. Oxford.

Godden, Malcolm, ed. 1979. *Ælfric's Catholic Homilies: The Second Series. Text.* Early English Text Society, s.s. 5. Oxford.

Sherley-Price, Leo, trans. 1990. *Bede: Ecclesiastical History of the English People.* Ed. and intro. D. H. Farmer. Penguin Classic. London.

Skeat, Walter W., ed. and trans. 1966. *Ælfric's Lives of Saints.* Early English Text Society, o.s. 76, 82, 94, 114. London, 1881–1900. Repr. 2 vols. London.

Sweet, H. 1970. *Sweet's Anglo-Saxon Reader in Prose and Verse.* Rev. Dorothy Whitelock. Oxford.

Whitelock, Dorothy, rev. 1967. *Sweet's Anglo-Saxon Reader in Prose and Verse.* Oxford.

Wilcox, Jonathan, ed. 1994. *Ælfric's Prefaces.* Durham Medieval Texts 9. Durham.

Wrenn, C. L., ed. 1973. *Beowulf.* Rev. W. F. Bolton. London.

Secondary sources

Barthes, Roland 1986. 'The Death of the Author'. *The Rustle of Language*, pp. 49–55. Trans. Richard Howard. Oxford.

Brown, Michelle P. 1991. *Anglo-Saxon Manuscripts.* London.

Chaplais, P. 1985. 'The Royal Anglo-Saxon "Chancery" of the Tenth Century Revisited'. *Studies in Medieval History Presented to R. H. C. Davis*, pp. 41–51. Eds H. Mayr-Harting and R. I. Moore. London.

Clemoes, P. A. M. 1959. 'The Chronology of Ælfric's Works'. *The Anglo-Saxons: Studies in Some Aspects of their History and Culture Presented to Bruce Dickins*, pp. 212–47. Ed. Peter Clemoes. London.

Foucault, Michel 1977. 'What Is an Author?'. *Language, Counter-Memory, Practice: Selected Essays and interviews*, pp. 113–38. Ed. Donald F. Bouchard. Trans. Donald F. Bouchard and Sherry Simon. Oxford.

Frantzen, Allen J. 1990. *Desire for Origins: New Language, Old English, and Teaching the Tradition.* New Brunswick, NJ, and London.

Hill, Joyce. 1985. 'Ælfric's "Silent Days"'. *Leeds Studies in English* n.s. 16: 118–31.

——1992. 'Ælfric and Smaragdus'. *Anglo-Saxon England* 21: 203–37.

——1994. 'Ælfric, Authorial Identity and the Changing Text'. *The Editing of Old English: Papers from the 1990 Manchester Conference*, pp. 177–89. Eds D. G. Scragg and Paul Szarmach. Cambridge.

——1998. *Bede and the Benedictine Reform.* Jarrow Lecture. Jarrow.

Holub, Robert C. 1984. *Reception Theory: A Critical Introduction.* London and New York.

Jauss, Hans Robert 1982. *Towards an Aesthetic of Reception.* Trans. Timothy Bahti. Minneapolis.

Ker, Neil 1949. 'Old English Notes Signed "Coleman"'. *Medium Ævum* 18: 28–31.

Keynes, Simon 1990. 'Royal Government and the Written Word in Late Anglo-Saxon England'. *The Uses of Literacy in Early Mediaeval Europe*, pp. 226–57. Ed. Rosamond McKitterick. Cambridge.

Kristeva, Julia 1986. 'Word, Dialogue and Novel'. *The Kristeva Reader*, pp. 34–61. Ed. Toril Moi. Oxford.

Lees, Clare A. 1991. 'Working with Patristic Sources: Language and Context in Old English Homilies'. *Speaking Two Languages: Traditional Disciplines and Contemporary Theory in Medieval Studies*, pp. 157–80. Ed. Allen J. Frantzen. Albany, NY.

O'Keeffe, Katherine O'Brien 1994. 'Editing and the Material Text'. *The Editing of Old English*, pp. 147–54. Eds D. G. Scragg and Paul E. Szarmach. Cambridge.

Pasternack, Carol Braun 1997. 'Post-structuralist Theories: The Subject and the Text'. *Reading Old English Texts*, pp. 170–91. Ed. Katherine O'Brien O'Keeffe. Cambridge.

Roberts, Jane and Christian Kay, with Lynne Grundy 1995. *A Thesaurus of Old English.* 2 vols. London.

Scragg, D. G. 1992. 'An Old English Homilist of Archbishop Dunstan's Day'. *Words, Texts and Manuscripts: Studies in Anglo-Saxon Culture Pre-*

sented to Helmut Gneuss on the Occasion of his Sixty-fifth Birthday*, pp. 181–92. Ed. Michael Korhammer. Cambridge.

——1999. *Dating and Style in Old English Composite Homilies*. H. M. Chadwick Memorial Lectures 9. Cambridge.

——and Paul E. Szarmach, eds 1994. *The Editing of Old English*. Cambridge.

Swan, Mary 1998. 'Memorialised Readings: Manuscript Evidence for Old English Homily Compilation'. *Anglo-Saxon Manuscripts and their Heritage*, pp. 205–17. Eds Phillip Pulsiano and Elaine Treharne. Aldershot.

Szarmach, Paul E. 1997. 'The Recovery of Texts'. *Reading Old English Texts*, pp. 124–45. Ed. Katherine O'Brien O'Keeffe. Cambridge.

Wilcox, Jonathan 1991. 'Napier's "Wulfstan" Homilies XL and XLII: Two Anonymous Works from Winchester?'. *Journal of English and Germanic Philology* 90: 1–19.

5
Audience(s), Reception, Literacy
Hugh Magennis

An outline of the range of the surviving literature from pre-Conquest England has already been presented in this book, and subsequent chapters will explore that range in detail. The literature of the Anglo-Saxons comprises writings in Latin and the vernacular. It ranges from the serious to the trivial and from abstract scholarship to material that is in a distinctly popular register. In approaching this literature in its historical context, it is relevant to consider what is known about its audience(s) and reception, and, since the literature we have exists as written texts in manuscripts, what is known about who might have read such manuscripts in the period. Obvious questions to start with would seem to be: what *was* the audience of Anglo-Saxon literature, and who read it? These questions turn out to be in some respects less straightforward than they might appear at first sight.

Audience

The word 'audience' has normally been used by Anglo-Saxonists in a somewhat hypo-thetical and imprecise way to refer to the people in the period who might have directly experienced the literature in question, either by reading it or hearing it. Often the use of the word denotes a specifically aural and communal context (Bragg 1991: 27–8), but 'audience' is vague enough not to imply any particular stance on the issue of the 'orality' of Old English poetry. Some Anglo-Saxon works identify their audiences reasonably clearly. With the homilist Ælfric (*c*.955–*c*.1010), for example, it is evident that different of his works were aimed at different audiences, some secular or mixed in character, others specifically monastic (Wilcox 1994: 12, 20–1, 50–2). Even with Ælfric, however, it is clear that many of his writings were appropriated outside his own circle and used in new contexts both in the Anglo-Saxon period and later (Swan 1997, 2000). And Ælfric himself, though ostensibly addressing some of his writings to individuals, also intended them as public documents to be circulated more widely. He begins his Old English preface to his collection *Lives of Saints* (Skeat 1966) by addressing his patron Æthelweard (d. *c*.998) in the second person singular (lines 35–6) but ends up by asking people (not just Æthelweard) who may recopy the book to do so carefully (lines 74–5). Close study of manuscripts can offer revealing indications of their use or uses. For example, a recent detailed analysis of annotations and additions to one particular late tenth- or early eleventh-century manuscript of monastic texts shows its continued use over a long period both for public reading in the monastery's chapter-house and for private study (Graham 1998).

There has been much disagreement as to who the audience of Old English *poetry* was, with discussion ranging from the construction of some kind of homogeneous, monolithic but unspecified 'Anglo-Saxon audience' or 'original audience', usually of high literary competence, to speculation about the specific target audience or 'intended' audience of individual works. *Beowulf* has particularly attracted speculation about its audience (Bjork and Obermeier 1997) and has been viewed, in the past twenty years or so alone, as fitting into reception contexts from Northumbria (Wormald 1978) to Wessex (Lapidge 1982a), via Mercia (Schneider 1986) and East Anglia (Newton 1993), as intended for a secular audience (Busse and Holtei 1981) and a monastic one (Cassidy 1982), as existing in an educated milieu (Bolton 1978) and a 'sub-literary' one (Clemoes 1995: 30–66), and as dating from various times from the seventh century to the eleventh (Chase 1981).

With such a bewildering array of views the best response, though not perhaps the most comforting, is surely one of open-mindedness about audience. A more fruitful question than what was the original audience of *Beowulf* might be what could *Beowulf* have been used for in Anglo-Saxon England. Not all people were the same in Anglo-Saxon England any more than they are now, and a poem like *Beowulf* would have had more than one audience. It was probably composed a considerable length of time before it was copied into its unique surviving manuscript in the early eleventh century. We can attempt to reconstruct what it might have meant to previous generations but are on more promising ground when we consider it in its early eleventh-century reception context, the period to which we can definitely connect the text of the poem. There still remains the certainty of heterogeneity of response even in the eleventh century, as the poem could be appropriated, or 'collaborated with' (O'Keeffe 1990: 193; Pasternack 1995: 26–8; Magennis 1996: 73–5), to produce meaning in different ways, but *Beowulf* should be seen in the first place as a particular text in a particular manuscript. It may be possible to move out from this central fact to consider wider aspects of the way a poem might have been received and appropriated by different kinds of audience, though there are theoretical problems about projecting back from a single manuscript (Pasternack 1995: 200). Awareness of different kinds of audience in Anglo-Saxon England, however, might help us to avoid reductionist and oversimplified views of the meaning of Old English literature in its period.

Latin Literacy

Early medieval literature was received in a context in which reading seems normally to have meant reading *aloud*, whether alone (Leclerq 1961: 23–6) or, more usually, publicly (Bragg 1991: 28; on early medieval reading practices see Parkes 1997: 6–10). As we shall see below, texts in manuscripts were accessible not only to those who could read for themselves but also to those who might be read to, provided they could understand the language. This latter consideration itself points to the fact that the answers to questions about the audience of literature in Anglo-Saxon England and who 'read' it will not be the same for Latin as for literature in Old English. At the risk of oversimplification, it is reasonable to say that, although in practice the people who 'received' Latin writings must inevitably have been at various levels of linguistic competence, such writings were aimed by definition at those in the period to whom the term *litteratus* could be applied. *Litterati* were 'literate' in Latin (Grundmann 1958: Bäuml 1980). Unlike their counterparts in Romanized areas of the continent in the Merovingian and even Carolingian periods (McKitterick 1989; Nelson 1990; Wright 1991), *litterati* in England had acquired Latin wholly academically, as a foreign language. They were predominantly, but not universally, men, and they would normally have been in religious or clerical life. Latin literacy was not an attribute necessary to the exercise of secular power but it was empowering spiritually, ecclesiastically and intellectually: it gave access to the writings that contained the mysteries of Christian faith and worship, it provided admission to participation in the full community of the church, and it made possible engagement with intellectual tradition.

It should be added that literacy did not necessarily imply mastery of writing. People who could read did not normally bother to perfect the craft of writing (Clanchy 1979: 97–102) (any more, perhaps, than most people bother today to master the craft of touch-typing). King Alfred (r. 871–99) could read, but he seems to have relied on others to write things down for him. For example, his biographer Asser says that the king got him to copy material into the commonplace book that he was compiling (*De rebus gestis Ælfredi*, ch. 88; Stevenson 1959). Alfred was also a major (vernacular) 'writer', of course, but, as was the normal practice in the early Middle Ages, he would have composed by dictation rather than having to do the actual writing himself. As M. T. Clanchy says, the only significant exceptions to the rule that authors dictated their works were some monks: 'Monks wrote more of their own works because they were expected to be humble and also because some had training in a *scriptorium*' (1979: 97).

Latin literacy was not confined to men. With regard to women, it is notable that while there is a significant dearth of positive evidence from the *later* Anglo-Saxon period, i.e. the period leading up to and including the time of the Benedictine Reform, there is considerable evidence from the earlier period (Fell 1984: 109–28; Neuman de Vegvar 1996: 62–5). In earlier Anglo-Saxon England we even have evidence of the manufacture of books in female religious houses (Brown 2001). In this earlier period there seems to have been nothing surprising about the existence of communities of religious women who could partake in Latin culture in a sophisticated way. From the seventh and eighth centuries we have Latin works addressed to women and written by women, many of which imply a high level of Latinity. Aldhelm (d. 709/10) addressed his syntactically and lexically demanding work, the prose *De virginitate*, to a group of nuns, who had already been in correspondence with him (in Latin). The eighth-century abbess Leoba, who was, according to her biographer, 'trained from childhood in the rudiments of grammar and the study of other liberal arts' and had become 'extremely learned' (ch. 11; Waitz 1887; Talbot 1954: 215), was among a number of female correspondents of the famous missionary Boniface, while her contemporary Hugeburc, or Hygeburg, was the writer of a Latin hagiographical narrative about the travels of the Anglo-Saxon saint Willibald. From the ninth century there is evidence of Latin prayer-books being owned by women and of the tailoring of the contents of such books to suit a female readership (Brown 2001).

In the later Anglo-Saxon period we see religious material being made available for women in the vernacular, as indeed was also the case for men, but there is not the same kind of evidence of female literacy as exists for previous centuries. Whereas Ælfric addresses his monks in Latin, as in his *Letter to the Monks of Eynsham* (Jones 1998), it is clear that women in religious life were among the intended audience of his translations. Jon Wilcox comments, for example, noting the reference to nuns as well as monks in Ælfric's Preface to his translation of the *Admonitio ad filium spiritualem*: 'The explicit mention of nuns may provide a clue to Ælfric's reason for translating such a specifically monastic work into English' (1994: 52); and Ælfric addresses his paraphrase of the Book of Judith (Assmann 1889) directly to a female audience (lines 429–45). According to 'An Account of Edgar's Establishment of the Monasteries' (Whitelock et al. 1981), the Old English translation of the *Regula Benedicti* by Ælfric's mentor Bishop Æthelwold (d. 984) was undertaken in the first place, among other reasons, because a vernacular version was 'necessary for unlearned laymen' ('niedbehefe ungelæredum woruldmannum'), who chose to give up secular life (151; see Gretsch 1992: 146); but Æthelwold's text was also adapted for nuns. The version for nuns has not survived but its existence is indicated by the remnants of feminine terminology and pronouns in manuscripts of the translation (Gretsch 1973: 195–8, 1992: 142–3). To the extent that women seem to have participated less in Latin literacy in the later period, they would have had less access to the kinds of empowerment it brought, as outlined above.

There is some evidence of lay Latin literacy in Anglo-Saxon England. For example, King Alfred's educational programme at the end of the ninth century, as announced in his Preface to his Old English translation of Gregory the Great's *Cura pastoralis* (Mitchell and Robinson 1992), included the intention of providing Latin teaching for those sons of freemen who were able to continue in learning, having first been taught to read English (lines 61–3; Crossley-Holland 1984: 200). According to Asser, Alfred himself learned Latin in adulthood (*De rebus gestis Ælfredi*, ch. 87) and, assisted by his clerical associates, he translated a number of Latin works into the vernacular. In the late tenth century the layman Æthelweard (according to the ascription of the preface to the work) translated a version of the *Anglo-Saxon Chronicle* into Latin. Æthelweard exemplifies lay Latin literacy in later Anglo-Saxon England, although, as Simon Keynes and Michael Lapidge comment, 'Æthelweard had little command of Latin grammar' despite 'immense stylistic pretentions, particularly when it came to obscure, learned-sounding words' (1983: 334; see also Winterbottom 1967).

Laypeople literate in Latin would have been rare individuals in Anglo-Saxon England, however, and it is clear that whatever community of *litterati* existed was overwhelmingly constituted by the ecclesiastical ranks (Wormald 1977: 105, 113–14). As noted above, the *Regula Benedicti* was translated in late Anglo-Saxon England partly for the benefit of 'unlearned laymen'.

The standard of Latin literacy among those in ecclesiastical ranks was an issue for discussion in the Anglo-Saxon period itself and has been the subject of much debate among modern commentators. A key – but equivocal – document for this debate is King Alfred's Preface to the Old English translation of the *Cura pastoralis*, mentioned above, in which he extols the learning of the Anglo-Saxon past (having in mind, no doubt, the reputations of writers such as Bede, Aldhelm and Alcuin), laments its sad decline in the present and announces an educational strategy for improving matters in the future. He comments that so general has been the decay of Latin learning that there were very few in his day in the country who could translate a letter from Latin into English. 'There were so few of them', he insists, 'that I cannot remember a single one south of the Thames when I came to the throne' (lines 18–19; Crossley-Holland 1984: 219). It is likely that Alfred presents something of an exaggerated picture. His low estimation of the state of Latinity can be seen as counterbalanced to some extent by his own comment that 'it is uncertain how long there will be such learned bishops as now, thanks be to God, there are nearly everywhere' (lines 78–9; Crossley-Holland 1984: 220). Alfred's assessment can also be seen as counterbalanced by the degree of Latin learning implicit in the Preface itself, which is an extremely sophisticated literary composition (Morrish 1986), and by the fact that we know also of roughly contemporary literary activity emanating from Mercian tradition, of a kind that presumes significant Latin literacy (Cross 1986; Roberts 1986; Brown 1996: 151–61, 2001). As Allen Frantzen writes: 'The term "Mercian" remains a vague and unsatisfactory designation of texts not written by Alfred, but we cannot doubt that Mercia occupied a position of intellectual leadership when Alfred came to the throne' (1986: 110).

None the less, it is clear that both the standard and the extent of Latin literacy in Alfred's time, even among ecclesiastics, were at a low ebb. Clerical ignorance of Latin had become a problem in earlier generations too (Kelly 1990: 59), and Alfred presents a picture in the ninth century of ecclesiastical centres containing books but of a clergy who 'could not understand anything of them, because they were not written in their own language' (lines 32–3; Crossley-Holland 1984: 219). Nor do Alfred's educational measures appear to have improved things significantly with regard to Latin literacy, since the following generations are remarkably lacking in evidence of a flourishing Latin culture. Leaders of the monastic reform of the later tenth century received their intellectual stimulation from abroad, from centres like Fleury and Ghent, and scholars from the continent, skilled in Latin, came to England to assist the project (Hohler 1975: 71–3). Ælfric became a leading figure of this reform but he reports in his *Preface to Genesis* (Mitchell and Robinson 1992) that he himself received his early education from a poorly educated mass-priest (lines 1–13) and he writes anxiously of 'unlearned priests' who understood only 'some little part' of books in Latin (lines 23–4). As his *Grammar* and *Colloquy* testify, Ælfric himself was actively involved in the teaching of Latin in the monastery, and he produced literary works in Latin as well as English. A revealing insight into the teaching of Latin in a monastic context in late Anglo-Saxon England is provided in the *Colloquies* of Ælfric's younger contemporary Ælfric Bata (see Gwara and Porter 1997: 9–10, 15–19). Despite the work of teachers such as Ælfric (of Eynsham) and Ælfric Bata, however, generally a low standard of clerical learning and even literacy seems to have persisted in the reform period (for a particularly severe assessment, see Hohler 1975: 71–6). The later Anglo-Saxon period saw a remarkable flowering of the literature of Christian teaching, but this was to a great degree writing in English, not Latin.

Latin works could be studied privately (Lapidge 1982b), or recited to a group audience as in a monastic chapter-house or refectory, but even the latter would be of benefit only to *litterati*. The audience of Latin literature in Anglo-Saxon England is thus to be seen as to some extent always an academic one, given the place of Latin as the key to any medium of developed Christian education and intellectual discourse. It was an audience with training in *grammatica*, 'the discipline that governed literacy, the study of literary language, the interpretation of texts, and the writing of manuscripts' (Irvine 1991: 184–5). The quality and extent of Latin literacy varied in the Anglo-Saxon period, but literacy was always essential to the church's institutional life, since the church relied on books, and the books that mattered were in Latin.

Vernacular Literacy

The questions of whom Anglo-Saxon *vernacular* literature was for and who read it are somewhat more complicated than is the case with Latin literature. For one thing, literature in the vernacular was accessible to the non-literate as well as to the literate. We know that some Old English literature was purely oral, and even that which was written down could be delivered orally to a non-literate as well as a literate audience by someone who could read. Some written literature, indeed, was clearly targeted at an audience which included the non-literate. Ælfric, for example, tells us that he wrote his *Catholic Homilies* for readers and listeners (*legentium vel audientium*, Latin Preface to the First Series; Clemoes 1997: line 8), and Wulfstan's famous sermon *ad Anglos*, 'to the English', is addressed to the people as a whole, not just the minority who could read.

An important distinction to be borne in mind with regard to Old English writings therefore is that between *literature* and *literacy*, and hence between the reception of literature and the actual reading of it. Literature and literacy do not necessarily go together. Individual literacy was not at all a precondition for experiencing even some 'learned' literature in the vernacular, as it was for Latin. Of course, not all Old English writing would have been suitable for reciting aloud (glosses, recipes and reference handbooks with extensive use of diagrams, tables and other visual information, like Byrhtferth's *Enchiridion*, are examples of non-oral texts), but much of it was recitable, and indeed much of it was clearly designed for oral performance.

The existence of written Old English literature presupposes individuals who could read. Even if they could not read Latin, the clergy that Alfred refers to in his Preface were literate in English: the reason they were unable to read books in their possession was 'because they were not written in their own language' (lines 32–3; Crossley-Holland 1984: 219). Literacy in the vernacular predates King Alfred's project, as he puts it, of translating 'into the language which we can all understand' books which are 'most needful for all men to know' (lines 55–6; Crossley-Holland 1984: 220) and of teaching the sons of wealthier freemen 'to read English writing well' (line 61; Crossley-Holland 1984: 220). Old English works were copied in pre-Alfredian scriptoria (Kelly 1990: 54), and Bede's pupil Cuthbert reports that at the time of his death his master had been working on English translations of the first six chapters of the Gospel of St John and the *De natura rerum* of Isidore of Seville (*Epistula de obitu Baedae*; Colgrave and Mynors 1969: 582). It was the existence of literacy in the vernacular in a context of widespread illiteracy in Latin that made possible and desirable Alfred's programme of translation and that opened the way to the subsequent proliferation of Old English texts in the last century of the Anglo-Saxon period. And in this period vernacular literacy was used not only for the obvious purpose of reading English texts but also as an aid to learning Latin, as evidenced by Ælfric's *Grammar* and perhaps by the existence of copies of Latin texts like *Regularis concordia* glossed in English (Kornexl 1995: 116–17).

It is impossible to know for sure how widespread vernacular literacy was. Literacy in English, as in Latin, may have been 'something of a clerical monopoly' throughout the period (Wormald 1997: 113), though evidence for a 'literate mentality' among the laity has been emphasized in recent scholarship (Lowe 1998: 179–80). We may wish to distinguish between what Seth Lerer refers to as 'elite traditions' of literacy (1991: 198), on the one hand ('ones that privilege spiritual commitment, linguistic training, or runic skill'), and popular and 'pragmatic' literacy, on the other, but certainly in later Anglo-Saxon England laypeople in authority were making increasing use of vernacular literacy in public administration. As Simon Keynes writes, 'It would seem reasonable to conclude that royal government in the tenth and eleventh centuries depended to a very considerable extent on the use of the written word, and that late Anglo-Saxon society was well accustomed to such manifestations of "pragmatic literacy"' (1990: 255). Whether relying largely on clerical knowledge, however, or benefiting also from 'pragmatic literacy' and education among people in secular life, the uneducated were not completely debarred from an appreciation of the written word. As long as they could make use of individuals who could read, whether clerical or lay, they were able to partake in literate culture at least to a limited extent.

In the Middle Ages, indeed, even people who could read often preferred to have manuscripts read to them than to read them themselves (Clanchy 1979: 214–20; cf. Nelson 1976–7). Later, this included the (literal) 'auditing' of monetary accounts. King Alfred is reported to have spent much time reading books for himself but, according to Asser, 'he was also in the habit of listening eagerly and attentively to Holy Scripture being read out' (*De rebus gestis Ælfredi*, ch. 76; Keynes and Lapidge 1983: 91). Asser says that he himself used to read to the king, for it was Alfred's habit 'either to read books aloud himself or to listen to others doing so' (ch. 81; Keynes and Lapidge 1983: 97). As described by Asser, Alfred in his childhood, before he learned to read, was already 'a careful listener, by day and night, to English poems, most frequently hearing them recited by others, and he readily retained them in his memory' (ch. 22; Keynes and Lapidge 1983: 75).

Orality and Textuality

In considering the reception of literature in the Middle Ages, scholars have widely adopted, and adapted, the concept of 'textual communities' first introduced by Brian Stock in his study of literacy in the post-Conquest period (1983: 90–2). To partake in textual culture, individuals did not have to be able to read books for themselves as long as they had access to and could interact with texts through mediators and interpreters. As Martin Irvine puts it, 'medieval textual communities were formed of literate, semiliterate, and illiterate members: those unable or just learning to read were expected to participate in textual culture, having the necessary texts, and their interpretation, read to them' (1991: 185; on textual communities see also Irvine 1994 *passim*). The non-literate laity were taking part in textual culture when they listened to a sermon, for example, or heard an account of a saint's life. Their preacher may or may not have been reading directly to them from a written text but in any case was drawing upon written texts he had read.

The textual communities associated with Anglo-Saxon monasteries could include experienced scholars but also uneducated people. In Bede's story of the poet Cædmon we see a humble cowherd being absorbed into a textual community, as the illiterate Cædmon is received into the monastery and instructed by learned men reading to him the events of sacred history: 'He learned all he could by listening to them and then, memorizing it and ruminating over it, like some clean animal chewing the cud, he turned it into the most melodious verse: and it sounded so sweet as he recited it that his teachers became in turn his audience (*auditores*)' (*HE* IV.24; Colgrave and Mynors 1969: 419). After Cædmon, vernacular Biblical poetry began to be written down and transmitted scribally. Thus, 'textualized' scriptural poetry in the tradition of Cædmon itself provided material for Anglo-Saxon textual communities, bringing edification as it was read aloud to its *auditores*. Written Old English literature can be seen as having been received in textual communities, which would have been able to draw on knowledge of vernacular oral tradition and to exploit the attributes of textual culture, with its foundation in *grammatica*.

In the light of the preceding discussion it is apparent that a key concept with regard to the Anglo-Saxon reception of written Old English literature, along with literacy, is textuality. Latin literature obviously has its existence in the context of textuality. Once Old English literature begins to be written down, it too enters the realm of textuality, whose social and aesthetic implications are different from those of orality (Ong 1975; Bäuml 1980; Schaefer 1991). Recent criticism has highlighted the 'self-conscious textuality of medieval literature and culture' (Lerer 1991: 7) and has explored the nature of that textuality.

But all the Old English poetry preserved in our manuscripts is the heir of oral poetry. A major focus of Old English literary studies in recent decades, but especially since the early 1990s, has been the questions of the transition from orality to textuality and of the relationship of the vernacular poetic texts of the Anglo-Saxon period to the oral literature from which they developed (see especially O'Keeffe 1990; Doane and Pasternack 1991; Lerer 1991; Pasternack 1995; Head 1997). Might Old English poetic texts simply be transcribed oral performances? Such a scenario is implied by Bede in his account of the poet Cædmon, who is presented as engaging in spontaneous oral composition. That Bede is able to render Cædmon's *Hymn* in his Latin text (*HE* IV.24) is ostensibly due to the fact that someone recorded it in writing as the illiterate Cædmon spoke it, or copied it down from memory soon afterwards. On the other hand, *written* composition seems likely for many surviving Old English poems, some of which, indeed, must have been created by poets working with Latin books open in front of them (Benson 1966; on literate poets, see also Kendall 1996). But even where composed in writing, Old English verse works in an oral-derived formulaic tradition. The very characteristics of that tradition, which of course could have had no concept of an autonomous text, raise difficult questions about the status of the individual poetic text and its transmission. Some of these questions will be explored below, while others are taken up elsewhere in this volume.

When the Anglo-Saxons first came to Britain in the fifth century their culture was in essential respects one of 'primary' orality (Havelock 1963; Goody and Watt 1968; Ong 1982; Street 1984). The settlers lived lives in which tradition, knowledge and belief had their existence in memory and utterance rather than in writing. Primary oral culture, as has been famously said, is a culture where no one has ever 'looked up' anything (Ong 1982: 21), where words have no visual presence, being evanescent events in time. Though the early Anglo-Saxons made use of runes, inscribed on wood and other hard surfaces, that system of writing was employed for highly restricted purposes. Runes seem to have represented esoteric knowledge and were used perhaps for magic, as well as for brief statements of commemoration and ownership (Kelly 1990: 36–8; Lerer 1991: 11–12). With the introduction of 'Roman writing', Anglo-Saxons continued to make specialized use of the cryptic possibilities of runes within vernacular literary texts. Perhaps the most famous Old English runic text is the crucifixion poem inscribed on the monument at Ruthwell (in Dumfriesshire). In pre-Christian times, however, runes seem not to have been used as a medium of developed textual discourse.

Beowulf, set in the pre-Christian society of the Germanic tribes, portrays a world of primary orality. In the poem knowledge is passed on by those who can remember traditions from far back, like the *scop* ('minstrel') who sings in the hall Heorot of God's creation of the world (though his account of the creation anachronistically follows the Genesis rather than pre-Christian Germanic tradition): 'Sægde, se þe cuþe / frumsceaft fira feorran reccan' (lines 90b–1; 'He spoke, who knew how to relate from far back the creation of men'). Knowledge of old traditions also enables minstrels to fashion new poetic compositions, improvising in the inherited language of poetry. Thus one of Hrothgar's retainers performs an impromptu poem in praise of Beowulf:

> Hwilum cyninges þegn,
> guma gilphlæden,   gidda gemyndig,
> se ðe ealfela   ealdgesegena
> worn gemunde,   word oþer fand
> soðe gebunden;   secg eft ongan
> sið Beowulfes   snyttrum styrian
> ond on sped wrecan   spel gerade,
> wordum wrixlan.
>
> (lines 867b–74a)

At times a thane of the king, filled with high-sounding words, with a memory for songs, a man who remembered a great multitude of ancient traditions, devised new words, properly linked together; he began skilfully to rehearse again Beowulf's exploit and fluently to relate an apt narrative, varying his words.

The thane also goes on to relate the story of the hero Sigemund, retelling what he has heard about him: 'Welhwylc gecwæð / þæt he fram Sigemunde secgan hyrde' (lines 674b–5; 'He spoke of nearly everything he had heard tell concerning Sigemund'). In primary oral culture a central function of the *scop* is to keep alive a people's memory of its past and values and to interpret the present in terms of those values, as the thane does in *Beowulf* (Niles 1998). The Exeter Book poem *Widsith* consists largely of a catalogue of names of individuals and peoples, whose memory the poem perpetuates. The speaker in *Widsith* refers to the treasury of words (*wordhord*, line 1) about the past that the *scop* has at his disposal. According to this speaker, the *scop* is someone who commemorates tribal tradition and addresses as his audience the inheritors of that tradition. His audience in turn should reward him for the valuable service he provides and thereby they themselves may merit to be absorbed into the material of his song, as he praises them also:

Swa scriþende   gesceapum hweorfað
gleomen gumena   geond grunda fela,
þearfe secgað,   þoncword sprecaþ,
simle suð oþþe norð   sumne gemetað
gydda gleawne,   geofum unhneawne,
se þe fore duguþe wile   dom aræran,
eorlscipe æfnan,   oþþæt eal scæceð,
leoht ond lif somod;   lof se gewyrceð,
hafað under heofonum   heahfæstne dom.

(lines 135–43)

Thus, travelling, the minstrels of men by fate wander through many lands, declare their need, speak words of thanks; always, south or north, they meet someone knowledgeable about songs, not stingy in his gifts, who in front of the retainers wishes to exalt his reputation and enhance his nobility, until all passes away, light and life together; he brings about praise, and has lasting glory below the heavens.

As well as portraying an oral culture in their content, *Beowulf* and other Old English poems display features in their form that have been identified as distinctive of oral literature. Grammatically and stylistically, oral poetry is additive rather than subordinative, avoiding elaborate sentence structure; it is aggregative rather than analytic, carrying 'a load of epithets and other formulary baggage which high literacy rejects as cumbersome and tiresomely redundant' (Ong 1982: 38); indeed, generally, redundancy or 'copiousness' is a feature of oral literature, which uses repetition, variation and recapitulation as means of making sure the audience does not get left behind. Other recognized characteristics of oral literature are that it is traditionalist, agonistic (embodying competition and conflict), empathetic (the attitude to what is described is not neutral), homeostatic (meanings come out of the present use of words, not their history: society keeps itself in equilibrium by sloughing off memories which no longer have present relevance), and situational rather than abstract (on these characteristics, see Ong 1982: 41–57).

Many of these features are clearly evident in the passage from *Widsith* quoted above, and one would not have to look far to find them in other poems too. But, of course, *Widsith* exists in a manuscript. It was received as a text by the readers of the Exeter Book. These readers would not have been like the traditional tribal audience implied in *Widsith* itself, nor – presumably – would they have had the knowledge of the 'minutiae of Germanic tribal lore' (Hill 1985: 315) that scholars have blithely assumed for that 'original' audience (but which must have been doubtful even for the latter; Hill 1984: 312–13). *Beowulf* and *Widsith* present themselves as the products of oral culture, their speakers adopting the stance of the minstrel, passing on orally the things they have heard about. In a textual context, however, the audience addressed in these poems becomes fictionalized, as does the figure of the narrator, who is now absent (Baüml 1980). These poems give the impression of being oral utterances of a minstrel, spontaneous performances, presumably delivered in the hall, which is implicitly evoked as the traditional setting for Germanic verse. *Beowulf*, like other Old English verse texts, begins with the conventional call for attention in speech, *Hwæt!*, and continues in its opening sentence with the inclusive pronoun *we* accompanied by a verb suggestive of hearing, *gefrignan*: 'Hwæt! We Gardena in geardagum, / þeodcyninga, þrym gefrunon' (lines 1–2; 'Listen, we have heard of the glory of the Spear-Danes in days gone by, of the kings of the people'). In *Beowulf* we are in an oral communal world, which is not the world of the *Beowulf*-manuscript. *Beowulf*, as we have it, was doubtless recited aloud to an audience, but such a reception is very different from that of the primary orality represented in the poem and its pre-literate tradition. Textuality changes the nature of the audience in literature and of the 'speaker'. The latter circumstance is particularly significant in a literature which shows considerable preoccupation with its speakers and with levels of speaker within a single text (cf. Head 1997: 27–53). In *Widsith*, for example, the figure of Widsith is someone whose travels are recounted but who never could have existed as presented, since he has visited people who lived generations apart. And the poem has a 'speaker' who is not Widsith, but neither is he, of course, the person speaking every time the poem is recited or read. The speaker, as opposed to the actual reciter, has to be imagined, as he relays (fictionally) the words of Widsith in a 'dramatic' rendition (cf. Schaefer 1991: 124–5). What the text called *Widsith* presents is a layered recreation of Germanic tradition, as embodied in the imagined poets of that tradition.

Aurality and the Seen Text

The vocabulary of speaking and hearing, as opposed to seeing on the page and writing, is favoured in Old English texts in their address to the people receiving those texts. Whether in the opening words of *Beowulf*, just quoted, or in religious texts like *The Dream of the Rood* or the corpus of prose homilies, an oral, usually public, context is assumed. Even in those writings discussed below which *do* present themselves as texts on the page, the oral dimension is also strongly emphasized. Doubtless, some texts would have been read privately but, as suggested above, even private reading does not necessarily imply silent reading.

A characteristic quality of Old English literature, which reflects its oral dimension and ultimately its oral origin, is its concern with the dimension of sound. Of course, Old English poetry is structurally alliterative: alliteration, accompanied by the metrical patterning of stressed and unstressed syllables, is built into every line of verse, making it difficult indeed, even for today's constitutionally silent readers, to read without enunciating it. The alliteration is inherent but can also be used 'artfully' (Orchard 1995), and the verse exploits other kinds of sound patterns too, like repetition, rhythmic variation and occasional rhyme.

Aural features associated with Old English verse, principally alliteration and pronounced rhythm, were adopted by writers of prose, often at the level of local rhetorical embellishment but also in a more systematic way. It is likely that there was influence from Latin tradition on some of the rhetorical practices of prose writers, but the influence of vernacular poetic tradition contributed a characteristic rhythmic quality to much prose writing. The homilist Wulfstan bases his distinctive prose on units of two-stress alliterating phrases of a kind derived from the structure of the verse half-line (McIntosh 1950). And the 'rhythmical prose' of Ælfric, with its use of systematic alliteration and stress, develops its basic structural principles from Old English poetry, though it is much looser than the latter and lacks its diction and tone (Pope 1967–8: 1.105–36). Aural techniques involving alliteration and rhythmical patterning are widely found both in the later Old English prose of Ælfric, Wulfstan and their contemporaries and immediate predecessors (such as the homilists of the Blickling and Vercelli collections) and in earlier writings (Orchard 1997: 109–14). To refer, for example, to one text discussed earlier, King Alfred's Preface to the *Pastoral Care* makes extensive use of two-stress alliterating phrases, particularly highlighting key themes in Alfred's discussion, like *lar* and *liornung* ('teaching' and 'learning', lines 10–11) and *wela* and *wisdom* ('prosperity' and 'wisdom', line 38), and the Preface generally reflects a preoccupation with sound. A later text, the anonymous *Legend of the Seven Sleepers* (Magennis 1994), is written in a mannered style which exploits many kinds of rhetorical balance and elaboration. At phrasal level these include the use of word-pairing and alliteration, often combined, as in 'holdode and . . . hricode' ('cut up and . . . cut to pieces', lines 64–5), 'ðafedon and þoledon' ('endured and suffered', line 111) and 'on myrhþe and on mærðe' ('in joy and in glory', line 129). Rhyme is also used, as in 'Mycel is me unbliss minra dyrlinga miss' ('Much is my sorrow at the loss of my dear ones', line 247), and syntactical and verbal repetition and variation are cultivated, especially in passages of emotional intensity (Magennis 1994: 27–8). The *Legend of the Seven Sleepers* is a text which shows a particularly developed interest in aural patterning, but similar points could be made about other works also.

Such features as those mentioned in the previous paragraphs point to the performative aspect of much Old English literature and indicate that it was designed for aural reception, having an intended audience of literal *audientes* ('listeners', to recall Ælfric's phrase). It is also true, however, that some Old English texts show consciousness of their *legentes* ('readers'), who are looking at letters and words in a manuscript. The brief entries of the early *Anglo-Saxon Chronicle*, preceded by the adverb *her*, 'here', reflect a tradition of terse jottings set out on the page for the eye, and the use of decoration and illustration highlights the visual dimension of a number of vernacular as well as Latin texts (Gameson 1995: 36–7). This visual dimension would not have been available to a group of listeners. Reading might have been a largely communal activity but, as Richard Gameson points out, writing of the reception of illustrated manuscripts in later Anglo-Saxon England, 'book illumination was essentially an intimate art' (1995: 56).

The idea of the seen text is particularly interesting with reference to Old English verse, a medium which was oral in origin and which retained characteristics of its oral heritage for as long as it was composed. Yet some Old English poetic texts have features accessible only to people who can see them – and read them – on the page, particularly texts that exploit letters and written words, often, though not always, through the incorporation of runes. One Old English poem, *The Rune Poem*, is made up of sections of from four to five lines, each beginning with a runic letter, the overall order following that of the runic alphabet. In this poem the runes represent their Anglo-Saxon names (*feoh*, 'money, property'; *ur*, 'bison, aurochs'; *þorn*, 'thorn'; etc.) and are incorporated into a series of riddle-like statements, relishing their own curiousness. There are, much later, rune poems in Old Norse (Dobbie 1942: xlvii–xlviii; Halsall 1981: 35–8) but *The Rune Poem* also recalls the clever abecedarian compositions of Latin tradition, such as Bede's hymn in praise of St Æthelthryth (Etheldreda; *HE* IV.20; Halsall 1981: 42–5). *The Rune Poem* is an ingenious work, combining learned and popular elements in a form that exploits both the visual and the aural. The cryptic nature of runes is also notably exploited in the Exeter Book poem *The Husband's Message*, in which a message in runes (the interpretation of which remains problematic) is conveyed to a loved one. The runic letters of the message are reproduced in the poem. Another 'message' in runes is to be found in the crucifixion poem of the Ruthwell monument, a seen text which is integrated into a larger visual scheme (Ó Carragáin 1987–8).

Runes also appear in the 'signatures' of Cynewulf, where they are worked into the text of a number of poems to spell out the name 'Cyn(e)wulf' (*The Fates of the Apostles*, *Elene*, *Christ II* and *Juliana*). In the surface meaning of the passages in question the runes stand for their name-words, but cryptically they function too as letters making up the word CYNEWULF or CYNWULF. The double meaning would hardly be discernible for a listener but stands out clearly on the page, being based on inscription as well as sound. And in one of the occurrences of the signature (in *The Fates of the Apostles*) the meaning is further concealed by the fact that the letters of the name are somewhat jumbled, in the sequence FWULCYN. It may be that the signatures are not intended to be noticed, or are intended to be noticed only by God, with whom the poet may find favour through being (unknowingly) commemorated by the audience of his poems. Whatever the purpose of the signatures, they are an interesting instance of the use of letters *as* letters in Old English literature.

The device of transposing letters in Old English texts is not confined to runic writing, though it is easy to see why this device might have been thought attractive to users of a writing system like runes which itself seems to have had associations of exclusivity, requiring special skill to be decoded. There is a simple example of letter transposition using not runes but the 'normal' (Roman) Anglo-Saxon alphabet in Riddle 23 of the Exeter Book, where the solution *boga* 'bow' is cryptically revealed in the riddle's first word, *Agof*, which, read backwards, gives *foga*, an earlier form of *boga*. The deciphering of this riddle is complicated by the unusual spelling *foga*, which may simply be an error by a scribe who did not understand what he or she was copying or may be a deliberately chosen archaic form.

Runic and Roman letter forms are exploited elsewhere in the Old English riddles. Riddle 24 contains a more difficult jumbling of the runic letters in its solution *higoræ*

(= *higore*, 'jay, magpie') and there are reversed runic spellings in Riddles 19 (and its companion piece 64), 42 and 75 (Williamson 1977: 188). In Riddle 42, indeed, the words *hana*, 'cock', and *hæn*, 'hen', overlap with each other, with several letters referring to both words. This riddle, as Seth Lerer explains, 'addresses issues in the "literate" interpretation of literary experience' (1991: 124). It is specifically addressed to those who know books ('þam þe bec witan', line 7). Riddle 36 contains a line, generally thought to be a defective later addition to the text (Orchard 1997: 114–17), in which the words *monn*, 'man', *wif*, 'woman', and *hors*, 'horse', are followed by their Latin equivalents, *homo*, *mulier* and *equus*, written in a code in which each vowel is represented by the consonant that follows it in the alphabet (the whole line is in the Roman alphabet). Unfortunately, the scribe has been defeated by the ingenuity of the line and has miscopied it: 'monn.hw.M.wiif.m.x.l.kf wf.hors. qxxs' (line 5). Such fascination with intellectual aspects of writing indicates a specialized readership for some surviving Old English poetry, a readership that clearly has much in common with the *litterati* whom we saw as receivers of Latin literature in Anglo-Saxon England. The overlap between the two groups is illustrated by the fact that one of the Exeter Book riddles (Riddle 90) is in Latin and by the existence of English–Latin macaronic verse in Anglo-Saxon England (as in *The Phoenix* and *A Summons to Prayer*) (see Irvine 1994: 423–4). Throughout this chapter I have hesitated – until the present paragraph – to use the word 'readership' at all, because of the questions that it begs. Much Old English poetry, including learned poetry, was certainly experienced aurally, but it is also evident that some vernacular literary works were received as seen texts.

REFERENCES

Primary sources

Assmann, Bruno, ed. 1889. 'Ælfric's Homilie über das Buch Judith'. *Angelsächsische Homilien und Heiligenleben*, pp. 102–16. Bibliothek der angelsächsischen Prosa 3. Kassel.

Clemoes, Peter, ed. 1997. *Ælfric's Catholic Homilies: The First Series*. Early English Text Society, s.s. 17. Oxford.

Colgrave, Bertram, and R. A. B. Mynors, eds and trans. 1969. *Bede's Ecclesiastical History of the English People*. Oxford.

Crossley-Holland, Kevin, trans. 1984. *The Anglo-Saxon World: An Anthology*. Oxford.

Dobbie, Elliott Van Kirk, ed. 1942. *The Anglo-Saxon Minor Poems*. Anglo-Saxon Poetic Records 6. New York and London.

Gretsch, Mechthild, ed. 1973. *Die Regula Sancti Benedicti in England*. Munich.

Gwara, Scott and David W. Porter, eds and trans.

1997. *Anglo-Saxon Conversations: The Colloquies of Ælfric Bata*. Woodbridge.

Halsall, Maureen, ed. 1981. *The Old English Rune Poem: A Critical Edition*. Toronto.

Jones, Christopher A., ed. 1998. *Ælfric's Letter to the Monks of Eynsham*. CSASE 24. Cambridge.

Keynes, Simon and Michael Lapidge 1983. *Alfred the Great: Asser's Life of King Alfred and Other Contemporary Sources*. Harmondsworth.

Magennis, Hugh, ed. 1994. *The Anonymous Old English Legend of the Seven Sleepers*. Durham Medieval Texts 7. Durham.

Mitchell, Bruce and Fred C. Robinson 1992. *A Guide to Old English*. 5th edn. Oxford.

Pope, John C., ed. 1967–8. *The Homilies of Ælfric: A Supplementary Collection*. Early English Text Society, s.s. 259–60. London.

Skeat, Walter W., ed. and trans. 1966. *Ælfric's Lives of Saints*. Early English Text Society, o.s.

76, 82, 94, 114. London, 1881–1900. Repr. 2 vols. London.

Stevenson, William Henry, ed. 1959. *Asser's Life of King Alfred, Together with the Annals of Saint Neots Erroneously Ascribed to Asser.* Oxford, 1904. Repr. intro. Dorothy Whitelock. Oxford.

Talbot, C. H., trans. 1954. *The Anglo-Saxon Missionaries to Germany.* London.

Waitz, G., ed. 1887. *Vitae Leobae abbatissae Biscofesheimensis auct. Rudolfo Fuldensi.* Monumenta Germaniae Historica, Scriptores 15.1: 118–31. Hanover.

Whitelock, D. M., M. Brett and C. N. L. Brooke, eds and trans. 1981. *Councils and Synods, with Other Documents Relating to the English Church. I. A.D. 871–1204.* Oxford.

Wilcox, Jonathan, ed. 1994. *Ælfric's Prefaces.* Durham Medieval Texts 9. Durham.

Williamson, Craig, ed. 1977. *The Old English Riddles of the Exeter Book.* Chapel Hill.

Secondary sources

Bäuml, Franz H. 1980. 'Varieties and Consequences of Medieval Literacy and Illiteracy'. *Speculum* 55: 237–65.

Benson, Larry 1966. 'The Literary Character of Anglo-Saxon Formulaic Poetry'. *Publications of the Modern Language Association* 81: 334–41.

Bjork, Robert E. and Anita Obermeier 1997. 'Date, Provenance, Author, Audiences'. *A Beowulf Handbook*, pp. 13–34. Eds Robert E. Bjork and John D. Niles. Lincoln, NE.

Bolton, Whitney F. 1978. *Alcuin and Beowulf: An Eighth-Century View.* New Brunswick, NJ.

Bragg, Lois 1991. *The Lyric Speakers of Old English Poetry.* Rutherford, CT.

Brown, Michelle P. 1996. *The Book of Cerne: Prayer, Patronage and Power in Ninth-century England.* London and Toronto.

——— 2001. 'Female Book-ownership and Production in Anglo-Saxon in England: The Evidence of the Ninth-century Prayerbooks'. *Lexis and Texts in Early English: Studies Presented to Jane Roberts*, pp. 45–67. Eds Christian Kay and Louise Sylvester. Amsterdam.

Busse, Wilhelm and R. Holtei 1981. '*Beowulf* and the Tenth Century'. *Bulletin of the John Rylands Society* 63: 285–329.

Cassidy, Frederic G. 1982. 'Knowledge of *Beowulf*

in its Own Time'. *Yearbook of Research in English and American Literature* 1: 1–12.

Clanchy, M. T. 1979. *From Memory to Written Record: England 1066–1307.* Oxford.

Clemoes, Peter 1995. *Interactions of Thought and Language in Old English Poetry.* Cambridge Studies in Anglo-Saxon England 12. Cambridge.

Chase, Colin, ed. 1981. *The Dating of Beowulf.* Toronto.

Cross, J. E. 1986. 'The Latinity of the Ninth-century Old English Martyrologist'. *Studies in Earlier Old English Prose*, pp. 275–99. Ed. Paul E. Szarmach. Albany, NY.

Doane, A. N. and C. B. Pasternack, eds 1991. *Vox Intexta: Orality and Textuality in the Middle Ages.* Madison.

Fell, Christine 1984. *Women in Anglo-Saxon England.* Oxford.

Frantzen, Allen J. 1986. *King Alfred.* Twayne's English Authors Series 425. Boston.

Gameson, Richard 1995. *The Role of Art in the Late Anglo-Saxon Church.* Oxford.

Goody, Jack and Ian Watt 1968. 'The Consequences of Literacy'. *Literacy in Traditional Societies*, pp. 27–68. Ed. Jack Goody. Cambridge.

Graham, Timothy 1998. 'Cambridge, Corpus Christi College 57 and its Anglo-Saxon Users'. *Anglo-Saxon Manuscripts and their Heritage*, pp. 21–69. Eds Phillip Pulsiano and Elaine M. Treharne. Aldershot.

Gretsch, Mechthild 1992. 'The Benedictine Rule in Old English: A Document of Bishop Æthelwold's Reform Politics'. *Words, Texts and Manuscripts: Studies in Anglo-Saxon Culture Presented to Helmut Gneuss on the Occasion of His Sixty-fifth Birthday*, pp. 131–58. Ed. Michael Korhammer, with the assistance of Karl Reichl and Hans Sauer. Cambridge.

Grundmann, Herbert 1958. '*Litteratus – Illiteratus*: Der Wandel einer Bildungsnorm vom Altertum zum Mittelalter'. *Archiv für Kulturgeschichte* 40: 1–65.

Havelock, Eric A. 1963. *A Preface to Plato.* Oxford.

Head, Pauline E. 1997. *Representation and Design: Tracing a Hermeneutics of Old English Poetry.* Albany, NY.

Hill, Joyce 1984. '*Widsith* and the Tenth Century'. *Neuphilologische Mitteilungen* 85: 305–15.

Hohler, C. E. 1975. 'Some Service Books of the Later Saxon Church'. *Tenth-century Studies*, pp.

60–83, 217–27. Ed. David Parsons. London and Chichester.

Irvine, Martin 1991. 'Medieval Textuality and the Archaeology of Textual Culture'. *Speaking Two Languages: Traditional Disciplines and Contemporary Theory in Medieval Studies*, pp. 181–210. Ed. Allen J. Frantzen. Albany, NY.

—— 1994. *The Making of Textual Culture: 'Grammatica' and Literary Theory 350–1100*. Cambridge Studies in Medieval Literature 19. Cambridge.

Kelly, Susan 1990. 'Anglo-Saxon Lay Society and the Written Word'. *The Uses of Literacy in Early Medieval Europe*, pp. 36–62. Ed. Rosamond McKitterick. Cambridge.

Kendall, Calvin B. 1996. 'Literacy and Orality in Anglo-Saxon Poetry: Horizontal Displacement in *Andreas*'. *Journal of English and Germanic Philology* 85: 1–18.

Keynes, Simon 1990. 'Royal Government and the Written Word in Late Anglo-Saxon England'. *The Uses of Literacy in Early Medieval Europe*, pp. 226–57. Ed. Rosamond McKitterick. Cambridge.

Kornexl, Lucia 1995. 'The *Regularis Concordia* and its Old English Gloss'. *Anglo-Saxon England* 24: 95–130.

Lapidge, Michael 1982a. '"Beowulf", Aldhelm, the "Liber Monstrorum" and Wessex'. *Studi Medievali* 3rd ser. 23: 151–92.

—— 1982b. 'The Study of Latin Texts in Late Anglo-Saxon England (I): The Evidence of Latin Glosses'. *Latin and the Vernacular Languages in Early Medieval Britain*, pp. 99–140. Ed. Nicholas Brooks. Leicester.

Leclerq, Jean 1961. *The Love of Learning and the Desire for God: A Study of Monastic Culture*. Trans. Catharine Misrahi. New York.

Lerer, Seth 1991. *Literacy and Power in Anglo-Saxon England*. Lincoln, NE, and London.

Lowe, Kathryn A. 1998. 'Lay Literacy in Anglo-Saxon England and the Development of the Chirograph'. *Anglo-Saxon Manuscripts and their Heritage*, pp. 161–204. Eds Phillip Pulsiano and Elaine M. Treharne. Aldershot.

Magennis, Hugh 1996. *Images of Community in Old English Poetry*. Cambridge Studies in Anglo-Saxon England 18. Cambridge.

McIntosh, Angus 1950. 'Wulfstan's Prose'. *Proceedings of the British Academy* 35: 109–42.

McKitterick, Rosamond 1989. *The Carolingians and the Written Word*. Cambridge.

——, ed. 1990. *The Uses of Literacy in Early Medieval Europe*. Cambridge.

Morrish, Jennifer 1986. 'King Alfred's Letter as a Source on Learning in England'. *Studies in Earlier Old English Prose*, pp. 87–107. Ed. Paul E. Szarmach. Albany, NY.

Nelson, Janet L. 1990. 'Literacy in Carolingian Government', pp. 258–96. Ed. Rosamond McKitterick. Cambridge.

Nelson, William 1976–7. 'From "Listen, Lordings" to "Dear Reader"'. *University of Toronto Quarterly* 46: 110–23.

Neuman de Vegvar, Carol 1996. 'Saints and Companions to Saints: Anglo-Saxon Royal Women Monastics in Context'. *Holy Man and Holy Women: Old English Prose Saints' Lives and their Contexts*, pp. 51–92. Ed. Paul E. Szarmach. Albany, NY.

Newton, Sam 1993. *The Origins of Beowulf and the Pre-Viking Kingdom of East Anglia*. Cambridge.

Niles, John D. 1998. 'Reconceiving *Beowulf*: Poetry as Social Praxis'. *College English* 61: 143–66.

Ó Carragáin, Éamonn 1987–8. 'The Ruthwell Crucifixion Poem in its Iconographic and Liturgical Contexts'. *Peritia* 6–7: 1–71.

O'Keeffe, Katherine O'Brien 1990. *Visible Song: Transitional Literacy in Old English Verse*. Cambridge Studies in Anglo-Saxon England 4. Cambridge.

Ong, Walter J. 1975. 'The Writer's Audience is Always a Fiction'. *Publications of the Modern Language Association* 90: 9–21.

—— 1982. *Orality and Literacy: The Technologizing of the Word*. London and New York.

Orchard, Andy 1995. 'Artful Alliteration in Anglo-Saxon Song and Story'. *Anglia* 119: 429–63.

—— 1997. 'Oral Tradition'. *Reading Old English Texts*, pp. 101–23. Ed. Katherine O'Brien O'Keeffe. Cambridge.

Parkes, M. B. 1997. '*Rædan, areccan, smeagan*: How the Anglo-Saxons Read'. *Anglo-Saxon England* 26: 1–22.

Pasternack, Carol Braun 1995. *The Textuality of Old English Poetry*. Cambridge Studies in Anglo-Saxon England 13. Cambridge.

Roberts, Jane 1986. 'The Old English Prose Translation of Felix's *Vita Sancti Guthlaci*'. *Studies in Earlier Old English Prose*, pp. 363–79. Ed. Paul E. Szarmach. Albany, NY.

Schaefer, Ursula 1991. 'Hearing from Books: The Rise of Fictionality in Old English Poetry'. *Vox Intexta: Orality and Textuality in the Middle Ages*, pp. 117–36. Eds A. N. Doane and Carol Braun Pasternack. Madison.

Schneider, Karl 1986. *Sophia Lectures on Beowulf*. Eds Shoichi Watanabe and Norio Tsuchiya. Tokyo.

Stock, Brian 1983. *The Implications of Literacy: Written Languages and Models of Interpretation in the Eleventh and Twelfth Centuries*. Princeton, NJ.

Street, Brian 1984. *Literacy in Theory and Practice*. Cambridge.

Swan, Mary 1997. 'Old English Made New: One Catholic Homily and its Reuses'. *Leeds Studies in English* n.s. 28: 1–18.

—— 2000. 'Ælfric's *Catholic Homilies* in the Twelfth Century'. *Rewriting Old English in the Twelfth Century*, pp. 62–82. Eds Mary Swan and Elaine Treharne. CSASE 30. Cambridge.

Winterbottom, Michael 1967. 'The Style of Æthelweard'. *Medium Ævum* 36: 109–18.

Wormald, Patrick 1977. 'The Uses of Literacy in Anglo-Saxon England and its Neighbours'. *Transactions of the Royal Historical Society* 5th ser. 27: 95–114.

—— 1978. 'Bede, *Beowulf* and the Conversion of the Anglo-Saxon Aristocracy'. *Bede and Anglo-Saxon England*, pp. 32–95. British Archaeological Reports 46. Ed. Robert T. Farrell. Oxford.

Wright, Roger, ed. 1991. *Latin and the Romance Languages in the Early Middle Ages*. London.

6

Anglo-Saxon Manuscript Production: Issues of Making and Using

Michelle P. Brown

Who was responsible for producing manuscripts in Anglo-Saxon England? As in the accompanying discussion of their audiences, the answer is multi-faceted. It is not, however, as open-ended as the assessment of who constituted 'readers' and 'textual communities' at their broadest extent. The production of writing during the Middle Ages was even more specialized in nature than its reception. This did not mean, of course, that it was restricted to those who actually composed texts. On the contrary, it has for some time been recognized that classical and medieval authors seldom penned their own works (Clanchy 1998: 125–6). Cicero dictated to his freedman secretary, Tiro, whose shorthand system, devised for the task, was still being partially utilized by the scribes who captured the words of Bede on their wax tablets.

One major advantage of the blurred distinctions between literacy and orality which prevailed during the period was that highly disciplined memories attuned to the oral preservation of group memory, and further enhanced in a Christian milieu by liturgical mnemonics and recitation, were predisposed towards both sustained mental composition and the recitation/dictation of texts. The adaptation to a Christian culture and to an ecclesiastical focus for learning did serve, however, to close the divide between the intellectual elite who generated knowledge and those who committed it to writing and preserved it (Wormald 1977). Although early medieval monastic rules make no specific provision for the copying of manuscripts, perhaps subsuming this under manual labour, they do specify reading and study, and monks and nuns were undoubtedly the key generators of books. With writing skills being acquired as part of a claustral education, and with humility in the undertaking of manual labour being a feature of the monastic regime (in whichever form), it would be surprising if some of the leading clerical authors of the Anglo-Saxon age did not on occasion take up the quill themselves. It is hard to credit that Bede, with his consuming interest in the detail and mechanics of knowledge and his assimilative and critical approach to research, would not have felt compelled to write notes himself, at the very least, even if the translation into Old English of John's Gospel with which he was occupied on his death-bed had perforce to be dictated to an amanuensis (related in Cuthbert's letter; Farmer 1990: 359).

We do not know of any survival of Bede's handwriting, but we do have the autographs of several other leading literary figures. That prolific letter-writer, the missionary Boniface (d. 754), has left us his annotations written in the margins of a seventh-century copy of Primasius' commentary *In Apocalypsin* (Oxford, Bodleian Library, MS Douce 140; see, for example, f. 59v; see Brown 1991a: pl. 19; Lowe 1934–72: 2, 237; for a visual overview of insular books, see Lowe 1934–72; Alexander 1978; Backhouse and Webster 1991; for the later Anglo-Saxon period, see Temple 1976; Backhouse et al. 1984; for the whole period, see Brown 1991a). These are written in a proficient insular cursive minuscule of a distinctive south-west English variety which was to prove influential in Continental scriptoria within Boniface's orbit, notably Fulda. Later in the Anglo-Saxon age two other prominent clerics, Wulfstan and Ælfric, used their own well-trained hands to edit and annotate their own works (see, for example, Ælfric's *First Series of Catholic Homilies* and Wulfstan's *Sermon of the Wolf to the English*, respectively London, British Library, Royal 7.C. xii and Cotton Nero A. i; see Brown 1991a: pls 20–1). Other autographs may remain to be identified. Alcuin, for example, would be a likely candidate for such a hands-on scribal/authorial/scholarly symbiosis.

Other examples of the handwriting of known figures have survived the massive losses of evidence that we know to have occurred. Around 700 Cuthswith, abbess of Inkberrow, Worcs., may well have penned her ownership inscription, which appears, in the vernacular and in a mixed half-uncial and uncial script, on the flyleaf of a fifth-century copy of Jerome, *In Ecclesiasten* (Würzburg, Universitätsbibliothek M.P.Th.Q.2, f.1; Lowe 1934–72: 9, 1430a; Sims-Williams 1976). Another lettered Englishwoman, Eadburh, abbess of Minster-in-Thanet, corresponded with Boniface and was instrumental in supplying books, probably copied by her and her nuns, for his use in the mission-fields. She may have started to inscribe her name with a stylus in the margins of an uncial copy of the Acts of the Apostles (Oxford, Bodleian Library, Selden Supra 30[3418]; see the New Palaeographical Soc. 2nd ser.: pl. 56; Lowe 1934–72: 2, 257). During the early ninth century a Mercian nobleman turned prelate, Archbishop Wulfred of Canterbury (805–32), not only conceived of a distinctive and elaborate cursive minuscule ('mannered minuscule') for use in his scriptorium at Christ Church, Canterbury, but also participated personally as part of the scriptorium team, using it to pen impressive legal instruments as part of his campaign to stave off Mercian royal encroachment and to regain rights alienated during Offa's reign (Brooks 1984: esp. 195–6; Brown 1987).

The authors and book producers mentioned so far have belonged to an ecclesiastical milieu. This was largely male, but nuns also played an important role, as indicated by the aforementioned cases of Eadburh and Cuthswith and that of Leoba (outlined below), who fostered learning and the copying of books within the communities under their charge, as presumably did others. Indications of female production and ownership of books are difficult to detect in the record, perhaps due to the nature of survival of material or to something of a 'degendered difference' which meant that it was not felt necessary to draw attention to gender when undertaking such efforts in the service of God. Some of the surviving books may have been made by women (Minster-in-Thanet may have played a part in producing some of the opulent gilded volumes of the Tiberius group which are commonly ascribed to Canterbury, whence much of Thanet's property was transferred in the eleventh century; McKitterick 1990; Brown 2001), and it is salutary to note that of the particularly depleted corpus of ninth-century books from Anglo-Saxon England several exhibit provocative signs of possible female production and use. These are three of a group of four prayer-books made in Mercia during the first four decades of the century (London, British Library, Harley 7653 and 2965 and Royal 2. A. xx). The personal nature of these manuals of private devotion facilitates the detection of any tell-tale clues, such as lapses into the feminine voice in mid-text (Brown 2001). One of these books, the Book of Nunnaminster (London, British Library, Harley 2965), is also likely to have been owned subsequently by a Mercian noblewoman, Ealhswith, wife of Alfred the Great. Another influential female book owner was his mother, Osburh, whose book of poetry with its attractive initials stimulated an urge in the young Alfred to memorize its text, even if he did later criticize parental neglect of his education. Female input is even harder to detect in the period of the monastic reform movement, although the patronage of women such as Queen Emma, Judith of Flanders and Margaret of Scotland is an important facet of eleventh-century book production, and women are known to have formed part of the audiences for works of religious instruction, from Aldhelm's *De Virginitate*, addressed to Hildelith and the nuns of Barking, to Ælfric's *Admonitio ad filium spiritualem* (the preface to which explicitly refers to nuns as well as monks, leading Jon Wilcox to speculate that female 'illiteracy', rather than more generally poor standards, may have prompted Ælfric to translate this specifically monastic work into English; Wilcox 1994: 52) and his paraphrase of the Book of Judith (Assmann 1889).

Writing was primarily the church's preserve, but it is likely that some laypeople could also write. Charlemagne attempted to acquire the skill quite late in life but, despite wearing a small set of wax tablets around his neck to allow him to practise, he never mastered the art (Einhard, *Vita Karoli*, ch. 25; Halphen 1967; Brown 1994: 8). Alfred the Great may have been more successful in acquiring such skills, but it is unlikely that he would have penned his own works, rather than dictating in established fashion. His own commonplace book, the most personal and informal of books, had items copied into it not by himself, but by Asser (*De Rebus Gestis Ælfredi*, ch. 88; Stevenson 1959). Alfred, of course, went on to use his literacy to become a leading scholar in his own right and promoted it as part of the spiritual armour not only of the English church but of its laity, advocating the education of the sons of his wealthier freemen (see the Preface to his Old English translation of Gregory the Great's *Cura Pastoralis*; Mitchell and Robinson 1992). Presumably, as throughout the Middle Ages, some families would have placed a greater value upon the education of certain of their members than would others. An education imparted by clerical teachers had long been available, whether in the cloister, as acquired by the young warrior turned saint, Guthlac, who studied under Abbess Ælfthryth of Repton (related in Felix's *Vita*; Colgrave 1956), and by Leoba, a young female relative of St Boniface who received a liberal education under Abbess Tette of Wimborne and/or Abbess Eadburh of Thanet (Whitelock 1979: no. 159; Talbot 1954: 215), or by a family chaplain, such as taught the young Alfred to recite the poems from a book owned by his mother. Not all the scions of noble houses, so educated, would have entered the cloister themselves and some may have had occasion to use their literacy skills in secular life. We do not, of course, know to what extent such skills incorporated the physical art of writing, whether in Latin or the vernacular.

It is also possible that some members of the laity learned to read and write for pragmatic purposes, perhaps needing such skills for aspects of local government, especially during the later Anglo-Saxon period when writs and other written instruments were becoming more prevalent. The production of charters and other legal documents was again the general responsibility of the church. Copies would usually be drawn up in a scriptorium on behalf of the recipient, or of the king as grantor, and would be archived by the church for future consultation (Stenton 1955; Lapidge et al. 1999: 94–5). In England clerics seem to have fulfilled this role, and even the royal chancery that emerged during the tenth century was staffed by priests attached to the royal household (Keynes 1990; Lapidge et al. 1999: 94–5). These could even be drawn out of the cloister, to judge from the case of Eadui Basan, a monk of Christ Church, Canterbury, during the early eleventh century, who seems to have been seconded to the court for a time and to have penned a number of royal documents. Estate management would also have benefited from literate administrative skills. A set of farming memoranda survives from Ely Abbey from the early eleventh century (London, British Library, Add. 61735; see Brown 1991a: pl. 46). These contain lists of livestock, rents, ships and the like and were compiled as working notes by four hands over a period of time. The writers were perhaps monks, but they might also have been lay servants of the abbey, educated for such a purpose. Some secular estates might also have utilized writing skills of this sort, although the services of clerics might again have been sought for these matters.

Other areas of life where written texts might be used remain equally ambiguous concerning the clerical/lay overlap. We do not know whether the leech, Bald, who owned one of several leechbooks or physician's handbooks (London, British Library, Royal 12. D. xvii; Brown 1991a: pl. 30), was a layman rather than a religious, but the book that he used was certainly produced in a monastic scriptorium in Winchester in the mid-tenth century (Cameron 1990). Other clear evidence of lay writing survives in the form of the numerous inscriptions, in Latin and in vernacular runes, which adorned public monuments, whether architectural or sculptural, and prestigious items of personal dress, such as scramasaxes, helmets (such as that found at Coppergate in York) and jewellery. Frequent mistakes in letterforms and the like indicate that the artisans were often copying and sometimes misunderstanding what was to be written. Scholars such as Elisabeth Okasha have deduced from this that their lay patrons were similarly ignorant of the mechanics of writing and that they simply respected its status and talismanic value, wishing to enhance their status or increase their protection by owning it without really understanding it (Okasha 1994). This may have been the case in many instances, but it cannot thereby be deduced that lay literacy per se did not exist in some measure. This having been said, professional book production remained firmly within the orbit of the church. When Æthelweard translated the *Anglo-Saxon Chronicle* into Latin during the late tenth century (as stated in the ascription to the work's Preface; see Campbell 1962; Keynes and Lapidge 1983: 334) it may have been with the aid of a clerical scribe, but does that make this layman with his pretensions as 'litteratus' (i.e. Latinate) any the less the generator of the book? Laypeople might, on occasion, be intimately involved in the production and consumption of writing, if rarely by comparison with their ecclesiastical counterparts. Similarly, it should be borne in mind that participation in such activities was the exception rather than the norm amongst religious, if the lamentations of Bede, Alfred and Ælfric on the poor levels of education and literacy prevalent amongst the clergy are to be given any credence.

How were manuscripts made, physically, during the period in question and what do we know about some of the scribes and artists who undertook the work?

Manuscripts were written upon prepared animal skins, either vellum (calf) or parchment (sheep or goat). These were de-fleshed in a bath of alum and lime, stretched on a frame and scraped, whilst damp, to the requisite thickness, with whitening agents such as chalk being added (Rück 1991). It is assumed that, until the rise of more specialized urban production from around 1200 onwards, stimulated initially by the universities, this preparation took place within monasteries, such as Jarrow, which has revealed production debris from excavations. Unless further evidence emerges from the increasingly exciting archaeological work in towns, this must continue to be viewed as usual practice. Larger volumes, such as the Ceolfrith Bibles or the great insular Gospel-books, could take many hundreds of skins. The impact of such projects upon the husbandry of a monastery's estates would be profound, especially given the other crucial domestic requirements for leather. Presumably an element of collaboration in the form of gifts from other institutions and patrons would have been involved. Skins were valuable and even those which exhibited blemishes, such as holes which opened up during stretching and which were the result of parasites biting the animal during its lifetime, would often be used in books, and the blemishes are sometimes even ornamented by the scribe. Only in the most de luxe projects could such materials be discarded in favour of those of uniformly high quality. A unique feature may be observed in the codicology of the Lindisfarne Gospels (London, British Library, Cotton Nero D. iv), where not only were the finest skins used, but they were selected and arranged in such a way that the spine ridges are aligned throughout to ensure uniformity when the surfaces distort and attempt to return to the original shape of the animal, as they will do unless kept at stable levels of temperature and humidity or unless compressed between heavy wooden binding boards with thongs or clasps.

Once the parchment or vellum was in the hands of the scribe, it was cut to size, pricked with a stylus or awl and ruled with a hard-point to provide the layout for text and, on occasion, image. From the early eleventh century, when extensive campaigns of illustration of the text were being increasingly experimented with, as in the Ælfric Hexateuch (London, British Library, Cotton Claudius B. iv) and the Harley Psalter (London, British Library, Harley 603), lead-point, the prototype of the pencil, was introduced in Anglo-Saxon England (these represent, to the best of my knowledge, the earliest experiments with this new implement, which does not enter into any measure of general use in England or elsewhere until the end of the century). This permitted greater flexibility of layout from page to page, to accommodate the integration of text and image, than the ridge and furrow effect produced by hard-point ruling, which often intrudes upon areas of illumination.

Methods of preparing writing surfaces to receive text and of assembling the sheets (bifolia) into gatherings (quires) varied in different times and places (Brown 1974; Brown 1990: 2–5; Rück 1991). Insular sheets were generally thicker than their late antique and continental counterparts, which were scraped thinner during production and which therefore exhibit a greater distinction between the whiter, velvety flesh-side and the smoother, yellower hair-side, which is also often speckled with hair follicles (Brown 1991b). The insular sheets are more uniform in appearance but can often appear darker and stiffer or cellulose in texture. At their best they have a suede-like nap and hold pigments and ink better than their counterparts. In a standard insular gathering, hair-sides face flesh-sides in an opening, whilst on the continent bifolia are laid down alternately, so that like faces like in an opening to present a more aesthetic appearance. Insular gatherings were also generally folded before they were pricked and ruled, with four bifolia being layered and folded to form a standard quire of eight leaves (although other quire lengths could occur, under special constraints of production or, for example, when emulating an antique quire of ten), which was then pricked and ruled from the outside, repeating the process inside if the impressions did not penetrate throughout. Continental bifolia were pricked and ruled whilst open, with ruling extending across what was to become the gutter (spine edge) of the book. Ruling each sheet thus was more time consuming, but was sometimes accelerated by the use of a template.

An examination of such codicological practices can assist in determining where works may have originated. They are particularly valuable in assessing whether, for example, an insular scribe's work was exported to the continent, perhaps to the mission-fields, or whether the scribe himself or herself actually travelled there and used locally prepared materials or practices. Conversely, antique or continental codicological practices were sometimes specifically adopted within insular scriptoria, probably as conscious statements of perceived 'romanitas' (Brown 1974, 1984; Brown 1991b). The Romanizing scriptoria of Wearmouth–Jarrow and Canterbury predictably exhibit these preferences, and such experiments were also applied to manuscript production as part of the reforms initiated by Alfred and his successors. Malcolm Parkes has identified such features as part of the endeavours of a revived scriptorium operating at Winchester during the early tenth century, responsible for works such as the Parker Chronicle (Cambridge, Corpus Christi College, 173; Parkes 1976, 1983), and perhaps consisting of a collaborative team composed of both monks and nuns (Brown 2001). Such tendencies were not, as aforementioned, a completely new phenomenon, nor were they uniformly employed thereafter, but suffice it to say that during the course of the tenth century Anglo-Saxon codicology increasingly came to resemble the continental (Brown 1991b).

The history of scripts in Anglo-Saxon England similarly traversed a two-way street (Bischoff 1990; Brown 1990; Brown 1993). The early insular system of scripts, which was heavily indebted to developments in Ireland and in the continental mission-fields, resembled its late Roman forebear in that it was hierarchical and geared form to function. This was basically stimulated by the recognition that it was inappropriate to use the same script for a list or letter as for a Gospel-book. Thus cursive minuscule scripts were developed for pragmatic records, for less formal books and for major publishing drives, such as that mounted by Wearmouth–Jarrow in response to the demand for copies of Bede's works (Parkes 1982), whilst insular half-uncial (sometimes termed majuscule) and, in England, more Romanizing uncial scripts were adopted for scripture and for some patristic texts. Capitals were retained for display scripts and decoration. By the ninth century the perception of the status of minuscule scripts was beginning to change, probably in response to experiments in the Carolingian orbit to find a universal script, Caroline minuscule, which could be written quickly as part of a programme of dissemination of 'authorized' texts and which would replace the diversity of local scripts throughout the amorphous empire. The influence of insular scripts and personnel, such as Alcuin of York, had also played its part in this process. The elevated status of minuscule script within charter production, promoted by Archbishop Wulfred, may also have contributed to the growing willingness to employ insular minuscule scripts for even the most formal works, notably the Royal Bible (London, British Library, Royal 1. E. vi) which was made at Canterbury *c*.820–40 and which also exhibits Carolingian influence in its illumination and codicology (Budny 1985; Brown 1996: 162–72).

The Alfredian revival drew upon such earlier ninth-century models, coupled with a direct reference to Carolingian practices. The insular hierarchy of scripts was replaced by an English universal script, Anglo-Saxon minuscule, with uncials and capitals being reserved for use in titles, rubrics and decoration. Its initial pointed appearance (aspect) was indebted to earlier ninth-century scripts, but during the course of the tenth century it assumed a square aspect and by the early eleventh century a rounded aspect, under increased Caroline influence (Dumville 1987, 1993, 1994). During the later tenth century, as an adjunct of the monastic reform movement, it gradually became accepted that Caroline minuscule was the appropriate script for works in Latin, whilst Anglo-Saxon minuscule was retained for vernacular texts (Bishop 1971). The two often appear side by side in bilingual translations and documents of the period. This novel solution survived the Conquest until an assimilation of native and

Norman practices had effectively evolved and been subsumed into a more international Protogothic script by the twelfth century (Ker 1960; Brown 1990).

The decoration of books was one of the outstanding cultural achievements of the insular and later Anglo-Saxon ages. The appearance of the page was to be transformed for the remainder of the Middle Ages. The deep-rooted social context of art in both the Celtic and Germanic cultures, whether ornamental or symbolic and with its overtones of status and power, engendered a wish to apply such decoration to the new medium of the written word. It must have seemed a natural process to apply these signals of authority to the new symbol of ultimate authority – the Word of God. So the cross-carpet pages of the great insular Gospel-books assume an iconic status as complex symbolic manifestations of the godhead (Nordenfalk 1977; Henderson 1987; Webster and Brown 1997: 211–12; Brown 1991a, 1998: 72–3, 2001). The incipit pages accompanying them likewise grow into images in their own right, their ornate initials and display scripts spreading across the whole of the page. Smaller initials mark other important sections of text, for one of the primary functions of manuscript decoration is the articulation of the text. The process of learning Latin as a foreign language and becoming familiar with the art of writing may well have fostered such innovation in an insular orbit, akin to the stimulus which led Irish scribes to introduce word separation and to extend the use of punctuation (Parkes 1987, 1992).

The other major strand to illumination was that of figural imagery and narrative. Late antique and early Christian book art had already begun to experiment with cycles of illustration (Weitzmann 1977), some of which were probably imported to Britain (such as the Augustine Gospels, Cambridge, Corpus Christi College, 286). Whilst other world cultures struggled with the implications of idolatory, the approach in the West was moulded by Gregory the Great's injunction that 'in images the illiterate read'. Nowhere was this taken more to heart than in the insular world, where text and image were interwoven in a process of mutual validation and elucidation. Not by chance was the historiated or story-telling initial an insular invention, first encountered around the 720s in the Kentish Vespasian Psalter (London, British Library, Cotton Vespasian A. i; Lowe 1934–72: 2, 193). Images of the evangelists and the miniatures of the Book of Kells go far beyond the narrative in their subtle layering of multivalent meaning and their inbuilt intertextuality, reliant upon a supporting raft of exegesis (Henderson 1987; Webster and Brown 1997: 211–12, 241–2; Brown 1996: 68–122; Farr 1997). Such trends exerted a formative influence upon late Merovingian and Carolingian book production, and by the end of the insular era the sumptuous appearance and narrative images of Charlemagne's court school manuscripts and the Tours Bibles were echoed in the large Bible made in Canterbury (London, British Library, Royal 1. E. vi), which is now, alas, deprived of its full-page illustrations.

The whimsical initials of earlier ninth-century Southumbrian 'Tiberius Group' manuscripts (which take their name from a key member, the Tiberius Bede, London, British Library, Cotton Tiberius C. ii) survived the Viking onslaught to reappear in

Alfredian and tenth-century books. Their beast heads are now furnished with exotic fronds of acanthus to munch upon, in continental fashion, and their variants have been categorized (Wormald 1984). With the return to a more opulent ornamental display page as part of the 'Winchester style' which accompanied the reform movement, major initials (including the distinctive Beatus initials) again assumed elaborate interlaced forms with zoomorphic elements, accompanied by elegant square capitals as display script and by exuberant frames embellished with acanthus, as seen in the Benedictional of St Æthelwold (London, British Library, Add. 49598), the Ramsey Psalter (London, British Library, Harley 2904) and the late tenth- to eleventh-century Gospelbooks. The heavily painted and gilded Winchester style could also assume a lighter form as tinted or outline drawings.

These elegant drawings assumed an added popularity with the introduction of the 'Utrecht Psalter' style, an animated, agitated and spontaneous style indebted to the Carolingian Reims school of illumination, of which the Utrecht Psalter was a masterwork (van der Horst et al. 1996). During the early eleventh century the scriptorium of Christ Church, Canterbury, came into possession of this influential Carolingian book, which may have been obtained by the archbishop in order to have a copy made for his own use. Not only did its style of drawing prove influential, but also the sophisticated way in which it accomplished a sustained programme of integrated text and image, with its picture poems literally illuminating the Psalms, threw the scriptorium into a fever of stimulation and controversy. The exemplar, always a key component in any major book project of the time, was disbound in order to understand better how it had been put together and to assist in the imposition of text required in making the 'copy' which also survives as the Harley Psalter (London, British Library, Harley 603; Noel 1997). It should be remembered that when a scribe laid a bifolium out on the writing board he or she would not be writing continuous text across the sheet, as it was to be folded with others into a quire. Instead of writing pages one and two of a text across an outer bifolium, for example, the scribe would be writing pages sixteen and one. The number of words to the page had to be carefully calculated beforehand, with reference to the exemplar. In this case, however, the text employed at Canterbury differed from that of the diocese of Reims. The 'point size' of the script also varied, the Utrecht Psalter being written in rustic capitals and the Harley Psalter in English Caroline minuscule. Presumably because the programme of illustration was seen as so crucial in this project, the unusual step was taken of allowing the artists to lay out the pages. The scribes obviously experienced great difficulty in accommodating their text in the allocated spaces and one can almost see before one on the pages the points at which they rebelled, the colourful Eadui Basan being amongst them, and regained the initiative. From that point onwards the artists were in trouble. The project continued to occupy the scriptorium sporadically until the twelfth century and was never finished.

This preoccupation with producing sustained picture cycles to illustrate texts can also be observed in works such as the herbal (London, British Library, Cotton Vitellius C. iii; Brown 1991a: pl. 29) and the Ælfric Hexateuch (London, British Library,

Cotton Claudius B. iv; Brown 1991a: pl. 54), in which an essentially early Christian cycle is adapted to an Old English text. The complex interrelationship between *traditio* and *innovatio* is a perpetual consideration in early medieval art and is reminiscent of the legal law of precedent, in which, as with Alfred's law-code, earlier elements are discovered and assembled to form something essentially innovative. This is nowhere better illustrated than in the Harley Psalter, where the Utrecht Psalter's imagery, itself probably reliant upon an early Christian prototype, is adapted to accommodate details of Anglo-Saxon military and agricultural implements, as if to site them within the Biblical landscape, and is also geared to emphasize different theological points.

In addition to transforming earlier picture cycles, later Anglo-Saxon illumination also featured some important experiments with new iconographies, notably its ruler images such as those of Edgar in the New Minster Charter (London, British Library, Cotton Vespasian A. viii: Brown 1991a: pl. 14) and the *Regularis Concordia* (London, British Library, Cotton Tiberius A. iii; Brown 1991a: pl. 13), and of Cnut and Emma in the *Liber Vitae* (London, British Library, Stowe 944; Brown 1991a: pl. 15), which, although indebted to Carolingian and Ottonian royal iconography, placed art at the service of the partnership of church and state epitomized in the reform movement itself (Deshman 1976; Gameson 1995). Similarly, on the eve of the Conquest, experiments with Christological and Davidic iconography, seen in the influential prefatory cycle of images in the Tiberius Psalter (London, British Library, Cotton Tiberius C. vi; Brown 1991a: pl. 76), continue the insular fascination with King David as the ideal of kingship first exhibited in works such as the eighth-century Vespasian Psalter and the Durham Cassiodorus (Durham, Cathedral Library, B. II. 30; Brown 1991a: pls 58, 59; Webster and Brown 1997: 224–30). The monumental mannered style of the Tiberius Psalter, combining both 'Winchester' and 'Utrecht' styles, also prefigures the English contribution to the development of Romanesque art.

The Harley Psalter was an exceptional project. The sequence of work in the scriptorium generally took the form of scribal layout, writing of the main text, rubrication (writing of titles, headings, instructions for use, chapter or section numbering etc.), then decoration, starting with initials and other elements designed to articulate the text. Miniatures and display openings, which needed extra time to execute and to dry, might be worked on concurrently or separately. Any campaign of correction might be conducted at the end of the project or after the initial writing campaign. Finally the gatherings would be sewn together, usually upon supports consisting of leather cords, although the earliest extant English binding, which still protects the St Cuthbert Gospel (London, British Library, Sloane 74; Brown 1991a: pl. 48; Brown et al. 1969), adopts an unsupported sewing technique. This is known as Coptic sewing, from its southern and eastern Mediterranean origins, and relies upon sewing with two needles working in a figure of eight to attach the gatherings to one another. The loose ends of the support cords or the sewing thread were then laced through holes drilled in the hardwood binding boards and pegged into place with wooden dowels. The boards were then covered with leather and perhaps adorned by tooling or with metalwork, ivories and ties (Lapidge et al. 1999: 70–1). Although extant Anglo-Saxon bindings are rare (others include the Fulda Codex (Fulda, Codex Bonifatianus I) and the Tollemache Orosius (London, British Library, Add. 47967), the latter retaining its Anglo-Saxon boards under later refurbishments; see Pollard 1975), much can be adduced concerning the original and subsequent bindings from holes relating to the sewing stations (sewing around the support cords) in the gutter and from corrosion marks from metalwork attachments (for a test case, see Brown 1996: 33–44). It should be remembered, however, that less prestigious volumes would have commanded less ostentatious or complex bindings, and that some may even have circulated as unbound gatherings or pamphlets, or have required only limp vellum covers. Library books, like their later medieval successors, are likely to have been bound within wooden boards, but these may have been covered only with leather or alum tawd (a supple sheepskin), if at all.

The composition of working teams might vary in accordance with the project or the scriptorium. Smaller, more personal books might well be written by one hand, or compiled from pamphlets or from a number of extracts gathered over a period of time (in copybook fashion, of the sort compiled by Asser for Alfred), whereas the more elaborate undertakings usually occupied teams of scribes and artists taking their turn at the scriptorium benches, probably under the supervision of a master. Scribal colophons are rarer in England than on the continent (Benedictines of Le Bouveret 1965–79), or indeed in Ireland, and the earliest extant female colophon does not occur until the twelfth century, in a book from the Nunnaminster in Winchester (a copy of Smaragdus, *Diadema Monachorum*, Oxford, Bodleian Library, Bodley 451; Robinson 1997), a centre which yields valuable earlier evidence of copying by women (Brown forthcoming). Where they do occur they generally record the name of only one member of a team, perhaps the master or even the patron, as in the 'ora pro uuig-baldo' inscription in the Barberini Gospels (Vatican, Barb. lat. 570; Lowe 1934–72: 1, 63), which is actually written by four hands.

The way in which labour was expended on a project may tell us something valuable about perceptions of the nature of the work. For example, library books produced in the scriptorium of Lindisfarne around 700, such as the Vatican Paulinus (Vatican, Pal. lat. 235; Lowe 1934–72: 1, 87; Brown 1989), are the work of a number of hands, whereas what is probably the most resource-consuming product of that monastery, the Lindisfarne Gospels, is the work of one artist-scribe. This represents an amazing commitment of time and energy on the part of one extremely gifted individual (whom the controversial later tenth-century colophon by Aldred names as Eadfrith, who became bishop of Lindisfarne in 698) and probably embodies their *opus dei* in an even more specific form than more usual scriptorium work. There may have been something of a particularly Celtic spiritual predisposition towards such solitary working patterns, consistent with a heightened eremitic approach to monasticism, to judge from the evidence found in the Book of Armagh (Dublin, Trinity College Library, 52; Lowe 1934–72: 2, 270). This was made in Armagh around 807 and records the name of its most flamboyant artist-scribe, Ferdomnach, one of a team of four (Brown 1989,

1990: pl. 19). Each of these artist-scribes worked exclusively on their own gatherings, laying them out, writing, decorating and undertaking a preliminary tacket sewing prior to binding. This was the exception, however; teams elsewhere (even in Celtic areas, to judge from projects such as the Book of Kells; Dublin, Trinity College Library, 58; Lowe 1934–72: 2, 274) seem not to have worked in isolation but to have collaborated. Whatever the scriptorium practice, undertaking the copying of the scriptures, especially when producing what was probably intended as a major cult item of iconic status, is likely to have been seen as a protracted act of prayer, as with the Byzantine icon painter, and exhortations such as Cassiodorus' injunction to faithful copying and his assertion that each word written was a wound on Satan's body would have placed such work in the spiritual 'front line', bestowing upon the scribe the role of *miles Christi*.

The programme of study of *grammatica* within the cloister would reveal the novices' aptitude as *lectores* or *scriptores*, and presumably those so gifted would be expected to hone their scribal skills by spending additional 'manual labour' or 'study' time in the scriptorium (Porter 1994). Wax tablets probably played a part in their learning process and were certainly used for drafting texts (as indicated by a later life of St Boniface, which records that the eighth-century version by Willibald was composed upon wax tablets and submitted for the approval of Archbishops Lull and Megingoz, before being copied onto parchment; Brown 1994: 10) and to assist in memorizing texts, as in the case of the Springmount Bog Tablets in the National Museum of Ireland, which carry extracts from the Psalms which were probably being used to assist an Irish priest in becoming *psalteratus* when they were lost during the late sixth or early seventh century. Learning also took place on the job. The frequent changes of hand, often for just a few lines' duration, in the Royal Bible (London, British Library, Royal 1. E. vi; Lowe 1934–72: 2, 244), suggest that more experienced scribes were intervening in the work of trainees, or vice versa, in order to show them how it should be done. The aforementioned volume containing the Cuthwith inscription also shows that the Anglo-Saxon scribe of around 700 who was filling a lacuna in the fifth- to sixth-century text of Jerome's *Commentary on Ecclesiastes* was learning her or his uncial script from that of the text being expanded.

The verses composed by Ælfric Bata at Christ Church, Canterbury, during the early eleventh century speak not only of the training of apprentice scribes and of the bargaining for payment with the potential patron of a missal, but of scribes who leave the cloister to earn fame beyond its walls, instead of staying and teaching as they ought (Ælfric Bata, *Colloquia*, chs 14, 24; Gwara 1996). A fitting candidate for such reproaches was Eadui Basan (Eadui the Fat), a monk of Christ Church at that time (for a 'self-portrait' see London, British Library, Arundel 155, f. 133; see Brown 1991a: pl. 24). In addition to participating in major projects of the scriptorium, such as the making of the Harley Psalter (London, British Library, Harley 603; Noel 1997; van der Horst et al. 1996), Eadui also caught the eye of the key patrons of the period, Cnut and Emma. Eadui seems to have spent time travelling with the court and was responsible for penning some of Cnut's documents, as already mentioned. The gift-giving which played such an important role in securing Cnut's newly won throne extended beyond the realm of land-grants and privileges to the presentation of luxurious works of art, such as the golden cross which he and Emma are depicted presenting to Hyde Abbey in its *Liber Vitae* (London, British Library, Stowe 944, f. 6; see Brown 1991a: pl. 15). Eadui was responsible for producing some of the most opulent Gospel-books of the age, such as the Grimbald Gospels (London, British Library, Add. 34890; Temple 1976: no. 68), and it is possible that some of these may have originated at Cnut and Emma's behest for similar purposes (Heslop 1990; Brown and Lovett 1999: 75–7).

Mobility beyond the cloister is again demonstrated by the work of the artist of the Ramsey Psalter (London, British Library, Harley 2904; see Brown 1991a: pl. 75), which he worked on at Winchester in the late tenth century. He seems to have travelled widely on the continent, perhaps in the entourage of a leading prelate, and to have 'sung for his supper' by participating in projects in a number of continental scriptoria, such as Fleury, where he provided the elegant tinted drawings for a copy of Cicero's *Aratea* (London, British Library, Harley 2506; see Brown 1991a: pl. 26), and St Bertin, where he worked on the Boulogne Gospels (Boulogne, Bibl. Mun., 11; Brown and Lovett 1999: 75–7). Other monastic scribes seem to have produced for their own immediate communities or their members, such as the Winchester monk Godeman, who records in a gilded verse his commissioning by Bishop Æthelwold, in the 970s–80s, to pen the Benedictional for his personal use (London, British Library, Add. 49598; see Brown 1991a: pl. 72; Deshman 1995).

The volumes discussed so far were mostly designed for public liturgical or private devotional use. What of other types of book, especially those in the vernacular? There was a secular impetus working along with the church in the production of texts in the vernacular from the very beginning. The authority of writing, presumably moulded by perceptions of the Word in the context of conversion to Christianity, seems to have appealed rapidly to secular authorities as a means of consolidating their rule and of bestowing upon it the legitimacy of association with their Roman pre-cursors (Webster and Brown 1997: 208–12, 219–20). Thus the earliest written manifestation of Old English is thought to be the Laws of King Æthelberht I of Kent, produced by Augustine and his fellow missionaries around 602–3 but preserved only in a twelfth-century Rochester compilation, the *Textus Roffensis* (Rochester, Cathedral Library, A. 35; Webster and Brown 1997: 220; Wormald 1995). The production of works in their native tongue remained an intermittent concern of influential religious and lay figures alike, be they Bede, Ælfric and Wulfstan or Alfred and Æthelweard. The use of the vernacular as an essential adjunct to Latin literacy in promoting knowl-edge of the faith and spiritual well-being amongst clerical and lay audiences alike was acknowledged in varying measure throughout the Anglo-Saxon age and was not the exclusive preserve of either sphere (see Magennis in this volume).

The physical task of producing works in the vernacular, whether of an overtly reli-gious or more ambiguous literary character, probably remained in clerical circles. The origins of the surviving manuscripts containing masterpieces of vernacular poetry such as *Beowulf* (London, British Library, Cotton Vitellius A. xv part II; Brown 1991a: pl. 37), the Exeter Book (Exeter, Cathedral Library, 3501; Brown 1991a: pl. 38) and the Vercelli Book (Vercelli, Biblioteca Capitolare CXVII) remain uncertain and hotly debated. Whoever their original owners or communities of readership, they are likely to have been penned by clerics trained in the scriptorium. Their physical manufacture does not notably single them out from other books of the period. At one level they appear to represent compilations of material which, whether undertaken by an author (as Kiernan controversially suggests in the case of *Beowulf*; Kiernan 1984, 2000) or for an individual (such as the canon whom Ó Carragáin, again controversially, favours as the compiler of the Vercelli Book; Ó Carragáin 1981), are perhaps best viewed in the context of the drive to gather and codify knowledge exhibited by the Anglo-Saxon church during the later tenth and early eleventh centuries. Much the same spirit may have inspired Byrhtferth of Ramsey to compile his computistical miscellany, the *Computus*, and to compose his *Enchiridion*. It may likewise have stimulated the production of the scientific miscellany now known as London, British Library, Cotton Tiberius B. v, part I, which includes a bilingual Latin/Old English copy of the *Marvels of the East*, along with computistic material, the *Aratea* and material relating to pilgrimage, such as Sigeric's itinerary and the Anglo-Saxon world map (Brown 1991a: pls 31, 33). Thus the clerical scribes of the later Anglo-Saxon age worked to stock the shelves of the monastic library and to fulfil the study needs of the individual, as well as continuing the work of their earlier brethren in supplying the essential liturgical and devotional tools of their faith and in committing the new literary compositions of their culture to the safe-keeping of writing.

REFERENCES

Alexander, Jonathan J. G. 1978. *Insular Manuscripts, 6th to the 9th Century*. London.

Assmann, Bruno, ed. 1889. 'Ælfric's Homilie über das Buch Judith'. *Angelsächsische Homilien und Heiligenleben*, Bibliothek der Angelsächsischen Prosa 3: 102–16. Kassel.

Backhouse, Janet M. and L. Webster, eds 1991. *The Making of England, Anglo-Saxon Art and Culture AD 600–900*. London. Catalogue of a British Museum/British Library exhibition 1991–2.

Backhouse, Janet M., D. Turner and L. Webster, eds 1984. *The Golden Age of Anglo-Saxon Art, 966–1066*. Catalogue of British Museum/British Library exhibition, 1984, London.

Benedictines of Le Bouveret 1965–79. *Colophons des manuscrits occidentaux des origines aux xvie siècle*. Spicilegii Friburgensis Subsidia. 2–6. Fribourg.

Bischoff, Bernhard 1990. *Latin Palaeography*.

Antiquity and the Middle Ages. Trans. D. Ó Cróinín and D. Ganz. Cambridge.

Bishop, T. A. M. 1971. *English Caroline Minuscule*. Oxford.

Brooks, Nicholas 1984. *The Early History of the Church of Canterbury*. Leicester.

Brown, Michelle P. 1987. 'Paris, BN lat. 10861 and the Scriptorium of Christ Church, Canterbury'. *Anglo-Saxon England* 15: 119–37.

——1989. 'The Lindisfarne Scriptorium from the Late Seventh to the Early Ninth Century'. *St Cuthbert, his Cult and his Community to AD 1200*. Eds G. Bonner et al. Woodbridge.

——1990 (repr. 1993, 1999). *A Guide to Western Historical Scripts from Antiquity to 1600*. London and Toronto.

——1991a. *Anglo-Saxon Manuscripts*. London.

——1991b. 'Continental Symptoms in Insular

Codicology: Historical Perspectives'. *Pergament*, pp. 57–62. Ed. P. Rück. Sigmaringen.

——1994. 'The Role of the Wax Tablet in Medieval Literacy: A Reconsideration in Light of a Recent Find from York'. *British Library Journal* 20, 1: 1–17.

——1996. *The Book of Cerne: Prayer, Patronage and Power in Ninth-Century England*. London and Toronto.

——1998. *The British Library Guide to Writing and Scripts: History and Techniques*. London and Toronto.

——2001. 'Female Book-ownership and Production in Anglo-Saxon England: The Evidence of the Ninth-century Prayerbooks'. *Lexis and Texts in Early English: Studies Presented to Jane Roberts*. Eds Christian Kay and Louise Sylvester. Amsterdam.

——and Patricia Lovett 1999. *The British Library Source Book for Scribes*. London and Toronto.

Brown, T. Julian 1974. 'The Distribution and Significance of Membrane Prepared in the Insular Manner'. *Colloques Internationaux du Centre National de la Récherche Scientifique*, no. 547: 127–35. Repr. Brown 1993: 125–40.

——1984. 'The Oldest Irish Manuscripts and their Late Antique Background'. *Irland und Europa: die Kirche im Frühmittelalter*. Eds P. Ní Chatháin and M. Richter. Stuttgart. Repr. Brown 1993: 221–41.

——1993. *A Palaeographer's View. Selected Writings of Julian Brown*. Eds J. Bately, M. P. Brown and J. Roberts. London.

——et al., eds 1969. *The Stonyhurst Gospel of St John*. London.

Budny, M. O. 1985. 'London, British Library MS Royal I. E. VI: The Anatomy of an Anglo-Saxon Bible Fragment'. PhD dissertation, London University.

Cameron, M. Laurence 1990. 'Bald's Leechbook and Cultural Interactions in Anglo-Saxon England'. *Anglo-Saxon England* 19: 5–12.

Campbell, Alistair, ed. 1962. *Chronicle of Æthelweard*. London.

Clanchy, M. 1998. *From Memory to Written Record*. Oxford.

Colgrave, Bertram, ed. 1956. *Felix's Life of St Guthlac*. Cambridge.

Deshman, Robert 1976. *Christus Rex et Magi Reges. Kingship and Christology in Ottonian and Anglo-Saxon Art*. Berlin.

——1995. *The Benedictional of Æthelwold*. Princeton, NJ.

Dumville, David N. 1987. 'English Square Minuscule Script: The Background and Early Phases'. *Anglo-Saxon England* 16: 147–79.

——1993. *English Caroline Script and Monastic History: Studies in Benedictinism, AD 950–1030*. Woodbridge.

——1994. 'English Square Minuscule Script: The Mid-Century Phases'. *Anglo-Saxon England* 23: 133–64.

Farmer, David H. ed. 1990. *Bede: Ecclesiastical History of the English People*. London.

Farr, Carol A. 1997. *The Book of Kells, its Function and Audience*. London.

Gameson, Richard 1995. *The Role of Art in the Late Anglo-Saxon Church*. Oxford.

Gwara, Scott, ed. 1996. *Latin Colloquies from Pre-Conquest Britain*. Toronto.

Halphen, L. ed. 1967. *Eginhard. Vita Karoli*. Paris.

Henderson, George 1987. *From Durrow to Kells. The Insular Gospelbooks*. London.

Heslop, Thomas A. S. 1990. 'The Production of De Luxe Manuscripts and the Patronage of King Cnut and Queen Emma'. *Anglo-Saxon England* 19: 151–95.

Ker, Neil R. 1960. *English Manuscripts in the Century after the Norman Conquest*. Oxford.

Keynes, Simon 1990. 'Royal Government and the Written Word in Late Anglo-Saxon England'. *The Uses of Literacy in Early Medieval Europe*, pp. 226–57. Ed. Rosamond McKitterick. Cambridge.

——and M. Lapidge 1983. *Alfred the Great*. Harmondsworth.

Kiernan, Kevin S. 1984. *'Beowulf' and the 'Beowulf' Manuscript*. New Brunswick, NJ.

——2000. *The Electronic 'Beowulf'*. London.

Lapidge, M., J. Blair, S. Keynes and D. Scragg eds 1999. *The Blackwell Encyclopaedia of Anglo-Saxon England*. Oxford.

Lowe, Elias A. 1934–72. *Codices Latini Antiquiores*. 11 vols and suppl. Oxford.

McKitterick, Rosamond, ed. 1990. *The Uses of Literacy in Early Medieval Europe*. Cambridge.

Mitchell, Bruce and Fred C. Robinson eds 1992. 'Alfred the Great's Preface to his Translation of Gregory's *Pastoral Care*'. *A Guide to Old English*, pp. 204–7. 5th edn. Oxford.

Noel, William 1997. *The Harley Psalter*. Cambridge.

Nordenfalk, Carl 1977. *Celtic and Anglo-Saxon Painting*. London.

Ó Carragáin, Éamonn 1981. 'How did the Vercelli Collector Interpret *The Dream of the Rood?*'. *Studies in Language and Literature in Honour of Paul Christophersen*, pp. 63–104. Ed. P. Tilling. Occasional Papers in Linguistics and Language Learning 8. Coleraine.

Okasha, Elisabeth 1994. 'The Commissioners, Makers and Owners of Anglo-Saxon Inscriptions'. *ASSAH* 7: 71–7.

Parkes, Malcolm B. 1976. 'The Palaeography of the Parker Manuscript of the *Chronicle*, Laws and Sedulius, and Historiography at Winchester in the Late Ninth and Tenth Centuries'. *Anglo-Saxon England* 5: 149–71. Repr. Parkes 1991: 143–69.

—— 1982. *The Scriptorium of Wearmouth–Jarrow*. Jarrow Lecture.

—— 1983. 'A Fragment of an Early Tenth-century Anglo-Saxon Manuscript and its Significance'. *Anglo-Saxon England* 12: 129–40. Repr. Parkes 1991: 171–85.

—— 1987. 'The Contribution of Insular Scribes to the Seventh and Eighth Centuries to the "Grammar of Legibility" '. *Grafia e interpunzione del latino nel medioevo*, pp. 15–30. Ed. A. Maierù. Rome.

—— 1991. *Scribes, Scripts and Readers*. London.

—— 1992. *Pause and Effect: An Introduction to the History of Punctuation in the West*. Aldershot.

Pollard, Graham 1975. 'Some Anglo-Saxon Bookbindings'. *Book Collector* 24: 130–59.

Porter, D. 1994. 'The Latin Syllabus in Anglo-Saxon Monastic Schools'. *Neophilologus* 78: 1–20.

Robinson, Pamela R. 1997. 'A Twelfth-Century Scriptrix from Nunnaminster'. *Of the Making of Books: Medieval Manuscripts, their Scribes and Readers: Essays Presented to M. B. Parkes*, pp. 73–93. Eds P. R. Robinson & R. Zim. Aldershot.

Rück, Peter, ed. 1991. *Pergament*. Sigmaringen.

Sims-Williams, Patrick 1976. 'Cuthswith, Seventh-century Abbess of Inkberrow, near Worcester, and the Würzburg Manuscript of Jerome on Ecclesiastes'. *Anglo-Saxon England* 5: 1–21.

Stenton, Frank M. 1955. *The Latin Charters of the Anglo-Saxon Period*. Oxford.

Stevenson, William Henry, ed. 1959 (1906). *Asser's Life of King Alfred, Together with the Annals of St Neots Erroneously Ascribed to Asser*. Repr. intro. D. Whitelock. Oxford.

Talbot, C. H. 1954. *The Anglo-Saxon Missionaries in Germany*. London.

Temple, Elzbieta 1976. *Anglo-Saxon Manuscripts 900–1066*. London.

van der Horst, Koert et al., eds 1996. *The Utrecht Psalter in Medieval Art*. Hes.

Webster, Leslie and Michelle P. Brown, eds 1997. *The Transformation of the Roman World*. London.

Weitzmann, Kurt 1977. *Late Antique and Early Christian Book Illumination*. London.

Whitelock, Dorothy, ed. 1979. *English Historical Documents*, I. London.

Wilcox, Jonathan, ed. 1994. *Ælfric's Prefaces*. Durham Medieval Texts 9. Durham.

Wormald, Francis 1984. 'Decorated Initials in English Manuscripts from A.D. 900 to 1100'. Repr. *Francis Wormald, Collected Writings*, I, pp. 47–75. Eds J. J. G. Alexander, T. J. Brown & J. Gibbs. London.

Wormald, Patrick 1977. 'The Uses of Literacy in Anglo-Saxon England and its Neighbours'. *Transactions of the Royal Historical Society*, 5th ser. 27: 95–114.

—— 1995. '*Inter Cetera Bona Genti Suae*: Lawmaking and Peace-keeping in the Earliest English Kingdoms'. *Settimane* 42: 963–96.

PART II
Readings: Cultural Framework and Heritage

7

The Germanic Background

Patrizia Lendinara

The Settlement of England

In the fifth century, Roman 'Britannia' was settled by Germanic-speakers, who are called by their collective name, the Anglo-Saxons. The Germanic migration to the British Isles was quite different from the other 'Barbarian' invasions, above all in its results. The so-called *Völkerwanderungen*, which changed the face of Europe to begin with in the middle of the fourth century, involved all the Germanic peoples (Schwarz 1956; Wolfram 1988), who took part in different types of migrations, from a full-scale migration of an entire people (such as the Gothic migration to the Black Sea) to the displacement of a small but powerful elite, a chieftain or royal family with their retainers. In the case in point only one part of more than one group of Germanic people (Saxons, Angles and other minor groups, including Frisians) moved from the continent to settle in England, leaving their homeland at different times and, possibly, for different reasons.

Moreover, the settlement of Britannia has a unique result and a different pattern from the rest of Europe, because, for once, the 'Barbarian culture' of the newcomers did not succumb to the indigenous culture. Anglo-Saxons came to an island populated by the Celts, and which was once a part of the Roman Empire, but, in England, the Germanic culture was not subdued either by the remains of the Roman civilization or by the Celtic inhabitants of Britain. The Germanic settlers did not entirely replace the Celtic British, but became a significant part of the population of Britain. Celtic people did not mix with the newcomers; they left their homeland and went to the west and north – to Wales and Scotland – and the Germanic peoples rapidly spread through the country. The native Britons and the Anglo-Saxons were, almost everywhere, in competition and, as a result, the two peoples, Celtic and Germanic, developed their culture quite separately, at best in parallel, with very limited interferences. The English language, with its extremely low number of ancient Celtic loanwords, provides undeniable evidence for the independent development of the two cultures.

The migration is the starting point and the background against which a study of the links of the Anglo-Saxons, their language and literature to the wider Germanic world must be set. Everyone – with the exception of scholars – is free to remain faithful to the old theory based on Bede's words about the arrival of Germanic tribes in the British islands around the middle of the fifth century. According to this tradition, the first Germanic war-band arrived in Britain about the year 449 to serve as mercenaries at the invitation of Vortigern:

> In the year of our Lord 449 . . . the race of the Angles or Saxons, invited by the aforesaid king [Vortigern], came to Britain in three warships and by his command were granted a place of settlement in the eastern part of the island, ostensibly to fight on behalf of the country, but their real intention was to conquer it. (Bede, *HE* I.15)

When those ruling the British failed in their agreement to supply the Anglo-Saxons with what they had promised, the foreign troops revolted and the first Germanic settlers invited their relatives from overseas to join them. There are few written sources for the end of Roman Britain and the migration: the principal 'insular' sources are *De excidio Britanniae*, written by Gildas in the mid-sixth century, the *Historia ecclesiastica gentis Anglorum* by Bede, and *The Anglo-Saxon Chronicle*; there is also much interesting material in the *Historia Brittonum* by Nennius. Gildas described the political crash following the withdrawal of Roman forces: Scots and Picts pressed on the former frontier and raided in Britain. An appeal for aid was sent, in vain, to Aetius in Gaul and, as a last resort, the British rulers arranged for a Saxon war-band under Hengest and Horsa to settle in England as federates.

All the sources give a mid-fifth-century date for the beginning of the migration of Germanic groups either after being invited by the British authorities as in Kent, or on their own as in Sussex and Wessex. These traditional dates are arbitrary: literary sources place the 'Adventus Saxonum' around 450, and present it as the beginning of the Germanic settlement in Britain. On the contrary, though, archaeological evidence indicates that by the mid-fifth century, the migration process was already under way, and thus proves the presence of Germanic troops well before the fifth century. Ceramic discoveries in Thanet support the presence of an early Germanic settlement in Kent, a settlement that was reinforced by the addition of the settlers' relatives from across the sea. Not much is known about the provenance of the Germanic peoples who occupied Kent and the Isle of Wight and who were supposed to be originally inhabitants of Jutland.

Bede (*HE* I.15) divides the Anglo-Saxons into their component groups, speaking of Saxons, Angles and Jutes; he bases the legend of their origin on the historical view accepted by the eighth century and their geographical dislocation in the British Isles. He also sketched the continental background of the English as he understood it. The Saxons, after establishing themselves in the south and east of England (now Sussex and Essex), founded a great kingdom in the west, which progressively absorbed almost the whole country south of the Thames (Wessex). The Angles founded the kingdoms of East Anglia (Norfolk and Suffolk), Mercia (the Midlands), Deira (Yorkshire) and Bernicia (the kingdom further north).

Another Germanic people that should be given more space in the early history of England and its Germanic background is outlined by Procopius. In his historical conflation, *Wars* VIII, 20, 8–10, he provides information about the Merovingians who claimed overlordship in southern England in the 550s, and the king of the Franks, Theudebert, who sent an embassy to the Emperor Justinian, seeking to establish his claim that England was under his rule. A possible Frankish hegemony in Kent and East Anglia has been surmised by several scholars (Stenton 1971: 59–60; Wallace-Hadrill 1975: 119–21) and has recently been proposed again by Wood. King Æthelberht had married Charibert I's daughter, Bertha, and Æthelberht's son, Eadbald, married a Frankish woman, Emma (Wood 1992: 240); undeniable also is the Frankish influence on the early English church (Wood 1994).

The Conversion

The years between the collapse of the Roman government in Britain and the arrival of St Augustine at the end of the sixth century were a period of significant change, but it was Christianity that was to play the major role in the transformation of Germanic tribal society. The conversion of the pagan English to Christianity is traditionally regarded – this is, again, Bede's conception – as a process beginning with the arrival of St Augustine in 597 (*HE* I.25). This conversion was gradual, and involved several missions from Rome, ending in the 680s with the conversion of the Isle of Wight (*HE* IV.16). A significant role in the conversion is given by Bede to Pope Gregory and the enlightened English rulers, first of all the Frankish princess Bertha, who had brought a Frankish bishop with her as chaplain. The monks headed by Augustine landed in Thanet and were received at the Kentish court: before the end of the century Kent had been converted and before the end of the next century the whole of England had forsaken its gods and its pagan practices (Mayr-Harting 1991).

Paganism

The Germanic invaders were pagan and illiterate. Their religion was the same as that of the other Germanic peoples, a religion whose features have more often been guessed at by scholars than known for certain in all its varied aspects. A lengthy chronological gulf separates the Anglo-Saxon pagan period (that is, less than three centuries after the migration) from the account of Tacitus's *Germania* on the one hand, and from the much later Old Norse mythology on the other (Lendinara 1989).

Some placenames preserve the names of the pagan deities: Tiw, Woden, Thunor and Frig. Their locations are in the east and south, where the earliest settlements are found, but in these instances it would be too rash to speak of pagan Saxon worship sites (Gelling 1961). Survivals of paganism in medical practices (Bonser 1963: 117–57) and in other aspects of Anglo-Saxon life and literature are difficult to prove (see Stanley 1975). Pagan Anglo-Saxon England had its stone carving, such as the images on the whetstones from Sutton Hoo and Hough on the Hill. There was a gradual transition from cremation to inhumation under the influence of British customs and the introduction of Christianity. Pagan inhumation burials were generally supplied with grave goods which provide excellent sources of information.

Archaeology

Archaeology supplies a considerable amount of information about the transition period and shows how the economic decline of the former Roman province was over by the sixth century. Pottery, brooches, buckles and spearheads have been classified in sequences (see, for example, Hines 1997) and provide invaluable evidence of the date and (the continental homelands) origin of immigrant groups. The shape and type of decoration of works of art and objects of personal adornments like brooches, buckles and wrist-clasps varied between tribal groups. In the fifth century, the quoit brooch style, a decorative style based on crouching animals and geometric motifs, developed in Kent (Suzuki 2000). Its origin is disputed, but Suzuki rightly sees it as an important step in the process of construction of a new group identity.

Placename studies provide additional information regarding the new emergent groups' identities in post-Roman society and their interaction, including their relationship with the British. These studies, however, must be used carefully to supplement other data and cannot be used without further support in order to prove the early origins of a village or town.

By the end of the sixth century, large parts of England witnessed the flourishing of a new 'warrior' culture. One well-known burial site, Sutton Hoo, provides evidence for the strong links of the newcomers with Scandinavia and France in the seventh century, but, at the same time, witnesses the receptivity and the power of assimilation of Anglo-Saxon culture. The cemetery, extending from the east bank of the river Deben in Suffolk, has a number of mounds and other smaller burials (see the fundamental works by Bruce-Mitford 1975–83; Carver 1986, 1998). The most famous burial is Mound 1, discovered in 1939, which contained a ship twenty-seven metres long. Within the ship was a funerary chamber, preserving an amazing variety of treasures, vessels, metalworks and weapons (the ship-burial is a cenotaph rather than an actual burial). It is inevitable, perhaps, that scholars in recent decades have subsequently linked this important archaeological discovery to the ship-burial of King Scyld in the opening sequence of *Beowulf.*

Writing

Anglo-Saxons used both the runic and the Latin alphabets and England experienced a long coexistence of the two kinds of writings. The former script was introduced from the continent by the Germanic invaders and was shared with many, if not all, of the Germanic peoples. The runic alphabet is also called *futhark*, because *f, u, th, a, r* and *k* are the first six letters, an order which must have had some mnemonic function (there are several inscriptions which contain the entire rune-row in the same fixed order). Though the origin of *futhark* is still debated, its connection with the Italic alphabets (including the Latin one) is certain. The number of the letters (the earliest *futhark* consisted of twenty-four letters) varied from place to place and changed to meet the phonetic exigencies of the different Germanic languages. In England new letters were added (*y, ea* and – limited to the north – *ĝ, k* and *k̂*), and other ones were adapted to reflect the sound-changes of Old English language: the original *a*-rune (the fourth letter of the rune-row, which became *futhorc* in Old English) was replaced by three different runes for *o, a* and *æ* (now the twenty-fifth and twenty-sixth letters, respectively). English inscriptions contain, all in all, thirty-one different letters: the runes for *o* and *a* have a parallel in the Anglo-Frisian runic corpus.

The oldest English inscription, found at Caistor-by-Norwich (Norfolk), dates from the beginning of the fifth century and was cut on a roe-deer's astragalus, probably used as a playing-piece. Some fifteen inscriptions date to the pagan period and, altogether, there are seventy Anglo-Saxon runic 'monuments' (excluding the inscriptions on coins) (see Page 1973, 1995). Each rune had a name which, in the majority of cases, began with the sound represented by the rune, that is the *f*-rune had the name *feoh* 'money, cattle' in Old English (the Old Norse name was *fé* and so on, as the names descended from a common Germanic form); the rune *w* was called *wynn* 'joy' and the rune *m man* 'man'.

The names of the runes, as well as their use, have been linked to the pagan Germanic religion, and runes have been seen as possessed of magical properties; actually runes were designated for inscriptional use (being usually inscribed on metal, stone or wood) and, from the beginning, were used as a writing system for practical purposes. They should not be considered as either magic or religious symbols with a purpose different from linguistic communication, but they are, nevertheless, an important feature of the Germanic inheritance in England (the Anglo-Frisian relationships need careful assessment), which was preserved and treasured by the Anglo-Saxons. In England runes were not given up for centuries, but were kept alongside the Roman letters and made their appearance also within the context of manuscripts (see Derolez 1954); the two runes *thorn* and *wynn* were themselves added to the Latin alphabet.

Old English Language

The term 'Anglo-Saxon' was used at first to distinguish the insular Saxons from the Old Saxons of continental Europe, but is commonly employed in reference to all Germanic inhabitants of England before the Norman Conquest. Extensively used until the early twentieth century, the term 'Anglo-Saxon' (an early seventeenth-century translation of the Latin *Anglo-Saxonicus*) is now often replaced by 'Old English', especially in reference to the language (for the advantages of the latter term, see Malone 1929, and on its origin in the sixteenth century, see Stanley 1995a, 1995b). Anglo-Saxons called their language *englisc* and their country *Engla land*.

Old English is one of the Germanic languages. It is differentiated from the others by developments in phonology, morphology and lexicon, but, at the same time, it preserves all the characteristic features of the so-called Germanic dialect. Anyone occupied with the history of Germanic or Indo-European will acknowledge the importance of the study of Old English and its significant role in comparative linguistics. The Germanic languages are conventionally divided into three groups: East (Gothic), North (Old Norse) and West Germanic (Old High German, Old Low Franconian, Old Frisian, Old Saxon and Old English) (for a more elaborate division, see, for example, Kufner 1972). West Germanic languages shared a number of linguistic features such as the gemination of consonants in front of *j*, *l*, *r*, *w*, *m* and *n* (contrast, for example, Gothic *halja* 'hell' and OE *hel(l)*, Old Saxon *hellia*, Old Frisian *helle* and Old High German *hella*), and the loss of final *-z* (from Indo-European *-s*), which had relevant morphologic consequences. By the same token, West Germanic people shared a number of relevant events, not least the date of the first vernacular documents: eighth century for Old English and Old High German, ninth century for Old Saxon and Old Low Franconian. The majority of Old English words and many compounds have cognates in other languages of the sub-group.

The historical context is of major importance in the development of a language. Old English was the language of the migrants – Saxons, Angles and the other people who first lived in northern Germany and later moved to the British Isles. The rate and degree of language change are closely related to historical context (see van Coetsem 1994): the more a society is in flux, the more also is the language spoken by the members of that society. This was true too of Common Germanic, which, during the transition from the Bronze Age to the Iron Age, underwent radical changes that may be related to the mobility of the Germanic tribes. The same can be said of Old English, which shows many innovative features related to historical context; namely the migrations of the Angles and Saxons which eventually brought them to England (van Coetsem 1994: 185). Old English language, for example, occupies the last place among the five West Germanic languages in complexity for the inflection of both the substantives and the verbs. At the same time Old English phonology underwent significant changes that included various mutations: vowel mutations, like *i*-mutation and others, are characteristic in the language; and new diphthongs were formed by breaking and other related processes.

Old English shared with the Germanic languages its accentual system (see Bennett 1972), which had undergone several changes from its origins in Indo-European: the Germanic accent was based on stress (and not on pitch) and primary stress had become fixed on a root syllable. The first syllable of a word was stressed at the expense of the other syllables; these, by progressive weakening, underwent reduction or were lost. In Old English the first syllable in all simple words is stressed: *cýningas* 'kings', *síngan* 'sing', as well as the prefixes of nominal compounds, *fórgiefenes* 'forgiveness' (with the exclusion of the proclitic *ge-*, which is always atonic). Verbal compounds have the accent on the root of the verb, that is, for example, as in *forgíefan* 'forgive'.

Old English is prolific in coining new lexical units, such as compounds, or in modifying existing lexemes. Three historical components, separated from each other by their origin, make up the Old English lexicon: the words inherited from Indo-European; the borrowings from other Indo-European languages (Celtic, Latin, Greek – mediated through Latin – and, beginning at the end of the tenth century, also French) and from other Germanic languages (in particular Old Norse); and items of unknown etymology (which cannot all be ascribed to a non-Indo-European substratum). The first group of original Germanic words comprises the majority and includes the lexicon that was used in everyday life.

The study of loanwords in Old English should begin with the period preceding the landing of Anglo-Saxons in Britain: a share of the loanwords that appeared in the language after leaving the continent had been borrowed before their sailing to Britain. Such common Germanic loanwords as Old English *win* 'wine' are found in more than one Germanic language and are thus called 'continental borrowing'. The majority of Latin words penetrated into Old English from the fifth century, thanks to the continuous relationship with Rome and the influence of Latin culture. By contrast, there was little interaction and reciprocal accommodation between the Anglo-Saxons and the non-Germanic tribes.

Language was not uniform throughout the country but fell into four dialects: Northumbrian, Mercian, West Saxon and Kentish; and it is West Saxon that is most commonly reflected in the writings of the Anglo-Saxons (and thus employed in modern Old English grammars).

The Germanic Inheritance in Old English Poetry

The potential afforded by the study of a language such as Old English, which has a corpus so large and differentiated, has attracted generations of linguists, whereas Old English literature has been for two centuries the object of philologists and literary historians. Traditional textual analysis, studies of manuscripts and sources have always been among the prevailing trends of research in the field of Anglo-Saxon studies, and the last two seem now to have dominating roles. None of these lines of research addresses the question of the Germanic background of Old English literature; it is not so with one of the predominant modes of twentieth-century criticism, that is the close examination of individual texts and analysis of diction and imagery. The New Critical close reading, which dominated the criticism of Old English poetry in the 1960s and early 1970s (see, for example, Greenfield 1966, 1972), laid great stress on the priority, the precedence and the naturalness of Old English poetry, which 'grew up naturally from Germanic roots in England' (Wrenn 1967: 195). This view cannot be maintained any longer, but the Old English poems' substratum of Germanic culture is now running the serious risk of being minimized or forgotten, the more so owing to the fuller appreciation of the Latin background and the enthusiasm for emphasizing Christian sources. The teaching of Old English language and literature continues, in most countries – Italy providing, for once, a lucky exception to this rule – in isolation from other Germanic languages and in connection, at best, with Celtic and Latin. This contributes to the hindrance of the recognition and the evaluation of common Germanic features in both the form and content of Old English literature.

Anglo-Saxon studies have also changed in other respects: Anglo-Saxon poetry is no longer seen as a product of the *Volkgeist*, or the poet trying to express his feelings, and the past is no longer a place of refuge where original virtue could be found. The extreme individualism of the attitude towards Old English literature has been abandoned, and texts are now studied as both product and mirror of a social reality, though far away in time.

In recent decades, scholars of oral-formulaic theory have focused on the repetition of verbal and syntactic structures throughout the corpus of Old English poetry and even beyond into all Germanic poetry (Kellogg 1965). The poet at work in England, and elsewhere in the medieval Germanic world in addition to other cultures and periods, drew upon established formulas or created new formulas on the patterns of the old. The oral-formulaic analyses that prevailed in the 1950s and 1960s have now virtually run their course, and the attempts to prove not only the oral-formulaic nature of Old English poetry, but also the oral provenance of all formulaic poetry, are over. With a more balanced judgement, Old English poetic texts are now seen as transitional texts, that is, written poetry embodying the traditional oral formulas (Benson 1966; Lawrence 1966).

The Old English verse form was that common to all the Germanic peoples and was certainly rooted in an oral tradition. The verse was regularly composed in the alliterative metre that is also found in Old Saxon and Old High German. None of the methods of scansion proposed to date by prosodists may be considered as definitive, and the nature of Old English metrics is still a hotly debated question, because our notion is based on modern analyses of the surviving texts (Anglo-Saxon scribes copied poetry in continuous lines). The first accepted theory of Old English metre was that of Eduard Sievers (1893), who distinguished five basic types of alliterative patterns: type A is the most common. John C. Pope (1942) used a musical notation to provide a definition of Old English metre. In recent times several studies on metre have appeared, drawing also on linguistic theories (Kendall 1991; Russom 1987).

The basic unit is a four-stress alliterative line, similar to that found in the other Germanic languages. A line is made up of two parts (half-lines a and b): each part contains two strongly stressed syllables and a variable number of lightly stressed ones. The foundation of this system lies in the alternation of stressed and unstressed syllables, and in the alliteration of the initial sounds of words in metrical position. Each consonant alliterates with itself: *w–w* / *s–s*, in the following example:

Ic seah wrætlice   wuhte feower
samed siþian;   swearte wæran lastas (*Riddle* 51, 1–2)

(I saw four wondrous creatures
travelling together. Black were their tracks)

All vowels alliterate with one another (in the following example, *e* alliterates with *a*):

Ic wat eardfæstne   anne standan (Riddle 49, 1)

(I know of one standing steadfast on the ground)

The solutions, for those who have been intrigued by the opening lines, are, respectively, 'quill pen and fingers' and either 'book-case' or 'bake-oven'.

The key-syllable within the verse line is the first stressed syllable in the second half-line: the word which receives this stress is often the most relevant for the meaning of the entire line:

Hræfen wandrode,
sweart and sealobrun.   Swurdleoma stod,
swylce eal Finnsburuh   fyrenu wære (*Battle of Finnsburh*, 34b–36)

(. . . The raven circled,
dusky and dark brown. There was the gleaming of swords
as if all Finnsburh was in flames)

West Germanic poetry developed long, wordy lines with a syntactic break in the middle, called the caesura; North Germanic developed short, minimal lines with medium-length stanzas and internal rhyme. East Germanic has left us no poetry. The bulk of Old English poetry is made up of pluri-lineal units, run-on links, with sentences that tend to go on from one line to the next, though there are examples of lines ending with a syntactical pause, every sentence making up either one line or one couplet.

Rhyme may occur within the long line (the best study is still that by Kluge 1884). The half-lines may rhyme, accidentally, with each other, as in *Beowulf*, line 1014: 'fylle **gefægon**, fægere **geþægon**' (gladly feasted, mannerly drank), where the use of two plural preterites causes the rhyme. Longer batches of rhyming lines are found elsewhere, though relatively rarely, as in *The Riming Poem*.

Stylistic devices such as the kenning, the *heiti* and variation all have a Germanic background. Anglo-Saxon poets make use of a large stock of poetic words, which never, or only infrequently, occurs in prose. A special place among poetic terms is occupied by synonyms for concepts like 'sea' or 'man' (for the former, see, for example, *The Wanderer* and *The Seafarer*; for the latter, see *Beowulf*, among other texts). Abundant also throughout Old English poetry is the use of compound words, not necessarily always kennings. Latin literary practice and the theories underlying it had an important influence on Old English literature (Campbell 1967). Much of Old English poetry was influenced by the Christian-Latin tradition; and, significantly, the development of religious verse in England has no parallel in the Germanic world.

The corpus of Old English poems has come down to us without clear evidence of date or place of origin: all the texts included in the four great codices of Anglo-Saxon poetry – the Exeter Book, the Vercelli Book, the *Beowulf*-manuscript and the Junius Book – are copies of earlier, pre-existing material, and a century-old attempt by scholars to establish a chronology for the large number of Old English poems has produced meagre results (see Busse 1987).

In terms of learning, the eighth century is the one when England led the civilized world in intellectual pursuits. An emergent 'national' identity is evident in the contemporary texts. Anglo-Saxon authors were conversant with Latin traditions of poetry, as well as with the Germanic tradition, and their literary output was of a very high standard. Literacy is associated with power in this society making the transition from oral to written culture. The social role of poetry is connected with the social role of the poet. *Scops* possibly had an important position within the community, and lived close to their lords, but very little is known of these poets, although several sources (such as Sidonius Apollinaris) provide records of their kind of performance. One may track the origins of Old English literature to the days of Tacitus and the songs on Mannus (the 'carmina antiqua': *Germania*, ch. III). According to Chadwick (1912) and Whitelock (1952) there is no break in tradition between Tacitus' first-century Germanic tribes and the Anglo-Saxons. It is not safe, however, to hypothesize about these earliest centuries, because the beginning of Anglo-Saxon poetry is connected with letters and books: the monastic scriptorium is more important than the banqueting hall.

The desire to search for the pristine Germanic tradition within this Anglo-Saxon literary production is alluring, but hard to deal with, without committing errors: much easier to follow are the paths of the other literary coupling, the Latin-Christian. Fortunately, perhaps, the overwhelmingly Christian interpretations of Old English literature that belonged to the allegorical school of critical thought some half-century ago has yielded place to a more objective attitude towards both poetry and prose. The Germanic elements too are now generally played down significantly, whereas the pagan elements have recently been seen in a different light. Edward Irving, for example, has pointed out that the word 'pagan' can be used with three different meanings: literal, vestigial and ethical (Irving 1996: 177–80), categories which include all paganism's manifestations in Anglo-Saxon England.

Common Genres

The Germanic tradition offered not only a common poetic medium but also a complete catalogue of material for stories with subjects from the Germanic heroic past.

Scenes from Germanic legends appear in the left section of the front panel of the Franks Casket: Weland the Smith holds with tongs one cup (made of the skull of one of the sons of King Nidhhad that he had previously killed) and offers the other to the king's daughter, Beaduhild. Anglo-Saxon heroic poetry has a continental counterpart, the *Hildebrandslied*; and the corpus also includes *Widsith*, *The Battle of Finnsburg*, *Waldere* and *Deor*, all of which concern continental heroes and events. The nature of the short, elegiac *Wulf and Eadwacer* is still open to debate. *Widsith* is a monologue where the singer tells his adventures, providing information about Eormanaric and the Goths. Some parts of *Widsith*, notably the 'Catalogue of Kings' (a mnemonic portion of the text in pre-classical style), have claims to great antiquity, whereas the poem as it stands in the Exeter Book has grown by gradual accretion. In *Deor* the singer names Germanic figures such as Weland and Eormanaric. Each exemplum ends with the refrain 'þæs ofereode, þisse swa mæg' (that passed away, so may this).

German scholars who created Anglo-Saxon studies in the nineteenth century were, in part, searching for the Germanic past in Old English literature, which is itself the oldest and most extensive Germanic literature. Secular heroic poetry was said to reflect the ideals of a warrior society, the lifestyle and value of warriors. The questions have been raised of whether Germanic heroism was an ongoing, live tradition, or a commonplace, or the product of deliberate antiquarianism. Roberta Frank (1991a) has argued that the use of Germanic legend in Old English literature is not an indication of a survival from the continental period, denying the existence of 'a pan-Germanism that never was' (Frank 1991a: 95). At the same time it is undeniable that the Anglo-Saxons themselves were curious about their origins and were exploring the beginnings of their culture, the age antecedent to theirs. A self-conscious use of the Germanic past is evident in *Beowulf*, the early dating of which has been challenged, but which undoubtedly draws on earlier tradition (see Chase 1981). The theory of a number of earlier scholars that the majority of Old English poems, including *Beowulf*, had been composed originally by a pagan *scop*, and reworked in subsequent centuries by a Christian monk, has been abandoned. It is now evident that the Anglo-Saxon (Christian) poets attempted to examine the values of the Germanic-heroic world as they are set against the whole history of mankind.

There are a few other shared genres that may be considered 'inherited'. 'Sayings' or gnomic verse is one of these. Gnomic poetry is concerned with understanding and spoken wisdom, but most of that which survives in Old English (*Precepts*, *Maxims* I and *Maxims* II) is Christian-Latin wisdom literature. There are also individually occurring proverbs, very much in line with medieval Latin proverbial collections. Whereas the *Precepts*, with their marked monastic provenance, contain generalized warnings against women, *Maxims* I and proverbial or sentential passages may reflect a native tradition of gnomic statements about women in contrast to the Latin tradition (Deskis 1994); for example the passages on motherhood (*Maxims* I, 23a–6, and *Fortunes of Men*, 1–3a).

Only literary riddles are preserved from Anglo-Saxon England, similar to the Latin riddles of Symphosius and Aldhelm on the one hand and, on the other, akin to poetic compositions on a set theme. Charms, the practical side of wisdom (remedies against a dwarf, a sudden stitch, the loss of cattle), may give us glimpses of the much-looked-for Germanic culture, coinciding, in this as well as in other instances, with what was genuine Anglo-Saxon. To speak of pagan remains in this literature is reductive, if not wholly inappropriate, and one should pay careful attention to the interplay of Germanic and Christian elements, even in the charms. Here, as elsewhere in Old English culture, there was no dramatic confrontation of Germanic and Christian ideas, and the worn-out series of dichotomies (not least the story of Aldhelm singing his songs on the bridge to attract people to his church as written about by William of Malmesbury) should be definitively abandoned.

Conclusions

Bede, in his *Historia ecclesiastica* (I.1), offered this definition of England:

> Britain, once called Albion, is an island of the ocean and lies to the north-west, being opposite Germany, Gaul, and Spain, which form the greater part of Europe, though at a considerable distance from them.

The distance between England and the rest of Europe, whence the Anglo-Saxons came, was not, indeed, that big, and a continuous net of relationships anchored the 'island' to the continent throughout the seven centuries of the Old English period, reinforcing the ties with North Sea neighbours or other Germanic peoples.

In the seventh century, there was a revival of trade across the Channel and the North Sea, which did not cease in the following centuries (Derolez 1974). Viking raids from the eighth century were followed by the permanent establishment of North Germanic people in England. The advent of another Germanic power, the Norman empire, was also a political upheaval for England, and effectively put an end to the Anglo-Saxon period. In several instances, because of these cultural interactions, it is not easy to decide if a certain 'Germanic' feature is a common inheritance of Germanic western Europe, or the result of the relations of England with the rest of north-western Europe. The poet using a certain literary topos (such as the 'ideal of the men dying with their lord' in *The Battle of Maldon*, for which see Frank 1991b) or the engraver at work on a stone sculpture in tenth-century Northumbria (Bailey 1980) did not necessarily look backwards to *Germania*, but, rather, around the corner, to Europe.

REFERENCES

Primary sources

Dewing, H. B., ed. 1914–28. *Procopius, 1–5: Wars.* Cambridge, MA.

Klaeber, Frederick, ed. 1950. *Beowulf and the Fight at Finnsburg.* 3rd edn. Boston.

Muir, Bernard J. 1994. *The Exeter Anthology of Old*

English Poetry: An Edition of Exeter Dean and Chapter MS 3501. 2 vols. Exeter.

Secondary sources

Bailey, R. N. 1980. *Viking-Age Sculpture in Northern England*. London.

Bennett, William H. 1972. 'Prosodic Features in Proto-Germanic'. *Toward a Grammar of Proto-Germanic*, pp. 99–116. Eds Frans van Coetsem and Herbert L. Kufner. Tübingen.

Benson, Larry D. 1966. 'The Literary Character of Anglo-Saxon Formulaic Poetry'. *Publications of the Modern Language Association* 81: 334–41.

Bonser, Wilfrid 1963. *The Medical Background of Anglo-Saxon England*. London.

Bruce-Mitford, Rupert L. S. 1975–83. *The Sutton Hoo Ship Burial*. 3 vols. London.

Busse, Wilhelm 1987. *Altenglische Literatur und ihre Geschichte. Zur Kritik des gegenwärtigen Deutungssystem*. Studia Humaniora 7. Düsseldorf.

Campbell, Jackson J. 1967. 'Knowledge of Rhetorical Figures in Anglo-Saxon England'. *Journal of English and Germanic Philology* 66: 1–20.

Carver, Martin O. H. 1986. 'Anglo-Saxon Objectives at Sutton Hoo, 1985'. *Anglo-Saxon England* 15: 139–52.

——1998. *Sutton Hoo: Burial Ground of Kings?*. London.

Chadwick, H. M. 1912. *The Heroic Age*. Cambridge.

Chase, Colin, ed. 1981. *The Dating of Beowulf*. Toronto Old English Series 6. Toronto.

Derolez, René 1954. *Runica Manuscripta*. Bruges.

——1974. 'Cross-Channel Language Ties'. *Anglo-Saxon England* 3: 1–14.

Deskis, Susan E. 1994. 'The Gnomic Woman in Old English Poetry'. *Philological Quarterly* 73: 133–49.

Frank, Roberta 1991a. 'Germanic Legend in Old English Literature'. *The Cambridge Companion to Old English Literature*, pp. 107–25. Eds Malcolm Godden and Michael Lapidge. Cambridge.

——1991b. 'The Ideal of Men Dying with their Lord in the *Battle of Maldon*: Anachronism or *Nouvelle Vague*'. *People and Places in Northern Europe 500–1600. Essays in Honour of Peter H. Sawyer*, pp. 95–106. Eds Ian Wood and Niels Lund. Woodbridge.

Gelling, Margaret 1961. 'Place-Names and Anglo-Saxon Paganism'. *University of Birmingham Historical Journal* 8.1: 7–25.

Greenfield, Stanley B. 1966. *A Critical History of Old English Literature*. London.

——1972. *The Interpretation of Old English Poems*. London.

Hines, John 1997. *A New Corpus of Anglo-Saxon Great Square-Headed Brooches*. Woodbridge.

Irving, Edward B. Jr 1996. 'Christian and Pagan Elements'. *A Beowulf Handbook*, pp. 175–92. Eds Robert E. Bjork and John D. Niles. Exeter.

Kellogg, Robert L. 1965. 'The South Germanic Oral Tradition'. *Franciplegius: Medieval and Linguistic Studies in Honor of F. P. Magoun Jr.*, pp. 66–74. Eds J. B. Bessinger Jr. and R. P. Creed. New York.

Kendall, Calvin B. 1991. *The Metrical Grammar of Beowulf*. CSASE 5. Cambridge.

Kluge, Frederick 1884. 'Zur Geschichte des Reimes im Altgermanischen'. *Beiträge zur Geschichte der deutschen Sprache und Literatur* 9: 422–50.

Kufner, Herbert L. 1972. 'The Grouping and Separation of the Germanic Languages'. *Toward a Grammar of Proto-Germanic*, pp. 71–97. Eds Frans van Coetsem and Herbert L. Kufner. Tübingen.

Lawrence, R. F. 1966. 'The Formulaic Theory and its Applications to English Alliterative Poetry'. *Essays on Style and Language: Linguistic and Critical Approaches to Literary Style*, pp. 166–83. Ed. Roger Fowler. London.

Lendinara, Patrizia 1989. 'Un popolo privato dei suoi dei. Notizie sul paganesimo nelle prime opere anglo-latine'. *MYTHOS* 1: 103–26.

Malone, Kemp 1929. 'Anglo-Saxon: A Semantic Study'. *Review of English Studies* 5: 173–85.

Mayr-Harting, Henry 1991. *The Coming of Christianity to Anglo-Saxon England*. 3rd edn. Philadelphia.

Page, R. I. 1973. *An Introduction to English Runes*. London.

——1995. *Runes and Runic Inscriptions: Collected Essays on Anglo-Saxon and Viking Runes*. Woodbridge.

Pope, John C. 1942. *The Rhythm of Beowulf*. New Haven, CT.

Russom, Geoffrey 1987. *Old English Meter and Linguistic Theory*. Cambridge.

Schwarz, Ernst 1956. *Germanische Stammeskunde*. Heidelberg.

Sievers, Eduard 1893. *Altgermanische Metrik.* Halle.

Stanley, Eric G. 1975. *The Search for Anglo-Saxon Paganism.* Cambridge.

——1995a. 'Old English = "Anglo-Saxon"'. *Notes and Queries* n.s. 42: 168–73.

——1995b. 'Old English = "Anglo-Saxon": William Lambard's Use in 1576'. *Notes and Queries* n.s. 42: 437.

Stenton, Frank M. 1971. *Anglo-Saxon England.* 3rd edn. Oxford.

Suzuki, Seiichi 2000. *The Quoit Brooch Style and Anglo-Saxon Settlement. A Casting and Recasting of Cultural Identity Symbols.* Woodbridge.

van Coetsem, Frans 1994. *The Vocalism of the Germanic Parent Language. Systemic Evolution and Sociohistorical Context.* Heidelberg.

Wallace-Hadrill, J. M. 1971. *Early Germanic Kingship in England and on the Continent.* Oxford.

——1975. 'Rome and the Early English Church: Some Questions of Transmission'. *Early Medieval History*, pp. 115–37. Oxford.

Whitelock, Dorothy 1952. *The Beginnings of English Society.* Harmondsworth.

Wolfram, Herwig 1988. *The History of the Goths.* Los Angeles.

——1992. 'Frankish Hegemony in England?'. *The Age of Sutton Hoo*, pp. 235–41. Ed. Martin Carver. Woodbridge.

——1994. *The Merovingian Kingdoms 450–751.* London.

Wrenn, Charles L. 1967. *A Study of Old English Literature.* London.

8
Religious Context: Pre-Benedictine Reform Period

Susan Irvine

The phrase 'pre-Benedictine Reform period', which defines a particular era in Anglo-Saxon England by reference to subsequent improvement, carries undeniably pejorative implications. Such implications are not entirely unjust. It is clear that the Benedictine Reform of the mid-tenth century did offer a much-needed revitalization of Anglo-Saxon religious life, particularly through its overhaul of the monasteries, which, largely as a result of the Danish invasions, had long failed to live up to their founding ideals. 'All available evidence from the reign of Alfred', argues David Knowles, 'points to a complete collapse of monasticism by the end of the ninth century' (Knowles 1963: 33).

Yet in literary terms at least, the pre-Reform period cannot be dismissed as being no more than a precursor to the considerable achievement of later writers such as Ælfric and Wulfstan. The century before the Reform witnessed the composition of some of the most distinguished prose literature in the vernacular to emerge from Anglo-Saxon England. The impetus for such literary endeavours can be traced in particular to one man, Alfred the Great, king of England from 871 to 899. Alfred used his royal authority to implement an educational programme including a series of English translations of Latin works which had a lasting impact on succeeding generations of writers. Some of these works are thought to have been translated by Alfred himself (Gregory's *Cura pastoralis*, Boethius's *De consolatione Philosophiae*, Augustine's *Soliloquia*, and probably the prose psalms of the Paris Psalter); translations of other works are thought to have been commissioned by him (Gregory's *Dialogi*, Orosius's *Historiarum adversus paganos libri septem*, Bede's *Historia ecclesiastica*). Two other vernacular works, the Old English *Martyrology* and the *Anglo-Saxon Chronicle* to 890, may also have been composed in response to Alfred's programme. Despite the decline of the monasteries, Alfred never seems to have lost sight of the ideal of a nation united by Christian faith and learning, and his literary programme represented a significant step towards achieving that end.

Alfred and his circle were apparently not alone in composing in English in the century before the Reform. Other works survive which are thought to be Anglian in origin and unconnected with Alfred's court. These works, listed by Janet Bately, are the *Apocalypse of Thomas*, the *Epistola Alexandri ad Aristotelem*, *St Chad*, *St Guthlac*, *The Wonders of the East* and the Christopher homily; a series of medical works; the Blickling collection of homilies and some items in the Vercelli Book; and 'a number of separate items, such as Napier XL and the *Vita Malchi* in Assmann XVIII' (1988: 99–100). Dating such works, however approximately, is by no means straightforward: Bately notes the 'virtual non-existence of texts . . . to which a date of composition in the period *c*.900 to *c*.970 can be securely assigned' (1988: 108–9). Whether these works were composed earlier than Alfred, contemporary with him, or later than his time cannot be easily ascertained, though all qualify as 'pre-Benedictine Reform' compositions.

What circumstances brought about this renaissance of prose writing in Old English before the Benedictine Reform? What do the nature and content of the works themselves indicate about the interests of their authors and audiences? In particular, how does the religious perspective underlying so many of these works contribute to and reveal itself in their composition? In this chapter I will address these questions first through a consideration of the cultural context for literary production and then through an examination of some of the writings, historical, philosophical and more strictly doctrinal.

In Anglo-Saxon England, books and religion were integrally bound up with one another. Books were copied and kept at religious centres: the extant manuscripts owe their survival to their being stored in monastic or cathedral libraries. Alfred, in an important prefatory letter to his translation of Gregory's *Cura pastoralis*, recalls how before the Viking invasions and consequent destruction, 'ða ciricean giond eall Angelcynn stodon maðma 7 boca gefyldæ' ('the churches throughout all England were filled with treasures and books'; translations are my own unless otherwise stated) (Sweet 1871: 5). In the same preface, Alfred points to the setting of the monastery as the appropriate destination for the initial copies of his own vernacular writings. In his opening words Alfred addresses individually each of the bishops who is intended to receive a copy of the work. The copy in Oxford, Bodleian Library, Hatton 20, for example, is headed 'Ðeos boc sceal to Wiogora Ceastre' ('this book must go to Worcester'), followed by the personal address 'Ælfred kyning hateð gretan Wærferð biscep his wordum luflice' ('King Alfred sends greetings to Bishop Waerferth with loving words'; Sweet 1871: 3). A seventeenth-century transcript of another manuscript of the Old English translation of *Cura pastoralis*, British Library, Cotton Tiberius B. xi, shows that a blank was left where 'Wærferð biscep' is written in the Hatton copy: presumably the copy was never sent out. The same Tiberius copy also contained a note 'Plegmunde arcebiscepe is agifen his boc 7 Swiðulfe biscepe 7 Werferðe biscepe' ('Archbishop Plegmund has been given his book, and Bishop Swithulf and Bishop Waerferth'; Sisam 1953: 142). At the end of the Preface, Alfred explicitly states his intention of sending a copy of his work to each bishopric (along with a valuable *æstel*, probably a bookmarker), and requests that this copy should always remain at the monastery unless the bishop wishes to have it, or it is out on loan, or it is being copied. Alfred assumes that the books associated with his programme of learning in the vernacular have their rightful place in the religious centres of his kingdom. If, moreover, the *æstel* does denote a bookmarker, this indicates not just how closely Alfred linked wealth and wisdom (Shippey 1979; Nelson 1986a), but also that Alfred viewed the monasteries as places where the books would be read rather than merely venerated.

Alfred's association between the manuscripts of his vernacular writings and the church was not new. Evidence of an early interest in writing in the vernacular in English churches has been traced to the school of Canterbury under Theodore of Tarsus, archbishop of Canterbury 669–90. Some of the students taught by Theodore and his colleague Hadrian, comments Bede, knew Latin and Greek just as well as their native language ('Latinam Grecamque linguam aeque ut propriam, in qua nati sunt, norunt'; Plummer 1896: I, 205), presumably a reference to the writing of these three languages rather than just the speaking of them (Wormald 1991: 8). Glossaries originating in Theodore's school have also been shown to rely frequently on vernacular translation (Lapidge 1986: 53–62). The first Christian poetry in the vernacular also owes its survival to its transcription by ecclesiastical scholars. When, as Bede recounts in book IV, ch. 24, of his *Historia ecclesiastica*, Cædmon miraculously found himself composing Christian poetry in English, he immediately made his way to the abbey at Whitby, where he recited his poem and then rendered into verse other scriptural material that was taught to him. Interestingly it is the Old English translator of Bede who, independently of the source, records that Cædmon's words were written down in the abbey. Where Bede notes only that through his beautiful song his instructors became his auditors ('in carmen dulcissimum conuertebat, suauiusque resonando doctores suos uicissim auditores sui faciebat'; Plummer 1896: I, 260), the Old English translator adds that his teachers wrote down his verses: 'Ond his song 7 his leoð wæron swa wynsumu to gehyranne, þætte seolfan þa his lareowas æt his muðe wreoton ond leornodon' ('And his song and his verses were so delightful to listen to that his very teachers wrote and learned from his mouth'; Miller 1890–8: I, 346). The act of writing in the vernacular in the seventh century is a matter worthy of special record to this anonymous Anglo-Saxon author writing in the vernacular about a century-and-a-half later.

That Alfred, as king, should see himself as duty-bound to provide books to be housed in monasteries might seem surprising. But such a response would be to underestimate the close interaction between court and church in the period. Augustine's mission to convert the English people had depended on the support of Anglo-Saxon kings, and the relationship between ecclesiastical and secular leaders became an integral part of the government of the country (Stenton 1971: 238). Alfred, in a well-known passage on the requirements for good government which he adds to the original in his translation of Boethius' *De consolatione Philosophiae*, includes clerics as an essential element in society: a king 'sceal habban gebedmen 7 fyrdmen 7 weorc-men' ('must have clergy and soldiers and labourers'; Sedgefield 1899: 40). Alfred's division of society into three orders, although it has Frankish analogues, is the first recorded use of this idea in Anglo-Saxon England (Powell 1994). The close relationship between the church and court in the pre-Reform period had considerable financial implications, as Asser in his contemporary biography of Alfred attests: in his reorganization of the expenditure of tax revenue, Alfred nominated half the income to the church, and the other half to the state (Stevenson 1904: 85–9).

It was not in England alone that royal and ecclesiastical concerns were seen as interdependent. The Frankish king Charlemagne (768–814) had taken a substantial interest in his kingdom's spiritual well-being, reforming church practices and ordering the production of religious books. Alfred is recognized to have modelled his kingship in many respects on that of his Carolingian counterparts (Wallace-Hadrill 1971, 1975; Nelson 1986b, 1993). Indeed Alfred's programme of learning may owe much to the precedent of Charlemagne, who, a century earlier, had instituted a similar regime, exhorting his ecclesiastics to devote themselves to the study and teaching of learning (Bately 1980: 10). Richard Gameson (1995) has shown that a considerable number of early medieval monarchs sponsored book production and scholarship: it was seen as the responsibility of the Christian monarch to provide the church with its resources, and these included books. Gameson argues further that the use of translation is also not in itself unique to Alfred. What is remarkable in Alfred's case is his energetic circulation of vernacular translations by which he aimed to make available essential Christian learning to as many of his subjects as possible, lay and clerical, in order to maximize the bestowal of God's favour upon his kingdom.

The housing of manuscripts in monasteries, the close relationship between king and church, and the influence of continental book production are all important aspects of the religious context underlying vernacular literature written in the pre-Benedictine Reform period. An awareness of, and an attempt to promote, the identity of England as rooted in a religious past also seem to be factors which underlie some of the literature of the period. Alfred, in his preface to the translation of *Cura pastoralis*, presents his educational programme as part of a revival of the Christian learning in England which had been taken for granted in the past. Alfred's nostalgic recollection of England's pre-eminence in learning at the beginning of his preface shows how closely he connects his kingdom's prestige with the extent of its learning. England's glorious past, Alfred proceeds to argue, has been blighted by the lassitude of its inhabitants in learning, leading to a ubiquitous and profound ignorance. In his eagerness to exhort his subjects to learning, Alfred even attributes the Viking invasions to God's punishment on the English for their lack of either learning or its dissemination: 'Geðenc hwelc witu us ða becomon for ðisse worulde, ða ða we hit nohwæðer ne selfe ne lufodon ne eac oðrum monnum ne lefdon: ðone naman anne we lufodon ðæt[te] we Cristne wæren, 7 swiðe feawe ða ðeawas' ('Think what punishments then afflicted us in this world, when we neither loved it [learning] ourselves nor bequeathed it to other people; we loved the name alone that we were Christian, and very few [loved] the virtues'; Sweet 1871: 5).

Whether or not Alfred's depiction of the parlous state of learning in contemporary England should be accepted as accurate has been energetically debated by scholars. According to one view, Alfred deliberately exaggerates the situation for purposes of propaganda. The preface, argues Alfred P. Smyth, shows 'the rhetorical use of exaggeration to paint as bleak a picture as possible in order to underline Alfred's personal achievement and in order also to persuade the bishops to take action' (1995: 549). Jennifer Morrish, who similarly finds Alfred's statements about past and present learning 'persuasive rather than factual', suggests that a decline in teaching rather than learning may account for Alfred's programme (1986: 90). It is certainly true that the preface cannot be read as a spontaneous stream of consciousness on Alfred's part. It is a carefully structured and rhetorically aware document (Huppé 1978). Alfred's use of such devices, however, may have been in his view the most effective means of conveying an accurate picture. The relatively small number of manuscripts produced in England itself in the ninth century before Alfred's reign has led Helmut Gneuss, and more recently Richard Gameson, to argue for the credibility of Alfred's representation of the conditions in England in his preface (Gneuss 1986; Gameson 1995).

For Alfred, his country's material and spiritual welfare was dependent on its ability to recreate the glorious age of learning taken for granted by past generations. This interest in the past is reflected by three historical works from the pre-Reform period which, though not ascribed to the king himself, are all associated with his programme of learning: the Old English *Orosius*, the Old English *Bede* and the *Anglo-Saxon Chronicle*. A concern to place England firmly within Christian history, from both a national and international perspective, seems to have inspired these writings.

Bede's *Historia ecclesiastica* exemplifies the literary achievement which Alfred associated with England's past. Written in 731 AD in the monastery of Wearmouth–Jarrow in Northumbria, the work charts the development of Christianity in England, starting with Julius Caesar's attempt to invade in 60 BC and ending at the date of its composition. The work's focus on England as a pivot of the Christian church must have appealed to a period around one and a half centuries later when the ideal of England as a Christian nation renowned for wisdom and learning was emerging. For Bede, as for Alfred and his circle, the very identity of England as a nation is bound up with the Christian faith of its people. Bede, for example, in book II, chapter 1, recounts a story in which Pope Gregory, as a result of responses to his enquiries about the origin of boys he saw for sale at a Roman market, posits an innate connection between the English people and Christianity (Plummer 1896: I, 79–80). The Old English translator faithfully renders this passage from Bede:

Eft he frægn, hwæt seo þeod nemned wære, þe heo of cwomon. Ondswarede him mon þæt heo Ongle nemde wæron. Cwæð he: Wel þæt swa mæg: forðon heo ænlice onsyne habbað, 7 eac swylce gedafonað, þæt heo engla æfenerfeweardas in heofonum sy. þa gyt he furðor frægn 7 cwæð: Hwæt hatte seo mægð, þe þa cneohtas hider of lædde wæron. þa ondswarede him mon 7 cwæð, þæt heo Dere nemde wæron. Cwæð he: Wel þæt is

cweden Dere, *de ira eruti*; heo sculon of Godes yrre beon abrogdene, 7 to Cristes mildheortnesse gecegde. Ða gyt he ahsode hwæt heora cyning haten wære: 7 him mon
ondswarade 7 cwæð, þætte he Æll haten wære. Ond þa plegode he mid his wordum to
þæm noman 7 cwæð: Alleluia, þæt gedafenað, þætte Godes lof usses scyppendes in þæm
dælum sungen sy.

Again he asked what the nationality from which they came was called. They answered
that they were called English. He said: 'That is appropriate because they have unique
looks and it is also fitting that they should be joint-heirs with the angels in heaven'.
Then he inquired further, saying: 'What is the name of the province from which the
boys were brought?' Then they answered him, saying that they were called Deiri. He
said: 'Deiri is an appropriate term, *de ira eruti*; they shall be removed from God's anger
and called to Christ's mercy'. He asked moreover what their king was called: and they
answered saying that he was called Aelle. And then he punned on the name, saying;
'Alleluia, it is fitting that praise of God our Creator should be sung in those places'.
(Miller 1890–8: I, 96)

The unique appearance of the English boys, and the linguistic significance of the
proper names associated with them, all suggest that in some way England is specially
destined to become a Christian nation. It is worth noting that the word *ænlice* with
its connotations of singularity is the Old English author's own: Bede's phrase *angeli-
cam habent faciem* merely prepares the way for the parallel with angels which follows
(Plummer 1896: I, 80). The Old English author is apparently concerned to emphasize in his rendering the distinctive nature of the relationship between the English
people and the Christian church.

The Old English translator provides a close translation of another well-known
episode from the *Historia ecclesiastica*: in the first part of book II, ch. 13, King Edwin's
advisors explain to him why they advocate acceptance of the Christian faith (Plummer
1896: I, 111–12). For Cefi, the powerlessness of the pagan gods is suggested by his
own failure to receive any special favours from the king in this world. The appealing
comparison, drawn by another advisor, of man's life on earth to the sparrow's temporary respite from wintry conditions as it flies through a hall encapsulates the attrac-
tiveness of the Christian faith to the English people. The Old English translator makes
effective use of vocabulary to evoke the contrast between the wintry storms and the
hall basking in warm firelight. His independent addition of the phrase *an eagan brhytm*
('the twinkling of an eye') to his translation of the Latin *paruissimo spatio* ('in the lit-
tlest space') has been much praised for adding vividness to the account. But through
his use of this phrase, the translator also reminds us of another time when a sudden
change will occur, not for a sparrow this time but for human beings, and one which
will carry enormous implications for mankind as a whole. The translator seems to be
alluding to I Corinthians 15, 52, where the phrase *in ictu oculi* refers to the moment
at which all mankind will be changed on Doomsday. Into a minor episode of English
history, the translator has inserted a reminder of universal Christian history and
England's central role within it.

The gradual but incessant consolidation of the Christian faith in England which Bede depicts was apparently to be recognized by participants in Alfred's programme as fitting into a much wider Christian scheme encompassing the entire world. The *Historia aduersus paganos libri septem*, written by Paulus Orosius in 417–18 and translated freely by an anonymous Old English writer in the pre-Reform period, covers the whole of world history from the Creation to 417. Orosius' work is informed throughout by its Christian perspective: for Orosius the whole of history is to be seen as working towards a peaceful Roman Empire which had been prearranged for the coming of Christ. That a Christian purpose lay behind all history was clearly a view congenial to the Old English translator. Many of the translator's omissions from his source, as Dorothy Whitelock has shown, relate to his concern to emphasize the close relationship between history and the coming of Christianity (Whitelock 1966: 90). The translator also introduces his own particular focus on the birth of Christ and the coming of Christianity: special emphasis, notes Bately in her edition of the Old English *Orosius*, 'is given to Christ's birth as the dividing point, separating a past of unrelieved misery from a present characterized by universal manifestations of mercy and peace and an undeniable improvement in man's lot' (1980: xciv).

It has always been assumed that Orosius' primary aim, to prove to his contemporary pagan audience that the sack of Rome by the Goths in 410 was not a result of the desertion of the old gods, would not have been one of particular relevance to late ninth-century Anglo-Saxon England. It is possible, however, that this very aim, outlined by Orosius in his prologue, may account for the Old English translator's attraction to the work. Not only had the gradual conversion to Christianity in England entailed the repudiation of the pagan gods which the Anglo-Saxons had previously worshipped (the second part of *Historia ecclesiastica*, book II, chapter 13, provides a striking example of such repudiation), but also the Danish invasions of the second half of the ninth century must have exposed the English anew to paganism and opened up the possibility of reversion to old beliefs. The Old English author, in translating this work, indirectly suggests that desertion of pagan gods is no more the cause for the attacks by the Danes than it was for the sack of Rome by the Goths. This threat to England's status as a Christian nation which the Danes represented extended well beyond the pre-Reform period. An explicit denunciation of the Danish gods, probably at least partly motivated by the same fear of backsliding, is found in Ælfric's sermon *De falsis diis* (Pope 1968: 667–724) and in Wulfstan's reworking of part of that sermon (Bethurum 1957: 221–4). If, for Orosius, the sack of Rome by the Goths ultimately served as evidence for Rome's place within the universal Christian scheme, so, implies the Old English translator, the Viking attacks on Anglo-Saxon England can be viewed as part of God's long-term plan establishing England's role as a glorious Christian nation.

The impact of the Danish invasions on England is one that the third historical work from the pre-Reform period, the *Anglo-Saxon Chronicle*, makes abundantly clear. The *Anglo-Saxon Chronicle* consists of a series of annals covering collectively the history of England from 60 BC (when Julius Caesar invaded Britain) to 1154. The *Chronicle* is in effect a compilation surviving in a variety of versions, all of which relate to one another in extremely complex ways (Keynes and Lapidge 1983: 275–81; Smyth 1995: 455–64). Evidence from the manuscripts, which all offer similar material up to the early 890s (scholars disagree about the precise *terminus ad quem*), suggests that the *Chronicle* was first issued as a single text at that time. This single text, however, itself consisted of a number of contributions by different authors, as Bately's study of the vocabulary of this part of the *Chronicle* has shown (1978: 93–129). Curiously Asser, who draws on the *Chronicle* for his *Life of Alfred*, only used material from it up to 887: either his copy stopped at this point, or he deliberately changed his focus (at ch. 87) from contemporary historical context to the more personal achievements of Alfred himself. To the core text were added groups of annals up to 1042, variously reproduced, augmented or omitted in the main versions of the *Chronicle* that survive. Only one of the manuscripts, known as the Peterborough Chronicle, extends the *Chronicle* into the twelfth century.

One of the most controversial issues relating to the production of the *Anglo-Saxon Chronicle* is the question of to what extent, if at all, Alfred was responsible for the production and contents of the *Chronicle* entries dating from his own reign. Alfred, argue some scholars, commissioned the *Anglo-Saxon Chronicle* in order to glorify his own achievements. One of the most rigorous proponents of the case for Alfred's active involvement is Alfred Smyth: 'When we bear in mind that the *Anglo-Saxon Chronicle* focuses first on Alfred's own dynastic ancestors and later concentrates almost exclusively on his own personal exploits against the Danes, there can scarcely be much doubt about the king's personal association – directly or indirectly – with the work' (Smyth 1995: 515).

The exact nature of Alfred's role in the production of the *Chronicle* is difficult to ascertain. There is, for example, a curious lack of information in the *Anglo-Saxon Chronicle* on events of the 880s in which Alfred took part. This objection is countered by Smyth with a speculation that the events may not have been written up until *c*.897: 'Common sense points to 896–7 as the time when the first proto-booklet of the *Anglo-Saxon Chronicle* was produced, and we should see it as being produced simultaneously with the set of annals covering Alfred's Last War' (Smyth 1995: 505). Other evidence, however, points strongly to a break in the composition of the *Chronicle* in 891–2 (Keynes and Lapidge 1983: 278–9). The conspicuous focus on Alfred and his motives in the final annals dating from his reign, those for 891–6, may, but need not, indicate a more direct involvement by Alfred in their production. Linguistic evidence attests to their composite nature: Bately's analysis suggests that there is no one chronicler responsible for the 891–6 section but rather 'an 896 annalist, responsible for the material now in annals 893 to 896 part 1 but actually referring as far back as autumn 892, with annals 892 and 896 parts 2 and 3 composed by other hands' (Bately 1985: 19). The 891–6 annals may, in the light of Bately's examination, be seen as a composite composition which one of its annalists works into an existing *Chronicle* framework.

Whatever the extent of Alfred's own involvement in the *Anglo-Saxon Chronicle*, it is clear that England's identity as a Christian nation is an assumption underlying its production. The opening annals of the *Chronicle* (excluding the varied Prefaces) focus on the earliest link between Britain and Rome, the unsuccessful attempt at invasion by Julius Caesar. Christ's birth is then recorded, followed by a series of annals for significant events in early Christian history. Amongst these is included for the year 47 an annal recording the emperor Claudius' more successful invasion of Britain. Then in 409 the annalist pronounces closed that period of Roman influence over Britain: 'Her Gotan abrecon Romeburg, 7 næfre siþan Romane ne ricsodon on Bretone' ('In this year the Goths stormed the city of Rome, and never afterwards did the Romans rule in Britain'; Bately 1986: 15). The beginnings of Christianity in Britain are recorded in the annal for 565: the annal in MS A (the Parker Chronicle) referred originally to the ministry of the Irish priest Columba and to his monastery on Iona: this was augmented (in MS A after deletion) to include a reference to Gregory's sending of baptism to Britain at this time, and further details about Columba and the conversion of the Picts. In the annal for 596 (transferred to 595 in MS A), Augustine's mission to Britain is recorded, and the annals thereafter, with varying degrees of detail, record events indicative of the assimilation of Christianity into the life of the English people, alongside other information of military, historical and genealogical significance. In this context, the wars against the Danes, which occupy so much of the chroniclers' attention in the *Chronicle*, can be seen as representing the perennial battle of Christians against pagans, and hence of good against evil. Repeatedly the terms *hæþen men* or *hæþen here* define the invaders, as the annals for 793 (MS E: the Peterborough Chronicle), 794 (MS E), 832, 838 (MS A), 851, 852 (MS E)/853 (MS A), 855 and 865 exemplify (Plummer 1892–9). The English are fighting a *justum bellum* in which by implication their very identity as a Christian nation is under threat. In the *Anglo-Saxon Chronicle*, just as in the Old English *Bede* and the Old English *Orosius*, England's status as a Christian nation is bound up with how it fits into a religious past.

The relationship between England and Christian world-history was an important stimulus for Old English writers of the pre-Reform period. One other work based on events of the Roman Christian past attracted attention in this period. The work itself, Boethius' *De consolatione Philosophiae*, is primarily philosophical rather than historical in its interests, and its confrontation of complex philosophical issues accounts for its appeal to Alfred, who is generally accepted as its Old English translator. But Alfred begins by adding independently of his source a historical summary of the events which led up to Boethius' imprisonment. The historical summary begins at the point where the translator of the OE *Orosius* leaves off, that is, with the sacking of Rome by the Goths. The perspective of the two authors, however, is very different. For the translator of the OE *Orosius*, the sacking of Rome by Alaric is a sign of God's mercy in that the Romans' misdeeds are so lightly avenged; in his final chapter (entitled 'Hu God gedyde Romanum his mildsunge' ('How God showed his mercy to the Romans')) he explains: 'God gedyde his miltsunge on Romanum, þa þa he hiora misdæda wrecan let, þæt hit þeh dyde Alrica se cristena cyning 7 se mildesta, 7 he mid swa lytle niþe abræc Romeburg þæt he bebead þæt mon nænne mon ne sloge' ('God showed his mercy to the Romans when he had their wrongful deeds avenged, in that the most merciful Christian king Alaric performed it, and he conquered Rome with so little harm that he commanded that no man should be slain'; Bately 1980: 8, 156). For Alfred, however, the sacking of Rome by Alaric (and, according to Alfred, by Rada-gaisus, also linked with Alaric by the *Orosius* translator in his penultimate chapter) is the first of a series of events culminating in the unjustified imprisonment of Boethius. Alfred's attitude is more clearly conveyed in the verse rendering of his original prose version: the advancing Goths he describes as 'monig . . . Gota gylpes full, guðe gelysted' ('many a Goth full of boasting, desiring battle'); the defeated Romans are 'seo wealaf' ('the woeful remnant'), and 'giomonna gestrion sealdon unwillum eþel-weardas, halige aðas; wæs gehwæðeres waa' ('defenders of the homeland unwillingly gave up ancestors' treasure [and] holy oaths; it was an affliction in both respects'; Sedgefield 1899: 151–2). The accession of Theodoric provides only a temporary and false respite. For Alfred there is no justification for the presence of the Goths in Rome, and Boethius is presented as the upholder of Christianity against an unrighteous usurper. In his approval for Boethius, it has been suggested, Alfred may have had in mind his own attempt to uphold a Christian kingdom against foreign invaders (Godden 1981: 419; Irvine 2001a).

De consolatione Philosophiae is not an explicitly Christian work. Unsurprisingly, however, given that Boethius himself was a Christian, nothing in the work is incom-patible with Christian doctrine. By Alfred's time, various Latin commentaries had already interpreted the work from a Christian perspective. The question of whether or not Alfred had available to him a commentary which he drew on for his transla-tion has been the subject of much scholarly debate (Wittig 1983): the answer may yet lie in the vast number of Latin commentaries on *De consolatione Philosophiae* which remain unedited.

Alfred translated Boethius' work with considerable freedom. Many of his changes can be attributed to the Christian meaning which he sees as the heart of the work. God is specifically the Christian God, who 'gelde ælcum men be his gewyrhtum' ('repays each man according to his deeds'; Sedgefield 1899: 144). The idea of Chris-tian wisdom is particularly important in Alfred's interpretation of Boethius (Otten 1964). Alfred explicitly links Christ and wisdom: 'Crist eardað on þære dene ead-modnesse 7 on þam gemynde wisdomes' ('Christ dwells in the valley of humility and in the memory of wisdom'; Sedgefield 1899: 27). Boethius's Lady Philosophy is fre-quently designated as 'se Wisdom' in Alfred's rendering and ultimately wisdom is equated with God: 'se wisdom is God' states Alfred unequivocally (Sedgefield 1899: 145). Just as God and Wisdom are one and the same, so also is wisdom the highest virtue that man can strive to attain on earth: 'Swa swa wisdom is se hehsta cræft, 7 se hæfð on him feower oðre cræftas; ðara is an wærscipe, oðer gemetgung, ðridde is ellen, feorðe rihtwisnes' ('Thus wisdom is the highest virtue and it encompasses within it four other virtues: one of them is prudence, the second moderation, the third courage and the fourth justice'; Sedgefield 1899: 62).

For Alfred wisdom is the quality required to undertake any task successfully. Wisdom is integral to his ideology of kingship, as he makes clear in his discussion of a ruler's requirements: 'Forþam ælc cræft 7 ælc anweald bið sona forealdod 7 forsugod, gif he bið buton wisdome; forðæm ne mæg non mon nænne cræft bringan buton wisdome; forðæmþe swa hwæt swa þurh dysig gedon bið, ne mæg hit mon næfre to cræfte gerecan' ('Therefore every skill and power is straightaway worn out and never heard of if it is without wisdom; for no one can show any skill without wisdom; because whatever is done in folly can never be considered a skill'; Sedgefield 1899: 40–1). The 'cooperation between *cræft* and *wisdom*', writes Peter Clemoes, was for Alfred 'the key to the moral achievement and the destiny of the Christian soul' (Clemoes 1992: 237).

For Alfred, wisdom has as its reward both earthly honour in this world and eternal life, as his resounding address to the wise demonstrates:

> Wella, wisan men, wel; gað ealle on þone weg þe eow lærað þa foremæran bisna þara godena gumena 7 þara weorðgeornena wera þe ær eow wæron. . . . Forðæm hi wunnon æfter weorðscipe on þisse worulde, 7 tiolodon goodes hlisan mid goodum weorcum, 7 worhton goode bisne þæm þe æfter him wæron. Forðæm hi wuniað nu ofer ðæm tunglum on ecre eadignesse for hiora godum weorcum.

> Oh wise men, go, all of you, on the path which the famous examples of the good men and of those eager for honour who preceded you teach you. . . . For they strove after honour in this world, and aimed for a good reputation through good deeds, and set a good example for those who followed them. Therefore, because of their good deeds, they now dwell above the stars in eternal bliss. (Sedgefield 1899: 139)

Alfred's *wisan men* replace the *fortes* ('strong men'/ 'brave men') who are the subject of Boethius' corresponding address at the end of book IV, metre 7 (Bieler 1957: 88). Alfred omits Boethius' specific examples of the pagan heroes Agamemnon, Ulysses and Hercules, presumably because although their strength is not in question their wisdom might be (Irvine 2001b).

Alfred elsewhere, however, far from eschewing the pagan material incorporated by Boethius, amplifies it and clarifies its relationship to his religious theme (Irvine 1996). Pagan stories, though themselves mendacious, could be a means of expressing truths: 'Ne fo we no on ða bisna 7 on ða bispel for ðara leasena spella lufan, ac forðæmðe we woldon mid gebecnan þa soðfæstnesse, 7 woldon ðæt hit wurde to nytte ðam geherendum' ('We do not use exempla for love of those false stories, but because we wish to signify the truth with them, and wish it to be of use to listeners'; Sedgefield 1899: 101). Alfred accordingly concludes his adaptation of Boethius' account of Orpheus and Eurydice with an explicitly Christian moralization which exhorts men to seek the light of God rather than hell's darkness and even offers the possibility of repentance for one's sins (Sedgefield 1899: 103). Boethius' reference to the myth of Jove and the giants is considerably expanded by Alfred, who also compares it to the Biblical story of the Tower of Babel and interprets it from an explicitly Christian perspective: 'Swa gebyreð ælcum þara þe winð wið ðæm godcundan anwalde; ne gewyxð him nan weorð-scipe on ðæm, ac wyrð se gewanod þe hi ær hæfdon' ('Thus it happens to each of those who strives against the divine power; their honour does not increase, and what they had before is diminished'; Sedgefield 1899: 99). In the case of Hercules, Alfred is even prepared to concede that his acts, whilst performed in ignorance of God, might conform to a Christian moral code: Hercules drowns Bosiris 'swiðe rihte be Godes dome' ('very rightly in God's judgement'; Sedgefield 1899: 37).

A religious perspective informs all the pre-Reform literature, historical and philo-sophical, that I have examined hitherto. A further body of works from the period draws on works primarily concerned with Christian doctrine. The inspiration for much of this writing in English seems to have been patristic, but links between these and non-patristic works are also helpful for indicating other areas of literary interest in the period. Gregory the Great provides the inspiration for two works. A translation of Gregory's *Dialogues*, written in 593, was, according to Asser, commissioned by Alfred from Bishop Werferth of Worcester (Stevenson 1904: 62). The work, trans-lated fairly literally into Old English, consists of a series of miracle stories told by Gregory to his deacon Peter. For Alfred the work seems to have been a convenient collection of saints' lives; in a Preface which he added to the translation he refers to it as 'be haligra manna þeawum 7 wundrum . . . þas æfterfylgendan lare' ('this fol-lowing teaching about the virtues and miracles of holy men'; Hecht 1901: 1). Many of the saints discussed are obscure, but two, Paulinus of Nola and St Benedict, were widely venerated in Anglo-Saxon England. Other pre-Reform literature reflects this interest in saints: English saints seem to have attracted particular interest. The Mercian *Life of St Chad*, probably composed in the second half of the ninth century, draws ultimately on Bede's *Historia ecclesiastica* for its account of the Mercian Bishop Chad (Vleeskruyer 1953; Bately 1988). The Anglian *Life of Guthlac*, again probably composed in the later ninth century, translates Felix of Crowland's *Vita Sancti Guth-laci* (Gonser 1909; Roberts 1986; Bately 1988). The Old English *Martyrology*, assigned with some certainty to the second half of the ninth century, may have been connected with Alfred's scheme (Kotzor 1981). This prose collection draws on a variety of sources to offer notices of around two hundred saints, including English ones. Günter Kotzor notes the compiler's 'tendency towards including narrative entries on "rare" saints of mainly local interest', such as St Pega (Guthlac's sister), St Cedd (Chad's brother) and St Higebald of Lindsey (Kotzor 1986: 322, 332). For English authors of the pre-Reform period, saints offered important reminders of God's power at work in the world, most significantly in England itself.

The second work drawing on Gregory the Great is an Old English rendering of his late sixth-century *Cura pastoralis*, thought to be the first translation undertaken by Alfred himself. In contrast to his later translations, Alfred follows his source relatively closely here. The popularity of Gregory's work within the English church accounts in itself for Alfred's choice of it for translation: its advice on the qualities necessary for a bishop and how he should go about his tasks had made it an essential manual for the clergy. Alfred may also have been attracted to the work, however, because so much of it was relevant for a secular as well as an ecclesiastical ruler. Alfred's vision of his own role as a Christian king reflects much of the advice offered to bishops by Gregory.

Another work, non-patristic in its source, may also have been selected for translation because of a combination of its high profile in church teaching and its affinity to Alfred's situation. The first fifty psalms of the Paris Psalter again were apparently translated by Alfred himself (Bately 1982); this version offers a fairly free rendering including additional exegetical commentary. It is likely, as Keynes and Lapidge have suggested, that Alfred, given his troubles with the Vikings, found particularly congenial King David's lamentations at oppression by enemies and his assertions of the need to embrace religious learning (1983: 32). Scriptural material is seen to have its own relevance to ninth-century England.

In addition to Gregory, another patristic author, St Augustine, provided material for an important pre-Reform work. His *Soliloquia* (written 386–7) was translated by King Alfred himself, probably soon after his translation of Boethius' *De consolatione Philosophiae* (Whitelock 1966: 76). As with the latter, Alfred is extremely free with his patristic source. Augustine, in his unfinished *Soliloquia*, presented in two books a dialogue between his own mind and Reason on the subject of the soul's immortality. Although Alfred's translation follows book I of the *Soliloquia* and the first part of book II, he also produces independently a third book drawing largely on another of Augustine's works, *De videndo Deo*, which has as its focus the life of the soul after death.

In a preface which Alfred attached to this work he gives a fascinating insight into his literary endeavours. He draws a lengthy comparison between the gathering of wood for building and the compilation of excerpts from the church Fathers (specifically Augustine, Gregory and Jerome) (Carnicelli 1969: 47–8): just as living comfortably in this present life entails selecting the finest timbers so constructing an eternal home depends on accumulating knowledge of the most illuminating Christian writings. Alfred is characteristically concerned that others should benefit from and build on his knowledge: everyone should, he advises, go to the same forest to fetch more timber for constructing their own splendid dwellings. The recognition that his writing entails a process of selection is also reflected in another concrete image by which he introduces book II of his translation of Augustine: 'Her onginð seo gadorung þære blostmena þære æftran bec' ('Here begins the collection of blossoms of the second book'; Carnicelli 1969: 83). The natural image suggests perhaps Alfred's awareness of the precarious position of such learning in his society; in an earlier passage added to Augustine's prayer to God, Alfred emphasizes how natural objects are subject to a cyclical process: 'Ac cumað oðre for hy, swa swa leaf on treowum; and æpla, (and) gears, and wyrtan, and treowu foraldiað and forseriað; and cumað oðer, grenu wexað, and gearwað, and ripað, for þat hy eft onginnað searian' ('But others come in their place, as leaves on trees; and apples and grass and plants and trees grow old and wither;

and others come and turn green and grow and ripen, whereupon they proceed to wither again'; Carnicelli 1969: 53). In his Preface to the *Cura pastoralis* discussed above, Alfred shows how literature and learning have become subject to the transience so prevalent in nature. For Alfred, the production of works in English is a means of arresting that process. With his translation of the *Soliloquia*, he both passes on Christian learning and interprets it so as to make it more accessible to his ninth-century audience.

Patristic material underlies another collection of literature not associated with Alfred's court but which may be defined as 'pre-Benedictine Reform'. These are the collections of sermons referred to as the Blickling and Vercelli Homilies, whose provenances and dates of composition remain so elusive (Morris 1874–80; Scragg 1979, 1985, 1992; Gatch 1989; Bately 1988). Homiletic writing in English clearly existed in the late ninth and early tenth century, though its extent and the circumstances of its composition and use cannot be ascertained. As Greenfield and Calder note of these collections, 'they represent the synthetic tradition of vernacular preaching before the watershed of the monastic revival, although that rebirth may have inspired their transcription' (1986: 71). These homilies attest to the beginnings of Christian homiletic writing in the vernacular before the Reform and foreshadow the work of homiletic authors such as Ælfric and Wulfstan, who were to play such an important part in the development of English literature after the Reform.

REFERENCES

Primary sources

Bately, Janet M., ed. 1980. *The Old English Orosius.* Early English Text Society, s.s. 6. London.

——, ed. 1986. *The Anglo-Saxon Chronicle: A Collaborative Edition. Vol. 3: MS A.* Cambridge.

Bethurum, Dorothy, ed. 1957. *The Homilies of Wulfstan.* Oxford.

Bieler, Ludwig, ed. 1957. *Anicii Manlii Severini Boethii Philosophiae Consolatio.* Corpus Christianorum Scriptorum Latinorum 94. Turnhout.

Carnicelli, Thomas A., ed. 1969. *King Alfred's Old English Version of St Augustine's Soliloquies.* Cambridge, MA.

Gonser, P. 1909. *Das angelsächsischen Prosa-Leben des hl. Guthlac.* Heidelberg. 1966. Repr. Heidelberg.

Hecht, Hans, ed. 1900–7. *Bischof Waerferths von Worcester Übersetzung der Dialoge Gregors des Grossen.* 2 vols. Bibliothek der Angelsächsischen Prosa 5. Leipzig.

Kotzor, Günter, ed. 1981. *Das altenglische Martyrologium.* Bayerische Akademie der Wissenschaften, Philosophisch-historische Abteilung, Neue Forschung 88. 1–2. Munich.

Miller, Thomas, ed. and trans. 1890–8. *The Old English Version of Bede's Ecclesiastical History of the English People.* 2 vols. Early English Text Society, o.s. 95, 96, 110, 111. London.

Morris, Richard, ed. 1874–80. *The Blickling Homilies of the Tenth Century.* Early English Text Society, o.s. 58, 63, 73. London.

Plummer, Charles, ed. 1892–9. *Two of the Saxon Chronicles Parallel.* 2 vols. Oxford.

——, ed. 1896. *Venerabilis Baedae Opera Historica.* 2 vols. Oxford.

Pope, John C., ed. 1967–8. *Homilies of Ælfric: A Supplementary Collection.* Early English Text Society, o.s. 259, 260. London.

Scragg, D. G., ed. 1992. *The Vercelli Homilies and Related Texts.* Early English Text Society, o.s. 300. London.

Sedgefield, Walter J., ed. 1899. *King Alfred's Old English Version of Boethius De Consolatione Philosophiae.* Oxford.

Stevenson, W. H., ed. 1904. *Asser's Life of King Alfred*. Oxford. 1959. Repr. with an article by D. Whitelock. Oxford.

Sweet, Henry, ed. 1871. *King Alfred's West-Saxon Version of Gregory's Pastoral Care*. Early English Text Society, o.s. 45, 50. London.

Vleeskruyer, R., ed. 1953. *The Life of St Chad*. Amsterdam.

Secondary sources

Bately, Janet M. 1978. 'The Compilation of *The Anglo-Saxon Chronicle*, 60 BC to AD 890: Vocabulary as Evidence'. *Proceedings of the British Academy* 64: 93–129.

——1980. *The Literary Prose of King Alfred's Reign: Translation or Transformation?*. University of London.

——1982. 'Lexical Evidence for the Authorship of the Prose Psalms in the Paris Psalter'. *Anglo-Saxon England* 10: 69–95.

——1985. 'The Compilation of the *Anglo-Saxon Chronicle* Once More'. *Leeds Studies in English* n.s.16: 7–26.

——1988. 'Old English Prose Before and During the Reign of Alfred'. *Anglo-Saxon England* 17: 93–138.

Clemoes, Peter 1992. 'King Alfred's Debt to Vernacular Poetry: The Evidence of *ellen* and *cræft*'. *Words, Texts and Manuscripts: Studies in Anglo-Saxon Culture Presented to Helmut Gneuss on the Occasion of his Sixty-fifth Birthday*, pp. 213–38. Ed. Michael Korhammer with the assistance of Karl Reichl and Hans Sauer. Cambridge.

Gameson, R. G. 1995. 'Alfred the Great and the Destruction and Production of Christian Books'. *Scriptorium* 49: 180–210.

Gatch, Milton McC. 1989. 'The Unknowable Audience of the Blickling Homilies'. *Anglo-Saxon England* 18: 99–115.

Gneuss, Helmut. 1986. 'King Alfred and the History of Anglo-Saxon Libraries'. *Modes of Interpretation in Old English Literature: Essays in Honour of Stanley B. Greenfield*, pp. 29–49. Eds Phyllis Rugg Brown, Georgia Ronan Crampton and Fred C. Robinson. Toronto, Buffalo and London.

Godden, Malcolm 1981. 'King Alfred's Boethius'. *Boethius: His Life, Thought and Influence*, pp. 419–24. Ed. Margaret Gibson. Oxford.

Greenfield, Stanley B. and Daniel G. Calder 1986. *A New Critical History of Old English Literature*. With a survey of the Anglo-Latin background by Michael Lapidge. New York and London.

Huppé, Bernard F. 1978. 'Alfred and Ælfric: A Study of Two Prefaces'. *The Old English Homily and its Backgrounds*, pp. 119–37. Eds Paul E. Szarmach and Bernard F. Huppé. Albany, NY.

Irvine, Susan 1996. 'Ulysses and Circe in King Alfred's *Boethius*: A Classical Myth Transformed'. *Studies in English Language and Literature: 'Doubt Wisely': Papers in Honour of E. G. Stanley*, pp. 387–401. Eds M. J. Toswell and E. M. Tyler. London and New York.

——2001a. 'The Anglo-Saxon Chronicle and the Idea of Rome in Alfredian Literature'. *Proceedings of the Southampton and London Alfred Conferences September and October 1999*. Ed. T. Reuter. Aldershot.

——2001b. 'Wrestling with Hercules: King Alfred and the Classical Past'. *Court Culture in the Early Middle Ages: Proceedings of the First York Alcuin Conference 17–20 July 1998*. Ed. C. Cubitt. Turnhout.

Keynes, Simon and Michael Lapidge, trans. 1983. *Alfred the Great*. Harmondsworth.

Knowles, Dom David 1963. *The Monastic Order in England*. Cambridge.

Kotzor, Günter 1986. 'The Latin Tradition of Martyrologies and the *Old English Martyrology*'. *Studies in Earlier Old English Prose*, pp. 301–33. Ed. Paul E. Szarmach. Albany, NY.

Lapidge, Michael 1986. 'The School of Theodore and Hadrian'. *Anglo-Saxon England* 15: 45–72.

Morrish, Jennifer 1986. 'King Alfred's Letter as a Source on Learning in England in the Ninth Century'. *Studies in Earlier Old English Prose*, pp. 87–107. Ed. Paul E. Szarmach. Albany, NY.

Nelson, Janet L. 1986a. 'Wealth and Wisdom: The Politics of Alfred the Great'. *Kings and Kingship*, pp. 31–52. Ed. J. Rosenthal. State University of New York Acta 11. New York.

——1986b. ' "A King Across the Sea": Alfred in Continental Perspective'. *Transactions of the Royal Historical Society* 36: 45–68.

——1993. 'The Political Ideas of Alfred of Wessex'. *Kings and Kingship in Medieval Europe*, pp. 125–58. Ed. Anne J. Duggan. King's College London.

Otten, Kurt 1964. *König Alfreds Boethius*. Tübingen.

Payne, F. A. 1968. *King Alfred and Boethius*. Madison, WI.

Powell, Timothy E. 1994. 'The "Three Orders" of Society in Anglo-Saxon England'. *Anglo-Saxon England* 23: 103–32.

Roberts, Jane 1986. 'The Old English Prose Translation of Felix's *Vita Sancti Guthlaci*'. *Studies in Earlier Old English Prose*, pp. 363–79. Ed. Paul E. Szarmach. Albany, NY.

Scragg, D. G. 1979. 'The Corpus of Vernacular Homilies and Prose Saints' Lives Before Ælfric'. *Anglo-Saxon England* 8: 223–77.

—— 1985. 'The Homilies of the Blickling Manuscript'. *Learning and Literature in Anglo-Saxon England: Studies Presented to Peter Clemoes on the Occasion of his Sixty-fifth Birthday*, pp. 299–316. Eds Michael Lapidge and Helmut Gneuss. Cambridge.

Shippey, T. A. 1979. 'Wealth and Wisdom in King Alfred's *Preface* to the Old English *Pastoral Care*'. *English Historical Review* 94: 346–55.

Sisam, Kenneth 1953. *Studies in the History of Old English Literature*. Oxford.

Smyth, Alfred P. 1995. *King Alfred the Great*. Oxford.

Stenton, F. M. 1971. *Anglo-Saxon England*. 3rd edn. Oxford.

Wallace-Hadrill, J. M. 1971. *Early Germanic Kingship in England and on the Continent*. Oxford.

—— 1975. 'The Franks and the English in the Ninth Century: Some Common Historical Interests'. *Early Medieval History*, pp. 201–16. Oxford.

Whitelock, Dorothy 1966. 'The Prose of Alfred's Reign'. *Continuations and Beginnings: Studies in Old English Literature*, pp. 67–103. Ed. E. G. Stanley. London.

Wittig, Joseph S. 1983. 'King Alfred's *Boethius* and its Latin Sources: A Reconsideration'. *Anglo-Saxon England* 11: 157–98.

Wormald, Patrick 1991. 'Anglo-Saxon Society and its Literature'. *The Cambridge Companion to Old English Literature*, pp. 1–22. Eds Malcolm Godden and Michael Lapidge. Cambridge.

9

The Benedictine Reform and Beyond

Joyce Hill

If there is a particular event which can be said to mark the beginning of the Anglo-Saxon Benedictine Reform, it is King Eadmund's appointment of Dunstan as abbot of Glastonbury, sometime between 940 and 946. Dunstan had been a member of the royal household for a long time but, in honouring at court his commitment to the regular ecclesiastical life begun in his youth at Glastonbury, he had made enemies as well as friends and, according to the English priest 'B', who wrote the earliest life of Dunstan *c*.995 × 1004 (Lapidge 1992), various malicious intrigues made Eadmund decide to strip him of his secular rank and exile him beyond the boundaries of the kingdom. The very next day, so the hagiography goes, the king had a narrow escape from death when hunting in the Mendips near Cheddar and, in thanks to God as well as in repentance for his attitude towards Dunstan, he immediately appointed him as abbot of Glastonbury. It was undeniably convenient, for Eadmund had thereby put at a distance a troublesome member of the court. But it was also advantageous in a religious sense because by this appointment he had honoured a man marked out as committed to a holy life, who was now in control of the greatest monastic foundation in Wessex.

With the hindsight of the hagiogapher, B had already identified Dunstan as a reformer by describing how, when he was taken to Glastonbury by his parents in his youth, he had had a vision of the monastic buildings he would erect, a prophecy borne out by the major reorganization of the abbey in the tenth century and the definition of a claustral layout. More significant in the present context of studies on Anglo-Saxon literary culture is his initiation of a reform of the communal life on the model of the Rule of St Benedict. But it was a gradualist and pragmatic approach in that the secular clerks who had formed the community were not ejected or compelled to become monks, with the result that a dissatisfied group of younger members, under the leadership of Æthelwold, moved to Abingdon. There a more rigorous monastic regime was established in accordance with the traditions of the Carolingian reforms of the ninth century, when a clear distinction had been drawn between the monks, who followed the Benedictine Rule, and the secular clergy, who, if they lived a communal and regulated life, did so according to other regimes, such as the Rule of Chrodegang.

Dunstan remained at Glastonbury until 956, when he again fell from grace, supposedly because of his intransigent attitude towards Eadwig's sexual indulgences on the day of his consecration as king, and this time his exile took effect. He was received by Count Arnulf I of Flanders and installed in the monastery of St Peter's in Ghent, where, according to Adelard of Ghent, who wrote one of the later lives of Dunstan, he set an example of light to be imitated. At the same time, however, it was a period of significant learning for Dunstan, because under the patronage of Count Arnulf the monastic life of St Peter's had been restored by Gerard of Brogne (d. 958), so that Dunstan was able to observe and experience at first hand the practices of continental reformed monasticism as established in the Carolingian period and reinvigorated by this more recent Lotharingian revival of the early tenth century. He was recalled to England by Eadwig's younger brother Eadgar, who became king of the Mercians in the summer or autumn of 957, while Eadwig remained in control of the patrimonial lands south of the Thames. Quite soon after his return, when vacancies occurred in quick succession, Eadgar appointed him to the bishoprics of Worcester and London. In 959 Eadwig died, which to B seemed nothing more than divine justice, and the kingdom was thus reunited under Eadgar. He immediately restored Dunstan to the abbacy of Glastonbury and then, before the end of the year, installed him in place of Eadwig's nominee as archbishop of Canterbury, where he remained until his death in 988 (Brooks 1992).

Æthelwold, whose dissatisfied departure from Glastonbury marked him out quite early on as a more decisive reformer than Dunstan, pursued a rather different line. He had been born of a wealthy and eminent Winchester family – much more eminent than that of Dunstan – and had been a member of the royal household of King Athelstan in his youth before being ordained priest on the same day as Dunstan by Bishop Ælfheah of Winchester, who was Dunstan's uncle. Æthelwold went to Glastonbury under Dunstan, and there he became a monk, but it was not many years before he developed a wish to travel abroad in order to advance his knowledge of the scriptures and, as Wulfstan of Winchester's *Vita Sancti Æthelwoldi* put it, 'monastica religione perfectius informari', 'to receive a more perfect grounding in a monk's religious life' (Lapidge and Winterbottom 1991: 18, 19) – more perfect, no doubt, than Æthelwold considered he had access to under Dunstan's regime. But Eadred, who was king at this time (946–55), at the insistence of his mother Eadgifu refused permission for him to leave the country and instead made him abbot of the derelict monastery of Abingdon. There, as noted above, Æthelwold instigated his own reforms, building up his community with men from Glastonbury, Winchester and elsewhere, and taking his inspiration from the Benedictine community of Fleury-sur-Loire, where he sent one of his monks to study at first hand the monastic life as recently reformed there by Odo of Cluny, whose monastic ideals were faithful to those of the Carolingians (Thacker 1988; Wormald 1988). Æthelwold's exacting reformist aspirations were thus already well in evidence, but the rigour with which he was prepared to pursue them was fully revealed in 964, the year after his appointment as bishop of Winchester, when, with the support of the pope and King Eadgar, he expelled the clerks from the Old and New Minsters and replaced them by monks brought from Abingdon. He remained bishop of Winchester until his death in 984.

The other leading first-generation reformer in England was Oswald, who was bishop of Worcester 961–92 and archbishop of York 971–92 (Bullough 1996; Nightingale 1996). He came of a wealthy Anglo-Danish family and was related in some way to Oscytel, his predecessor at York. More important is the fact that he was brought up in the household of his uncle Oda, who was archbishop of Canterbury 941–58, and received his early education from the continental scholar Frithegod, renowned for his esoteric Latin (Lapidge 1988b). Oda had been tonsured at Fleury, perhaps in 936 when he was abroad on royal business, and it is consequently not surprising that Oswald also went to Fleury sometime in the early 950s, where he received the tonsure and remained as a member of the community until shortly after Oda's death. Fleury was a strong influence in Oswald's monastic foundations, most notably at Ramsey (established 966), where Abbo of Fleury taught from 985 to 987, before returning to Fleury to become abbot in 988. But there is some doubt about the thoroughness with which Oswald effected a monastic reform in his Worcester see, since the evidence of leases of land suggests that clerks continued to be part of the community (Sawyer 1975; Barrow 1996). Perhaps Oswald saw the need to proceed cautiously when dealing with an established community which was, after all, associated with a bishopric and was not intrinsically a monastic foundation. In this fundamental respect it differed from his purely monastic foundations such as Ramsey and Westbury-on-Trym. Superficially we might suppose that a Fleury-trained monk would be eager to reform Worcester, but the monastic see, which we associate with the reform in England, was not a continental phenomenon, and it might well be that it was precisely his familiarity with the purely monastic, non-episcopal traditions of Fleury which held him back in this instance; what was desirable in one ecclesiastical sphere might not have seemed so compelling in another.

The ideal of uniformity of observance within monastic foundations came to be a defining feature of the Anglo-Saxon Benedictine Reform once developments were under way, as it had also been in Carolingian Francia under Louis the Pious (emperor 814–40) and Benedict of Aniane (Bullough 1975). The key text in England was the *Regularis Concordia*, drawn up as the standard reform consuetudinary in a council held at Winchester under the auspices of King Eadgar at some time in the years 970 × 973 (Symons 1953; Symons et al. 1984; Kornexl 1993, 1995). By this date the three leading reformers were well established in the key posts within the English church: Dunstan in the metropolitan see, Æthelwold in the royal city of Winchester, and Oswald in Worcester (one of the richest sees, certainly the richest in Mercia) and actually or about to be archbishop of York. They had also personally reformed or founded 'families' of monasteries, over which they retained considerable influence and sometimes even authority, and from these other Benedictine foundations were to spring

(Hill 1981: 151). The consuetudinary that the Council of Winchester produced was intended not to supplant the Benedictine Rule, but to supplement it with elaborated detail about liturgical and para-liturgical observance and the general conduct of life within the monastic community. Its models were continental consuetudinaries, and in view of the careers of the leading figures, it is not surprising that there were representatives from Lotharingia and Fleury at the council. But although it stands firmly within the continental traditions (Symons 1941, 1975; John 1960), the *Regularis Concordia* is eclectic in its particular details and is unique in its inclusion of prayers for the royal family, a mark of the extent to which the Reform owed much of its initial impetus to secular support.

There is good reason to believe that Æthelwold was the main compiler of this central text, and in the proem, written in the voice of King Eadgar, the allusion to 'a certain abbot' who is said to have tutored the king is probably a reference to Æthelwold (Symons 1953: 1). Certainly, Æthelwold's vernacular account of the monastic Reform, now known as 'Edgar's establishment of the monasteries' (Whitelock et al. 1981: 142–54), which seems to have been intended to serve as a preface to Æthelwold's own translation of the Benedictine Rule when it was put into circulation, gives full credit to King Eadgar. Æthelwold was well placed to foster the king's enthusiasm in Winchester, where the Old Minster, the New Minster, Nunnaminster and the king's and bishop's palaces were juxtaposed in the south-west corner of the town (Biddle 1975). There is no better image of the interweaving of royal and religious interests than the miniature which prefaces the copy of the *Regularis Concordia* in London, British Library Cotton Tiberius A. iii, where a scroll, symbolizing the text, entwines and so unites the figure of a monk with King Eadgar, before whom the monk kneels, and the figures of Archbishop Dunstan and Bishop Æthelwold, who are seated on either side of the king (Deshman 1995: pl. 138).

In addition to the *Regularis Concordia*, the other foundation text for the Reform was, of course, the Benedictine Rule itself. This has come down to us in three recensions: the *textus purus*, which derives from St Benedict's original and preserves his vulgar Latin; the *textus interpolatus*, from *c*.600, in which the Latin has been normalized; and the *textus receptus*, which was a product of the Carolingian reform under Benedict of Aniane. At a very early stage in the Anglo-Saxon Reform, probably in the 940s or 950s, Æthelwold produced an accurate and idiomatic English translation of the *textus receptus*, although there is evidence that, in interpreting it, he also made use of the commentary on the Rule by Smaragdus, abbot of St Mihiel and a reforming associate of Benedict of Aniane (Schröer 1885–8; Gretsch 1973, 1974, 1992; Lapidge and Winterbottom 1991: li–lx). The fact that there are four Anglo-Saxon manuscripts in which the Latin and Old English texts alternate chapter by chapter suggests that text and translation were meant to be studied side by side. Æthelwold may have been a more uncompromising reformer than Dunstan or Oswald, but he was alert to the need to overcome the linguistic barrier presented by Latin as the language of the church. As he put it in 'Edgar's establishment of the monasteries' (Whitelock et al. 1981: 152):

Wel mæg dug[an hit naht] mid hwylcan gereorde mon sy gestryned 7 to þan soþan geleafan gewæmed, butan þæt an sy þæt he Gode gegange. Hæbban forþi þa ungelære-den inlendisce þæs halgan regules cyþþe þurh agenes gereordes anwrigenesse, þæt hy þe geornlicor Gode þeowien and nane tale næbben þæt hy þurh nytennesse misfon þurfen.

It certainly cannot matter by what language a man is acquired and drawn to the true faith, as long only as he comes to God. Therefore let the unlearned natives have the knowledge of this holy rule by the exposition of their own language, that they may the more zealously serve God and have no excuse that they were driven by ignorance to err.

Recourse to the vernacular was not a feature of the Carolingian reforms of the ninth century because the emerging vernacular, as yet still perceived as 'rustic Latin', existed on a continuous spectrum with the Latin of the *eruditi* (Banniard 1995). That was not true in Anglo-Saxon England, of course, where the linguistic milieu was Germanic and knowledge of Latin was a hard-won skill. Æthelwold's willingness to use English where necessary is remarked upon by Wulfstan of Winchester in his *Vita Æthelwoldi*, and it is a detail which another of Æthelwold's pupils, the homilist Ælfric, thought important enough to preserve in his abridgement (Lapidge and Winterbottom 1991: 46–9, 77). Whether Æthelwold, as a good Latinist, ever had any qualms about using the vernacular, of the kind that Ælfric sometimes voiced, is not known. This linguistic flexibility, however, brought into being by a strong didactic and reformist impulse, meant that the Anglo-Saxon Benedictine Reform fostered both Old English and Latin literature, and that, as a direct result of Æthelwold's use of English in teaching, a recognizable 'Winchester vocabulary' developed, in which particular vernacular words were favoured by those who had been trained within the Winchester tradition (Gneuss 1972; Hofstetter 1987, 1988; Gretsch 1999). One can readily envisage this lexical bias developing in a context where pupils were drilled in translation from one lan-guage to the other, paradoxically a context in which the primary aim was the acqui-sition of a high standard of Latin.

Of the three leading reformers, it was Æthelwold who had the greatest direct impact on late Old English and Anglo-Latin literature, although some of the monas-tic communities which Dunstan and Oswald variously founded or reformed became major centres of book collection, manuscript production and learning in late Anglo-Saxon England, with Worcester being the last bastion of Old English scholarship well into the Norman period (Franzen 1991). Oswald himself, however, was celebrated by his biographer, Byrhtferth of Ramsey, not as a scholar but as an exemplar of reformed monastic ideals, and there are only three brief Latin writings by him which survive (Lapidge 1975: 78). Dunstan, by contrast, was renowned as a scholar even in his youth, as B makes eminently clear, and we have several manuscripts which are annotated in his hand, as well as a difficult acrostic poem by him, which all confirm his abilities as a Latinist (Lapidge 1975: 108–11, 1980, 1991: 976–7). Yet there are no substan-tial texts associated with him, no 'school', and no corpus of writings by others which can be attributed to his influence. Surprisingly little is known about his period as archbishop, except for his involvement in the production of the *Regularis Concordia*, his regular participation in the king's council, and his endowment of a number of monasteries, although he seems to have used his position well in ensuring that reformers were appointed to bishoprics and monasteries, even though this meant that, for a time, until the appropriate people could be found, he held a number of posts in plurality – an uncanonical situation which we should probably interpret as another sign of his pragmatism.

At Winchester Æthelwold expended a great deal of energy on enhancing the prestige of the Old Minster by increasing its endowments, rebuilding the cathedral on a scale which was grand even by European standards, and raising the status of St Swithun, the relatively insignificant local saint, by means of a splendid translation to a lavish new shrine (Quirk 1957; Biddle 1975). In this he demonstrated his appreciation of the importance of ecclesiastical power as defined by outward display financed by wealth in the form of treasures and landholdings, which in turn made publicly evident the extent to which the reformed foundations were supported by royal and aristocratic donors. But at the same time he was a rigorous teacher and fostered traditions of scholarship which were admired by those who knew him (Lapidge 1988a). His own literary monuments, chiefly the translation of the Rule (for men, with a modified version for women) and the *Regularis Concordia*, together with the vernacular tract on the reforming of the monasteries, a number of charters, and some letters which are probably his, demonstrate his mastery of Latin. We also need to take note of an interlinear translation of the Psalter and a vast corpus of glosses to Aldhelm's prose *De virginitate*. These are now (Gretsch 1999) confidently assigned to Æthelwold and his circle, and testify to an interest both in the vernacular and in stylistic refinement. We can, though, go farther than this and see, in his penchant for flamboyant vocabulary and stylistic embellishments such as alliteration, characteristics of that rather esoteric style known as hermeneutic Latin which was fashionable in learned reform circles in the second half of the tenth century and the early eleventh (Lapidge 1975).

The Frankish scholar Frithegod, Oswald's tutor at Canterbury, produced as a commission from Archbishop Oda the *Breviloquium Vitae Wilfridi*, a long metrical version of Stephen of Ripon's prose life of Wilfrid, rich in the archaic words, neologisms and Graecisms which define the hermeneutic style (Lapidge 1975: 77–81), and these are also features of the style of the grammarian Ælfric Bata, who was active at Canterbury early in the eleventh century. Dunstan, when still at Glastonbury, wrote in this style (though little survives), and so did his biographer 'B' (Lapidge 1975: 95–7). At Ramsey the chief exponent was Byrhtferth, the evidence being the Latin parts of his *Enchiridion*, a computistical treatise written between 1010 and 1012, the *Vita S. Oswaldi* and the *Vita S. Ecgwini*, both anonymous but now attributed to Byrhtferth, and the early sections of Simeon of Durham's *Historia regum*, which again are attributed to Byrhtferth chiefly on stylistic grounds (Lapidge 1975: 90–5, 1979, 1981). But it is from Winchester that we have the greatest concentration: Godeman's poem in praise of Æthelwold which stands as a preface to the *Benedictional of Æthelwold*, one of the most lavishly illuminated manuscripts of the Benedictine Reform; the *Trans-*

latio et Miracula S. Swithuni, written by the continental scholar Lantfred to celebrate the translation of Swithun's remains to the new cathedral in 971; the various Latin works of Wulfstan the Cantor, a pupil of Æthelwold; and some anonymous poems composed at Winchester in the late tenth century, two of them being a debate between a master and a pupil, which probably relates quite directly to local pedagogic practices, and one on the problem of free will addressed to Æthelwold himself (Lapidge 1972, 1975: 85–90). The prestige of contexts and content suggests that the hermeneutic style had high status, whilst the direct and indirect compliments to Æthelwold in these works, when taken together with what we know of Æthelwold's own use of hermeneutic traits, lead one to assume that he actively fostered this style at Winchester. It also seems to have been his intention to foster it at Peterborough (Medehamstede), one of his new foundations, because the books that he sent there included several items that would support the acquisition of obscure Latin vocabulary: *Expositio Hebreorum nominum* (probably that of Jerome); *Sinonima Isidori*; *Descidia Parisiace polis* (the *Bella Parisiacae Urbis* of Abbo of Saint-Germain-des-Prés, the third book of which was an important study-text) (Lapidge 1975; Lendinara 1986); and *De litteris Grecorum* (probably a Greek–Latin glossary) (Lapidge 1985: 52–5). It is particularly striking, then, that the homilist Ælfric, despite his reverence for Æthelwold, his own linguistic capacities and the pervasive stylistic fashion, studiously avoided the hermeneutic style whenever he wrote in Latin, keeping instead to something more straightforward (Jones 1998b).

Ælfric was at first educated by a priest who 'cuðe be dæle Lyden understandan' (Crawford 1922: 76). This may mean that he had an imperfect knowledge of Latin, understanding it only in part ('be dæle'), or that he knew the technicalities of Latin, understanding it according to its parts of speech ('be dæle'), but not knowing the principles of exegetical interpretation which would have allowed him to move beyond the literal, particularly when reading those parts of the Old Testament which were at odds with the teaching of the New. The second of these two interpretations is the more likely, because Ælfric used *dæl* in grammatical contexts to mean 'part of speech', and because the immediate context of the statement about his first teacher is in his *Preface to Genesis* at the point where he discusses the difficulty of coming to terms with the information that Jacob had four wives. We do not know when it was that Ælfric went on to Winchester, just as we also do not know when it was that he was born (c.950?) or when he died (c.1010?), but in various prefaces he presents himself, with gratitude, as an *alumnus* of Winchester and a pupil of Æthelwold (Wilcox 1994: 7–8). He remained at Winchester until 987, when he was sent by Æthelwold's successor Ælfheah, at the request of the thane Æthelmær, son of Æthelweard, ealdormann of the Western Provinces, to the monastery of Cerne Abbas, which Æthelmær had just refounded. Æthelweard and Æthelmær were strong supporters of the Benedictine Reform and patrons of Ælfric; it was at their insistence, as well as that of certain other equally enthusiastic seculars, that Ælfric produced some of his vernacular works, making available in English materials normally accessible only to well-trained ecclesiastics (usually those with monastic backgrounds) who could read Latin. The prefaces and some passing comments within his works give us what are, for this early period, unusual insights into the author's intentions and the immediate circumstances of some of his output, so that we can be reasonably confident about the order in which his writings were produced and can even determine the actual dates within fairly close limits (Clemoes 1959). On the basis of this evidence, we can see that most of his writings were produced when he was monk and mass-priest at Cerne, where he remained until 1005, the year in which he became the first abbot of Æthelmær's newly founded monastery of Eynsham in Oxfordshire, not far from Abingdon.

Ælfric's first works, produced between 989 and 994, were the *Catholic Homilies*. These two sets of predominantly exegetical homilies, originally forty in each series, were organized according to the liturgical year and based on the lections – mainly the Gospel lections – for the day (Thorpe 1844–6; Clemoes 1997; Godden 1979). Their purpose was to make accessible to secular clergy and thus to their lay congregations the Biblical and doctrinal teaching that had come into England with the Reform, which was encapsulated in the Carolingian Latin homiliaries that Ælfric must have known at Winchester and that he evidently had available at Cerne: the homiletic anthology of Paul the Deacon, and the homiliaries of Smaragdus and Haymo of Auxerre (Smetana 1959, 1961; Hill 1992b, 1997, 1998b). Paul's patristic anthology gave the name of the author at the head of each item, and Ælfric used a manuscript of Smaragdus' homiliary in which the patristic passages making up the interpretation of each lection had letter-abbreviations in the margin identifying the original author. This enabled Ælfric to identify by name in the course of his homilies the great authorities – such as Augustine, Jerome, Bede and Gregory – who were his ultimate sources and thus the validators of his orthodoxy. It was a technique which placed him squarely within the Carolingian traditions on which he drew, representing him as heir to patristic authority and defining him as a scholar. But it also served to define him as a reformer, one who set himself apart, and wished to remain apart, from those who indulged in using more popular, apocryphal and sometimes downright unreliable materials for preaching. His stance is clear in the letters written to Archbishop Sigeric of Canterbury to accompany copies of the First and Second Series of the *Catholic Homilies*; in various comments within the body of the homilies, as when he refuses to relate the standard apocryphal narrative for the Feasts of the Nativity and the Assumption of the Virgin; and in the prayer at the end of the Second Series, when he begs that his work will not be mingled with the work of others in subsequent manuscript copies (Hill 1993). It was not intellectual arrogance, but a self-conscious and in many respects polemical commitment to a particular tradition within reformed monasticism, coupled with a corresponding desire to avoid – and in fact to replace – what in his view were the unreliable vernacular homilies of the kind which survive now in collections such as those of the Blickling and Vercelli manuscripts.

The extension of the reform into the secular church, which inspired the *Catholic Homilies*, was a recurrent thread in Ælfric's work, and it has to be understood in the context of other evidence that the monasteries were not isolated from worldly concerns. The sees which were reformed on monastic lines – Canterbury, Winchester,

Worcester and Sherborne – were channels for the permeation of Reform ideals and ideas into the secular church. The dominance of monks in episcopal appointments in late Anglo-Saxon England, another consequence of the Reform, was a further means by which ideas could be transmitted. Moreover, the roles of leading ecclesiastics as advisors to kings, and of archbishops, bishops and abbots as signatories to royal char-ters, underline the direct involvement of the monastic as well as the secular church in the affairs of the kingdom. Dunstan and Æthelwold were much involved in royal politics, not necessarily on the same side (Yorke 1988b), and it is unlikely that Oswald would have been appointed to the archbishopric of York if he had not been politically competent, although we know practically nothing about him in this respect. Even Æthelmær's refoundation of Cerne Abbas may have resulted from an essentially secular reorganization of inherited estates (Yorke 1988a), and it is difficult not to see the foun-dation of Eynsham as an expedient move by Æthelmær to provide an acceptable retreat for himself when his political fortunes changed and he was obliged to retire from the court (Keynes 1980: 209–13). None of this detracts from Æthelmær's religious com-mitment, any more than does the political involvement of Dunstan or Æthelwold, but it helps define for us a world in which commitments and motives – and ulti-mately the progress of the Reform – were not quite as simple or as clear cut as the Reform's hagiographical apologists would have us believe. Ælfric's involvement with the secular world was more straightforward than that of some, in that, from his posi-tion as monk and abbot, he focused his attention on providing materials for the improvement of priestly life and priestly teaching. He was, however, aware of the moral state of the nation and of the requirements of kingly authority (Pope 1967: 372–7; Godden 1985: 95–7; Clayton 1993), and his commitment to Æthelwold and his patronage by Æthelmær, especially at the time of his appointment as abbot of Eynsham, put him in a particular political as well as a particular reformist camp. None of the reformers was in a position divorced from larger political and secular concerns, and although the Reform was a monastic movement, confined for reasons of history, politics and economics to the southern part of England, its impact cannot be assessed by considering the affairs of the monasteries alone.

In addition to providing the *Catholic Homilies*, which he continued to modify and supplement throughout the rest of his career (Pope 1967–8), Ælfric engaged directly with the condition of the secular church in his *Pastoral Letters*, regulatory public addresses written at the request of and in the name of two bishops with monastic backgrounds and reforming tendencies (Fehr 1914; Hill 1992a). The first, in English, was for Wulfsige, when he was bishop of Sherborne, 992–1002; the other two, written in Latin and then rewritten in English (not simply translated), were for Archbishop Wulfstan of York, *c*.1005, when Ælfric was an abbot. Wulfsige, who reformed Sher-borne as a monastic see, may well have turned to Ælfric for assistance because the monastery of Cerne was within his diocese. Wulfstan of York knew Ælfric's work well enough to use some of it in producing his own vernacular writings and had previ-ously had a correspondence with Ælfric, in Latin, on regulatory matters before com-missioning the public letters, which seem to have been drawn up by Ælfric in Latin before he prepared the Old English versions for sending out. The content of the letters, painstakingly informative on basic elements of doctrinal history, the proper conduct of priestly life and the execution of liturgical ritual, evoke images of a secular church staffed by ill-educated clergy; yet the aspirations they express are for a regulated and liturgically complex life modelled to some degree on that of reformed monasticism and supported by personal possession of a modest library of texts, which the priests were directed to check for accuracy of copying. This requirement seems particularly unrealistic. We should see it perhaps as one of the more extreme examples within the Letters of the reformist stance, although it may be a reflex of Ælfric's own scholarly preoccupation with the need for accurate copying in the interests of doctrinal reliability; a concern which he expresses in a number of his prefaces and which he may have acquired from the Carolingians, for whom textual accuracy was of paramount importance.

Works produced by Ælfric in direct response to requests from seculars include: the *Lives of Saints* for Æthelweard and Æthelmær, a vernacular version of saints' lives from the monastic legendary (now identified as the Cotton-Corpus legendary) (Skeat 1881–1900; Zettel 1982; Jackson and Lapidge 1996); a translation of part of Genesis, also for Æthelweard, but only up to the story of Isaac, because Æthelweard had the rest in a translation made by someone else (Crawford 1922); a treatise on the Old and New Testament for a certain Sigeweard, which reviews the sweep of Christian history and demonstrates how much Biblical writing is available in English (a good deal of it being Ælfric's own) (Crawford 1922); a letter to someone called Wulfgeat of Ylmandun on how to live a moral life (Assmann 1889: 1–12); and one to a certain Sigefyrth, mainly on clerical celibacy (Assmann 1889: 13–23). There is, in all of these, an irresistible urge to teach, to respond finally to the sometimes insistent demands of those who wish to know more about their faith; but there is always present an unresolved tension, since Ælfric the Latinist, monk, mass-priest and then abbot, is constantly anxious about the wisdom of making complex material directly available in the vernacular to those who might not have the framework of learning which would enable them properly to interpret the inner meaning.

Materials prepared for use within monastic circles did not, of course, give rise to these concerns, even though Ælfric followed Æthelwold's example in sometimes using the vernacular. In any case, some of what he wrote for this context was instructional or regulatory, so that questions of textual interpretation or doctrinal orthodoxy were not a fundamental issue. Among the first works of this kind was his *Grammar*, which was to remain popular until the twelfth century (Zupitza 1880). For Ælfric, as for the Carolingians, grammar was the key which unlocked the understanding of the scriptures. As with the *Catholic Homilies* and *Lives of Saints*, his primary source was a Carolingian compilation, as yet unpublished, which is designated in manuscripts as the *Excerptiones de Prisciano* (Law 1987). Despite its apparently descriptive title, this was not an ad hoc compilation from the grammatical works of Priscian, but an intermediate-level grammar which fused together material from Priscian, the *Ars Minor* of Donatus, and at least one other unidentified medieval source. Ælfric modified his source somewhat (as he also modified his Carolingian sources elsewhere in reaching out to his audience), but the real novelty is the startling innovation of teaching Latin through the medium of English (Bullough 1972). The emergence of Winchester vocabulary, which we have noted above, suggests that Æthelwold may also have used English in teaching Latin, but the *textual* medium seems to have been the Latin *Excerptiones*, which Ælfric says was used in Æthelwold's school, and which he now 'translates'. To accompany it, he also produced a Latin–English *Glossary* (Zupitza 1880), which commonly circulated with the *Grammar*, and a skilfully constructed practice conversation, known as the *Colloquy* (Garmonsway 1939). This latter seems to have been little used, perhaps because it avoids the hermeneutic vocabulary which is characteristic of most of the other colloquies surviving from this period (Hill 1998a). The *Colloquy*, like the *Grammar*, stands within a classical tradition which was taken up in modified form by the Carolingians, but Ælfric's is unusual in engaging the boys in role-play which takes them beyond the schoolroom. It is one of the best known of Ælfric's works because of the novelty of the subject and its dramatic form, but it is commonly the Old English interlinear gloss-translation which is referred to rather than the Latin text. This gloss is not by Ælfric but was added later, perhaps by Ælfric's pupil Ælfric Bata, who also produced an augmented version of the *Colloquy*, which – in common with the abstruse colloquies which are wholly his own – flaunts the esoteric Latin vocabulary Ælfric generally avoided (Stevenson 1929: 75–102; Gwara 1996; Gwara and Porter 1997).

Other works which are clearly monastic are the Latin *Letter to the Monks of Eynsham* (Nocent et al. 1984; Jones 1998a), which is a condensed and adapted version of the *Regularis Concordia* with additional material from the *De ecclesiasticis officiis* of Amalarius of Metz, another Carolingian textual source for the English Benedictine Reform; an abridgement of Wulfstan of Winchester's *Vita Sancti Æthelwoldi* (Lapidge and Winterbottom 1991); and a translation into English rhythmical prose (such as Ælfric also used for his *Lives of Saints*) of the *Admonitio ad filium spiritualem* (Norman 1848), a work of moral instruction for monks and nuns attributed to Basil of Caesarea, which would have been significant for the reformers because St Benedict alludes to it in support of his Rule. This translation seems to have been intended for a monastic context in which a high level of proficiency in Latin could not be relied upon. That being so, and bearing in mind that the level of Latinity was such that even the Benedictine Rule circulated with Æthelwold's English translation, we may imagine that vernacular works by Ælfric which were not initially produced expressly for monastic use may nevertheless have been drawn upon in such contexts. It is similarly not easy to determine who might have benefited from other of his vernacular works that, though not esoteric, would have appealed only to those of a more thoughtful and scholarly turn of mind, whether inside the monastery or outside. These works are the translations of parts of the Old Testament (Crawford 1922); the *De Temporibus Anni* (Henel 1942), on time and the nature of the world; the *Hexameron* (Crawford 1921), on the six days of creation; and the *Interrogationes Sigewulfi in Genesin* (MacLean 1883–4), based selectively on Alcuin's question-and-answer commentary on Genesis.

In the context of this chapter, it is worth looking at Ælfric's work in some detail. This is not simply because his is the largest identifiable corpus of vernacular writings from this period, but especially because, through his work, we can easily identify some of the key features of the Anglo-Saxon Benedictine Reform: the desire to achieve uniformity in religious observance in monasteries, regularize and raise the standards of the secular church, strengthen the knowledge of Latin, guarantee the quality of texts, and re-establish an authoritative orthodoxy as defined by the patristic tradition. The mediators and the models were chiefly the works of the Carolingian reform, which were influential across the full range of instructional, regulatory and interpretative writings represented by the Ælfrician corpus. But it has to be admitted that Ælfric's reformist position, for all the humanity of his writings, was more extreme than that of others, even including, in some respects, his revered teacher Æthelwold. No other writer begged for his work to be kept apart from that of others, made such insistent pleas for correct copying, or deployed such a range of devices for establishing his orthodoxy and identifying the authority tradition within which he worked. He was also clearer than anyone else in stating the limits of what he would and would not do (although he sometimes allowed himself to be persuaded otherwise), and the line that he took was often an independent one. For example, Ælfric's refusal to treat Marian apocrypha, which is referred to above, is indicative of a more rigorous position than that found within Reform circles; even Æthelwold's *Benedictional* illustrates a scene known only from the apocryphal legends (Clayton 1986, 1990: 210–66; Deshman 1995: 132–6). Similarly, he had doubts about sensational elements in the narratives of St Thomas and St George, despite the fact that these details were present in the Benedictine Reform legendary which was his authoritative source-text (Hill 1989 for 1985, 1993: 29–34). In fact, the purity of his position was one that was not sustained, because homily collections were soon made which brought together items by Ælfric and anonymous authors, and composite homilies were produced, even in Winchester, which mixed Ælfric's work with that of others within the framework of a single homiletic text (Godden 1975). The extent to which Ælfric at once exemplifies the Benedictine Reform and yet is a quite distinctive author of decided views confirms what we have already seen in different ways in respect of Dunstan, Oswald and Æthelwold. The Reform was not a simple, uniform development, but was one which was responded to and carried forward in various ways, having diverse effects in different times and places.

One manifestation of that diversity is the fact that we regard Oswald's foundation of Ramsey as distinctive for its scientific scholarship – an important aspect of the Reform which is not well represented elsewhere. The major influence here was Abbo of Fleury, who took many books with him when he went there for his 'exile', including his own Computus and a number of other works, amongst them Macrobius' Commentary on Cicero's *Somnium Scipionis*, a foundation text for scientific instruction in Carolingian schools. Abbo was a scholar of international renown and his relatively brief period of residence at Ramsey had a profound influence, most notably on Bryhtferth, who compiled his own computus during the years 988–96. This now has to be reconstructed from twelfth-century manuscripts, but we have his *Enchiridion*, which is in the main a commentary on the computus in Latin and English (Baker and Lapidge 1995). A computus proper – several of which were produced in late Anglo-Saxon England – contains arithmetical tables, formulas and rules for calculating the moveable religious feasts (chiefly Easter, to which the other feasts are tied in fixed relationships). Byrhtferth's *Enchiridion* deals with the 'science' underlying these calculations, but in his characteristically eclectic and erudite fashion it also includes extensive material on metre, rhetoric, weights and measures, and arithmology. The pedantic bent that is evident here is also apparent in Byrhtferth's historical writings, referred to earlier; for example, in the *Vita Sancti Ecgwini* we see him filling out a rather thin body of information with spurious charters, hagiographical commonplaces, allegory and arithmology (Lapidge 1979).

Byrhtferth was prolific and was one of the most learned men of his day, but in modern times he has suffered in comparison with Ælfric because he wrote on relatively inaccessible subjects and mostly in quite difficult Latin. Different again was Wulfstan (Jost 1950; Bethurum 1966), bishop of London 996–1002, bishop of Worcester 1002–1016, and archbishop of York 1002–23. He probably had a monastic background, and he certainly attempted to promote the standards associated with the Reform through the Pastoral Letters prepared for him by Ælfric. His spheres of influence, though, were the secular church and the affairs of the state, spanning the troubled times of Æthelred the Unready and the break in the West Saxon dynasty that came with the accession of the Danish Cnut, whose successful establishment as a Christian king in England probably owed a good deal to Wulfstan's counsels (Whitelock 1942, 1948). In his most famous homily, 'The Sermon of Wulf to the English' (*Sermo Lupi ad Anglos*), written in 1014, Wulfstan exploited to the full his idiosyncratic two-stress rhythmical and alliterative style (McIntosh 1950; Orchard 1992) to produce an impassioned denunciation of the moral state of the English, which he believed was responsible for bringing upon them the wrath of God in the form of the Viking depredations, begun again in 991 (Whitelock 1939). Unlike Ælfric's exegetical interpretations of the lections or his devotional hagiographies, this is very much the pronouncement of a public figure, preoccupied with his responsibilities in the church and the nation at large. He revised the homily a number of times for use on other occasions, and there are several other homilies which have some common ground with the *Sermo Lupi* in addressing political and moral issues, the theme of Antichrist and the Last Days. But there are homilies which more narrowly reflect Wulfstan's teaching function (on the Creed, Baptism, the gifts of the Holy Spirit, the Christian life, punishment for sin, false gods), and yet others which relate to his role as archbishop (the reconciliation of penitents, negligent priests, the consecration of a bishop, the dedication of a church) (Bethurum 1957). Several law-codes of Æthelred and Cnut are attributed to him on stylistic grounds, and he was also the author of the *Institutes of Polity* (Jost 1959), an analysis of the roles of authority in church and state; the *Canons of Edgar* (Fowler 1972), directed at the secular clergy; the prose portions of the so-called *Old English Benedictine Office* (Ure 1957; Clemoes

1960); and probably, at least in part, the *Gerefa* and the *Rectitudines* (Liebermann 1903: 444–55), on the management of a large estate. His principal sources were not the patristic authorities, but continental authors of the Carolingian reform and later who wrote regulatory works. In some of the major manuscript compendia from the eleventh century, which have been identified as reflexes of Wulfstan's 'commonplace book', we can see evidence of the way in which he worked in assembling the materials relevant to his wide range of interests (Bethurum 1942; Whitelock 1942; Fowler 1963; Sauer 1980; Cross 1992).

By the time Wulfstan's career came to an end, or perhaps even by the end of Æthelred's reign a few years earlier, the Benedictine Reform can be said to have played itself out. It had not been carried forward with the rigour shown by Æthelwold or Ælfric, and even the *Regularis Concordia* was not followed in reformed monasteries with the degree of uniformity originally envisaged; Ælfric's modifications in the *Letter to the Monks of Eynsham* show that this was the case, and it is obvious that some of the complexity of its liturgical and community life could not be fully sustained in small houses, where the scholarly standards, including the standards of Latin, were lower than Dunstan and Æthelwold would have desired. But monastic life – at least in the south of England – had been regularized and enriched, foundations had been established which would continue and in some cases flourish, some attempt had been made to improve the standards of the secular church (although the monastic bias of most of the evidence makes it difficult to judge the situation fairly), and the reforming impulse had led to the importation of continental manuscripts and a vigorous tradition of manuscript production, which continued through the eleventh century. Although most of the output was in Latin and was for ecclesiastical use, not everything was. In English there were medical texts and legal documents of various kinds; the *Anglo-Saxon Chronicle* was continued (sometimes in a decidedly homiletic or moralistic tone); some new literature was translated, such as *Apollonius of Tyre* (Goolden 1958), the first example of the romance genre in English; and it was in the late tenth and early eleventh centuries that scribes wrote out the four codices which contain most of the surviving Old English poetic corpus.

We should also not overlook the rich legacy of Benedictine Reform art, particularly in manuscript illumination and in small artefacts such as ivories and various forms of metalwork (Backhouse et al. 1984). Ecclesiastical architecture will also have been a continuing witness to the effects of the Reform throughout the eleventh century, although the medieval habit of rebuilding the cathedrals and greater churches means that much of the evidence is lost for us (Taylor 1975; Fernie 1982).

One further impact of the Reform, which can easily be overlooked but which will have been very obvious in late Anglo-Saxon society, was the extent to which ecclesiastical endowment through bookland, which was held in perpetuity, reshaped the pattern of landholding in late Anglo-Saxon England and set monasteries in particular on the path which led to some of them becoming major economic forces in the land. It was precisely this large-scale removal of land from secular hereditament that led to a backlash against the Reform after the death of Eadgar, when some nobles made manipulative efforts to appropriate ecclesiastical property in their own interests (Fisher 1952; Keynes 1980: 176–86), but the reversal was not long-lived and by the time of Domesday Book (1086) there were seven monastic houses with gross annual incomes of between £500 and £900, a further seven between £200 and £500, and six between £100 and £200 (Hill 1981: 154).

The Anglo-Saxon church from the time of Cnut was relatively undistinguished and in some respects increasingly old-fashioned, although there was a modest injection of new ideas from the continent in the reign of Edward the Confessor with the appointment to bishoprics of such figures as Robert of Jumièges, Herman from Lotharingia and Leofric, probably of English or Celtic descent but educated in Lotharingia. In Leofric's case the removal of the Devon see from Crediton to Exeter in 1050 was in accordance with the continental expectation that sees should be in an urban centre; he was also reformist in introducing a Rule for the canons of the episcopal *familia* – probably the enlarged Rule of Chrodegang – and in building up a respectable library and scriptorium such as his continental experience would have led him to expect (Barlow 1972; Conner 1993; Gameson 1996). But further changes of a wide-ranging kind were not to occur until after the Norman Conquest, and then, under Lanfranc, archbishop of Canterbury 1070–89, the developments were quite unlike those of the tenth-century Benedictine Reform.

REFERENCES

Primary sources

Assmann, Bruno, ed. 1889. *Angelsächsische Homilien und Heiligenleben*. Bibliothek der angelsächsischen Prosa 3. Kassel. Repr. intro. Peter Clemoes. 1964. Darmstadt.

Baker, Peter S. and Michael Lapidge, eds and trans. 1995. *Byrhtferth of Ramsey: Enchiridion*. Early English Text Society, s.s. 15. Oxford.

Bethurum, Dorothy, ed. 1957. *The Homilies of Wulfstan*. Oxford.

Clemoes, Peter, ed. 1997. *Ælfric's Catholic Homilies: The First Series*. Early English Text Society, s.s. 17. Oxford.

Crawford, Samuel J., ed. 1921. *Exameron Anglice, or the Old English Hexameron*. Bibliothek der angelsächsischen Prosa 10. Hamburg.

——ed. 1922. *The Old English Version of the Heptateuch, Ælfric's Treatise on the Old and New Testament, and his Preface to Genesis*. Early English Text Society, o.s. 160. London, New York, Toronto.

Fehr, Bernhard, ed. 1914. *Die Hirtenbriefe Ælfrics*. Bibliothek der angelsächsischen Prosa 9. Hamburg. Repr. intro. Peter Clemoes. Darmstadt, 1966.

Fowler, Roger, ed. 1972. *Wulfstan's Canons of Edgar*. Early English Text Society, o.s. 266. London, New York and Toronto.

Garmonsway, G. N., ed. 1939. *Ælfric's Colloquy*. London. Reissued Exeter. 1978.

Godden, Malcolm, ed. 1979. *Ælfric's Catholic Homilies. The Second Series*. Early English Text Society, s.s. 5. Oxford.

Goolden, Peter, ed. 1958. *The Old English Apollonius of Tyre*. London.

Gwara, Scott 1996. *Latin Colloquies from Pre-Conquest Britain*. Toronto Medieval Latin Texts 22. Toronto.

——and David W. Porter, eds and trans. 1997. *Anglo-Saxon Conversations: The Colloquies of Ælfric Bata*. Woodbridge.

Henel, Heinrich, ed. 1942. *Ælfric's De Temporibus Anni*. Early English Text Society, o.s. 213. London.

Jost, Karl, ed. 1959. *Die 'Institutes of Polity, Civil and Ecclesiastical'. Ein Werk Erzbischof Wulfstans von York*. Swiss Studies in English 47. Bern.

Kornexl, Lucia, ed. 1993. *Die Regularis Concordia und ihre altenglische Interlinearversion*. Munich.

Lapidge, Michael and Michael Winterbottom, eds 1991. *Wulfstan of Winchester: The Life of St Æthelwold*. Oxford.

Liebermann, F., ed. 1903. *Die Gesetze der Angelsächsen* I. Leipzig.

MacLean, George E. 1883–4. 'Ælfric's Version of Alcuini Interrogationes Sigeuulfi in Genesin'. *Anglia* 6: 425–73; 7: 1–59.

Nocent, Hadrianus, Kassius Hallinger and Candida Elvert, eds 1984. 'Aelfrici Abbatis Epistula ad monachos Egneshamnenses directa'. *Corpus Consuetudinum Saeculi X/XI/XII Monumenta Non-Cluniacensia* Ed. Kassius Hallinger. *Corpus Consuetudinum Monasticarum VII/3*, pp. 149–85. Siegburg.

Norman, Henry W., ed. 1848. *The Anglo-Saxon Version of the Hexameron of St Basil or, Be Godes six daga weorcum. And the Anglo-Saxon Remains of St Basil's Admonitio ad filium spiritualem*. London and Oxford.

Pope, John C., ed. 1967–8. *The Homilies of Ælfric: A Supplementary Collection*. 2 vols. Early English Text Society, o.s. 259, 260. London, New York and Toronto.

Schröer, Arnold, ed. 1885–8. *Die angelsächsichen Prosabearbeitungen der Benediktinerregel*. Bibliothek der angelsächsischen Prosa, 2. Kassel. Repr. with suppl. H. Gneuss. Darmstadt. 1964.

Skeat, Walter W., ed. and trans. 1881–1900. *Ælfric's Lives of Saints*. Early English Text Society, o.s. 76, 82, 94, 114. Repr. 2 vols. London, 1966.

Stevenson, W. H., ed. 1929. *Early Scholastic Colloquies*. Oxford.

Symons, Thomas, ed. 1953. *Regularis Concordia Anglicae Nationis Monachorum Sanctimonialiumque: The Monastic Agreement of the Monks and Nuns of the English Nation*. London, Edinburgh, Paris, Melbourne, Toronto and New York.

——, Sigrid Spath, Maria Wegener and Kassius Hallinger, eds 1984. 'Regularis Concordia Anglicae Nationis'. *Corpus Consuetudinum Saeculi X/XI/XII Monumenta Non-Cluniacensia*. Ed. Kassius Hallinger. *Corpus Consuetudinum Monasticarum VII/3*, pp. 61–147. Siegburg.

Thorpe, Benjamin, ed. 1844–6. *The Homilies of the Anglo-Saxon Church*. 2 vols. London.

Ure, James, ed. 1957. *The Benedictine Office: An Old English Text*. Edinburgh.

Whitelock, Dorothy, ed. 1939. *Sermo Lupi ad Anglos*. London. Reissued Exeter. 1976.

——, M. Brett and C. N. L. Brooke, eds 1981. *Councils and Synods with Other Documents Relating to the English Church, I: A.D. 871–1205. Part I: 871–1066*. Oxford.

Wilcox, Jonathan, ed. 1994. *Ælfric's Prefaces*. Durham Medieval Texts 9. Durham.

Zupitza, Julius, ed. 1880. *Ælfrics Grammatik und Glossar*. Berlin. Repr. pref. Helmut Gneuss. 1966. Berlin.

Secondary sources

Backhouse, Janet, D. H. Turner and Leslie Webster 1984. *The Golden Age of Anglo-Saxon Art: 966–1066*. London.

Banniard, Michel 1995. 'Language and Communication in Carolingian Europe'. *The New Cambridge Medieval History: Volume II c.700–c.900*, pp. 695–708. Ed. Rosamond McKitterick. Cambridge.

Barlow, Frank 1972. 'Leofric and his Times'. *Leofric of Exeter: Essays in Commemoration of the Foundation of Exeter Cathedral Library in A.D. 1072*, pp. 1–16. Eds F. Barlow, K. M. Dexter, A. M. Erskine and L. J. Lloyd. Exeter.

Barrow, Julia 1996. 'The Community of Worcester, 961–c.1100'. *St Oswald of Worcester: Life and Influence*, pp. 84–99. Eds Nicholas Brooks and Catherine Cubitt. London and New York.

Bethurum, Dorothy 1942. 'Archbishop Wulfstan's Commonplace Book'. *Publications of the Modern Language Association of America* 57: 916–29.

——1966. 'Wulfstan'. *Continuations and Beginnings: Studies in Old English Literature*, pp. 210–46. Ed. Eric Gerald Stanley. London.

Biddle, Martin 1975. '*Felix Urbs Winthonia*: Winchester in the Age of Monastic Reform'. *Tenth-Century Studies: Essays in Commemoration of the Millennium of the Council of Winchester and Regularis Concordia*, pp. 123–40. Ed. David Parsons. London and Chichester.

Brooks, N. P. 1992. 'The Career of St Dunstan'. *St Dunstan: His Life, Times and Cult*, pp. 1–23. Eds Nigel Ramsay, Margaret Sparks and Tim Tatton-Brown. Woodbridge.

Bullough, D. A. 1972. 'The Educational Tradition in England from Alfred to Ælfric: Teaching *utriusque linguae*'. *La scuola nell'occidente latino del-*

l'alto medioevo, pp. 453–94. Settimane de studio del centro italiano di studi sull'alto medioevo 19. Spoleto. Repr. D. A. Bullough, *Carolingian Renewal: Sources and Heritage*, pp. 297–334. Manchester. 1991.

—— 1975. 'The Continental Background of the Reform'. *Tenth-Century Studies: Essays in Commemoration of the Millennium of the Council of Winchester and Regularis Concordia*, pp. 20–36. Ed. David Parsons. London and Chichester. Repr. D. A. Bullough, *Carolingian Renewal: Sources and Heritage*, pp. 272–96 [revised title 'The Continental Background of the Tenth-century English Reform']. Manchester. 1991.

—— 1996. 'St Oswald: Monk, Bishop and Archbishop'. *St Oswald of Worcester: Life and Influence*, pp. 1–22. Eds Nicholas Brooks and Catherine Cubitt. London and New York.

Clayton, Mary 1986. 'Ælfric and the Nativity of the Blessed Virgin Mary'. *Anglia* 104: 286–315.

—— 1990. *The Cult of the Virgin Mary in Anglo-Saxon England*. CSASE 2. Cambridge.

—— 1993. 'Of Mice and Men: Ælfric's Second Homily for the Feast of a Confessor'. *Leeds Studies in English* n.s. 24: 1–26.

Clemoes, P. A. M. 1959. 'The Chronology of Ælfric's Works'. *The Anglo-Saxons: Studies in Some Aspects of their History and Culture presented to Bruce Dickins*, pp. 212–47. Ed. Peter Clemoes. London.

—— 1960. 'The Old English Benedictine Office, Corpus Christi College, Cambridge, MS 190, and the Relations between Ælfric and Wulfstan: A Reconsideration'. *Anglia* 78: 265–83.

Conner, Patrick W. 1993. *Anglo-Saxon Exeter: A Tenth-Century Cultural History*. Studies in Anglo-Saxon History 4. Woodbridge.

Cross, J. E. 1992. 'A Newly-identified Manuscript of Wulfstan's "Commonplace Book," Rouen, Bibliothèque Municipale, MS 1382 (U. 109), fols 173r–198v'. *Journal of Medieval Latin* 2: 63–83.

Deshman, Robert 1995. *The Benedictional of Æthelwold*. Princeton, NJ.

Fernie, Eric 1982. *The Architecture of the Anglo-Saxons*. London.

Fisher, D. J. V. 1952. 'The Anti-Monastic Reaction in the Reign of Edward the Martyr'. *Cambridge University Journal* 10: 254–70.

Fowler, R. G. 1963. '"Archbishop Wulfstan's Commonplace-Book" and the Canons of Edgar'. *Medium Ævum* 32: 1–10.

Franzen, Christine 1991. *The Tremulous Hand of Worcester. A Study of Old English in the Thirteenth Century*. Oxford.

Gameson, Richard 1996. 'The Origin of the Exeter Book of Old English Poetry'. *Anglo-Saxon England* 25: 135–85.

Gneuss, Helmut 1972. 'The Origin of Standard Old English and Æthelwold's School at Winchester'. *Anglo-Saxon England* 1: 63–83.

Godden, M. R. 1975. 'Old English Composite Homilies from Winchester'. *Anglo-Saxon England* 4: 57–65.

—— 1985. 'Ælfric's Saints' Lives and the Problem of Miracles'. *Leeds Studies in English* n.s. 16: 83–97.

Gretsch, Mechthild 1973. *Die Regula Sancti Benedicti in England und ihre altenglische Übersetzung*. Munich.

—— 1974. 'Æthelwold's Translation of the *Regula Sancti Benedicti* and its Latin Exemplar'. *Anglo-Saxon England* 3: 125–51.

—— 1992. 'The Benedictine Rule in Old English: A Document of Bishop Æthelwold's Reform Politics'. *Words, Texts and Manuscripts. Studies in Anglo-Saxon Culture Presented to Helmut Gneuss on the Occasion of his Sixty-fifth Birthday*, pp. 131–58. Ed. Michael Korhammer, with the assistance of Karl Reichl and Hans Sauer. Woodbridge.

—— 1999. *The Intellectual Foundations of the English Benedictine Reform*. CSASE 25. Cambridge.

Hill, David 1981. *An Atlas of Anglo-Saxon England*. Oxford.

Hill, Joyce 1989 for 1985. 'Ælfric, Gelasius and St George'. *Mediaevalia* 11: 1–17.

—— 1992a. 'Monastic Reform and the Secular Church: Ælfric's Pastoral Letters in Context'. *England in the Eleventh Century: Proceedings of the 1990 Harlaxton Symposium*, pp. 103–17. Ed. Carola Hickes. Stamford.

—— 1992b. 'Ælfric and Smaragdus'. *Anglo-Saxon England* 21: 203–37.

—— 1993. 'Reform and Resistance: Preaching Styles in Late Anglo-Saxon England'. *De l'homélie au sermon: histoire de la prédication médiévale*, pp. 15–46. Eds Jacqueline Hamesse and Xavier Hermand. Publications de l'Institut d'Études Médiévales: Texts, Études, Congrès 14. Louvain-la-Neuve.

—— 1997. *Translating the Tradition: Manuscripts, Models and Methodologies in the Composition of Ælfric's Catholic Homilies.* The Toller Memorial Lecture. Manchester. Also *Bulletin of the John Rylands University Library of Manchester* 79: 43–65.

—— 1998a. 'Winchester Pedagogy and the *Colloquy* of Ælfric'. *Leeds Studies in English* n.s. 29: 137–52.

—— 1998b. *Bede and the Benedictine Reform.* The Jarrow Lecture. Jarrow.

Hofstetter, Walter 1987. *Winchester und der spätaltenglische Sprachgebrauch: Untersuchungen zur geographischen und zeitlichen Verbreitung altenglische Synonyme.* Munich.

—— 1988. 'Winchester and the Standardization of Old English Vocabulary'. *Anglo-Saxon England* 17: 139–61.

Jackson, Peter and Michael Lapidge 1996. 'The Contents of the Cotton-Corpus Legendary'. *Holy Men and Holy Women: Old English Prose Saints' Lives and their Contexts*, pp. 131–46. Ed. Paul E. Szarmach. Albany, NY.

John, Eric 1960. 'The Sources of the English Monastic Reformation: A Comment'. *Revue Bénédictine* 70: 197–203.

Jones, Christopher A. 1998a. *Ælfric's Letter to the Monks of Eynsham.* CSASE 24. Cambridge.

—— 1998b. '*Meatim sed et Rustica*: Ælfric of Eynsham as a Medieval Latin Author'. *Journal of Medieval Latin* 8: 1–57.

Jost, Karl 1950. *Wulfstanstudien.* Swiss Studies in English 23. Bern.

Keynes, Simon 1980. *The Diplomas of Æthelred 'The Unready' 978–1016: A Study in their Use as Historical Evidence.* Cambridge.

Kornexl, Lucia 1995. 'The *Regularis Concordia* and its Old English Gloss'. *Anglo-Saxon England* 24: 95–130.

Lapidge, Michael 1972. 'Three Latin Poems from Æthelwold's School at Winchester'. *Anglo-Saxon England* 1: 85–137.

—— 1975. 'The Hermeneutic Style in Tenth-century Anglo-Latin Literature'. *Anglo-Saxon England* 4: 67–111.

—— 1979. 'Byrhtferth and the *Vita S. Ecgwini*'. *Mediaeval Studies* 41: 331–53.

—— 1980. 'St Dunstan's Latin Poetry'. *Anglia* 98: 101–6.

—— 1981. 'Byrhtferth of Ramsey and the Early Sections of the *Historia Regum* Attributed to Symeon of Durham'. *Anglo-Saxon England* 10: 97–122.

—— 1985. 'Surviving Booklists from Anglo-Saxon England'. *Learning and Literature in Anglo-Saxon England. Studies Presented to Peter Clemoes on the Occasion of his Sixty-fifth Birthday*, pp. 33–89. Eds Michael Lapidge and Helmut Gneuss. Cambridge.

—— 1988a. 'Æthelwold as Scholar and Teacher'. *Bishop Æthelwold: His Careeer and Influence*, pp. 89–117. Ed. Barbara Yorke. Woodbridge.

—— 1988b. 'A Frankish Scholar in Tenth-century England: Frithegod of Canterbury/Fredegaud of Brioude'. *Anglo-Saxon England* 17: 45–65.

—— 1991. 'Schools, Learning and Literature in Tenth-Century England'. *Il secolo di ferro: mito e realtà del secolo X*, pp. 951–1005. Settimane de studio del centro italiano di studi sull'alto medioevo 38. Spoleto.

—— 1992. 'B. and the *Vita S. Dunstani*'. *St Dunstan: His Life, Times and Cult*, pp. 147–59. Eds Nigel Ramsay, Margaret Sparks and Tim Tatton-Brown. Woodbridge.

Law, Vivien 1987. 'Anglo-Saxon England: Ælfric's *Excerptiones de arte grammatica anglice*'. *Histoire Épistémologie Langage* 9: 47–71. Repr. Vivien Law, *Grammar and Grammarians in the Early Middle Ages*, pp. 200–23. London and New York. 1997.

Lendinara, Patrizia 1986. 'The Third Book of the *Bella Parisiacae Urbis* by Abbo of Saint-Germain-des-Prés and its Old English Gloss'. *Anglo-Saxon England* 15: 73–89.

McIntosh, Angus 1950. 'Wulfstan's Prose'. *Proceedings of the British Academy* 35: 109–42.

Nightingale, John 1996. 'Oswald, Fleury and Continental Reform'. *St Oswald of Worcester: Life and Influence*, pp. 23–45. Eds Nicholas Brooks and Catherine Cubitt. London and New York.

Orchard, A. P. McD 1992. 'Crying Wolf: Oral Style and the *Sermones Lupi*'. *Anglo-Saxon England* 21: 239–64.

Quirk, R. N. 1957. 'Winchester Cathedral in the Tenth Century'. *Archaeological Journal* 114: 28–69.

Sauer, Hans 1980. 'Zur Überlieferung und Anlage von Erzbischof Wulfstans "Handbuch"'. *Deutsches Archiv für Erforschung des Mittelalters* 36: 341–84.

Sawyer, P. H. 1975. 'Charters of the Reform Movement: The Worcester Archive'. *Tenth-century Studies: Essays in Commemoration of the Millennium of the Council of Winchester and Regularis Concordia*, pp. 84–93. Ed. David Parsons. London and Chichester.

Smetana, Cyril L. 1959. 'Ælfric and the Early Medieval Homiliary'. *Traditio* 15: 163–204.

——1961. 'Ælfric and the Homiliary of Haymo of Halberstadt'. *Traditio* 17: 457–69.

Symons, Thomas 1941. 'Sources of the Regularis Concordia'. *Downside Review* 59: 14–36, 143–70, 264–89.

——1975. 'Regularis Concordia: History and Derivation'. *Tenth-century Studies: Essays in Commemoration of the Millennium of the Council of Winchester and Regularis Concordia*, pp. 37–59. Ed. David Parsons. London and Chichester.

Taylor, H. M. 1975. 'Tenth-century Church Building in England and on the Continent'. *Tenth-century Studies: Essays in Commemoration of the Millennium of the Council of Winchester and Regularis Concordia*, pp. 141–68. Ed. David Parsons. London and Chichester.

Thacker, Alan 1988. 'Æthelwold and Abingdon'. *Bishop Æthelwold: His Careeer and Influence*, pp. 43–64. Ed. Barbara Yorke. Woodbridge.

Whitelock, D. 1942. 'Archbishop Wulfstan, Homilist and Statesman'. *Transactions of the Royal Historical Society* 4th ser. 24: 25–45.

——1948. 'Wulfstan and the Laws of Cnut'. *English Historical Review* 63: 433–52.

Wormald, Patrick 1988. 'Æthelwold and his Continental Counterparts: Contact, Comparison, Contrast'. *Bishop Æthelwold: His Careeer and Influence*, pp. 13–42. Ed. Barbara Yorke. Woodbridge.

Yorke, Barbara 1988a. 'Aethelmaer, the Foundation of the Abbey at Cerne and the Politics of the Tenth Century'. *The Cerne Abbey Millennium Lectures*, pp. 15–25. Ed. Katherine Barker. Cerne Abbas.

——1988b. 'Æthelwold and the Politics of the Tenth Century'. *Bishop Æthelwold: His Careeer and Influence*, pp. 65–88. Ed. Barbara Yorke. Woodbridge.

Zettel, Patrick H. 1982. 'Saints' Lives in Old English: Latin Manuscripts and Vernacular Accounts: Ælfric'. *Peritia* 1: 17–37.

10

Legal and Documentary Writings

Carole Hough

Introduction

A substantial corpus of legal and documentary writings survives from Anglo-Saxon England in the form of law-codes, royal diplomas and writs, and non-royal charters such as leases, records of dispute settlements, memoranda and wills. Produced for different purposes and at different times and places, this heterogeneous body of material comprises a range of different types of evidence. The law-codes, issued by English kings from the seventh to the eleventh centuries, are essentially prescriptive, tabulating legal norms or aspirations which may or may not reflect actual contemporary practice. Diplomas, writs and other charters are more descriptive, illustrating various aspects of the working of the legal system as it applied in particular situations. Most evidence relating to criminal law is preserved in law-codes and records of dispute settlements, while civil matters such as land ownership and grants of privileges appear in diplomas, writs and leases. As regards social class, the law-codes make provision for all ranks of society from king to slaves, whereas diplomas and writs deal primarily with the upper classes, as to a lesser extent do wills. Diplomas are characteristically written in Latin, laws, writs and wills in the vernacular; but not all are extant in their original form, and some survive only in much later copies or translations. Each of these major categories of source material presents its own difficulties, but each preserves important and unique insights into the structure of law and society during the Anglo-Saxon period.

Law-codes

The earliest Anglo-Saxon legislation is represented by three law-codes produced in Kent during the seventh century and uniquely preserved in the twelfth-century *Textus Roffensis* manuscript (Rochester, Cathedral Library A. 3. 5; Sawyer 1957). The first was issued by King Æthelberht (r. *c.*580–616) following his conversion to Christianity, a legislative act inspired by the Roman mission under Augustine according to Bede's account in *Historia ecclesiastica* II.5:

> Qui inter cetera bona quae genti suae consulendo conferebat, etiam decreta illi iudiciorum iuxta exempla Romanorum cum consilio sapientium constituit; quae conscripta Anglorum sermone hactenus habentur et obseruantur ab ea. In quibus primitus posuit, qualiter id emendare deberet, qui aliquid rerum uel ecclesiae uel episcopi uel reliquorum ordinum furto auferret, uolens scilicet tuitionem eis, quos et quorum doctrinam susceperat, praestare.

> Among other benefits which he conferred upon the race under his care, he established with the advice of his counsellors a code of laws after the Roman manner. These are written in English and are still kept and observed by the people. Among these he set down first of all what restitution must be made by anyone who steals anything belonging to the church or the bishop or any other clergy; these laws were designed to give protection to those whose coming and whose teaching he had welcomed. (Colgrave and Mynors 1969: 150–1)

The phrase *iuxta exempla Romanorum* 'after the Roman manner' has caused some problems since the extant code shows no signs of Roman influence; but it has been suggested that Bede was referring either to the Roman practice of written law, a cultural innovation introduced through the medium of the Church (Chaney 1962: 151), or to the Romano-Christian ideology responsible for establishing the king's role in maintaining law and order and enforcing religious standards (Wormald 1995). Most recently, D. R. Howlett (1997: 257–62) presents an analysis of the code as a ten-part structure 'presumably in imitation of the Decalogue', and argues that the arrangement of Æthelberht's laws exhibits Biblical style attributable to the influence of the missionaries. Apart from the first section, which deals with offences against the new religion, the code may have been based largely on earlier, oral legislation, issued for the first time in written form. The hierarchical structure, progressing in sequence through laws relating to the church, the king, *eorl* and *ceorl*, followed by a personal injury tariff and sections dealing with women, servants and slaves, suggests a codification of existing law rather than legislation in the initial stages of enactment, while close parallels with continental Germanic law testify to a common origin in an established legal tradition. An oral origin may also help to explain the lack of chapter numbers in the extant manuscript. Whereas later Anglo-Saxon law-codes are divided into numbered clauses in the *Textus Roffensis* as in other manuscript witnesses, the Kentish laws are written consecutively, with clause divisions indicated by the use of initials. This may reflect an original conception not as a written text but as a spoken utterance, where the visual clues provided by chapter numbers would be irrelevant.

A temporal link between the promulgation of the laws in written form and the arrival of the missionaries is supported not only by Bede's statement, but by references to the church in the opening sequence of clauses and by a rubric assigning the laws to the time of Augustine. Although the rubric is not original, it may, as J. M. Wallace-Hadrill (1971: 39) suggests, derive from a lost prologue similar to the pre-ambles preceding other English and continental legislation, and would therefore suggest a *terminus ad quem* of 604 or 609, depending on alternative traditions of the date of Augustine's death. The issue of the appropriate penalty for robbing a church, the topic of the opening section of Æthelberht's code, is raised in question 3 of the *Libellus responsionum*, a letter purportedly written by Gregory the Great in 601 in response to questions raised by Augustine (*HE* I.27), and this is usually taken to indi-cate that the laws were then in the process of being drawn up. F. Liebermann (1903–16: 3.2) therefore dated the code to *c.*602/3.

This dating was challenged by H. G. Richardson and G. O. Sayles (1966: 1–9) on the grounds that with the exception of the first article, the code shows no signs of Christian influence and could well pre-date the arrival of Augustine. Dismissing the opening section as an interpolation and claiming that Æthelberht was never actu-ally converted to Christianity, they proposed that the laws may have been issued earlier in his reign, belonging to the late sixth century rather than the early seventh. Their hypothesis is not widely accepted by present-day scholars, but the suggestion that the opening section may be spurious is regularly revived, most recently by Patrizia Lend-inara (1997: 236). Supporting evidence is generally adduced from stylistic differences between Æthelberht 1 and the rest of the code, and from the fact that theft from the church is penalized more heavily than theft from the king, requiring higher amounts of compensation than are compatible with Gregory's instructions to Augustine in *Libellus responsionum* 3, where simple restitution alone is required. Neither point, however, stands up to scrutiny. First, provisions relating to compensation for the church and its officials cannot have been drawn up until after the arrival of the mis-sionaries, so they would inevitably be written in a different style from laws that were already in existence orally. Second, excessive amounts of restitution to the church are a recurrent feature of early legislation. Chapter 6 of the second series of Alamannic laws, issued during the early eighth century, demands restitution of twenty-seven times the amount stolen from a church (Lehman 1966: 74), while ch. 1.3 of the mid-eighth-century Bavarian laws demands restitution of between nine and twenty-seven times (von Schwind 1926: 270–2). In England, the early-eighth-century *Theodore Penitential* book 1, sect. 3.2, directs that money stolen from a church is to be repaid fourfold, from a layman twofold, again contravening Gregory's instructions (Haddan and Stubbs 1869–73: 3.179). Æthelberht's code is therefore far from exceptional in this respect. It should also be noted that although numbered as a single clause in modern editions, regulations regarding restitution to the church are set out in the manuscript as seven separate provisions, whose cumulative weight is less easy to set aside than an isolated edict. The fact that this section was already present in the copy of Æthelberht's laws available to Bede in the early eighth century further reduces the likelihood that it is not original.

It may be helpful to approach the discrepancy between Æthelberht 1 and *Libellus responsionum* 3 from another angle. Rather than playing a part in the drafting of Æthelberht's laws, Gregory's ruling on theft may have been issued in response to the unacceptable provisions of the opening section, a possibility raised briefly by Wallace-Hadrill (1971: 40). Recent work on the *Libellus* itself, addressing the issue of why Augustine asked the questions to which Gregory sends his considered answers, may support this view. In an important article on the implications of the *Libellus* for missionary activity in southern England, Rob Meens (1994) points out that Augustine is unlikely to have been unfamiliar with church doctrine on matters such as ritual purity, the topic of questions 8 and 9, and suggests that the questions were raised because of points of difference between the British and Roman churches. A similar explanation may underlie question 3 on theft from a church. It is equally unlikely that Augustine would have been unfamiliar with church doctrine concerning theft, so it seems reasonable to deduce that here too what he required was not information but authority. Whether this was also necessitated by a challenge from the British church, or by an excess of enthusiasm on the part of the compilers of the opening section of Æthelberht's code, the logical conclusion is that the *Libellus* in fact postdates the promulgation of this sequence of laws. I would therefore suggest that the code as a whole must have been issued before rather than after 601, the most likely dating parameters being *c.*599–600.

The second series of Kentish laws represents the only legislation to survive in the joint names of two Anglo-Saxon kings: Hlothhere, who succeeded his brother Egbert (664–73) to reign from 637 or 674 to 685, and Egbert's son Eadric, who defeated his uncle in battle in February 685 but held the throne only until an invasion by Cædwalla of Wessex in the following year. It is uncertain whether the laws were actually issued jointly. Alternative possibilities are that Eadric may have reissued during his own reign laws previously drawn up by Hlothhere, or that the extant series was compiled later from laws originally issued separately by each king. However, since there is evidence to support a tradition of joint kingship in Kent (Yorke 1983; Kelly 1995: 195–203), it is perhaps most likely that Eadric was associated with his uncle for part of the latter's reign, and that the laws were issued during a period of amity between the two rulers.

It is clear from the preamble that the laws of Hlothhere and Eadric were intended not as a self-contained code but as a supplement to the existing body of Kentish legislation:

Hloþhære 7 Eadric Cantwara cyningas ecton þa ǽ, þa ðe heora aldoras ær geworhton, ðyssum domum þe hyr efter sægeþ. (Liebermann 1903–16: 1.9)

Hlothhere and Eadric, kings of the people of Kent, augmented the laws which their predecessors had made by these decrees which are stated hereafter.

Æthelberht's laws were therefore still in force. The new series is again largely concerned with financial compensation, providing fuller details of procedural matters the earlier code. The opening sequence, dealing with manslaughter committed ˻ᵃ *esne* (chs 1–4), follows almost directly on from clauses concerning the unfree towards the end of Æthelberht's code. A widow's right to custody of her children, briefly alluded to in Æthelberht 79 (Hough 1994), is here reaffirmed with additional information on the age of majority and the role of the paternal kin (ch. 6). Information is provided on the value of the Kentish *wergild* (chs 1 and 3), as well as on procedures for law-suits (chs 5, 7–10) and on violations of a householder's *mund* (chs 11–14). Introduced for the first time is a concern with trade, relating both to merchants and others visiting Kent, and to Kentish men buying goods in London (chs 15–16).

Æthelberht's code was further supplemented by a third series of Kentish laws issued by King Wihtred (691–725) in 695. In contrast with the essentially secular legislation of Æthelberht and of Hlothhere and Eadric, the emphasis throughout Wihtred's code is on establishing Christian principles and strengthening the position of the church. The church is exempted from taxation and allocated a *mundbyrd* equal to that of the king (chs 1 and 2). Illicit cohabitation is prohibited (chs 3–6), penalties are established for working on the Sabbath or eating during a fast (chs 9–11, 14–15), and for the first time, laws are issued forbidding heathen practices, that is, making offerings to devils (chs 12 and 13). In chs 16–24, the legal status of different ranks of the clergy is specified, and a communicant is allowed to swear an oath of greater value than a non-communicant.

The Kentish laws offer many difficulties of interpretation, partly because they represent a stage of the language for which little other evidence survives. Æthelberht's code comprises not only the beginning of legislative tradition in Anglo-Saxon England, but the earliest extant text in Old English. As Patrick Wormald (1995: 969–70) demonstrates, its simplicity of syntax corresponds to a very primitive state of prose writing, with some 75 per cent of clauses representing simple conditionals. A more sophisticated phraseology is found in the laws of Hlothhere and Eadric and of Wihtred, reflecting a developing prose style which offers little support for a recent suggestion (Lendinara 1997) that the extant version of all three codes may represent a translation from an original Latin text. Given, however, that the continental Germanic law-codes are in Latin, it remains uncertain why the vernacular was used in England. Wormald (1977: 115) suggests the possibility that 'in England (as in Ireland) there was no one with the knowledge of Latin to bridge the gap between local custom and Latin vocabulary'; but as Susan Kelly (1990: 57) points out, Theodore and/or Hadrian were resident in Kent at the time when the later seventh-century law-codes were produced. The archaic vocabulary of all three codes, containing a high proportion of *hapax legomena*, presents a number of interpretational cruces, and these are exacerbated by the cryptic wording of the laws, which assume a preexisting knowledge of the circumstances and tend to state baldly the amount of compensation due in a particular situation without specifying who is to pay it or to whom. This lack of clarity has led to much uncertainty concerning the application of individual laws, and is in part responsible for the current polarization of opinions concerning the position of women in early Anglo-Saxon England, with one group of scholars believing that women paid and received compensation on their own behalf, while another concludes that a male relative or guardian must have been responsible for all such transactions.

Roughly contemporary with Wihtred's legislation are the laws of the West Saxon king Ine (688–725/6), extant only as an appendix to the late-ninth-century *domboc* of Alfred the Great, but originally issued between 688 and 694. These are much less coherently structured than the Kentish codes, with several topics treated more than once; and it is possible, as Wormald (1995: 977–83) suggests, that the extant compilation represents six individual sets of laws. In this case, the dating evidence, based on a reference in the preamble to a bishop known to have died by 694 (Bishop Erconwald), would apply only to the first set (chs 1–27), so that Ine's other laws may have been issued at any time up to the end of his reign in 725 or 726. It is uncertain to what extent they were edited by Alfred prior to inclusion within the composite *domboc*, but since a number of provisions are included which clash with Alfred's own (Hough 1997: 2–3), there is a reasonable probability that Ine's laws have been reproduced in their entirety. A degree of co-operation between the kingdoms of Wessex and of Kent is reflected in a clause which appears in almost identical form in Ine 20 and Wihtred 28, stating that a stranger who leaves the road and neither shouts nor blows a horn may be killed with impunity on the assumption that he is a thief. Although sometimes taken as evidence of borrowing from one code to another (Richardson and Sayles 1966: 13), the fact that the clause is concerned with travellers, possibly from one kingdom to another, seems rather to reflect a reciprocal agreement between the two rulers.

No other regional law-codes have survived; and unless some of Ine's laws do indeed date from the latter part of his reign, no Anglo-Saxon legislation is extant from the eighth century or the first three-quarters of the ninth. From the late ninth century onwards, however, Anglo-Saxon kings became prolific legislators. The first national code was issued *c.*887–93 by Alfred the Great, and survives in six manuscripts, the earliest being the mid-tenth-century Cambridge, Corpus Christi College 173. It is possible that, like Alfred's translation of Pope Gregory's *Cura pastoralis*, copies were distributed to various parts of his kingdom for consultation by the local authorities (Keynes 1990: 232). This would account for a number of references to the *domboc* in later codes, to which Simon Keynes (1990: 223) draws attention. Its practical value, none the less, must have been very limited. In all extant manuscripts, the combined laws of Alfred and Ine are prefaced by a lengthy translation of Mosaic law and are divided into 120 chapters to reflect, as Wormald (1977: 132) argues, a symbolic unity between the Israelites and the Anglo-Saxons as the chosen races of God. The chapter-divisions are illogical in terms of subject matter, and would have made it difficult to use the *domboc* for any practical purpose; but the symbolic value of 120 as the age of Moses the Lawgiver and as the number of members of the early church evidently took precedence over functional considerations. There is in fact reason to believe that the Anglo-Saxon law-codes were not primarily intended for practical use. Not only are they highly selective and occasionally inconsistent, as with the discrepancies between the Alfred/Ine sections of the *domboc*, but there is little evidence that they were actually consulted in courts of law. Wormald (1977: 122) points out that none of the Anglo-Saxon charters recording judicial decisions makes any reference to the written texts, and Katherine O'Brien O'Keeffe (1998: 228–9) draws attention to two documented cases where the written law was evidently not put into effect. The law-codes do not represent legislation in the modern sense, but served a symbolic purpose, establishing the role of the king as law-giver. As Simon Keynes and Michael Lapidge (1983: 39) comment in connection with Alfred's *domboc*, 'The act of law-making was a public display of a king's royal power, and provided an opportunity for him to express his political and ideological aspirations in legal form.' It was a matter not simply of legislative content but of image-building.

The symbolic function of law-making helps to explain why so many Anglo-Saxon kings issued law-codes, even when they were essentially reiterating existing legislation. The extant body of Anglo-Saxon law is highly repetitive, with many clauses reproduced either exactly or in modified form in later codes, and it is likely that the preservation of early texts was often due to their potential use in the drafting of new laws. At least two series of laws were issued by Alfred's son Edward the Elder (*c*.900–25), six by Alfred's grandson Æthelstan (*c*.925–39), three by Edmund (*c*.939–46), four by Edgar (*c*.959–63), ten by Æthelred (*c*.978–1014), and two by the Danish conqueror Cnut (*c*.1020–3), many of whose laws, like those of his predecessor Æthelred, were drafted by Archbishop Wulfstan of York (Whitelock 1948, 1955). Not all represent royal codes as such (Keynes 1990: 235–42), and not all survive in their entirety. For instance, fragments only are extant of IX and X Æthelred, while III and IV Æthelstan, III Edmund and IV Æthelred are preserved only in an early twelfth-century Latin translation of Anglo-Saxon law known as *Quadripartitus*, recently discussed in detail by Wormald (1994). Some codes have been lost altogether. These include treaties relating to the northern and eastern parts of England mentioned in II Edward 5.2, and laws issued to enforce the Christian religion by Æthelberht's grandson Eorcenberht (r. 640–64), now known only from a passing reference by Bede in *Historia ecclesiastica* III.8.

No legislation is extant from the kingdoms of Mercia or Northumbria, although Alfred claims in the Preface to his own law-code to have drawn on the laws of Offa of Mercia as well as those of Æthelberht of Kent and Ine of Wessex:

> 49.9 Ic ða Ælfred cyning þás togædere gegaderode 7 awritan het, monege þara þe ure foregengan heoldon, ða ðe me licodon; 7 manege þara þe me ne licodon ic áwearp mid minra witena geðeahte, 7 on oðre wisan bebead to healdanne. Forðam ic ne dorste geðristlæcan þara minra awuht fela on gewrit settan, forðam me wæs uncuð, hwæt þæs ðam lician wolde ðe æfter ús wæren. Ac ða ðe ic gemette awðer oððe on Ines dæge, mines mæges, oððe on Offan Mercna cyninges oððe on Æþelbryhtes, þe ærest fulluhte onfeng on Angelcynne, þa ðe me ryhtoste ðuhton, ic þa heron gegaderode, 7 þa oðre forlét. (Liebermann 1903–16: 1.46)
>
> I then, King Alfred, gathered these together and ordered to be written many that pleased me of those which our forefathers kept; and I rejected many of those that did not please

me with the advice of my councillors, and ordered them to be kept in a different way. I did not dare presume to set in writing many at all of my own, because I did not know what would please those who should come after us. But I collected herein those that I found which seemed to me most just, either from the time of my kinsman Ine, or of Offa, king of the Mercians, or of Æthelberht, who first received baptism among the English, and I omitted the others.

No trace of Offa's laws has survived, unless, as Wormald (1991) suggests, Alfred was referring not to a vernacular law-code but to an extant Latin capitulary of twenty canons dating from 786 (Dümmler 1895: no. 3). The capitulary was presented by papal legates to a synod held by Offa under their auspices, and has a number of points in common with some of Alfred's own laws. For instance, there are striking parallels between the treatment of marriage and inheritance in the fifteenth and sixteenth canons and in Alfred 8, one of three clauses in the *domboc* to contain Mercian vocabulary (Whitelock et al. 1981: 1.18). This in itself, however, seems to point to the existence of an intermediate text in the vernacular. Furthermore, Wormald's suggestion that Offa's laws may have taken a different form from 'a code in the mould of Æthelberht's, Ine's and Alfred's own' (1991: 43) may allow insufficient weight to the political value of such a code. Wormald himself has done much to demonstrate the prestige-value of early legislation as a reflection of 'the ideological aspirations of Germanic kinship' (1977: 106); and since both Kent and Wessex had already produced written legislation, it would be surprising if Mercia had not taken the opportunity to do the same. Although some at least of the Mercian laws mentioned in Alfred's Preface may have borne a close resemblance to the capitulary of 786, this does not preclude the existence of a separate law-code. Possibly the papal legates took existing legislation into consideration when drafting their canons for the Mercian people: alternatively, as Whitelock, Brett and Brook (1981: 1.18) suggest, the laws of Offa may well have been influenced by the legatine decrees.

Apart from any of Offa's laws that may be represented in the 786 capitulary or in Alfred's *domboc*, the only records of either Mercian or Northumbrian legislation are preserved in short texts known as *Norðleoda laga* 'Law of the North People' and *Mircna laga* 'Law of the Mercians'. These form part of a group of unofficial texts concerned with social rank and *wergild* values, apparently compiled by Archbishop Wulfstan during the early eleventh century. In the same group are *Geþyncðo* 'Rank', *Að* 'Oath', and *Hadbot* 'Compensation for offences against people in holy orders'. Marriage law is documented in another unofficial text known as *Be wifmannes beweddunge* 'On the betrothal of a woman', also generally dated to the late tenth or early eleventh century despite close parallels with a sequence of laws dealing with the marriage contract in the seventh-century code of Æthelberht. Both state that a payment is to be made by the prospective bridegroom (Æthelberht 77; *Wif* 2); both refer to the *morgengifu*, or property granted by the bridegroom to the bride (Æthelberht 81; *Wif* 3); both specify the amount of property to which the woman will be entitled if her husband dies first (Æthelberht 78; *Wif* 4); and both stipulate that the widow's inheritance rights are to be reduced on remarriage (Æthelberht 80; *Wif* 4). Comparison of the two texts would suggest that marriage law remained remarkably stable throughout the Anglo-Saxon period.

The same cannot be said of Anglo-Saxon law in general. In other respects, there are fundamental differences between the seventh-century law-codes and those of later kings. Crimes are increasingly regarded as offences against society rather than against individuals, leading to a change of emphasis from the compensation of victims to the punishment of offenders. The principle of straightforward financial redress which underlies much of Æthelberht's legislation is replaced by punitive fines, capital punishment and mutilation. Thus whereas the penalty for theft in Æthelberht's code ranges from twofold to twelvefold restitution depending on the status of thief and victim (chs 1, 4, 9, 28, 90), the same offence under Wihtred is punishable by slavery or death (chs 26–8), and under Ine by slavery, death or mutilation (chs 7, 12, 37). By the time of King Alfred, anyone who stole from a church might lose his hand (ch. 6), while IV Athelstan 6 provides for a thief to face death by drowning if a free person, and by stoning or burning if a slave. An effective illustration of changing attitudes is provided by the treatment of adultery in seventh- and eleventh-century law. According to Æthelberht 31, the adulterer has to pay a *wergild* (whether his own or that of the woman or her husband is unclear), and also to meet the financial costs of acquiring a second wife for the wronged husband. Under II Cnut 53, on the other hand, the guilty woman forfeits all her property to her husband, and loses her nose and ears.

Charters

Like the practice of written legislation, charters were introduced to England by the church during the seventh century. Characteristically written in Latin on a single sheet of parchment, their initial purpose was to record a grant of land or of privileges by the king to a religious house, and to act as the title-deed for the estate of 'bookland' thereby created. These royal grants are known as 'diplomas', a term which also includes confirmations of earlier grants by later kings. Gradually, however, charters came to be used for a wider range of purposes, including grants to laymen, records of dispute settlements, memoranda, and over a hundred extant leases, some of which are in the vernacular. The vernacular was also used for the boundary clauses of diplomas, identifying the extent of the estates granted and exchanged. These are of the first importance in the study of land use and administration, and often contain early forms of placenames otherwise recorded only in post-Conquest sources.

Out of *c.* 1,100 extant diplomas, about two hundred survive in their original single-sheet form, preserving crucial evidence for the study of Anglo-Saxon script and manuscript production. The rest comprise later copies, often entered into cartularies, and these can be difficult to distinguish from forgeries fabricated in support of a spurious claim to land or privileges, some of which may include genuine elements. Indeed, the authenticity even of single-sheet versions can only be verified through close study of palaeographic, linguistic and diplomatic features (Chaplais 1968). Scholarly opinion in respect of individual charters is summarized by P. H. Sawyer (1968), whose total of 1,539 entries (excluding bounds and lost or incomplete texts) includes not only the royal diplomas issued in Latin by Anglo-Saxon kings, but also the various other types of charters to be discussed below. A new edition of the entire corpus is currently in progress (Campbell 1973; Sawyer 1979; O'Donovan 1988; Kelly 1995, 1996). All will be cited by the number assigned to them in Sawyer's catalogue, abbreviated as S.

The date at which charters were first produced in England is uncertain. The earliest authentic examples date from the 670s, but display a variety of formulas which suggests that the charter tradition was already well established and beginning to diversify. It is fully possible that earlier documents may have been lost, and although circumstantial evidence points to Archbishop Theodore as the instigator, a case has also been made for Augustine (Chaplais 1965, 1969). It is even possible that the origins of the charter tradition are to be sought outside the Roman mission. As with the law-codes, the majority of early records are from the south of England, weighting the evidence in favour of a connection with the Italian church; but Wormald (1984: 13–19) argues for a more diverse origin, including both Frankish and Celtic influences, and this view may be supported by recent work highlighting the role of the Frankish and British churches in the conversion process (Meens 1994; Wood 1994).

The structure of the royal diploma is heavily formulaic, characteristically beginning with an invocation, followed by a religious proem, the grant itself, a sanction, boundary-clause, dating-clause and witness-list. There are many variations from this norm, however, and distinctive groups of charters have been identified, such as the 'alliterative' type of the 940s and 950s, and the 'Dunstan B' type of the mid-tenth century. Characteristic features of the former include a rhythmical style with much alliteration, the use of the third person rather than the first, and some unusual inclusions in the witness-lists. This group appears to be associated with Bishop Cenwald of Worcester, who appears in all examples with full witness-lists. The 'Dunstan B' charters, produced between about 951 and 975 and using a diplomatic protocol apparently developed by Abbot Dunstan for the Glastonbury scriptorium, begin with a dating-clause instead of an invocation or proem, and share a preference for particular formulas to introduce the boundary-clause and witness-list, and for the attestation (Keynes 1994a).

By the later Anglo-Saxon period, writs had also come into use. Generally much shorter than diplomas and written in the vernacular, these were sealed letters intended to be read out to the shire court or other official meeting, announcing changes in land ownership and the like. Some 120 writs survive, six of them in their original form. Characteristic features include an opening protocol which names the sender and the addressee(s) and contains a greeting. Although writs are extant only from the eleventh century, the occurrence of a similar protocol at the beginning of King Alfred's Preface to his translation of Pope Gregory's *Cura pastoralis* suggests that they were already current in England by the late ninth, and this is confirmed by a reference to an *ærendgewrit* in a passage interpolated by Alfred into his translation of St Augustine's *Soliloquia* (Harmer 1952: 10–11).

Up to the end of the ninth century, royal charters appear to have been drawn up at religious houses by ecclesiastical scribes acting on behalf of the beneficiaries. Thus, Kentish charters were produced at Rochester and at Christ Church, Canterbury, and Mercian charters at Worcester. The situation during the tenth and eleventh centuries is less clear. There is evidence for some form of centralized production from the 930s and 940s, and much discussion has focused on the putative existence of a royal chancery. On the one hand, the case that charters continued to be produced in ecclesiastical scriptoria has been strongly made by Pierre Chaplais (1965, 1966, 1985). On the other hand, the view that a central agency attached to the king's household was responsible for the production of royal diplomas and writs is developed by Keynes (1980, 1988), who also suggests that such an agency may already have been emerging in ninth-century Wessex (1994b).

Charters shed additional light on various aspects of Anglo-Saxon law and society, supplementing the information preserved in the law-codes. Despite the non-survival of written legislation from the early kingdom of Merica, for instance, charter evidence attests to the existence of an organized system of law and administration. In S 98, King Æthelbald of Mercia (r. 716–57) grants remission of the taxes due on two ships to Bishop Milred and the church of Worcester. This shows that a toll system was already in operation, although the earliest extant legislation on this subject dates from the late tenth century (IV Æthelred 2). Remission of the toll due on two ships is also granted to Abbess Sigeburga by King Eadberht of Kent *c.*761 (S 29), while S 91 records a grant of half the toll due on a ship to Abbess Eadburga by King Æthelbald in 748. The earliest extant Anglo-Saxon diploma to refer to the public duties of bridge and fortress building is S 59 dating from 770, a grant of land by Uhtred, sub-king of the Hwicce, endorsed by King Offa of Mercia. Of particular interest is a grant of land by Offa to Worcester Cathedral between 793 and 796 (S 146), which details the amount of taxes that could be raised from the estate. As well as constituting 'the only surviving statement of the amount the king could draw from an estate as his farm' (Whitelock 1979: 507), this suggests that the position of the church was less strong in Mercia than in Kent, where according to Wihtred 1 it was exempted altogether from taxation.

A substantial minority of extant charters are issued or witnessed by women, providing eloquent testimony to the legal autonomy of women in Anglo-Saxon England (Hough 1993: 174–203). The grantees of many early diplomas are also female, testifying to the position of women as rulers of religious communities during the seventh and eighth centuries; while later grants and leases to laywomen, either in their own right or in association with husbands or other relatives, illustrate the role of women as land-holders throughout the Anglo-Saxon period. Charter evidence also confirms that women were considered to be 'oath-worthy' (Hough 1997: 6–7), and indeed that they played a part in the administration of justice. As Frank Stenton (1971: 495) points out, whereas the 'earliest unequivocal reference to the exercise of jurisdiction by a lord of lower rank than the king' (i.e., the granting of *sacu* and *socn*) occurs in a charter of 956 in favour of the archbishop of York (S 659), the second such grant three years later concerns the allocation of similar rights over Howden and eight dependent villages in south Yorkshire to a woman named Quen (S 681). This has obvious implications for the legal status of women during the mid-tenth century.

Charters also constitute a primary source of evidence for Anglo-Saxon case-law. Wormald (1988) identifies a corpus of 178 cases drawn from a variety of sources including charters, chronicles, saints' lives and Domesday Book. Many contain details of legal procedure; and several instances of disputes which turned on the possession of diplomas or other forms of documentation are discussed by Wormald (1986) and Keynes (1990: 248–51). This section will conclude with a brief examination of a case involving criminal law, in order to consider how far the course adopted corresponds to provisions within the law-codes.

The case is no. 27 in Wormald (1988), and is recorded in S 362, a grant to Æthelwulf of an estate at Wylye in Wiltshire by Edward the Elder. The grant includes a reference to an earlier forfeiture of the estate by Wulfhere and his wife, which resulted from Wulfhere's desertion under King Alfred:

> Ista vero prænominata tellus primitus fuit . præpeditus á quodam duce nomine Wulhere. et ejus uxore quando ille utrumque et suum dominum regem Ælfredum . et patriam ultra jusjurandum quam regi et suis omnibus optimatibus juraverat sine licentia dereliquit. Tunc etiam cum omnium juditio sapientium Geuisorum et Mercensium . potestatem et hereditatem dereliquit agrorum. (Birch 1885–93: 2.243)

> Truly this afore-named estate was originally forfeited by a certain ealdorman, Wulfhere by name, and his wife, when he deserted without permission both his lord King Alfred and his country in spite of the oath which he had sworn to the king and all his leading men. Then by the judgment of all the councillors of the Gewisse and of the Mercians he lost the control and inheritance of his lands. (Whitelock 1979: 542)

To some extent this is in line with the law-codes. Ine 51, which, as part of the composite *domboc* issued by King Alfred, was presumably in force at the time of Wulfhere's desertion, states that a nobleman was to forfeit all his land for neglecting military service:

> Gif gesiðcund mon landagende forsitte fierd, geselle CXX scill. 7 ðolie his landes; unlandagende LX scill.; cierlisc XXX scill. to fierdwite. (Liebermann 1903–16: 1.112)

> If a man of *gesith* rank who owns land neglects military service, he is to pay 120 shillings and forfeit his land; one who does not own land, 60 shillings; one of *ceorl* rank, 30 shillings as a fine for neglecting military service.

Forfeiture continued to be the penalty for desertion throughout the later Anglo-Saxon period, appearing again in the eleventh-century laws of Cnut. II Cnut 77 reads as follows:

> 77. 7 se man, þe ætfleo fram his hlaforde oððe fram his geferan for his yrhþe, si hit on scipfyrde, si hit on Landfyrde; þolige ealles þæs þe he age 7 his agenes feores; 7 fo se hlaford to þam æhtan 7 to his lande, þe he him ær sealde.
>
> 77.1. 7 gyf he bocland hæbbe, ge *þæt* þam cingce to handa. (Liebermann 1903–16: 1.364)
>
> 77. And the man, who flees from his lord or from his companions because of his cowardice, whether it is on a naval or military expedition, is to forfeit all that he possesses and his own life; and the lord is to succeed to the possessions and to his land, which he had given him.
>
> 77.1 And if he has bookland, it is to pass into the king's hands.

The reference to King Alfred in S 362 may suggest that Wulfhere deserted from an army under the personal command of the king. This situation is dealt with in VI Æthelred 35:

> 7 gif hwa of fyrde butan leafe gewende, þe cyning [sylf on] sy, plihte his are. (Liebermann 1903–16: 1.256)
>
> And if anyone deserts an army where the king himself is present, he to forfeit his property.

There is also another point to be considered. Wulfhere's crime was not simply that he deserted, but that he contravened his sworn oath to king and country. This topic is covered by the opening chapter of Alfred's code, which deals with the keeping of oaths and shows that in extreme instances, oath-breaking could result in the forfeiture of property. According to Alfred 1.4, an oath-breaker who refused to submit to punishment would be liable for such a penalty:

> Gif hine mon togendan scyle, 7 he elles nylle, gif hine on gebinde, þolige his wæpna 7 his ierfes. (Liebermann 1903–16: 1.48)
>
> If he will not submit unless force is used, and he is bound, he is to forfeit his weapons and his property.

Thus Wulfhere could have forfeited the estate at Wylye on either count.

There is, however, one aspect of this case that appears to be at odds with written legislation. This concerns the reference to Wulfhere's wife. According to S 362, the estate was forfeited by Wulfhere and his wife because of his desertion. The extent of his wife's involvement, if any, is quite unclear, and she is not even named in the charter. In general, the law-codes define precisely the limits of a married woman's liability. For instance, Wihtred 12 distinguishes between the case of a husband who secretly makes offerings to devils and one who does so in collaboration with his wife. In the first instance, the husband alone is to forfeit his possessions and his *healsfang*; in the second, both husband and wife are to forfeit their possessions and *healsfang*. Ine 7 stipulates that a woman is implicated in a theft perpetrated by her husband only if she knows about it; and Ine 57 specifically exonerates a married woman from responsibility for her husband's theft of cattle, allowing her to retain her third of the joint property if she declares on oath that she has not eaten the stolen meat. Similarly in VI Æthelstan 1, a married woman is allocated a third of the goods forfeited by a husband convicted of theft, provided she has not acted as accessory to the crime. Here, on the other hand, Wulfhere's wife seems to have forfeited her share of the estate for a crime committed by her husband alone. In this respect, the scrupulous division of responsibility implied by the law-codes does not appear to have been carried out in practice.

Wills

The testamentary dispositions of nearly seventy Anglo-Saxon men and women are recorded in vernacular charters dating from the mid-ninth century onwards. The corpus is established by Lowe (1998b), who identifies a total of sixty-four vernacular wills, about a third of them extant in single-sheet charters datable to the eleventh century or before, and the rest in post-Conquest copies. Forty-six are by men (including two kings – Alfred and Eadred), thirteen by women, and five in the joint names of husband and wife. Other wills have been lost, including that of King Æthelwulf of Wessex (839–58), referred to in the will of his son Alfred the Great; and several are known only from Latin translations or abstracts preserved in the *Historia Ramesiensis*, the *Liber Eliensis* and the St Albans cartulary. In some instances, wills were made orally in the presence of witnesses, as with the dispositions of Æthelric, son of Æthelmund (S 1187), and these may not always have been committed to writing (Whitelock 1930: xvi–xviii).

The extant wills fall into two main categories: the bequest or *post obitum* gift, and the multi-gift will. Three types of *post obitum* bequest are represented: the *precaria oblata* (*traditio cum reservatione usufructus*), where the property was first given to the donee but was then reacquired for one or more lives; the *precaria remuneratoria* (*census pro investitura*), whereby the donor paid rent to the donee in acknowledgment of the latter's right to the property; and the *precaria data* (*traditio post obitum*), whereby the property continued to belong to the donor until death without payment of any fee. Multi-gift wills include a number of bequests, but seldom dispose of the testator's entire possessions. Although there are at least three accounts of death-bed wills (Whitelock 1968: 19–20), the majority of dispositions appear to have been made while the testator was alive and well, and they could be added to, emended and even revoked (Lowe 1998b: 36–8).

Unlike diplomas, which functioned as title-deeds, wills were often produced in duplicate or triplicate so that copies could be held by the testator and principal beneficiaries. King Alfred, in revising his earlier testamentary dispositions, declares that he had entrusted copies to many witnesses and has now burned all that he could find:

> þonne hæfde ic ær on oðre wisan awriten ymbe min yrfe þa ic hæfde mare feoh 7 ma maga 7 hæfde monegum mannum þa gewritu oðfæst 7 on þas ylcan gewitnesse hy wæron awritene. þonne hæbbe ic nu forbær'n'ed þa ealdan þe ic geahsian mihte. Gif hyra hwylc funden bið, ne forstent þæt naht, forþam ic wille þæt hit nu þus sy mid Godes fultume. (Harmer 1914: 18)

> Now I had made other arrangements in writing concerning my inheritance, when I had more money and more kinsmen, and had committed the documents to many men, with whose cognisance they had been drawn up. I have now burnt the old ones which I could hear of. If any of these is found, it shall be of no value, since these are the arrangements which I now desire should stand, with God's help. (Harmer 1914: 52)

Some wills were produced as chirographs, documents copied in duplicate, triplicate or quadruplicate on a single sheet of parchment and cut into separate parts after the word CYROGRAPHVM had been written across the whole. Each of the interested parties could then retain a part. Lowe (1998a) establishes a corpus of sixty-four pre-Conquest charters produced as chirographs, and comments that the device 'seem[s] to have been almost exclusively reserved for recording contracts between parties' (171). Of these sixty-four examples, no fewer than twelve are vernacular wills, while the remainder are mostly leases, agreements and records of dispute settlements.

Concluding Remarks

Any study of Anglo-Saxon legal and documentary writings must bear in mind the intensely fragmentary and unbalanced nature of the surviving material. Early law-codes are extant from one area of the country only, and deal with a very limited range of topics. Records of case-law belong primarily to the reigns of Alfred, Edgar and Æthelred, with a preponderance of early records from Kent. Writs appear to have been in use by the late ninth century, but survive only from the eleventh, while the royal diplomas attested from the 670s onwards may represent either the beginning of the Anglo-Saxon charter tradition or the continuation of a practice inaugurated almost seventy years before. The majority of extant wills are preserved in the archives of Bury St Edmunds, Christ Church, Canterbury, and the Old and New Minsters, Winchester, suggesting heavy losses from other parts of the country. Certain areas of the law are unrepresented in any of the known sources, and it is not always clear whether the relevant evidence has been lost or never existed in written form. A case in point is suggested by the boundary clauses of diplomas and leases of land, over a thousand of which are extant. It is axiomatic that penalties must have been in place for interfering with the boundary markers establishing the legal perimeters of the estates, but no trace of legislation or case-law on this topic survives. Comparison with continental law-codes confirms that such penalties were customary under Germanic law. Chapter 55 of the Burgundian code issued by King Gundobad during the late fifth century is concerned with disputes over boundaries, stipulating in 55.6 that a freeman who moved or destroyed a boundary marker was to lose his land, while a slave guilty of the same offence was to be killed (de Salis 1892: 90–1). According to chapters 236–41 of the laws issued by the Lombard King Rothair during the seventh century, a freeman would incur financial penalties for digging out boundary markers, cutting down marked trees, or making false marks on other trees, with mutilation or death as the corresponding punishment for a slave (Bluhme 1869: 59). Chapter 12 of the mid-eighth-century Bavarian laws also contains lengthy provisions relating to deliberate or accidental interference with boundary markers, and to disputes over boundary markers (von Schwind 1926: 398–405), as does book 10, chapter 3, of the Visigothic Code (Zeumer 1902: 396–9). Similar regulations must have been in force in England to safeguard the integrity of estate boundaries, and it is highly unlikely that no disputes ever turned on such a point; but this is an area of jurisprudence for which documentary evidence is entirely lacking. It serves as a salutary reminder that despite the range and variety of the material discussed in this chapter, there are many aspects of Anglo-Saxon government and administration on which the sources are completely silent.

REFERENCES

Primary sources

Attenborough, F. L. 1922. *The Laws of the Earliest English Kings*. Cambridge.

Birch, Walter de Gray, ed. 1885–93. *Cartularium Saxonicum*. 3 vols and index. London.

Bluhme, F., ed. 1869. *Leges Langobardorum*. Monumenta Germaniae Historica, Leges 4. Hanover.

Campbell, A., ed. 1973. *Charters of Rochester*. Anglo-Saxon Charters 1. London.

Colgrave, Bertram and R. A. B. Mynors, eds. 1969. *Bede's Ecclesiastical History of the English People*. Oxford Medieval Texts. Oxford.

de Salis, L. R. ed. 1892. *Leges Burgundionum*. Monumenta Germaniae Historica, Legum Sectio I, 2.1. Hanover.

Dümmler, E., ed. 1895. *Alcuini Epistolae*. Monumenta Germaniae Historica, Epistolarum Karolini Aevi 2. Frankfurt.

Haddan, Arthur West and William Stubbs, eds.

1869–73. *Councils and Ecclesiastical Documents Relating to Great Britain and Ireland*. 3 vols. Oxford.

Harmer, F. E., ed. 1914. *Select English Historical Documents of the Ninth and Tenth Centuries*. Cambridge.

——, ed. 1952. *Anglo-Saxon Writs*. Manchester.

Kelly, S. E., ed. 1995. *Charters of St Augustine's Abbey Canterbury and Minster-in-Thanet*. Anglo-Saxon Charters 4. Oxford.

——, ed. 1996. *Charters of Shaftesbury Abbey*. Anglo-Saxon Charters 5. Oxford.

Lehman, Karl, ed. 1966. *Lex Alamannorum*. Monumenta Germaniae Historica, Legum Sectio I, 5.1. Rev. ed. Karl August Eckhardt. Hanover.

Liebermann, F., ed. 1903–16. *Die Gesetze der Angelsachsen*. 3 vols. Halle.

O'Donovan, M. A. 1988, ed. *Charters of Sherborne*. Anglo-Saxon Charters 3. Oxford.

Robertson, A. J. 1925. *The Laws of the Kings of England from Edmund to Henry I*. Cambridge.

Sawyer, P. H., ed. 1957. *Textus Roffensis: Rochester Cathedral Library Manuscript A.3.5. Part 1*. Early English Manuscript in Facsimile 7. Copenhagen.

—— 1968. *Anglo-Saxon Charters: An Annotated List and Bibliography*. Royal Historical Society Guides and Handbooks 8. London.

——, ed. 1979. *Charters of Burton Abbey*. Anglo-Saxon Charters 2. London.

von Schwind, Ernst, ed. 1926. *Lex Baiwariorum*. Monumenta Germaniae Historica, Legum Sectio I, 5.2. Hanover.

Whitelock, Dorothy, ed. 1930. *Anglo-Saxon Wills*. Cambridge

——, ed. 1968. *The Will of Æthelgifu: A Tenth Century Anglo-Saxon Manuscript*. Oxford.

——, ed. 1979. *English Historical Documents c.500–1042*. 2nd edn. London.

——, M Brett and C. N. L. Brooke, eds. 1981. *Councils and Synods with Other Documents Relating to the English Church: I. AD 871–1204*. 2 vols. Oxford.

Zeumer, K., ed. 1902. *Leges Visigothorum*. Monumenta Germaniae Historica, Legum Sectio I. 1. Hanover.

Secondary sources

Chaney, William, A. 1962. 'Aethelberht's Code and the King's Number'. *American Journal of Legal History* 6: 161–77.

Chaplais, Pierre 1965. 'The Origin and Authenticity of the Royal Anglo-Saxon Diploma'. *Journal of the Society of Archivists* 3: 48–61. Repr. *Prisca Munimenta*, pp. 28–42. Ed. Felicity Ranger. London, 1973.

—— 1966. 'The Anglo-Saxon Chancery: From the Diploma to the Writ'. *Journal of the Society of Archivists* 3: 160–76. Repr. *Prisca Munimenta*, pp. 43–62. Ed. Felicity Ranger. London, 1973.

—— 1968. 'Some Early Anglo-Saxon Diplomas on Single Sheets: Originals or Copies?'. *Journal of the Society of Archivists* 3: 315–36. Repr. *Prisca Munimenta*, pp. 63–87. Ed. Felicity Ranger. London, 1973.

—— 1969. 'Who Introduced Charters into England? The Case for Augustine'. *Journal of the Society of Archivists* 3: 526–42. Repr. *Prisca*

Munimenta, pp. 88–107. Ed. Felicity Ranger. London, 1973.

—— 1985. 'The Royal Anglo-Saxon "Chancery" of the Tenth Century Revisited'. *Studies in Medieval History Presented to R. H. C. Davis*, pp. 41–51. Eds Henry Mayr-Harting and R. I. Moore. London.

Hough, Carole 1993. 'Women and the Law in Early Anglo-Saxon England'. Unpublished PhD dissertation, University of Nottingham.

—— 1994. 'The Early Kentish "Divorce Laws": A Reconsideration of Æthelberht, chs. 79 and 80'. *Anglo-Saxon England* 23: 19–34.

—— 1997. 'Alfred's *Domboc* and the Language of Rape: A Reconsideration of Alfred ch. 11'. *Medium Ævum* 66: 1–27.

Howlett, D. R. 1997. *British Books in Biblical Style*. Dublin.

Kelly, Susan 1990. 'Anglo-Saxon Lay Society and the Written Word'. *The Uses of Literacy in Early Mediaeval Europe*, pp. 36–62. Ed. Rosamond McKitterick. Cambridge.

Keynes, Simon 1980. *The Diplomas of King Æthelred 'The Unready' 978–1016: A Study in their Use as Historical Evidence*. Cambridge.

—— 1988. 'Regenbald the Chancellor (*sic*)'. *Anglo-Norman Studies* 10: 185–222.

—— 1900. 'Royal Government and the Written Word in Late Anglo-Saxon England'. *The Uses of Literacy in Early Mediaeval Europe*, pp. 226–57. Ed. Rosamond McKitterick. Cambridge.

—— 1994a. 'The "Dunstan B" Charters'. *Anglo-Saxon England* 23: 165–93.

—— 1994b. 'The West Saxon Charters of King Æthelwulf and His Sons'. *English Historical Review* 109: 1109–49.

—— and Michael Lapidge, trans. 1983. *Alfred the Great: Asser's 'Life of King Alfred' and Other Contemporary Sources*. London.

Lendinara, Patrizia 1997. 'The Kentish Laws'. *The Anglo-Saxons from the Migration Period to the Eighth Century: An Ethnographic Perspective*, pp. 211–43. Ed. John Hines. Woodbridge.

Lowe, Kathryn A. 1998a. 'Lay Literacy in Anglo-Saxon England and the Development of the Chirograph'. *Anglo-Saxon Manuscripts and their Heritage*, pp. 161–204. Ed. Phillip Pulsiano and Elaine M. Treharne. Aldershot.

—— 1998b. 'The Nature and Effect of the Anglo-Saxon Vernacular Will'. *Journal of Legal History* 19: 23–61.

Meens, Rob 1994. 'A Background to Augustine's Mission to Anglo-Saxon England'. *Anglo-Saxon England* 23: 5–17.

O'Keeffe, Katherine O'Brien 1998. 'Body and Law in Late Anglo-Saxon England'. *Anglo-Saxon England* 27: 209–32.

Richardson, H. G. and G. O. Sayles 1966. *Law and Legislation from Æthelberht to Magna Carta*. Edinburgh.

Stenton, Frank 1971. *Anglo-Saxon England*. 3rd edn. Oxford.

Wallace-Hadrill, J. M. 1971. *Early Germanic Kingship in England and on the Continent*. Oxford.

Whitelock, Dorothy 1948. 'Wulfstan and the Laws of Cnut'. *English Historical Review* 63: 433–52. Repr. *History, Law and Literature in 10th–11th Century England*. London, 1981.

—— 1955. 'Wulfstan's Authorship of Cnut's Laws'. *English Historical Review* 70: 72–85. Repr. *History, Law and Literature in 10th–11th Century England*. London, 1981.

Wood, Ian 1944. 'The Mission of Augustine of Canterbury to the English'. *Speculum* 69: 1–17.

Wormald, Patrick 1977. '*Lex Scripta* and *Verbum Regis*: Legislation and Germanic Kingship, from Euric to Cnut'. *Early Medieval Kingship*, pp. 105–38. Ed. P. H. Sawyer and I. N. Wood. Leeds.

—— 1984. *Bede and the Conversion of England: The Charter Evidence*. Jarrow Lecture.

—— 1986. 'Charters, Law and the Settlement of Disputes in Anglo-Saxon England'. *The Settlement of Disputes in Early Medieval Europe*, pp. 149–68. Eds Wendy Davies and Paul Fouracre. Cambridge.

—— 1988. 'A Handlist of Anglo-Saxon Lawsuits'. *Anglo-Saxon England* 17: 247–81.

—— 1991. 'In Search of King Offa's "Law Code"'. *People and Places in Northern Europe 500–1600: Essays in Honour of Peter Hayes Sawyer*, pp. 25–40. Eds Ian Wood and Niels Lund. Woodbridge.

—— 1944. '*Quadripartitus*'. *Law and Government in Medieval England and Normandy: Essays in Honour of Sir James Holt*, pp. 111–47. Eds George Garnett and John Hudson. Cambridge.

—— 1995. '"Inter cetera bona . . . genti suae": Law-Making and Peace-keeping in the Earliest English Kingdoms'. *Settimane di studiio del centro italiano di studi sull'alto medioevo* 42: 963–93.

Yorke, B. A. E. 1983. 'Joint Kingship in Kent c.560 to 785'. *Archæologia Cantiana* 99: 1–19.

11
Scientific and Medical Writings
Stephanie Hollis

Computistica and Scientific Writings

When Theodore arrived in England in 669, Bede reports, he taught the art of metre, astronomy and 'arithmeticae ecclesiasticae disciplinam' (Colgrave and Mynors 1969: 332), that is, 'the study of ecclesiastical arithmetic', usually known as *computus*, a term which is applied both to the study of time-reckoning and to texts relating to that study. Inevitably, the production of tables that accurately predicted the date of Easter and other moveable feasts in any given year of the Julian calendar was the practical focus of early medieval computus. As the timing of Easter is determined by reference to the luni-solar cycles, study of astronomy was fundamental to computus. Aldhelm, one of the first Anglo-Saxons to study at the Canterbury school established by Theodore and Hadrian, wrote to his bishop in Wessex of the 'intense disputation of computation' at the Canterbury school, of the 'profound study' of 'the circle of the twelve signs [the Zodiac] that rotates at the peak of heaven', as well as 'the complex reckoning of the horoscope', by which he presumably meant a sun-dial or some kind of tabulated data (Lapidge and Herren 1979: 152).

Subsequently, some time before Aldhelm became bishop of Sherborne *c*.706, he produced his own table for calculating Easter. The 'Cyclus Aldhelmi', based on a lunar period of twenty-nine and a half days, survives in six manuscripts dating from the ninth to the twelfth centuries. Like many early medieval tables, the 'Cyclus Aldhelmi' employed a lunar period derived from data which only co-ordinated the appearance of sun and moon (synodical time). Bede's major scientific achievement was to recognize that tables based on synodical time were less accurate than those employing a lunar period of twenty-seven days and eight hours, based on data which co-ordinated the appearance of sun and moon with reference to the position of the stars (sidereal time). He also developed a scientific theory of tides (Stevens 1995a, 1995b).

The Easter controversy at the synod of Whitby in 664, as is well known, resulted in a victory for the Roman faction led by Wilfrid, who appears to have been familiar with the Victurian system based on the Alexandrian nineteen-year cycle, over Coleman and his followers, who were using an eighty-four-year cycle attributed to Anatolius, brought from Iona by Aidan. Nor were practices uniform within either the Celtic or the Roman church. Stimulated by this state of affairs, and presumably by contact with the teachings of Theodore, Northumbrian computus was so far advanced by *c*.706 that Bede's teacher Ceolfrith could boast of a multitude of mathematicians, some of whom were able to continue the Easter cycles 'so that the succession of the sun, the moon, the month and the week returns in the same order as before' (Colgrave and Mynors 1969: 547).

Bede's two earliest scientific works, *De natura rerum, c*.701, and *De temporibus, c*.703, were both written as schoolbooks (Jones 1943, 1975). *De natura rerum* gives particular attention to matters which have bearing on time-reckoning, but as its title suggests ('On the Nature of Things'), it is an account of cosmology and natural phenomena, an introduction to the scientific context in which serious computistical study could take place. *De natura rerum* draws chiefly on a work of the same name by Isidore, as well as on Pliny's *Historia naturalis*, books II and VII, but incorporates information from a number of other sources (DiPilla 1992). Bede's *De temporum ratione* (Jones 1943), *c*.725, is a more sophisticated work, the product of long study and empirical observation aided by the sun-dial that Bede constructed at Jarrow (Stevens 1995a). In this work, he offered his own calendar table ('pagina regularum'), accompanied by an explanation of sidereal time. Bede's 'pagina regularum' was much copied over the next four centuries, often without its accompanying explanation. Although Bede recognized its inadequacies and invited others to improve upon it, no significant advance in the study of sidereal time, and hence the accuracy of Bede's table, was made until the time of Abbo of Fleury, who took temporary refuge in England *c*.985 (Stevens 1995b).

Although Bede's *De natura rerum*, together with Isidore's work of the same name, was the basis of elementary scientific instruction throughout the Anglo-Saxon period, no pre-Conquest copy of any of Bede's scientific works survives in England (Stevens 1995b: 133). The computistical sources used by Bede at Jarrow, however, survive in an eleventh-century copy, probably of Vendôme provenance, Oxford, Bodleian Library, Bodley 309 (Jones 1943: 105–13). Bede was fortunate in possessing a library based upon the cartloads of books Biscop Benedict brought from Rome. Bodley 309 includes Spanish and African computistical texts which reached him from Ireland.

Some forty-five computus manuscripts written in England before 1200 have been identified to date, which include sixty-two independent *computi* (Stevens 1995b: 143). The majority of these, as is to be expected, date from the eleventh and twelfth centuries. Of particular interest for the Alfredian period is Oxford, Bodleian Library, Digby 63. The opening folios were copied *c*.867 by a Frankish scribe, Raegenbold, who brought them with him to England, but the remainder of the manuscript appears to represent texts which were circulating in England at the time. Digby 63 contains some of the Spanish and African computistical texts found in Bodley 309, as well as a sidereal table. The manuscript was in use at Winchester *c*.1000. Rabanus Maurus' *De computo*, however, composed at Fulda *c*.820, and well known in Carolingian schools, did not explain the difference between synodical and sidereal lunar months; the earliest English copy of Rabanus' work is found in an Exeter manuscript (Exeter, Cathedral Library 3507), written *c*.960–86; it also contains Isidore's *De natura rerum*, a collection of computistical verses and geographical texts of interest for scientific study (Stevens 1995b: 134–6).

The arrival of Abbo of Fleury *c*.985 brought the monastic school at Ramsey, where he taught for two years, into contact with one of the leading scholars of the time. In the eleventh century, another visiting scholar, Gerland, taught for twenty years in England, and wrote his *Computus Bedam imitantis* there before leaving for Besançon in 1057 (Stevens 1995b: 140). Abbo is presumed to have brought many books to England when he fled from Fleury, but the only one which was certainly transmitted by him was his edited version of Helperic's *De computo ecclesiastico* (dated before 903), of which there are several English copies (McGurk 1974). Between 988 and 996, Abbo's pupil, Byrhtferth of Ramsey, assembled a collection of Latin computistical texts, which formed the basis for his *Enchiridion*, a vernacular instruction manual probably completed in 1013. Byrhtferth's Latin computus survives in Oxford, St John's College 17, an early twelfth-century copy made at Thorney (Baker 1981); less complete copies are found in two other later manuscripts. Byrhtferth's *Enchiridion* is primarily a commentary on three texts, Bede's *De temporum ratione*, Rabanus' *De computo* and Hilperic's *De computo ecclesiastico*. The *Enchiridion* also draws on Bede's *De natura rerum*, and Isidore's work of the same name, as well as some minor computistical sources (Baker and Lapidge 1995: lxxxvi–xciv).

Byrhtferth also drew on a short vernacular treatise by Ælfric, *De temporibus anni* (Henel 1942), completed at Cerne Abbas, *c*.995. It draws principally on Bede's *De natura rerum*, and perhaps also on Bede's two tracts on time and Isidore's *De natura rerum*. *De temporibus anni* is a brief introduction to cosmology, intended for interested laymen and for priests, who were required, before ordination, to satisfy an examining bishop of their practical working knowledge of the liturgical calendar. *De temporibus anni* deals in part with matters of immediate concern to priests, such as the calculation of Easter and other moveable feasts, divisions of time and information about the beginning of the year. Interwoven with this are 'scientific' accounts of natural phenomena such as thunder and lightning, and the whole is given a moral and theological perspective by an opening account of the creation of the world and occasional references to religious symbolism (Godden 1983).

Byrhtferth's *Enchiridion* is an instruction manual for priests and monastic oblates; it is primarily a work on computus, giving specific and detailed instruction on time-reckoning and the divisions of time as well as the practical knowledge required of priests. It also contains a section on rhetoric, and concludes with a section on number symbolism and the six Ages of the World. This, like the treatment of weights and measures, reflects the tendency of computus to attract all aspects of knowledge, particularly those involving number and measurement (Borst 1993: 6–41). The underlying conception of knowledge the *Enchiridion* reflects is best expressed by Byrhtferth's opening affirmation that God at the creation arranged 'all things in measure, and number and weight' (Baker and Lapidge 1995: 7), and in his 'diagram of the four-fours', which originally figured in the *Enchiridion*, but is preserved only in St John's College 17 and a related manuscript (Singer and Singer 1917–19). The diagram embodies the relationship of microcosm and macrocosm, connecting *inter alia* the four humours of the human body to the four elements.

The gulf between Bede's Latin schoolbooks and the vernacular treatises of Ælfric and Byrhtferth has been taken as symptomatic of a general decline in the scholarship of the late Anglo-Saxon period. But whereas Bede wrote for men eager to join him at the cutting edge of scientific advance, the vernacular treatises of Ælfric and Byrhtferth reflect a reform movement aimed at raising the level of education among the laity and parish priests. Neither *De temporibus anni* nor the *Enchiridion* refers to sidereal time, but the extent of Byrhtferth's actual knowledge is evinced by St John's College 17.

There are few signs that Byrhtferth's *Enchiridion* was known outside Ramsey, but vernacular study of computus is reflected in the appearance of Old English notes on practical information relating to the use of the liturgical calendar (Henely 1934). Typically these notes relate to epacts, concurrents, ferial regulars and rules for finding moveable feasts. Five of the manuscripts containing Old English computus notes also contain all or part of Ælfric's *De temporibus anni*. In a number of manuscripts, computus notes occur in combination with notes on biblical persons and events of numerical significance, such as the Ages of the World and the age of the Virgin; such matters, as Byrhtferth's *Enchiridion* shows, were closely associated with computus (Hollis and Wright 1992: 185–90, 60–1).

Substantial clusters of Old English computus notes are found in five different manuscripts dating from the eleventh century. Three of these are liturgical books, all associated with Winchester (Ker, *Catalogue*). In these books (Ælfwine's Prayerbook, the Vitellius Psalter and the Red-book of Darley), the computus and related notes are attached, as we would expect, to a calendar. In London, British Library, Caligula A. xv, they form part of a vernacular miscellany headed by tables for the year and annals of Christ Church, Canterbury. London, British Library, Harley 3271, however, has more of the appearance of a manuscript used in a monastic school, since the computus notes follow a copy of Ælfric's *Colloquy*. More strikingly, in all five manuscripts, the Old English computus and related notes are preserved with a wide variety of vernacular prognostic texts; in Ælfwine's Prayerbook, the prognostics, like the computus and related notes, are mostly in Latin. Another manuscript, London, British Library, Tiberius A. iii, which like Caligula A. xv probably originated at Christ Church, Canterbury, contains only two Old English notes on computus, but computus-related notes are found in combination with a large number of prognostic texts. In two mid-twelfth-century manuscripts, London, British Library, Vespasian D. xiv, and Oxford, Bodleian Library, Hatton 115, prognostics are preserved with vernacular homilies. Old English prognostics also appear in another eleventh-century liturgical book, from Worcester, the so-called 'Portiforium of St Wulfstan' (Cockayne 1965: 3.144–6, 150–214).

Many of the prognostic texts found in these manuscripts are based on the lunar month. They include medical prognostics, which predict the chances of recovery from an illness depending on the time when it was contracted, as well as nativity prognostics, which predict the character and fortunes of a child according to the age of the moon at the time of birth. Other sets of prognostics list propitious days for particular activities according to the day of the lunar moon or the day of the week in which the new moon appears. Some employ thunder as an omen, predicting events according to the time it was heard or its compass direction. Others make predictions for the year ahead based on the occurrence of wind and sunshine on the first twelve days after Christmas; others again base predictions on the day of the week midwinter mass is celebrated, or on the day of the week that the kalend of January falls. There are also 'Dreambooks', some quite lengthy, which interpret dream images as portents of future events; in some versions, the phase of the moon at the time of the dream is regarded as critical to the outcome. Tables of lucky and unlucky days also occur. There are tables of propitious birth days, inauspicious days for blood-letting, and also a table of twenty-four unlucky days in the year (Hollis and Wright 1992: 257–69).

The appearance of prognostic texts in conjunction with computus notes runs parallel to the inclusion of magical cures employing popular and pagan beliefs in Anglo-Saxon medical literature (see below). The prognostic texts represent, in effect, a popular or 'superstitious' analogue to computus study, since they employ time-keeping and the observation of natural phenomena as a means to predict the future. All forms of divination, however, were condemned by orthodox writers and prohibited by canon law, on the grounds that it contravened both the Christian doctrine of human free will and the doctrine of divine providence, and was contrary to the exercise of faith. Divination was also deeply embedded in pagan beliefs. In his *De temporibus anni*, Ælfric particularly condemns pagan beliefs and practices relating to the moon, and his explanations of natural phenomena offer a rationalist or 'scientific' means of combating such beliefs. Elsewhere, he condemns the belief that days are inherently propitious or not , as well as a whole range of divinatory practices, which, Audrey Meaney (1984, 1985) argues, are not merely echoed from patristic condemnations, but represent customs actually practised in late Anglo-Saxon England.

The preservation of popular superstitions in late Anglo-Saxon manuscripts has been regarded as one of the signs that the intellectual standards of monasteries were in a state of decline on the eve of the Conquest. More recently, Valerie Flint (1991: 301–28) has connected the appearance of such material with the monasteries' increasing involvement in pastoral ministry in the late Anglo-Saxon period. She regards it as a reflection of a willingness on the part of some reformist churchmen, particularly those actively engaged in ministering to the laity, to accommodate popular and pagan practices; to some, it appeared wiser either to assimilate pagan practices to a Christian framework, or to provide acceptable alternatives modelled on them, than to attempt the task of eradicating all of the beliefs and customs that the strictly orthodox condemned.

The manuscripts containing prognostics can plausibly be connected either with pastoral ministry (the liturgical books and the two twelfth-century manuscripts containing vernacular homilies) or with the education of priests (Harley 3271, Caligula A. xv and Tiberius A. iii). Most of the prognostic texts relate to belief in 'the magic of the heavens', which Flint regards as the most easily accommodated, and they are more closely adjacent to the legitimate observation of natural phenomena by farmers and sailors which Augustine distinguished from prohibited practices than is, for instance, the employment of birds' cries as auguries. Lunar medical prognosis, relatively speaking, was innocuous; the moon was understood to exert a powerful effect, and the ultimately Greek belief in the body as a microcosm of the universe, enshrined in Byrhtferth's 'diagram of the four-fours', enabled Isidore to advocate consideration of the phases of the moon in medical diagnosis. Belief in divinatory dreams, though more problematic, could also be legitimated. Lot-casting, however, represented by the alphabet divination in Ælfwine's Prayerbook, appears to have been more seriously condemned (Flint 1991: 87–172, 217–26).

Unlike Anglo-Saxon medical literature, then, which accommodates at least some identifiably pagan Germanic customs among its popular elements, Anglo-Saxon divinatory impulses and lunar beliefs appear to have been catered for by the substitution of popular beliefs of classical origin. In the last resort, presumably, even the alphabet divination in Ælfwine's Prayerbook (Günzel 1993: 121), which was at least based on a written Latin source, was preferable to the use of rune-sticks. But although the vernacular prognostic texts undoubtedly derive ultimately from Latin sources, the exact sources have in many cases not been identified, and further study of these surprisingly neglected texts might reveal instances of a more direct accommodation of Germanic beliefs (Hollis and Wright 1992: 261–2). The means used by priests actually ministering to the laity can scarcely have been acceptable to an orthodox educator like Ælfric, and are in marked contrast to the rationalist means he employs in *De temporibus anni*, conceivably preserved in some manuscripts containing prognostics as an example of ecclesiastical best practice. But the fact that a number of prognostic texts found in more than one manuscript appear to derive from a common source, as do the duplicated clusters of computus notes (Henel 1934: 66–70), suggests that material was disseminated from a single monastic centre concerned to equip priests for the task of ministering to the laity.

Abbo may have introduced to England the *quadrivium* which had been part of the Carolingian curriculum since the ninth century, consisting of geometry, arithmetic, astronomy and musical theory, for which the basic texts were Boethius' *De consolatione Philosophiae*, Martianus Capella's *De nuptiis philologiae et Mercurii*, Macrobius' commentary on Cicero's *Somnium Scipionis* and Calcidius' commentary on Plato's *Timaeus*. Of these, Alfred and the scholars who assisted his educational revival translated only Boethius; copies of the three other elementary texts begin to make an appearance in eleventh-century manuscripts. It therefore appears that the *quadrivium* was not taught in England until the late tenth century and then only fitfully (Baker and Lapidge 1995: lxxxiv–vi). There are, however, some seventy pre-twelfth-century English manuscripts whose contents pertain to study that may be described loosely as 'scientific' (Stevens 1995b: 134).

Of particular interest is London, British Library, Tiberius B. v, dated *c.*1050, a predominantly Latin manuscript with some Old English entries; it includes material originating at Glastonbury, but was probably produced at Christ Church, Canterbury. Its lavish illustrations include three picture cycles, as well as a zonal map and a *mappa mundi*. Its generally secular character has been remarked upon; it may be a presentation copy designed for a lay patron, but nothing is known of the motive of its production. An attempt has been made (McGurk et al. 1983: 107–9) to categorize its contents as scientific (comprising computus notes, Ælfric's *De temporibus anni*, and the *Aratea*), historical (genealogies and lists of bishops, kings, etc.), geographical (the Old English translation of *Marvels of the East*, with accompanying Latin, the account of Sigeric's journey to Rome, the stations at Rome and Priscian's translation of *Periegesis*) and ecclesiastical (the calendar and the lost *De laude crucis* of Rabanus Maurus). But the essential feature of Tiberius B. v is that it is not conceived in terms of the categories known either to the modern scholar or to the medieval student of the *quadrivium*. It is a celebration of knowledge as conceived by students of computus, whose encyclopaedic tendencies are embryonically discernible, in very different ways, in *De temporibus anni* and Byrhtferth's *Enchiridion*; embedded in the study of the cosmos, computus could embrace all forms of knowledge (Wallis 1995). Tiberius B. v is a graphic representation of the continued dominance of a curriculum defined by computus. Like Alfred's educational revival, Tiberius B. v may be short on hard science, but demonstrates a wealth of eclectic curiosity.

Medical Writtings

A substantial corpus of vernacular medical literature survives from the Anglo-Saxon period, including three major collections of remedies, *Bald's Leechbook*, *Leechbook III* and *Lacnunga* (Cockayne 1965). All of it, with the exception of a single fragment, is preserved in manuscripts dating from the mid-tenth century onwards. But it derives from a long tradition of study and translation of classical literature, which may have originated with Archbishop Theodore. It also preserves, in largely indefinable ways, healing practices and knowledge current before the arrival of Theodore in 669.

No medical work belonging to Theodore has been positively identified, but confirmation is beginning to emerge in support of the long-standing supposition that medical works, possibly in Greek, were among the books that he brought to England (Stevenson 1995: 47–55). Bede does not mention medicine among the subjects taught by Theodore at the school he and Hadrian established at Canterbury, but Aldhelm, who was educated there, twice includes *medicina* when he lists the *fisicae artes* (Lapidge and Herren 1979: 42, 96), and a few of his *Aenigmata* show signs of acquaintance with classical medicine (Cameron 1993: 25–6), although this could reflect the influence of the Irishmen who were his first teachers. Theodore's own knowledge of medicine, presumably acquired at Constantinople, is reflected in exegetical commentaries which include discussion of fever and the relation of lunacy to phases of the moon. As these commentaries suggest, Anglo-Saxons who studied the scriptures must have developed very early on some understanding of classical diagnosis of diseases and their vernacular equivalents. Bede, in his commentary on Acts of the Apostles, quotes from Cassius Felix's *De medicina* to explain a reference to dysentery. Classical medical theory related to computus, particularly the doctrine of the humours and lunar influence on the human body, was also introduced at an early stage, as is shown by Bede's report of John of Beverley rebuking the nuns of Watton for undertaking phlebotomy at a time contrary to Theodore's teaching on the correct time of the lunar month (Colgrave and Mynors 1969: 460). In his discussion of the four humours in *De temporum ratione*, Bede quotes from two other identifiable medical works (Cameron 1993: 28).

Some of the *medici* referred to in early Northumbrian sources can be assumed to have gained acquaintance with classical medicine through men taught by Theodore. Several of the *medici* referred to in Bede's *Historia ecclesiastica* are associated with John of Beverley. From *c.*690, if not before, there were skilled *medici* at Lindisfarne, according to the earliest Life of Cuthbert (Colgrave 1985: 136), and their presence may account for the Lindisfarne author's occasional use of Latin medical terms. Bede, too, appears to have been familiar with a class of Latin-educated *medici*. He refers, for instance, to 'a disease which *medici* call dysentery' (Colgrave 1985: 182), and his occasional descriptions of medical practice suggest men trained in the classical tradition; he relates, for instance, how the *medici* at Lindisfarne treated a tumour by applying a poultice and the disagreement among them on the advisability of resorting to surgery (Colgrave and Mynors 1969: 448).

Not all of the medical knowledge and practice attested in early Northumbrian sources, however, is traceable to Theodore; the nuns at Watton, for instance, evidently had some knowledge of phlebotomy, almost certainly of Irish origin, and the *medici* located at Bedesfeld *c.*685 are likely to have been Celtic (Colgrave 1985: 254). The influence of Irish learning, pervasive in the West Country as well as in Northumbria, is less easy to detect in Old English medical compilations than are popular beliefs of Celtic origin (Bonser 1926), but may be assumed to have been transmitted along with the Irish incantations (generally very corrupt), including one described in *Bald's Leechbook* (Cockayne 1965: 2.10) as *scyttisce* (Scottish) (Meroney 1945–6). Archaeological evidence of successful trepanation in fifth- and sixth-century East Anglia suggests the lingering influence of Romano-British practices (Parker 1989). Anglo-Saxon settlers brought with them their own medical traditions; the schedules of compensation for injury in the two earliest Kentish law-codes, like early Frankish and Burgundian codes, evince a degree of anatomical knowledge, and assume the availability of treatment for injuries (Liebermann 1960: 1.5–7, 9).

Anglo-Saxon study of classical medicine is documented in a letter from Cyneheard, bishop of Winchester, to the Anglo-Saxon missionary Lull at Mainz in 754.

Cyneheard asked Lull to keep him in mind if he acquired any books on the 'secular science' of medicine. 'We have some medical books', he explained, 'but the foreign ingredients we find prescribed in them are unknown to us and difficult to obtain' (Tangl 1995: 247). Cyneheard's letter reveals the underlying basis of Winchester's later development as an important medical centre – the early availability of both medical books and the Mediterranean plants they prescribed, which missionaries on the continent obtained from Rome; others were brought to England by pilgrims to Rome and the Holy Land (Voigts 1979). But over a decade before Cyneheard wrote, ingredients used in classical medicine had already been sent by Lull to Latin-educated abbesses in England (Tangl 1955: 80, 143). The Anglo-Saxons in contact with the mission were principally located in Wessex and on the Mercian border. The female communities of double monasteries in Wessex and neighbouring Mercia may therefore have contributed to the sources drawn on by *Bald's Leechbook*, as well those underlying *Lacnunga*, which has a more evident connection with early double monasteries.

Bald's Leechbook and *Leechbook III* are found in a handsome mid-tenth-century manuscript, London, British Library, Royal 12 D. xvii (Wright 1955). The manuscript was written by a single scribe, presumably at Winchester (Old Minster), since the Parker annals for 925–55 are in the same hand (Ker, *Catalogue*). *Lacnunga* is preserved in London, British Library, Harley 585, together with an Old English translation of a sixth-century Latin medical compilation known as the *Herbarium* of Pseudo-Apuleius. Harley 585 is a late tenth- or more probably early eleventh-century manuscript. Early medical historians made much of the 'superstitious' and 'decadent' character of *Lacnunga*; it is therefore noteworthy that it is preserved in the same manuscript as a 'respectable' classical work, and that both texts, except for the last few folios of *Lacnunga*, were written by the same scribe. The provenance of Harley 585 is unknown; the style of some decorated capitals suggests that it originated at a centre influenced by Winchester (Doane 1994).

Two other translations of the *Herbarium* are found in eleventh-century manuscripts, Oxford, Bodleian, Hatton 76, and London, British Library, Cotton Vitellius C. iii. Hatton 76 was at Worcester from at least the thirteenth century. Vitellius C. iii is a presentation copy (D'Aronco and Cameron 1998); the text is accompanied by coloured illustrations of the plants and animals whose medical uses are described, and it is preceded by a dedication page and a full-page illustration which announces the work's classical-pagan associations, since it depicts Apuleius receiving a book from Aesculapius, the god of medicine, and his mentor Chiron the Centaur (Voigts 1977, 1978). The style of the illustrations suggests that it was copied at one of the East Anglian monasteries, such as Peterborough or Ely (Voigts 1976). Spaces have been left for illustrations in Hatton; their omission from Harley 585 is in keeping with the functional character of the manuscript, which, however, does contain a few zoomorphic and other drawings.

Other vernacular medical literature is found in a number of manuscripts, all but one dating from the eleventh and twelfth centuries (Hollis and Wright 1992: 230–70). Two groups of remedies, which may be fragmentary survivals of more substantial compilations, have close parallels with *Bald's Leechbook*, but do not derive from it (Meaney 1984a). A collection of some fifty remedies, tending to group by topic, survives only in Laurence Nowell's mid-sixteenth-century transcript. The collection was copied in the early eleventh century by a Winchester scribe, but it may have originated in Mercia (Torkar 1976). The Omont Fragment, consisting of a single leaf, contains a group of eleven remedies, eight for feet, thighs and loins, and three for paralysis, written on the recto on specially ruled lines (Schauman and Cameron 1977). This fragment, which came to light only in the 1970s, is the earliest surviving copy of Old English remedies. It was dated to the second half of the ninth century by its editors, but to the early tenth century by Ker (*Catalogue*). It too probably originated in Mercia. Six groups of remedies and diagnostic material relating to the 'half-dead disease', found in London, British Library, Harley 55, correspond to one of the chapters which are now missing from *Bald's Leechbook*, owing to the loss of a quire, but which are described in a table of contents accompanying the work (Cockayne 1965: 2.280–8). Harley 55 was probably copied directly from Royal 12 D. xvii. It is a fragment of an eleventh-century manuscript belonging to Archbishop Wulfstan (d. 1023), whose handwriting appears in annotations to one of the two legal items which flank the chapter on the 'half-dead disease' (Ker, *Catalogue*).

Some manuscripts associated with pastoral ministry, referred to above in the description of computistica, contain lunar medical prognostics and blood-letting tables, as well as other entries related to medical practice, chiefly popular cures and liturgical healing formulas (commonly classified as 'charms'). Of these manuscripts, Ælfwine's Prayerbook contains a single vernacular remedy of the classical type (commonly termed 'recipes') (Günzel 1993: 157). In the Vitellius Psalter (London, British Library, Cotton Vitellius E. xviii), a cluster of charms relating to bees, crops and the recovery of livestock includes two vernacular recipes for treating diseases in cattle and sheep (Cockayne 1965: 388). The manuscript also contains the *Sphera Apulei* (or 'Sphere of Pythagoras'), a circular diagram employed in medical prognosis. The vernacular prognostics in London, British Library, Cotton Tiberius A. iii, include 'Omens on Pregnancy', as well as a short account of the development of the human foetus (Cockayne 1965: 3.144–6) ultimately derived from Hippocrates (Talbot 1976: 20). Tiberius A. iii also contains the Old English *Lapidary*, which incorporates some information on the medical use of stones (Kitson 1978). In London, British Library, Cotton Caligula A. xv, too, clusters of Old English and Latin healing charms are found among the prognostic texts (Cockayne 1965: 1.384–404, 3.286–90, 294–5).

One other cluster of medical material which may be associated with pastoral ministry is recorded in the margins of Cambridge, Corpus Christi College 41. The marginal additions, probably originating in the Glastonbury area, include a number of Old English and Latin charms for healing, the *Sator Arepo* formula used for childbirth, and a recipe for treating eyes, as well as Old English metrical charms for bees, for safety when journeying and for the recovery of stolen cattle (Grant 1978). Unlike the manuscripts associated with pastoral ministry previously referred to, these marginal additions contain no computistic or prognostic material, but other material with which they are preserved – vernacular homilies and extracts from a missal – suggest that the manuscript copied into the margins of CCCC 41 was used by a priest ministering to the laity. Healing charms in Latin and Old English, and a few vernacular recipes, are found in a dozen or so other manuscripts, mostly as late additions (Hollis and Wright 1992: 234–50). Of these manuscripts only three contain more than a single recipe. The Galba Prayerbook, probably from Nunnaminster at Winchester, includes two recipes from a source drawn on by *Bald's Leechbook* (Muir 1988: 150). The Wellcome Fragment, found in the binding of a volume published in Antwerp in the mid-sixteenth century, records five recipes (Napier 1890). London, British Library, Cotton Faustina A. x, has four recipes, added in two separate groups to a glossed copy of the Rule of Benedict (Cockayne 1965: 3.292).

Bald's Leechbook, as it appears in Royal 12 D. xvii, is evidently a copy, because *Leechbook III* begins without a break on the same page as the concluding colophon from which *Bald's Leechbook* takes its name. (The colophon reads in part: 'Bald owns this book, which he ordered Cild to write: earnestly here I pray all in the name of Christ that no person should take this book from me. Because no treasure is so dear to me as the dear books which the grace of Christ attends.') The exemplar is dated *c*.900 on linguistic grounds (Quirk 1955). *Bald's Leechbook* thus appears to have taken the form in which we have it either shortly before or after the death of King Alfred; an incompletely preserved chapter towards the end of the work, containing remedies for 'inward tenderness', claims to record advice sent to King Alfred by the Patriarch of Jerusalem, whose correspondence with the king is mentioned in Asser's Life of King Alfred. Asser also mentions the presence at Alfred's court of physicians who attempted to cure a mysterious illness suffered by the king (Keynes and Lapidge 1985: 101, 88–9). The presence of trained *medici* among Alfred's advisors is reflected in the compensation-for-injury schedule in his law-code, which shows a marked increase in medical knowledge over earlier law-codes (Liebermann 1960:1.78–88).

Bald's Leechbook is divided into two books, devoted respectively to 'outer' and 'inner' diseases. The two books consist of chapters organized according to topic, and each book is preceded by a table of contents. The first book consists of remedies for specific parts of the body, organized in head-to-toe order, followed by remedies for 'outer' diseases, which, by and large, are associated with the body as a whole rather than a specific part. *Bald's Leechbook* is remarkable for its methodical and highly practical organization. Its organization reflects the influence of classical models, although division into 'outer' and 'inner' diseases is extremely rare (Cameron 1993: 42). The concluding chapters of the first book, however (from Cockayne 1965: 2.148), appear somewhat random, and consist chiefly of single items. In the second book, the section which runs from the chapter on female conditions to the conclusion includes remedies for head and eyes, already covered in the first book, as well as remedies for 'elf-shot', a chapter on the medical uses of agate and one on weights and measures. Owing to the loss of a quire, the chapter on female ailments and some of the remedies described in the table of contents are missing, so that the section in question now begins in the middle of the Patriarch's advice to Alfred (Cockayne 1965: 2.172–4).

A concluding 'miscellaneous' section is characteristic of the classical models the work reflects, but the seeming disorder towards the end of the two books, combined with the appearance of remedies different in kind from those which make up the bulk of the collection, may suggest that *Bald's Leechbook* comprises an original compilation to which later additions were made at the end of each book.

Audrey Meaney's study of the textual relations of Old English remedies reveals the full extent of the organizational feat achieved by the compiler(s) of *Bald's Leechbook*, who drew on a variety of sources, and very probably used a filing system based on small scraps of vellum. Even *before* the reign of Alfred, she concludes, small clusters of remedies, in both Latin and Old English, were already circulating. She deduces that the Nowell transcript remedies were copied by the Winchester scribe from one of the sources drawn on by the compiler of *Bald's Leechbook*. Of the fifty or so remedies contained in the Nowell transcript, all but seven are found in *Bald's Leechbook*, not as a group, but under their appropriate chapter heading. The Omont remedies also derive from one of the sources drawn upon and reorganized by the compiler of *Bald's Leechbook*. The Omont remedies and their parallels in *Bald's Leechbook* appear to derive from a common distant ancestor, which may have been in English. Like the Nowell transcript, the Omont Fragment shows that there was a tendency, from a very early date, for remedies relating to the same topic to be grouped together in small clusters (Meaney 1984a).

Leechbook III reflects, somewhat loosely, the organization of the first of the two books which comprise *Bald's Leechbook*. *Leechbook III* is preceded by a list of chapters describing their contents, but it does not distinguish 'inner' and 'outer' diseases, and the topical division of chapters as well as the head-to-toe ordering is less methodical. The fact that only a very few of its remedies have parallels in *Bald's Leechbook* may suggest that it was originally compiled at another centre. It is conceivable that *Leechbook III* is a later compilation, loosely modelled on *Bald's Leechbook*, and the overall character of the remedies might support that view; but both *Leechbooks* could equally well reflect the currency of classical models of organization. *Lacnunga* has no table of contents; it begins with remedies for specific parts of the body, with some semblance of the head-to-toe ordering, and its remedies throughout tend to group in clusters, but there is no discernible principle of organization, and there are signs of confusion and disarray. *Lacnunga* contains a number of remedies with parallels in *Bald's Leechbook*; these, too, do not derive from *Bald's Leechbook* but from sources drawn upon by that work. It is conceivable that *Lacnunga* did not achieve the precise form in which we have it until it was recorded in Harley 585. The corrupt form of some of *Lacnunga's* material, however, as well as the material it has in common with prayer-books dated to the late eighth or early ninth century, is reason to conclude that *Lacnunga* is drawn substantially from sources much older than the manuscript in which it appears.

The three vernacular compilations represent to differing degrees the assimilation of classical medical literature to Anglo-Saxon beliefs and practices. Classical medicine is found in a relatively undiluted form in *Bald's Leechbook*, particularly in the second book, which contains a high proportion of remedies from identifiable classical sources, interspersed with diagnostic material. Remedies derived from or modelled on classical sources reflect the structure of the classical *receipt* (rubric, indications, prescription and administration), often in a simplified form. They generally involve direct treatment of the body, either by the administration of compounds, salves, poultices and surgery, or by dietary recommendations. The underlying aetiology, explicitly or implicitly, is natural (Meaney 1992). Disease is a disruption in the body's normal state and the body is therefore treated to restore it to that state, or to restore the balance of the humours, a classical theory pervasive in Anglo-Saxon medical literature (Ayoub 1995).

'Popular' practices, more common in *Leechbook III* and *Lacnunga* than in *Bald's Leechbook*, typically do not involve direct treatment of the body; treatment tends to be displaced, sometimes with the evident intention of displacing the symptoms or causes of the ailment. Popular aetiology is supernatural; conditions are attributed to external agents such as elves, dwarfs or demons, and also to human malevolence, although the last is not often explicitly named. Vernacular formulas ('charms') are employed in combination with other practices; some remedies consist solely of a formula to be intoned or written. Six metrical charms, consisting of passages of Old English alliterative verse, some quite long, are found in *Lacnunga*, and one, for water-elf disease, occurs in *Leechbook III*. These charms, much anthologized, have attracted considerable attention because of their pagan allusions and associations, which are particularly a feature of the charm for 'Sudden Stitch' and the 'Nine-Herbs Charm' (Storms 1948: 140–2, 186–90). There is also a strong strain of liturgical healing, which includes prayers and liturgical formulas, both spoken and written, rituals, particularly masses and blessings, and ingredients such as holy water and oil.

Remedies employing only one of these types of healing occur in all of the three major compilations, but many, particularly in *Leechbook III* and *Lacnunga*, combine the characteristics of two or all three types. Popular and liturgical healing practices are particularly closely intertwined, especially, as we might expect, in combating pagan supernatural agents such as elves. Remedies based on the classical model often include holy water in the prescription, and the administration is sometimes accompanied by prayers. Popular practices do occur, though less frequently, in the classical remedies in *Bald's Leechbook*; at least some of these practices derive from classical medical sources. Noticeably, however, liturgical healing practices are not much in evidence in *Bald's Leechbook*, and in the second book are almost entirely confined to the concluding section. *Leechbook III* is considered to be 'the least contaminated by Mediterranean medical ideas' and 'as close as we can get to ancient Northern European medicine' (Cameron 1993: 35). Its remedies are generally shorter and simpler than those of *Bald's Leechbook* and contain fewer imported ingredients, but it could equally well represent a later compilation in which classical sources have been more fully assimilated and are therefore not susceptible to identification.

In *Lacnunga*, we find liturgical healing in an undiluted form. A number of remedies consist purely of Latin prayers or liturgical formulas, distinguished only from conventional prayer by a rubric or instruction defining them as efficacious for specific conditions such as toothache or 'flying venom'. This type of remedy is not character-istic of the *Leechbooks*, but it occurs frequently in manuscripts associated with pastoral activity. *Lacnunga* has material in common with four prayer-books compiled at double monasteries in the West Country in the late eighth or early ninth century (Sims-Williams 1990: 273–327). It includes, for instance, a remedy against poison and a lorica (once attributed to Gildas) also found in the Book of Nunnaminster, and the theme of Christ the *medicus* which dominates the early prayer-books is reflected in *Lac-nunga* in an extraneous quotation from Matthew xi, 28 (Grattan and Singer 1952: 128–46, 188). A prayer for protection against pestilence for 'male and female servants of God' occurs towards the end of *Lacnunga*. A possible explanation for the disorder of *Lacnunga* is that the compiler was selecting relevant material (not always very care-fully) from prayer-books originating at early double monasteries, which may also have contained remedies entered in blank spaces and in the margins.

For early medical historians, particularly Charles Singer, the assimilation of classi-cal learning to popular and liturgical beliefs represented 'a final pathological disinte-gration of the great system of Greek medical thought', and *Lacnunga* typified the low intellectual standard of late Anglo-Saxon monasteries (Grattan and Singer 1952: 94). Subsequent study has shown that a considerable number of the Latin works and Latin epitomes of Greek works which were in use elsewhere in Europe were known to Anglo-Saxons, including Oribasius' *Synopsis* and *Euporistes*, Vindicianus' *Epistula ad Pentadium nepotem* and *Epitome altera*, Marcellus' *De medicamentis*, Alexander of Tralles' *Latin Alexander*, *Passionarius Galeni* and the so-called *Practica Petrocelli* (Cameron 1982), as well as the *Physica Plinii* (Adams and Deegan 1992). Study of the use of classical sources in *Bald's Leechbook* reveals that it is not, as Singer supposed, a record of surgical operations beyond the meagre skills of Anglo-Saxons and preparations exceeding their limited resources, but the work of an experienced physician picking out what he had found useful in his practice (Cameron 1983). Fuller knowledge of classical writings available in Anglo-Saxon England waits upon the identification and dating of Latin medical manuscripts, both in England and on the continent. To date, few Latin medical manuscripts of Anglo-Saxon origin are known to have survived, particularly from the early period, but medical works taken by Anglo-Saxon mis-sionaries to the continent may have included a compilation based on the *Practica Petrocelli* and drawn on by *Bald's Leechbook* (Talbot 1965).

One Latin work that was widely known is the *Herbarium* of Pseudo-Apuleius. It consists of two separate groups of texts; the second of these, called *Medicina de quadru-pedibus*, includes Sextus Placitus' collection of remedies employing animal ingredi-ents. None of the surviving Old English translations, which are all from a common source, can be confidently assigned to a date earlier than the first quarter of the eleventh century. A case has been made, though not a very strong one, that *Medicina de quadrupedibus* was first translated in the eighth century and that this original trans-lation was of Anglian origin (de Vriend 1984: lxviii–lxxix, lxxxii); it is possible that the surviving translations of the *Herbarium* originated in the latter part of the tenth century with a translation made for Bishop Æthelwold (D'Aronco 1994–5). However, remedies derived from the *Herbarium* appear in all three compilations, and these include remedies (whether in Latin or Old English) which were among the sources drawn on by the compiler of *Bald's Leechbook c.*900 (Meaney 1984a: 250). The Galba Prayerbook may testify to the early existence of vernacular remedies adapted from the *Herbarium*, since it preserves two remedies from a source drawn on by *Bald's Leechbook* together with one adapted from *Medicina de quadrupedibus* (Hollis and Wright 1994). The Latin text on which the Old English translations were based was highly unusual in a number of ways, particularly as it included the short or 'A-Text' of Sextus Placitus. Correspondences between the Latin text underlying the Old English translation and a ninth-century continental manuscript (Herten, Westphalia 192), as described before its destruction (Sudhoff 1917), suggest that the distinctive form of the Old English *Herbarium* may be a sign that the work was transmitted to England at a very early date. A number of English copies of the 'standard' text of the Latin *Herbarium* survive; the earliest appears to be London, British Library, Additional 8926, *c.*1000.

As was noted in the above discussion of computistica, Valerie Flint regards the recording in late Anglo-Saxon manuscripts of popular practices prohibited by orthodox churchmen not as Singer did – as evidence of the ill-educated and superstitious ethos of Anglo-Saxon monasteries – but as evidence of the monasteries' increasing involvement with the laity during the Benedictine Reform period. She considers that the vernacular medical codices, as well as manuscripts such as Ælfwine's Prayerbook, the Vitellius Psalter and Tiberius A. iii, reflect the willingness of some reformers to assimilate paganism to a Christian framework, to accommodate or if necessary modify popular practices, rather than to attempt the eradication of everything condemned by the strictly orthodox (Flint 1991: 301–28). Karen Jolly (1996) similarly regards *Lacnunga* and the *Leechbooks* as a reflection of the church's interaction with the laity in the late Anglo-Saxon period, although she rejects Flint's view that the process was overseen by a monastic intelligentsia in favour of a 'grass-roots' development of 'popular religion', mediated by parish priests, who to a high degree shared the world-view of the laity they served.

Bald's Leechbook, however, was already in existence by *c.*900. Its explicit connection with King Alfred has been interpreted in two ways. It has been suggested that *Bald's Leechbook* had a place in the Alfredian programme of educational revival, although it has little in common with the works known to have been translated by Alfred and his associates. It has also been linked to the attempts made by Alfred's physicians to cure the king's mysterious illness, and the attention given to 'inner' diseases in *Bald's Leechbook* appears suggestive in this context (Meaney 1975, 1978). *Lacnunga*, too, and probably *Leechbook III*, draw substantially on earlier sources. In so far as the medical compilations do record remedies formed in the course of the church's interaction with laity, then, they principally record an interaction that pre-dates the Benedictine Reform period; ninth-century monasteries in Wessex and Mercia, as well as Northumbrian monasteries in the age of Bede, faced the same pressures to respond to lay expectations of healing by the accommodation of popular and pagan beliefs.

Undoubtedly, however, Royal 12 D. xvii and Harley 585 were being used as medical codices throughout the period of Benedictine Reform, and for some time after. So too were the translations of the *Herbarium* in Vitellius C. iii and Hatton 76 (Voigts 1979). Later additions to *Lacnunga*, for instance, include a Latin tract on urine and a remedy in French. Royal 12 D. xvii may even have been copied at Winchester in the time of Æthelwold, who replaced the secular canons there with reformed monks shortly after his installation as bishop in 963. Æthelwold evidently encouraged the study of medicine in monasteries, since the books sent by him to Peterborough included one called *Medicinalis* (Lapidge 1994: 118). Orthodox reformers, however, were more likely to promote classical healing practices. Ælfric, educated at Winchester under Æthelwold and active in the lay education programme associated with the Benedictine Reform, would have found much to condemn in Royal 12 D. xvii; he acknowledges a legitimate form of medical treatment involving herbs, but condemns all accompanying practices except prayer (Meaney 1984b). His *De temporibus anni* embodies his own preference for combating paganism by 'scientific' means; Archbishop Wulfstan's possession of a rational account of 'the half-dead disease' from *Bald's Leechbook* points in the same direction. The *Herbarium* in Vitellius C. iii may even be an East Anglian copy of a translation originally made for Æthelwold (D'Aronco 1994–5); if so, the classical-pagan significance of the illustrated title page surely passed him by (Voigts 1977). The fact that there are three eleventh-century copies of the *Herbarium*, but none of Royal 12 D. xvii and *Lacnunga*, may well mean that it commanded a higher degree of orthodox approval. It is also a possible explanation of the preservation of *Bald's Leechbook* with *Leechbook III* in Royal 12 D. xvii, the *Herbarium* with *Lacnunga* in Harley 585, that both manuscripts were designed to cater to both orthodox and popular preferences.

Overridingly, however, Royal 12 D. xvii and Harley 585 have the appearance of books used by professional medical practitioners, not priests ministering to the laity. They are essentially different from the largely vernacular compilations in manuscripts such as the Vitellius Psalter and Tiberius A. iii, where a few remedies, generally of a popular or liturgical kind, are included among material seemingly designed to equip pastors to meet a variety of contingencies encountered in working among the laity. One of the most noticeable characteristics of *Bald's Leechbook* is its professionalism. Its prescriptions, often involving a great deal of time and labour, and its treatments, often calling for lengthy and repeated attention to the patient, as well as specialized equipment, give the impression of a paid practitioner attending upon an extremely wealthy clientele. The high proportion of imported, and therefore expensive, prescription ingredients likewise suggest the possibility that *Bald's Leechbook* was originally compiled for a court physician, perhaps even one of the *medici* who attended King Alfred (Keynes and Lapidge 1985: 88–9).

Although treatments are generally simpler and imported ingredients relatively less frequent in *Leechbook III* and *Lacnunga*, their social penetration is also open to question. The veterinary remedies included in these compilations have been taken to indicate an ethos of rural poverty and unsophistication; but most are for horses, which were in general owned only by wealthy landowners (Liebermann 1960: 1.176), and one of *Lacnunga*'s remedies involves a herd of cattle so large that the owner is instructed to have it valued before paying a tithe to the church (Grattan and Singer 1952: 178). It is conceivable that both Royal 12 D. xvii and Harley 585 were owned by lay physicians, and that some remedies derived from professional laymen (Rubin 1987). Such manuscripts, however, are more likely to have been owned by the Anglo-Saxon counterparts of the professional monastic *medici* of Norman origin, whose presence in England is first recorded in the reign of Edward the Confessor. Documentation relating to Anglo-Saxon physicians is rare in the pre-Conquest period; post-Conquest documentation suggests that the lay/monastic distinction may oversimplify the actual variety of professional *medici* (or 'leeches') who practised in the Anglo-Saxon period. One of the *medici* consulted by Henry I, for instance, was a hermit called Wulfric, who had formerly been an ordained secular priest; he knew French and Latin and owned a library (Kealey 1981: 44).

At least until the transmission of Salernitan and Arab influences to England, Norman *medici* relied upon medical books compiled both before and after the Conquest by Anglo-Saxons (Kealey 1981: 2–6). As noted above, Royal 12 D. xvii and Harley 585 continued to be used and added to throughout the eleventh and twelfth centuries, and so also were the translations of the *Herbarium* in Vitellius C. iii and Hatton 76. But there are few signs that Latin medical literature was being studied throughout the eleventh century. Doubtless much has been lost. London, British Library, Cotton Galba ii and iii, now burnt, contained medical literature in Latin as well as in Old English and Norman French (Ker, *Catalogue*). The Wellcome Fragment is the sole survivor of what was, presumably, a significant amount of Anglo-Saxon material among the medical manuscripts sold in enormous quantities to book-binders in Antwerp following the dissolution of the monasteries (Napier 1890). Other material known to have been lost is a 'Leechbook' (*lece boc*) in the possession of a priest at Bury St Edmunds in the time of Abbot Baldwin, who was one of the Norman physicians of Edward the Confessor; a Latin medical book appears to have been among those taken to the continent shortly after the Conquest by the abbot of Bath (Lapidge 1994: 147, 127).

There are, however, two Latin compilations dating from the early twelfth century which were used and probably assembled by Anglo-Saxons; they contain tracts on blood-letting, diet and the humours as well as recipes. The medical material found in Oxford, St John's College 17, was added at Thorney to a copy of a computistical compilation made in the late tenth century by Abbo of Fleury's pupil, Byrhtferth of Ramsey, and might therefore have been available in England before the Conquest. But Byrhtferth's *Enchiridion* offers no reason to suppose that medical study received any impetus from the arrival of Abbo of Fleury; what little there is of medical import in the *Enchiridion*, apart from the 'diagram of the four-fours', is derived from the discussion of the humours in Bede's computistical writings. The Canterbury Classbook includes texts related to the study of Greek medical terms, which might perhaps have been introduced by Theodore (Cameron 1993: 48–58).

Other evidence of Anglo-Saxon use of post-Conquest Latin manuscripts is found in a copy of the *Herbarium*, from Bury St Edmunds, dated *c.*1100 (Gunther 1925). It contains illustrations of plants labelled in Old English, and a case has been made that the Latin text is based, for the most part, on one of the surviving Old English translations (de Vriend 1972: xlvi–lii). As late as *c.*1200, we find another vernacular version of the *Herbarium*, in London, British Library, MS Harley 6258B; it is based on one of the surviving Old English translations, but has alphabetical ordering. Accompanying this reorganized translation of the *Herbarium* is a vernacular medical treatise in the same hand, entitled *Peri Didaxeon* (Löweneck 1896), which, like *Bald's Leechbook*, is based on *Practica Petrocelli*. The manuscript also contains a group of remedies (headed *De beta*); some of these have parallels in *Bald's Leechbook*, and are seemingly drawn from the same source (Meaney 1984a). Irrespective of whether the language of this manuscript is technically Middle rather than Old English (Hollis and Wright 1992: 315–16, 3227–8), it is an important testimony to the endurance and creative vitality of the Anglo-Saxon medical tradition.

REFERENCES

1 Computistica and scientific writings

Primary sources

Baker, Peter S. and Michael Lapidge, eds and trans. 1995. *Byrhtferth of Ramsey: Enchiridion*. Early English Text Society, s.s. 15. Oxford.

Cockayne, Oswald, ed. 1965. *Leechdoms, Wortcunning and Starcraft in Early England*. 3 vols. Rolls Series 35. London 1864–6. Repr. Wiesbaden. Rev. edn with new intro. Charles Singer. 3 vols. London, 1961.

Colgrave, Bertram and R. A. B. Mynors, eds 1969. *Bede's Ecclesiastical History of the English People*. Oxford Medieval Texts. Oxford.

Günzel, Beate, ed. 1993. *Ælfwine's Prayerbook (London, British Library, Cotton Titus D. xxvi + xxvii)*. Henry Bradshaw Society 108. London.

Henel, Heinrich 1934. *Studien zum altenglischen Computus*. Beiträge zur englischen Philologie 26. Leipzig.

——, ed. 1942. *Ælfric's De Temporibus Anni*. Early English Text Society, o.s. 213. London.

Jones, Charles W., ed. 1943. *Bedae Opera de temporibus*. Medieval Academy of American Publications 41. Cambridge, MA.

——, ed. 1975. *Bedae Venerabilis Opera: Opera Didascalica, 1*. Corpus Christianorum, Series Latina, 123A. Turnhout.

McGurk, P., D. N. Dumville, M. R. Godden and Ann Knock, eds 1983. *An Eleventh Century Anglo-Saxon Illustrated Miscellany: British Library Cotton Tiberius B. V Part I. Together with Leaves from British Library Cotton Nero D. II*. Early English Manuscripts in Facsimile 21. Copenhagen.

Secondary sources

Baker, Peter S. 1981. 'Byrhtferth's *"Enchiridion"* and the Computus in Oxford, St John's College 17'. *Anglo-Saxon England* 10: 123–42.

Borst, Arno 1993. *The Ordering of Time: From the Ancient Computus to the Modern Computer*. Trans. Andrew Winnard. Cambridge and Chicago. First pub. as *Computus: Zeit und Zahl in der Geschichte Europas*. Kleine kulturwissenschaftliche Bibliothek 28. Berlin 1990.

DiPilla, Alessandra 1992. 'Cosmologia e uso delle fonti nel *De natura rerum* di Beda'. *Romanobarbarica* 11: 129–47.

Flint, Valerie I. J. 1991. *The Rise of Magic in Early Medieval Europe*. Princeton, NJ.

Godden, M. R. 1983. 'Ælfric's *De Temporibus Anni*'. *An Eleventh Century Anglo-Saxon Illustrated Miscellany: British Library Cotton Tiberius B. V Part I. Together with Leaves from British Library Cotton Nero D. II*, pp. 59–64. Eds P. McGurk, D. N.

Dumville, M. R. Godden and Ann Knock. Early English Manuscripts in Facsimile 21. Copenhagen.

Hollis, Stephanie and Michael Wright 1992. *Old English Prose of Secular Learning*. Annotated Bibliographies of Old and Middle English Literature 6. Cambridge.

Lapidge, Michael and Michael Herren 1979. *Aldhelm: The Prose Works*. Cambridge and Totowa.

McGurk, P. 1974. 'Computus Helperici: Its Transmission in England in the Eleventh and Twelfth Centuries'. *Medium Ævum* 43: 1–5.

Meaney, Audrey L. 1984. 'Ælfric and Idolatry'. *Journal of Religious History* 13: 119–35.

——1985. 'Ælfric's Use of his Sources in his Homily on Auguries'. *English Studies* 66: 477–95.

Singer, Charles and Dorothea Singer 1917–19. 'A Restoration: Byrhtferð of Ramsey's Diagram of the Physical and Physiological Fours'. *Bodleian Quarterly Record* 2: 47–51.

Stevens, Wesley M. 1995a. *Bede's Scientific Achievement*. The Jarrow Lecture, 1985. Newcastle-upon-Tyne, 1986. Repr. with revisions *Cycles of Time and Scientific Learning in Medieval Europe*. Ed. Wesley M. Stevens. Variorum Collected Studies Series, CS 482. Aldershot and Brookfield.

——1995b. 'Sidereal Time in Anglo-Saxon England'. *Voyage to the Other World: The Legacy of Sutton Hoo*, pp. 125–52. Eds Calvin B. Kendall and Peter S. Wells. Medieval Studies at Minnesota 5. Minneapolis, 1992. Repr. *Cycles of Time and Scientific Learning in Medieval Europe*. Ed. Wesley M. Stevens. Variorum Collected Studies Series, CS 482. Aldershot and Brookfield.

Wallis, Faith 1995. 'Medicine in Medieval Calendar Manuscripts'. *Manuscript Sources of Medieval Medicine: A Book of Essays*, pp. 105–44. Ed. Margaret R. Schleissner. Garland Medieval Casebooks. Garland Reference Library of the Humanities 1576. New York and London.

2   *Medical writings*

Primary sources

Cockayne, Oswald, ed. and trans. 1965. *Leechdoms, Wortcunning and Starcraft of Early England*. 3 vols. Rolls Series 35. London, 1864–6. Repr.

Wiesbaden. Rev. edn with new intro. Charles Singer. 3 vols. London, 1961.

Colgrave, Bertram, ed. and trans. 1985. *Two Lives of Saint Cuthbert*. Cambridge, 1940. Repr. Cambridge.

——and R. A. B. Mynors, eds 1969. *Bede's Ecclesiastical History of the English People*. Oxford Medieval Texts. Oxford.

D'Aronco, Maria Amalia and M. L. Cameron, eds 1998. *The Old English Illustrated Pharmacopoeia: British Library Cotton Vitellius C. III*. Early English Manuscripts in Facsimile 27. Copenhagen.

Grant, Raymond J. S., ed. 1978. *Cambridge, Corpus Christi College 41: The Loricas and the Missal*. Costerus, n.s. 17. Amsterdam.

Grattan, J. H. G. and Charles Singer, eds. 1952. *Anglo-Saxon Magic and Medicine Illustrated Specially from the Semi-Pagan Text 'Lacnunga'*. Publications of the Wellcome Historical Medical Museum, n.s. 3. London, New York and Toronto.

Gunther, Robert T., ed. 1925. *The Herbal of Apuleius Barbarus, From the Early Twelfth-Century Manuscript Formerly in the Abbey of Bury St. Edmunds (MS. Bodley 130)*. Roxburghe Club Publication. Oxford.

Günzel, Beate, ed. 1993. *Ælfwine's Prayerbook (London, British Library, Cotton Titus D. xxvi + xxvii)*. Henry Bradshaw Society 108. London.

Kitson, Peter 1978. 'Lapidary Traditions in Anglo-Saxon England: Part I, the Background; the Old English Lapidary'. *Anglo-Saxon England* 7: 9–60.

Liebermann, F., ed. 1960. *Die Gesetze der Angelsachsen*. 3 vols. Halle, 1903–16. Repr. Aalen.

Löweneck, Max, ed. 1896. *Peri Didaxeon, eine sammlung von rezepten in englischer sprache aus dem 11./12. Jahrhundert*. Erlanger Beiträge zur Englischen Philologie und Vergleichenden Literaturgeschichte 12. Erlangen.

Muir, Bernard James, ed. 1988. *A Pre-Conquest English Prayer-Book (BL MSS Cotton Galba A.xiv and Nero A.ii (ff. 3–13))*. Henry Bradshaw Society 103. Woodbridge and Wolfeboro, NH.

Napier, A. 1890. 'Altenglische Miscellen'. *Archiv für das Studium der neueren Sprachen und Literaturen* 84: 323–7.

Schauman, Bella and Angus Cameron 1977. 'A Newly-found Leaf of Old English from Louvain'. *Anglia* 95: 289–312.

Storms, G., ed. 1948. *Anglo-Saxon Magic*. The Hague.

Tangl, Michael, ed. 1955. *Die Briefe des heiligen Bonifatius und Lullus*. 1st edn Berlin, 1916. Monumenta Germaniae Historica, Epistolae Selectae, 1. 2nd. edn Berlin.

Torkar, Roland 1976. 'Zu den ae. Medizinaltexten in Otho B. XI und Royal 12 D. XVII: Mit einer Edition der Unica (Ker, No. 180 art. 11a–d)'. *Anglia* 94: 319–38.

Vriend, Hubert Jan de, ed. 1972. *The Old English Medicina de Quadrupedibus*. University of Groningen dissertation. Tilburg.

——, ed. 1984. *The Old English Herbarium and Medicina de Quadrupedibus*. Early English Text Society, o.s. 286. London.

Wright, C.E., ed. 1955. *Bald's Leechbook (British Museum Royal Manuscript 12.D.xvii)*. With an appendix by Randolph Quirk. Early English Manuscripts in Facsimile 5. Copenhagen.

Secondary sources

Adams, J. N. and Marilyn Deegan 1992. '*Bald's Leechbook* and the *Physica Plinii*'. *Anglo-Saxon England* 21: 87–114.

Ayoub, Lois 1995. 'Old English *wǣta* and the Medical Theory of the Humours'. *Journal of English and Germanic Philology* 94: 332–46.

Bonser, Wilfrid 1926. 'The Dissimilarity of Ancient Irish Magic from that of the Anglo-Saxons'. *Folklore* 37: 371–88.

Cameron, M. L. 1982. 'The Sources of Medical Knowledge in Anglo-Saxon England'. *Anglo-Saxon England* 11: 135–55.

——1983. '*Bald's Leechbook*: Its Sources and their Use in its Compilation'. *Anglo-Saxon England* 12: 153–82.

——1993. *Anglo-Saxon Medicine*. Cambridge Studies in Anglo-Saxon England 7. Cambridge.

D'Aronco, Maria Amalia 1994–5. 'L'erbario anglosassone, un'ipotesi sulla data della traduzione'. *Romanobarbarica* 13: 325–66.

Doane, A. N. 1994. *Anglo-Saxon Manuscripts in Microfiche Facsimile* 1. Medieval and Renaissance Texts and Studies 136. Binghamton, NY.

Flint, Valerie I. J. 1991. *The Rise of Magic in Early Medieval Europe*. Princeton, NJ.

Hollis, Stephanie and Michael Wright 1992. *Old English Prose of Secular Learning*. Annotated Bibliographies of Old and Middle English 6. Cambridge.

——1994. 'The Remedies in British Library MS Cotton Galba A.xiv, fos 139 and 136r'. *Notes and Queries* n.s. 41: 146–7.

Jolly, Karen Louise 1996. *Popular Religion in Late Saxon England: Elf Charms in Context*. Chapel Hill and London.

Kealey, Edward J. 1981. *Medieval Medicus: A Social History of Anglo-Norman Medicine*. Baltimore.

Keynes, Simon and Michael Lapidge 1985. *Alfred the Great: Asser's Life of King Alfred, and Other Contemporary Sources*. Harmondsworth 1983. Repr. Harmondsworth.

Lapidge, Michael 1994. 'Surviving Booklists from Anglo-Saxon England'. *Learning and Literature in Anglo-Saxon England: Studies Presented to Peter Clemoes on the Occasion of his Sixty-fifth Birthday*, pp. 33–89. Eds Michael Lapidge and Helmut Gneuss. Cambridge 1985. Repr. with corrections *Anglo-Saxon Manuscripts: Basic Readings*, pp. 87–167. Ed. Mary P. Richards. Basic Readings in Anglo-Saxon England: Garland Reference Library of the Humanities 1434. New York and London.

——and Michael Herren 1979. *Aldhelm: The Prose Works*. Cambridge and Totowa.

Meaney, Audrey 1975. 'King Alfred and his Secretariat'. *Parergon* 11: 16–24.

——1978. 'Alfred, the Patriarch and the White Stone'. *AUMLA: Journal of the Australasian Universities Language and Literature Association* 49: 65–79.

——1984a. 'Variant Versions of Old English Medical Remedies and the Compilation of Bald's *Leechbook*'. *Anglo-Saxon England* 13: 235–68.

——1984b. 'Ælfric and Idolatry'. *Journal of Religious History* 13: 119–35.

——1992. 'The Anglo-Saxon View of the Causes of Disease'. *Health, Disease and Healing in Medieval Culture*. Eds Sheila Campbell, Bert Hall and David Klausner. Toronto.

Meroney, Howard 1945–6. 'Irish in the Old English Charms'. *Speculum* 20: 172–82.

Parker, S. J. 1989. 'Skulls, Symbols and Surgery: A Review of the Evidence for Trepanation in Anglo-Saxon England and a Consideration of the Motives behind the Practice'. *Superstition and Popular Medicine in Anglo-Saxon England*, pp. 73–84. Ed. D. G. Scragg. Manchester.

Quirk, Randolph 1955. 'Language of the

Leechbook'. *Bald's Leechbook (British Museum Royal Manuscript 12.D.xvii)*, Appendix [n.p.]. Ed. C. E. Wright. Early English Manuscripts in Facsimile 5. Copenhagen.

Rubin, Stanley 1987. 'The Anglo-Saxon Physician'. *Medicine in Early Medieval England*, pp. 7–15. Eds Marilyn Deegan and D. G. Scragg. Manchester.

Sims-Williams, Patrick 1990. *Religion and Literature in Western England, 600–800*. Cambridge Studies in Anglo-Saxon England 3. Cambridge.

Stevenson, Jane 1995. *The 'Laterculus Malalianus' and the School of Archbishop Theodore*. Cambridge Studies in Anglo-Saxon England 14. Cambridge.

Sudhoff, Karl 1917. 'Codex Medicus Hertensis (Nr. 192)'. *Archiv für Geschichte der Medizin* 10: 265–313.

Talbot, C. H. 1965. 'Some Notes on Anglo-Saxon Medicine'. *Bulletin of Medical History* 9: 156–69.

—— 1967. *Medicine in Medieval England*. Olbourne History of Science Library. London.

Voigts, Linda Ehrsam 1976. 'A New Look at a Manuscript Containing the Old English Translation of the *Herbarium Apulei*'. *Manuscripta* 20: 40–60.

—— 1977. 'One Anglo-Saxon View of the Classical Gods'. *Studies in Iconography* 3: 3–16.

—— 1978. 'The Significance of the Name *Apuleius* to the *Herbarium Apulei*'. *Bulletin of the History of Medicine* 52: 214–27.

—— 1979. 'Anglo-Saxon Plant Remedies and the Anglo-Saxons'. *Isis* 70: 250–68.

12
Prayers, Glosses and Glossaries
Phillip Pulsiano

Prayers

Latin and Old English prayers are found in numerous codices (see appendix), of which five constitute prayer-books for private devotion and meditation: (1) Cambridge, University Library Ll. 1. 10 (Book of Cerne; s. ix; Kuypers 1902); (2) London, British Library, Cotton Galba A. xiv + Nero A. ii, fols 3–13 (s. xi; Muir 1988); (3) London, British Library, Royal 2 A. xx (s. viii; see Birch 1889: 101–13); (4) London, British Library, Harley 2965 (Book of Nunnaminster; s. viii/ix; Birch 1889); (5) London, British Library, Harley 7653 (s. viii/ix), a single quire comprising part of a litany (Lapidge 1991) followed by seven prayers (Warren 1893–5: 2.83–97; Birch 1889: 114–19; Bestul 1986 adds Oxford, Bodleian Library, Seldon Supra 30 [s. viii], which contains two prayers). The early compilations typically begin with lessons from the Gospels, and variously include hymns, excerpts from the psalms (the Book of Cerne contains a breviate Psalter), and occasional charms. The later (and much damaged) Galba/Nero prayer-book does not include lessons, but like Harley 7653 includes litanies (Muir 1988; Lapidge 1991); also, the manuscript contains a calendar and computistical material in addition to its *c*.100 prayers. Ælfwine's Prayerbook (London, British Library, Cotton Titus D. xxvi + xxvii; s xi; Günzel 1993), while it does contain a large number of prayers (including private devotional prayers), stands apart from the other compilations in that it contains a collectar and a number of offices (e.g., of the Trinity, the Cross, the Virgin Mary), in addition to a calendar, computistical texts, prognostics and more, and cannot strictly be classed among prayer-books (see Gneuss 1985; Günzel 1993: 5). Along with the extensive corpus of Latin prayers stand roughly 250 vernacular prayers extant in twenty-three manuscripts written or owned in Anglo-Saxon England, and some thirty manuscripts containing renderings of the Creed and Pater Noster, certainly the two most fundamental and ubiquitous prayers from the period. The contexts within which the vernacular prayers exist include prayer-books, penitentials, pontificals, homily collections, psalters and Bibles (for the

Creeds and Pater Noster), in addition to manuscripts containing Boethius' *De conso-latione Philosophiae*, Ælfric's *Grammar* and *Glossary*, the *Regula Benedicti*, Augustine's *Soliloquia* and medical texts, such as Pseudo-Apuleius' *Herbarium*.

The early prayer-books show no precise contemporary continental analogues, although Irish and continental influence can be traced for many of the prayers. Bishop, in his appendix to Kuypers' (1902) edition of the Book of Cerne, argues also for Spanish influence via Ireland, but as Brown (1996; see Hilgarth 1961, 1962; Dumville 1973) notes such influence may have been transmitted through Gaul. Bestul (1986) argues for the presence of Italian influence through Northumbria. Sources remain unidentified for numerous prayers (Cerne, for example, contains seven prayers found nowhere else). What is clear, of course, is that such prayer-books reflect compilations drawn from a great variety of sources and also show connections among themseves. For example, the famous 'Lorica of Lodgen/Laidcenn' ('Suffragare trinitas [or 'trini-tatis'] unitas uanitatis miserere'), attributed to Laidcenn, an Irish monk of Clonfert-Mulloe, d. 661 (see Herren 1973), is found in CUL Ll. 1. 10, fols 43r–44v, London, British Library, Harley 585, fols 152r–157v, and Harley 2965, fols 38r–40r (the first two with a continuous Old English gloss); CUL Ll. 1. 10 and Royal 2 A. xx have in common 'Sanctam ergo unitatem trinitatis' (fols 40v–41v and 18r–19v, respectively), 'Mecum esto (domine deus) saboath mane cum (re)surrexero intende ad me' (fols 45r–46r and 22rv, and which also occurs in Harley 7653, fols 2v–3r), 'Ambulemus in prosperis huius diei luminis' (fols 46rv and 25r), 'Auxiliatrix esto (in nomine) mihi sancta(e) trinita(ti)s' (fols 60rv and 46r, with variation in the Sacramentary of Echter-nach, *c*.895–8, where it is ascribed to Augustine; Hen 1997: 81), 'In primis obsecro supplex obnixis pr(a)ecibus' (fols 67rv and 17rv) and 'Deus iustitiae te depr(a)ecor' (fols 73r–74r and 47r–49r). Harley 2965 has another seventeen prayers in common with CUL Ll. 1. 10 and Harley 7653 has four (see Kuypers 1902: xxii–xxiii). The later Galba/Nero prayer-book, which has been localized to Winchester during the period 1029 x 1047 (Muir 1988: xv), also contains prayers found in a number of other manuscripts, including the earliest prayer-books. The prayer 'Dominator domine deus omnipotens' (fols 39r–45r) is found, for example, in CUL Ll. 1. 10, fols 52r–53v, Harley 2965, fols 16v–18v, and London, British Library, Cotton Otho A. viii (lost but described by Smith 1696 and Wanley 1705 and containing an Old English gloss); 'Domine iesu christi qui dedisti potestatem apostolis tuis' (fols 28v–36r) is found (twice) in CUL Ll. 1. 10, fols 64r–66r and 82r–83v, and in London, British Library, Arundel 155, fols 184r–185v (Arundel Psalter), where it is glossed in Old English (on relations to Galba, see Muir 1988: xxviii–xxxi; for a broader treatment of rela-tions, see Bestul 1986).

Among vernacular prayers agreements are few. For example, four prayers in London, British Library, Royal 2 B. v (Regius Psalter), are also found in London, British Library, Cotton Tiberius A. iii, and one of these occurs also in Cambridge, Corpus Christi College 391 ('Drihten for þinre þære miclan midheortnesse', pp. 601–3); Tiberius C. i contains a prayer ('ic andette þe drihten ælmihtig god 7 sancta marian', fol. 161rv) found also in CCCC 190. The prayer 'ic andette ælmihtigum gode 7 minum scrifte' occurs in both Tiberius A. iii (fols 55v–56r) and CCCC 201 (pp. 115–17; *Regularis concordia*). Arundel 155 contains a series of prayers to Christ and the Cross at fol. 172rv, glossed in Old English, two of which also occur in Galba A. xiv, fols 111r–113r (Old English only), as part of another sequence of prayers to Christ and the Cross. The same series as in Arundel 155 (fol. 172r/7–172v/19) occurs in the *Regularis concordia* (Latin only; Symons 1953: 43), with the exception of those in Arundel 155 at fol. 172r/17–20 (wanting in Symons' base text) and fol. 172v/15–19; much the same sequence occurs in the same order in CCCC 391, pp. 611–13, although the latter includes additional prayers before and after 'Domine iesu christe gloriossime'. Yet the exact series in the *Regularis concordia* is also found in the Book of Cerne (fols 58v–59r) as part of a series under the rubric 'Oratio sancta ad dominum' (beginning at fol. 57v), and a number of the prayers are found too in a Carolingian prayerbook in Paris, Bibliothèque Nationale, lat. 13388 (Wilmart 1940: 142). Significantly, as Bestul (1986: 115) observes, the series also occurs in the Æthelstan Psalter (Galba A. xviii, fol. 22r), a ninth-century continental work brought to Winchester in the tenth century (the section containing the prayers in the Book of Cerne dates to *c*.820–40). The series of prayers to the Cross is instructive in that it offers a glimpse of the complex relations among prayers and the difficulties of tracing their transmission within England and from the continent while also raising questions about the movement of such prayers into the vernacular.

The use of prayers was not confined to liturgy and private devotion, but also served a function within a broad range of curative formulas and charms. In the entry for St Tibertius in the *Old English Martyrology* (11 August), we read that the saint's belief in God was so perfect that 'if he sang his Creed and Pater Noster over a sick man, he was immediately cured'. The border separating (popular) religion and superstition is at times little more than a veil of gossamer. In both Tiberius A. iii, fol. 59rv, and CCCC 391, pp. 617–18, as a later addition in an originally blank space, there are written nearly identical charms in the form of an invocation to the cross, in Old English and Latin, for protection from an enemy, and providing clear directions on the ritual: 'If you think that the enemy adversely oppresses you, then go to a more fitting place and invoke the cross for protection.' Comprised of invocations to the Cross, *incipits* to psalms and prayers, and punctuated by directions ('stand up then for a little while and sing this psalm . . . and after that this prayer'), the composition reminds us that prayer need not operate within traditionally conceived categories, but can move apart from liturgy and meditation or devotion to effect specific and immediate results within a secular context. In the charm for making a holy salve (Storms 1948: no. 19) five herbs are mixed into butter made from milk of a cow that is of one colour; the names of the four evangelists are inscribed on the stick with which the mixture is to be stirred. As this is done, psalm verses, the Creed, the Pater Noster, a litany, a list of holy names and more are recited, followed by the recitation nine times of some incantatory gibberish, after which the individual must spit and breathe on the mixture. Then follow a number of prayers (in Latin): 'Domine me, rogo te pater, te deprecor fili', which invokes the Trinity to cast out the devil ('Therefore, evil one, know your sentence and give honour to God and go away from the servant of God'); the second prayer ('Domine sancte pater omnipotens aeterne deus') calls upon God the Creator to free the soul of the servant (who would then insert his name into the prayer). The sequence of prayers and petitions continues thus in its invocation of God to drive out evil and cure the individual.

The 'Lorica of Lodgen/Laidcenn', particularly in its second part, certainly pertains to the genres of both prayer and charm. The first part of the prayer calls upon the Trinity, Michael, Gabriel and the orders of angels, the patriarchs and prophets, and all virgins, widows and confessors for defence against enemies and all evil. The second part calls for protection from the darts of demons as it enumerates, in learned and often arcane diction, 119 body parts. The prayer concludes with a petition for protection from disease and pain so that the speaker may reach old age and erase sin with good deeds in anticipation of God's kingdom. There are, however, numerous analogues within the corpus of prayers that employ the enumerative method in the construction of a petition for spiritual and physical protection (see Hughes 1970). The prayer 'Mecum esto (domine deus) saboath' in CUL Ll. 1. 10, Harley 7653 and Royal 2 A. xx calls for protection of the mouth, eyes, feet and hands; the prayer in CUL Ll. 1. 10 entitled 'Confessio sancta penitentis' (fols 40v–48v) includes a confessional catalogue listing, among other items, skin, mouth, tongue, lips, throat, teeth, hair, spit and brain. A catalogue in praise of God (using the formula 'tuus es X') and of sins (using the formula 'peccavi per X') occurs also in CUL Ll. 1. 10, fols 48r–50r. Still another prayer in the same manuscript (fols 54v–56r) is entitled 'Oratio utilis de membra Christi', in which the petitioner details Christ's body parts as he asks for protection, cleansing, mercy and the like. This prayer, while within the enumerative tradition, points as well to the meditative tradition in which Christ's body is dismembered through the language of prayer, creating a new text to be read – the body itself – as a locus for meditation and petition that privileges the body and the petitioner's reading of it.

Prayer also occupied a position of some significance in the literary compositions of the period. Stanley (1956) locates the poem *Resignation* within a broad penitential tradition of confessional prayer, although no direct source can be posited. Bestul (1977) places the poem within the period of monastic revival in the tenth century against the background of private devotional prayers contained in CUL Ll. 1. 10, Royal 2 A. xx, Harley 2965 and Harley 7653, along with prayers treating penitential and confessional themes in the Arundel, Regius and Vespasian Psalters (London, British Library, Cotton Vespasian A. i), the Galba/Nero prayer-book, Tiberius A. iii (which contains the *Regula Benedicti* and the *Regularis concordia*) and the Paris Psalter (Paris, Bibliothèque Nationale, lat. 8824). In a study that treats the invocation of the Trinity in such works as *Judith*, *Christ*, *Juliana*, *Azarias* and the 'Journey Charm', Hill (1981) looks to Celtic Christianity for the origins of the convention and in particular the *loricae*, concluding that Old English writers thoroughly assimilated the trope. And Stanley (1994: 218–43) addresses prayer in *Beowulf*.

Bzdyl (1982) offers a focused study of prayer in Old English narratives, noting, as one would expect, that prayers appear frequently in Ælfric's *Lives of Saints*, in sections of the *Old English Martyrology*, in saints' legends, and in Biblical verse, such as *Genesis*, *Daniel*, *Christ and Satan*, *Andreas*, *Elene*, *Juliana* and *Judith*, but also in secular works, such as *The Battle of Maldon* and *Beowulf*. And when works such as *The Seafarer*, *The Wanderer*, *The Dream of the Rood* and *The Lord's Prayer*, for example, are added to the corpus, it becomes clear that the majority of literary compositions in Old English operate within a religious context to varying degrees, and many incorporate prayers in various forms. Indeed, it becomes a far easier task to segregate those works that are lacking in such associations, such as *The Ruin*, *Durham*, *Waldere*, *Widsith* or *Apollonius of Tyre*, to name a few. In all, the body of literature attests to the pervasiveness of Christian thought, and the search in the literature for reflexes of pre-Christian, pre-Cædmonian, Anglo-Saxon paganism must stand as sharply qualified within a broader, deeply Christian, monastic and aristocratic literary tradition shaped by hundreds of years of nurturing influence.

Glosses and Glossaries

Roughly 225 manuscripts written or owned in Anglo-Saxon England contain vernacular glosses and glossaries, or approaching half the entire corpus of extant manuscripts containing Old English (see Ker, *Catalogue*: Index 1 for the range of glossed texts). When Latin–Latin glosses and glossaries are added to the mix, the number of manuscripts is even more staggering, so pervasive was the practice of glossing and glossary-making during the period. Glosses provide aids to learning vocabulary, parts of speech, syntax, etc., offer interpretation, provide commentary, attest to filiations with earlier authorities, establish a text as within particular traditions of copying, and more. Glosses take on a variety of forms and functions. They may be lexical, particularly, but not exclusively, in supplying synonyms; grammatical, such as indicating case or tense, etc.; syntactical, often through the use of 'paving letters' (see below), overdotting or, more commonly, underdotting; provide interpretation or commentary; and, of course, present straightforward translations (a Latin word glossed by an Anglo-Saxon word, or vice versa) (see Wieland 1985). Texts may be glossed sporadically, partially or continuously; they may be entered in ink or written in 'dry-point' (also called 'scratched' glosses). Typically, glosses are interlined, being written above the lemmata they gloss, although glosses may be written in the margins as well (as is often the case with commentary glosses). Texts may or may not be ruled for glosses. Generally, glosses are written in a smaller hand than the main text (an interesting exception is the gloss to the Cambridge Psalter [Cambridge, University Library, Ff. 1. 23], written in red ink, and the same size as the main hand).

Glossaries, too, have their own terminology. The three types are *glossae collectae*, class glossaries and alphabetical glossaries. *Glossae collectae*, as the term explains, are compilations drawn from one or more source texts and written in the order in which they occur in the source. Class glossaries pertain to various subject fields, as, for example in Brussels, Bibliothèque Royale 1828–30, which contains sections such as 'Nomina uolucrum' ('Names of birds', drawn ultimately from the *Hermeneumata Pseudo-Dositheana*, a Greek–Latin schoolbook composed *c*.AD 200), 'Nomina piscium' ('Names of fish'), 'Nomina herbarum Grece et Latine' ('Names of herbs in Greek and Latin') and the like. Alphabetical glossaries can be written in 'a-order', where items are arranged according to their first letter (as in the Épinal-Erfurt Glossary, Épinal, Bibliothèque Municipale 72 + Erfurt, Stadtbücherei, Amplonianus fol. 42), 'ab-order', where they are arranged according to their first two letters (as in the Harley Glossary, London, British Library, Harley 3376), or, in their later development, abc-order (on the terminology, see Lapidge 1986: 53–4; Gneuss 1990: 19).

Continuously glossed texts are found in just over thirty manuscripts, and include such items as Psalters and canticles (Ker, *Catalogue*: nos 13, 79, 91, 107, 129, 134, 160, 199, 203, 208, 224, 249, 271, 280, 335, 379), Boethius' *De consolatione Philosophiae* (no. 51), the Durham Ritual (no. 106), prayers (nos 135, 280), hymns (nos 160, 208), Gospels (nos 165, 292), *Regula Benedicti* (no. 186), *Regularis concordia* (no. 186), prognostics (no. 186), Ælfric's *Colloquy* (no. 186), Prosper's *Epigrammata* and *Versus ad coniugem* (no. 189), *Liber scintillarum* (no. 256), Isidore's *De miraculis christi* (no. 308), Abbo of St Germain's *Bella Parisiacae urbis* (no. 362), and more. In addition to the continuously glossed texts, others contain large repositories of glosses, most important among them the various manuscripts of Aldhelm's prose *De virginitate*, of which thirteen are glossed. Of these the early eleventh-century manuscript, Brussels, Bibliothèque Royale 1650 (Goosens 1974), with its five strata of glosses, preserves some 5,400 Old English glosses; that in Oxford, Bodleian Library, Digby 146, contains over 5,000, some of which were copied from the Brussels text. (The relationship among the various glossed texts is immensely complex; see Gwara 1993, 1997, 1998; Gretsch 1999a: 132–84.)

Psalter glosses also reflect a complex tradition of relations. The earliest glosses are found in the eighth-century Vespasian Psalter (London, British Library, Cotton Vespasian A. i) and in the Blickling Psalter (red glosses only; New York, The Pierpont Morgan Library, M. 776). Those in Vespasian (which are termed 'A-type' glosses), in turn, are copied from an earlier, lost, exemplar. A-type Vespasian glosses were copied, for example, into the Junius Psalter (Oxford, Bodleian Library, Junius 27). A second main tradition (called 'D-type') is represented by the tenth-century Regius Psalter (London, British Library, Royal 2 B. v); this manuscript provided glosses for a number of other manuscripts, including the Tiberius Psalter (London, British Library, Cotton Tiberius C. vi) and the Salisbury Psalter (Salisbury, Cathedral Library 150), as well as the later glosses in the Blickling Psalter. An independent gloss (although also with relations to the main traditions) is found in the Lambeth Psalter (London, Lambeth Palace 427); and independent glosses can be found too in the twelfth-century Eadwine Psalter (Cambridge, Trinity College, R. 17. 1). (The most comprehensive discussion of gloss relations among the psalters can be found in Sisam and Sisam 1959; see also

Pulsiano 1995. On the Lambeth Psalter, see O'Neill 1991; on the Eadwine Psalter, see Gibson et al. 1992. An exceptional and essential study of, among other subjects, the Regius Psalter gloss and the Aldhelm glosses is Gretsch 1999a.)

For the purposes of providing examples of the different types and functions of glossing, I shall selectively cull from a few manuscripts of the period. Translation glosses are perhaps the most common type when considering an Old English gloss to a Latin text; generally, the gloss is entered as a word-for-word translation. Thus, in the Salisbury Psalter, Psalm 76.2 '[V]oce mea ad dominum clamaui' ('I called out to the Lord with my voice') is glossed 'stefne minre to drihten ic clypude', where normal Old English syntax would yield 'ic clypude to drihten (mid) minre stefne'. Old English texts can also carry a Latin gloss, as in Cambridge, Corpus Christi College 201, p. 87, where an eleven-line section ('Be cinedome') of the *Institutes of Polity* on the eight pillars that sustain a kingdom is partially glossed; for example: 'Soðfætnes 7 modignes 7 rumheortnes 7 rædfæstnes' ('Truth and greatness of soul and generosity and reasonableness'), etc. glossed 'ueritas, patientia, largitas, persuasibilitas', etc.; 'And sixte þæt he godes circan forðige 7 friðige' ('And sixth that he contribute to and protect the church of God'), glossed 'ecclesiam dei adiuuare et defendere'. In London, British Library, Cotton Nero A. i, fol. 71r, the list is presented in Latin and glossed in Old English. A random example of interpretative glossing can be drawn from manuscripts containing Persius' *Satires*. Satire II.64 reads 'Haec sibi corrupto casiam dissoluit oliuo'. In one of the manuscripts, 'haec sibi' is glossed 'scillicet una mulier', indicating that it is the woman who corrupts the flesh just as olive oil is spoiled by mixing it with cinnamon (*casia*); and 'casiam' is itself given an explanatory gloss: 'casia herba aromatica. cassia frutex liquore'. The same manuscript also offers examples of lexical glossing, as then 'pappare' (III.17) is given two alternative verbs, 'manducare' and 'comedere' ('eat, devour').

Syntactical glossing appears variously in the manuscripts. Notable examples are London, British Library, Cotton Tiberius A. iii and the Lambeth Psalter (London, Lambeth Palace 427). Tiberius A. iii makes extensive use of 'paving-letters', that is, letters (a, b, c, d, etc.) written above the lemmata and gloss to indicate order. For example:

```
b        c        d        b      a
se forma        eadmodnesse stape   is
[the first step of humility is]
Primus   itaque humilitatis   gradus est
                (Logeman 1888: 28)
```

The system of construe marks (dots, cedillas, wavy lines, hyphens) in the Lambeth Psalter is far more sophisticated, as this system pertains to both the Latin text and its Old English gloss. Patrick O'Neill (1992), responding to earlier articles by Fred C. Robinson (1973) and Michael Korhammer (1980), provides a number of pointed examples that illustrate the method. At Psalm 75.12 we read:

ealle   ge   ymbhwyrfte; on his þe offriaþ   lac
omnes qui in   circuitu   eius   affertis   munera.
     .   ,   , ...

As O'Neill explains, word-for-word translation makes little sense, since 'ge' cannot gloss 'qui' nor can 'on his' gloss 'eius'. The construe marks here reorder the Old English gloss, yielding 'ealle ge þe offriaþ lac on his ymbhwyrfte' (the semicolon after 'ymbhwyrfte' indicates that this word is the last in the syntactical unit). Glosses can also exist as meregraphs (abbreviated forms), as in Paris, Bibliothèque Nationale, nouv. acq. lat. 586 (see Ker 1957: no. 371, art. b).

It should not be assumed that glossing is simply the art of rote copying of earlier sources. Each new transmission brings accretions, some from other sources, some certainly independent (i.e. scribal). British Library, Royal 5 E. xi, offers an unusual snapshot of a glossator at work. The manuscript, comprising Aldhelm's prose *De virginitate*, contains two leaves, now fols 1 and 120, that evidently formed part of the original contents of the codex, coming after fol. 115. Because of poor preparation of the leaves, combined with slits and tears (later sewn) that disrupted both the aspect and writing of the text, they were excised and relegated to their present position as flyleaves. In their place two new leaves were copied by the same scribe, now standing as fols 116 and 117. Since the same scribe wrote both sets of leaves and within absolute proximity, perhaps even shortly after the quire was completed, we might rightly expect exact duplicates. In fact, while there are many points of agreement, the glosses on these leaves show substantive differences. The lemmata and their glosses are given below, with parentheses used to indicate scratched glosses ('.i' is an abbreviation for 'id est', .s. for 'scillicet'):

	fols 116–117	*fols 1 and 120*
foenus	.i. lucrum	.i. lucrum
fascis	.i. moræ	yldinge
descriptio	ł re	gengewrit
stipulatio		.i. confirmatio
transfretauerint	yn	
minime	s. q*uo*d	s. quod
retatibus	(on)	
itidentidem	(efte)	ædniwan
ac	s. si	s. si
parcarum	gewyrda	gewyrda
tricauerit	gelet	let
exametrorum	(leð)	
uelut	(swylce)	
parietibus	wagu[m]	wagu*m* ('woge' in a later hand)
metrorum	([ ]isse)	
inponam	on	in

sciscitandi	.i. interrogandi	.i. interrogandi
scribendi	(writende)	
totidiem	wel oft	wel oft
lepida	.i. iocunda	
urbanitatis facundia		wom:a gewyrdi ∷ nesse
merebamini	(ge ge)	s. meme[]
opusculi	.i. libri	bec
sarcina	(seame)	
lasescere	.i. fatigare	.i. fatigare
stilum	(boc)	
leporis	.i. iocundantis	iocundantis
disertitudinis	.i. sagacitatis	sagacitatis
eloquentia	.i. urbanitatis	urbanitatis
discrepent	.i. diuidant	diuid[an]t
quantu	s. distast[]	distæt
dulcis [s]apa	.i. ream win	ream win
témeto	wine	win
toracidas	.i. imagines	
liniamenta	.i. simulationis	simulationis
tamen	(þonne)	
opifices		.i. artifices
iconisma	[a]nlicny[s]se seo ss g:g:e	
stemmate	.i. corona	corona
ad	to (late hand)	
litus	warode (late hand)	
adhuc	(nu)	

It can be assumed and demonstrated that the glossator was working from a model. The glosses *moræ, lucrum, confirmatio, quod, gewyrda, interrogandi, gewyrdinesse, iocunda, fatigare, iocundantis, sagacitatis, urbanitatis, diuidant, distæt,* (*ream*) *win, wine, corona,* for example, occur variously in other manuscripts of *De virginitate*: Oxford, Bodleian Library, Digby 146; London, British Library, Royal 6 A. vi and Royal 6 B. vii, for instance. The fact of copying, however, does not exclude the possibility that the individual glossator shaped the gloss. Consider the gloss to *fascis*, which on the replacement leaves is given as *moræ* 'delay' but which is given in Old English on the original leaves: *yldinge*. This type of diglossa appears also in the glosses to *opusculi*, which on the original leaves is given as Old English *bec* 'books' but on the replacement leaves as *libri*. The Old English glosses in these instances do not appear in the other Aldhelm manuscripts, which suggests that the glossator, even as he read his Latin source, purposely or instinctively rendered the glosses into Old English or perhaps selectively drew from his sources. The replacement leaves show a number of scratched glosses, although none appears on the original leaves (given the poor condition and the mesh used in the conservation of the leaves, they might simply not be visible any longer).

Only one of these glosses occurs elsewhere in manuscripts of *De virginitate*: *sarcina*: *seame*. Finally, the syntactical under- and overdotting differs for both leaves. The leaves would thus seem to offer a fortuitous moment in which a scribe is 'caught in the act' of glossing, a process that moved beyond rote copying and which entailed editorial decisions.

Among the numerous glossaries found in Anglo-Saxon manuscripts (see Index A in Ker, *Catalogue*), the most important ones containing Old English are found in: Cambridge, Corpus Christi College 144; Épinal, Bibliothèque Municipale 72, fols 94–107; London, British Library, Cotton Cleopatra A. iii; London, British Library, Cotton Otho E. i; London, British Library, Harley 3376 + Oxford, Bodleian Library, Lat. Misc. a. 3, fol. 49; Erfurt, Stadtbücherei, Amplonianus F. 42; Leiden, Rijksuniversiteit, Vossianus lat. 4° 69; Werden, Pfarrhof + Münster, Universitätsbibliothek, Paulinianus 271 (719) + Munich, Bayerische Staatsbibliothek, Cgm. 187 (e. 4).

Relations among the glossaries are various and complex. The main (or second) glossary in Corpus 144 (s. viii/ix; Hessels 1890; Lindsay 1921) derives, as Ker (1957) states, from a 'fuller version of those in the Épinal and Erfurt manuscripts . . . making greater use of the glossary material and rearranging the material into an AB order' (49). The Épinal-Erfurt glossary derives from a lost archetype of the late seventh century. Pheifer (1974) is more exact in assessing the relationship among these three manuscripts, noting that the Corpus Glossary combines most of the entries from Épinal-Erfurt with roughly an equal amount of new material (xxviii): 'Corpus thus provides what is virtually a third text of the Épinal-Erfurt glossary, and one which derives from the archetype independently of the common exemplar of Épinal and Erfurt' (xxix; for a facsimile of these glossaries see Bischoff et al. 1988). The Cleopatra Glossary (s. x med.; Wright and Wülcker 1884) contains three Old English glossaries: an alphabetical glossary from A to P mainly in a-order (fols 5r–75v; First Cleopatra Glossary, or Cleopatra I), a combined subject and alphabetical glossary (fols 76r–91v; Second Cleopatra Glossary, or Cleopatra II) and an interlinear glossary to Aldhelm's *De virginitate* (fols 92r–117r). Material related to Cleopatra I and II can be found in Épinal-Erfurt; however, the extent of the debt to these and other glossaries cannot fully be assessed until a new edition and full study are published. About two-fifths of the material in Cleopatra can be found in British Library, Harley 3376 + Lat. Misc. a 3, fol. 49 (s. x/xi; Harley Glossary; Oliphant 1966, Old English only). In turn, Brussels, Bibliothèque royale 1828–30 (s. xi in.; Brussels Glossary), in the first three of its subject lists follows Cleopatra II, while the fourth list ('nomina herbarum') is found in Épinal-Erfurt. Otho E i (s. x/xi; Otho Glossary; unedited) closely follows Cleopatra (the manuscript was burnt in the Cotton fire of 1731, but is still largely legible); and the glossary in Bodley 730 (s. xii; Hunt 1981) likewise is related to Cleopatra. A minute sampling from the subject list of bird names from Cleopatra ('De auibus', Wright and Wülcker 1884: 1.260/2–20), Bodley and Brussels, along with (alphabetical) entries in the Corpus and Épinal-Erfurt glossaries, provides some sense of relations:

cucu(rata) : hleapewince Cl (WW 260.2), leopewinke Bo 151, hleapewince Br (curcu-rata, WW 285.11), lepewince Co C951 (cucuzata)

bicoca : hæferblæte Cl (WW 260.3), heuenblete Bo 152 (bicota), haebreblete Co B96, hraebrebletae Ép 124, hebrebletae Er 124

fasianus (fusianua) : worhana Cl (WW 260.4), wirþorn Bo 153, worhanna Br (fursianus, WW 285.13), worhona Co F22, uuorhana Ép 424, uuorhona Er 424 (fassianus)

rusunia : nihtegale Cl (WW 260.5), nitegale Bo 154 (ruscina), nitegala uel achalantida Br (luscinia, WW 285.14), naectegale Co L230 (luscinia), naectegale Co R201 (roscinia), nectaegalae Ép 857 (roscinia), necegle Er 857 (roscinia)

columba : culfre Cl (WW 260.6), culure Bo 155, culfre Br (WW 286.1)

palumba : cusceote Cl (pudumba, WW 260.7), cuiste id est wudeculure Bo 156, columba Co P103, cuscote uel culfre Br (WW 287.2), cuscutan Ép 829 (palumbes)

coruus : hrefn Cl (WW 260.8), hræfn uel corax Br (WW 286.3), hraefn Co C735 (corax), hraebn Er 285 (corax)

cornix : crawe Cl (WW 260.9), crawe Br (WW 286.4), crawe Co C653, crauua Er 308

grallus : hroc Cl (WW 260.10), roc Bo 157, hroc Br [WW 286.6, order is *cornicula*, *grallus*], hrooc Ép-Er 469

cornicula : cio Cl (WW 260.11), schoha Bo 158, cyo uel graula Br (WW 286.5), crauue Co C652 (cornacula), chyae Ép 240, ciae Er 240

beatica : stearn Cl (WW 260.12), Co B61, stern Bo 159 (beattica), tearn Br (WW 286.7), stearno Ép 125, stærn Er 125

sternus : ster Bo 160

mursopicus (marsopicus) : fina Cl (WW 260.13), Co M35, Ép 648, fine Bo 161, pina ER 648 (marpicus)

picus : higere Cl (WW 270.14), hiwere Bo 162, higere uel gagia Br (WW 286.19), higre fina Co P424, fina uel higrae Ép-Er 808

noctua : ule Cl (WW 260.15), hule Bo 163, ule uel strix uel cauanna Br (WW 286.10), ulula, ule Co N138, naechthraebn ali dicunt nectigalae Ép 673, nechthraebn alii dicunt nacthegelae Er 673

ulula : ule Cl (WW 260.16), idem Bo 164 [i.e., hule], ulae Co U238

rubesca : seltra Cl (WW 260.17), spichmase Bo 166, salthaga uel ruddic Br (rubisca, WW 286.11), sealtna Co R256 [order of lemmata in Bo is *parra, rubesca, parrula*; *sigitula* omitted]

fringilla : finc Br (WW 286.12)

sigitula : frecmase Cl (WW 260.18), Co L91 (laudariulus), fæcmase Br (sigatula, WW 286.13)

parra : cummase Cl (WW 260.19), colmase Bo 165, colmase Br (WW 286.14)

par(r)ula : colmasse Cl (WW 260.20), þe lesse blake mase Bo 167, spicmase Br (WW 286.15), mase Co P128, masae Ép-Er 806

One can detect here as well something of the process of editing in Bodley 730, where the copyist sought to distinguish more clearly between *colmase* and *cummase* 'coal tit-mouse' by glossing *parrula* as þe *lesse blake mase* ('the less black mouse') and glossing *parra* as *colmase* rather than *cummase* as in Cleopatra.

Significant for the study of glossaries is the Leiden Glossary (Leiden, Bibliotheek der Rijksuniversiteit, Vossianus Lat. 4° 69). The manuscript is a composite text in six parts; part 2 (fols 7–47), dating from *c.*800 (except for the text on fols 46v–47v, which dates to the end of the ninth century) and written at St Gall, contains a glossary at fols 20r–36r which includes some 255 Old English glosses. The original English collection (see Lindsay 1921b: 2) dates from between *c.*650 and *c.*700 (Lapidge 1986: 55, 58), and was first in England before travelling to the continent (affirmed by the presence of Old English glosses in numerous 'glossae collectae'; see Lapidge 1986: 67–72 for the list of continental 'Leiden family' manuscripts). Michael Lapidge argues that the original collection can be assigned to the school of Theodore (602–90) and Hadrian (d. 709 or 710) in Canterbury, on the basis of the fact that '[a] number of manuscripts of the Leiden family independently assign various explanations of individual words by name to Theodore and Hadrian' (1986: 58). The continental glossaries (most of which remain unprinted) may thus cast light on the books and learning that existed at this early school.

APPENDIX
VERNACULAR PRAYERS AND LATIN PRAYERS WITH VERNACULAR GLOSSES

Not included are versions of the Pater Noster and Creed. These can be found in (a) Cambridge, University Library, Gg. 3. 28 and Ii. 2. 11; (b) Cambridge, Corpus Christi College 140 + 111, pp. 7, 8, 55–6, and MS 201; (c) Cambridge, Trinity College R. 17. 1; (d) Blickling Hall, Norfolk, 6864; (e) London, British Library, Additional 37,517, Arundel 60; Arundel 155, Cleopatra B. xiii, Nero D. iv, Otho C. i, Tiberius A. iii, Tiberius C. i, Vespasian A. i, Vitellius A. xii, Vitellius E. xviii, Harley 863, Royal 1 A. xiv, Royal 2 A. xx, Royal 2 B. v, Stowe 2; (f) London, Lambeth Palace Library 427; (g) Oxford, Bodleian Library, Auct. D. 2. 19, Bodley 441, Hatton 38, Hatton 113, Junius 121; (h) Salisbury, Cathedral Library 150; (i) and the poetic versions of the Lord's Prayer in Exeter, Cathedral Library 3501 and Oxford, Bodleian Library, Junius 121. Note that the *Durham Collectar* (Durham, Dean and Chapter Library, A. IV. 19, ed. Lindelöf 1927) is not included in the list below; the text, with its numerous prayers, carries a continuous Old English gloss. Abbreviations used are as follows: HG = Gneuss 1981; Ker = Ker, *Catalogue*; FC = Frank and Cameron 1973.

1   *Cambridge, University Library Gg. 3. 28*
    (*Ælfric, Catholic Homilies*) {*HG 11*}

fol. 255r [Ker 15.92, FC B1.2.50] **Oratio** 'Ic ðancige þam ælmihtigum scyppende mid ealre heortan' (Thorpe 1844–6: 2.594).
Series of ten prayers under the rubric **Gebedu on englisc** (Thorpe 1844–6: 2.598, 600; Bzdyl 1977: 99–101) [Ker 15.94, FC B12.3.1]:
fol. 262r 'þú ælmihtiga 7 ðu eca god'.
fol. 262r **Item** 'We biddað þe drihten þæt ðu geíce þinne geleafan on us'.
fol. 262r **Item** 'Drihten god ælmihtig fæder gebletsa us'.

fol. 262r **De sapientia** 'Eala ðu ælmihtiga god þu ðe þurh ðinum euenecum wisdome'.
fol. 262r **De patientia** 'Eala ðu ælmihtiga god þu ðe dydest þæt ðin leofa sunu'.
fol. 262r **Oratio** 'Eala ðu ælmihtiga god þu ðe awritst mid þinum fingre on urum heortum'.
fol. 262v **Item** 'þu ælmihtiga wealdend alys ure heortan fram costnunge yfelra geðohta'.
fol. 262v 'God ælmihtig gemiltsa me synfullum'.
fol. 262v 'Ic bletsige me mid bletsunge þæs ælmihtigan fæder'.
fol. 262v 'Eala ðu halige ðrynnys fæder 7 sunu 7 halig gast'.

2 Cambridge, University Library L1. 1. 10 (Book of Cerne) {HG 28}

fols 43r–44v [Ker 27b, FC C83] *Lorica*: **Hanc luricam loding cantauit ter in omne die**. 'Suffragare trinitati unitas unitatis miserere' [gloss:] 'gemiltsa sio þrynes sio annes þære annesse gemiltsa' (Cockayne 1864: 1.lxviii–lxxiii; Sweet 1885: 172–4 [older glosses]; Kuypers 1902: 85–8; Leonhardi 1905a: 175–93; see Leonhardi 1905b).

fol. 57r [Ker 27c, FC C91.1] Glosses to 'Domine iesu christe qui in hunc mundum': (a) 'de protoplasto : fram þam frumcennedan'; (b) 'qui consuetus est : þe gewuna is' (Kuypers 1902: 113; Ker 1957: 40).

3 Cambridge, Corpus Christi College 190 (Penitentials, Ælfric: Pastoral Letters, etc.) {HG 190}

p. 365 [Ker 45B.13, FC B11.9.1] 'Ic andette þe drihten ælmihtig god 7 sanctam marian' (Wanley 1705: 111–12; Förster 1942b: 14–18 [collated with London, British Library, Cotton Tiberius C. i, fol. 161rv].

4 Cambridge, Corpus Christi College 201 {pp. 1–178} (Regularis concordia, Homilies, etc.) {HG 65}

pp. 116–17 [Ker 49B.50(b), FC B11.4] 'Ic andette ælmihtigum gode' 7 minum scrifte' (Wanley 1705: 145; Thorpe 1840: 403–4).

5 Cambridge, Corpus Christi College 303 (Homilies)

p. 94 [Ker 57.21, FC B12.4.8] Prayer following homily: 'Uton biddan ealle eadmodlice þæs halgan apostolas' (Ker 1957: 101).

6 Cambridge, Corpus Christi College 391 (Portiforium of Wulfstan) {HG 104}

pp. 601–3 [Ker 67a, FC B12.4.3.1] **Anglice** 'Drihten for þinre þære miclan mildheortnesse'

(Zupitza 1890: 327–8; Hughes 1956–60: 2.14–15).

pp. 611–15 [Ker 67b, FC B12.4.4] Series of prayers to Christ and adorations to the Cross, alternating Latin and Old English, under the rubric **Item alię orationes latine et anglice** (Zupitza 1892: 361–4; Hughes 1956–60: 2.20–2):

p. 611 'Kyrrieleyson. christeleison kyrrieleison. Adhoramus te christe et benedicimus tibi' **Anglice** 'We gebiddað þe drihten 7 ðe gebletsiað'.

p. 611 **Latine** 'Domine iesu christe adoro te in cruce ascendentem' **Anglice** 'Drihten hælend crist ic bidde ðe on rode astigende'.

p. 611 'Domine iesu christe adoro te in cruce uulneratum' **Anglice** 'Drihten hælend crist ic bedde þe on rode gewundadne'.

pp. 611–12 **Latine** 'Domine iesu christe adoro te in sepulchro positum' **Anglice** 'Drihten hælend crist ic gebidde þe on byrigenne geledne'.

p. 612 'Domine iesu christe adoro te descendentem ad inferos' **Anglice** 'Drihten hælend crist ic gebidde ðe adune to helwarum astigende'.

p. 612 **Latine** '[D]omine iesu christe adoro te resurgentem ab inferis' **Anglice** 'Drihten hælend crist ic gebidde þe arisende fram helwarum'.

p. 612 **Hoc prosequitur latine** 'Domine iesu christe adoro te uenturum et iudicaturum' **Anglice** 'Drihten hælend crist ic gebidde ðe toweardne deman'.

p. 612 'Crucem tuam adoramus domine' **Anglice** 'Drihten þine halgan rode we geeadmedað'.

p. 612 'O crux benedicta quę sola fuisti digna portare regem celorum et dominum' **Anglice** 'Hala þu gebletsode rod þu ðe ana wyrðe to beorenne heofona cyning 7 hlaford'.

pp. 612–14 **Oratio** 'Domine iesu christe gloriossime conditor mundi' 'Drihten hælend crist se wuldorfullesta middaneardes scyppend'.

p. 614 'Tuam crucem adoramus domine' 'Drihten ðine halgan rode we geeadmedað'.

p. 614 'Salua nos christe saluator per uirtutem sancte crucis' 'Eala hælend crist gehæl us ðurh ðinre halgan rode'.

p. 614 'Ne derelinquas me domine pater et dominator' 'Eala ðu drihten fæder 7 wealdend'.

p. 615 'Domine iesu christe adoro te in cruce ascendentem' '[D]rihten helend crist ic geadmede þe on rode astigende'.

7   Cambridge, Corpus Christi College 421

p. 2 [Ker 68.16, FC B12.4.8] 'Uton nu biddan ealle eadmodlice [`t an'] þysne [`þas'] halgan [`haligan'] apostol [`t las'] (Förster 1942b: 49).

8   London, British Library, Arundel 155 (Arundel Psalter) {HG 306, FC C23.1}

fol. 171r/19–171v/8 [Ker 135.1] **Oratio ad personam patris** 'Domine deus omnipotens. aeterne et ineffabilis' [gloss:] 'eala drihten god ælmihtig ece 7 unasecgendlic' (Holthausen 1941: no. 1).

fol. 171v/8–16 [Ker 135.2] **Oratio ad personam filii** 'Domine iesu christe rex uirginum' [gloss:] 'eala drihten hælend crist cyning fæmnena' (Holthausen 1941: no. 2).

fol. 171v/16–172r/6 [Ker 135.3] **Oratio ad personam spiritus sancti** 'Spiritus sancte deus omnipotens. ex utroque patre & filio procedens' [gloss:] '. . . god ælmihtig of ægðrum fæder 7 suna forðstæppende' (Holthausen 1941: no. 3).

fol. 172r/7–172v/19 Sequence of petitions for the veneration of the Cross:

fol. 172r/7–10 [Ker 135.4] 'Domine iesu christe adoro te in cruce ascendentem' [gloss:] 'eala drihten hælend crist ic geeadmede þe on rode astigende' (Holthausen 1941: no. 4).

fol. 172r/10–12 **Alia** 'Domine iesu christe adoro té in cruce uulneratum' [gloss:] 'la drihten ic geeadmede þe on rode gewundudne' (Holthausen 1941: no. 5).

fol. 172r/12–14 **Alia** 'Domine iesu christe adoro té in sepulchro positum' [gloss:] '. . . on byrgene geledne' (Holthausen 1941: no. 6).

fol. 172r/14–17 **Alia** 'Domine iesu christe adoro té descendentem ad inferos' [gloss:] '. . . nyðerastigendne to hellwarum' (Holthausen 1941: no. 7).

fol. 172r/17–20 **Alia** 'Domine iesu christe adoro té a mortuis resurgentem' [gloss:] '. . . fram deadum arisendne' (Holthausen 1941: no. 8).

fol. 172r/20–172v/1 **Alia** 'Domine iesu christe adoro té uenturum & iudicaturum' [gloss:] '. . . toweardne 7 to demenne' (Holthausen 1941: no. 9).

fol. 172v/2–14 [Ker 135.5] 'Domine iesu christe gloriossime conditor mundi' [gloss:] 'eala drihten hælend crist wuldorfullusta

scyppend middaneardes' (Holthausen 1941: no. 10).

fol. 172v/15–19 [Ker 135.6] 'Deus omnipotens iesu christe. qui tuas sanctas manus propter nos is cruce extendisti' [gloss:] 'eala god ælmihtig þu ðe þine haligan handa for us on rode aðenudest' (Holthausen 1941: no. 11).

fols 172v/20–13r/3 [Ker 135.7] 'Domine iesu christe qui pro humano genere crucis patibulum sustinuisti' [gloss:] 'þu þe for menniscum cynne rode galgan þoludest' (Holthausen 1941: no. 12).

fol. 173r/4–12 [Ker 135.8] **Ante crucem domini. oratio sancta** 'Per gloriam & uirtutem sanctę crucis tuę domine iesu christe' [gloss:] 'þurh wuldor 7 mægen haligre rode þinre . . .' (Holthausen 1941: no. 13).

fol. 173r/22–173v/12 [Ker 135.9] **Alia** 'Omnipotens dilectissime deus. sanctissime atque amantissime saluator' [gloss:] 'eala ælmihtiga 7 lufwendusta god la haligusta 7 lufigendusta hælend' (Holthausen 191: no. 14).

fol. 173v/13–174r/2 **Oratio ad crucem cum .vii. petitionibus** [Ker 135.10] (Holthausen 1941: no. 15):

fol. 173v/13–15 'Domine iesu christe pro sancta cruce tua' [gloss:] '. . . for haligre rode þinre'.

fol. 173v/15–17 **Alia** 'Domine iesu christe pro benedicta cruce tua' [gloss:] '. . . for gebletsudre rode þinre'.

fol. 173v/17–18 **Alia** 'Domine iesu christe pro beata cruce tua' [gloss:] '. . . for eadigre rode þinre'.

fol. 173v/18–19 **Alia** 'Domine iesu christe pro gloriosa cruce tua' [gloss:] '. . . wuldorfulre rode þinre'.

fol. 173v/19–21 **Alia** 'Domine iesu christe pro ueneranda cruce tua' [gloss:] '. . . for arwurðre rode þinre'.

fol. 173v/21–22 **Alia** 'Domine iesu christe pro laudanda cruce tua' [gloss:] '. . . for herigendlicre rode þinre'.

fols 173v/23–174r/2 **Alia** 'Domine iesu christe pro magnifica cruce tua' [gloss:] '. . . for mærre rode þinre'.

fols 174r/2–175v/13 [Ker 135.11] **Oratio Sancti gregorii. quicumque hanc orationem in die cantauerit sicut ipse sanctus gregorius dixit.**

quod nec malus homo. Nec diabolus numquam nocere poterit 'Domine exaudi orationem meam. quia iam cognosco' [gloss:] 'gehyr gebed min þæt eallunga ic oncnawe' (Holthausen 1941: no. 16).

fols 175v/14–177v/9 [Ker 135.12] **Oratio Sancti augustini. Quicumque hanc orationem cotidie coram deo deote orauerit. & in presenti saeculo beatus erit. & in futuro cum sanctis gaudebit** 'Deus inestimabilis misericordię. Deus inmensę pietatis' [gloss:] 'eala god untwynigendre mildheortnesse . . . ormætre arfæstnesse' (Logeman 1889a: 115–19).

fols 177v/10–179v/1 [Ker 135.13] **Incipit inquisitio Sancti augustini de ista oratione. In quacumque die cantauerit aliquis istam orationem non nocebit illi diabolus. neque ullus homo impedimentum facere potest** 'Domine iesu christe qui in hunc mundum propter nos' [gloss:] 'eala drihten hælend crist þu on þysne middaneard for us' (Holthausen 1941: no. 18).

fols 179v/2–180r/7 [Ker 135.14] 'Confiteor tibi domine quia ego peccaui nimis coram té & coram angelis tuis' [gloss:] 'ic andette þe drihten forþi ic syngude ðearle beforan þe 7 beforan englum þinum' (Holthausen 1941: no. 19).

fol. 180r/8–17 [Ker 135.15] **Confessio ad dominum** 'Confitebor tibi domine deo cęli omnia peccata mea' [gloss:] 'ic andette þe drihtne gode heofenes ealle synna mine' (Holthausen 1941: no. 20).

fol. 180r/18–21 [Ker 135.16] 'Spiritus sanctus septiformis super mé ueniat' [gloss:] 'gast halig seofonhiwe ofer cume' (Holthausen 1941: no. 21).

fol. 180r/21–180v/18 [Ker 135.17] **Confessio coram altare** 'Confiteor tibi domine omnia peccata mea' [gloss:] 'ic andette þe drihten ealle synna mine' (Holthausen 1941: no. 22).

fols 180v/19–181v/4 [Ker 135.18] 'Clementissime deus. qui mé inutilem famulum tuum' [gloss:] 'eala mildesta god þu unnyte þeow þinne' (Holthausen 1941: no. 23).

fol. 181v/5–7 [Ker 135.19] **Oratio pro semetipso** 'Domine deus meus qui non habes dominum' [gloss:] 'drihten god min þu ðe næfst hlaford' (Holthausen 1941: no. 24).

fols 181v/14–182r/1 [Ker 135.20] **Alia** 'Deus qui és iustorum gloria & peccatorum misericordia'

[gloss:] 'god þu eart rihtwisra wuldor 7 synnfulra mildheortnes' (Holthausen 1941: no. 25).

fol. 182r/1–12 [Ker 135.21] **Alia** 'Suscipiat pietas tua domine deus meus humilitatis meę preces' [gloss:] 'underfo arfæstnes þin drihten god min eadmodnesse minre bena' (Holthausen 1941: no. 26).

fol. 182r/13–182v/17 [Ker 135.22] **Oratio de tribulatione temptationum** 'Salua me domine rex ęternę glorię' [gloss:] 'gehæl drihten cyning eces wuldres' (Holthausen 1941: no. 27).

fols 182v/17–183r/11 [Ker 134.23] **Oratio de sancta maria** 'Sancta & gloriosa dei genetrix semperque uirgo MARIA' [gloss:] 'la þu halige 7 wuldorfulle godes moder 7 simble mæden . . .' (Holthausen 1941: no. 28 Campbell 1963: no. 28).

fol. 183r/11–183v/4 [Ker 135.24] **Oratio de sancto michahele** 'Sancte Michahel archangele domini nostri iesu christi' [gloss:] 'la þu haliga . . . heahengel' (Campbell 1963: no. 29).

fol. 183v/4–12 [Ker 135.25] **Oratio de sancto Iohanne baptista** 'Sancte Iohannes baptista intercede pro peccatis meis' [gloss:] 'la þu haliga . . . fulluhtere foreþinga for synnum minum' (Campbell 1963: no. 30).

fols 183v/12–184r/4 [Ker 135.26] **Oratio de sancto petro. Et paulo** 'Deus qui elisos erigis' [gloss:] '. . . þu ðe nyþeraworpene uparæst' (Campbell 1963: no. 31).

fol. 184r/5–185v/15 [Ker 135.27] **Oratio ad .xii. apostolos** 'Domine iesu christe qui dedisti potestatem' [gloss:] 'drihten hælend þu sealdest anweald' (Campbell 1963: no. 32).

fols 185v/15–186r/1 [Ker 135.28] **Oratio de sancto Stephano** 'Sancte stephane protomartyr domini gloriose. primitia sancta' [gloss:] 'la þu haliga . . . se æresta drihtnes wuldorfulla frumsceat halig' (Campbell 1963: no. 33).

fol. 186r/1–14 [Ker 135.29] **Oratio de sancto mauricio** 'Sancti martyres dei dignissimi. Maurici' [gloss:] 'la ge haligan . . . wurþustan' (Campbell 1963: no. 34).

fols 186r/14–187r/16 [Ker 135.30] **Oratio de santo ælfhego** 'Cogitationum & uoluntatum mearum' [gloss:] 'geþanca 7 lusta oþþe willena minra' ['ælfhego' glossed 'thoma' throughout in 12c hand] (Campbell 1963: no. 35).

fol. 187r/17–187v/7 [Ker 135.31] **Oratio ad sanctos martyres** 'Deus caritatis & pacis. qui pro salute generis humani' [gloss:] 'go[d] soþre lufe 7 sibbe þu for hæle cynnes mennisces' (Campbell 1963: no. 36).

fol. 187v/7–20 [Ker 135.32] **Oratio de sancto Benedicto abbate** 'Obsecro té beatissime BENEDICITE dilecte dei' [gloss:] 'ic halsige eadigosta . . . gecorena' (Campbell 1963: no. 37).

fols 187v/20–188v/2 [Ker 135.33] **Oratio de sancto dunstano** 'Sancte ac beatissime dom[i]ne & pater Dunstane' [gloss:] 'la haliga 7 eadigostiga hlaford 7 fæder . . .' (Campbell 1963: no. 38).

fol. 188v/2–12 [Ker 135.34] **Oratio ad sanctos confessores** 'Obsecro uos beatissimi confessores' [gloss:] 'ic halsige eow la eadigustan andetteras' (Campbell 1963: no. 39).

fols 188v/12–189v/12 [Ker 135.35] **Oratio ad sanctam ceciliam** 'Corde & ore. atque omni confidentia' [gloss:] 'on heortan 7 on muþe 7 ælcum getruwan' (Campbell 1963: no. 40).

fol. 189v/12–22 [Ker 135.36] **Oratio ad sanctas uirgines** 'Omnes sanctę uirgines & gloriosę' [gloss:] 'ealle . . . mædene 7 wuldorfulle' (Campbell 1963: no. 41).

fols 189v/22–190v/16 [Ker 135.37] **Oratio de omnibus sanctis** 'Per merita omnium sanctorum tuorum' [gloss:] 'ðurh geearnunga ealra haligra þinra' (Campbell 1963: no. 42).

fol. 190v/16–181v/3 [Ker 135.38] **Oratio ad omnes sanctos** 'Succurrite mihi queso omnes sancti dei' [gloss:] 'gehelpað ic bidde ealle . . .' (Campbell 1963: no. 43).

fols 191v/4–192v/6 [Ker 135.39] **Oratio post psalterium uel orationum** 'Liberator animarum mundique redemptor' [gloss:] 'alysend sawla middaneardes alysend' (Campbell 1963: no. 44).

9   *London, British Library, Cotton Galba A. xiv + Nero A. ii, fols 3–13 (Prayerbook, Collectar) {Ker 157, HG 334}*

fols 4v–6v [FC B12.4.6] 'Æla þu drihten æla þu ælmihtiga god' (Galba fols 3r–4v, Nero fol. 11v) (Birch 1885–93: 333, no. 657 (OE), 333, no. 656 (Lat); Muir 1988: 30 (OE), 29 (Lat.)).

fols 27r, 34r [FC C91.2] Glosses to 'Peccaui

domine et nimis peccaui' and 'Domine iesu christe qui dedisti potestatem' (Ker 1957: 200; Muir 1988: 46, 51).

fols 104r–105r [FC B12.4.5] 'In naman [þære hal] gan þrynesse þ[æt i]s fæder [7 sunu 7 se] halga gast god ælmihtig' (Banks 1965: 209; Braekman 1965: 272–3; Muir 1988: 136–7).

fol. 105v [FC B12.4.5] 'Min drihten hælend crist ic do þe þancas [ea]lra þara goda' (Banks 1965: 210; Braekman 1965: 273; Muir 1988: 138).

fols 1–5v–106r [FC B12.4.5] 'Min drihten þu gefyldest me' (Banks 1965: 210; Braekman 1965: 273–4 (reading 'gesyldest'); Muir 1988: 138).

fol. 106r [FC B12.4.5] 'Min drihten hælend crist godes sunu. on þinum noman ic mine hande up ahebbe' (Banks 1965: 210–11; Braekman 1965: 274; Muir 1988: 138).

fol. 106v [FC B12.4.5] 'Min drihten hælend crist þu þe on þa ðriddan [tide d]æges' (Banks 1965: 211; Braekman 1965: 274; Muir 1988: 138).

fol. 106v [FC B12.4.5] 'Min drihten hælend crist þu þe on þa sixtan tide dæges' (Banks 1965: 211; Braekman 1965: 274; Muir 1988: 139).

fol. 107r [FC B12.4.5] 'Min drihten hælend crist þu þe on rode galgan ahangen wære' (Banks 1965: 212; Braekman 1965: 274; Muir 1988: 139).

fol. 107v [FC B12.4.5] 'þancas ic þe do [min drihten] ælm[ihtig] god þæt þu me ges[undne] þurh þisses dæges ryne to þisse æfentide becuman lete' (Banks 1965: 212; Braekman 1965: 274–5; Muir 1988: 139).

fol. 107v [FC B12.4.5] 'Min drihten waldend 7 gescyldend þu þe leoht fram þystrum ascyredest' (Banks 1965: 212; Braekman 1965: 274–6; Muir 1988) [Ker 1957: 199 and Banks read 'hælend' where Braekman reads 'wældend' and Muir 'waldend'].

fol. 107v [FC B12.4.5] 'Drihten god almih[tig] þu þe to fruman þisses dæges' (Banks 1965: 213; Braekman 1965: 274–5; Muir 1988: 139).

fols 111r–112r [FC B12.4.4] 'Drihten hælend crist ic gebidde þe on rode astigende' (Muir 1988: 144).

fols 112v–113r [FC 12.4.4] 'Drihten hælend crist se wuldorfullesta middaneardes scippend' (Muir 1988: 145–6).

fol. 114r [FC B12.4.4] 'God ælmightig hælend cyning' (Banks 1965: 208; Muir 1988: 146) [for Latin, see Logeman 1891: 419–21; Symons 1953: 43–4; Banks 1965: 208; Muir 1988: 146].

10   London, British Library, Cotton Julius A. ii (Ælfric: Grammar, Glossary) {HG 336}

fols 136r–137r [Ker 159.1, FC A28] 'Æla drihten leof æla dema god' (Thomson 1849: 213–25; Bouterwick 1854: 190–2, 328–31; Grein 1858: 290–2; Grein and Wülker 1881–98: 2.211–17; Williams 1909: 72–4 [ll. 21–79]; Dobbie 1942: 94–6).

11   {London, British Library, Cotton Otho A. viii} {Ker 169, HG 348}

fols 88–90 [FC C23.2] (lost: account from Smith 1696; Wanley 1705; Ker 1957) 'drihten woldend god ælmihtig þu ært þrine an feder on sunu 7 in feder mid ðæam halgan gast . . . ic eam unwyrþe 7 ungeselig mon hwa gefreolsaþ me of deaþes lichoman þissa synna butan gefe usses drihtnes hælendes cristes' (Dominator dominus deus omnipotens qui es trinitas una . . . nisi gratia domini nostri christi) [described by Smith as 'Oratio S. Gregorii Papæ, cum interlineari glossa Saxonica'; followed by glossed prayer attributed to Bede, described by Smith as "Fragmentum orationis bedæ Presbyteri, itidem Saxonice interlineatum. F. 90.b.' and by Wanley as 'Super tres hujusce *Bedæ Presbyteri* Orationis versus priores, interlineatim scripta sunt verba quædam Saxonica, quæ sunt quasi continuatio Orationis Gregorianæ, nequamquam ad hanc Bedæ Orat. spectantia'.].

12   London, British Library, Cotton Tiberius A. iii (Regula S. Benedicti) {Ker 186, HG 363}

fols 44r–45r [Ker 186.9a, FC B11.9.3] **Confessio et oratio ad deum** 'Eala þa ælmihtiga god unasecgendlicere mildheortnesse' (*Grammar*, ending at 'gylpes cepte 7 wolde beon ge-', see

Pulsiano 1989; Pulsiano and McGowan 1994: 206–8; transcript by Francis Junius, Oxford, Bodleian Library, Junius 63, pp. 1–4; see Logeman 1889a: 112–14; Förster 1942a: 54–5).

fols 45r–46r [Ker 186.9b, FC B12.4.3.2] 'Man mot hine gebidden swa swa he mæg 7 cán . . . Ic eom andetta ælmihtigan gode 7 eac minum scrifte' (Förster 1908: 45–6, 1942b: 8–11; see Fehr 1921: 55n).

fols 46v–47r [Ker 186.9d, FC B12.4.3.1] 'Min drihten leof for þinre þære mycelan mildheortnysse' (Pulsiano and McGowan 1994: 209–10; see Logeman 1889b; Zupitza 1890: 327–8).

fols 47r–48r [Ker 186.9e, FC B11.9.3] 'Min drihten god ælmihtig ic þe eom ándetta minra synna' (Pulsiano and McGowan 1994: 210–12; see Logeman 1889b: 501–3; Hallander 1968: 100–2).

fols 48r–50v [Ker 186.9f, FC B12.4.3.3] 'Din [*recte* Min] drihten ælmihtig god si ðe wuldor 7 þanc' (Pulsiano and McGowan 1994: 212–16; see Logeman 1889b: 504–11; Hallander 1968: 102–10).

fols 50v–51v [Ker 186.9g, FC B9.4] 'Drihten þu eart scippend ealra gescefta' [extract from King Alfred's translation of St. Augustine's *Soliloquia*] (Logeman 1889b: 511–13; see Hargrove 1902: 4/21–6/10, 11/20–14/8; Endter 1922: 4/11–5/1, 11/15–14/7; Carnicelli 1969: 50/10—17, 54/22–56/9).

fols 55v–56r [Ker 186.9k, FC B11.4] 'Ic andette ælmihtigum gode 7 minum scrifte' (Thorpe 1840: 402–4; Fowler 1965: 17/35–19/81).

13   London, British Library, Cotton Tiberius C. i (Pontifical, Homilies) {Ker 197, HG 376}

fols 159v–160r [Ker 197.d, FC B12.4.3.4] 'Ic bidde ðe min drihten on ðæs acennedan godes naman' (Logman 1889a: 101).

fols 160r–161r [Ker 197.e, FC B11.9.4] 'Ic eom þe ealra 7 dettende 7 þinum englum' (Logeman 1889a: 101–2, Förster 1942b: 31–6).

fol. 161rv [Ker 197.f, FC B11.9.4] 'Ic andette þe drihten ælmihtig god 7 sancta marian' (Logeman 1889a: 102–3; see Förster 1942b: 14–20).

14 London, British Library, Cotton Vespasian D. xx (Penitential Texts) {Ker 212, HG 395}

fols 87r–90v [FC B12.4.3.5] 'Dryhten þu halga god þu eart ælmihtig 7 ece god' (Logeman 1889a: 97–100; Förster 1942b: 27–36 [partial parallel text based on Logeman]).

15 London, British Library, Cotton Vitellius A. xv (Augustine: Soliloquia, Gospel of Nicodemus)

fols 7v–14v [Ker 215.1, FC B9.4] 'Drihten þu ðe eart scypend ealra gesceafta' (Cockayne 1864–70: 165–71; Hulme 1893: 333/40–337/1; Hargrove 1902: 4/21–14/8; Endter 1922: 4/11–14/7; Carnicelli 1969: 50/10–56/9).

16 London, British Library, Harley 585 (Ps.-Apuleius: Herbarium, etc.) {HG 421}

fols 152r–157r [Ker 231.2, FC C22] *Lorica*: 'Suffragare trinitas unitas unitatis miserere' [gloss:] 'gefultimge seo þrinis seo annis ðære annisse gemildsa me' (Cockayne 1864: lxxiii–lxxiv; Leonhardi 1905b: 175–93; Grattan and Singer 1952: 130–46; Herren 1987: 76–89).

17 London, British Library, Royal 2 A. xx (Prayerbook) {HG 450}

fol. 13r [Ker 248.a (iv), FC C54] 'Deus omnipotens et dominus noster' [gloss:] 'god almahtig 7 drihten ur' (Zupitza 1889: 61).
fol. 19r [Ker 248.a (viii), FC C54] Scattered glosses to 'Inprimis obsecro' (Zupitza 1889: 64).

18 London, British Library, Royal 2 B. v (Regius Psalter) {HG 451}

fol. 6r [Ker 249.c, FC B12.4.3.1] 'Min drihten leof for þinre þære micelan midheortnysse' (Logeman 1889b: 499–501).
fols 190v–192r [Ker 249.d, FC B11.9.3] 'Myn drihten god ælmihtig ic þe eom andetta minra synna' (Logeman 1889b: 501–3; Hallander 1968: 100–2).
fols 192r–196v [Ker 249.e, FC B12.4.3.3] 'Min drihten ælmihtig god si þe wuldor 7 þanc

[< þonc]' (Logeman 1889b: 504–11; Hallander 1968: 100–10).
fols 197r–198r [Ker 249.g, FC B11.9.3] Confessio et oratio 'Eala þu ælmihtig god unasecgendlicre mildheortnesse' (Logeman 1889a: 112–15 [variants from Tiberius A. iii, fol. 44]).

19 London, Lambeth Palace 427 (Lambeth Psalter) {HG 517}

fols 141r–142r [Ker 290.3, FC C91.4] Partial gloss to prayer 'O summe deus miserorum consolator omnium' (Förster 1914: 328–9).
fol. 183v [Ker 280.4, FC A28] 'Æla drihten leof æla dema god' (see Grein and Wülker 1881–98: 2.211–12; Dobbie 1942: 94–5).

20 Oxford, Bodleian Library, Bodley 180 (2079) (Boethius: De consolatione Philosophiae)

fol. 94r [Ker 305, FC B12.4.7] 'Drihten ælmihtiga god wyrhta 7 wealdend ealra gesceafta' (Sedgefield 1899: 149).

21 Oxford, Bodleian Library, Laud Misc. 482 (1054) (Penitential Texts, Offices) {HG 657}

fol. 54rv [Ker 343.18, FC B12.5.11] 'Geþeaf 7 gecnæwe ic eom' (Fehr 1921: 55–6, Förster 1942b: 10–11).

22 Salisbury, Cathedral Library 150 (Salisbury Psalter) {Ker 379, HG 740}

fol. 138r [FC C23.3] 'Omnipotens et misericors deus clementiam tuam suppliciter deprecor' [gloss:] 'ælmihtig 7 mildheort go[d] arfæstnesse þine eadmodlice ic bidde' (Sisam and Sisam 1959: 284–5).

23 York, Minster Library (Documents, Sermons)

fol. 161v [Ker 402.e, FC B12.4.2] 'Wutan we gebiddan god ealmihtine' (Henderson 1875: 220; Simmons 1879: 62, 3212; Stevenson 1912: 10; *New. Pal. Soc.* 1926: 2, opp. pl. 165a).

REFERENCES

Prayers

Bestul, T. 1977. 'The Old English *Resignation* and the Benedictine Reform'. *Neuphilologische Mitteilungen* 78: 19–20.

—— 1986. 'Continental Sources of Anglo-Saxon Devotional Writing'. *Sources of Anglo-Saxon Literary Culture*, pp. 103–26. Ed. Paul E. Szarmach. Studies in Medieval Culture 20. Kalamazoo.

Birch, Walter de Gray, ed. 1889. *An Ancient Manuscript of the Eighth or Ninth Century Formerly Belonging to St. Mary's Abbey, or Nunnaminster, Winchester.* Hampshire Record Society. London and Winchester.

Brown, Michelle P. 1996. *The Book of Cerne: Prayer, Patronage and Power in Ninth-Century England.* British Library Studies in Medieval Culture. London and Toronto.

Bzdyl, Donald G. 1982. 'Prayer in Old English Narratives'. *Medium Ævum* 51.2: 135–51.

Constantinescu, Radu 1974. 'Alcuin et les "Libelli Precum" de l'époque carolingienne'. *Revue d'Histoire de la Spiritualité* 50: 17–56.

Dumville, David N. 1973. 'Biblical Apocrypha and the Early Irish: A Preliminary Investigation'. *Proceedings of the Royal Irish Academy* 73C: 299–338.

Gneuss, Helmut 1985. 'Liturgical Books in Anglo-Saxon England and their Old English Terminology'. *Learning and Literature in Anglo-Saxon England: Studies Presented to Peter Clemoes on the Occasion of His Sixty-fifth Birthday*, pp. 91–141. Eds Michael Lapidge and Helmut Gneuss. Cambridge.

Günzel, Beate, ed. 1993. *Ælfwine's Prayerbook (London, British Library, Cotton Titus D. xxvi + xxviii).* Henry Bradshaw Society 108. London.

Hen, Yitzhak, ed. 1997. *The Sacramentary of Echternach (Paris, Bibliothèque Nationale, MS. lat. 9433).* Henry Bradshaw Society 110. London.

Herren, M. W. 1973. 'The Authorship, Date of Composition and Provenance of the So-called *Lorica Gildae*'. *Ériu* 24: 35–51.

Hilgarth, J. N. 1961. 'The East, Visigothic Spain and the Irish'. *Studia patristica* 4: 442–56.

—— 1962. 'Visigothic Spain and Early Christian Ireland'. *Proceedings of the Royal Irish Academy* 62C: 167–94.

Hill, Thomas D. 1981. 'Invocation of the Trinity and the Tradition of the *Lorica* in Old English'. *Speculum* 56: 259–67.

Hughes, Kathleen 1970. 'Some Aspects of Irish Influence on Early Private Prayer'. *Studia Celtica* 5: 48–61.

Kuypers, A. B., ed. 1902. *The Prayer Book of Aedeluald the Bishop Commonly Called the Book of Cerne.* Cambridge.

Lapidge, Michael, ed. 1991. *Anglo-Saxon Litanies of the Saints.* Henry Bradshaw Society 106. London.

Muir, Bernard James, ed. 1988. *A Pre-Conquest English Prayer-Book (BL MSS Cotton Galba A. xi and Nero A. ii (ff. 3–13)).* Henry Bradshaw Society 103. Woodbridge.

Smith, Thomas 1696. *Catalogue of Manuscripts in the Cottonian Library 1696 (Catalogus librorum manuscriptorum bibliothecae Cottonianae).* Ed. C. G. C. Tite. Suffolk.

Stanley, E. G. 1956. 'Old English Poetic Diction and the Interpretation of *The Wanderer, The Seafarer* and *The Penitent's Prayer*'. *Anglia* 73: 413–66.

—— 1994. 'Prayers, Praise, and Thanksgiving in Old English Verse'. *In the Foreground: Beowulf*, pp. 218–43. Cambridge.

Storms, G., ed. 1948. *Anglo-Saxon Magic.* The Hague.

Symons, T., ed. and trans. 1953. *Regularis Concordia Anglicae Nationis Monachorum Sanctimonialiumgne: The Monastic Agreement of the Monks and Nuns of the English Nation.* London.

Wanley, Humfrey 1705. *Librorum vett. septentrionalium, qui in Angliæ bibliothecis extant.* Oxford.

Warren, F. E., ed. 1893–5. *The Antiphonary of Bangor.* 2 vols. Henry Bradshaw Society 4, 5. London.

Wilmart, A. 1940. *Precum Libelli Quattuor Aevi Karolini.* Rome.

Glosses and glossaries

Primary sources

Bischoff, Bernhard, Mildred Bundy, Geoffrey Harlow, M. B. Parkes and J. D. Pheifer, eds

1988. *The Épinal, Erfurt, Werden and Corpus Glossaries.* Early English Manuscripts in Facsimile 22. Copenhagen.

Goosens, Louis, ed. 1974. *The Old English Glosses of MS. Brussels, Royal Library 1650 (Aldhelm's De Laudibus Virginitatis).* Brussels.

Hessels, J. H., ed. 1890. *An Eighth-century Latin–Anglo-Saxon Glossary Preserved in the Library of Corpus Christi College, Cambridge (MS. No. 144).* Cambridge.

Hunt, Tony 1981. 'The Old English Vocabularies in MS. Oxford, Bodley 730'. *English Studies* 62: 201–9.

Lindsay, W. M., ed. 1921a. *The Corpus Glossary.* Cambridge.

Logeman, H. 1888. *The Rule of S. Benet: Latin and Anglo-Saxon Interlinear Version.* Early English Text Society, o.s. 90. London. Repr. Millwood, 1981.

Oliphant, R. T., ed. 1966. *The Harley Latin–Old English Glossary, Edited from British Museum MS Harley 3376.* Janua Linguarum, Series Practica 20. The Hague.

Pheifer, J. D., ed. 1974. *Old English Glosses in the Épinal-Erfurt Glossary.* Oxford.

Sisam, Celia and Kenneth Sisam, eds 1959. *The Salisbury Psalter, Edited from Salisbury Cathedral MS. 150.* Early English Text Society, o.s. 242. London. Repr. 1969.

Wright, Thomas and R. P. Wülcker, eds 1884. *Anglo-Saxon and Old English Vocabularies.* 2 vols. London.

—— 1997. 'Glosses to Aldhelm's "Prosa de virginitate" and Glossaries from the Anglo-Saxon Golden Age, ca. 670–800'. *Studi Medievali* 3rd ser. 38: 561–645.

—— 1998. 'The Transmission of the "Digby" Corpus of Bilingual Glosses to Aldhelm's *Prose de uirginitate*'. *Anglo-Saxon England* 27: 139–68.

Korhammer, Michael 1980. 'Mittelalterliche Konstruktionshilfen und altenglische Wortstellung'. *Scriptorium* 34: 18–55.

Lapidge, Michael 1986. 'The School of Theodore and Hadrian'. *Anglo-Saxon England* 15: 43–72.

Lindsay, W. M. 1921b. *The Corpus, Épinal, Erfurt and Leyden Glossaries.* Publications of the Philological Society 8. Oxford.

O'Neill, Patrick P. 1991. 'Latin Learning at Winchester in the Early Eleventh Century: The Evidence of the Lambeth Psalter'. *Anglo-Saxon England* 20: 143–66.

—— 1992. 'Syntactical Glosses in the Lambeth Psalter and the Reading of the Old English Interlinear Translation as Sentences'. *Scriptorium* 46: 250–6.

Pulsiano, Phillip 1995. 'Psalters'. *The Liturgical Books of Anglo-Saxon England*, pp. 61–85. Old English Newsletter, Subsidia 23. Kalamazoo.

Robinson, Fred C. 1973. 'Syntactical Glosses in Latin Manuscripts of Anglo-Saxon Provenance'. *Speculum* 47: 443–75.

Wieland, Gernot 1985. 'Latin Lemma – Latin Gloss: The Stepchild of Glossologists'. *Mittellateinisches Jahrbuch* 18: 91–9.

Secondary sources

Gibson, Margaret, T. A. Heslop and Richard W. Pfaff, eds 1992. *The Eadwine Psalter: Text, Image and Monastic Culture in Twelfth-century Canterbury.* Publications of the Modern Humanities Research Association 14. London and University Park.

Gneuss, Helmut 1990. *The Study of Language in Anglo-Saxon England.* The Toller Memorial Lecture. Manchester. Repr. from *Bulletin of the John Rylands University Library of Manchester* 72.1 (1990).

Gwara, Scott 1993. 'Literary Culture in Anglo-Saxon England and the Old English and Latin Glosses to Aldhelm's *Prosa de virginitate*'. Unpublished PhD dissertation, University of Toronto.

Appendix

Banks, R. A. 1965. 'Some Anglo-Saxon Prayers from British Museum MS. Cotton Galba A. XIV'. *Notes and Queries* 210: 207–13.

Birch, Walter de Gray, ed. 1885–93. *Cartularium Saxonicum: A Collection of Charters Relating to Anglo-Saxon History.* London.

Bouterwick, K. W., ed. 1854. *Cædmon's des angelsahischen biblischen Dichtungen.* Vol. 1. Gütersloh.

Braekman, W. 1965. 'Some Minor Old English Texts'. *Archiv für das Studium der neuern Sprachen und Literaturen* 202: 271–6.

Bzdyl, Donald G. 1977. 'The Sources of Ælfric's Prayers in Cambridge University Library MS. Gg. 3.28'. *Notes and Queries* 222: 98–102.

Campbell, Jackson J. 1963. 'Prayers from MS. Arundel 155'. *Anglia* 81: 82–117.

Carnicelli, Thomas A., ed. 1969. *King Alfred's Version of St. Augustine's Soliloquies.* Cambridge, MA.

Cockayne, Oswald, ed. 1864. *Leechdoms, Wortcunning, and Starcraft of Early England.* Vol. 1. London.

Cockayne, Thomas O. 1864–70. *The Shrine: A Collection of Occasional Papers on Dry Subjects.* London.

Dobbie, Elliot Van Kirk, ed. 1942. *The Anglo-Saxon Minor Poems.* Anglo-Saxon Poetic Records 6. New York and London.

Endter, W. 1922. *König Alfreds des Grosen Bearneitung der Solioquien des Augustinus.* Hamburg.

Fehr, Bernhard 1921. 'Altenglische Ritualtexte für Krankenbesuch, heilige Ölung und Begräbnis'. *Texte und Forschungen zur englischen Kulturgeschichte: Festgabe für Felix Liebermann zum 20. Juli 1921,* pp. 20–67. Eds Heinrich Boehmer et al. Halle.

Förster, Max 1908. 'Beiträge zur mittelalterlichen Volkskunde III'. *Archiv für das Studium der neuern Sprachen und Literaturen* 121: 30–46.

——1914. 'Die altenglischen Beigaben des Lambeth Psalters'. *Archiv für das Studium der neuern Sprachen und Literaturen* 132: 328–35.

——1942a. 'Zu den ae. Texten aus Ms. Arundel 155'. *Anglia* 66: 52–5.

——1942b. 'Zur Liturgik der angelsächsischen Kirke'. *Anglia* 66: 1–51.

Frank, Roberta and Angus Cameron 1973. *A Plan for the Dictionary of Old English.* Toronto.

Gneuss, Helmut 1981. 'A Preliminary Handlist of Manuscripts Written or Owned in England up to 1100'. *Anglo-Saxon England* 9: 1–60.

Grein, W. M., ed. 1858. *Bibliothek der angelsächsischen Poesie in kritische bearbeiteten Texten und mit vollständigem Glossar.* vol. 2. Göttingen.

——and Richard Wülker, eds 1881–98. *Bibliothek der angelsächsischen Poesie.* 3 vols. Leipzig.

Hallander, Lars-G. 1968. 'Two Old English Confessional Prayers'. *Studier i modern Språkvetenskap* n.s. 3: 87–110.

Hargrove, Henry Lee, ed. 1902. *King Alfred's Old English Version of St Augustine's Soliloquies.* New York.

Henderson, G., ed. 1875. *Catholic Church Ritual (York). Manuale et processionale ad usum insignis exlesiae Eboracensis.* Surtees Society 63. Durham.

Holthausen, F. 1941. 'Altenglische Interlinearver-sionen lateinischer Gebete und Beichten'. *Anglia* 65: 230–54.

Hughes, Anselm, ed. 1956–60. *The Portiforium of Wulfstan (Corpus Christi College Cambridge, MS 391).* Henry Bradshaw Society 89, 90. Leighton Buzzard.

Hulme, William H. 1893. '"Blooms" von Köning Aelfred'. *Englische Studien* 18: 331–56.

Ker, N. R. 1957. *A Catalogue of Manuscripts Containing Anglo-Saxon.* Oxford. Repr. with supplement 1990.

Kuypers, A. B., ed. 1902. *The Prayer Book of Aedeluald the Bishop Commonly Called the Book of Cerne.* Cambridge.

Leonhardi, Günther, ed. 1905a. *Kleinere angelsächsische Denkmäler I.* Hamburg.

——1905b. *Die Lorica des Gildas.* Hamburg.

Lindelöf, U., ed. 1927. *Rituale Ecclesiae Dunelmensis. The Durham Collectar.* Durham.

Logeman, H. 1889a. 'Anglo-Saxonica Minora. I.' *Anglia* 11: 97–120.

——1889b. 'Anglo-Saxonica Minora'. *Anglia* 12: 497–518.

Logeman, W. S. 1891. 'De Consuetudine Monachorum'. *Anglia* 13: 365–454.

——1893. 'De Consuetudine Monachorum'. *Anglia* 14: 20–40.

Muir, Bernard James, ed. 1988. *A Pre-Conquest English Prayer-Book: BL MSS Cotton Galba A. xiv and Nero A. ii (ff. 3–13).* Henry Bradshaw Society 103. Woodbridge and Wolfeboro, NH.

New Pal. Soc. 1926. *New Palaeographical Society. Facsimiles of Ancient Manuscripts.* Ser. 2, pts x, xi. London.

Pulsiano, Phillip 1989. 'A *Gothic Grammar* with a Transcript of Anglo-Saxon Prayers (Columbia University)'. *Old English Newsletter* 23.1: 40–1.

——and Joseph McGowan. 1994. 'Four Unedited Prayers in London, British Library, Cotton Tiberius A. iii'. *Mediaeval Studies* 56: 189–216.

Sedgefield, W. J., ed. 1899. *King Alfred's Old English Version of Boethius De Consolatione Philosophiae.* Oxford.

Simmons, Thomas Frederick, ed. 1879. *The Lay Folks Mass Book.* Early English Text Society, o.s. 71. London.

Sisam, Kenneth and Celia Sisam, eds 1959. *The Salisbury Psalter, Edited from Salisbury Cathedral Ms. 150.* Early English Text Society, o.s. 242. London.

Smith, Thomas 1696. *Catalogue of Manuscripts in*

the Cottonian Library 1696 (Catalogus librorum manuscriptorum bibliothecae Cottonianae). Ed. C. G. C. Tite. Suffolk.

Stevenson, W. H. 1912. 'Yorkshire Surveys and Other Eleventh-century Documents in the York Gospels'. *English Historical Review* 27.105: 1–25.

Sweet, Henry, ed. 1885. *The Oldest English Texts.* Early English Text Society, o.s. 82. London.

Thomson, E., ed. 1849. *Godcunde Lár and þeódóm. Select Monuments of the Doctrine and Worship of the Catholic Church in England before the Norman Conquest.* London.

Thorpe, Benjamin, ed. 1840. *Ancient Laws and Institutes of England.* London.

——ed. 1844–6. *The Homilies of the Anglo-Saxon Church. The First Part.* 2 vols. London.

Wanley, Humfrey 1705. *Librorum Vett. Septentrionalium, qui in Angliæ Bibliothecis extant.* Oxford.

Williams, O. T. 1909. *Short Extracts from Old English Poetry.* Bangor.

Zupitza, Julius 1889. 'Mersisches aus der Hs. Royal 2 A 20 im Britischen Museum'. *Zeitschrift für deutsches Altertum* 33: 47–66.

——1890. 'Eine weitere Aufzeichnung der Oratio pro peccatis'. *Archiv für das Studium der neueren Sprachen und Literaturen* 84: 327–30.

——1892. 'Kreuzandacht'. *Archiv für das Studium der neueren Sprachen und Literaturen* 88: 361–4.

PART III
Genres and Modes

13

Religious Prose

Roy M. Liuzza

According to the Venerable Bede, the conversion of the English was set in motion by an act of mistranslation. Bede recounts a story of how the future Pope Gregory was inspired to evangelize the island when he saw a group of Angle slaves 'with fair skin, fine features, and hair of outstanding beauty' for sale in a Roman marketplace. Impressed by their beauty but dismayed to learn of their paganism, Gregory indulges in a bit of pious wordplay: the slaves say they are 'Angles', and Gregory says they are 'angeli'; they are from 'Deira', to which Gregory replies they are 'de ira eruti' (plucked from the wrath of God); their king is 'Ælla', and Gregory shouts 'Alleluia' (Colgrave and Mynors 1991 [hereafter *HE*]: II.1). The language of the slaves is English, but the language of Christian salvation is Latin. The story leaves little doubt which language is proper – though their angelic appearance made them fit for salvation, the tongue of the English 'knew nothing but to gnash the teeth barbarously', Bede says, and needed to be trained and translated to a more appropriate language.

The Christian faith had established outposts among the English even before Augustine, his companions and their Frankish interpreters arrived on the island in 597, but there is virtually no evidence for sustained religious prose in the vernacular before the end of the ninth century. The missionary activity of the early English church necessarily involved vernacular instruction; a monastic education must have begun with some gloss on a Biblical passage, as early surviving word-lists attest (see Lindsay 1921; Pheifer 1974; Lapidge 1986; Bischoff and Lapidge 1994), and preaching to the laity could hardly have been effective except in their native language. Yet there is no evidence that such teachings were committed to writing. Bede is said to have been translating the Gospel of John 'ad utilitatem ecclesiae' on his death-bed, and by his own report had translated the Lord's Prayer and Creed for the use of unlearned clergy, but no trace of these has survived. The history of Old English religious prose, then, begins nearly three centuries after the beginnings of English Christianity.

This scarcity of early vernacular religious writing may be due to the winnowing effects of time – it is generally assumed that most manuscripts were either read to tatters or eventually thrown out as rubbish – but it is more likely to be a reflection of the general lack of written English of any kind from the earlier periods. Fewer than a dozen manuscripts from before the tenth century contain any English at all (Brown 1995: 116), and several of these are glossaries, not continuous texts. They indicate the persistence of a vernacular teaching tradition but only the beginnings of vernacular literacy. The history of Old English religious prose may thus be viewed against the gradual development of a textual practice; the fact of translation is ancient but the practice of committing such translations to writing is a relatively late phenomenon. It has been suggested that Bede's homilies on the Gospels, though written in Latin, were delivered in English to a mixed monastic and lay audience (Thacker 1992: 141); his homily for Holy Saturday (Hurst 1955: 2.6) refers to members of the audience who are not yet baptized. Latin was the language of *auctoritas*; English was oral, utilitarian and ephemeral, and developed only belatedly into a literary form. For Bede, it is Latin that unifies the different tribes and tongues of Britain (*HE* I.1) and links the monasteries of the Northumbrian hinterland to the centre of the universal church in Rome. The scriptoria of the great abbeys which 'made the eastern coast of Northumbria from Lindisfarne to Whitby a veritable monastic Riviera' (Riché 1976: 378) produced magnificently decorated Latin manuscripts like the Lindisfarne Gospels, not translations.

If writing in English was rare, however, teaching in English must have been widespread, not only for the laity but among the clergy as well, for the learning of Latin is arduous and not all priests and monks were equal to the task. We may indeed wonder whether many priests in Bede's day, especially those far from the monastic centres of learning, would have been competent to translate a Latin text into English for a lay audience. Bede's *Letter to Ecgbert* urges that priests who do not know Latin must be taught the Creed and the Lord's Prayer in their own tongue. The 747 Council of *Clofesho* likewise stipulates that priests – apparently those who were ignorant of Latin – must be able to expound the Creed and the Lord's Prayer in their own language (Cubitt 1992, 1995). Such priests must have had some instruction in English, but little manuscript evidence has survived showing how this instruction was transmitted. In any case preaching and teaching to the laity must have been entirely in English. Bede's story of Cædmon (*HE* IV.24) suggests that Christian doctrine might also have been taught through poetry and performance. When Cædmon's miraculous poetic gift is recognized, he is taken up into the monastic life and taught sacred history; he learns all he can by hearing ('cuncta quae audiendo discere poterat') and makes songs so sweet that 'doctores suos vicissim auditores sui faciebat' ('his teachers in turn became his listeners'). What is notable in the present context is that the whole process, from inspiration to performance, takes place without the medium of writing. Nobody teaches Cædmon to read the sacred history for himself, or to write down his poetic paraphrases; instruction in Christian doctrine takes place as an oral exchange, not a textual production.

In the late ninth-century Old English version of Bede (Miller 1890–8), the last-quoted phrase of the story is translated 'þa seolfan his lareowas æt his muðe *wreoton* and leornodon' (emphasis added). The addition is significant: the translators of Bede assumed that Cædmon's works were transcribed. This indicates that the status of English was changing, and the vernacular was becoming 'an alternative literary and documentary language' (Kelly 1990: 51), in this case for the preservation of sacred poetry. The beginnings of this change are difficult to discern. The writing of writs and charters in English undoubtedly prepared the way for more literary uses of the vernacular, as did the practice of word-for-word glossing of Latin texts, as seen in the ninth-century interlinear glosses added to the eighth-century Vespasian Psalter (London, British Library, Cotton Vespasian A. i). A vernacular *Martyrology* (essentially a calendar-like account of the miracles and deaths of the saints) survives in two early fragments (London, British Library, Add. 23211 and 40165A) from the end of the ninth century but probably originated in Mercia somewhat earlier (Herzfeld 1900; Sisam 1953; Kotzor 1981; Cross 1986); some early works of Old English prose such as the *Life of St Chad* may survive only in copies from later centuries (Vleeskruyer 1953). The growth and development of Old English prose began in earnest, however, in the last decade of the ninth century with the educational initiatives of Alfred the Great.

After making peace with the Vikings Alfred turned his attention to the improvement and unification of his own kingdom, including the redevelopment of intellectual life. He recruited scholars from outside and abroad; he established a palace school; Asser's *Life of Alfred* records that the king's sons studied books in both Latin and English (Keynes and Lapidge 1983: 90); the king himself is said to have struggled to learn Latin so that he might contribute directly to this educational reform. Alfred's more-or-less explicit imitation of Charlemagne had a significant innovation from its continental model – the promotion of the vernacular as the medium of this educational reform. The most famous statement of Alfred's intentions is found in the letter, addressed to his bishops, which accompanies his translation of Gregory the Great's *Regula Pastoralis*, a manual for bishops widely used in the instruction of parish priests (Sweet 1871). Alfred calls it *Hierdeboc* or 'shepherd's book'; it was an appropriate work with which to begin the task of clerical and educational reform. Alfred's letter (generally but not quite accurately called his 'Preface' to the *Pastoral Care*) accompanied the translation and announced its purpose. In it he laments the decay of learning in England in the wake of a century of Danish invasions; the land had once stood full of books and treasure, he says, but men in their sloth had lost both wisdom and wealth. He remembers that when he became king 'swiðe feawa wæron behionan Humbre ðe hiora ðeninga cuðen understondan on Englisc oððe furðum an ærendgewrit of Lædene on Englisc areccean; ond ic wene ðætte noht monige behiondan Humbre næren' (Sweet 1871: 3) 'there were very few on this side of the Humber who could understand their services in English or even translate a letter from Latin into English, and I think there were not many beyond the Humber'. To stem the decline of literacy Alfred outlines a programme of education in English which provides for translations of certain texts 'most necessary for all men to know' and free education for freeborn boys: he was concerned to create both the supply and the demand for English prose, both a body of vernacular literature and a public to read it (Morrish 1986: 89; see also Szarmach 1982).

Alfred undoubtedly had in mind the improvement of public life, to say nothing of the smooth functioning of royal power, when he began his promotion of English literacy and literature, but in the preface he attached to Werferth's version of Gregory's *Dialogues* (a collection of miracle stories about Italian saints) he describes his purposes in terms of personal piety:

> Ic Ælfred geofendum Criste mid cynehades mærnysse geweorðod, habbe gearolice ongyten and þurh haligra boca gesægene oft gehyred, þætte us, þam þe God swa micle heanesse worldgeþingða forgifen hafað, is seo mæste ðearf, þæt we hwilon ure mod betwix þas eorþlican ymbhigdo geleoðigen and gebigen to ðam godcundan and þam gastlican rihte. and forþan ic sohte and wilnade to minum getreowum freondum, þæt hi me of Godes bocum be haligra manna þeawum and wundrum awriten þas æfterfyl-gendan lare, þæt ic þurh þa mynegunge and lufe gescyrped on minum mode betwih þas eorðlican gedrefednesse hwilum gehicge þa heofonlican. (Hecht 1900–7: 1)

> I, Alfred, by the grace of Christ honoured with the greatness of kingship, have surely perceived and often heard in the statements of holy books, that for us, to whom God has given such great exaltation of worldly position, there is the greatest need that we sometimes relax our mind among these earthly concerns and turn it to divine and spir-itual laws. Therefore I have sought and desired of my loyal friends that they should write for me the following teaching from God's books about the virtues and miracles of holy men, so that through them I might, my mind whetted by that admonition and love, among these earthly troubles sometimes think of heavenly things.

Among the works which can be associated with Alfred's programme are English versions of the *Regula Pastoralis* and Gregory's *Dialogues*, Boethius' *De consolatione Philosophiae*, Augustine's *Soliloquia*, Orosius' *Historiae adversum paganos* and Bede's *Historia ecclesiastica*, a code of laws and a prose version of the first fifty Psalms of the Roman Psalter. Not all were done directly at Alfred's request – the *Dialogues*, trans-lated by Werferth, bishop of Worcester, and the OE Bede are probably Mercian in origin – but Alfred himself had a hand in the translation of the Psalms, Augustine's *Soliloquies*, the *Boethius* and the *Regula Pastoralis*. These works constitute a broad but eclectic library of wisdom: world and English history, advice on pastoral care and moral instruction, stories of saints and metaphysical debate on the nature of fate and free will. As translations, most of them are somewhat free; the Boethius and the *Soliloquies* are considerably rewritten for an English audience (Whitelock 1966; Bately 1980; Godden 1981; Gatch 1986).

The generation after Alfred seems not to have continued his programme of English translation with much vigour; in the tenth century the impetus for vernacular works of religious instruction came from monastic and cathedral schools rather than the royal household (Lapidge 1991a). Some of the surviving OE homilies probably come from the earlier and middle decades of the century; two manuscripts in particular, the Vercelli Homilies (Vercelli, Biblioteca Capitolare, CXVII, ed. Scragg 1990, facsimile edn Sisam 1976) and the Blickling Homilies (Princeton University Library, W. H. Scheide Collection 71, ed. Morris 1874–80, facsimile edn Willard 1960), may reflect the nature of English religious writing in these years. Both are miscellaneous collections of works by various anonymous authors; the latter is arranged roughly according to the liturgical year (Scragg 1985). Most of the items in these two collections are general exhortations and expositions of basic Christian instruction; many rely on the uncritical and unsystematic borrowing of sources, as well as on the vivid and sensational stories found in popular apocrypha of questionable orthodoxy (Gatch 1989). The Blickling sermon on the dedication of St Michael's church, for example, ends with an account of the archangel showing St Paul around the precincts of Hell, a theologically dubious scene but one of compelling horror, with echoes of the description of Grendel's Mere in *Beowulf* (Malone 1958):

Swa Sanctus Paulus wæs geseonde on norðanweardne þisne middangeard, þær ealle wætero niðergewitað, 7 he þær geseah ofer ðæm wætere sumne harne stan. 7 wæron norð of ðæm stane awexene swiðe hrimige bearwas, 7 ðær wæron þystrogenipo, 7 under þæm stane wæs niccra eardung 7 wearga. 7 he geseah þæt on ðæm clife hangodan on ðæm isigean bearwum manige swearte saula be heora handum gebundne. 7 þa fynd þara on nicra onlicnesse heora gripende wæron, swa swa grædig wulf. 7 þæt wæter wæs sweart under þæm clife neoðan. 7 betuh þæm clife on ðæm wætre wæron swylce twelf mila. 7 ðonne ða twigo forburston þonne gewitan þa saula niðer þa þe on ðæm twigum hangodan, 7 him onfengon ða nicras. ðis ðonne wæron ða saula þa ðe her on worlde mid unrihte gefyrenode wæron, 7 ðæs noldan geswican ær heora lifes ende. Ac uton nu biddan Sanctus Michael geornlice þæt he ure saula gelæde on gefean, þær hie motan blissian abuton ende on ecnesse. (Morris 1874–80: no. 17, lines 237ff)

As Saint Paul was looking toward the northern part of this world, where all waters descend, he also saw over the waters a grey stone. And north of the stone had grown very frosty groves, and there were gloomy mists, and under the stone was the dwelling-place of sea-monsters and evil spirits. And he saw that on the cliff many black souls were hanging in the icy groves, bound by their hands, and devils in the shape of sea-monsters were clutching at them like greedy wolves. And the water was black under the cliff below, and from the cliff to the water was about twelve miles. And when the boughs broke, the souls that hung on the twigs fell down, and the sea-monsters seized them. These were the souls of those who had sinned here in this world, and would not cease from it before their life's end. But let us now eagerly ask St Michael that he lead our souls to bliss, where they might rejoice without end in eternity.

The origins and audiences of these homiletic works are not clear, but they do indicate some earlier tenth-century interest in providing bodies of writing in English for pastoral or devotional use. The writing of English religious prose and the translation of Latin works began again in earnest, however, during the revival of Benedictine monasticism in the last decades of the tenth century. Æthelwold's school at the Old Minster in Winchester is credited with establishing and teaching a 'Standard Old

English' language with a relatively uniform vocabulary (Gneuss 1972; Hofstetter 1987, 1988); this suggests that from the beginning of the reform English was being regarded as a suitable literary medium. Indeed, the most striking feature of the reform movement, along with and perhaps not unrelated to the amount of royal support it enjoyed, is its use of the vernacular; the continental reforms in Ghent and Fleury on which Dunstan and Æthelwold and Oswald modelled their own efforts hardly depended on vernacular translation. Æthelwold's defence of translation, appended to his OE version of the *Benedictine Rule*, is forthright: although 'keen-witted scholars' do not need translations, he admits, it is no less necessary for 'ungelæredum worold-monnum' ('unlearned laymen') to turn from their sins and choose 'the holy service of this rule':

> Wel mæg dugan hit naht mid hwylcan gereorde mon sy gestryned and to þan soþan geleafan gewæmed, butan þan an sy þæt he Gode gegange. Hæbben forþi þa ungelære-den inlendisce þæs halgan regules cyþþe þurh agenes gereordes anwrigenesse, þæt hy þe geornlicor Gode þeowien and nane tale næbben þæt hy þurh nytennesse misfon þurfen. (Whitelock et al. 1981: 151–2)

> It certainly cannot matter by what language a man is acquired and drawn to the true faith, so long as he come to God. Therefore let the unlearned natives have the knowl-edge of the holy rule by the exposition in their own language, that they may the more zealously serve God and have no excuse that they were driven to err by ignorance.

From this promotion of English as an alternative language of religious instruction arose the two best-known writers of Old English prose, Ælfric and Wulfstan. Ælfric was born somewhere in the middle of the tenth century; he was at first unhappily educated by a half-learned priest (as he remarks in the Preface to his translation of Genesis), but was later trained by Æthelwold at Winchester (Hurt 1972 offers a bio-graphical study; see also Clemoes 1959, 1966; Wilcox 1994: 1–15; see also Hill's chapter in this book). He was made master of novices at Cerne Abbas in Dorset in 987, and later abbot of Eynsham in 1005. He wrote most of his works at Cerne, partly as a consequence of his pedagogical responsibilities: the religious works include two series of forty sermons (the *Catholic Homilies*) for Sundays and major feast days, a series of *Lives of the Saints*, and translations of parts of the Old Testament. As abbot, Ælfric continued to write works of a more pragmatic nature such as pastoral letters (Hill 1992b), a monastic rule for the monks at Eynsham, and writings of instruction such as the Letter to Sigeweard 'On the Old and New Testaments' (Oxford, Bodleian Library, Laud Misc. 509), a synopsis of Christian history which appears elsewhere extracted as a homily.

Ælfric's contemporary Wulfstan was less directly a product of the monastic revival; rather he was a legislator and reformer, a leading figure of the English church in a time of crisis – the reigns of Æthelred 'Unræd' and the Danish Cnut. Wulfstan became bishop of London in 996, and later held the sees of impoverished York and wealthy Worcester in plurality. His career is that of a statesman rather than a scholar; his body of work is smaller than Ælfric's and his sermons are more episcopal in character, falling broadly into two categories: catechetical explanations of Christian doctrine (baptism, the Creed, the duties of a Christian) meant to regularize the practice of parish priests and assist them in the administration of sacraments, and vigorous calls for moral reform to a sinning people. Wulfstan was a public figure in a way that Ælfric was not, and his prose is more suitably public as well, dealing with contemporary matters and designed to exhort and inspire a large mixed audience. Wulfstan died in 1023 and is buried at Ely near ealdorman Byrhtnoth, who fell at the Battle of Maldon (see further Bethurum 1957, 1966).

Though Æthelwold writes of his concern for the 'ungelæred woroldmon', the promotion of English must be viewed at least partly as a concession to the perennial problem of clerical illiteracy. Among the secular clergy outside the monasteries, most evidence indicates that the ability to read Latin was the exception rather than the rule (see Hohler 1975: 74). Echoing Alfred's letter to his bishops, Ælfric laments the decline of learning in the preface to his *Grammar*; only a few years earlier, he says, 'nan englisc preost ne cuðe dihtan oððe asmeagean anne pistol on leden, oðþæt Dunstan arcebisceop and Aðelwold bisceop eft þa lare on munuclifum arærdon' (Zupitza 1880: 3), 'no English priest could compose or interpret a letter in Latin, until Archbishop Dunstan and Bishop Æthelwold restored learning to the monastic life.' Elsewhere he writes in a pastoral letter for Wulfstan, 'Us bisceopum gedafenæð, þæt we þa boclican lare þe ure canon us tæcð and eac seo Cristes boc, eow preostum geopenigen on Engliscum gereorde; forþam þe ge ealle ne cunnon þæt leden understandan' (Fehr 1966: II.2), 'It behoves us bishops that we should reveal in the English language the scholarly learning which our canon teaches us and also the Gospels for you priests, because you do not all know how to understand Latin.' Priests were trained alongside monks in some monastic classrooms, and may have been regarded as second-class students; the eleventh-century schoolmaster and scholar Byrhtferth of Ramsey makes a jocular reference to the 'uplendiscum preostum' ('hillbilly priests') who will understand less than his 'iungum munecum' ('young monks'; Baker and Lapidge 1995: II.3.239–40). The Latinity of the secular clergy was apparently always doubtful, from Bede's day to Ælfric's; competent translations of liturgical and pastoral works were a necessity if the reform was to have any benefits beyond the walls of the monasteries.

The need for English books among the secular clergy was paralleled by a demand for religious works from pious ealdormen and women. Æthelwold translated the Benedictine Rule at the request of King Edgar and his wife (Gneuss 1964; Gretsch 1974), and more than one nobleman apparently sought to imitate monastic liturgical observances in lay life. Several of Ælfric's works are addressed to lay patrons – the *Lives of the Saints* was composed at the request of ealdorman Æthelweard and his son Æthelmær, so that laymen might have the same readings as monks (Skeat 1966; see also Moloney 1984); Æthelweard requested a copy of the first series of *Catholic Homilies*; another ealdorman, Sigeweard, entreated Ælfric for copies of his works in English. London, British Museum, Cotton Claudius B. iv, an illustrated copy of the

OE *Hexateuch* (a translation of several books of the Old Testament including portions by Ælfric), may have been made for a lay patron (Dodwell and Clemoes 1974: 58). Ælfric's preface to his translation of *Genesis* begins:

> Ælfric munuc gret Æðelweard ealdormann eadmodlice. þu bæde me, leof, ðæt ic sceolde ðe awendan of Lydene on Englisc þa boc Genesis: ða þuhte me hefigtime þe to tiþienne þæs, and þu cwæde þa þæt ic ne þorfte na mare awendan þære bec buton to Isaace, Abrahames suna, for þam þe sum oðer man hæfde awend fram Isaace þa boc oþ ende. (Crawford 1922: 76)

> Ælfric monk humbly greets Æthelweard ealdorman. You asked me, lord, to translate the book of Genesis for you from Latin into English. It seemed burdensome to me to undertake that, and you said that I need only translate the book to 'Isaac, Abraham's son', because some other man had translated the book from 'Isaac' to the end.

Æthelweard apparently had other sources than Ælfric for his devotional reading; these lines suggest a considerable lay interest – at least at the highest levels of society – in works of religious instruction.

The decades surrounding the millennium saw a remarkable range of religious writings. Substantial parts of the Bible had been translated; prose and verse renderings of the Psalms already existed, the former done in Alfred's court (Bately 1982), and Ælfric contributed, though by his own account reluctantly, to a translation of parts of the Old Testament. An anonymous translation of the four Gospels survives in six eleventh-century and two twelfth-century copies (Liuzza 1994); one of the eleventh-century manuscripts (CUL Ii. 2. 11) has been systematically marked for liturgical reading, perhaps as a homiletic aid, and is accompanied by a translation of the apocryphal Gospel of Nicodemus. One may also find a relative abundance of manuscripts containing vernacular catechetical texts such as expositions of the Lord's Prayer and Creed, prayers connected with penance (on which see Frantzen 1983) and directions for confessors. Many of these translate Latin works; some may pre-date the Benedictine reform. The mid-eleventh-century London, British Library, Cotton Tiberius A. iii, a monastic miscellany whose various texts were probably collected together in Christ Church, Canterbury, is one among many indications that English and Latin texts were used side by side: the *Life of St Margaret* and the 'Devil's Account of the Next World' beside a glossed copy of the Benedictine Rule, directions for confessors and penitential prayers alongside a Latin book of dream interpretations and the monastic Office of the Blessed Virgin (Gneuss 1997).

By far the majority of surviving works, however, are the relatively brief exegetical or catechetical texts known as homilies. These form a complex body of material which has only recently begun to be studied systematically. Contrary to the modern associations of the word, not every homily, whether Latin or English, was intended for oral delivery to a lay congregation on a particular occasion; some may have been collected for private devotional reading, or recitation on Sundays during the monastic night office. Nor did every mass contain a homily; regular preaching at mass is a relatively late phenomenon which developed only slowly (Gatch 1977: 27–39). Preaching was an episcopal duty in the early church, but was later enjoined upon the parish priest. Wulfstan mandates that 'preostas ælce sunnandæge folce bodigan and aa wel bisnian' ('priests should preach to the people every Sunday and always teach by a good example'; Fowler 1972: 37); Ælfric's pastoral letter composed for Wulfsige, bishop of Sherborne, urges that:

> Se mæssepreost sceal secgan sunnandagum and mæssedagum þæs godspelles angyt on englisc þam folce. And be þam pater nostre and be þam credan eac, swa he oftost mage, þam mannum to onbryrdnysse, þat hi cunnon geleafan and heora cristendom geheald. Warnige se lareow wið þæt, þe se witega cwæð: *Canes muti non possunt latrare*; þa dumban hundas ne magon beorcan. We sceolon beorcan and bodigan þam læwedum, þe læs hy for larlyste losian sceoldan. (Whitelock et al. 1981: I.208)

> On Sundays and mass-days the priest should relate the meaning of the Gospel to the people in English, and also concerning the Paternoster and the Creed, as often as he can, to inspire the people to know their faith and hold their Christianity. Let the teacher beware of what the prophet said: *Canes muti non possunt latrare*; dumb dogs cannot bark. We ought to bark and preach to the unlearned, lest they be lost for lack of learning.

The fact that such pastoral letters often reiterate this requirement suggests, perhaps, that it was not universally observed; it is in fulfilment of this mandate, apparently, that Ælfric produced the bulk of his writings.

Public preaching could take many forms depending on the intended audience and the liturgical occasion. The church year unfolds in two overlapping cycles, the *temporale* and the *sanctorale*; the former is a sequence of moveable feasts – Lent, Easter, Ascension, Pentecost – tied to the date of Easter, which differs each year, while the latter is a series of celebrations occurring on fixed days – Christmas, Epiphany, the memorials and feasts of the saints (Lapidge 1991b, 1996). The relation between these two cycles differs each year; readings and prayers are assigned for each Sunday and feast of the church year (for a study of such readings in Anglo-Saxon England see Lenker 1997). A preacher may comment on the gospel reading, called a *pericope*, usually drawing his explanations from the writings of the church Fathers; his work is then called a 'homily'. He may tell the life (or *legend*) of a saint – his or her birth, death and miracles – whose feast is celebrated on a given day. He may give general moral advice or catechetical explanation, which is properly called a 'sermon', though the distinction is seldom maintained by either modern scholars or medieval authors. Calls to penance were especially frequent during Lent and the Rogation Days, the three days before Ascension Thursday called in OE 'gangdagas' from the custom of processing through the parish with the cross, Gospel and relics of the saints (Bazire and Cross 1989). A substantial body of anonymous sermons and saints' lives has survived, scattered in a number of manuscripts and fragments (Scragg 1979, 1996; Bately

1993; Whatley 1996); prominent among these are the Vercelli and Blickling Homily collections already mentioned. Most manuscript collections mingle anonymous sermons from diverse sources with works by Ælfric and Wulfstan.

In his capacity as archbishop and royal advisor Wulfstan produced some of the most energetic prose in Old English. Like his law-codes for Æthelred and Cnut, Wulfstan's homilies show his stern moral fervour and concern for social order; with the conviction of a prophet he denounces the sin and corruption that have caused the kingdom's troubles. His prose, like his person, 'presents a figure of abounding energy and concentrated purpose' (Bethurum 1966: 241); at its most artful it is analogous to the form of OE poetry, consisting of a series of strongly marked two-beat phrases, linked by alliteration and sometimes rhyme, characterized by repetition and semantic pairing, the powerful placement of rhetorical questions, and the frequent use of intensifiers such as *wide, swiðe, georne, ofer ealle, oft and gelome* (McIntosh 1949; Funke 1962; Hollis 1977). Wulfstan's prose is fundamentally a style for oral delivery and for the pulpit – it is written to be heard, and to move the hearer to action. His most widely known work, the *Sermo Lupi ad Anglos* written in 1014 during a crisis of Danish invasion, is one of the most forceful paraenetic works in English; piling detail upon detail, it moves the audience by the concatenation of sound and the accumulation of emotion rather than the flow of logic. Wulfstan's message is that political and spiritual degeneration, moral decline and military defeat, are one and the same:

> Nis eac nan wundor þeah us mislympe, forðam we witan ful georne þæt nu fela geara men na ne rohton foroft hwæt hi worhton wordes oððe dæde. Ac wearð þes þeodscipe, swa hit þyncan mæg, swyðe forsyngod þurh mænigfealda synna and þurh fela misdæda: ðurh morðdæda and ðurh mandæda, ðurh gytsunge and þurh gifernesse, ðurh stala and þurh strudunga, ðurh mansylene and þurh hæðene unsida, þurh swicdomas and þurh searocræftas, ðurh lahbrycas and ðurh æswicas, ðurh mægræsas and þurh manslihtas, ðurh hadbrycas and þurh æwbrycas, ðurh sibgelegeru and ðurh mistlice forlegeru. And eac synd wide, swa we ær cwædon, þurh aðbrycas and þurh wedbrycas and þurh mistlice leasunga forloren and forlogen ma þonne scolde, and freolsbrycas and fæstenbrycas wide geworhte oft and gelome. (Bethurum 1957: 264–5)

> It is no wonder that misfortune should befall us, because we know full well that for many years now men have not cared what they did in word or deed. Rather it seems this nation has become thoroughly corrupted through manifold sins and many misdeeds: through acts of murder and evil, through avarice and greed, through theft and thievery, through slavery and pagan abuses, through treachery and trickery, through the breach of law and order, through mayhem upon kinsmen and manslaughter, through the breaking of holy orders and law, through incest and various fornications. And everywhere, as we said before, by the breaking of oaths and by various lies many more than should be are lost and betrayed, and breaches of feasts and fasts are widely and frequently committed.

Ælfric, in contrast, developed a more restrained and expository style for the systematic exegesis of the Gospels. He composed eighty-four homilies for liturgical occasions and thirty-four sermons on the saints, collected into three sets of readings. The two series of *Catholic Homilies* contain forty homilies each, arranged around the cycle of the liturgical year; the *Lives of the Saints*, despite its modern title, contains material for the *temporale* as well as the *sanctorale*. Ælfric was concerned that laymen would misunderstand the 'naked narrative' of scripture if it were not interpreted for them: he comments to Æthelweard in the preface to *Genesis* that the danger of a translation is that 'þonne þincþ þam ungelæredum þæt eall þæt andgit beo belocen on þære anfealdan gerecednisse, ac hit ys swiþe feor þam' ('it will seem to the unlearned that all the sense is locked in the simple narrative, but it is very far from that'; Crawford 1922: 77). Existing homilies, he felt, provided no surer guidance; in the preface to the first series of *Catholic Homilies* he complains of the 'mycel gedwyld' ('great error') he has found in many English books, 'þe ungelærede menn þurh heora bilewitnysse to micclum wisdom tealdon' ('which the unlearned in their simplicity consider great wisdom'); he regrets that 'hi ne cuþon ne næfdon þa godspellican lare on heora gewritum, butan þam mannum anum ðe þæt leden cuðon, and buton þam bocum ðe Ælfred cyning snoterlice awende of ledene on Englisc, þa synd to hæbbene' (Clemoes 1997: 174), 'they [i.e. the English] did not know and did not have the Gospel teachings among their writings, except for those who knew Latin, and except for the books which King Alfred wisely translated from Latin to English, which are available'. In his expositions of scripture Ælfric made careful and selective use of orthodox authorities; he avoided the colourful but questionable sources used by anonymous authors collected in the Vercelli and Blickling manuscripts, pointedly omitting, for example, any recounting of the apocryphal *Visio Pauli* which was one of the sources for the Blickling sermon already quoted: 'Humeta rædað sume men ða leasan gesetnysse ðe hi hatað Paulus gesihðe, nu he sylfe sæde þæt he ða digelan word gehyrde, þe nan eorðlic mann sprecan ne mot?' ('How can some men read the false composition which they call the "Paul's Vision," when Paul himself said that he heard secret words, which no earthly man may speak?'; Godden 1979: 332; see also Healey 1978). Instead he drew ultimately upon the writings of the church Fathers – Gregory, Bede, Augustine, Jerome – and more directly upon the Carolingian homiliaries of Smaragdus, Haymo of Auxerre, and Paul the Deacon which collected these writings (Ælfric's sources are discussed by Smetana 1959, 1961, 1978; Godden 1978; Clayton 1985; Hill 1992a, 1993, 1996).

Ælfric describes his writings as translations, but he adapted and edited his sources, omitting some of the more esoteric allegorical implications of obscure Biblical passages in consideration of the limitations of his audiences; in a homily on Job addressed to a monastic audience (Gatch 1985: 359), he begins:

> Mine gebroðra. We rædað nu æt godes ðenungum be ðan eadigan were IOB. nu wille we eow hwæt lytles be him gereccan. for ðan þe seo deopnys ðære race oferstihð ure andgit. and eac swiðor þæra ungelæredra; Man sceal læwedum mannum secgan be heora andgites mæðe. swa þæt hi ne beon ðurh ða deopnysse æmode. ne ðurh ða langsumnysse geæðrytte. (Godden 1979: no. 30)

My brethren, we read now at God's services about the blessed Job. Now we will tell only a bit about him, because the profundity of the story exceeds our understanding, and even more so that of the unlearned. One ought to speak to simple people according to the measure of their understanding, so that they may not be disheartened by profundity, nor wearied by length.

The opening words of many of Ælfric's homilies indicate that he intended them to be read at mass after the Gospel; at the same time he saw his homiliaries as devotional reading – his patron Æthelweard had a copy – and as a reference work: in a homily for Pentecost he omits a long explanation of John 14, 23–31, with the excuse that 'We habbað gesæd swutellicor be þisum on þam oðrum spelle þe her to gebyrað, on þam man mæg gehyran be þam Halgan Gaste, se ðe hit rædan wyle, oþþe rædan gehyrð' (Pope 1967–8: I.396–405) ('we have discussed this more clearly in another writing concerning this, in which anyone may learn about the Holy Spirit who wishes to read it or hear it read'). In his letter to Sigeweard he apologizes for abbreviating the discussion of Christ's life by saying 'Ic secge þis sceortlice, for ðan þe ic gesett hæbbe of þisum feower bocum wel feowertig larspella on Engliscum gereorde and sumne eacan ðærto, þa þu miht rædan be þissere race on maran andgite, ðonne ic her secge' (Crawford 1922: 56), 'I say this briefly, because I have composed from these four books [i.e. the Gospels] nearly forty sermons in English and some more, which you can read on this matter with more insight than I could say here.' Manuscript evidence indicates that Ælfric took care to arrange, correct and improve his texts; his concern with his writings as a body of work, with their copying and circulation, their use as source and reference, and the orthodoxy and integrity of his teaching, is rare in a medieval literary culture where anonymity and textual instability are generally the hallmarks of vernacular writing. With Ælfric it is clear that writing in English is no mere concession to necessity, no makeshift solution to the problem of clerical illiteracy, but a finely developed intellectual practice.

Ælfric's Gospel homilies generally follow the patristic model of a 'continuous gloss' to a text, close translation interrupted by frequent commentary, moral instruction, and the citation of parallel or related passages (Szarmach 1989). Like Augustine's *De doctrina Christiana*, Ælfric moves quite naturally from *lectio* to *praedicatio* as inseparable parts of the same process; his homilies are a second-person address to an audience, a discourse rather than a text, aiming at the *ræd* which is at the root of OE verb *rædan* (see Howe 1993: 66–7), the 'teaching' that is an inseparable part of 'reading'. His homily for the Ninth Sunday after Pentecost (Godden 1979: 235–40) may be taken as a typical performance. Ælfric first translates the text, Matthew 7, 15–21, then returns to it phrase by phrase for explication; he explains the spiritual significance of the literal words – the trees which produce good or evil fruit, he says, are not literally trees but represent 'rational men who have understanding, and work by their own will good or evil. . . . Let us be fruitful in good works, lest the Lord find us fruitless, and command us to be cut down with the axe of death, and then thrown into the eternal fire.' He considers the theme of planting in several scriptural passages, quotes the parable of the vinedresser (Luke 13, 6–9), and concludes with a moral exhortation:

þæt treow bið bedolfen. and mid meoxe beworpen. þonne se cristena man mid soðre ead- modnysse his synna behreowsað; þæs treowes ymbgedelf is seo eadmodnys. þæs behre- owsiendan mannes; þæt meox is þæt gemynd his fulan dæda. on ðære dædbote; Hwæt is fulre ðonne meox? And swa ðeah gif ðu his wel notast. hwæt bið wæstmbærre? Awend þine heortan mid soðre dædbote. and ðin weorc bið awend; Awyrtwala grædignysse of ðinre heortan. and aplanta þæron ða soðan lufe; Seo grædignys is. swa swa se apostol Paulus cwæð wyrtruma ælces yfeles. and seo soðe lufu is wyrtruma ælces godes; ... Hwæt fremað þe þæt ðin cyst stande ful mid godum. and ðin ingehyd beo æmtig ælces godes? ðu wilt habban god. and nelt ðe sylf beon god; Sceamian ðe mæg þæt ðin hus hæbbe ælces godes genoh. and hæbbe þe ænne yfelne; Soðlice nelt ðu nan ðing yfeles habban. on ðinum æhtum; Nelt ðu habban yfel wif. ne yfele cild. ne yfele ðeowemen. ne yfel scrud. ne furðon yfele sceos. and wylt swa ðeah habban yfel lif; Ic bidde þe þæt ðu læte huru ðe ðin lif deorre. þonne ðine sceos; þu wilt habban ealle fægere ðing and acorene. and wilt ðe sylf beon waclic and unwurð; ðine æhta mid stylre stemne. wyllað þe wregen to ðinum drihtne; Efne ðu forgeafe þisum men þus fela goda. and he sylf is yfel; Hwæt fremað him þæt þæt he hæfð. þonne he ðone næfð þe him ða god forgeaf þe he hæfð?

The tree is dug around and heaped with dung when the Christian man repents his sins with true humility. The tree's surrounding trench is the humility of the penitent man, the dung is the memory of his foul deeds in penance. What is fouler than dung? And yet if you use it well, what is more fruitful? Turn aside your hearts with true penance, and your works will be turned around. Root up greed from your heart, and plant therein true love. Greed is, as the apostle Paul says, the root of every evil [I Tim 6:10], and true love is the root of all good. . . . What good does it do you if your coffer stands full of goods, and your conscience is empty of all good? You wish to have good, and will not yourself be good. It may shame you that your house should have enough of every good thing, and you should have only evil. Truly, you do not wish to have any evil thing in your possessions: you do not want an evil wife, nor evil children, nor evil servants, nor evil clothes, nor even evil shoes, and yet you would have an evil life. I ask you, indeed, to consider your life more precious than your shoes. You would have all things fair and well-chosen, and will yourself be trifling and worthless. Your possessions, with a steely voice, will accuse you to your lord: 'Behold, you gave to this man so many goods, and he himself is evil. What good does all that he has do him, when he does not have Him who gave him that which he has?'

Many of Ælfric's later works, such as many of the *Lives of the Saints*, are written in a rhythmical prose which, like Wulfstan's, consists of pairs of two-beat phrases linked by alliteration. In these rhythmical pieces and elsewhere, however, his prose is in a lower register than Wulfstan's, and unlike Wulfstan Ælfric uses sentence structure as a rhetorical device, conveying his point through figures of thought as well as figures of sound and speech.

The manuscript evidence attests to the popularity of Ælfric's works; Malcolm Godden notes twenty-four manuscripts drawing on the *Catholic Homilies*, nine fragments possibly from larger collections, and six manuscripts containing only one or two items (Godden 1978: 110). Ælfric apparently wanted to keep his works whole and apart from other writings of questionable orthodoxy; at the end of the second series of *Catholic Homilies* he adds a prayer asking that if anyone wishes to write more homilies or Gospel translations, 'ðonne bidde ic hine, for Godes lufon, þæt he gesette his boc onsundron fram ðam twam bocum ðe we awend habbað, we truwiað þurh Godes diht' (Godden 1979: 345), 'then I ask him, for the love of God, to keep his books separate from the two books which we have translated, we trust, with God's help'. His request was not honoured, however, and subsequent compilers excerpted, adapted and collected his homilies alongside anonymous works; only a few manuscripts contain purely Ælfrician material. This is a sign of their popularity and wide circulation, but Ælfric's innovation – the presentation of carefully orthodox Gospel exegesis tied to the cycle of the liturgical year – seems not to have caught on. This is perhaps not surprising: Gospel homilies may be used only on a particular day of the year, while moral exhortation and instruction in the streamlined basics of the Christian life are more flexible and adaptable.

Devotional, liturgical and catechetical writings obviously found an audience among both the clergy and the laity, and collections of homilies and other writings continued to be read and copied throughout the eleventh and twelfth centuries. Oxford, Bodleian Library, Bodley 343, from the middle of the twelfth century, contains pieces by Ælfric and Wulfstan as well as anonymous works (Irvine 1993); another mid-twelfth-century manuscript, London, British Library, Cotton Vespasian D. xiv, contains Ælfrician and anonymous homilies alongside translations of post-conquest sermons (Warner 1917; Handley 1974). A copy of the Old English Gospels found in Oxford, Bodleian Library, Hatton 38, may have been written as late as 1185 (Liuzza 1994: xxxvi). The scribes of these manuscripts modernized their language, adapted their texts and rearranged their copies, suggesting that Old English religious prose continued to be read throughout the century after the Norman Conquest – the scribes' interest in these works was not merely antiquarian. A number of eleventh-century manuscripts have glosses and annotations by a thirteenth-century glossator whose distinctively shakey hand has led him to be known as the 'Worcester Tremulous' scribe (Franzen 1992; see also Cameron 1974). These late readers recognized the value of vernacular religious prose. The precociously modern use of the vernacular for serious works of religious instruction began as a necessity, but had become a virtue; the distinctive styles of writers as different as Ælfric and Wulfstan show the flexibility of Old English prose as an instrument of serious and consciously artful expression, adaptable to a broad range of subjects and occasions. The confidence and competence of these authors, and others such as the anonymous translators of the Gospels, is a striking witness to the strength of Anglo-Saxon literary culture. Christianity changed the landscape and culture of the Anglo-Saxons, but the native traditions of the English changed the nature and expression of the church as well; the vernacular enriched and was enriched by the complex reciprocal interchange of Latin and English literary cultures.

REFERENCES

Primary sources

Baker, Peter S. and Michael Lapidge, eds and trans. 1995. *Byrhtferth of Ramsey: Enchiridion*. EETS, s.s. 15. Oxford.

Bazire, Joyce and J. E. Cross, eds 1989. *Eleven Old English Rogationtide Homilies*. King's College London Medieval Studies 4. London.

Bethurum, Dorothy, ed. 1957. *The Homilies of Wulfstan*. Oxford.

Bischoff, B. and M. Lapidge 1994. *Biblical Commentaries from the Canterbury School of Theodore and Hadrian*. Cambridge Studies in Anglo-Saxon England 10. Cambridge.

Clemoes, Peter, ed. 1997. *Ælfric's Catholic Homilies: The First Series*. EETS, s.s. 17. Oxford.

Colgrave, B. and R. A. B. Mynors, eds 1991. *Bede's Historia Ecclesiastica Gentis Anglorum*. Oxford.

Crawford, S. J. 1922. *The Old English Version of the Hexateuch, Ælfric's Treatise on the Old and New Testament and his Preface to Genesis*. EETS, o.s. 160. Repr. with additions N. R. Ker. 1969.

Dodwell, C. R. and Peter Clemoes, eds 1974. *The Old English Illustrated Hexateuch, British Museum Cotton Claudius B. IV*. Early English Manuscripts in Facsimile 18. Copenhagen.

Fehr, B., ed. 1966. *Die Hirtenbriefe Ælfrics*. Bibliothek der angelsächsischen Prosa 9. Repr. with suppl. P. Clemoes. Darmstadt.

Fowler, Roger 1972. *Wulfstan's Canons of Edgar*. EETS, o.s. 266. Oxford.

Godden, Malcolm, ed. 1979. *Ælfric's Catholic Homilies: The Second Series*. EETS, s.s. 5. Oxford.

Healey, Antonette diPaolo 1978. *The Old English Vision of St Paul*. *Speculum* Anniversary Monographs 2. Cambridge, MA.

Hecht, H. 1900–7. *Bischof Waerferths von Worcester Übersetzung der Dialoge Gregors des Grossen*. Bibliothek der angelsächsischen Prosa 5. Leipzig. Repr. Darmstadt, 1965.

Herzfeld, George 1900. *An Old English Martyrology*. EETS, o.s. 116. London.

Hurst, D., ed. 1955. *Bedae Venerabilis opera III: Opera homiletica*. Corpus Christianorum, Series Latina 122. Turnhout.

Irvine, Susan 1993. *Old English Homilies from MS Bodley 343*. EETS, o.s. 302. Oxford.

Keynes, Simon and M. Lapidge 1983. *Alfred the Great: Asser's Life of King Alfred and Other Contemporary Sources*. Harmondsworth.

Kotzor, Günter 1981. *Das altenglische Martyrologium*. Bayerische Akademie der Wissenschaften, Philosophisch-historische Klasse, Abhandlungen, 88, nos. 1 and 2. 2 vols. Munich.

Lindsay, W. M. 1921. *The Corpus, Épinal, Erfurt, and Leiden Glossaries*. Publications of the Philological Society viii. London.

Liuzza, R. M. 1994. *The Old English Version of the Gospels, vol. I: Text and Introduction*. EETS, o.s. 304. Oxford.

Miller, T. 1890–8. *The Old English Version of Bede's Ecclesiastical History of the English People*. EETS, o.s. 95–6, 110–11. Oxford. Repr. 1959–63.

Morris, R., ed. 1874–80. *The Blickling Homilies of the Tenth Century*. EETS, o.s. 58, 63, 73. London.

Pheifer, J. D. 1974. *Old English Glosses in the Épinal-Erfurt Glossary*. Oxford.

Pope, John C. 1967–8. *Homilies of Ælfric: A Supplementary Collection*. EETS, o.s. 259–60. London.

Scragg, D. G. 1990. *The Vercelli Homilies and Related Texts*. EETS, o.s. 300. Oxford.

Sisam, Celia 1976. *The Vercelli Book*. Early English Manuscripts in Facsimile 19. Copenhagen.

Skeat, Walter W., ed. and trans. 1966. *Ælfric's Lives of Saints*. EETS, o.s. 76, 82, 94, 114. London, 1881–90. Repr. as 2 vols. London.

Sweet, H. 1871. *King Alfred's West-Saxon Version of Gregory's Pastoral Care*. EETS, o.s. 45 and 50. Oxford.

Vleeskruyer, R. 1953. *The Life of St Chad: An Old English Homily*. Amsterdam.

Warner, Ruby D.-N. 1917. *Early English Homilies from the Twelfth Century MS. Vespasian D. xiv*.

EETS, o.s. 152. London.

Whitelock, Dorothy, M. Brett, and C. N. L. Brooke, eds 1981. *Councils and Synods with Other Documents Relating to the English Church, vol. i: A.D. 871–1204*. Oxford.

Wilcox, Jonathan 1994. *Ælfric's Prefaces*. Durham Medieval Texts 9. Durham.

Willard, R. ed. 1960. *The Blickling Homilies*. Early English Manuscripts in Facsimile 10. Copenhagen.

Zupitza, Julius 1880. *Ælfrics Grammatik und Glossar, pt I: Text und Varianten*. Berlin.

Secondary sources

Bately, Janet 1980. *The Literary Prose of King Alfred's Reign: Translation or Transformation?*. Inaugural Lecture, King's College, University of London. London.

——1982. 'Lexical Evidence for the Authorship of the Prose Psalms in the Paris Psalter'. *Anglo-Saxon England* 10: 69–95.

——1993. *Anonymous Old English Homilies: A Preliminary Bibliography of Source-Studies*. Binghamton, NY.

Bethurum, Dorothy 1966. 'Wulfstan'. *Continuations and Beginnings: Studies in Old English Literature*, pp. 210–46. Ed. E. G. Stanley. London.

Brown, George 1995. 'The Dynamics of Literacy in Anglo-Saxon England'. *Bulletin of the John Rylands Library* 77: 109–42.

Cameron, Angus 1974. 'Middle English in Old English Manuscripts'. *Chaucer and Middle English Studies in Honour of Rossel Hope Robbins*, pp. 218–29. Ed. Beryl Rowlands. London.

Clayton, Mary 1985. 'Homiliaries and Preaching in Anglo-Saxon England'. *Peritia* 4, 207–42.

Clemoes, Peter 1959. 'The Chronology of Ælfric's Works'. *The Anglo-Saxons: Studies in some Aspects of their History and Culture presented to Bruce Dickins*, pp. 212–47. Ed. Peter Clemoes. London. Rpt. with corrections *The Chronology of Ælfric's Works*. Old English Newsletter Subsidia 5. Binghamton, NY, 1980.

——1966. 'Ælfric'. *Continuations and Beginnings: Studies in Old English Literature*, pp. 176–209. Ed. E. G. Stanley. London.

Cross, J. E. 1986. 'The Latinity of the Ninth-Century Old English Martyrologist'. *Studies in*

Earlier Old English Prose, pp. 275–299. Ed. P. E. Szarmach. Albany, NY.

Cubitt, Catherine 1992. 'Pastoral Care and the Conciliar Canons: The Provisions of the 747 Council of *Clofesho*'. *Pastoral Care Before the Parish*, pp. 193–211. Eds J. Blair and R. Sharpe. London.

——1995. *Anglo-Saxon Church Councils c.650–850*. London.

Frantzen, A. J. 1983. *The Literature of Penance in Anglo-Saxon England*. New Brunswick, NJ.

Franzen, C. 1992. *The Tremulous Hand of Worcester*. Oxford.

Funke, O. 1962. 'Some Remarks on Wulfstan's Prose Rhythms'. *English Studies* 43: 311–18.

Gatch, M. McC. 1977. *Preaching and Theology in Anglo-Saxon England: Ælfric and Wulfstan*. Toronto.

——1985. 'The Office in Late Anglo-Saxon Monasticism'. *Learning and Literature in Anglo-Saxon England. Studies Presented to Peter Clemoes on the Occasion of his Sixty-fifth birthday*, pp. 341–62. Eds Michael Lapidge and Helmut Gneuss. Cambridge.

——1986. 'King Alfred's Version of Augustine's *Soliloquia*: Some Suggestions on its Rationale and Unity'. *Studies in Earlier Old English Prose*, pp. 17–45. Ed. P. E. Szarmach. Albany, NY.

——1989. 'The Unknowable Audience of the Blickling Homilies'. *Anglo-Saxon England* 18, 99–115.

Gneuss, Helmut 1964. 'Die Benediktinerregel in England und ihre altenglische Übersetzung'. *Die angelsächsischen Prosabearbeitungen der Benediktinerregel*. Ed. A. Schröer. Bibliothek der angelsächsischen Prosa 2. 2nd edn. Darmstadt.

——1972. 'The Origin of Standard Old English and Æthelwold's School at Winchester'. *Anglo-Saxon England* 1: 63–83.

——1997. 'Origin and Provenance of Anglo-Saxon Manuscripts: The Case of Cotton Tiberius A.III'. *Of the Making of Books: Medieval Manuscripts, their Scribes and Readers. Essays Presented to M. B. Parkes*, pp. 13–48. Eds P. R. Robinson and Rivkah Zim. Aldershot.

——1978. 'Ælfric and the Vernacular Prose Tradition'. *The Old English Homily and its Backgrounds*, pp. 99–117. Eds Paul Szarmach and Bernard Huppé. Albany, NY.

——1981. 'King Alfred's Boethius'. *Boethius: His*

Life, Thought, and Influence, pp. 419–29. Ed. Margaret Gibson. Oxford.

Gretsch, Mechthild 1974. 'Æthelwold's Translation of the *Regula Sancti Benedicti* and its Latin Exemplar'. *Anglo-Saxon England* 3: 125–51.

Handley, Rima 1974. 'British Museum MS. Cotton Vespasian D.xiv'. *Notes & Queries* 21: 243–50.

Hill, Joyce 1992a. 'Ælfric and Smaragdus'. *Anglo-Saxon England* 21: 203–37.

—— 1992b. 'Monastic Reform and the Secular Church: Ælfric's Pastoral Letters in Context'. *England in the Eleventh Century: Proceedings of the 1990 Harlaxton Symposium*, pp. 103–17. Ed. Carola Hicks. Stamford.

—— 1993. 'Reform and Resistance: Preaching Styles in Late Anglo-Saxon England'. *De l'homélie au sermon: histoire de la prédication médiévale*, pp. 15–46. Ed. J. Hamesse and X. Hermand. Louvain-sur-Neuve.

—— 1996. 'Ælfric's Sources Reconsidered: Some Case Studies from the *Catholic Homilies*'. *'Doubt Wisely': Papers in Honour of E. G. Stanley*, pp. 362–86. Eds M. J. Toswell and E. M. Tyler. London.

Hofstetter, Walter 1987. *Winchester und der Spätaltenglische Sprachgebrauch*. Munich.

—— 1988. 'Winchester and the Standardization of Old English Vocabulary'. *Anglo-Saxon England* 17: 139–61.

Hohler, C. E. 1975. 'Some Service-books of the Later Saxon Church'. *Tenth-Century Studies: Essays in Commemoration of the Millennium of the Council of Winchester and* Regularis Concordia, pp. 60–83. Ed. David Parsons. Chichester.

Hollis, S. 1977. 'The Thematic Structure of the *Sermo Lupi*'. *Anglo-Saxon England* 6: 175–95.

Howe, Nicholas 1993. 'The Cultural Construction of Reading in Anglo-Saxon England'. *The Ethnography of Reading*, pp. 58–79. Ed. Jonathan Boyarin. Berkeley, CA.

Hurt, James R. 1972. *Ælfric*. Twayne's English Authors Series 131. New York.

Jeffrey, J. E. 1989. *Blickling Spirituality and the Old English Vernacular Homily: A Textual Analysis*. Studies in Medieval Literature 1. New York.

Kelly, Susan 1990. 'Anglo-Saxon Lay Society and the Written Word'. *The Uses of Literacy in Early Medieval Europe*, pp. 36–62. Ed. Rosamund McKitterick. Cambridge.

Lapidge, Michael 1991a. 'Schools, Learning and Literature in Tenth-Century England'. 'Il secolo de ferro: Mito e realtà del secolo X'. *Settimane de studio del centro italiano di studi sull'alto medioevo* 38: 951–1005.

—— 1996. 'Ælfric's *Sanctorale*'. *Holy Men and Holy Women: Old English Prose Saints' Lives and their Contexts*, pp. 115–29. Ed. Paul E. Szarmach. Albany, NY.

Lenker, Ursula 1997. *Die westsächsische Evangelienversion und die Perikopenordnungen im angelsächsischen England*. Munich.

Malone, Kemp 1958. 'Grendel and his Abode'. *Studia Philologica et Litteraria in Honorem L. Spitzer*, pp. 297–308. Eds A. G. Hatcher and K. L. Selig. Bern.

McIntosh, Angus 1949. 'Wulfstan's Prose'. *Proceedings of the British Academy* 34, 109–42.

Moloney, Bernadette 1984. 'Be Godes Halgum: Ælfric's Hagiography and the Cult of the Saints in England in the Tenth Century'. *Literature and Learning in Medieval and Renaissance England: Essays Presented to Fitzroy Pyle*, pp. 25–40. Ed. John Scattergood. Dublin.

Morrish, J. 1986. 'King Alfred's Letter as a Source on Learning in England in the Ninth Century'. *Studies in Earlier Old English Prose*, pp. 87–107. Ed. P. E. Szarmach. Albany, NY.

Riché, Pierre 1976. *Education and Culture in the Barbarian West: Sixth through Eighth Centuries*. Tr. John J. Contreni. University of South Carolina Press.

Scragg, D. G. 1979. 'The Corpus of Vernacular Homilies and Prose Saints' Lives before Ælfric'. *Anglo-Saxon England* 8: 223–77.

—— 1985. 'The Homilies of the Blickling Manuscript'. *Learning and Literature in Anglo-Saxon England. Studies Presented to Peter Clemoes on the Occasion of his Sixty-fifth Birthday*, pp. 299–316. Eds Michael Lapidge and Helmut Gneuss. Cambridge.

—— 1996. 'The Corpus of Anonymous Lives and their Manuscript Context'. *Holy Men and Holy Women: Old English Prose Saints' Lives and their Contexts*, pp. 209–30. Ed. Paul E. Szarmach. Albany, NY.

Sisam, Celia 1953. 'An Early Fragment of the Old English *Martyrology*'. *Review of English Studies* 4, n.s. 15: 209–20.

Smetana, Cyril 1959. 'Ælfric and the Early Medieval Homiliary'. *Traditio* 15: 163–204.

—— 1961. 'Ælfric and the Homiliary of Haymo of Halberstadt'. *Traditio* 17, 457–69.

—— 1978. 'Paul the Deacon's Patristic Anthology'. *The Old English Homily and its Backgrounds*, pp. 75–97. Eds Paul Szarmach and Bernard Huppé. Albany, NY.

Szarmach, P. 1982. 'The Meaning of Alfred's *Preface* to the *Pastoral Care*'. *Medievalia* 6: 57–86.

—— 1989. 'Ælfric as Exegete: Approaches and Examples in the Study of the *Sermones Catholici*'. *Hermeneutics and Medieval Culture*, pp. 237–47. Eds Patrick J. Gallacher and Helen Damico. Albany, NY.

Thacker, Alan 1992. 'Monks, Preaching, and Pastoral Care in Early Anglo-Saxon England'. *Pastoral Care Before the Parish*, pp. 137–70. Eds J. Blair and R. Sharpe. London.

Whatley, E. Gordon 1996. 'An Introduction to the Study of Old English Prose Hagiography: Sources and Resources'. *Holy Men and Holy Women: Old English Prose Saints' Lives and their Contexts*, pp. 3–32. Ed. Paul E. Szarmach. Albany, NY.

Whitelock, Dorothy 1966. 'The Prose of Alfred's Reign'. *Continuations and Beginnings: Studies in Old English Literature*, pp. 67–103. Ed. E. G. Stanley. London.

14

Religious Poetry

Patrick W. Conner

The present essay endeavours to examine the body of Old English poetry where it intersects with religion, seeking to describe the cultural space occupied by religious and poetic discourses during the Anglo-Saxon period and – in so doing – striving to enlarge the interpretative horizons of expectation for the postmodern reader, who is very often unacquainted with the forms and functions of religion in the Anglo-Saxon period. As a category, Old English religious poetry transcends the philosophically unexamined, ideologically constrained moralizations which the modern label 'religious' too often suggests to uninformed readers, but – after a thousand years – the core of this poetry remains as powerful as that of any other period of English poetry, and it begs to be read on its own terms.

I shall not try to explain systematically here the specific doctrinal, liturgical or dogmatic issues which scholars sometimes see operating in one poem or another, and I do not seek either to confirm or refute those ingenious archaeological approaches to our poetry (almost never made by archaeologists themselves) which identify the strata of Christian rite and dogma lying atop older varieties of pre-Christian cultural production.

To say that a poem is religious is to say that it participates in religious discourse, but as generations of philosophers, anthropologists and sociologists have shown, a definition of religion itself is hard to come by, and it is even harder to specify the ways in which religion (not to mention magic) and culture interact (see Cunningham 1999). While it is generally useful in cultural matters to empathize with the practices and forms of other places and other times even if they are not congenial to us, the subset of religious cultural matters – especially overtly Christian practice – often creates a resistance to such empathy for the Western reader in the twenty-first century. This is due to a myriad of ongoing, overlapping processes in the West, including the renewed politicization of religious values, issues of cultural and gender identity contested by the hegemonic religious denominations, the continuing validation in science of truths which appear antithetical to accepted religious dogma and a growing international pressure to reduce ethnic divisions traditionally affirmed in religious belief. Any analysis today of religious poetry of any period which does not take into account our determined indeterminacy respecting religion will be regarded as ingenuous at best or, worse, repressive. The days of Robertsonian patristic exegesis presenting, in the main, a programme of Christian apologetic are past.

Since Émile Durkheim's *The Elementary Forms of Religious Life* in 1915, the problem of how to confront religious forms in the study of unfamiliar cultures has been a preoccupation of anthropology. Before Durkheim, Max Weber, Herbert Spencer, J. G. Frazer, Sigmund Freud and Bronislaw Malinowski, to mention only the best-known names, concerned themselves with non-denominational definitions of religion and religiosity, distinguishing between what is sacred and what is secular or profane, but the problem of the subject position which Durkheim and other structuralists had begun to articulate necessarily led to new definitions of religion more focused on issues of semiotics and language, and it is these which I find to be useful in approaching the religious nature of Old English poetry. American anthropologist Clifford Geertz offers a definition of religion which may help us to understand better the nature of the religious impulse in Old English poetry:

> A religion is (1) a system of symbols which acts to (2) establish powerful, pervasive, and long-lasting moods and motivations in men by (3) formulating conceptions of a general order of existence and (4) clothing these conceptions with such an aura of factuality that (5) the moods and motivations seem uniquely realistic. (Geertz 1973: 90)

An advantage of this definition is that it addresses social structure, systematics of culture and individual personality, all of which must be considered in any account of textual practice as well as in the practice of religion.

Geertz atomizes his definition as follows. That religion is first of all a system of symbols requires his Saussurean definition of symbol as 'any object, act, event, quality, or relation which serves as a vehicle for a conception – the conception is the symbol's "meaning"' (Geertz 1973: 91). The semiotician will recognize the signifier in this, but Geertz makes the additional point – clearly relevant to religion but probably to poetry as well – that such symbolic systems and the culture systems embracing them 'have an intrinsic double aspect: they give meaning, that is objective conceptual form, to social and psychological reality both by shaping themselves to it and by shaping it to themselves' (Geertz 1973: 93).

Karen Louise Jolly demonstrates how this worked in Anglo-Saxon religious practice in her introduction to *Popular Religion in Late Saxon England* (1996: 6–34). The double nature of the bond between systems of signifiers and social and psychological reality allows her to assert reciprocal relationships between popular and formal modes of religion; whereas scholars for a very long time assumed the primacy of the formal mode, by which Jolly means the scholarly, intellectual strand of early Christian practice which is usually taken to articulate orthodoxy of the whole, she asserts that the whole is more properly identified with the adjective 'popular':

These two categories, popular and formal, are overlapping spheres, with the formal nestled almost completely within the popular. The popular is the more comprehensive and yet more amorphous sphere, incorporating the widest population and practice. The formal sphere is smaller and tighter, making up a self-defined dominant minority within the total practice of religion. Since 'secret' doctrines or rituals are antithetical to the Christian tradition, it is hard to locate any formal church practices that would fall outside the popular religion – perhaps certain abstruse theological constructs. In general, all doctrine and ritual technically belonged to the entire Christian community, whether presented formally in Latin or explained in the vernacular for lay persons. Likewise, the formal church did not exist in isolation from the culture it inhabited; churchmen and scholars were Anglo-Saxons too. A common Christian worldview was shared by both popular religion and the formal religion. (Jolly 1996: 18–19)

In fact, what Jolly labels 'popular religion' is, from Geertz's point of view, religion unqualified, and – with this proviso in mind – her study of Anglo-Saxon religion is an important correction to those works which exploit the formal church's self-conscious propaganda to the neglect of the church's more inclusive popular system of signifiers.

The second point in Geertz's definition is that systems of religious signifiers 'establish powerful, pervasive, and long-lasting moods and motivations' in people. Doubtless, he carefully chose the phrase 'moods and motivations', if only because it also needs to do other work at the end of this definition. The work of Raymond Williams, Louis Althusser and Fredric Jameson has helped elucidate literary works as the products and means of cultural ideologies, and in this definition, Geertz places religion in the same category. From a Marxian point of view, 'powerful, pervasive, and long-lasting moods and motivations' may be rewritten then as 'ideology.' (See Williams 1977: 110, wherein 'hegemony' is defined synonymously with 'ideology': 'It is a whole body of practices and expectations, over the whole of living: our senses and assignments of energy, our shaping perceptions of ourselves and our world. It is a lived system of meanings and values – constitutive and constituting – which as they are experienced as practices appear as reciprocally confirming. It thus constitutes a sense of reality for most people in the society.') The head of the phrase, 'moods and motivations', is further defined by Geertz:

A motivation is a persisting tendency, a chronic inclination to perform certain sorts of acts and experience certain sorts of feelings in certain sorts of situations, the 'sorts' being commonly very heterogeneous and rather ill-defined classes. (Geertz 1973: 96)

The moods that sacred symbols induce, at different times and in different places, range from exultation to melancholy, from self-confidence to self-pity, from an incorrigible playfulness to a bland listlessness – to say nothing of the erogenous power of so many of the world's myths and rituals. No more than there is a single sort of motivation one can call piety is there a single sort of mood one can call worshipful. (Geertz 1973: 97)

While Geertz is careful not merely to specify Judaeo-Christian passions and actions with which we are already familiar in the West in his definitions of 'moods and motivations', it is clear that they are at the heart of an ideology we should identify as religious in nature:

> But perhaps the most important difference, so far as we are concerned, between moods and motivations is that motivations are 'made meaningful' with reference to the ends toward which they are conceived to conduce, whereas moods are 'made meaningful' with reference to the conditions from which they are conceived to spring. We interpret motives in terms of their consummations, but we interpret moods in terms of their sources. (Geertz 1973: 97)

That moods and motivations arising from the system of signifiers are 'pervasive' and 'long-lasting' is particularly important for our attempt to apply this definition to Anglo-Saxon religious culture. As Jolly points out in her comments on Augustine and his successors' conversion of the Anglo-Saxons, the new Christian system did not simply replace a now-disavowed pre-Christian or pagan system. Either the Germanic religion which preceded Christianity possessed a system of symbols which acted to establish powerful, pervasive and long-lasting moods and motivations in people, or – by the definition we are using – it was not a religion. In other words, religious syncretism, which is well documented in Anglo-Saxon sources, is evidence for an ongoing religious system embedded in the culture. If such things as sacred wells and groves and other indications of pre-Christian Germanic animism were maintained long into the Christian period, as Jolly indicates, this is not necessarily an indication of the psychological or sociological fitness of these particular signifiers so much as it is an indication of the enduring nature of the contents of any religious system. By our definition, an ideology must be pervasive and long-lasting to be a religious ideology. To be pervasive, it must interact with the whole culture in the manner already stated: it shapes the culture and the culture shapes it. The difference between what may be called 'cults' and what qualifies as religion is specified in this part of the definition. Individuals are capable of specifying systems of signifiers which fulfil all of the conditions of this definition, but if these systems are not pervasive and they do not last, then they do not rise to the status of a religion. The fact of Anglo-Saxon syncretism is, perhaps, itself evidence of a genuine religious tradition in pre-Christian Anglo-Saxon England. Such a tradition might well have had numerous local variations (as did liturgies and other practices of the Christian Church before the thirteenth century), but the shadowy contents of these pre-Christian practices which are preserved in bits of our poetry – nowhere so well, perhaps, as in *Beowulf* – mainly indicate that the Anglo-Saxons had an adequate religious tradition before Christianity that could not and would not be easily shuffled off when Christianity arrived, because it was in fact a self-sufficient religion. That the Anglo-Saxons appear in the main not merely to have accepted certain basic tenets of Christianity, but to have embraced them, does not invalidate the pervasive and long-lasting nature of their former creeds. Nor does it entitle those creeds to any particular regard from pride of place. We are confronted here, as we are in many places, with the dialectic of social change: dominant ideologies become residual, emergent ideologies become dominant.

The third point in Geertz's definition is that systems of religious signifiers which establish enduring ideologies do so by 'formulating conceptions of a general order of existence'. This is a point that does not need to be belaboured. The ideological power of a religion lies in the appearance of the order of existence it espouses. Coifi's famous allegory of the swallow flying from the winter storm into the hall and back out as the order of our existence before our births and after our deaths stresses the power of this general order of existence:

> This sparrow flies swiftly in through one door of the hall, and out through another. While he is inside, he is safe from winter storms; but after a few moments of comfort, he vanishes from sight into the wintry world from which he came. Even so man appears on earth for a little while; but of what went before this life or of what follows, we know nothing. Therefore, if this new teaching has brought any more certain knowledge, it seems only right that we should follow it. (Bede, *HE* II.13; Sherley-Price 1990: 129–30)

Moreover, the general order of existence is confronted in all cultures, as Geertz notes, with the interrelated problems of the suffering of innocents and the existence of evil:

> The strange opacity of certain empirical events, the dumb senselessness of intense or inexorable pain, and the enigmatic unaccountability of gross iniquity all raise the uncomfortable suspicion that perhaps the world, and hence man's life in the world, has no genuine order at all – no empirical regularity, no emotional form, no moral coherence. And the religious response to this suspicion is in each case the same: the formulation, by means of symbols and of an image of such a genuine order of the world which will account for, and even celebrate, the perceived ambiguities, puzzles, and paradoxes in human experience. (Geertz 1973: 107–8)

Boethius' *De consolatio Philosophiae* is the best-known early medieval tract on this very theme, and indeed Boethius both accounts for and celebrates the ambiguities, puzzles and paradoxes of human experience, using the methods of a Platonic dialogue to establish the logic of what is, in fact, the general order of existence for orthodox Christianity. Furthermore, the format of the *Consolatio*, wherein the narrator despairs at his bad fortune only to have Lady Philosophy provide him with an account of existence which establishes within him a new mood and imbues him with positive intentions for the future, is rather a rehearsal of religion at work according to the Geertzian definition.

Fourth, Geertz's definition asserts that 'conceptions of a general order of existence' are supplied with an 'aura of factuality', by which he means to characterize ritual:

> It is in some sort of ceremonial form – even if that form be hardly more than the recitation of a myth, the consultation of an oracle, or the decoration of a grave – that the

moods and motivations which sacred symbols induce in men and the general conceptions of the order of existence which they formulate for men meet and reinforce one
another. (Geertz 1973: 112)

The 'aura of factuality' refers then to the way in which religions create texts out of
religious conceptions and symbols. Such texts may be highly verbal and literate, and
thus they are 'myths', or they may be purely performative, and thus constitute liturgies and the rubrics thereof. Or they may fall somewhere in between, as do prayers,
ceremonies like baptism, and the verbal elaborations of the Eucharist. In any case,
such texts represent significant content of the religion, and the 'aura of factuality'
Geertz posits in them derives from the necessity for interpretation with which they
are imbued. When such forms make their way into poetry, the reader is obliged to
recognize their religious interpretations even if eventually she or he desires to subvert
such interpretations. The adoration of the cross and the centrality of the crucifixion
to Christian thought cannot reasonably be ignored in an interpretation of *The Dream
of the Rood*, because these are 'facts' of the dominant ideology of both the poem and
the society which created it. The crucifixion is always the sacrifice at the centre of
Christian thought, and the cross is always both the instrument of torture and the
means of salvation. The elements of the Eucharist are always the body and the blood
of Christ, whatever else they may be, and Ælfric's Eucharistic sermon makes clear how
profoundly factual these things are, even before the Fourth Lateran Council legislated
the facts of Christian forms.

Finally, Geertz notes that 'the moods and motivation seem uniquely realistic'. By
'realistic', he apparently means that what is dramatized in ceremony atemporally is
manifested in the faithful's behaviour in the temporal world:

> The dispositions which religious rituals induce thus have their most important impact
> – from a human point of view – outside the boundaries of the ritual itself as they reflect
> back to color the individual's conception of the established world of bare fact. (Geertz
> 1973: 119)

The major function of the religious dimension in Old English poetry is to reference
the ceremonial and ineffable from the position of the temporal and the commonplace.
One of the best examples of this is found in the so-called Old English elegies, where
the final few lines enact a religious application to the foregoing text in such a way
that the elegiac portrayal of hardship is transformed explicitly into the religious mood
of suffering and endurance. In *The Wanderer* this application occupies only one and
one-half metrical lines, yet its purpose in a religious reading of the poem is clear; the
interpretation it initiates for the preceding 113 and one-half metrical lines of the
poem would seem inescapable:

> Wel bið se þam þe him are seceð
> frofre to fæder in heofonum,   þær us eal seo fæstnung stondeð.
> (Krapp and Dobbie 1936: 137, lines 114b–115)

Well will it be for the person who seeks mercy and comfort from the Father in Heaven, where there is protection for us all.

These lines follow the poet's proclamation that:

> Eall is earfoðlic   eorþan rice,
> onwendeð wyrda gesceaft   weoruld under heofonum.
> Her bið feoh læne,   her bið freond læne,
> her bið mon læne,   her bið mæg læne,
> eal þis eorþan gesteal   idel weorpeð!
>   (Krapp and Dobbie 1936: 137, lines 106–10)

Everything is troubled in the earthly kingdom, circumstance alters the created world under Heaven. Here possessions are short-lived; here friends are short-lived; here human beings are short-lived; here dynasties are short-lived. All of the edifice of earth will become empty.

The whole poem presents the troubles of living on this earth from the point of view of one who has travelled much, and whose conclusions identify the temporal nature of the world in which we all live (see Fell 1991). But the short application at the end of the poem, gnomically styled to present an unchallengeable religious tenet, both recognizes the factuality of the *earfeþa*, or 'hardships', described in the poem and, by tying the realism implicit in the presentation of suffering to Christian ideology which reifies suffering by offering its antithesis in Heaven, shows how it is that Anglo-Saxon religious poetry functions not only to formulate conceptions of a general order of existence appropriate to the dominant religious ideology, but also to mediate between the ceremonial and ordinary existence here above ground.

Ezra Pound's (1957: 18–21) decision not to translate the application in his renowned modernization of *The Seafarer* notwithstanding, the remarkable group of Exeter Book poems known as the Old English elegies (which I consider to include also *The Rhyming Poem* and *Resignation A* and *B*) all employ a clearly Christian application – as do many other Old English poems – whose purpose, often explicitly avowed, is to constrain a Christian reading (see Klinck 1992; Mora 1993). These applications offer the modern reader a means of approaching the religious dimension of the poem as a discursive strategy for enlarging the symbolic inventory of a traditional poetic through the dominant religious ideology. It is inappropriate, however, to oppose pre-Christian religions in England to post-Augustinian Christian orthodoxy, for that is not what is implied in the religious dimensions of most Old English poems. The tension, instead, is between varieties of Christian expression, where, for example, a tendency to favour cultural syncretism encourages pre-/non-Christian materials whose interpretation is constrained by Christian applications (e.g. *Deor* or *Widsith*), where renewed Benedictinism proclaims superiority to an older monastic poetic (e.g. *Guthlac A*; see Jones 1995), or perhaps liturgical hermeneutics asserts a more symbolically complex perspective, thus subverting the simple narrative line of the Gospel (e.g. *Christ I* [*The Advent Lyrics*]). There are texts (and some of them are poems) where a Christian ethic appears mainly to be grafted on to a non-Christian one (the Charms come to mind) or where a Christian poet constructs a non-Christian ethos in order to display its weakness (*Beowulf* is a good example). In both cases, however, the system of symbols supposed to represent a residual pre-Christianity is completely manipulated by the dominant ideology of the poet. On close examination of what we suppose to be residual materials, we find that we simply do not have sufficient remnants to construct a coherent pre-Christian ideology (see Fell 1991: 172–89). The conceptions of a general order of existence which remain in Old English poetry are those of the Christianized Roman world with, I dare say, no exceptions. The factuality which clothes the Charms is the reality of the church, of placing barren soil on the altar to make it 'live', or of invoking Christ's name in the proceeding, not as the result of syncretistic processes with two religions on equal footings vying for hegemony, but as a result of a shift in the source of the origin of numinous power. The realistic terror of the unbaptized Danes and Geats of *Beowulf* is of course manipulated by the ideology of the poet, who, albeit sympathetic to their pagan predicament, is clearly aware of another system of symbols which acts to establish its own powerful, pervasive and long-lasting moods and motivations in people.

The religious dimension of Old English poetry resides in the way the mundane asserts itself as part of a Christian system of symbols. The very language of antique Christianity differentiated itself from Roman rhetoric by asserting a humble vocabulary and exalting it in a sacred context. So it is that this poetry creates its grandest effect in Old English. The assertion of the mundane in the service of the mystical can be demonstrated in almost any Old English poem which evinces more than a casual interest in the things pertaining to religion and piety.

There is not space in a chapter of this sort to examine an extensive catalogue of examples of poetic religious expression, but the student of Old English will find that such passages and allusions are pervasive, and it is in interpreting them that we find ourselves confronted with the necessity to engage a more formal methodology to deal with religious content in the poetry. I shall try to sketch the merest outline of considerations for that formal methodology.

Religious poetry extends to all the domains of religion itself and is contextualized by those same domains. Some of this poetry, such as the vernacularizations of the Pater Noster and the Creed, are tied quite closely to the formal practices of religion; other poems, such as *Judgment Day* and *Soul and Body*, participate as commentaries on doctrine and dogma; still other poems, such as saints' lives and Biblical poems, rehearse the myth and history of the religion. It may be useful, then, to focus a reading of an Old English religious poem in terms of one of the following four modes: the doctrinal, the ceremonial, the personal or the social. Each mode embraces a different kind of cultural work undertaken by the poem being examined, and, of course, the authority of the reader granted by most recent approaches to critical theory presupposes that postulating a mode for one interpretation will not require the same mode to be postulated for a different reading of the same poem. What follows is not an attempt to schematize or classify so much as it is an attempt to help a reader account for a variety of foci used in religious poetry.

Doctrinal religious Old English poetry is centred on the first three parts of the Geertzian definition of religion: '(1) a system of symbols which acts to (2) establish powerful, pervasive, and long-lasting moods and motivations in men by (3) formulating conceptions of a general order of existence'. Shorn of the rest of the definition, these three ideas assert the hegemonic tendencies of religion, or at least of early Christianity. If we remember that most of what survives of Old English poetry was a product of monasticism, wherein the ideal required (and requires) vows of poverty, chastity and obedience, we can easily imagine that the religious semiotic was destined in such a context to overwrite the symmetrical exchange systems of economy, sexuality and political power which are necessarily hobbled by adherence to these monastic vows. Of course, religious communities found (and, no doubt, find) ways to mediate these three, too, within a religious context, but religious signifiers constructing textual support for a general order of existence within a monastic context should not be surprising. Sometimes the implied subject of an Old English poem is a reflection of or upon what is virtuous not only in a Christian culture, but in a specific monastic context (e.g. Jones 1995: 259–91; Ure 1957; Anderson 1983: 164).

A number of Old English poems focus on the doctrine or dogma which informed the culture contextualizing that poem. In many cases, this is blatant, as in *Christ and Satan*, *Christ II*, *Christ III*, the homiletic fragments, *Solomon and Saturn* and the Bestiary poems of the Exeter Book (including *The Phoenix*). Such poems demand an intertextual reading that recognizes scriptural and non-scriptural sources, commentaries on the sources, and the purpose of these texts in monastic culture. From the anthropologist's point of view, a doctrinal reading of the poem, such as I am describing here, seeks to explain what is getting said about a specific problem in the nature of existence. Christianity, the avowed religion of the Anglo-Saxons during the literate period of their existence, inherited the notion of the 'book' as authority from its Judaic roots, and the formal discussion of the religion has always involved a layering of texts, one commenting on the other (see Gatch 1971: 94–100; Lerer 1991: 127–57). The Gospel invokes Mosaic law; even Jesus alludes to Psalms and earlier texts in his comments. Augustine, Jerome, Bede, Cassiodorus, Isidore and a host of others filled codices with commentaries on the texts that they had inherited. When a poem takes up an idea from scripture or dogma or moral theology, what is almost always getting said is conveyed not only in the words the poet chooses for the issues he or she wants to explain or describe, but also in the texts chosen to which the poet alludes. Thus, both Cynewulf in *Christ II* and the poet of *The Battle of Brunanburh* allude unselfconsciously to the authority of *bec* – 'books' – in their respective poems, the former because his intention is to teach doctrine and he needs to reference his authority for the oppression of the faithful under the heathen in former days (lines 701b–705), and the latter because the poet wished to use as authority for Æthelstan's triumph the trope of the wisdom of ancient books fashionable in Latin poetry (lines 68–73). The rhetoric of the latter example is itself drawn from the stock expressions of doctrinal poetry, I suspect, even though *The Battle of Brunanburh* cannot easily be considered a doctrinal poem.

The kind of religious poem we are labelling 'doctrinal' involves multiple layers of textual allusions; this layering or cascade of allusions has the effect of constantly deferring responsibility for any given statement of dogma to the poet's source or the source of a source. Some poems, like *Christ and Satan* and *Solomon and Saturn*, dramatize the dialogic reasoning behind religious mystery. Others, like the homiletic poems, assert instead the voices of religious authority: 'þæt word þe gecwæð wuldres ealdor' (Muir 1994: 277, line 2; 'the message which the Prince of Glory spoke') tags most of the surviving text of *Homiletic Fragment III* in the Exeter Book.

Finally, there are the doctrinal poems of Oxford, Bodleian Library, Junius 11, *Genesis*, *Exodus* and *Daniel*, all related in differing ways to the Biblical canon. But these poems are no mere translations or metric paraphrases of the Bible. One of the most interesting aspects of Old English religious poetry – especially of the sort we are calling 'doctrinal' – is its amalgamation of materials from other sources. The most recent scholar to illustrate this for the Junius manuscript is Paul Remley:

> We have now surveyed the various circumstances under which Anglo-Saxon Christians are known to have encountered the texts of the Bible. We still do not know precisely how the poets of the verse of Junius 11 learned about the contents of the Old Testament, but we can be quite sure that each poet will have gained access to biblical knowledge in one or more of the ways outlined above: from an interlocutor, whether in the context of a systematic course of biblical paraphrase or in informal exchanges with other Christians; in the classroom or in private study, most probably while engaged in a programme of elementary or intermediary instruction; or in the fulfilment of liturgical and devotional obligations. (Remley 1996: 90–1)

Not only is a vernacular poem in the doctrinal mode essentially didactic, but it is largely based on didactic materials as well. It represents a cascade of religious texts. The business of a poem with such a genealogy is to establish a tradition of belief, or, in other words, to assert orthodoxy as it is perceived by the poet.

The doctrinal dimension of religious poetry inheres in all of the other kinds of Old English religious poetry we might examine, both among those kinds I have chosen to describe and among other formalizations of religious poetry. What essentially makes a poem a religious poem is its realization in poetic form of some part of the system of signifiers through which a culture constructs its religion. There are poems which never do this. *Waldere* is certainly one, and *The Battle of Maldon* may well be another, although it is always possible that we have lost the key to identifying the doctrinal base of poems originating in a society so far removed from our own as that of Anglo-Saxon England. I shall take up this issue again in discussing the mode of the social religious poem.

Just as dependent upon an intertextual base as what we have termed the doctrinal religious poem is the personal religious poem. But such poems focus on the behavioural concept of religion expressed in part two of the Geertzian definition: 'to (2) establish powerful, pervasive, and long-lasting moods and motivations in men' by using the lives of individuals to model significant behaviours generally approved by the religion's 'general order of existence'. By 'personal', however, is meant not the kind of description of ordinary intercourse Augustine comments upon in his *Confessions*, but rather the actions ascribed to individuals which are particularly exemplary of the grandest gestures afforded by the religious system; that is, personal religious poems employ the heroic mode in a religious context. Cynewulf's *Fates of the Apostles* provides distillations of these in a series of epitomes dedicated to each of Christ's apostles. Each epitome describes how each apostle died in his effort to promulgate Christian doctrine in cultures hostile to it, and each implies that such a death serves the greater good of the Christian world. We generally call such narratives, whether in poetry or prose, hagiography. The subjects of hagiography confront the enemies of the religion's order of existence in its most basic forms. Andreas resists non-believers who do not merely refuse his message, but whose cannibalism may be a demonic inversion of the central symbol of Christianity, the mystery of the Eucharist which signifies the potential to incorporate Christ himself into the person of the believer. Elene challenges men who hold the most sacred sign of religion, the original cross and its nails, within their domain and yet refuse to understand the power of these signs. Guthlac wrestles with demons in order to assert the power of Christian holiness symbolically and commits the remainder of his life to maintaining the possibility of a sanctity of place. Juliana defies a demon and leads him to confession, a sign of the extent of commitment of the ideal of religious revolution. To shrive the devil is heroic work.

I would moreover classify *Judith* as a hagiographic work in this respect, although clearly the source of the text is the canonical but apocryphal book Judith. The poem, however, focuses not on the text as a source of doctrine, but on the narrative as a tale of the triumph of innocence. The Old English poem *Vainglory* takes up the demonic nature of the same excesses of which Holofernus is guilty in a doctrinal mode, and it is easy to assume that he represents just such a sign of the God-forsaken in the personal mode as the drunken thane in *Vainglory* represents in the doctrinal mode. But the poem is centred on Judith, whose ability to assert the power of her religion is akin to that in the myriad of narratives of noble Roman virgin martyrs, including Saints Juliana, Catherine, Cecelia, Agatha and many others. The relics of those virgin martyrs were kept (or so believers believed) throughout England during this period, and it is reasonable to suppose that the power of hagiographic writings – in both poetry and prose – was virtually unquestioned during the Anglo-Saxon period.

This leads us to a major distinction between doctrinal poetry and personal poetry. Personal religious poetry functions in the realm of what has been analysed by Michel Certeau as 'festive' texts:

> Tales of the saints' lives bring a festive element to the community. They are situated on the side of relaxation and leisure. They correspond to free time, a place set aside, a

spiritual and contemplative respite; they do not belong in the realm of instruction, pedagogical norms, or dogma. They 'divert.' Unlike texts that must be practised and believed, the Saints' Lives oscillate between the believable and the marvellous, advocating what one is at liberty to think or do. From both points of view they create an area of 'vacation' and of new conditions outside of everyday time and rule. (Certeau 1988: 273–4)

Saints were celebrated with feast days; doctrine was memorialized through fasting. Doctrine was propounded in the pulpit and the chapter house. Saints' Lives were read in the refectory and during one's leisure time; indeed 'to listen willingly to holy reading' is, according to the *Regula Benedicti*, one of 'the instruments of good works' (Verheyen 1949: ch. 4). The narrative fabric of hagiography, whether rendered as poetry or as prose, is in fact the superhuman, the marvellous and the fanciful. While such narratives are often filled with preposterous acts of violence that function to set off the saints' virtues within a framework of the depravity of others, it should not be forgotten that the genealogy of such violence is to be found in Peseistratus' eyeball stuck on a lance beneath Ilium's wall in Homer, in Aeneas' final, angry dispatch of Turnus in Virgil, in the gruesome excesses of the Senecan tragedy, and similarly in a variety of venues whose major aim was to reinforce the common morality. At the same time, the effect thrills. Enduring torture, encountering forces of evil, finding the iconic gesture at the point of death – these are not only the stuff of *Star Wars*.

If all Saints' Lives generally point to 'new conditions outside of everyday time and rule' as Certeau suggests, what is the particular advantage of rendering some of them as poetry? With the exception of *Aldhelm* and Cynewulf's *Fates of the Apostles*, which belong to the mode of hagiography, if not to the genre of *vita sancti*, we have only five hagiographical Old English poems: *Andreas, Elene, Guthlac A, Guthlac B* and *Juliana*. Two (or three, depending on how we ascribe authorship to *Guthlac B*) are by Cynewulf. As a group, however, the verse Saints' Lives differ from the Old English prose Lives:

> The Old English life, instead of relating the entire life of a saint and thus embracing a broad, historically determined set of conventions, centres on the moment of greatest emotional and spiritual turmoil for the saint. It distils the fact of sainthood into the particulars of an individual moment or event so that a certain Christian truth can be told. Focusing on truth in this way is perhaps not unique to the Old English life, since hagiography generally, as Jean Leclercq observes, 'advances a moral thesis and a religious idea', but the Old English life goes further in trimming away extraneous fact or religious fantasy than does the Latin life. It tends to highlight the moral that usually derives from the climactic encounter with the devil, and it also paradoxically individualizes a saint with preserving his place in Christ's body. (Bjork 1985: 126–7)

Old English religious poetry in the personal mode supplements, in fact, poetry in the doctrinal mode. It appealed, we may suppose, to readers who admired hagiographical narrative generally. However, these poems function to link the 'powerful, pervasive, and long-lasting moods and motivations in men' in Geertz's definition more closely to 'formulating conceptions of a general order of existence' than usually is the case in doctrinal religious poetry (see Bjork 1985: 125–31).

The mode of ceremonial religious Old English poetry emphasizes the fourth part of the Geertzian definition of religion: 'clothing these conceptions with such an aura of factuality'. Geertz's discussion of this part of his definition is particularly relevant here:

> It is this sense of the 'really real' upon which the religious perspective rests and which the symbolic activities of religion as a cultural system are devoted to producing, intensifying, and, so far as possible, rendering inviolable by the discordant revelations of secular experience. It is, again, the imbuing of a certain specific complex of symbols – of the metaphysic they formulate and the style of life they recommend – with a persuasive authority which, from an analytic point of view, is the essence of religious action.
>
> Which brings us, at length, to ritual. For it is in ritual – that is, consecrated behavior – that this conviction that religious conceptions are veridical and that religious directives are sound is somehow generated. It is in some sort of ceremonial form – even if that form be hardly more than the recitation of a myth, the consultation of an oracle, or the decoration of a grave – that the moods and motivations which sacred symbols induce in men and the general conceptions of the order of existence which they formulate for men meet and reinforce one another. In a ritual, the world as lived and the world as imagined, fused under the agency of a single set of symbolic forms, turn out to be the same world, producing thus that idiosyncratic transformation in one's sense of reality. . . . (Geertz 1973: 112)

Anglo-Saxon culture abounded with religious ritual. Christianity, as it was practised in the tenth century (the earliest period for our manuscripts containing Old English poetry), provided an elaborate cycle of public ritual in the liturgy. The Christian liturgy as practised in the Anglo-Saxon church not only concerned itself with the annual cycle of masses, sung daily and distributed according to a complex calendrical system oriented for different purposes to both the solar and lunar calendars, but included too the 'Divine Office', the special liturgy performed six times a day in both male and female religious communities, also with variations determined by the church calendar. Christian ritual was ubiquitous in Anglo-Saxon society, not restricted to monastic houses. The church calendar (or kalendar) operated as the civic calendar which continually reminded the non-coenobitic, non-priestly classes of ritual times and opportunities. Monasteries were among the largest land owners, and their activities therefore affected all those, religious or not, who laboured on their estates. As early, perhaps, as the period of King Alfred's civic reforms, the Anglo-Saxon Church began the process which eventually was known as the 'Benedictine Reformation', which David Dumville (1992: 185–205) has characterized as nothing short of a revolution, beginning with the reforms of King Alfred. Certainly, part of that revolution was concerned with the practice of ritual, and its culminating document, the *Regularis concordia* (Symons 1953), is very nearly completely taken up with matters of liturgical practice. Clearly, as Geertz suggests, matters of authority inhere in ritual, and 'it is in some sort of ceremonial form . . . that the moods and motivations which sacred symbols induce in men and the general conceptions of the order of existence which they formulate for men meet and reinforce one another'.

We are hardly surprised, then, to find that there is a considerable body of poetry with roots in the liturgy. It is not always clear whether any of the Old English paraphrases of liturgical texts might actually have been substituted for the Latin text in some ceremony, although it is much more likely that the context for making such a substitution would have occurred in a popular ritual context, such as the 'Æcerbot' or 'field remedy' charm which Jolly (1996: 618) analyses. But whether any of these poems actually functioned in ritual contexts – popular or otherwise – is beside the point. The point is that Christian ritual inspired a category of religious poetry; knowing that is germane to reading the poems.

Old English translations and paraphrases of Latin texts used in the liturgy include *The Creed, Lord's Prayer I, II, III, The Gloria I, II*, the Psalter and Psalm fragments, and *A Prayer*, to list those printed in the Anglo-Saxon Poetic Records, the edited corpus of all surviving Old English poetry. They confirm most clearly the presence of the liturgy as a clear influence on the poetry. Other poems in the ceremonial mode, however, are more interesting in the way they transform the symbolic language of the rite into Old English lyricism. *Christ I* is based on a sequence of antiphons for the Divine Office at Advent; *Exodus* is dependent on the complex traditions of the Great Vigil Mass of Easter, as is the *Descent into Hell*; *Azarias* and *Daniel* both reflect the canticle 'Canticum trium puerorum', one of the liturgical songs regularly appended to the psalter. A source in the liturgy does not in itself guarantee a viable mode of religious poetry. Indeed, both *Daniel* and *Exodus* could be read in the doctrinal mode with a cascade of traditions and sources behind the text, of which the liturgy was one. What, then, makes an Old English poem classifiable in the ceremonial mode?

Ritual is the means of 'clothing these conceptions with such an aura of factuality', to cite the definition again. The language of ritual must make its referents present; its words and its tone must establish the factuality of the ideas about which it speaks. When this idea of factuality is transferred from the liturgy into poetry, the poetry thus created fuses the world as lived and the world as imagined. A portion of *Christ I* serves to demonstrate:

> Eala earendel,   engla beorhtast,
> ofer middangeard   monnum sended,
> ond soðfæsta   sunnan leoma,
> torht ofer tunglas,   þu tida gehwane
> of sylfum þe   symle inlihtes!
> Swa þu, god of gode   gearo acenned,
> sunu soþan fæder,   swegles in wuldre

butan anginne   æfre wære,
swa þec nu for þearfum   þin agen geweord
bideð þurh byldo,   þæt þu þa beorhtan us
sunnan onsende,   ond þe sylf cyme
þæt ðu inleohte   þa þe longe ær,
þrosme beþeahte   ond in þeostrum her,
sæton sinneahtes;   synnum bifealdne
deorc deaþes sceadu   dreogan sceoldan.
(Krapp and Dobbie 1936: 6, lines 104–18)

O Morning Star, brightest of messengers
Send to this earth, and to men, truest
Radiance of the eternal Sun, clear
And glorious beyond all stars, in every
Season glowing with Your own light!
God Himself brought You forth,
God creating God, heaven's
Glory knowing no beginning. Now
God's other creation calls to you, needing You,
Hoping You will hear us, send us Your holy
Light, praying for Your shining truth
To burn where darkness has covered us over
Here in our long night, crouching
In unending blackness, wrapped in our sins,
Enduring the evil shadows of death. (Gatch 1971: 95)

This is taken from the fifth lyric of the *Advent Lyrics* or *Christ I*, which is based on the antiphon, 'O Orient, splendour of the eternal light and sun of justice: come and enlighten those who sit in darkness and in the shadow of death.' The voice of the poet is in the present. 'Now', as he says, 'God's other creation' – i.e. we – 'call to you.' The prototypical liturgical texts are the Psalms, supposedly in the voice of David calling to God. The recitation of the Psalter was the core of the Divine Office, and the atemporality of the Psalms ultimately coloured liturgical language. The poet of *Christ I* tends to create psalms out of the antiphons which inspired him.

The final mode to be discussed is that of the social mode of Old English religious poetry, which stresses the second and fifth parts of the Geertzian definition of religion: 'to (2) establish powerful, pervasive, and long-lasting moods and motivations in men . . . [which] (5) . . . seem uniquely realistic'. There is a difference between 'clothing in factuality' and seeming 'uniquely realistic'. The former has to do with the world of ritual symbols which are introduced as if they were facts to embrace and navigate. The latter constitutes another world, one often closer to us, as Geertz observes:

But no one, not even a saint, lives in the world religious symbols formulate all of the time, and the majority of men live in it only at moments. The everyday world of common-sense objects and practical acts is . . . the paramount reality in human experience – paramount in the sense that it is the world in which we are most solidly rooted, whose inherent actuality we can hardly question (however much we may question certain portions of it), and from whose pressures and requirements we can least escape. A man, even large groups of men, may be aesthetically insensitive, religiously unconcerned, and unequipped to pursue formal scientific analysis, but he cannot be completely lacking in common sense and survive. The dispositions which religious ritual induce thus have their most important impact – from a human point of view – outside the boundaries of the ritual itself as they reflect back *to color the individual's conception of the established world of bare fact*. . . . Religion is sociologically interesting not because, as vulgar positivism would have it, it describes the social order (which, in so far as it does, it does not only very obliquely but very incompletely), but because, like environment, political power, wealth, jural obligation, personal affection, and a sense of beauty, it shapes it. (Geertz 1973: 119)

Old English religious poetry in the social mode does not necessarily even look like religious poetry. We have already mentioned how the religious application at the end of *The Seafarer* was regarded by Ezra Pound as an inferior addition to the poem which he need not render in his translation. Pound liked the realism in the Seafarer's voyage and apparently did not realize that, for a tenth-century Anglo-Saxon, seafaring was very likely to be the way the world of bare fact reflects rituals of transition and transformation. The prayer at the end of the poem is not an unrelated addition, but a commentary and a proof that the poet's world of common sense was shaped by the metaphors of his or her religion.

Not only the Old English elegies, but *Widsith, Deor*, often the riddles and, of course, *Beowulf* (among other poems) all belong to this mode of Old English religious poetry. It is the poetry of people who had lives beyond the cloister wall, but it is not the poetry of people uninfluenced by dogma and liturgy. Interpreting religious poetry in this mode, however, can be a complex undertaking. Such poetry does not readily yield its sources (and probably does not have any exact sources in most cases), although scholars find no paucity of analogues; nevertheless source studies, which provide the basis for doctrinal, personal or ceremonial reading, are not often available for a reading of a religious poem in the social mode. It is, therefore, difficult to characterize this poetry further as a category. Poems we should ascribe to the social mode constitute a diverse set of texts, and ultimately each of these texts demands its own reading in ways that do not generalize to the others.

The analysis of Old English religious poetry is not a religious exercise, but an analytical one. The desire of the postmodern reader of this poetry is not to share in revelation – it is not a pursuit of the ecstatic – but to comprehend the discourse through which Anglo-Saxons encountered the existential dilemmas with which their cultures and their lives presented them.

REFERENCES

Primary sources

Klinck, Anne L., ed. 1992. *The Old English Elegies: A Critical Edition and Genre Study*. Montreal.

Krapp, George Philip and Elliott Van Kirk Dobbie, eds 1936. *The Exeter Book*. Anglo-Saxon Poetic Records 3. New York and London.

Muir, Bernard James, ed. 1994. *The Exeter Anthology of Old English Poetry: An Edition of Exeter Dean and Chapter MS 3501*. 2 vols. Exeter.

Pound, Ezra 1957. *Selected Poems of Ezra Pound*. New York.

Sherley-Price, Leo, trans. 1990. *Bede: A History of the English Church and People with Bede's Letter to Egbert and Cuthbert's Letter on the Death of Bede*. Penguin Classics. Baltimore.

Symons, Dom Thomas, ed. 1953. *Regularis Concordia*. London.

Ure, James M., ed. 1957. *The Benedictine Office: An Old English Text*. Edinburgh University Publications in Language and Literature 11. Edinburgh.

Verheyen, Boniface, trans. 1949. *The Holy Rule of Our Most Holy Father Benedict*. Atchison, KS.

Secondary sources

Anderson, Earl 1983. *Cynewulf: Structure, Style, and Theme in His Poetry*. Rutherford.

Bjork, Robert E. 1985. *The Old English Verse Saints' Lives*. Toronto.

Certeau, Michel 1988. *The Writing of History*. Trans. Tom Conley. New York.

Cunningham, Graham 1999. *Religion and Magic: Approaches and Theories*. New York.

Dumville, David N. 1992. *Wessex and England from Alfred to Edgar*. Woodbridge.

Fell, Christine 1991. 'Perceptions of Transience'. *The Cambridge Companion to Old English Literature*, pp. 172–89. Eds Malcolm Godden and Michael Lapidge. Cambridge.

Gatch, Milton McC. 1971. *Loyalties and Traditions: Man and his World in Old English Literature*. New York.

Geertz, Clifford 1973. *The Interpretation of Cultures*. New York.

Jolly, Karen Louise 1996. *Popular Religion in Late Saxon England: Elf Charms in Context*. Chapel Hill, NC.

Jones, Christopher A. 1995. 'Envisioning the *Cenoebium* in the Old English *Guthlac A*'. *Medieval Studies* 57: 259–91.

Lerer, Seth 1991. *Literacy and Power in Ango-Saxon Literature*. London.

Mora, Maria José 1993. 'Modulation and Hybridization in the Old English Elegies'. *Papers from the IVth International Conference of the Spanish Society for Medieval English Language and Literature*, pp. 203–11. Ed. Teresa Fanego Lema. Oviedo.

Remley, Paul G. 1996. *Old English Biblical Verse: Studies in Genesis, Exodus and Daniel*. Cambridge.

Williams, Raymond 1977. *Marxism and Literature*. Oxford.

15
Secular Prose
Donald G. Scragg

The term 'secular prose' has historically been used primarily of the limited range of creative and pseudo-scientific writings which survives from the Anglo-Saxon period, the romance literature and the tales of the fabulous encountered by distant travellers. But there is also a further and substantial body of writings from the period which is secular in content; for example, legal material and chronicles, administrative texts, medical and scientific handbooks, and school texts which deal with the trappings of secular life. This chapter will therefore range widely over texts which have secular content but which are not covered by other chapters in this book.

However, the first question to ask in a chapter dealing with secular prose is what is meant by secular in relation to the Old English period. Everything that we know about the origin, use and transmission of the majority of surviving Anglo-Saxon manuscripts leads us to suppose that they were monastic. For a clearer sense of what we mean by secular, we first of all need to look closely at the manuscript context for those writings which are to be classified as secular. The most startling example is the prose romance known as *Apollonius of Tyre*, which could hardly be more secular in its story-line, since it describes the adventures of a young nobleman of an eastern Mediterranean kingdom who was forced into exile and subsequently lost both his wealth and his status, but who then won the heart and the hand of the daughter of the king of another land, which he subsequently inherited. But even after he had become king his troubles were not at an end, for by a series of misadventures he lost both his wife and their daughter, and only at the end of the tale was reunited with them. This is the stuff of romance and the story remained popular in English in the later medieval period, to be recreated for modern audiences in Shakespeare's *Pericles*. The Old English version, translated during the tenth century from a Latin, ultimately Greek, text, survives in a single manuscript copy, Cambridge, Corpus Christi College 201, where it follows a large collection of sermons and comparable religious material closely associated with Archbishop Wulfstan, together with laws and related legal documents generally assumed to have been collected for or written by the archbishop. Although this particular manuscript is of the mid-eleventh century and so represents a late copy of texts assembled by or for Wulfstan, a single scribe copied the sermons, the laws and *Apollonius*. The manuscript foliation suggests that the scribe copied the collection continuously up to and including *Apollonius*, and that he then (assuming a male copyist) intended to end the book, although he and others added more material subsequently. This points to whoever wrote the Cambridge manuscript having found the romance together with the homiletic and legal material in the copy-text, and means that at least two scribes thought that *Apollonius* was suitable to be included in this particular collection.

Critics have long been puzzled about why both the person who assembled this set of texts and at least one later scribe thought that a chivalric tale set in the Near East was an appropriate addition to a set of homilies and laws. It may be that there is a clue in the one significant change that the translator made to the Latin which he had before him. He added a codicil asking the reader not to censure the translation but to disguise any faults in it. Such self-deprecation on the part of a translator was traditional, but it implies someone who assumed a learned reader for the text, presumably a monastic one. Since within the educational system which was widespread amongst monasteries of the period, including those of Anglo-Saxon England, a reader was expected to correct imperfections which he found in his text, it may be that there is more than the manuscript context to suggest an association of this text with a monastic environment. Indeed the Latin version of the tale is found widely copied throughout Europe in manuscripts which are clearly meant for monastic use (Archibald 1991). The *Apollonius* story is one that would serve as a moral exemplum for a clerical audience, and it is almost certainly with this use in mind that the English version was included in the collection now surviving in the Cambridge manuscript. Thus although the story-line is secular, the broader context for it and other similar texts may not be.

The story opens with an account of Antiochus, king of Antioch, who conceived such a desire for his own daughter that he was impelled early one morning to enter her bed-chamber, send away his retainers, and rape her. Such an overturning of the natural order is a clear case for moral instruction. The girl, distraught at her situation in having nowhere to turn for redress, is an obvious subject for a modern character study, but the medieval writer has a different agenda. After displaying her distress in a pathetic exchange with her nurse, the author makes her disappear from the story, and turns instead to the device by which the king ensured that he could continue to satisfy his lust. Suitors for her hand are denied marriage until they solve a riddle which exposes the incest, whilst failure to solve it means death. Apollonius interprets it correctly, but the king denies the validity of his solution, with the result that the hero narrowly escapes with his life. The author's lack of interest in the potential for character development in the king's daughter should alert us to the danger of seeking for modern interests in the tale as a whole. During his wanderings as an exile, Apollonius, having been reduced to destitution, arrives at the court of another king and attracts the attention of both him and his daughter. She falls in love with him, and begs her father to allow them to marry. The episode has been seen as significant in revealing a new type of heroine in English, one who is much more modern than those of earlier vernacular prose and verse (Riedinger 1990). But this approach is too solidly based in a modern perspective. Arcestrate, Apollonius' future wife, remains through-out the story a Mediterranean citizen and has no English trait, any more than Apol-lonius is an Englishman in any more than his title of *ealdorman*. His disdain for social inferiors is Roman, not English, and her ruse to have him housed at court must be seen as part of the mechanics of plot rather than character study. It is in the context of a moral tale that her schemes to bring Apollonius into close contact with her, first in his lodging at court and next as her tutor, although they result immediately in their marriage, are to be seen as balanced by their spending much of their life apart. Arcestrate's actions, like so much in this text, are a basis for moral instruction.

The piece has lexical interest which the reader should be alert to. Many modern commentators have used unwarranted superlatives to describe this early English venture into the romance genre. In fact the text remains faithful to its classical source, in both story-line and characterization, even though it has to be admitted that no very close source in Latin has been found. Yet despite the foreignness of many of the ideas expressed, the translator appears to have made changes which do show some English influence without greatly altering the broad outline of the narrative. Since almost every reading in the Old English can be confirmed in one of the large number of Latin versions that survive (Goolden 1958; Archibald 1991), it is possible to reconstruct the Latin which the translator had before him, and to see what he did with it. Words and phrases such as *bridgifta* for *legitimum nuptiarum* (§2), *fostormodor* for *nutrix* (§2), *sloh ut on ða sæ* for *tradidit . . . pelago* (§6), and *sæ Neptune* for *Neptune* (§12) reveal much about the translator's care in making intelligible concepts that might not be under-stood by his audience, and in the use of idiom which has rarely survived elsewhere. The text exhibits the confidence which many writers in the late Anglo-Saxon period felt in the ability of their language to convey foreign ideas clearly and well.

Although *Apollonius* is set in Mediterranean countries, these would not be entirely foreign to a monastic reader of the late Anglo-Saxon period who had available to him or her the works of Boethius and Orosius translated by King Alfred and his court circle and also a range of homiletic and hagiographic material with Near Eastern set-tings. There are also records of Anglo-Saxons themselves making pilgrimages to the Holy Land, and spices, herbs and silk were imported from as far as India. There is, then, interest in distant lands, and it is therefore perhaps not surprising to find two prose works of fiction set in such a context. The first is a *Letter to Aristotle* purporting to come from his pupil Alexander the Great while on an expedition to India, describ-ing the many wonders that he encountered there. Again, this is a tale which was highly popular throughout the medieval period, and the Old English version is the earliest of many translations from Latin into vernacular languages. In Old English it survives in only one copy, in London, British Library, Cotton Vitellius A. xv, imme-diately before *Beowulf* and copied by the first scribe of the poem. Comparison with Latin redactions of the text reveals the translation to be highly selective, and the nature of the selection creates a distinctive adaptation, presumably one which was made in England even if it was first made in a lost Latin antecedent. Much of the critical commentary on this text is disparaging, based particularly on the assumption that the translator should be seen as incompetent. But the most recent and fullest critique (Orchard 1995) sees alteration of the original as part of a deliberate strategy, the English version building a picture of Alexander displaying 'self-absorption' and 'disturbing arrogance'. The epistolary framework and first-person narrative, with references to the king's mother and sisters as well as to his relationship with the recipient of the letter, Aristotle, focus attention on the king, and the English text, unlike any which survive in Latin, ends abruptly at the point where he hears the prophecy of his own death. In the conclusion, which is not drawn from any surviving Latin text, Alexander laments that he had achieved less than he would have wished but that nevertheless his glory and his honour were greater than those possessed by any other earthly king. The reader's attention would surely be drawn to the word *eorðcyning*. If this, like the *Apollonius*, is a work that was read for contemplation, the moral is clear: whatever the fictional Alexander may have thought, the power and glory of earthly kings is transitory, whereas that of the heavenly king is not. Alexander thus becomes a recognizable type figure, an exemplum for a medieval Christian reader.

In his letter, Alexander characterizes himself as a fearsome commander, ruthless to those who confront or deceive him but careful of the men who are loyal to him and of the animals they made use of in their campaign. His military tactics are made believable, such as frightening off marauding elephants with a herd of pigs and having to kill a crocodile with hammers because its tough skin was impervious to spears. There is a literary tradition too, though. The episode in which he visits the camp of his enemy in disguise to learn of their plans is remarkably like the twelfth-century William of Malmesbury's description of both King Alfred amongst his Danish foes and Anlaf visiting the English camp before Brunanburh (Sisam 1953: 88), presumably because they share a source. Amongst the text's most informative aspects is its illustration of a medieval mind-set which describes incredible animals, strange humans and magical encounters without any sense of their not being real. Elephants, hippopotami, tigers and leopards roam across the pages alongside two-headed monster snakes with poisonous breath, rough-haired and naked men and women nine feet tall, and a priest who is ten feet tall and three hundred years old, while the prophecy of Alexander's death comes from oracular speaking trees. For an Anglo-Saxon, there is a very blurred distinction between the natural and the supernatural worlds. The *Letter* is presented as a realistic catalogue of wonders from distant lands.

It would be wrong, however, to dismiss the text as a catalogue in form. The focus on Alexander himself and his account to Aristotle of his adventures in chronological sequence creates a strong narrative structure, bounded by the prophecy of his death. In this sense, the text is quite unlike a second Eastern tale in Old English, although the two are regularly linked in literary histories of the period. This piece, known variously as *The Wonders of the East* or *The Marvels of the East*, survives in two copies, one of them being found immediately before the *Letter* in the *Beowulf* manuscript, thus providing the basic link between them. This text too originally had an epistolary form but it is not found in the Old English and had perhaps been lost before the text reached the Latin version used to translate it, leaving it as a simple catalogue of the wonders to be found in the flora, fauna and races of the Middle East and India, with an even greater emphasis on the grotesque; for example, the ants as big as dogs that dig for gold and the wiles of the intrepid men that steal it from them. The *Marvels* survives in a second copy in an elaborate and beautifully written codex of the first half of the eleventh century which contains a miscellany of English and classical and late Latin texts, London, British Library, Cotton Tiberius B. v. In this manuscript the text is written in Latin, divided into unnumbered sections, each of which is followed by the Old English translation.

In both copies of the *Marvels* a set of elaborate coloured drawings accompanies the text. Textual differences between the two versions are minor except that Vitellius (the *Beowulf*-manuscript copy) lacks a sentence or so from the middle of Tiberius and also several wonders from the end. The omission of the sentence in the middle might be deliberate, since its content is technical, but the revision of the conclusion is probably to be explained as a linking device with the following text, the Alexander *Letter*, since the Vitellius conclusion contains one of three references to Alexander to be found in the *Marvels*. Though there is little in common between the two sets of drawings, the textual similarity means that there can be no doubt that both surviving Old English copies derive from a common ancestor which was illustrated. This is a text, then, which ought not to be read without reference to the illustrations, and it is therefore unfortunate that the most widely available editions are of the text alone: the Tiberius text (collated with readings from Vitellius) with the Latin antecedent is in Orchard 1995, and the Vitellius text (with selected variants from Tiberius) in Rypins 1924. Both manuscripts have, however, been reproduced in full in the series Early English Manuscripts in Facsimile, vols 12 and 21 (Malone 1963; McGurk et al. 1983).

There is one more difference between the two copies. The Tiberius version has a final paragraph, unusually long for the text, but linked by its manuscript presentation and by the drawing which accompanies it. What marks it off even more radically, however, is that this paragraph is not another in the list of currently available marvels but a reference to figures from the Old Testament, the Egyptian sorcerers Jamnes (or Jannes) and Mambres who confronted Moses (Exodus, 7 and 8; the sorcerers are not named in the Old Testament but are in 2 Timothy 3, 8; see Biggs and Hall 1996). We are told that after Jamnes' death, Mambres used magic to raise his brother's soul from hell, whereupon it preached a mini-sermon warning of the terror of damnation. The paragraph begins with the formula *Her segð* ('It says here'), which is not in the Latin and which is nowhere else in the *Marvels*. But this phrase (or some variation upon it) occurs very many times as the opening of homilies and saints' lives, especially pre-Ælfrician ones, and the paragraph has other linguistic marks of an origin as a preaching exemplum; for example, the direct invocation to his brother and the description of the torments of hell. It is, then, more than possible that the Jamnes and Mambres piece existed separately before it was added to the *Marvels*, probably by the scribe of the Tiberius manuscript, because it seemed a fitting addition to the catalogue as part of the matter of Egypt. Whatever its textual history, it points to the fact that a text such as the *Marvels*, although in origin secular, might have religious material added to it during transmission, and this forces us to consider again the question of the epithet 'secular' attached to this text.

In style, as against the organization of the material, the *Marvels* and the *Letter to Aristotle* are both close to their respective sources, and therefore to a large extent detailed comment on their literary qualities – that the former is for the most part fairly formulaic while the latter has passages of more extended imaginative description – is superfluous in a review of Old English literature. What can and should be observed is the flexibility of the medium used for the translations. In them, late Old English appears as a resourceful and adaptable language, and their author/translators are more than capable of producing clear, idiomatic and flowing prose. Even more significant is the light shed on Anglo-Saxon culture by these texts. Their existence links late Anglo-Saxon England firmly into a European cultural tradition. The many Latin manuscripts and the number of translations into vernacular languages throughout the medieval period testify to a great appetite for such stories. But most of the Latin manuscripts are post-Conquest and continental, and the translations into the vernacular are of the thirteenth century onwards. What is distinctive about the Anglo-Saxon prose is that it is so early. The Old English translations, the earliest into any vernacular, are symptomatic of an insular tradition far ahead of European counterparts. Such translations will not reappear in English until the thirteenth century. Furthermore, both texts exhibit unique adaptations which we should consider a distinctively English addition to the history of ideas.

The way in which one copy of the *Marvels* appears to have been expanded with a Biblical example leads us to other prose texts which are religious in origin but which have been expanded with secular material. The next two texts to be considered again fall into the category of lists, but in this case they are arranged in question-and-answer form. The prose *Solomon and Saturn* is a series of fifty-nine questions posed by Saturn and answered by Solomon, although neither 'character' appears in more than the heading to the text, and the work is unrelated to the poems of the same name. The dialogue, as it is usually but imprecisely known, survives only as the final item in a twelfth-century manuscript which was attached to the *Beowulf* codex, London, British Library, Vitellius A. xv, by Sir Robert Cotton in the sixteenth century. The language is entirely formulaic, each question beginning 'Tell me' and each answer 'I tell you'. The subjects covered are mostly learned and scriptural, and it is possible that the lists were used as memoranda of 'facts' for preachers. The primitive dialogue form has many Latin analogues, especially the *Joca monachum*, which is a source for many of the items. Related to *Solomon and Saturn* is a 'dialogue' of the same form (with many shared items) between *Adrian and Ritheus*, with forty-eight questions. In both texts there are a few questions and answers, such as why the sun is red in the morning, which superficially look secular but which on close examination appear to be drawn from the patristic tradition (Cross and Hill 1982).

Both of these texts survive in unique copies in very late manuscripts, and though they depend heavily on similar Latin lists, they undoubtedly were added to during the course of copying. The way in which these lists were compiled and supplemented may be illustrated from a single example in *Solomon and Saturn*. The two lists have four verbal parallels with the tenth-century sermon known as Vercelli Homily XIX. Since we have the direct Latin sources for the homily, it is clear that the question-and-answer lists borrowed from the sermon rather than the other way round. But in one case we have a further surviving parallel. An estimation of the years spent by Adam in Hell (5,228), which is included in *Solomon and Saturn* question 11 and is drawn from the homily, also appears independently in a scribbled note at the end of a manuscript now in the Bodleian Library in Oxford, shelfmark Hatton 115. It looks as if this is something culled from the homily which circulated as an independent piece of information perhaps to be incorporated in the question-and-answer lists. This takes us into the area of notes and scribbles, large numbers of which were added to Anglo-Saxon manuscripts during the eleventh and twelfth centuries. Most of them have been published but many are scattered in essays in periodicals, and collectively they have largely been overlooked. If they were all brought together in one place and compared with the frequency with which manuscripts were glossed in Old English, they would create a new awareness of the wide currency of the written vernacular in the post-Conquest period, and of the freedom with which a large number of writers annotated manuscripts in their native language and felt that they had reason to do so.

It is logical to move from the so-called dialogues to scholastic colloquies, lively conversations in Latin about everyday subjects between a teacher and his pupils designed to give the latter a wide vocabulary and an ability to converse in the universal language of the church. The earliest is by Abbot Ælfric, with others by one of his pupils, also named Ælfric but given the sobriquet Bata, probably a pejorative by-name meaning 'the Fat' (Garmonsway 1939; Gwara and Porter 1997). Ælfric Bata is responsible for expanded versions of Ælfric's colloquy surviving in some manuscripts. But it is Ælfric's original colloquy which has attracted the greatest attention, for two reasons. First Ælfric, to ensure that his pupils had a complete Latin vocabulary of ordinary life, got each of them to take on the role of workers such as the farmer, the hunter, the fisherman, the merchant and the cobbler, and to respond to questions from their master about their daily life. Together these offer a fascinating window on the proletariat of Anglo-Saxon England, a class of whom we generally hear little. It also tells us something about the education of oblates within a monastic community. But the second reason why this colloquy is important is that some time in the middle of the eleventh century, in a community where, presumably, grasp of Latin had slipped to such an extent that the colloquy was no longer fully intelligible, the version of the colloquy which survives in Cotton Tiberius A. iii, a manuscript from Christ Church, Canterbury, was given an interlinear word-for-word gloss in English. Because it follows Latin syntax and word-order, the continuous gloss when abstracted from the

Latin is not idiomatic Old English, even though it consists of a string of Old English words. But the content of this text has proved so useful to modern scholars, and so attractive to those wishing to teach Old English at an elementary level, that in the late nineteenth century, the philologist Henry Sweet revised the gloss into what he believed would have been natural to native speakers, and Sweet's prose subsequently has become very widely anthologized (Sweet 1897), giving readers a false sense of the existence of a colloquy in the vernacular where clearly it would have no purpose.

The wide range of scientific and medical writings in Old English in general falls outside the scope of this chapter. Many works of science are monastic in origin, although they have much secular content. Byrhtferth of Ramsey's *Enchiridion*, a large compendium of scientific material written to accompany his work on the computus (important for calculating the date of Easter), might be called an encyclopaedia of numbers, consisting of everything from the days of the months to the metre of verse (Baker and Lapidge 1995). His older contemporary Abbot Ælfric wrote a short treatise on the earth, the heavens and the weather, *De temporibus anni*, largely translated from a careful selection of the works of Bede following Ælfric's usual fashion (Henel 1942). It is a valuable introduction to Anglo-Saxon attitudes to the nature of the universe, beautifully articulated. On the edge of the medical writings are texts that straddle the boundary between medicine and folklore. In Cotton Tiberius A. iii, a large miscellany of writings from the mid-eleventh century, immediately before a short text describing the stages of growth of the foetus which itself combines anatomical knowledge with folklore elements, is a series of prognostications on how man will be affected when a new moon occurs on each of the days of the week. Although both of these texts are somewhat repetitive in language, especially in sentence structure, the fact remains that their authors show competence in representing a series of fairly complex ideas. The audience intended for such material is harder to assess, although there is no doubt that the surviving witness, the Tiberius manuscript, is a monastic production.

Amongst a variety of administrative documents in vernacular prose, one of the most interesting, in terms of both content and style, is a text concerned with English agricultural life which survives uniquely in a late manuscript containing copies of the Old English laws, Cambridge, Corpus Christi College 383, a text known today as *Gerefa* or *Be gesceadwisan gerefa*, 'The wise reeve', to use the title supplied by a twelfth-century annotator of the manuscript (Liebermann 1903–16). This is an account of the duties and responsibilities of a manorial steward, ranging from management of men and women on the estate, through the various tasks that need to be performed at different times of year, to a long list of tools and equipment necessary for the farm workers. It gives us a unique insight into the running of a great estate in the period. Despite its technical content, it is far from being a mundane administrative document. Its style is accomplished, with many rhetorical flourishes such as sequences of pairs of patterned phrases, often alliterative or rhymed, e.g. *ge on tune and dune, ge on wuda ge on wætere, ge on felda ge on falde, ge inne ge ute* ('in yard and hill, in wood and stream, in field and pen, inside and out'). This device, plus the use of intensives such as *to soðe ic secge* ('in truth I say'), has resulted in the linking of the text with Archbishop Wulfstan, the best exponent of such rhetoric in the period, but it is more likely that their appearance is the result of the popularity of Wulfstan's style than that he himself wrote this text (McIntosh 1949). What is clear is that a confident writer might put such an elaborate style to a wide variety of uses including the purely technical. Again, though, we have to guard against too simple a reading of secular. Monasteries were great land owners in the eleventh century, and although there is nothing in the text to suggest that it was in any way religious, its survival in its manuscript environment suggests that it was written by someone concerned with the management of a monastic estate.

Gerefa has long been associated with the text which precedes it in the manuscript, *Rectitudines singularum personarum*, which in fact is more concerned with the rights of different classes of society and is in content closer to a work which is certainly by Wulfstan, the *Institutes of Polity* (Jost 1959). *Polity* defines the duties and responsibilities of every class of society of England in the eleventh century, both eccelesiastic and lay (in that order), stressing their orderly arrangement. It discusses the relationship between religious orders and laymen, as well as the source of royal power in the three supports to the throne, those that pray, those that work and those that fight (*Oratores, Laboratores, Bellatores*). The work survives in two versions, the second, made towards the end of the archbishop's life in 1023, including some references which throw light on contemporary conditions (Whitelock 1963). In sum, it is one of the most important political treatises to have survived from the medieval period, and certainly the most significant in English.

Arguably the most important prose work to survive in Old English is the series of texts known collectively as the *Anglo-Saxon Chronicle* (= *ASC*, Thorpe 1861). In it we have a set of annals which relates the major events of Britain from the Roman invasion to, in the case of the latest manuscript, the second half of the twelfth century. For the early entries, which are sparse, the original compiler relied heavily on Bede's *Ecclesiastical History*, supplemented after Bede's death by lists of the southern kings. With the exception of the long entry for 755, which tells of the reign of King Cynewulf and his death at the hands of the princeling Cyneheard, the *ASC* proper begins with the ninth-century entries leading up to the Danish invasions in the middle of that century and the success of King Alfred against them. It would appear from linguistic tests that, although a number of writers may have worked on early entries, the *ASC* as we have it was compiled initially up to the year 892 and subsequently added to periodically. Seven manuscripts survive, varying in both content and reliability, and produced in different monastic centres; this includes one which was burnt in the fire in the Cotton Library in 1731, although a copy of it had been made in the sixteenth century. A single-page fragment of an eighth survives from the twelfth century. The original material common to the full texts, the so-called 'common stock', is presumed to be that which was issued by a central authority, but it is occasionally supplemented with local information which enables us to localize the manuscript copies or gives information about their transmission. The earliest copy, designated A and also known as the Parker Chronicle because it was given by Archbishop Matthew Parker to Corpus Christi College, Cambridge, in 1575, is written continuously up to 892 and then has additions periodically up to 1070, supplemented by large numbers of marginal and interlinear notes in other hands (Bately 1986). It was at Winchester until 1001, when it was moved to Canterbury. In some ways this is the most reliable text, because its entries for the tenth century were made closest to the events described, but it is throughout a copy and subject to all the errors that any copy has. The dating of the annals in other manuscripts, for example, is sometimes shown by external evidence to be more reliable. The large number of hands in A provides a marked contrast to the situation in B, a manuscript which was copied all at one time in or around 977, at which point it ends, and which is therefore the least contemporary (Taylor 1983). Version C is often assumed to be closely related to B (both may have connections with Abingdon, though it should be noted that a direct B–C link is now thought less likely) but was written entirely in the eleventh century. C ends at 1066 (Earle and Plummer 1892–9). D, again written in the eleventh century, ends at 1079 (Cubbin 1996). This version has material which suggests a particular interest in, or knowledge of, the north, and it probably originated either in the diocese of York or in Worcester, which was linked to York throughout the eleventh century. The E version, known as the Peterborough Chronicle, was copied at Peterborough after a fire destroyed their library. It was made in 1121, and the scribe who copied it later added further material to 1131. A final long entry in 1154 describes in the starkest terms the troubled reign of King Stephen, and is seen linguistically as the earliest Middle English text. It is clear from marginal annotations that this manuscript was widely read throughout the later medieval period; indeed, in a vacant space, a thirteenth-century scribe entered an extended chronicle of Britain in French, from Brutus to the accession of Edward I (1239). In other words, the tradition of a sequential annalistic chronicle in the vernacular established in the ninth century remained alive and important for many centuries after the Norman Conquest.

The other *Chronicle* manuscripts are less valuable textually but are of interest culturally. F, a Canterbury manuscript of the late eleventh century, is bilingual, each annal being followed by a Latin translation. Although its abbreviated entries limit its textual importance, the evidence it provides of interest in the *ASC* by those who worked in Latin is symptomatic of the post-Conquest period. It is in fact just one of many English documents to be translated in the Norman period. G is the burnt manuscript, our knowledge of which derives largely from the copy made by the antiquarian Laurence Nowell in 1562. It is a copy of A made at Winchester. Finally, H is a fragment written in the twelfth century and containing parts of annals for 1113–14. Although it has no obvious relationship with any other surviving text, it is important for the independent evidence it offers of the continuity of chronicle writing in English long after the Conquest.

There are other texts of importance in any consideration of *ASC*. Most significant is the Mercian Register, an account of the reign of Edward the Elder (899–924) which supplements the common-stock annals in B, C and D. Amongst Latin works which draw on the *ASC*, often on versions earlier than, and hence potentially more reliable than, those that survive are Asser's *Life of King Alfred* (Keynes and Lapidge 1983), a Latin translation of the *ASC* made by Æthelweard, ealdorman of the western shires, at the end of the tenth century (Campbell 1962), and the compiler of the so-called *Annals of St Neots* which survives in a post-Conquest manuscript (Dumville and Lapidge 1985). Æthelweard is sometimes guilty of misreading or misrepresenting the Old English, but his text bears witness to a different and perhaps earlier version of the *ASC* than any that we have. Anglo-Norman chroniclers, again writing in Latin, also drew heavily on the *ASC*. In other words, this is a work of enduring significance. It influenced prose writers and poets in its own day, it was read and drawn upon by significant figures both before the Conquest and after, and it continues to be among the best-known and most widely read works in Old English. Selections from it were published as early as 1644 and a comprehensive edition was available by the end of that century, and it has continued to be re-edited at regular intervals since then. Because it was compiled by many hands over three centuries from the late ninth until the twelfth, its style and its focus change considerably. In the ninth century, its focus is very firmly King Alfred and his success in defeating the Danes. In the tenth century, although the annals for the middle years are briefer, the focus remains glorification of the military achievements of the house of Alfred, the failures being understated. But during the reign of Æthelred at the end of that century, when annals are full again, the emphasis switches to the failures of the aristocracy to perform their duty in the defence of the realm, until during the early years of the eleventh century we find swingeing attacks on authority. It may be observed, however, that the Alfredian annals which applaud the king are recorded within his lifetime, whereas the criticism of Æthelred occurs only in manuscripts written long after his death. The style changes too, from staccato formulaic entries in the mid-ninth century, through longer accounts that include cause and effect in the last decade of Alfred's reign, to highly rhetorical passages in Æthelred's reign, influenced by the prose styles of homiletic writers of that period (Clark 1971).

Ostensibly this again is a secular work, in that it records historical events, but in origin it is undoubtedly clerical. Its progenitors are notes added by monks to tables used to calculate the date of Easter, and also significant Latin texts which were widely read in monasteries, such as those by Bede, Isidore and Jerome (Bately 1988). We must view this series of texts as a clerical production, perhaps produced in response to an initiative from Alfred's court, but certainly created, continued and maintained in monasteries throughout the land. One need point only to the type of information included: the lives and deeds of kings, of course, but also the recording of the deaths of bishops and abbots and the succession to the episcopal sees and monasteries. Even that most apparently secular of early entries, the contest between Cynewulf and Cyneheard under annal 755, with its seeming endorsement of the comitatus ideal (the loyalty of a lord's companions to him above all other ties), may be read as a clerical presentation of the importance of loyalty to God (Scragg 1997).

Throughout this chapter it has been emphasized that the term 'secular' must be viewed with suspicion in Old English studies. Finally we must turn to the other word used in the chapter title, for the *ASC* in the tenth and eleventh centuries has a few entries which fall into the rhythmical units of verse, and which, in some cases, have diction and imagery associated with heroic poetry. The best and longest of these verse annals (for 937) is the poem *The Battle of Brunanburh*, which survives in versions A, B, C and D. The appearance of verse within an essentially prose work is less surprising in an Anglo-Saxon context than might at first be supposed, for the line between prose and verse in Old English is nowhere as clear as it is today. In composing homilies and saints' lives, writers like Ælfric and Wulfstan, as well as the anonymous preachers that preceded them, utilized some of the rhetorical tricks associated with verse, such as consistent patterns of alliteration or two-stress phrases linked by alliteration or rhyme. In early anonymous homilies, the register occasionally shifts into verse mode, as in the first half of Vercelli Homily II, or, more briefly, in Vercelli Homily X, while in Vercelli Homily XXI a poem, *Exhortation to Christian Living*, has been incorporated into the text. It has already been noted that the *Beowulf*-manuscript contains prose as well as verse, with its juxtaposition of the *Marvels* and *Alexander's Letter* with *Beowulf* itself. This does not mean that Anglo-Saxon writers and readers failed to recognize verse and prose as different modes, but does mean that there were degrees between the two that make the separate categorization implied in the title to this chapter an unfortunate one (McIntosh 1949). A useful example of the blurred distinction between the two modes is in a collection of proverbial sayings usually known as the *Distichs of Cato*, a translation of the late Latin tract the *Disticha Catonis*, which became a standard primer in the monastic schools, but which in its Old English form incorporates some secular material. The vernacular text consists of a series of brief general truths or maxims (Cox 1972), and should be linked with wisdom poetry such as *Precepts* and passages of elegiac verse such as are found in *The Wanderer*. To divorce consideration of the prose text from that of poetry is to distort.

Surviving in Old English are a few scattered examples of many prose genres: romance, tales of the fabulous, wisdom literature, folklore, together with technical monastic instruments and administrative, historical and legal documents. It is impossible to know if some of these categories represent the tip of an iceberg the rest of which is submerged in the sea of time or if they were unique experiments, but given all that we know about the culture of late Anglo-Saxon England, the former is the more likely. With the exception of the *ASC*, almost all of the texts considered in this chapter can be shown to draw directly or indirectly upon Latin sources. The spread of the texts gives evidence of an interest during the late Anglo-Saxon period in a wide diversity of Latin material, and the success of the translations supports the view of the native language as a flexible, resourceful, versatile and adaptable medium, capable of expressing a wide range of concepts. Not until the sixteenth century will English once again be put to such a range of uses.

References

Primary sources

Baker, P. and M. Lapidge, eds and trans. 1995. *Byrhtferth of Ramsey: Enchiridion*. Early English Text Society, s.s. 15. Oxford.

Bately, J., ed. 1986. *MS A. The Anglo-Saxon Chronicle: A Collaborative Edition*, 3. Cambridge.

Campbell, A., ed. 1962. *The Chronicle of Æthelweard*. Edinburgh.

Cox, R. S., ed. 1972. 'The Old English Distichs of Cato'. *Anglia* 90: 1–42.

Cross, J. E. and T. D. Hill, eds 1982. *The Prose 'Solomon and Saturn' and 'Adrian and Ritheus'*. Toronto.

Cubbin, G. P., ed. 1996. *MS D. The Anglo-Saxon Chronicle: A Collaborative Edition*. Cambridge.

Dumville, D. and M. Lapidge, eds 1985. *Annals of St Neots with the Vita Prima Sancti Neoti*. Cambridge.

Earle, J. and C. Plummer 1892–9. *Two of the Saxon Chronicles Parallel*. 2 vols. Oxford.

Garmonsway, G. N., ed. 1939. *Ælfric's Colloquy*. London.

Goolden, Peter 1958. *The Old English 'Apollonius of Tyre'*. Oxford.

Gwara, S. and D. W. Porter, eds 1997. *Anglo-Saxon Conversations: The Colloquies of Ælfric Bata*. Woodbridge.

Henel, H., ed. 1942. *Ælfric's De Temporibus Anni*. Early English Text Society, o.s. 213. London. Repr. 1970.

Jost, K., ed. 1959. *Die 'Institutes of Polity, Civil and Ecclesiastical'*. Bern.

Keynes, S. and M. Lapidge, eds 1983. *Alfred the Great: Asser's Life of King Alfred and Other Contemporary Sources*. Harmondsworth.

Liebermann, F., ed. 1903–16. *Die Gesetze der Angelsachsen*. 3 vols. Halle.

Malone, K., ed. 1963. *The Nowell Codex: British Museum Cotton Vitellius A. XV, Second MS*. Early English Manuscripts in Facsimile 12. Copenhagen.

McGurk, P., D. N. Dumville, M. R. Godden and A. Knock, eds 1983. *An Eleventh-century Illustrated Miscellany (British Library Cotton Tiberius B. V, Part I)*. Early English Manuscripts in Facsimile 21. Copenhagen.

Rypins, Stanley I., ed. 1924. *Three Old English Prose Texts in MS Cotton Vitellius A. xv*. Early English Text Society, o.s. 161. London. Repr. 1971.

Sweet, H. 1897. *First Steps in Anglo-Saxon*. Oxford.

Taylor, S., ed. 1983. *MS B. The Anglo-Saxon Chronicle: A Collaborative Edition*. Cambridge.

Thorpe, B., ed. 1861. *The Anglo-Saxon Chronicle*. 2 vols. London.

Whitelock, D., ed. 1963. *Sermo Lupi ad Anglos*. 3rd edn. London.

Secondary sources

Archibald, Elizabeth 1991. *Apollonius of Tyre: Medieval and Renaissance Themes and Variations*. Cambridge.

Bately, J. 1988. 'Manuscript Layout and *The Anglo-Saxon Chronicle*'. *Bulletin of the John Rylands University Library of Manchester* 70: 21–43.

Bethurum, D., ed. 1957. *The Homilies of Wulfstan*. Oxford.

Biggs, F. M. and T. N. Hall 1996. 'Traditions Concerning Jamnes and Mambres in Anglo-Saxon England'. *Anglo-Saxon England* 25: 69–89.

Clark, Cecily 1971. 'The Narrative Mode of *The Anglo-Saxon Chronicle* Before the Conquest'. *England Before the Conquest: Studies in Primary Sources Presented to Dorothy Whitelock*, pp. 215–35. Eds P. Clemoes and K. Hughes. Cambridge.

Hollis, Stephanie and Michael Wright 1992. *Old English Prose of Secular Learning*. Annotated Bibliographies of Old and Middle English Literature IV. Cambridge.

McIntosh, A. 1949. 'Wulfstan's Prose'. *Proceedings of the British Academy* 35: 109–42.

Orchard, A. 1995. *Pride and Prodigies: Studies in the Monsters of the Beowulf-Manuscript*. Cambridge.

Riedinger, A. R. 1990. 'The Englishing of Arcestrate: Women in *Apollonius of Tyre*'. *New Readings on Women in Old English Literature*, pp. 292–306. Eds H. Damico and A. Hennessey Olsen. Bloomington, IN.

Scragg, D. G. 1997. '*WifcyðDe* and the Morality of the Cynewulf and Cyneheard Episode in the *Anglo-Saxon Chronicle*'. *Alfred the Wise: Essays in Honour of Janet Bately*, pp. 179–85. Eds J. Roberts and J. L. Nelson with M. Godden. Cambridge.

Sisam, K. 1953. *Studies in the History of Old English Literature*. Oxford.

16

Secular Poetry

Fred C. Robinson

The term 'secular poetry' refers here to those works in the Old English verse corpus that are not concerned primarily with Christianity. A secular poem may include a reference to God or Heaven or salvation, but its primary subject is something other than scriptural narrative, a saint's life, prayer or the like. The ensuing survey is organized broadly according to subject matter. We shall begin by considering those poems which look back to the continental origins of the English, keeping alive in Anglo-Saxon England the names of lands and peoples, kings and queens, heroes and villains as well as some of the cultural values of the Germanic world. Next we shall consider poems dealing with specifically English people and events; and finally we turn to poems which use the traditional poetic style to treat non-religious subjects of no particular locale or time. Throughout our survey we shall be concerned with the way the Anglo-Saxon poets showed a pervasive awareness of their Germanic cultural heritage.

It is not surprising that Anglo-Saxon poets retained a keen interest in continental Germanic topics even long after the English had been Christianized and their attention redirected towards the contemporary Christian world in which they lived. Almost all the Germanic peoples take an interest in their pre-Christian origins even centuries after their conversion. Saxo Grammaticus in the early thirteenth century painstakingly reconstructs the history of the Danes because of his people's 'joy in recollecting their ancestors' and 'vaunting the fame of their achievements' (Fisher and Davidson 1979: 4). Similarly, Jordanes (Mierow 1915) memorializes the Goths, Widukind the Saxons (Hirsch and Lohmann 1935), Paul the Deacon the Lombards (Foulke 1907), Snorri Sturluson the old Norwegian kings (in *Heimskringla*; Hollander 1964) and the old Scandinavian myths (in the *Prose Edda*; Young 1964), and Bede the Anglo-Saxons (Colgrave and Mynors 1969). Even the latest-preserved of the early Germanic literatures, that of the Frisians, contains repeated references (in the laws; von Richthofen 1840) to the time when the Frisians were still pagan. Charlemagne, whose Christian zeal prompted him to conversions by the sword, was none the less so fond of 'the old vernacular songs that celebrated the deeds and wars of the ancient kings' that he had them recorded for posterity, and while dining he listened to 'the stories and deeds of olden time' (Einhard, chs 29 and 24, in Turner 1960). Asser (Keynes and Lapidge 1983) tells us that when King Alfred the Great was a boy he so coveted a book of *Saxonica carmina* that he learned the poems by heart in order to persuade his mother to give him the book. Earlier, Alcuin's famous letter of 797 reveals that even the clergy in some parts of Anglo-Saxon England were accustomed to hearing old songs about the heathen Germanic kings like Ingeld (Garmonsway and Simpson 1971: 242).

All this being so, it is hardly surprising that one Anglo-Saxon poet composes a poem devoted largely to sounding the names of pagan Germanic kings and peoples (*Widsith*) and that another emphasizes the lessons we can learn from the old Germanic legends (*Deor*). Or that other poets recall an ancient feud between Danes and Frisians (*The Battle of Finnesburh*) and the derring-do of the Germanic hero Waldere and his contemporaries. The same pattern of thought would explain the fact that a Christian Anglo-Saxon poet commits the longest-surviving Old English poem (*Beowulf*) to the celebration of pagan Germanic peoples on the continent. Memorializing their Germanic roots was clearly a major concern of the Christian poets of Anglo-Saxon England.

Wisdith, a wandering poet's monologue preserved in the tenth-century Exeter Book (facsimile, Chambers et al. 1933), clearly evinces this interest in pre-migration, continental Germanic culture. The major purpose of the poem would seem to be to suggest that (1) the Germanic world was rich with kings, cultures and heroes and (2) these kings and their peoples were of sufficient stature to be set alongside the greatest rulers and nations of antiquity – Alexander, Caesar, the Greeks and Romans, the Persians and Medes, the Egyptians and Jews – all of whom are included in the speaker's list of names. The chronology of the poem is mythic, not historical, ranging in time from Alexander and Caesar through the fourth-century historical figure Eormanric and the fifth-century Attila down to the sixth-century Langobardish king Alboin (Ælfwine). This list of ancient names is presented from a proto-Anglo-Saxon perspective. The *scop* Widsith is identified as a Myrging, and this nation appears to be a sub-group of the Saxons when they were still in their continental home (Malone 1962: 183–6). The lady Ealhhild, whom he escorts to the court of the mighty Gothic king Eormanric, is from Ongel. That is, she is from the tribe of the Angles while they were still in Schleswig, before they migrated to England. The Christian Anglo-Saxon audience of *Widsith* is given a tour of the people and nations of ancient Germania by a man who is one of their forebears with connections to both Angles and Saxons.

After introducing Widsith as a Myrging and Ealhhild as an Ongel, the poet allows Widsith himself to begin speaking in line 10, and we are treated to a traditional alliterative list (or *þula*, to use the Old Norse term for such a list) of Germanic kings and the people they ruled. In line 50 he boasts of how far he has travelled throughout the known world (the name *Widsith* means 'far journey'), and in line 57 he begins a second *þula* listing the various peoples whom he had visited, and this geographical survey of the Germanic world and beyond is as unrealistic as the chronological range of the first list. In line 112 he commences another list naming individual men whom he had visited. Widsith's monologue ends with line 134, and in the poem's remaining nine lines the poet, speaking in his own voice, says that Widsith is typical of the minstrels who wander through many lands singing the praises of leaders before their warrior bands and receiving rewards for their performances. The minstrel, it is implied, is the instrument of fame, for it is through his songs that the deeds of men are remembered.

In the verses separating his name-lists Widsith tells us of his travels and mentions certain leaders as being especially noteworthy and especially generous. He singles out Eormanric (the fourth-century Ostrogothic king) and his queen Ealhhild, both of whom enriched him before he returned to the service of his native Myrging king Eadgils. He says he received great praise when he performed with Schilling, which is probably the name of his musical instrument (*scil-* apparently means 'resounding like a harp'; cf. 'scyl wæs hearpe' in *The Rhyming Poem*, line 27, and 'schille harpe' in *The Owl and the Nightingale*, line 143). The characteristic personification of the harp in line 104 'for uncrum sigedryhtne' ('before our victorious lord') has misled some critics into assuming that Scilling is a companion singer, but such a personage appears nowhere else in the poem, while the harp is specifically mentioned in line 105.

The verses in which Widsith comments on himself and those in which the poet comments on him are in a prosodic style quite different from that of the lists themselves. The name-lists are in the most primitive prosodic form used by Germanic poets, end-stopped long lines in which verse-structure and sentence-structure coincide (Malone 1967: 26). Widsith's comments about himself are in the later style of Old English poets with ever-increasing enjambement. This contrast in style has led to the suggestion that the lists in *Widsith* were ancient, pre-existing Germanic elements which the *Widsith*-poet adapted to his purposes. Evidently the lists were not anciently closed: the second list has been expanded with references to Hebrews and Assyrians and the like – but always in the old end-stopped style.

What is remarkable is that these dry, archaic lists should have been of such importance to tenth-century Anglo-Saxons as to have earned preservation and sustained interest. We might surmise that the very fullness of the lists would have given the impression of a rich Germanic past peopled with heroes and kings bearing sonorous Germanic names. Roberta Frank has described vividly how long-Christianized Anglo-Saxons might have yearned for 'a proud history' (Frank 1991: 104). The surviving texts suggest a further possible reason for the Anglo-Saxons to preserve and expand the old end-stopped name-lists from century to century. The names probably suggested to the English audience stories involving the named characters and peoples. Widsith himself pauses at times to allude to deeds performed by the people he lists: the Goths' stand against Atilla, Ealhhild's marriage and her generosity (her Angle origins would have especially interested an English audience), Hrothulf and Hrothgar's long but temporary alliance (further elaborated in *Beowulf*) and a laudatory digression on Offa – especially noteworthy since the *Beowulf*-poet (lines 1949–62) similarly digresses at the mention of Offa's name. Other names merely mentioned by Widsith designate the actors in stories told or summarized by the *Beowulf*-poet (Breca, Ongentheow, Ingeld, Heathobards, Finn, Hama, etc.). Others named in *Widsith* turn up in *Waldere*, in texts from other Germanic traditions, or in *Deor*. When so many of the names in *Widsith*'s lists can be shown from our fragmentary remains to figure in known stories, it seems likely that others were similarly documented in the original corpus of Old English writings. And so *Widsith* attests to an Anglo-Saxon audience which valued its traditional stories even though these involved people who were both heroic and heathen (*Widsith* line 81).

That the heathen stories were thought to hold useful lessons for life is demonstrated by another poem in the Exeter Book, *Deor*, in which a court *scop* who has lost his post to a rival poet consoles himself by reviewing five Germanic heroic instances of men or women enduring misfortunes such as his and then living to see a positive outcome. Deor's mention of the ancient stories is sometimes cryptic. Information provided by other texts (Old English or Scandinavian) makes the relevance of each incident more or less clear. Where existing data do not enable us to establish the parallel with Deor's misfortune precisely, we should be hesitant to question the poet's skill or detect irony, for we cannot be sure of the exact form of the tale to which the poet alludes. A character who is heroic in one surviving narrative can be villainous in another (Hrothulf, Eormanric); a romantic abduction in one telling can be a brutal rape in another. Kemp Malone's brilliant solution to the previously puzzling Mæthhild and Geat stanza is exemplary: two late Scandinavian ballads give variant accounts of the story that, between them, explain the allusion (Malone 1960: 8–9).

Two leaves of a vellum manuscript written around 1000 (preserved now in the Kongelike Bibliotek in Copenhagen; facsimile, Robinson and Stanley 1991) were discovered and published in Denmark in 1860 with the title *Two Leaves of King Waldere's Lay* (Stephens 1860). The story of the Germanic hero Waldere is known from a variety of fragments and allusions but most completely from a Latin epic *Waltharius* written in the tenth century by a monk of St Gall. *Waltharius* tells how Atilla the Hun, after subduing his Germanic enemies, took hostages – Hagen from the Franks, Hildegund from the Burgundians and Walter (Old English Waldere) from the Aquitanians, the latter two being betrothed. Some years later Hagen escapes, returning to join his Frankish king Gunther. Subsequently Walter and Hildegund escape with a considerable amount of treasure, intending to return to their homes. But when they come to the Frankish realm, Gunther and his men attack Walter, wanting to plunder the treasure. Hagen is with Gunther, but being Walter's friend, he is reluctant to join in the attack. Protected in a narrow defile, Walter single-handedly kills all of Gunther's warrior's except Hagen, who now joins Gunther in attacking Walter, his (Hagen's) sister's son having fallen with the other Frankish warriors. After each of the three is seriously wounded, they strike a truce; Walter and Hildegund depart together and are later married, after which Walter enjoys a thirty-year reign as king of the Aquitanians.

The two fragments of the Old English version of *Waldere* are hard to fit precisely into the larger narrative but are remarkable for the prominence of traditional Germanic themes that are included in the sixty-three lines that survive. In one fragment Hildegund (the Old English form of which would have been Hildegyth, had she been named in the fragments) exhorts Waldere to fight – as Germanic women do from Tacitus' *Germania* to the late sagas of the Icelanders. She praises a sword named Mimming, 'the work of Weland', and comments on Waldere's defence of a narrow place (another old Germanic topos). She also alludes to Waldere's outstanding service to Atilla the Hun and to the lasting fame Waldere will achieve through his valour in fighting Gunther (Old English Guthhere). The second fragment is about heirloom swords and Walter's manly defiance of Gunther. Waldere refers to Hagen's role in the battle, Hagen being in the classic heroic predicament: torn between loyalty to his friend and loyalty to his lord Gunther. And Waldere boasts of wearing an heirloom corselet inherited from his father Ælfhere. Names found in Germanic legend are invoked: Weland the supernatural smith (again), his tormentor Nithhad, his son Widia and Theodoric the Ostrogoth. So many Germanic heroic topoi in such a brief space suggest that had *Waldere* survived entire rather than in fragments, we should have a full-blown epic poem about Germania, one to compare with *Beowulf*, which now stands in isolation as the only secular epic in Old English.

Also preserving several Old Germanic topoi in brief space is the even shorter (forty-eight lines) fragment *The Battle of Finnesburh*. The Lambeth Palace Library (London) leaf which contained these lines is lost, and so we must rely on the transcription which George Hickes published in his *Thesaurus* (1703–5: pt 1, 192–3). In this text we encounter the beasts of battle (a traditional description of the scavenging birds that devour the slain after a battle – a common motif in Old English battle poems), warriors responding eagerly to the call for them to 'contend in the vanguard' ('winnað on orde'), the defence of a narrow place at the hall entrances, a warrior defiantly identifying himself to his enemy, and a classic expression of the motif of warriors repaying their lord's generosity with courage on the field of battle:

> Ne gefrægn ic næfre wurþlicor   æt wera hilde
> sixtig sigebeorna   sel gebæran,
> ne nefre swetne medo   sel forgyldan
> ðonne Hnæfe guldan   his hægstealdas.
> (lines 37–40)

I have never heard of sixty triumphant warriors bearing themselves at a battle of men better, more honourably, nor of young men repaying the sweet mead better than his retainers repaid Hnæf.

We are able to place the fragment in the context of the story as a whole since the *Beowulf*-poet summarizes the entire narrative of *The Battle of Finnesburh* in *Beowulf*, lines 1068–159, where Hrothgar's *scop* sings the narrative of Finnesburh as part of the celebration of Beowulf's victory over Grendel. It is a story of Danish vengeance deferred and then vengeance gloriously taken (hence its appropriateness to the celebration of Grendel's defeat, a vengeance-taking for which the Danes had to wait for twelve years). It is also about conflicting loyalties and reciprocal obligations of retainers and the lord – the classic Germanic themes.

The Danish prince Hnæf with sixty retainers is visiting his sister Hildeburh (who is married to the Frisian lord Finn) when a group of Frisians launches a nocturnal attack on their Danish guests, who are sleeping in a meadhall which the Frisians had made available to them. Hnæf and many others on both sides are killed, and the two groups fight to a standoff. Finally Finn and Hengest (who has succeeded Hnæf as leader of the Danes) strike a truce whereby the Danes agree to acknowledge Finn as their leader and share equally with the Frisians in possession of the hall and distribution of treasure. For the Danes it is a humiliating disgrace to reach such an accommodation with the slayers of their lord Hnæf, but since winter has set in and they cannot sail home for reinforcements, the Danes must accept the situation. But with the coming of spring the Danes (apparently) recruit comrades to join in an attack on the Frisians in which Finn and his retainers are slain. With much booty and the lady Hildeburh the Danes return triumphantly to Denmark.

This is the story that Hrothgar's *scop* tells the Danes in *Beowulf*, and from what we can tell it conforms with the details of the fragment. But the *Beowulf*-poet, in his summary of the *scop*'s narrative, gives a different perspective on the events, and in doing so he shows how Christian Anglo-Saxon poets could turn the ancient tales to their own purposes. An examination of this adaptation of a pre-existing legend from pagan times to his own poetic purposes will provide a convenient segue into our examination of the central text in Old English secular poetry, *Beowulf* (preserved in London, British Library, Cotton Vitellius A. xv; facsimile, Malone 1963). The *Beowulf*-poet begins and ends his account of events by focusing on Hildeburh, the woman who suffered most from the tragedy, being torn between loyalty to her brother on the one hand and loyalty to her husband and son on the other. Death claims all three – brother, husband and son – by the end of the violence. Thus the *Beowulf*-poet implies an Anglo-Christian's judgement of the heroic age he is describing: to the characters in the poem revenge is a supreme imperative, and Hrothgar's *scop* and his audience would have exulted in the Danes' eventual success in avenging Hnæf's death. But the *Beowulf*-poet's attention to Hildeburh in his summary of the narrative forces us to contemplate the suffering which this culture of violence and revenge causes an innocent woman, and indeed implies a critique of that culture in general: 'We must admire the men of old without stint', the poet seems to say, 'but we must never wish to live as they did, for we know a better way now.'

This is a fair statement of the poet's perspective throughout the poem *Beowulf*, which is a long, admiring but not uncritical scrutiny of the culture whence the English had come. The men and women who lived on the continent in Germanic lands were glorious in their heroic bearing, their indomitable courage, their dignity in defeat and their unflinching acceptance of fate's hard decrees. The poem is primarily a celebration of these qualities and must have left its audience proud to be who they were and inspired by the example of their forebears. But all is tinged with the sadness of Christian retrospection on a culture pathetically ignorant of Christian truth. Yet this sadness has not deterred the Christian Anglo-Saxons from looking deeply into their pagan origins. Even as late as the year 1000, which is approximately the date when London, British Library, Cotton Vitellius A. xv (the manuscript containing *Beowulf*) was copied, there was this felt need for conjoining with the age before, this unwillingness to lose the old names and narratives that give their past its identity.

Beowulf begins with an exploration of origins. The ancient court of Hrothgar is where the narrative begins, but that is not ancient enough. The poet traces King Hrothgar's lineage back through Healfdene, Beowulf and Scyld to the time when there was no king. Similarly in treating the Geats the poet tells us about the reigning king Hygelac but also reverts again and again – nine times – to Hygelac's father Hrethel. The Grendelkin are repeatedly genealogized back to their ultimate origin – Cain. And when the dragon and his treasure are introduced, we are given elaborate accounts of how the treasure came into being in a remote area when even earlier races – 'gumena nathwylc' ('I know not what men', line 2233) – had gathered the treasure before dying out.

For an Anglo-Saxon listening to the story of Beowulf these names and places would have had a familiar resonance. The names of the early Danish kings found their way into the genealogies of West Saxon kings (as did the name of Woden and a god named Geat), and these are repeated in chronicles both Latin and Anglo-Saxon. Hygelac is referred to in the *Liber monstrorum*, thought to be of Anglo-Saxon provenance (Lapidge 1982: 165–7). Some of these names are also in *Widsith*, as we have seen above, Also, 'it is reasonable to assume that the audience which listened to [the *Beowulf*-poet's account of Offa] knew something of the deeds of Offa' (Whitelock 1951: 60). The land where Hrothgar ruled lay near to those lands which Bede says were left empty after the 'powerful Germanic tribes' which populated England had left the Continent (HE I.15). Cain and dragons and buried treasure were also familiar topics in the literature of Anglo-Saxon England. The poem unfolds amid names and allusions which were more familiar than exotic to the Anglo-Saxon audience.

The central subject of the poem is the triumphs of Beowulf, particularly his triumph over the Grendelkin in the first part of the poem and over the fire-breathing dragon in the second and last. His triumphs in conventional wars are described and alluded to throughout the poem, and, like the monster fights, they are always motivated by a concern for others' welfare – to save his country's Danish neighbours from a scourge, to protect his own people from foes natural and supernatural, to help his Swedish neighbours, to avenge his slain king. Interwoven with these events are descriptions of customs and rituals showing the dignity of the ancient civilization – banqueting, speech-making, gifts graciously given and graciously received, performances of poetry, funeral rites and the various activities of kings and queens. Likewise copious allusions to a rich history (some mythic, some actual) lend depth to the portrayal of the Germanic world. And the poet pauses repeatedly to comment on the actions he is describing, telling his audience that they should emulate the exemplary conduct of their forebears ('swa sceal geong guma . . .', line 26; 'swa sceal man don . . .', line 1534; 'swa sceal mæg don . . .', line 2166, etc.). The poem's dominant theme is pride of ancestry, and this is not surprising since most national epics are a celebration of a people's glorious past. What sets *Beowulf* apart from most other heroic celebrations is its poignant religious perspective, as has been suggested briefly above and as I have argued in some detail in Robinson (1985) *passim*, where I suggest that the religious perspective contributes significantly to the poem's high seriousness. It is true that some scholars have suggested that the Christian Anglo-Saxon audience of the poem would have been so caught up in the heroics of the poem and the deeds of derring-do that they would not have thought about the implications of the poem's pagan setting. But it is my firm belief that Christian Anglo-Saxons who were the least bit reflective and intelligent could not but sigh over such noble people as Beowulf and Wiglaf, Hrothgar and Wealhtheow, being cut off from the Christian truth which gave meaning and hope of salvation to the members of the Christian audience.

Turning from poems which deal with the ancient Germanic subjects to those which treat contemporary Anglo-Saxon matters, we might begin with a consideration of six poems from the *Anglo-Saxon Chronicle* (facsimiles of all manuscripts, Robinson and Stanley 1991). The titles which modern scholars have assigned to these poems are *The Battle of Brunanburh, The Capture of the Five Boroughs, The Coronation of Edgar, The Death of Edgar, The Death of Alfred* and *The Death of Edward*. Rooted firmly in English soil and treating events which occurred in (respectively) 937, 942, 973, 975, 1036 and 1065, these compositions would seem to be wholly concerned with English matters with no reference to the ancient past. And yet they do in varying degrees look back to the old Germanic origins even as they explore contemporary English subjects. *The Battle of Brunanburh* celebrates a bloody and decisive defeat by King Æthelstan's army of a coalition formed by the Norse king Anlaf. The poem gloats exultantly over the Anglo-Saxons' slaying of five young kings and seven earls and countless others in Anlaf's army, concluding with the climactic assertion that a greater slaughter of men had not occurred in England 'since the Angles and Saxons, proud war-makers, came hither over the broad sea from the east and attacked Britain; the vigorous noblemen overcame the Britons and seized the land' (lines 69b–73, 'siþþan eastan hider / Engle and Seaxe up becoman / ofer brad brimu Brytene sohtan, / wlance wigsmiþas, Wealas ofercoman, / eorlas arhwate eard begeatan'). A tenth-century victory can be fully appreciated, it would seem, only in the context of the ancient Anglo-Saxons' migration to Britain from Germania. The triumphant gesture to the nation's past is proudly made even though it undercuts the only moral justification of the poet's exultation over the defeat of Anlaf: it is defence of homeland against an overseas invader which entitles Anglo-Saxons to gloat over the killing they have done. But then the poem's backward look to the Germanic past acknowledges that the Anglo-Saxons were themselves overseas invaders.

When Edward the Elder subjugated Mercia in 924, he brought virtually all of England under the rule of one English king for the first time, but the Scandinavians subsequently regained control of the area. *The Capture of the Five Boroughs* commemorates King Edmund's restoration of Anglo-Saxon hegemony. Like the other *Chronicle* poems this is a panegyric (the verse 'Eadmund cyning' at the beginning and end of the poem frames a text devoted mainly to praising Edmund), and many scholars regard panegyric as the earliest form of Germanic poetry (see Heusler 1943: 123–43; Opland 1980: 12, 48, 63–4, *et passim*). And so, in a sense, the genre of all these *Chronicle* poems looks back to Germanic origins. *The Death of Edgar* is no exception. Twelve lines of correct and traditional verse commemorate the king's death with laudatory epithets. But then the verse trails off into a mechanical recitation of other events of the year 975, and this has no retrospective quality. *The Coronation of Edgar* commemorates the crowning of this king 'in the ancient city' ('in ðære ealdan byrig') of Bath just 927 years after the birth of Christ. *The Death of Alfred* praises this brother of Edward the Confessor, but combined with the praise is an indignant narration of how the innocent prince was brutally tortured and murdered by henchmen of the powerful Godwin – strictly contemporary matter. *The Death of Edward* eulogizes the king ('he lived in royal majesty, wise in counsels, the lord of heroes . . . splendid in his armour', etc.), but with an admixture of the hagiographic, which moves the poem away from its roots in Germanic praise-song.

The poem *Durham* is also eulogistic in its account of that city, but here the ancient Germanic form has been completely assimilated by Christian-Latin conventions. The poem follows closely the prescribed details of an *encomium urbis*, a literary exercise descended from the ancient classical schools of rhetoric (Schlauch 1941).

The Battle of Maldon was fought on the tenth or eleventh of August in 991, and so the poem of that name was composed after that date. One would expect that such a late composition would be far removed from its continental roots and well adapted to the Christian-Latin traditions which had taken hold in England. But in fact *The Battle of Maldon* (preserved in an eighteenth-century transcript of a now lost manuscript; facsimile, Robinson and Stanley 1991), though it narrates an event from late Anglo-Saxon history, is one of the most quintessentially Germanic, backward-looking poems in Old English. Its depiction of English warriors accepting death and defeat gloriously in their struggle against a larger force of Vikings rings the changes on all the ancient themes: manly defiance in the face of an arrogant, overconfident enemy; repeated declarations by the English warriors that they prefer to die trying to avenge their slain leader rather than return home without him; exhortations to repay with blood their leader's generosity in past years; hot condemnation of the vile cowardice shown by a treacherous few. Even details like the beasts of battle and the importance of the relationship of uncle to his sister's son are included. The most illuminating gloss on *The Battle of Maldon* is – incredibly – Tacitus' *Germania*, which again and again confirms as typically Germanic the behaviour of the warriors at Maldon. There are of course other elements in the poem and they combine with the strong Germanic tone to yield a poem of great power (Robinson 1993: 105–21), but most remarkable is the demonstrated tenacity with which Anglo-Saxons held to their ancient traditions.

Another verse text from a very specific moment in Anglo-Saxon history is the Old English proverb quoted in a Latin letter (facsimile, Robinson and Stanley 1991) from an unnamed monk to an unnamed cleric dated to the second half of the eighth century.

The letter-writer is encouraging the church dignitary to whom he is writing to carry out promptly the course of action which he has set for himself. 'Memento Saxonicum uerbum' ('remember the Saxon proverb'), he says, and then quotes: 'Oft dædlata dome foreldit / sigisitha gahuem; suuyltit thi ana' ('The one slow to act always delays [his pursuit] of fame in every victorious undertaking; for that he shall die alone'). '[I]t may be the oldest of all extant English verse' (Stanley 1987: 121), and what is remarkable about it is the reversion to old Germanic heroic folk wisdom in a context that is purely religious. Even the Christian intelligentsia of early England would not surrender their ancestral traditions.

Turning now to secular verse which treats subjects from no particular time or locale, we might begin with that miscellaneous group of meditative poems which some scholars have classified as 'elegies', a classification which Morton Bloomfield (1970: 77–80) called into question. Comparing the Old English poems with somewhat similar Old Norse poems, Joseph Harris (1983) has suggested that there was a 'Common Germanic heroic elegy' and that both Old English and Old Norse poems descend from that primitive form. The poems (all of which occur in the Exeter Book, although they are not together there) are *The Wife's Lament, The Wanderer, The Seafarer, The Ruin, Resignation* (actually fragments of two poems which modern editions have mistakenly fused [Bliss and Frantzen 1976]; only the second text, which begins at line 70, is a secular poem, called by critics *Resignation B*), *Deor, Wulf and Eadwacer, The Rhyming Poem* and *The Husband's Message*. These poems all draw from the traditional heritage such subjects as wandering or imprisoned exiles, daring seafarers, feuds and wars. After developing one or more of these subjects, the poems come to some sort of generalization or general attitude, sometimes a Christian truth (*The Wanderer, The Seafarer, The Rhyming Poem*), sometimes a view with no particularly Christian association (*The Wife's Lament, The Ruin, Wulf and Eadwacer, The Husband's Message, Resignation B* and *Deor*). *Deor*, it is true, mentions 'witig dryhten' ('wise Lord') in line 32, but the general view that things change in this world, sometimes for the better, sometimes for the worse, can hardly be regarded as deeply or specifically religious. Similarly *Resignation B* mentions God repeatedly, but the conclusion is simple stoic acceptance: 'Giet biþ þæt selast, þonne mon him sylf ne mæg / wyrd onwendan, þæt he þonne wel þolige' (lines 117–18, 'When one cannot himself change his fate, it is best that he endure it well'). Whatever the closing generalization, it is the elegies' subjects drawn from the Germanic cultural heritage – the royal *scop* of *Deor*, the exile bereft of his comitatus in *The Wanderer*, the woman caught up in family feuds in *The Wife's Lament*, the brave and resolute seafarer, the Anglo-Saxon meditating on 'enta geweorc' ('the work of giants') in *The Ruin* – that leave the deepest impression on the reader.

The metrical charms – magical incantations against various physical maladies or infertility of one's acreage or mishaps on a journey, etc. – have been called 'the oldest relics of Germanic literature, despite their Christianization in their Old English forms' (Greenfield and Calder 1986: 255). Recently, Richard North (1997: 105–6, 250–5) has provided analyses of two charms which draw on extensive connections with Germanic pre-Christian beliefs, and the fact that references to such figures as Woden and the earth mother appear in the charms seems indicative of dependence on ancient lore. The twelve surviving metrical charms are preserved in five separate manuscripts of the tenth and eleventh centuries, and this suggests that charms were a widespread, popular genre even at a late stage of the Anglo-Saxon period. Of course, Christianization induced charm-writers to include invocations of the Pater Noster, Sanctus, prayers to Mary, the Gospels, etc., but these coexist with quite a bit of ancient Germanic lore.

Another repository of ancient lore commingled with a few Christian sentiments is the two sets of texts called *Maxims I* (preserved in the Exeter Book) and *Maxims II* (preserved in London, British Library, Cotton Tiberius B. i, where the compiler has placed it immediately before the C-text of the *Anglo-Saxon Chronicle*). Typical passages from the latter poem are:

> wyrd byð swiðost.
> (line 5)

Wyrd is most powerful.

> Geongne æþeling sceolan   gode gesiðas
> byldan to beaduwe   and to beahgife.
> Ellen sceal on eorle,   ecg sceal wið hellme
> hilde gebidan.
> (lines 14–17a)

Good comrades must urge a young nobleman to battle and to the giving of rings; courage must be in the nobleman; sword-blade must experience war against the helmet.

> Draca sceal on hlæwe,
> frod, frætwum wlanc.
> (lines 26b–7a)

A dragon must be in a barrow, crafty and proud of his treasures.

> Cyning sceal on healle
> beagas dælan.
> (lines 28b–9a)

The king shall distribute rings in his hall.

These sentiments are characteristic of Anglo-Saxon thought of all periods, although mention of Wyrd, the importance of courage and comitatus, king's generosity and dragons guarding gold might suggest a gaze back to the old heroic days more than a contemporary Christian Anglo-Saxon perspective. Even the emphatically Christian conclusion to *Maxims II* suggests some of the uncertainty about future events which the pagan thane in Bede's story of Cædmon (*HE* IV.24) expresses more than a devout Christian view of things:

> Is seo forðgesceaft
> digol and dyrne;   drihten ana wat,
> nergende fæder.   Næni eft cymeð
> hider under hrofas,   þe þæt her for soð
> mannum secge   hwylc sy meotodes gesceaft,
> sigefolca gesetu,   þær he sylfa wunað.
>
> (lines 61b–66)

The future is hidden and secret; only the Lord, the salvific Father, has knowledge. No one comes back here under our roofs who may say to men with certainty what the Creator's dispensation is like [or] the seats of the victorious where he lives.

Maxims I has passages similar to these and in one section incorporates a verse from Psalm 95, 5, which one would think emphasizes the poet's contemporary Christian outlook. But in fact the poet's concern is to make clear the Psalter passage's relevance to Anglo-Saxon paganism (see North 1997: 88–90): 'Woden worhte weos, wuldor alwalda, / rume roderas' (lines 132–3a, 'Woden built idols, the Almighty [built] splendour, the spacious heavens'). Since aphorisms and sententious observations occur in virtually all the Germanic languages, it would appear that this form is a relic of the Germanic past. But the form was constantly being utilized for contemporary subjects. Thus the first two lines of *Maxims II* seem to document the Anglo-Saxons' amazement at the Roman structures in stone which they encountered after they occupied Britain: 'Ceastra beoð feorran gesyne, / orðanc enta geweorc' (lines 1b–2a, 'Cities are seen from afar, the cunning handiwork of giants').

The ninety-four-line *Rune Poem* preserves the ancient Germanic alphabet for a later Anglo-Saxon audience and explains in a three- to five-line stanza apiece the significance of each of the twenty-nine runes. (The text survives only in Hickes 1703–5: I, 135, the original manuscript being lost.) The letters given are the English *futhorc* (with the 'Anglo-Frisian' runes to accommodate sound changes in Old English and Frisian). The stanzas of the *Rune Poem* are also updated with several Christian references inserted (Niles 1991: 135–6), but the very subject of the runic alphabet is a turning back to the past. There are similar runic poems in Old Icelandic and Norwegian, and some of the phrasing in these echoes that in the Old English poem, suggesting that the three poems, in part at least, go back to some kind of *ur*-poem about runes in Germanic. Of the rune *hægl* 'hail' the Old English poet says, 'Hægl byþ hwitust corna' ('Hail is the brightest of grains'), while the Norwegian rune poem says, 'Hagell er kaldastr korna' ('Hail is the coldest of grains'), and the Old Icelandic poem says, 'Hagell er kaldakorn' ('Hail is a cold grain'). Evidently the comparison between hail and grain goes back to ancient Germanic rune-lore. Similarly in their stanzas for the rune *gear* '(fruitful) year' both the Old English and the Old Icelandic poems say that the fruitful year 'is a boon for men'. Amid innovations and diversions the rune poems all clearly retain at the same time relics from a common past.

Runes are used in other Old English poems as well. The husband's call to his wife in *The Husband's Message* is carved (presumably) in runes on a stick, and at the close of the message he lists five runes with which he seals the pledges the two had made in days of old. The precise meaning of the runic collocation is unclear (see the inconclusive discussion by Leslie 1961: 15–18), but the runes evidently were thought to have some kind of covenantal force.

Runes are also used in the somewhat mystifying poem *Solomon and Saturn*, which is preserved in fragmentary form in two manuscripts at the Parker Library, Corpus Christi College, Cambridge (facsimiles, Robinson and Stanley 1991). At one point in this exotic dialogue there is a disquisition on the magical properties of each of the letters used in the Latin Pater Noster, the prayer being regarded as a kind of spell with numinous powers. Somewhat incongruously the poet supplies these letters in runic form (with the equivalent letter in insular script standing alongside them), and he concludes by describing how these letters can insure a weapon's efficacy if they are carved on it. It is curious that a poem so imbued with the lore and magic of the East should call into play the old Germanic *futhorc*; for the poet, apparently, the concept of letters with special power evoked irresistibly the traditional writing system of his ancestors. One might also question the appropriateness of Cynewulf weaving his runic signature into the text of his explicitly Christian poems, but here runes are used with their letter-names punningly constituting part of the text's meaning. Letters of the Roman alphabet did not have meaningful names.

Verses written in beautifully carved runes appear on the Franks Casket, which also has a depiction of the story of Weland, the legendary Germanic smith. Runes are also used as part of the riddling apparatus in four verse riddles in the Exeter Book (numbers 19, 24, 64 and 75 in the Krapp–Dobbie numeration). The runes typically spell the answer to the riddle, but the order of the letters is usually scrambled in order to increase the difficulty of finding the solution. Riddle 24, for example, has for its solution the word *higoræ* 'magpie', but the order in which the runes are given is *gærohi*. Riddling is an ancient genre and some of those in the Exeter Book are probably remembered from continental times. Others are clearly Christian-Latin in origin, and so the riddles are a mix of old and new. The runes, like the alliterative form and the traditional diction, are relics from the Germanic past. The flexible expressiveness of the riddles and their variety of subject matter make them an especially interesting Old English genre (Adams 1965: 335–48). For an excellent discussion of the verse riddles' place in both Old English literature and Anglo-Saxon culture, see Niles (1998: 169–207, esp. 196–207).

The Old English verse translation of the *Metres of Boethius* could not possibly reference ancient Germanic motifs, one would assume, since their content is determined by the Latin base text. But even here there are backward glances to old Germanic culture. The preface to the *Metres* which the translator affixes to his translation is a detailed account of how the Goths under Alaric (d. 410) and Radagaisus overcame the Romans and how Theodoric, king of the Ostrogoths (d. 526), subsequently became ruler in Rome. Thus the translator places his verse rendering of Boethius squarely in the midst of the Germanic migration at approximately the time that Germanic tribes were migrating to Britain. And later, in a famous passage in *Metre* 10, lines 33–43, the Old English versifier substitutes the Germanic mythological smith Weland for Boethius' allusion to the Roman Fabricius. Other poems which are decidedly Christian in their orientation also have surprising moments of cultural retrospection. In the Metrical Preface to the *Pastoral Care*, for example, the versifier introduces the translation of the Gregorian text by referring to St Augustine of Canterbury's mission bringing Christianity to the pagan Anglo-Saxons, and the saint's life *Elene* opens with a thoroughly Germanic war scene with shield walls, beasts of battle, boar-helmets and all the panoply of the native heroic tradition. Another of Cynewulf's poems, *Fates of the Apostles*, also opens with a markedly Germanic-epic presentation of the Apostles. It is not just their secular poetry that refuses to let go of the ancestral past.

Starting around the middle of the twentieth century, great emphasis began to be laid upon the importance of Christian doctrine in Old English poetry. Patristic learning, Christian iconography and Christian allegory were zealously applied to the interpretation not only of the explicitly religious poems of the Anglo-Saxons but also of many of the poems to which this chapter is devoted. The undeniably profound Christian character of Anglo-Saxon culture at large has been emphasized, and long-neglected Christian-Latin writings of the Anglo-Saxons began receiving the attention they deserved. This was clearly a positive development in Anglo-Saxon studies, and much good has come of it. But sometimes the Christian dimension of Old English literature seems to have been stressed almost to the exclusion of any other elements, especially of the native Germanic features of that corpus. Scholars and students seemed to lose sight at times of what a deeply retrospective strain marks the poetry of the Anglo-Saxons, who seemed to cling persistently to their history and their cultural identity. This survey of the secular poetry of the Anglo-Saxons serves to remind us of how important a part of the unique character of Old English poetry is the strong historical sense which keeps the people of early England in constant touch with their Germanic past and in full awareness of their cultural identity.

REFERENCES

Primary sources

Chambers, R. W., Max Förster and Robin Flower, eds 1933. *The Exeter Book of Old English Poetry*. Bradford.

Colgrave, Bertram and R. A. B. Mynors, eds 1969. *Bede's Ecclesiastical History of the English People*. Oxford Medieval Texts. Oxford.

Fisher, Peter, ed., and Hilda Ellis Davidson, trans. 1979. *Saxo Grammaticus: The History of the Danes*. Exeter.

Foulke, William Dudley, trans. 1907. *History of the Langobards by Paul the Deacon*.

Garmonsway, G. N. and Jacqueline Simpson, eds and trans. 1971. *Beowulf and its Analogues*. New York.

Hickes, George 1703–5. *Linguarum vett. septentrionalium thesaurus grammatico-criticus et archæologicus*. Oxford. Facsimile repr. Menston, 1970.

Hirsch, P. and H. E. Lohmann, eds 1935. *Widukindi Monachi Corbeiensis Rerum Gestarum Saxonicarum Libri Tres*. 5th edn. Hanover and Leipzig.

Hollander, Lee, trans. 1964. *Snorri Sturluson: Heimskringla*. Trans. Lee Hollander. Austin, TX.

Keynes, Simon and Michael Lapidge, trans. 1983. *Alfred the Great: Asser's Life of King Alfred and Other Contemporary Sources.* Harmondsworth.

Leslie, R. F., ed. 1961. *Three Old English Elegies: The Wife's Lament, The Husband's Message, The Ruin.* Manchester.

Malone, Kemp, ed. 1960. *Deor.* 3rd edn. London.

——, ed. 1962. *Widsith.* 2nd edn. Copenhagen.

——, ed. 1963. *The Nowell Codex.* Early English Manuscripts in Facsimile, 12. Copenhagen.

Mierow, Charles, trans. 1915. *Jordanes: The Origin and Deeds of the Goths.* Princeton, NJ.

Mitchell, Bruce and Fred C. Robinson, eds 1998. *Beowulf: An Edition with Relevant Shorter Texts.* Oxford.

Muir, Bernard, ed. 1994. *The Exeter Anthology of Old English Poetry.* 2 vols. Exeter.

Richthofen, Karl von 1840. *Friesische Rechtsquellen.* Göttingen.

Robinson, Fred C. and E. G. Stanley, eds 1991. *Old English Verse Texts from Many Sources: A Comprehensive Collection.* Early English Manuscripts in Facsimile 23. Copenhagen.

Stephens, George, ed. and trans. 1860. *Two Leaves of King Waldere's Lay, A Hitherto Unknown Old English Epic of the Eighth Century, Belonging to the Saga-Cyclus King Theodoric and his Men.* Copenhagen.

Turner, Samuel Epes, trans. 1960. *Life of Charlemagne by Einhard.* New York.

Young, Jean I., trans. 1964. *The Prose Edda of Snorri Sturluson.* Berkeley, CA.

Secondary sources

Adams, John 1965. 'The Anglo-Saxon Riddle as Lyric Mode'. *Criticism* 7: 335–48.

Bliss, Alan and Allen J. Frantzen 1976. 'The Integrity of *Resignation'*. *Review of English Studies* n.s. 27: 385–402.

Bloomfield, Morton 1970. *Essays and Explorations.* Cambridge, MA.

Frank, Roberta 1991. 'Germanic Legend in Old English Literature'. *The Cambridge Companion to Old English Literature*, pp. 88–106. Eds Malcolm Godden and Michael Lapidge. Cambridge.

Greenfield, Stanley B. and Daniel G. Calder 1986. *A New Critical History of Old English Literature.* New York.

Harris, Joseph 1983. 'Elegy in Old English and Old Norse: A Problem in Literary History'. *The Old English Elegies*, pp. 46–56. Ed. Martin Green. London and Toronto.

Heusler, Andreas 1943. *Die altgermanische Dichtung.* 2nd edn. Potsdam.

Lapidge, Michael 1982. '"Beowulf", Aldhelm, the "Liber Monstrorum" and Wessex'. *Studi Medievali* 3rd ser. 23: 151–92.

Malone, Kemp 1967. 'The Middle Ages: The Old English Period (to 1100)'. *A Literary History of England*, pp. 1–105. Ed. A. C. Baugh, 2nd edn. New York.

Niles, John 1991. 'Pagan Survivals and Popular Belief'. *The Cambridge Companion to Old English Literature*, pp. 88–106. Eds Malcolm Godden and Michael Lapidge. Cambridge.

——1998. 'Exeter Book Riddle 74 and the Play of the Text'. *Anglo-Saxon England* 27: 169–207.

North, Richard 1997. *Heathen Gods in Old English Literature.* Cambridge.

Opland, Jeff 1980. *Anglo-Saxon Oral Poetry: A Study of the Traditions.* New Haven, CT.

Robinson, Fred C. 1985. *Beowulf and the Appositive Style.* Knoxville.

——1993. *The Tomb of Beowulf and Other Essays on Old English.* Oxford.

Schlauch, Margaret 1941. 'An Old English Encomium Urbis'. *Journal of English and Germanic Philology* 40: 14–28.

Stanley, Eric Gerald 1987. *A Collection of Papers with Emphasis on Old English Literature.* Toronto.

Whitelock, Dorothy 1951. *The Audience of Beowulf.* Oxford.

17

Anglo-Latin Prose

Joseph P. McGowan

Early medieval England's fame abroad rested upon the strength of its monastic schools and the learned missionaries who set about their work in the Low Countries and Germany (Levison 1946). English authors were known abroad when writing in Latin, the language of their schools and the *ecclesia*, which established them for the training of its clergy. Though England produced, particularly in the late Anglo-Saxon period, a vibrant vernacular literature, such literary activity was primarily domestic. Anglo-Saxon bishops maintained a lively correspondence with church officials throughout the West (and Theodore and Hadrian came to England, via Rome, from eastern Christendom) and with former students abroad, and Alcuin of York seems to have composed most if not all of his extensive poetic output on the continent. The literary remains of Anglo-Saxon England surviving in the Latin language are far more abundant than those in the vernacular; while students of political and ecclesiastical history give these documents their due notice, Anglo-Latin texts remain underappreciated by literary historians and critics. Of the Anglo-Latin corpus from the pre-Conquest period, the greater share naturally enough is found in prose: some of it strictly for ecclesiastic business, some even more workaday, but prose of a great diversity of forms and uses. The students in Ælfric's prose *Colloquium* ('Colloquy') ask to be taught how to *speak* proper Latin (*Nos pueri rogamus te, magister, ut doceas nos loqui latialiter recte*; Garmonsway 1947: 18), and they might agree with the master of Magdalen Grammar School in Oxford of the 1490s that 'all langage well nygh is but rude beside the latyne tonge' (Sharpe in Mantello and Rigg 1996: 317). Such sentiment, echoed in one form or another down the centuries since the Christianization of Anglo-Saxon England, gives a sense of the desire for proficiency in Latin. If not all early Anglo-Latin poets were highly accomplished metrists (though several – Aldhelm, Bede, Boniface and Tatwine – wrote on *ars metrica*), this far north-western outpost of Christianity produced a number of influential prose stylists, Bede foremost among them.

There can be a tendency to list as prose nearly any form of writing that does not scan properly, in addition to works of formal prose composition. Glosses in and of themselves are a distinct activity, but as they exist not in isolation, rather in conjunction with the lemmata standing in for passages either familiar or once known (even if forgotten to later redactors), they can be considered a form of prose activity too. Marginalia, lists, short notes, and the sort of very brief treatises often catalogued as 'miscellaneous pieces' (Ker, *Catalogue*) merit mention as well. Though many of these brief to very brief prose extracts may be deemed not injudiciously 'sub-literary', they often give a sense of the range of interests of medieval readers and perplex modern readers as to the rationale of their inclusion here and there in many manuscripts. One small example is provided in London, British Library, Harley 3271 (Ker, *Catalogue*: item 239), an early eleventh-century manuscript of Ælfric's *Grammar* that contains also a great variety of brief tracts with titles such as *De arca noe, De diebus malis, De diebus festis, De epactis, De initio creaturae*, as well as a tribal hidage and a six-line catalogue of ethnic tags that can be translated as:

> The triumphalism of the Egyptians. The invidiousness of the Jews. The wisdom of the Greeks. The cruelty of the Picts. The cunning or fortitude of the Romans. The liberality of the Lombards. The gluttony of the Gallic. The pride or overbearing of the Franks. The wrath of the Britons. The stupidity of the Saxons or English. The lust of the Irish (fol. 6v, ll. 23–8).

One relies on Ker's indispensable *Catalogue* for brief notices of such Anglo-Latin prose curiosities; Ker's aim was to describe the roughly five hundred and a score manuscripts containing Old English, so we have no way of knowing yet how many such tracts exist (compare the brief listings in Gneuss 1981). As with the case of Anglo-Latin saints' lives, many no doubt remain to be discovered.

Anglo-Latin prose will be surveyed by employing some very broad classifications: historical, hagiographical, liturgical, educational, scientific, literary, epistolary and the *varia* already alluded to. These are not meant as categorizations to be used with any great confidence, nor are they watertight compartmentalizations. Bede's *Historia ecclesiastica*, for example, is precisely what its title implies – a work of ecclesiastical history. It is also a rich if problematic source of secular history as well as a work combining hagiography, martyrology, epistolary and poetic extracts, biography and, very briefly (*HE* V.24), autobiography.

Historical

Bede's *Historia ecclesiastica gentis Anglorum* is undoubtedly the paramount work of Anglo-Latin prose. Bede's influence would extend beyond that of some fellow Anglo-Latin authors of the Anglo-Saxon age, such as Aldhelm or Felix, and the scope of design of his work draws on models set by Christian Latin and Roman predecessors. Bede (673–735) first and foremost engages scripture; by virtue of his scholarly output (Sharpe 1997: 70–6) and contemporary reputation (Brown 1987: 42–61), he was primarily an exegete. Bede is better known now as a historian, and he draws on Orosius and Gildas directly, Eusebius and Gregory of Tours and others Christian and classical indirectly. Gildas' history is in some respects a jeremiad, as the preface to the *De excidio Britanniae* invokes that prophet almost immediately: 'because of the sins of men, the voice of the holy prophets rose in complaint, especially Jeremiah's, as he bewailed the ruin of his city in four alphabetic songs' (Winterbottom 1978). The Britons, lulled by a time of peace following the defeat of the Saxons living in Britain, had become sinful and incautious: what Gildas has to bewail tearfully is a 'general loss of good, a heaping up of bad' (Winterbottom 1978: 13, 87). Gildas' work is divided into three parts: a history of Britain and its fall (chs 1–26); a complaint against its kings (chs 27–65); and a complaint against its priests, culminating in a prayer for good leaders of the flock (chs 66–110). Gildas was sometimes described by later authors as a prophet; he certainly casts his *De excidio Britanniae* and his own role in prophetic form (by rough count, Gildas cites the prophets some 140 times in the work, Jeremiah and Isaiah most frequently).

Bede was less the prophet and more the hagiographer (responsible for versions of lives of Sts Anastasius and Felix, as well as his *opus geminatum*, or 'twinned work', on Cuthbert) and the *HE* offers abundant evidence of Bede the hagiographer at work. Bede opens the *HE* with his dedication to Ceolwulf, king of Northumbria, borrowing phrases from Gregory the Great's *Dialogi*. Gregory naturally enough figures prominently in Bede's narrative: it was at his instigation that the conversion of the *Angli* began, and Bede drew on his *responsiones* in the *HE* (at I.27, and in his earlier *Vita S. Cuthberti*). Bede drew on an English adulation of Gregory that was particularly strong in Northumbria, for at Whitby was written the earliest *vita* of the pope and saint (Colgrave 1968) and both Bede and the anonymous Whitby life of Gregory record his encounter with *Angli* youths for sale in a slave-market in Rome. The story affords Gregory the opportunity for play etymologies – the Angle youths (*Angli*) have the faces of angels (*angeli*), and their homeland *Deira* he breaks into *de ira*, for the youths have been plucked from the wrath and called unto the mercy of Christ (*HE* II.1). The story is believed to derive from an oral tradition current at least in Northumbria and Bede believed he was justified in inserting the story into his history as it was a tradition from of old (II.1). Just how much of the *HE* is from Bede's first- and secondhand sources, or the oral traditions of English monasteries, is difficult to ascertain; the anecdotes and tales (particularly of native saints) help give the work its local character. Monks, abbots, ealdormen and kings of England have their place beside popes and their letters. The story is of England, but of an England converted and thus part of Christendom; Bede alludes to news of general concern to the churches at times, such as the Muslim invasions of Spain, Gaul and Christian Africa (V.23). In five books Bede covers the island's history from its Celtic antiquity through Roman and Germanic invasions to the present, completing this work of his maturity in 732: 'This is the state of the whole of Britain at the present time, about 285 years after the coming of the English to Britain, in the year of our Lord 731' (V.23).

The bulk of Bede's *HE* covers the period 597–731 – not a tremendous span for a chronicler or annalist to tackle, but as Bede was writing ecclesiastical history a number of episodes of the history required dilation. Bede makes room for the inclusion of numerous letters, as well as epitaphs, reconstructed discourse (Bede is in classical company with this device), and documents such as the synodal decisions of the Council of Hertford called by Archbishop Theodore in 673 (IV.5) or Ceolfrith's letter to King Nechtan (Naiton) of the Picts (V.21). Bede's focus may perhaps more generally be termed spiritual, with the *HE* as a whole of many parts (with a chronological recapitulation at V.24) detailing the unfolding of God's providence in the isle of Britain. The many hagiographic elements serve as proof-texts of a sort, whether involving the *passio* (St Alban I.7; King Oswald III.2, 9–12) or *vita* (St Germanus of Auxerre I.17–21; Edwin martyr II.20; St Aidan III.5, 15–17; St Fursa III.19; St Chad III.23, IV.3; St Wilfrid IV.12–13, V, 19; St Æthelthryth IV.19–20; St Cuthbert IV.27–32; St Ceolfrith V *passim*) of the particular saint or martyr. Saintly bishops in particular make their appearance in the *HE*: Germanus, Augustine, Mellitus (who prayed down a fire at Canterbury: II.7), Paulinus, Chad (one of four brothers who entered the clergy, two of them, Cedd and Chad, becoming bishops), Wilfrid, Cuthbert. Kings often appear as either resisting conversion, backsliding or – penitently converted – even actively propagating the faith. The process was not always a simple one but was usually cast as a victory for the struggling man of God who ventured his life amongst heathen peoples. Paulinus' conversion of King Edwin and the Northumbrians is treated in some detail in book II, and Bede tells us twice that Edwin would often sit apart alone debating in silence what action to take and what faith to follow (II.12).

Among the sainted and virtuous company of Bede's *HE* are a good many Irish. Though Bede seems to bear a particular grudge against the Irish clergy holding to their own Easter custom (as against the Roman custom that won out at the Synod of Whitby), it is nothing like the animus held towards the Britons: after Edwin's death at Hatfield Chase during Cædwalla's rebellion (supported by the heathen Penda of Mercia), Bede notes that the Britons ever since (thus to the time of writing of the *HE*) have spurned the faith and religion of the English and refused to share in anything with them any more than with heathens (II.20). The five books of the *HE* recount in part too the ecclesiastical history of the Irish (Palladius' mission I.13, the Easter question *passim*), and are framed by the 'matter of the Irish': book I closes with the battle of Degsastan in 603, in which Aédán mac Gabráin of the Dál Riata was defeated, and no Irish king in Britain, we are told, ever again dared make war on the English (I.34); Bede's prose narrative winds down with concluding observations of the time of writing: the Picts are now at home in the Catholic church and the Irish in Britain are resigned to their own holdings and offer up no further treachery against the English (V.23). In both cases, at opposite ends of Bede's grand history, the *gens Anglorum* is set in opposition to the *Scotti*, and the Irish are paired up with the daring to offer battle (*proelium*), treachery (*insidiae*) and deceit (*fraus*). Bede is often said to be 'perhaps the first to lay stress on the unity of all the smaller kingdoms in the one great English nation' – and thus at the expense of the native inhabitants – (Colgrave and Mynors 1969: xxx), but it may be just to say that reading the *HE* as a prose epic of nation-building is only of secondary interest. Bede is equally capable of treating equably the Irish contribution to the story of God's providence in Britain (as of an Aidan or Fursa or Colman; III.5, 19, IV.4) and the air clears for him when Britons or Picts or Irish accept the Roman custom for fixing the date of Easter (compare the view in Ó Cróinín 1983). Bede was additionally a scientific writer, a chronologist in particular (see now Wallis 1999), and the matter concerned him as a man of learning and especially as an active defender of the church's unity. The *HE* stands early in the Anglo-Latin tradition and pre-eminently; it is difficult to describe its nature any better than by Bede's own title, *historia ecclesiastica*. The *HE* in many ways set standards for subsequent Anglo-Latin prose, in terms of content, approach, use of sources, if not style: Bede is more straightforward and plain in the *HE* than in his *Life of St Cuthbert* and far plainer than Aldhelm's hermeneutic style.

Bede also compiled brief chronological tracts of world history, the *chronica maiora* and *chronica minora*, included in his *De temporum ratione* (Jones 1975b) and *De temporibus* (Jones 1980) and each organized in the familiar 'six ages of the world' (*sex aetates mundi*; Tristram 1985). These works may more properly belong to Bede's scientific corpus as they are connected to his computistical concerns – the proper fixing of the date of Easter seen so often and passionately in the *HE*. A history of the abbots of Wearmouth and Jarrow was composed by Bede too. A work of two brief books, the *Historia abbatum* is really a collection of *vitae* of the abbots Benedict Biscop (who founded Wearmouth in 674 and Jarrow some seven miles away in 681), Ceolfrid, Eosterwine, Sigfrid and Hwætberht. Bede gives us the tantalizing and celebrated (for the glimpse they give us of early Anglo-Saxon library-building and church-adorning) descriptions of the gifts Benedict Biscop brought back from Italy on his fifth and sixth journeys to Rome (chs 6, 9). Ceolfrid too travelled beyond Northumbria; he resigned from the abbacy to make a pilgrimage to Rome in 716, and we are given a touching portrait of his departure (ch. 17).

In addition to Bede's account of the abbots of Wearmouth and Jarrow, we have what has traditionally been labelled an anonymous Northumbrian *Historia abbatum* surviving in two manuscripts (London, British Library, Harley 3020, and Oxford, Bodleian Library, Digby 112) – a text more properly described as a *Vita Ceolfridi* and perhaps from Bede's pen. Bedan historical writing might be described as taking on two guises: the brief, annalistic format in his *chronica* and the fuller, discursive format of his *historiae*. The great masterwork of historical writing from pre-Conquest England, the *Anglo-Saxon Chronicle*, owes much to Bede. The *Anglo-Saxon Chronicle* grew out of the notes added to lines of Easter tables – the science of which Bede was the pre-eminent practitioner. It developed in the vernacular into one of the great achievements of Anglo-Saxon literature and, as such, is of primary consideration as Old English prose. But sections of the *Anglo-Saxon Chronicle* were transmitted in (or translated into) Latin too; there is for example the Canterbury bilingual chronicle (London, British Library, Cotton Domitian viii), which includes a text of the acts of Lanfranc (Ker 1957: item 148). Much of the early material in the *Chronicle* is indebted to Bede, and the *Chronicle* in turn served as a source of two other historical writers: Asser in Cambro-Latin (Stevenson 1959) and Æthelweard in Anglo-Latin (Campbell 1962).

The Welshman Asser hailed from St Davids, Dyfed, where he was a monk and possibly, by the time he met Alfred, bishop of that see. His name is from the Hebrew, for Asher (one of the sons of Jacob, by Leah's maid Zilpah), meaning 'happy, blessed' (thus the speculation that his Welsh name may have been the equivalent Gwyn). The monk (or bishop) from St Davids was among those men of learning – such as Wærferth, Plegmund, Æthelstan, Werwulf, Grimbald, John the Old Saxon (*De rebus gestis Ælfredi*, chs 78–9) – recruited by King Alfred for his programme of cultural renewal. After visits to Wessex 885–6, starting in 887 Asser agreed to Alfred's proposal to spend half a year with him and half back in Wales (Stevenson 1959: 64). Asser's picture of his time with the king is a pleasant one; he recounts hours spent reading to the wise ruler, who called attention to passages he wished to be taken down and added to his *vademecum* or *enchiridion* (Stevenson 1959: 73). Asser's biography of Alfred, the earliest surviving life of an English monarch, seems to have been intended for a Welsh audience, perhaps to sing the praises of the ruler to whom the Welsh lords had sworn loyalty. It survives now only in two sixteenth-century transcripts (which feeds occasional doubts of its authenticity), its sole surviving medieval witness, London, British Library, Cotton Otho A. xii, having been burnt in the fire of 23 October 1731.

Æthelweard's *Chronicon* (or the plural form now used, *Chronica*) is a work curious in its Latinity and historical status; in the main, it Latinizes good portions of the *Anglo-Saxon Chronicle*, with additions from Bede and a dedicatory epistle to Æthelweard's cousin Matilda, abbess of the continental house at Essen. But Æthelweard also includes significant material not in the *Chronicle* for the years 893–946 (Campbell 1962). As with Asser's 'Deeds of Alfred', we are dependent upon a transcript for the complete text of the *Chronicon*, published in the 1596 edition by Henry Savile from, as he tells us, Anglo-Saxon historians following Bede. Fragments of an early eleventh-century copy (perhaps 'the first fair copy made of the work'; Campbell 1962: xii) survive in BL, Cotton Otho A. x and Otho A. xii, taken from the original Otho A. x, which was severely damaged in the fire at Ashburnham House.

Æthelweard writes more in the Aldhelmian hermeneutic vein; his debt to Aldhelm is clear and seemingly acknowledged by the author himself in the entry for 709, the year of the poet's death: 'After a period of four years Aldhelm, the blessed bishop, died. Men read his works, which are composed with wondrous skill, and his bishopric was the province which is called Selwood by the common people' (Campbell 1962: 21–2). Æthelweard often tends towards the periodic sentences of Aldhelmian prose style, and his diction is peppered with Graecisms and Latin arcana of the hermeneutic sort (Winterbottom 1967). Rare for editions of Anglo-Latin texts, Campbell's Æthelweard examines the grammar, rhetoric and syntax of the *Chronicon* (this is the same scholar to whom investigators of Old English dialectology are much indebted for his *Old English Grammar*; Campbell 1959). Thus we are provided with examples of Æthelweard's hermeneutic vocabulary (Graecisms like *artemon* 'ship', *dromon* 'light ship', *stefos* 'crown'); 'curiously violent' tmesis (lit. 'cutting'; separation of elements of a compound by intervening word(s)), as in *ultra petunt marinas partes* for *ultramarinas petunt partes* ('they sought places beyond the sea'; Campbell 1962: lii); and varying and sometimes unusual handling in Latin of non-Latin (Celtic, English, Norse) names (Æthelweard gives a rare attestation of the river name *Sæfern* in the form *Sefern*; elsewhere the name component *Ælf*- appears as *Elf*-; Campbell 1962: xlv–lx). In his dedicatory epistle to Matilda, Æthelweard (perhaps wryly?) states that he 'dwell[s] in plain style' upon their ancestors *sine nexilitate exorno* ('without convoluted adorning'), with *nexilitas* perhaps another of his 'glossary words'.

If, as seems the case, the identification of Æthelweard the chronicler and Æthelweard the ealdorman of Dorset (who was a witness to charters surviving from 973 to 998) is correct, we have the remarkable instance of a layman composing a significant work in competent Latin. Æthelweard was also a patron of Ælfric (who mentions Æthelweard as keenly interested in his translation of saints' lives), involved in the national affairs of the late tenth century (he is mentioned in the *Anglo-Saxon Chronicle* in the entry for 994 as part of an embassy escorting Anlaf to King Æthelred), and a benefactor of the church, founding the abbey of Pershore (at least according to William of Malmesbury's *Gesta pontificum*). His son Æthelmær continued in his father's footsteps in this last respect, supporting the refoundation of Cerne Abbas as a Benedictine abbey in 987 (Brown 1996).

Æthelweard's prose can be difficult to follow, and the sense of what is included where and why is not always apparent (Campbell noted that his translation 'should not be read except in conjunction with the Latin. It amounts in hard passages only to a suggestion of a possible meaning'; Campbell 1962: vii). In the fourth and final book of the *Chronicon*, in the entry for 891, Æthelweard amplifies the account of the visit of three Irish *peregrini* to Cornwall and then Alfred's court:

> In the same year three chosen men, on fire with belief, withdrew from the Irish nation. They sewed a boat from bull's hide in secret, they provided a week's food for themselves, they kept sail up for seven days and seven nights, and they arrived in their boat in Cornwall. Leaving their boat, which had not been brought by tackle nor by ample shoulders, but rather by the nod of him who sees all things, they went to Ælfred, king of the English. And the witan rejoiced equally with the king at their arrival. Then they directed their course to seek Rome as Christ's teachers are wont frequently to do. Their minds proposed going thence to Jerusalem. Soon the more eminent of them departed this life. One brother set apart under guardianship the relics of his companion and associate, and it would be right to describe in this compendium all the great miracles performed. Another returned home, shaking the dust from his feet, and thus stated the names of the absent ones: first Dubhslaine, second Macbeathadh, and third Mælinmhein, a man blossoming in the arts, learned in literature, an eminent teacher of the Irish. (Campbell 1962: 48–9)

The three men in a boat stand in for the many *peregrini* from Ireland who wound up in England (like Fursa or Columba) or on the continent (Columbanus, Gall, many others); their currach takes them on a journey that leads to King Alfred's court (which king had recently complained of the lack of Latin learning in his kingdom), Rome and possibly Jerusalem. The episode also gives us an early attestation of the name to be borne by one of English literature's greatest characters: Macbeth (Ó Cróinín 1995: 222).

Hagiographical

Hagiographic texts seemingly promise to offer much of interest to contemporary literary critics with their interrogations of representations of power, gender, violence, the body and so forth. The texts, however, often seem to frustrate in their seemingly overwrought piety, singularity of purpose (God's glory manifested through select holy men and women), triumphalism and sentiment (such as in Bede's account of Ceolfrid's departure for Rome). Hagiography was one of the most productive genres in the medieval period and Anglo-Saxon England contributed more than its share; one estimate of the saints culted in Anglo-Saxon England puts the figure at over 300, another, local in scope, lists approximately eighty female Anglo-Saxon saints (Pulsiano 1999). Hagiography was also one of the great medieval influences upon the modern; for many Christians the world of the saints is still alive. For Roman Catholics in particular the landscape is still dotted with and demarcated by parishes bearing the names of saints; parochial schools bearing saints' names celebrate their patrons' feasts; saints' relics still circulate: a piece of the shawl of St Theresa of Avila or the cloak of St Martin de Porres; sombre effigies of saints still stand in the alcoves of churches; church calendars mark saints' feasts and parents name their young after saints; pilgrimages and processions to saintly shrines, such as St Anne de Beaupré in Québec, are facilitated now by tour buses; and *vitae* of saints, such as extracts from *Butler's Lives*, still form part of the curriculum in parochial schools. The appeal of saints, their intercessory power and their *vitae* to what social historians once termed 'the masses' has not changed, though extension of the cult of the saints to the laity in addition to clergy and royalty in Anglo-Saxon England may be a post-Viking raids phenomenon (Rollason 1989). What have changed are the attitudes of the elites (particularly scholars), a number of whom in the medieval period provided for the construction of churches and commissioned saints' lives or themselves penned them. We are not even sure how many pre-Conquest hagiographies exist: some or many await identification and editing in the manuscripts.

Some sense of the liturgical function of saints can be gleaned from the litanies of saints recently edited by Michael Lapidge (Lapidge 1991a). The litanies, surviving mainly in manuscripts of the tenth and eleventh centuries, usually begin and end with the Greek prayer *Kyrie eleison, Christe eleison* and consist of a readily expandable series of invocations and supplications (similar petitions, in expandable form, can still occur in the Roman rite). Fairly simple texts, the litanies are interesting for the saints mentioned and their possible insular origins for the Western church. One example is the litany in the eleventh-century manuscript miscellany London, British Library, Cotton Tiberius A. iii (Lapidge 1991a: 174–6). It contains a list of female saints in its final third, of note for its selection: among the early church martyrs and other holy women are two of the most popular Anglo-Saxon female saints: St Æthelthryth (or Etheldreda, Audrey; d. 679, feast 23 June), foundress of the abbey at Ely, and St Mildred (or Mildrith, d. *c.*700; feast 13 July). Two Irish female saints come at the end of the litany, natural enough considering the interaction between the churches in the early medieval period.

Recent research (Lapidge 1991a) has suggested that it may have been in the British Isles, Anglo-Saxon England in particular, that the litany of the saints began as a liturgical form for the Western church. Deriving from the Greek, the litany of the saints may have been transmitted from an Eastern Christian centre, such as Antioch, where the form was practised both as a type of private prayer (a litanic prayer appears in the famous *Book of Cerne*; Kuypers 1902) and in public processions. A plausible vehicle of transmission came in the form of Theodore, sent from Rome to Canterbury in 668 (Lapidge 1991a: 19–27). The earliest litany of the saints in Western Christendom occurs in the *Æthelstan Psalter* (London, British Library, Cotton Galba A. xviii), a ninth-century manuscript from Liège brought to King Æthelstan's court by the first decade of the tenth century (to judge by the additions made *c.*910–30s in Anglo-Saxon minuscule; Lapidge 1991a: 13–14). This manuscript contains a Greek litany and prayer copied into its final folios; it is plausible that the Greek material in the manuscript was assembled by Israel the Grammarian, a Breton scholar who sought asylum at Æthelstan's court (Lapidge 1991a: 13–16). The Greek texts may have already been introduced to Anglo-Saxon England in the late seventh century by Theodore; during the eighth they would be transmitted back to the continent (Lapidge 1991a).

While the litanies of the saints in themselves are not the most substantial of texts, we have none the less an instance of substantial liturgical innovation on the part of pre-Conquest Anglo-Latin literature. And we have further testimony to the innovative programme of the school of Theodore and Hadrian at Canterbury, which appears responsible for new liturgical forms, Biblical commentaries, a family of glossaries, and instruction in quantitative verse (Bischoff and Lapidge 1994). But it is from Northumbria that one of the earliest Anglo-Latin texts originates: an anonymous life of St Gregory by a religious of Whitby. The particular esteem in which the recently converted English – in Northumbria the seventh century had been tumultuous for the church – held Pope Gregory has already been alluded to. The 'Book of the Blessed and Praiseworthy man Gregory Pope of the City of Rome concerning his Life and Virtues' survives in one ninth-century manuscript from St Gall, Stiftsbibliothek MS 567. The Life of Gregory the Great was written sometime around 710 and served as one of the sources of John the Deacon's life of that saint. Dating to the abbacy of Ælfflæd at Whitby (680–714), the anonymous monk (or nun) at Whitby (which is referred to in ch. 19 as *nostrum coenobium*, 'our monastery'; Colgrave 1968: 104) apologizes (and judging by the content of this Life, unnecessarily) early on for an apparent variation on the usual theme of a saint's *vita*:

> We wish to write a book about him, though, in the record of his deeds, we have heard of few miracles: but we pray our readers not to feel distaste if we praise the great man somewhat exuberantly. For many are accustomed to judge the lives of saints by their miracles and to measure their merits and holiness by the signs they perform; nor is this unreasonable; for often God, who is glorious in his saints that he loves beyond other men, makes them shine above other men by the miracles they perform. (Colgrave 1968 76–7)

The story of Gregory and the Angle slaves on sale in Rome is recounted in more or less the same form as in Bede's *Historia ecclesiastica* II.1 (with an additional note concerning whether the Angles were *pulchros pueros* 'beautiful boys' or *crispos iuvenes et decoros* 'curly-haired, handsome youths': it is not clear whether the anonymous author here intends a substantive difference between *pueros* 'boys' and *iuvenes* 'young men'). In this recounting of what was apparently an oral tradition, the young slaves reply directly to Gregory. The philological puns (see chapter 2 in this volume) on *Angli, angeli, Aelli, Alleluia* recur, along with a somewhat strained play on Edwin's name: *Eduinus, cuius nomen tribus sillabis constans, recte sibi designat sancte misterium trinitatis* ('Edwin's name, consisting of three syllables, truly signifies the mystery of the Holy Trinity'; ch. 14, Colgrave 1968: 96–7).

The selection of stories (or, more properly in many cases, legends) about Gregory included is sometimes curious. Thus, in chapter 28, we are told of the fate of Sabinian, Gregory's successor as bishop of Rome; Sabinian was apparently jealous of the great adulation of Gregory by Roman citizens, and was miserly in his relief of their hunger from the papal grain storehouses (John the Deacon reports a different case, attributing the famine to Gregory's lavish spending, which provoked anti-Gregorian sentiment during the hunger; PL 75). Sabinian is reported to have said thrice that he could not possibly feed all of the people; St Gregory appears to him in warning:

> Each time he said it to those who very frequently urged upon him their need of such provisions as they had received from St Gregory, the saint appeared to him and is said to have asked him in far from gentle tones why he had judged his motives so wrongly when he had done it for the Lord's sake alone. Since Gregory was unable to silence him by his words, on the third occasion he kicked the man on the head. His successor died in a few days from the pain of the blow. (Colgrave 1968: 126–7)

The editor Colgrave felt moved enough by the anonymous author's inclusion of this episode to comment:

> it is a crude and unworthy tale in which Gregory's only motive is revenge. Nowhere in the Life does the Whitby author reveal more clearly the crudeness of his times. In fact

the dead saint's violent behaviour is reminiscent of northern tales told later on in the Norse sagas of the frightful havoc wrought by offended ghosts upon the living as in the *Grettissaga* or the *Eyrbyggja Saga*. (Colgrave 1968: 161)

It is difficult to say whether such an episode is typical of a sort of 'northernness', for Adomnán's 'Life of Columba' offers examples of the righteous anger of a saintly man and Gerald of Wales would later comment on the great number and vindictiveness of saints from early medieval Ireland (*Topographia Hiberniae*, cap. 83; O'Meara 1949).

Gentleness is one of the characteristics the *vitae* of St Cuthbert emphasize. Another of the earliest Anglo-Latin texts, perhaps the earliest (sometime fairly shortly after the saint's translation in 698), is the anonymous *Vita S. Cuthberti* by a monk of Lindisfarne. The monk used some of the standard hagiographical models of the time – Evagriu's Latin version of the *Vita Antonii* and Sulpicius Severus' *Vita Martini*. The anonymous Life is preserved in seven continental manuscripts, the oldest of which, Saint-Omer 267 (late ninth to early tenth century), is in an insular hand. The cult of Cuthbert, begun in Northumbria and promoted by Bede, spread to the rest of England and to the continent too with the Anglo-Saxon missions. Many copies of early Anglo-Latin works, including the anonymous lives of Gregory and Cuthbert (Levison 1946: 145–7), no doubt perished in Viking raids of the late eighth and ninth centuries, to be preserved on the continent in centres established or influenced by insular missionaries.

Cuthbert was born into a Northumbria troubled by strife, particularly at the hands of heathen Penda of Mercia. The Irishman Aidan had established the monastery at Lindisfarne in 635, approximately the time of Cuthbert's birth, and was enlisted by King Oswald in the repair of the Northumbrian church. Cuthbert was influenced more in his lifetime by the Irish monastic custom which prevailed in the north; he entered the monastery at Melrose after witnessing the soul of Aidan ascend into heaven (I.5; Colgrave 1940) – a common set piece in saints' lives (Cuthbert later sees the soul of a brother being transported into heaven after the man falls from a tree; IV.10). The anonymous Life provides extensive evidence of Cuthbert's holy works of healing and twice alerts the reader that various other miracles have been omitted (I.7, IV.18). Of note is Cuthbert's particular connection with the sea: two small sea-beasts offer him obeisance one night as the saint sings and prays along the shore: 'immediately there followed in his footsteps two little sea animals [Bede said they were otters, Ælfric seals], humbly prostrating themselves on the earth; and, licking his feet, they rolled upon them, wiping them with their skins and warming them with their breath' (II.3); on a journey to Pictland the Lord provides Cuthbert and his hungry companions with dolphin flesh to eat (II.4); Cuthbert retires, in Irish fashion, to the isle of Lindisfarne (for the anonymous author: *ad hanc insulam nostram que dicitur Lindisfarnae*, 'to this island of ours which is called Lindisfarne'; III.1) where his *sermo* was *sale conditus* ('seasoned with salt'; III.7).

Bede's *Vita Cuthberti* is the more expansive of the lives (forty-six chapters compared to the fifteen of the anonymous Life) and more scholarly, Bede noting that the particulars had been checked against reports of firsthand witnesses (such as Herefrith, former abbot of Lindisfarne and resident of Melrose). Bede had first composed a metrical *Vita S. Cuthberti* based on the anonymous prose Life sometime around 705 or slightly later (the anonymous Life was composed 698 × 705); he fashioned an *opus geminatum* by penning a prose version around 720. The three lives of Cuthbert did much to promote and validate the saint's growing cult. Born *c.*635, Cuthbert had entered Melrose in 651; he accompanied his abbot Eata first to Ripon, then Lindisfarne. In a pattern set by Irish monks of the time, Cuthbert retreated to a small isle off Lindisfarne (since then St Cuthbert's Isle), then further off to Farne, where, after a brief tenure as bishop of Lindisfarne beginning in 685, he expired 20 March 687. The spread of Cuthbert's cult was perhaps in response to controversies stirred by Bishop Wilfrid, who is defended vigorously in the Life penned by Stephen of Ripon.

Composed in the period 710 × 720, the *Vita Wilfridi* by Stephen of Ripon (or, formerly, Eddius Stephanus) surveys in sixty-eight brief chapters the troublesome career of Wilfrid, who, like Cuthbert, had connections to leading royal figures in Northumbria (Cuthbert and Eata left Ripon after Alhfrith installed Wilfrid as abbot; *Vita Wilfridi episcopi* ch. 8, Colgrave 1927). Cuthbert had been raised in a Northumbria firmly bearing the imprint of Irish monasticism, which included their method of fixing the date of Easter (they differed also in the form of their tonsure and baptismal formulas). Wilfrid took up the challenge of bringing Northumbria into line with the Roman custom, sparring with Bishop Colman (ch. 10); he had trouble too with Kings Ecgfrith and Aldfrith and Archbishop Theodore. Stephen doggedly defends his patron, as, one can imagine, the other members of the Ripon household wished him to (perhaps desiring a *vita* of their patron as Lindisfarne had for their Cuthbert); there can perhaps be said to be some rivalry, as Stephen's opening is patterned after that of the anonymous *Vita S. Cuthberti* (Colgrave 1927: 150; Howlett 1997). As biased as Stephen may be, he tells an interesting tale, as Wilfrid's life was an active one (spending more than half of his episcopate exiled from his see): travels to Gaul and Rome; miraculous healings; close encounters with heathens, including a brush with some South Saxons (ch. 13). Stephen recounts the dramatic event with a syntactically elegant flair: he has a love of balanced modifiers and structures (the tricolon *navem et homines relinquens, terras fugiens, litoraque detegens*, '[leaving] ship and men high and dry, [fleeing] from the land . . . laying the shores bare' [Colgrave 1927: 27], describing the action of the sea). Throughout the Life he employs frequent Biblical allusions; here the South Saxons have the hard-heartedness of Pharaoh, their *magus* stands against God's people like Balaam, and one of Wilfrid's monks *more Davidico* brings low the South Saxon Goliath. These are patterns that obtain throughout the Life, which would be given new form (and adorned in hermeneutic style) in the mid-tenth-century metrical *Breuiloquium vitae Wilfridi* composed by the Frankish Frithegod (Fredegaud of Brioude) at the request of Archbishop Oda of Canterbury, upon that see's acquisition of Wilfrid's remains in 948.

Among the other hagiographic works from Anglo-Saxon England before the onset of Viking raids (which would interrupt production of such texts for nearly a century and a half – at least in so far as we can judge from surviving manuscripts) were the anonymous *Vita Ceolfridi*, Bede's versions of lives of Sts Felix and Anastasius, and – from Mercia – Felix's *Vita S. Guthlaci*. That last hagiography would be of particular importance, as it helped generate vernacular versions that testify to the popularity of his cult: a prose Old English life and two incomplete poems (generally known as *Guthlac A* and *Guthlac B*, the latter of which is closer to the Life; Roberts 1979).

Virtually nothing is known of Felix. We are not even sure if he was an Englishman; the doubt is sown in chapter 10, an account of Guthlac's lineage in which Felix remarks that the etymology of his name (*Guth-lac, belli munus*, 'battle-reward') fits his character, 'as those knowlegeable of his people assert' (Colgrave 1956). His *Vita S. Guthlaci* can only help date the author and his work to the reign of King Ælfwald of the East Angles (713–49), who commisioned the Life. Guthlac provided an interesting saintly model for the time, as he was descended from a noble line (he is linked to Icel, known from Mercian royal genealogies) and spent nine years as a battle leader fighting along Mercia's western frontier with Wales. We are told of his martial spirit, inspired by the brave deeds of heroes of former times (ch. 16) and tempered in some way as if informed by divine providence (ch. 17: he is said to have returned one-third of plunder to his victims). Guthlac drew about him warriors of various races and from everywhere (ch. 17). We are, unfortunately, not told who these warriors were, but Guthlac had become familiar with the 'sibilant' tongue of the Britons while an exile among them (ch. 34). Discontented with the military life, Guthlac in the twenty-fourth year of his life entered the monastery at Repton. Two years later he sought greater solitude, and left with his companion Beccel for the fens of Crowland, where he remained for the rest of his days and struggled to fight off temptations and evil apparitions. Guthlac even more than Cuthbert becomes identified with nature; he is able to intervene (chs 38, 40) against the mischief of blackbirds or jackdaws (Colgrave takes *corvus* throughout as the *corvus monedula*), and swallows obey his command and express their affection for him (ch. 39: a pattern seen in *vitae* of Irish saints).

The Viking raids seem to have taken their toll on Anglo-Latin hagiography, as well they might: entries in the *Parker Chronicle* for 793, 832–3, 838–40, 845, 855, 860, 865–7, 870 (death of Edmund) and 871–8 (Alfred counterattacks) attest to the devastation. Texts might not be expected to be produced (or to survive if not transmitted to the continent) when monasteries were burned, altars stripped, monks slaughtered, even kings and bishops killed. But this gloomy picture is no doubt an exaggeration, as other types of texts continued to be produced (including such manuscript masterpieces as the *Royal Bible* and *Book of Cerne* – which, of course, may owe their survival to their very high value). The programme of cultural renewal undertaken by Alfred and his successors, and the intellectual renewal of the Benedictine Reform in the tenth century, revived the genre. Frithegod composed the hexametral *Breviloquium vitae Wilfridi* for Oda, and Lantfred composed *c.*975 the *Translatio et miracula S. Swithuni*, in celebration of the translation of Swithun's remains and effects to the Old Minster at Winchester organized by Æthelwold. Lantfred's prose was turned into hexameters *c.*996 in the *Narratio metrica de S. Swithuno* by one of Æthelwold's students, Wulfstan Cantor (Campbell 1950; Sharpe 1997: 824–5). Wulfstan also penned the *Vita S. Æthelwoldi*, commemorating the teacher-bishop behind the great school at Winchester. Wulfstan Cantor drew on preceding Anglo-Latin hagiographies for the Life of his teacher, including Bede and Lantfred. Like Bede's *Vita S. Cuthberti*, the work is comprised of forty-six chapters, a figure of numerological significance: it is the numerical value of the name of Adam in Greek, and the Temple of Jerusalem was constructed over forty-six years (Jn 2:20; Lapidge and Winterbottom 1991: cvi). Wulfstan's *Vita S. Æthelwoldi episcopi* was abridged by Ælfric of Eynsham 1004 × 1006.

Other late pre-Conquest Anglo-Latin hagiographical writings include: Abbo of Fleury's *Passio S. Eadmundi* for the *sanctus rex et martyr* (ch. 16) slain by the Danes (Winterbottom 1972); Byrhtferth of Ramsey's hagiographical writings – a *passio* of the brother martyrs Æthelred and Æthelberht included in the portions of Simeon of Durham's *Historia regum* attributed to Byrhtferth (Lapidge 1981a), and *vitae* of the bishops Oswald of York and Ecgwine of Worcester (Lapidge 1979); the *Vita S. Dunstani* attributed to B. (possibly a Byrhthelm) in exile at Liège; an anonymous *Vita prima S. Neoti* commemorating the acquisition by Eynesbury (later St Neots) of the relics of that Cornish saint; a *Passio* of St Indract (Indrechtach), an Irish pilgrim to Glastonbury killed there in the ninth century and commemorated along with other Irish saints into the twelfth (Lapidge 1982b); a *passio* of the eighth-century martyred King Æthelberht of East Anglia, whose remains were translated to Hereford Cathedral; and, from the time of the Conquest, lives of Sts Bertin, Botwulf (Botulph), Edward the Confessor and John of Beverley (Sharpe 1997: 116–17). After the Conquest Goscelin of Canterbury, like Folchard once a monk of Saint-Bertin, was a prolific hagiographical writer, turning out lives of: Augustine of Canterbury; Theodore and Hadrian; the early bishops Laurence, Mellitus, Justus, Honorius and Deusdedit; Sts Erkenwald and Kenelm (Love 1996); and, among some others, a number of female saints from Anglo-Saxon England: Æthelthryth, Edith, Hildelith, Mildburga, Mildred, Sexburga and Werburga (Sharpe 1997: 151–4; Pulsiano 1999). Late hagiographical works await editing, and others no doubt await discovery. The Anglo-Saxons on the continent also generated and produced hagiographical literature, such as Boniface's letter (*Epistola* 10; Tangl 1955) recounting the vision of a monk of Wenlock, or Willibald's *Vita S. Bonfatii* (Levison 1905). The lives, passions and litanies of saints produced in Anglo-Saxon England evidence the industriousness of its religious writers, all of whom strove to show God's glory made manifest through holy women and men and who, in doing so, like Bede, recorded ecclesiastical history.

Liturgical

Christians, like other 'peoples of the Book', have at the core of their beliefs the four Gospels forming the heart of the New Testament; Christianity in faith and liturgical practice is 'a book-based religion' (Backhouse 1997: 11). Anglo-Saxon Northumbria, for instance, produced the earliest complete copy of the Latin Bible in the West: the *Codex Amiatinus* (Florence, Biblioteca Medicea Laurenziana, Amiatino 1). The *Codex Amiatinus* is one of the three pandects or complete copies of scripture commissioned by abbot Ceolfrith (*tres pandectes*; Bede, *Historia abbatum* ch. 15; anonymous *Historia abbatum* ch. 20; Plummer 1896: 1): two Bibles were given to his houses at Jarrow and Monkwearmouth (one of which, later known as 'Offa's Bible', survives only in fragments: London, British Library, Additional 37,777 and 45,025); one was to be taken by Ceolfrith to Rome to be presented to St Peter's. Ceolfrith died along the route south at Langres in 716; the manuscript reached its destination and is now housed in Florence. It is a tremendously significant manuscript: in terms of the history of transmission of the Bible in the West and more specifically in the British Isles (Marsden 1995); as an example of Northumbrian cultural achievement in the Age of Bede; palaeographically, as a magnificent example of English uncial; and as a work of art (Bruce-Mitford 1967), its illuminations important in the insular tradition of iconography of the evangelists (Brown 1996).

Bibles and Gospel-books were produced in Anglo-Saxon England in de luxe presentation copies such as the *Codex Amiatinus*, the *Lindisfarne Gospels* (produced in honour of St Cuthbert, *c.*698, by Eadfrith; London, British Library, Cotton Nero D. iv), or the *Royal Bible* (s. viii, Canterbury, either St Augustine's or Christ Church; London, British Library, Royal 1 E. vi; Gneuss 1981: no. 448; Backhouse 1997: no. 4); in more workaday medium formats for use in services or for reading (and annotating) in monastic houses; and, as spectacular as the de luxe versions in their own way, as pocket Gospel-books: the Irish were famous for their production of these manuscript gems, such as the ninth-century *MacDurnan Gospels* into which were later tucked documents in Old English, including a writ of Cnut (London, Lambeth Palace 1370; McGurk 1956). As these manuscripts represent the transmission of an established text imported into the British Isles, they are of concern here in so far as the style of the Latin text (the *Vetus Latinus* and, most often, the Vulgate) influenced Anglo-Latin authors (and it was extensively: the sometimes copious Biblical allusions in hagiographies provide one witness) or generated commentary in full form or as Latin glosses and marginalia (these latter forms of commentary generally receive far less attention than their vernacular counterparts). Anglo-Saxon England also produced a number of psalters, fourteen of which were glossed in the vernacular (Pulsiano 2001). The copying, reading, interpreting and glossing of the Book of Psalms occupied an important place in the Anglo-Saxon ecclesiastical experience.

Some other types of liturgical texts bear more apparently the imprint of local innovation. Some of the types of liturgical texts in use may be briefly identified (Dumville 1992 provides examples and explanation):

- **benedictionals**: which contain the blessings a bishop gives during mass on Sundays and feast-days (Nelson and Pfaff in Pfaff 1995). The most famous from Anglo-Saxon England is London, British Library, Additional 49598, the *Benedictional of Æthelwold* (dated to approximately 971–84; Brown 1994), an ornately decorated manuscript given an additional flourish with a hermeneutic poem in gold capitals written by the manuscript's scribe Godeman, likely to have been Æthelwold's chaplain at Winchester (Lapidge 1975; Deshman 1995; Prescott 1987, 1988);

- **collectars**: three of these collections of collects – prayers recited at the end of the first seven of the eight liturgical offices (Corrêa in Pfaff 1995) – survive from Anglo-Saxon England: Durham, Cathedral Library A IV.19 (the Durham Collectar); London, British Library, Cotton Titus D. xxvi (Ælfwine's Prayerbook); London, British Library, Harley 2961 (the Leofric Collectar);

- **homiliaries**: collections of homilies, arranged as for Sundays or saints' feasts (Cambridge, Corpus Christi College 367, Old English homilies, with Latin rubrics, for saints' feasts [Ker, *Catalogue*: item 63]; Cambridge, Pembroke College 25, a Latin homiliary from Bury St Edmunds [Gneuss 1981: no. 131]);

- **lectionaries**: books of readings for church services during the liturgical year, such as gospel or mass or Office lectionaries (Worcester, Cathedral Library Q.78b [Gneuss 1981: no. 769]; Cambridge, Fitzwilliam Museum 218 [Gneuss 1981: no. 118]);

- **liber vitae**: manuscript lists of benefactors and *familiares* (community members) of monastic houses whose names were read out at prime. One of the most famous examples is the *Liber Vitae* of New Minster, Winchester, London, British Library, Stowe 944, which also contains a copy of the will of King Alfred (Brown 1994; Keynes 1996);

- **martyrologies**: lists of martyrs arranged in order of their feasts. Bede made advances in filling in the early martyrology and his model was adopted on the continent, such as in Paris, Bibliothèque Nationale lat. 3879 (Cambridge, Corpus Christi College 57, contains a martyrology from Abingdon; London, British Library, Cotton Vitellius C. xii, is from St Augustine's, Canterbury);

- **missals**: containing all of the prayers and responses necessary to the celebration of mass through the liturgical year, such as the Leofric Missal or the Missal of St Augustine's, Canterbury (Cambridge, Corpus Christi College 270; Pfaff 1995). Alcuin is known to have sent an abbreviated missal, a *chartula missalis*, to the monks of Fulda in 801 (London, British Library, Royal 4 A. xiv contains fragments of an eleventh-century missal);

- **passionals**: containing stories of the sufferings of saints and martyrs (Cambridge, Corpus Christi College 9, of the mid-eleventh century, contains saints' lives and passions arranged through the year);

- **penitentials**: or *libri paenitentiales*, handbooks for confessors detailing sins and apposite penances (Frantzen 1983a, 1983b; Dumville 1992);

- **pontificals**: one of the most perduring of liturgical books, the Roman pontifical remained relatively stable until changes made 1961–5. The pontifical traditionally consists of three parts, which serve to collect together the various rites reserved unto bishops: ordinations, consecrations of other bishops, anointing of kings and queens (comprising the part *de personis*); consecration of churches, altars and other liturgical objects (comprising the part *de rebus*); and a third part covering special rites, such as diocesan visits, synods, councils (an early example of this form comes from Anglo-Saxon England: the *Pontifical of Ecgberht*, bishop of York 736–66, contained in the Paris, Bibliothèque nationale lat. 10575, of the mid-tenth century [Gneuss 1981: no. 896]; for other examples, cf. Nelson and Pfaff in Pfaff 1995);

- **sacramentaries**: containing texts the celebrant needs in the service of the mass. Sacramentaries (in Latin the *Liber sacramentorum* or *Sacramentarium*) have a complex history, and Alcuin may have played a part in updating the *Hadrianum* sacramentary sent to Charlemagne (Cambrai, Bibliothèque Municipale, 164); in Anglo-Saxon England and insular-influenced continental centres Gelasian, eighth-century hybrids and later Gregorian sacramentaries were in use (the 'rede boke of darleye', Cambridge, Corpus Christi College 422 [Ker, *Catalogue*: item 70]; cf. also Pfaff 1995);

- **tropers**: generally, unofficial books of additions or interpolations to official texts of the liturgy (for the mass or Divine Office) involving music and poetry, such as new melodies, melodic extensions or new texts for existing chants (the *Winchester Troper*, Oxford, Bodleian Library, Bodley 775 [Gneuss 1981: no. 597] or the *Caligula Troper*, London, British Library, Cotton Caligula A. xiv, of the mid-tenth century [Gneuss 1981: no. 309]; cf. Teviotdale in Pfaff 1995).

A number of other types of 'paraliturgical' texts were of assistance: litanies of saints, hagiographies, metrical calendars (such as that in Oxford, St John's College 17), martyrologies and legendaries (such as London, Lambeth Palace 173, containing lives and visions of saints).

Private prayer-books allow to be discerned some sense of local innovation, and four survive from Southumbria around 800: the famous *Book of Cerne* (Cambridge, University Library Ll.1.10) and three British Library manuscripts: Harley 2965 (the *Book of Nunnaminster*) and Harley 7653 (which were apparently private prayer-books for women; Dumville 1992), and Royal 2 A. xx. The *Book of Cerne* is particularly renowned for its miniatures of the four evangelists and their iconographic symbols (Luke : ox, Matthew : man, Mark : lion, John : eagle; Brown 1996: I–IV). The manuscript includes among its contents an acrostic prayer (at fol. 21r) naming the author as *Aedeluald episcopus*, probably Aediluald bishop of Lindisfarne (successor of Eadfrith, responsible for the illuminations in the *Lindisfarne Gospels*, London, British Library, Cotton Nero D. iv), and a section of seventy-one prayers and hymns (fols 43–87), including the *Lorica of Laidcenn* (fols 43–4; Kuypers 1902 and the extensive recent study in Brown 1996). A later example of a prayer-book is *Ælfwine's Prayerbook* of the early eleventh century (London, British Library, Cotton Titus D. xxvi and D. xxvii), which contains also a copy of Ælfric's *De temporibus anni* and much computistical material (Günzel 1993). The manuscript begins with calendrical material, naturally enough since the liturgy commemorated moveable (such as Easter) and immoveable feasts (Christmas, Feast of the Circumcision [now Holy Family], Epiphany, and the Purification, Annunciation, Assumption and other feasts associated with Mary).

Though mostly in Latin, interspersed are passages in Old English (Ker, *Catalogue*: item 202); there are a variety of very brief texts (names of the Seven Sleepers, the Six Ages of the World; Günzel 1993: 109, 143–4), some 279 prayers, a collectar, a litany of the saints, and a good many prognostications. The last group is in keeping with such manuscript miscellanies containing liturgical material: the computistical material was scientific, the *prognostica* very often pseudo-scientific, other materials paramedical (such as *prognostica* for propitious days or moons for blood-letting; Günzel 1993: 110–11, 146–7).

The sheer number and variety of Anglo-Latin liturgical texts make anything more than a superficial sketch here impossible. The student interested in the texts has the invaluable assistance of the Henry Bradshaw Society (motto: 'Founded in the Year of Our Lord 1890 for the editing of Rare Liturgical Texts'); a number of pre-Conquest texts have appeared in the series, including the aforementioned Litanies of the Saints (Lapidge 1991a) and *Ælfwine's Prayerbook* (Günzel 1993), as well as the *Portiforium of Wulstan* (Hughes 1958–60), the *Leofric Collectar* (Dewick and Frere 1921), the *Durham Collectar* (Corrêa 1992) and the *Calendar of St Willibrord* (Wilson 1918).

Educational and Scientific

Included under this rubric are texts in any way meant as an aid to instruction, whether rudimentary (the colloquies) or more advanced (the computistical work of Bede and Byrhtferth). Scientific works of the time often sought to do what continues to be the goal of science: to explain phenomena by observation, experimentation, description and identification. Many of the significant advances in medieval scientific writing came after the eleventh century and thus after our period of concern, and much of the scientific and medical knowledge that circulated in Anglo-Saxon England now seems either quaintly or alarmingly wrongheaded. But other areas of investigation show an unexpected level of sophistication for a land at the edge of Western Europe, particularly in the fields of astronomy, geometry and chronology. Glossary evidence shows a keen if not fully proficient interest in botany (Bierbaumer 1975–9). Greek vocabulary that found its way into Anglo-Latin writing was often technical: glossary words utilized by authors in the hermeneutic vein, rhetorical and metrical terminology, names for flora and fauna, terms for Biblical exegesis, toponyms. The types of Anglo-Latin prose texts involved here are perhaps best surveyed in the order of the contemporary educational programme: trivial and quadrivial.

Instruction under the *grammaticus* ('teacher of grammar') and *rhetor* ('teacher of rhetoric') was expected in the classical system, and it persisted in part (that is, most students at least trained under *grammatici*) in the early medieval period. Gaul was particularly known for its teachers in late antiquity, Ireland gained its reputation soon after (whether because of an influx of Gaulish teachers fleeing strife on the continent or not – a matter still not certain; Meyer 1913; Stevenson 1989). Ireland produced significant grammatical writers prior to 700, such as Malsachanus and the *Anonymus ad Cuimnanum.* Anglo-Latin writers too fairly early on turned their attention to grammar, penning in particular works on accidence, orthography and metrics. Throughout the period, directly and indirectly (through the compiling of bilingual glossaries or occasional interlinear glossing), lexicology was a concern. Nearly the entire focus of these Anglo-Saxon grammatical writers was Latin (Law 1982, 1987). The early generation of grammatical writers – Aldhelm, Bede, Boniface and Tatwine – wrote at a time when insular grammarians were worthy of note throughout Europe.

Bede's grammatical treatises include the *De orthographia*, *De arte metrica* and *De schematibus et tropis* (Jones 1975a), the main source of which (as for much of early insular grammatical writing) was Donatus. The *De orthographia* is a relatively brief compendium of information on correct spelling and word choice, sense and history; the point is sometimes orthographical: *Teloneum, non theloneum, id est per .t. simplicem, non aspriatione addita. Est autem graece telon, latine uectigal* ('*Teloneum*, non *theloneum*, that is, with unaspriated *t*, not with aspiration added. In the Greek it is *telon*, in Latin *uectigal*'; Jones 1975a: 55). In other cases the point is grammatical: *transmigro uerbum duplicem significationem habet* ('The verb *transmigro* has two senses'; Jones 1975a: 54), or *Senex et senior superlatiuum gradum non habent* ('*Senex* [old] and *senior* [older] do not have a superlative form'; Jones 1975a: 51). Throughout, the work is a small treasury of lexical information, rewarding doubly the student's reading. The *De arte metrica* by Bede relies heavily upon Donatus and provides basic instruction in prosody over the course of twenty-five brief chapters. The work and its addendum on figures of speech and tropes (*De schematibus et tropis*) are dedicated to Cuthbert (Kendall 1975: 141), later abbot of Wearmouth and Jarrow and author of the letter recounting Bede's passing (*Epistola de obitu Baedae*; Sharpe 1997: 94). Bede begins in his metrical treatise with the basics of sounds (in his account, eight vowels and nineteen consonants), syllables (initial, medial, final, with a look at inflectional suffixes), types of metrical feet (pyrrhic, tribrach and so forth), types of meter (dactylic hexameter and pentameter, sapphic, iambic tetrameter, others), metrical devices (caesura, synaloepha, diaeresis), and occasions on which metrical rules might be violated (ch. 15; Kendall 1975: 127–9). The *De schematibus et tropis* covers some thirty or so figures of speech and tropes from classical and late classical grammar: prolepsis, zeugma, hypozeuxis, syllepsis, anadiplosis, anaphora, epanalepsis, epizeuxis, paronomasia, schesis, paromoeon, homoeoteleuton and so forth. Of the tropes, allegory receives the fullest treatment, naturally enough as for Bede it connects with his exegetical concerns: for him the trivial subjects, indeed, all educational training, aided in exegesis.

Aldhelm's *De metris et enigmatibus ac pedum regulis* (or *Epistola ad Acircium*) is a collection of three treatises explaining the basics of metre through an exposition of basic terminology and principles (the *De metris*, part of which is framed in a *magister et discipulus* dialogue: *Quot sunt genera versuum in dactilico metro? Quinque* ['How many types of verse are in dactylic metre? Five']; Ehwald 1919: 82); pragmatic demonstration in the form of a century of riddles or 'mysteries' based on those of Symphosius (*Aenigmata*); and a catalogue of examples of metrical feet (*De pedum regulis*: pyrrhic, spondee, iamb, trochee, tribrach, molossus, anapaest, dactyl, amphibrach, amphimacer, etc.).

Whereas Bede generally restricted his selection of illustrative quotations to Christian Latin poets (Sedulius, Prudentius, Arator, Prosper, Iuvencus), making exception for Virgil (*Aeneid* and *Georgics* are cited fairly frequently) and possibly Horace (*De arte metrica* I.vi), Aldhelm was the more eclectic reader and – from what we can judge of surviving verse (no doubt unfair in part since so little of Bede's verse survives) – the more sophisticated metrist. Aldhelm cites Virgil extensively, as well as Symphosius and other poets circulating in the *Anthologia latina*, Juvenal, Lucan, Lucretius, Persius, Seneca, Terence, and, via other grammarians, Cicero and Sallust.

Tatwine (d. 734) of Mercia, later archbishop of Canterbury, and Boniface (d. 755) from Southumbria, later bishop of Mainz, also composed *aenigmata* and grammatical treatises. Boniface helped establish the insular educational tradition on the continent during his German missions. The *ars Tatuini (de partibus orationis)* is a fairly comprehensive survey of the fundamentals of Latin accidence in order of the eight principal parts of speech (*partes orationis secundum grammaticos sunt octo* – namely, *secundum Donatum*, 'according to Donatus'; De Marco 1968: 3). The treatise is in orderly, textbook format; thus nouns are treated in their six classifications or markings: *qualitas* (personal nouns in the forms *praenomen, nomen, cognomen, agnomen*: Tatwine gives the example 'Puplius Cornelius Scipio Affricanus'; concrete, abstract, derivational, verbal, diminutive, patronymic and other distinctions); *conparatio* (positive, comparative, superlative forms of substantival adjectives: *doctus, doctior, doctissimus*); *genus* (*naturalia* and *artificialia*); *numerus* (singular and plural); *figura* (*simplex* and *conpositus*); *casus* (nominative, genitive, dative, accusative, vocative, ablative; De Marco 1968: 6–41). The last section on nominal case is the most extensive, involving long lists of declensional forms. Only the treament of verbs is more substantial (involving the combination of grammatical instruction with the long lists of conjugated verbs which sometimes circulated separately). Tatwine's grammar was written in England (possibly at Breedon), perhaps travelled with him to Canterbury in 731 (where glosses of the Canterbury school may have been added), and thence made its way to the continent.

Boniface (the adopted Latin name of Wynfreth or Wynfrid) was one of the leaders in the Anglo-Saxon missions to the continent and one of the most important figures in the epistolary literature of pre-Conquest Anglo-Latin. He too wrote a grammatical text (*ars grammatica*) and a very brief *ars metrica* surviving in four continental manuscripts of the eighth and ninth centuries. In the latter work Boniface briefly explains types of metrical feet, caesuras and some additional poetic terminology (epithalamium, epode, etc.; Gebauer and Löfstedt 1980). His *ars grammatica* begins with a dedicatory acrostic and surveys the parts of speech according to the Donatan schema. His range of quotations is not especially extensive, but of interest in the number of classical authors cited: Virgil, of course (*Aeneid, Eclogues, Georgics*) and Cicero (the Catilinarians, *Pro Milone, Pro Roscio Amerino*), the prophetic Roman poet Marcius, Persius, Sallust, Terence.

From late Anglo-Saxon England (the lack or gap in learning King Alfred lamented seems plausible at least in the case of grammatical writing) we have the grammatical work of Ælfric of Eynsham. His major linguistic work is the Latin textbook for

English speakers (the first such grammar of Latin in a European vernacular), the *Excerptiones de arte grammatica anglice* (or, *Ælfric's Grammar*; Zupitza 1880: 1–296). Ælfric drew heavily on Priscian (whose works were not fully available to the early grammarians), and we may have his preparatory notes in the *Excerptiones de Prisciano* attributed to Ælfric, which survives in three eleventh-century manuscripts (Law 1987). The Priscian excerpts are explained in Old English and the text is supplemented with a bilingual glossary (Zupitza 1880: 297–322), under such rubrics as *nomina membrorum* (parts of the body; followed by sections with names of family relationship, social class and trade, and other word classes); *nomina avium, piscium, ferarum, herbarum, arborum* (rounding out a physical world glossary class, names of birds, fish, wild animals, plant life); *nomina domorum* (a glossary of building types begins a miscellaneous word-list that comprises various *artificialia* ('things man-made') and closes with a class of things *synful*). It is difficult to say how ingenuous was Ælfric's note that the work was for *pueruli* ('little boys') – and difficult too to determine what we can read from the appearance in this late period of a grammar of Latin in English. Ælfric's *Colloquy* does bear out his concern for elementary Latin instruction, as do the colloquies of Ælfric Bata (Gwara 1996); these texts would have allowed for practice with accidence and aided in the acquisition of vocabulary and synonyms.

The students in Ælfric's *Colloquy* are asked what they desire, and they reply *Uolumus esse sapientes* ('we wish to be wise'): rhetoric and dialectic (or logic) were the trivial subjects designed to develop the ability to form arguments, to know the good ones from the sophistic, and to be convincing when right. Given the prominent role played by late medieval English philosophers and logicians, it may seem curious that either very little was written by the Anglo-Saxons on these subjects or little of what was written survives. One exception is Alcuin's *Disputatio de rhetorica et de virtutibus sapientissimi regis Karli et Albini magistri* (Halm 1863). While not a particularly innovative work, it at least records some of Alcuin's rhetorical and dialectical teachings prepared for the palace school at Aachen. It is cast as a dialogue between Albinus (Alcuin, present here not as Flaccus, the court poet role he adopted on the continent) and Karolus (or Karulus, Karlus), and the *disputatio* begins, after requisite flattery of the monarch, with the basics; the dialogue is an example of what it seeks to teach, and it is also a moral work intended for the monarch and his court.

In turning to the quadrivial subjects, two Anglo-Saxon authors stand out: Bede and Byrhtferth, both of whom had a strong interest in chronology and the science of the computus. Both too had a scientific interest in the nature of things. Bede's *De natura rerum* is comprised of fifty-one brief chapters, often with accompanying *rotae* (wheel-like charts) in the later manuscripts which were taken from Isidore; the main sources for this work were Isidore of Seville (his *De natura rerum* and *Etymologiae*) and Pliny the Elder (the *Naturalis historia*). Topics covered include the formation of the world (*de mundi formatione*), the course of the planets (*de cursu planetarum*), the twelve signs of the zodiac (*de .xii. signis*), solar and lunar eclipses (*de eclipsi solis et lunae*), comets, winds, thunder and lightning, clouds, rain and snow, tides (Jones 1975a: 189–234). Bede's chronological work includes the *De temporum ratione* (including his *chronica maiora*; Jones 1975b) and *De temporibus* (including his *chronica minora*; Jones 1980). The latter work is the earlier (dated to 703) and more basic, comprised of twenty-two chapters (chs 16–22, arranged in the 'six ages of the world' format, being the minor chronicle). The fuller *De temporum ratione* (dated to 725) is comprised of seventy-one chapters, the major chronicle beginning in ch. 66. Both works are concerned with explaining units of measurement of time (days, weeks, months in various systems of dating, such as Hebrew and Greek); setting out principles for proper alignment of systems of dating (in particular, the *bissextus*, or intercalary day, and *saltus lunae*, a lunar day 'leapt over' at the end of the nineteen-year paschal cycle to realign the solar and lunar cycles).

Byrhtferth of Ramsey's major work was computistical; he is believed to have compiled a *computus* – literally, mathematical calculation; essentially, a genre of early scientific compendia for determining the date of Easter regularly – during the period 988–96, which survives in good part in the early twelfth-century manuscript Oxford, St John's College 17 (Wallis 1985). Byrthferth's major prose treatise, the *Manual* or *Enchiridion*, is for the most part a commentary on the computus with additional related material (for instance, a version of the *sex aetates mundi*; Baker and Lapidge 1995: 232–41). The *Enchiridion* is a storehouse of early medieval knowledge astronomical, astrological, arithmetic and arithmologic (the study of the mystical properties or significances of numbers and numerical patterns; Baker and Lapidge 1995: lxi–lxxiv).

The *Enchiridion* is arranged much like a textbook: I.1 *De anno et partibus eius* ('On the year and its parts'; like much of the work, it is macaronic, occurring in Latin and Old English, with Old English predominating); I.2 *De concurrentibus, regularibus et epactis* ('On the concurrents, regulars and epacts', which introduces some computistical terminology; the epact, for instance, being an intercalary day used in harmonizing solar and lunar calendars); I.3 *De uersibus Bede* ('On Bede's verses', which includes the verse *Bis sena mensum uertigine uoluitur annus*, 'The year runs on the axis of twice-six months', which circulated in the *Anthologia latina* fascicles [Riese 1894: no. 680] as well as material that appeared also in the York metrical calendar; Lapidge 1984); I.4 *Argumenta de concurrentibus, regularibus et epactis* ('Instructions on the concurrents, regulars and epacts'); II.1 *De duodecim mensibus* ('On the twelve months'); II.2 *De septem embolismis* ('On the seven embolisms', another type of intercalation); II.3 *De anno et die et nocte et horis et eius partibus* ('On the year, the day, the night, the hours and their parts'); III.1 *De Pascha* ('On Easter'); III.2 *De ratione Pasche* ('On the reckoning of Easter') – these first two sections of book III come to the heart of the matter for Anglo-Saxon chronologists from Bede to Byrhtferth; III.3 *De plurimis* ('Concerning many things'), a fascinating brief encyclopaedia including: *de tribus generibus poematos* ('On the three types of poetry': dramatic, narrative, and 'mixed'); *de schematibus* ('on figures of speech': Bede's *De schematibus et tropis* is the major source); a table of 'lunar letters'; *de figuris accentum* ('On the figures of accents': a list of ten accents taken from Isidore's *Etymologiae*); *de notis sententiarum* ('on the marks of sense': a list of punctuation signals also from Isidore); *de ratione unciarum* ('on the reckoning of weights': a number of the terms introduced occur frequently in the glossaries); *de alphabetis* ('on alphabets': Latin,

Greek and Hebrew alphabets and their numerical values); *de numeris Latinorum* ('On Roman numbers'); IV.1 *De numerorum significationibus* ('on the meanings of numbers': an arithmological tract); IV.2 *de sex aetatibus mundi* ('on the six ages of the world'). Throughout the text are a number of diagrams (or *rotae*, familiar from illustrated Isidore manuscripts such as the ninth-century Zofingen, Stadtbibliothek P. 32) and tables. Baker and Lapidge (1995) print in an appendix a reconstruction of Byrhtferth's computus from material in Oxford, St John's 17, a magnificent illustrated miscellany also containing Bede's *De temporum ratione* (Ker, *Catalogue*: item 360). Bede's *computistica* was a significant source for Byrhtferth, as were the *De computo* of Hrabanus Maurus (one of Alcuin's students) and Ælfric's *De temporibus anni* (Henel 1942; itself abstracted from Bede).

As the most broadly learned of early Anglo-Latin writers, Bede no doubt had training in another of the quadrivial arts: music. A *Liber hymnorum* is attributed to him, though the extracts from Boethius' *De institutione musica* that circulated under the title *De musica theorica* are no longer so. Attributed to Wulfstan, precentor of Winchester, is the work *De tonorum harmonia*, which survives only as quotations in the *Breviloquium super musicam* (Lapidge and Winterbottom 1991: xvi–xvii). Much of the medical and pseudo-medical writing of the period appears in the vernacular. Other Anglo-Latin works of a scientific and educational nature no doubt remain to be identified, and the corpus of glossaries from the period (Latin–Latin and Latin–Old English) could serve as another source for the range of interests of Anglo-Saxon writers.

Literary

A classification such as 'literary' for this period of Anglo-Latin prose serves little purpose – Bede certainly sought to instruct and delight as well as edify with the *HE*; Anglo-Latin authors seem conscious, whether producing hagiographies, letters, wills, charters or chronicles, of engaging in *literary* production. But the label 'literary' might be pressed into service here for works in prose that do not fit comfortably under any other of the rubrics. Three specimens will serve as examples: one quite possibly an Anglo-Latin original composition (the *Liber monstrorum*), two others imports read, copied and redacted in England during the period spanning, roughly, the eighth to eleventh centuries (the *Historia Apollonii Regis Tyri* and the *Epistola Alexandri ad Aristotelem* and its sibling *De mirabilibus Orientis*).

'Apollonius of Tyre' and 'Alexander's Letter' are two of the most popular secular texts of the early medieval period, each deriving ultimately from late antiquity. Both may be, after a fashion, styled romances (Perry 1967), and both enjoyed a cycle of transmission in Britain. In fact, an insular strain of *Historia Apollonii* manuscripts (belonging to Recension C of the text) has been noted (Schmeling 1988). The manuscripts of this *circulus Anglicus* (including Cambridge, Corpus Christi College, 318 and 451; Oxford, Bodleian Laud misc. 247 and Rawlinson D.893) belong to the twelfth and thirteenth centuries, though they evidence a period of circulation in the British

Isles believed to have begun somewhere in the eighth or ninth century (Schmeling 1988). The 'Apollonius' was translated into Old English (Goolden 1958), an incomplete version surviving in one manuscript (Cambridge, Corpus Christi College 201) most probably based on a Recension C text earlier than those surviving in English collections (McGowan 1990).

The appearance of the Apollonius story in Anglo-Saxon England has provoked some curiosity (though it remains one of the most neglected texts from the period) and occasioned some puzzlement as to its place in the literature of Anglo-Saxon England. For one, it is a text that, however moralizing in its core tale of redemptive love, is pre-Christian and ambiguous in its reference to *dii* ('gods') and *deae* ('goddesses', namely Diana) on the one hand, and a *deus uiuus* ('living God', by whom Athenagoras, prince of Mytilene, swears in cap. 45, or which appears in ablative absolutes such as *deo fauente*). It is also a tale of incest, murder, pirates, brothels, gymnasia and triclinia. But, too, it is a story of the testing and preservation of the virginity of Apollonius' daughter Tarsia. That the text was available in multiple copies in Anglo-Saxon England is interesting; that it was translated into late West Saxon all the more so. If anything, in sentiment and topoi, it fits in most comfortably with the hagiographies, which too had their trials and sudden reversals, abandonments and restorations.

The popularity of 'Alexander's Letter to Aristotle' has also exercised literary critics. To be certain, the text participates in the exemplum tradition: Alexander as the dutiful student reporting his adventures to his great teacher (cap. 1); Alexander as the exemplary military leader who refused water while his own soldiers suffered dire thirst (cap. 12); Alexander as the doomed over-reacher, whose death at Babylon is prophesied by the Tree of the Moon: ' "Alexander", said the tree of the moon, "you have now the full reach of your lifetime. For in the following year in the ninth month you shall die in Babylon: by whom you least expect you shall be deceived" ' (ch. 38). The *Epistola Alexandri* is, like the 'Apollonius', a romance, an early appearance in England of the Alexander romance to blossom fantastically in medieval literature (Cary 1956). It is a text that has moved away from earlier *res gestae* ('books of deeds', such as the *Epitoma Metensis*) towards the epistolary travel narrative of the campaign against King Porus of India. Its richness in teratological detail (wonders animal and human are retailed, from hippopotami [compare *Liber monstrorum* II.9] to horned serpents [the *coluber cerastes; Liber monstrorum* III.15], from icthyophages [eaters of raw fish; compare *Liber monstrorum* I.15] to cynocephali [a dog-headed race; *Liber monstrorum* I.16]) is preserved without the epistolary framework in the *De mirabilibus Orientis*, in which in some three dozen chapters 'wonders' are enumerated. Both 'Alexander's Letter' and the 'Wonders of the East' were included in the *Beowulf* portion of British Library, Cotton Vitellius A. xv. The bilingual copy of the 'Wonders' in British Library, Cotton Tiberius B. v (of the eleventh century), and Latin text in Oxford, Bodleian Library, Bodley 614 (of the twelfth), are illustrated magnificently.

Matters teratological bring us to the *Liber monstrorum*. The *Liber monstrorum de diversis generibus* is divided into three books of monstrous wonders: *homines* (monstrous men or semi-human monstrosities: fauns, sirens, giants, *cynocephali* and many others); *beluae* (wild beasts or composite fabled beasts: lions, elephants, tigers, leopards, panthers, hippopotami, crocodiles, whales, giant mice [taken from 'Alexander's Letter']); *serpentes* (Hydra, salamander, horned serpents and others); the text has for some time been of note also for its mention of Hygelac from *Beowulf* at I.2. More recent attention has focused on the possibility of attributing the text to the school of Aldhelm (Lapidge 1982a; Orchard 1995). The manuscript witnesses point towards an insular origin by virtue of orthographical detail (Porsia 1976; Orchard 1995: 86–7); the appearance of Hygelac (I.2) and the type of learning displayed and sources utilized have led several scholars to conclude that it is an Anglo-Latin work (references in Orchard 1995: 87n.). Michael Lapidge has pressed the claim further, locating the text in the milieu of the Anglo-Saxon scholars influenced by the school of Theodore and Hadrian (including Aldhelm and his circle), and offering a dating of 650 × 750 (Lapidge 1982a). Though not usually considered, an Irish origin is not out of the question; the account of the giant girl in I.13 has Irish analogues (those extant being later than the *Liber monstrorum*; Orchard 1995: 106–10).

At any rate, the *Liber* merits attention for more than its mention of Hygelac; it is a curious compendium of learning, wit and lexical information – this last area of consideration has received recent notice in a study seeing links between the vocabulary of the *Liber* and the Biblical glossaries compiled by the school of Theodore and Hadrian (Lendinara 1996). The *Liber* in the main mines three principal sources: Christian ones such as Isidore's *Etymologiae* (a text recently published in 636, if the *Liber* is taken as an Anglo-Latin composition following from the Canterbury school) and Augustine's *De civitate Dei* book XVI; late antique Alexander material, such as the *Epistola Alexandri*; and Virgil (Orchard 1995: his appendix IIIc gives a convenient list of sources and analogues for the individual chapters). Beyond its exotic appeal, the *Liber* no doubt also offered a rich trove of vocabulary, of words arcane, even in the hermeneutic vein. And the use of such vocabulary in Anglo-Latin (such as Aldhelm's *Carmen de virginitate*, perhaps known to the compiler of the *Liber*; Whitbread 1974; Lapidge 1982a) is commonplace; so too the compilation of difficult and arcane lemmata. Digging at roots in the Isidorean vein was a well-established pursuit of Anglo-Saxon scholars.

Epistolary

The appeal of epistolary fiction such as 'Alexander's Letter' is rather natural amongst scholars and clerics, whose epistolary output is exemplary for the early medieval period. Boniface in particular left to us, happily, an extensive corpus of correspondence. A good many of the writers and correspondents in Anglo-Latin known by name are preserved in the Bonifatian corpus (Tangl 1955), as a surveying glance through Richard Sharpe's indispensable *Handlist* makes clear (Sharpe 1997). In fact, Boniface's correspondence – including letters to and from Lul, his assistant and successor to the see of Mainz – serves as a sort of onomasticon: Ælfflæd, abbess of Whitby (ep. 8);

Cuthbert, abbot of Wearmouth and Jarrow (epp. 116, 126–7), who also authored the *Epistola de obitu Baedae*; Cyneheard, bishop of Winchester (epp. 114, 123); and nearly a score of others. As with Aldhelm, Bede, Alcuin and Ælfric, Boniface's letters often concern matters of pastoral care and ecclesiastical administration. Boniface's letters are additionally important as signal witnesses to the peak of Anglo-Saxon missionary activity on the continent.

To some extent we can trace Boniface's career through letters to him, from him, and on his behalf. Four letters from Daniel, bishop of Winchester, survive in the corpus (epp. 11, 23, 39, 64), the earliest of which (ep. 11, from 718) was a letter of introduction written on behalf of the Anglo-Saxon missionary Wynfrith (later Boniface) 'To godly and merciful kings, all dukes, reverend and beloved bishops, priests and holy abbots and to all the spiritual sons of Christ' (Talbot 1954: 67). Papal letters of encouragement and direction were sent to Boniface during his work in Frisia and Germany (epp. 12, 17–19, 24–6 from Gregory II in 719–26; epp. 50, 68, 89 [which includes the charter for the house at Fulda] from Zacharias in 742–51); letters to and from kings survive too (ep. 22 in 723, at the request of Gregory II, Charles Martel places Boniface under his protection; ep. 107 in 753, concerning Boniface's ire with a brother Ansfrid, was addressed to Pippin, whom Boniface had consecrated in 752). Other letters concern items more modest in scale if no less needed: letters from Boniface addressed to Hwætbert (ep. 76 in 746–7) and Egbert (ep. 91 in 747–51) requesting copies of Bede's works; a letter from King Ethelbert of Kent (ep. 105) requesting falcons. Boniface's correspondence, in the main, concerns furtherance of the missionary activity on the continent (in ep. 73 of 746–7 he speaks particularly harshly of the Wends), and the welfare of friends and companions (a dedicatory epistle to Sigeberht is affixed to one of the manuscript copies of his *ars grammatica*, though it may have circulated separately: Law 1979). A letter to abbess Eadburg of Thanet (ep. 10) preserves the famous 'Vision of a Monk of Wenlock'; the abbess had asked Boniface to relate the man's vision of the afterworld, encountered upon his decease and revivification (*mortuus est et revixit*), and Boniface conducted an interview with the man in the presence of three brethren known to be faithful, true and worthy as witnesses to his account. Boniface's account participates in the tradition of visions of the otherworld and the Judgement, and provides too a *psychomachia* in epitome: the Monk of Wenlock recalls his own sins crying out in accusation, his virtues subsequently mounting a defence (Tangl 1955: 9–10).

Aldhelm and Bede have also left us letters (one can imagine the correspondence behind the *HE*); Cuthbert gave us the *Epistola de obitu Bedae*, which shows Bede to have been concerned with pedagogy to the very end (Dobbie 1937: 123). Alcuin too, in a letter to the monks of Wearmouth and Jarrow (*sanctissimis in Christo fratribus Viorensis eclesi<a>e et Gyruensis*; Chase 1975), speaks fondly of Bede's spirit:

> Think what a love for learning the elder Bede, the most notable teacher of our age, had as a boy, and how honoured he is now among men and even more gloriously rewarded by God. Liven sleepy minds with his example. Sit with your teachers, open your books,

study the text, grasp its sense, that you may find spiritual food for yourselves and for others. (Allott 1974: 40)

Letter writing in England is first evidenced by the Vindolanda tablets, the largely mundane correspondence of Roman soldiers and officers. Though influenced by classic epistolary models to an extent (Anglo-Saxon clerics wrote for one another *litterae commendaticiae*, letters of recommendation), the form in particular abundance from early medieval Anglo-Latin is the ecclesiastical or pastoral letter, Pope Gregory's correspondence being of especial influence. Ælfric's 'Letter to the Monks of Eynsham' (Jones 1998) employed an epistolary framework to transmit the abbot's reworking of the *Regularis concordia* into a monastic customary, that is, a book composed of the rules and customs of a monastery.

Letters can at times be counted among ephemera, but as often are meant to last: examples amply supplied by Cicero's correspondence, the Pauline epistles, papal letters and dedicatory epistles. The device of cloaking a treatise meant for circulation (Ælfric is, one way or another, with or without the epistolary frame, addressing his 'brothers in Christ') was not new, and had a model in Aldhelm's *De metris* or *Epistola ad Acircium*. The appeal of the epistolary form in the period – whether the fictive epistle of Alexander to Aristotle, or a Boniface or Alcuin writing *ad familiares*, or letters sent on church business (such as pastoral and penitential letters; Whitelock et al. 1981: nos. 40, 42) – is quite apparent. The particular contribution of Anglo-Saxons to the form and place of the epistolary in medieval Latin awaits fuller study.

Varia

A great many other types of texts in Anglo-Latin survive from the Anglo-Saxon period. Many of them, though not all, can be classed as sub-literary: law-codes, statutes, royal and ecclesiastical correspondence, conciliar documents, charters, writs, wills, manumissions, and an extensive body of epigraphic materials. Ecclesiastical materials, naturally enough, abound; many of the charters concern grants of lands to churches or monastic houses, and many of the letters and writs concern such matters as pastoral guidance, monastic discipline or episcopal succession. One such form is the episcopal profession; a single example from the tenth century, if not spurious, survives in Cotton Cleopatra E.i, the profession of Eadwulf (Athulf), bishop of the restored see of Elmham, to Oda, archbishop of Canterbury (951 × 955), to whom he professes devoted service, as a humble servant of Christ, so long as there should be the breath of life in him and living spirit in his nostrils (Whitelock et al. 1981: no. 22). Charters also often offer a profession of sorts in the granting of land, their tightly formulaic style calling to mind once more the uses officialdom had for Latin. The earliest of the charters of the see of Rochester, dated to 604 though evidently a later concoction (Levison 1946: 223–5; Campbell 1973: xxii), sought to establish a grant of land ('I hand over a little something of my land') to St Andrew's, Rochester, by Æthelbert of Kent, the first Christian English king (Campbell 1973: no. 1).

Among the briefest examples of Anglo-Latin prose, manumissions – often tucked or copied into blank leaves of Gospel-books, law-codes or other significant manuscripts – concerned *donationes* of another sort. A group of fifty-one manumissions occurs in London, British Library, Additional 9381, the *Bodmin Gospels*, with ten in Old English, the majority in Latin (Ker 1957: item 126). The manumitting of the slaves took place at the altar of St Petroc's, Bodmin, Cornwall – and many of the names of those manumitted were Celtic. That the altar was where the legal act occurred no doubt added to its solemnity (especially as the altar would have contained relics of the saint; Rollason 1989: 192–3); that the manumissions were copied into blank leaves of the Bodmin Gospel-book did so too. One of these manumissions in London, British Library, Additional 9381, fol. 1r, involves slaves freed by Bishop Wulfsige of Cornwall for the sake of King Edgar's soul (allowing a dating of 975 × 989): 'Bishop Wulfsige freed Iudprost with his sons for the soul of King Edgar and for his own soul before these witnesses: Brihtsige the priest, Electus the priest, Abel the priest, Morhatho the deacon, Canretheo the deacon, Riol the deacon' (Whitelock 1955: no. 145). The manumissions offer a picture not of grand events such as in chronicles, rather more of daily life; this brief tract of Anglo-Latin captures what must have been, at least for Iudprost and sons, an extraordinary day.

REFERENCES

References can be found at the end of chapter 2, 'An Introduction to the Corpus of Anglo-Latin Literature'.

PART IV
Intertextualities:
Sources and Influences

18
Biblical and Patristic Learning
Thomas Hall

Biblical study was a fundamental activity for the Anglo-Saxons, the central goal of all formal instruction in monastic schools, and the starting point for literary endeavours of virtually any kind. Chapter 48 of the Benedictine *Rule* mandates three to four hours of meditative *lectio divina* per day, a requirement ideally fulfilled by prayerful rumination on the Bible and select writings of the Fathers (Butler 1924: 279–81, 287). We consequently find repeated emphasis in Anglo-Saxon monastic writings on the centrality of Biblical study to the spiritual and intellectual life, which English monks pursued in part through rote memorization of the Psalter. Bede recalls with admiration in *Historia ecclesiastica* III.5 (hereafter *HE*) that members of the *familia* of St Aidan at Lindisfarne 'whether tonsured or laymen' were required to memorize the Psalter as part of their course of study (Colgrave and Mynors 1969: 226–7). Similar practices are described in the *Vita S. Wilfridi*, which claims that Wilfrid as a youth learned both the Roman and Gallican versions of the Psalter by heart (Colgrave 1927: 6–9), and in the anonymous eighth-century *Vita S. Ceolfridi*, which alleges that Ceolfrith routinely sang the Psalter twice a day, three times daily while travelling (Plummer 1896: 1.401). A regimen only slightly less rigorous is enjoined by the *Regularis concordia*, which specifies that the brethren should recite Psalms while engaged in physical labour (§32) and should sing the entire Psalter in chorus after Prime on each of the three days from Maundy Thursday to Holy Saturday (§64) (Symons et al. 1984: 91, 111), a practice enforced as well by Ælfric's *Letter to the Monks of Eynsham* (§34) (Jones 1998: 126–7).

To study the Bible, one had to have access to reliable copies of the text, and the Anglo-Saxons proved exceptionally skilled at collecting, copying, editing and illustrating the Latin Bible. Over half of the 138 extant Latin Gospel manuscripts produced before the ninth century originated in the British Isles, and of these the majority are English (McGurk 1961: 11). More than a hundred Bible manuscripts written or owned in England before the twelfth century survive, including the remains of eleven originally complete Bibles, six part-Bibles containing one or more Old Testament books, and fifty-nine more or less complete Gospel-books plus fragments of another nineteen (Marsden 1998: 169–76; cf. Gneuss 1996b: 106). When considered in relation to the pool of early medieval Bible manuscripts from outside the British Isles, these numbers may seem comparatively large, but if we can assume that at least one Bible – or at the very least one copy of the Psalter and a Gospel-book – must have been required as basic equipment in each of the two hundred churches that were in England by the end of the eighth century, then we begin to see how many such books must have perished and how active the market for Bibles and part-Bibles must have been (Marsden 1998: 155).

Thanks to devotional reading habits and liturgical requirements, the demand for certain books was naturally greater than for others, with the Gospels and Psalms ranking at the top of the list. Surviving copies of the Old Testament are much rarer than those of the New, particularly from the south: only eight manuscripts containing portions of the Old Testament survive from the mid-tenth century or earlier, of which the majority (six out of eight) were written in Northumbria (Marsden 1994a: 102–3, 123). Gospel-books count as the most sumptuously decorated class of luxury manuscripts, often accompanied by the elaborate initial pages, carpet pages and evangelist pages that are characteristic of a distinctively insular method of Gospel-book illumination, with particularly famous examples including the Lichfield Gospels, the Lindisfarne Gospels and the Gospels of Countess Judith of Flanders. From the early period the greatest single monument of Biblical production is surely the Codex Amiatinus, the only surviving member of the trio of massive pandects of the Vulgate completed at Wearmouth–Jarrow under the direction of Abbot Ceolfrith sometime before 716, and now the earliest complete Latin Bible in existence. The principal exemplars for Amiatinus were Italian Bibles acquired either by Ceolfrith or his predecessor Benedict Biscop during their several book-buying excursions abroad (Fischer 1985: 9–34, 67–9), and the Amiatinus text is so important that it was consulted for the Sixtine revision of the Vulgate in 1587–90. Only one other substantially complete Bible survives from the entire pre-Conquest period, namely the two-volume 'Royal Bible' in London, British Library, Royal 1. E. vii–viii (? southern England, late tenth century), which is complete save for the loss of Genesis 1, 1 to 29, 33 (Marsden 1995a: 321–78).

What people were reading when they were reading the Bible was in most cases essentially Jerome's Latin Vulgate, although once this general assertion is accepted a number of important qualifications need to be made. To begin with, the cost and physical labour involved in Bible production ensured that few people were ever likely to have access to a complete Bible containing all the books from Genesis to Revelation, and even if they did, that Bible was likely to comprise multiple volumes. The famous Ezra miniature in the Codex Amiatinus depicts the Jewish scribe Ezra seated before an open cupboard housing a Bible in nine volumes, and this number must not have been unusual. The vast majority of early English Bible manuscripts are of part-Bibles only – in most cases copies of a single book or of a set of books such as the Gospels or the minor prophets – which helps explain why a common medieval term for the Bible was *bibliotheca* 'the library' (Mundó 1950; Duchet-Suchaux and Lefèvre 1984: 13–15). Second, the textual history of the Latin Bible is vastly more complex than the oversimplified labels 'Vulgate' and 'Old Latin' tend to suggest, so that in practice any two Anglo-Saxon Bibles taken at random would have certainly contained variant readings and very possibly a different ordering of books. The sequence of books adopted by Ælfric in his *Libellus de veteri testamenti et de novo*, for instance, puts I and II Chronicles immediately after Kings (in agreement with Augustine and the Codex Amiatinus), but the tenth-century Royal Bible places Isaiah after Kings and inserts Chronicles over twenty books down the line (Marsden 1995a: 450). In seventh- and eighth-century Northumbria, moreover, the pervasiveness of Celtic influence on all aspects of British Christianity resulted in extensive borrowings from the distinctive Irish textual tradition, which at times diverged substantially from the Vulgate, particularly within the Gospels, the Psalms and Job (Marsden 1998: 148–9).

In addition, individual Old Latin readings, pre-dating the Vulgate, were kept in circulation throughout the period by quotations in patristic writings and liturgical texts such as canticles and Gospel pericopes. A short unpublished Latin sermon for Easter in an eleventh-century pontifical from Salisbury (London, British Library, Cotton Tiberius C. i, fols 176v–177v) contains a rare Old Latin quotation of Isaiah 26, 10, which reads *Tollatur impius, ne videat gloriam Dei* ('The impious one will be destroyed; he will not see the glory of God'), as opposed to the more common Vulgate reading, *Misereamur impio et non discet iustitiam; in terra sanctorum inique gessit et non videbit gloriam Domini* ('Let us have pity on the wicked, but he will not learn justice; in the land of the saints he has done wicked things, and he shall not see the glory of the Lord'). The shorter Old Latin form of this verse appears in very few extant Bibles, but it happens to be the reading favoured by Gregory the Great, who quotes it three times in his *Moralia in Iob* (IV.xi.58, VI.xxx.3, XX.iii.121), once in his second homily on Ezechiel and once in his thirteenth Gospel homily, so there is reason to think the author of the Salisbury sermon encountered this verse not in an Old Latin manuscript of Isaiah but in a copy of one of Gregory's works, which were far more plentiful. Ælfric likewise quotes (or translates) on occasion from an Old Latin text in his homilies, but in doing so he is almost always simply echoing the verse forms transmitted in his patristic sources rather than quoting directly from an Old Latin Bible (Pope 1967–8: 1.152; Marsden 1995a: 54, 398–9). The ever-scrupulous Bede is unusual among English writers for his habit of comparing Vulgate and Old Latin readings, as he does in *HE* V.21, where he quotes two variant readings of a verse from Genesis in order to take advantage of all available Biblical teachings concerning the dating of Easter in relation to the vernal equinox (Colgrave and Mynors 1969: 542–3).

For most Anglo-Saxons 'the Bible' necessarily meant a Bible in Latin. There never was a complete translation of the Bible into Old English, although on a number of occasions attempts were made to translate certain portions of the Bible, a process that began with Bede, who is said to have been occupied with a translation of the Gospel of John at the time of his death in 735 (Colgrave and Mynors 1969: 582–3). At some point probably in the tenth or early eleventh century an anonymous metrical translation of the Psalter was produced, of which the verses corresponding to Psalms 51–150:3 survive in the mid-eleventh-century Paris Psalter, where they are preceded by an Old English prose translation of Psalms 1–50, now believed to be by King Alfred (Bately 1982; Pulsiano 1995: 77–9). Also in the late tenth or early eleventh century the first complete English translation of the four Gospels was made, of which six full copies and a small number of fragments survive, attesting to a pattern of transmission that carried into the twelfth century. Although traditionally referred to as the West Saxon Gospels, these Old English Gospels point linguistically to a geographical origin somewhere in the south-east, possibly but not certainly Canterbury (Liuzza 2000: 49, 154). Because three of the earliest manuscripts closely mirror one another in their text as well as their spelling and punctuation, they appear to reflect a planned programme of publication. Glosses and corrections appear in every copy, and in one remarkable case liturgical directions have been added identifying the pericopes to be read on certain feast days, a sign that at least one of the translations was intended to function as a mass lectionary (Liuzza 1998, 2000: 208–14). Also in the very early eleventh century a group effort to translate portions of the Old Testament resulted in the Old English *Hexateuch* (or *Heptateuch*, since one manuscript adds a translation of Judges), a project to which Ælfric made significant contributions as the sole translator of Genesis 1–24, Numbers 13–36, and the abbreviated version of Joshua (plus the whole of Judges in the *Heptateuch* manuscript). Whoever translated the rest of the *Hexateuch* (Genesis 25–50, Exodus, Leviticus, Numbers 1–12 and Deuteronomy) remains unknown, but on stylistic grounds it is clear that more than one person was involved (Exodus alone had at least two translators), and the resulting compilation shows evidence of skilful editing, many selective omissions, and intermittent contamination from Old Latin, particularly within the portion of Genesis translated by Ælfric (Jost 1927; Raith 1952; Clemoes 1974; Marsden 1994b, 2000).

In addition to his work towards the Old English *Hexateuch*, Ælfric produced a large number of Biblical translations, many of which he incorporated into his homilies and saints' lives. In his *Libellus de veteri testamento et novo* Ælfric claims to have translated the first seven books of the Old Testament (Genesis to Judges) plus Maccabees and portions of Kings, Daniel, Job, Esther and Judith (Crawford 1969: 37, 47, 48, 51). In all such cases Ælfric's method of translation reveals much about his attitude to the Biblical text. Even though he cautions in his Preface to Genesis that a Biblical translator should adhere closely to the original and add nothing new ('we ne durron na mare awritan on Englisc þonne ðæt Leden hæfð, ne ða endebyrdnysse awendan'; Crawford 1969: 79; discussion by Marsden 1991: 322–4), his own translations are at times free enough to qualify as paraphrases, and it is not unusual for him to abridge or expand the Latin to clarify obscure passages, encourage certain interpretations, or bring the text into conformity with the prosodic and alliterative requirements of his own rhythmical prose. In translating Genesis 3, 6, which tells that Eve saw the Tree of Knowledge to be good for food and pleasing to the eyes, Ælfric interjects the laconic remark 'be ðam ðe hyre ðuhte' ('or so it seemed to her'; Crawford 1969: 88). And at Genesis 19, 26, on the transformation of Lot's wife into a pillar of salt, he adds the comment, here placed by Crawford in parentheses, that this was not a magic trick but an act of God intended as a warning to those who disobey him: 'þa beseah Lothes wif unwislice underbæc, 7 wearð sona awend to anum sealtstane (na for wiglunge, ac for gewisre getacnunge)' ('Then Lot's wife foolishly looked back and was immediately turned into a salt-stone – not out of sorcery but for a sure sign'; Crawford 1969: 134). The addition not only explains God's purpose in performing this miracle and fends off a superstitious interpretation but extends the pattern of alliteration on **w** in the sentence in the words *unwislice, wearð, awend, wiglunge* and *gewisre* (cf. Biggs 1991: 291).

In other cases Ælfric's renderings force a more precise meaning or even provide commentary. Where the Vulgate Genesis 1, 20, has God commanding the primordial waters to bring forth all creeping things that are living (*producant aquae reptile animae viventis*), Ælfric has the waters bringing forth 'swymmende cynn cucu on life' (Crawford 1969: 83), with 'swimming creatures' here standing for 'creeping things', a substitution that seems to be prompted by the practical observation that marine animals are more apt to swim than creep. Where Genesis 2, 13, mentions only that the name of the second river of paradise is Geon, Ælfric supplies the onomastic gloss 'seo is eac gehaten Nilus' ('which is also called the Nile'; Crawford 1969: 86), a detail he probably picked up from patristic commentary. Similarly, his translation of Genesis 3, 20, on Adam's naming of Eve, adds the definition 'Eua, ðæt is lif' ('Eve, that is, "life"'; Crawford 1969: 90), an equivalent of the patristic commonplace that *Eva* signifies *vita* (Marsden 1991: 338–9, 1994b: 239).

A vital product of Biblical study from virtually the moment Roman literacy came to England was the composition of verse Biblical paraphrases and scriptural commentaries, and in both areas English authors made important original contributions. In his account of the career of the poet Cædmon, Bede relates that after Cædmon joined Hild's monastery in the 680s he began making verse paraphrases concerning 'the creation of the world, the origin of the human race, and the whole history of Genesis, of the departure of Israel from Egypt and the entry into the promised land and of many other of the stories taken from the sacred Scriptures: of the incarnation, passion, and resurrection of the Lord, of His ascension into heaven, of the coming of the Holy Spirit and the teaching of the apostles' (Colgrave and Mynors 1969: 419). To this Bede adds that other poets in Cædmon's wake soon wrote religious poetry in the same manner, and some have deduced from this that an entire school of Cædmonian poets, all practising the art of verse Biblical paraphrase, was established in the late seventh century and following, a school now represented by the Old English Biblical poems of the Junius manuscript (Oxford, Bodleian Library, Junius 11). Bede himself authored over twenty Biblical commentaries plus a treatise on Biblical topography (the *De locis sanctis*), a set of fifty Gospel homilies, and a *collectaneum* of extracts from works by Augustine on the Pauline epistles (Ray 1982; Brown 1987: 51–65). Bede's *De schematibus et tropis*, a grammatical handbook for readers of scripture, is significant for its definitive presentation of the patristic theory of the fourfold sense of scripture (literal, typological, moral, mystical) which informed so much medieval exegesis. Bede also made a serious effort to master Greek in order to improve his knowledge of the Greek New Testament, and in fact the very copy of the bilingual Greek and Latin Acts of the Apostles which he consulted while engaged in his *Retractatio in Actus Apostolorum* is believed to survive in Oxford, Bodleian Library, Laud Graecus 35 (Italy [?Sardinia], s. vi or vii).

Independent of Bede, the most advanced and productive programme of biblical exegesis in England before the twelfth century was undertaken at the school established by Theodore and Hadrian at Canterbury in the 670s, where the study of the Latin Bible was bolstered by mastery of several ancillary disciplines including grammar, rhetoric, metrics, computus, astronomy and Roman law. The Canterbury commentaries on the Pentateuch and the Gospels reveal an extraordinary (if idiosyncratic) command of patristic learning in Latin and Greek as well as Syriac, and the recent publication of a portion of these texts has already begun to shed light on the scholarly activities of the Canterbury school, which the editors judge to represent 'the intellectual highpoint of Anglo-Saxon literary culture' (Bischoff and Lapidge 1994: 274).

It is important to remember that throughout the Middle Ages Biblical studies entailed more than the study of the sixty-six books that today make up the Protestant Bible. The six books now referred to customarily as deuterocanonical or intertestamental apocrypha – Tobit, Judith, Wisdom, Ecclesiasticus (or Sirach), and I and II Maccabees – were all equally well known and were generally accorded a canonical status on a par with that of Genesis or Matthew. All these books came to the Latin Bible from the Greek Septuagint (though Jerome was doubtful of their doctrinal value and left four untranslated, so the versions incorporated into the Vulgate are actually Old Latin), and all would have been regarded by early medieval readers as standard components of the Old Testament. In *De doctrina christiana* II.13 Augustine enumerates forty-four books of the Old Testament, including all six of the deuterocanonical books mentioned above, plus twenty-seven books of the New Testament. This is the same number and selection of books approved by the Council of Hippo (393) and the Third Council of Carthage (397), and the same adopted by Cassiodorus (*Institutiones* I.13) and Isidore (*Etymologiae* VI.ii.34–50), and this is consequently the Biblical canon most Anglo-Saxons would have recognized (Bruce 1983: 66–7). Irish theologians, by contrast, were partial to a canon of forty-five Old Testament books, since this number, when added to the twenty-seven New Testament books, yields a total of seventy-two, a favourite number among Irish exegetes. The Book of Lismore recension of the *Evernew Tongue* claims that there are not only seventy-two languages in the world but precisely this same number of human races; troops of angels; seats in God's mansion; wandering stars in the heavens; manners of torment in hell; species of birds, serpents, sea-beasts, fruits and animals of the forest; and kinds of melodies sung by the leaves and blossoms of the tree Nathaban in the land of the Hebrews to the south of Mount Zion (Stokes 1905: 118–19, 122–3, 126–7, 128–9, 132–3).

The deuterocanonical books, at any rate, were very much a part of the Anglo-Saxon Bible, and to judge from the frequency with which they were quoted and translated they received ample attention from English writers. Ælfric accordingly translated portions of Judith and Maccabees, Judith was rendered into Old English verse, Bede was the first Latin theologian anywhere to write a commentary on Tobit, and Ælfric's *Letter to the Monks of Eynsham* (§74) stipulates that Biblical lections for the Night Office in late September and early October are to be taken from Tobit, Judith, Esdras and Maccabees (Jones 1998: 146–7). It has even been argued that the Latin prologue to Sirach served as a model for the letter on educational reform which King Alfred affixed to his translation of the *Cura pastoralis*, since both texts discuss in a strikingly similar manner a period of glorious accomplishment in the nation's early history, a lamentable decline in learning, and the author's desire to initiate a programme of reform through an act of translation (Discenza 1998).

But apart from the size and constitution of the canon, the very concept of 'Biblical literature' was considerably more flexible in the early Middle Ages than it is today, so that many works now classed somewhat pejoratively as apocrypha or pseudepigrapha would have had a welcome place on an Anglo-Saxon bookshelf right next to the Psalter and the Gospels. In spite of the condemnations levelled against such books in the sixth-century as *Pseudo-Gelasian Decree* and Charlemagne's *Admonitio generalis* (789), apocryphal texts enjoyed a wide readership throughout the British Isles and were copied prolifically. The *Gospel of Nicodemus* and *Gospel of Pseudo-Matthew*, for instance, both products of the post-apostolic era that underwent extensive revision and elaboration in the early Middle Ages, were well known in England by the eleventh century, and both were translated into Old English on more than one occasion (Hall 1990, 1996; Clayton 1998: 18–23, 153–209). Multiple redactions of the *Visio Pauli*, a Latin version of the Greek *Apocalypse of Paul* that recounts St Paul's fantastic otherworld voyage, were likewise produced in Britain and Ireland, and an Old English translation survives in a mid-eleventh-century manuscript from Kent (Healey 1978).

In addition to works such as these which might be classed as Biblically inspired ecclesiastical fiction, there is also a substantial body of what might be termed para-Biblical material that was current in England at this time: isolated bits of pseudo-factual lore with putative links to the Bible but which circulated in patterns independent of Biblical books. The Old English prose *Solomon and Saturn* and *Adrian and Ritheus* dialogues are uncommonly rich repositories of such para-Biblical trivia, with surprising and decidedly non-Biblical answers to questions about matters such as the height of Adam (116 inches), the number of his children (thirty sons and thirty daughters), the name of the city where the sun rises in the morning (Iaiaca), the identity of the first person who spoke to a dog (St Peter) and the reason why the sea is salty (because when Moses threw the tablets containing the ten commandments into the sea, his salty tears flooded into it as well). A memorable example of this type of learning is the pair of questions in *Solomon and Saturn* 8–9 concerning the physical composition of Adam's body:

8. Tell me the substance from which Adam, the first man, was made.
    I tell you, from eight pounds' weight.

9. Tell me what they are called.

    I tell you, the first was a pound of earth from which his flesh was made. The second
    was a pound of fire; from this his blood was red and hot. The third was a pound of
    wind; from this his breath was given. The fourth was a pound of cloud; from this
    his instability of mind was given. The fifth was a pound of grace; from this was
    given his understanding and thought. The sixth was a pound of blossoms; from this
    was given the variety of his eyes. The seventh was a pound of dew; from this he got
    sweat. The eighth was a pound of salt; from this his tears were salty. (Cross and
    Hill 1982: 67–8)

This instance of the apocryphal theme known as 'Adam octipartite' or 'microcosmic
Adam' has its roots not in the canonical Christian scriptures, of course, but in the
Slavonic apocalypse known as *II Enoch*, a midrashic work of the first century AD which
may also be the ultimate source for the question immediately preceding this one in
the *Solomon and Saturn* dialogue on the derivation of Adam's name from four stars
whose Greek names begin with the letters A, D, A, M (in their semi-corrupt Latinized
forms Arthox, Dux, Arotholem, Minsymbrie). Questions like these which transmit
apocryphal learning of various kinds are positioned in the dialogue right next to questions involving legitimate Biblical knowledge (e.g. How long did Adam live? How
long did Noah's flood last?) with no attempt to distinguish between the two, a method
of arrangement that has the effect of annulling the distinction between 'Biblical' and
'apocryphal'.

In their efforts to master the Biblical text, English readers naturally turned to the
Fathers for assistance, but the patristic sources available for consultation in England
were generally quite limited before the late eleventh century, at least by comparison
with contemporary centres on the continent. Remarkably, fewer than two dozen manuscripts survive written in pre-Conquest Anglo-Caroline minuscule containing a
single work by Augustine, Ambrose, Jerome or Gregory (Ker 1960: 8), and even the
best-known library bequest of the post-Conquest period – the donation of sixty-six
books to Exeter Cathedral by Bishop Leofric in 1072 – includes no texts at all by the
first three of these four Latin Fathers (although it does include a copy each of Gregory's
Dialogi and *Cura pastoralis*) (Lapidge 1994: 132–9). There were of course particular
times and places where the absorption of patristic learning reached dramatic levels of
concentration – one thinks first of Bede's Wearmouth–Jarrow and Theodore's Canterbury, perhaps – but these are by no means the rule, and it is misleading to think
of any kind of sustained continuum of intellectual activity stretching across both sides
of the Humber from one end of the period to the other drawing on a standard reper-
tory of patristic literature. Instead it is closer to the truth to say that patristic learning developed fitfully and unevenly in England, attaining a sophisticated level only
in the hands of a few select individuals who had access to extraordinary book collections built up over time at great expense. One has only to realize that there are no
complete extant pre-Conquest English copies of Augustine's *De Genesi ad litteram* or
De civitate Dei, Jerome's *In Hieremiam* or *In Ezechielem*, or Ambrose's *De fide* or *In evan-*

gelium Lucae to appreciate that patristic scholarship was a restricted and difficult enterprise until the Norman restaffing of English scriptoria brought with it a redefinition of scholarly tastes and a fresh infusion of books from the continent.

A small problem with this set of claims is that a learned Anglo-Saxon such as Aldhelm or Æthelwold would not necessarily have used the phrase 'Fathers of the church' to apply exclusively to the four Latin doctors named above, since this narrow application of the category *patres* was not well established until after the Anglo-Saxon period, and early English writers would have certainly accepted as 'Fathers' other Greek and Latin authors who shared in the formation of Western theological and exegetical traditions. Bede, in his *Expositio in Lucae evangelium*, was apparently the earliest writer to fix upon Ambrose, Augustine, Gregory and Jerome as the four leading doctors of the church, but this list was not to become broadly canonized until late in the eleventh century, when it began to gain favour as an enumerative standard modelled on the four evangelists and the four major prophets (Hurst 1960: 7; Webber 1997: 193). Ælfric's acknowledgement in the Latin preface to his First Series of *Catholic Homilies* that the authors who exerted the greatest influence on him are Augustine, Jerome, Bede, Gregory, Smaragdus and to a lesser extent Haymo is intended not as an endorsement of a particular ranking of patristic authorities, but rather as an index of his major sources in the forms in which he encountered them, in this case individual sermons by the first four writers (mediated, probably, through Paul the Deacon's Homiliary) and the Frankish compilations of patristic materials by the last two writers (Hill 1992). To speak of 'church Fathers' at any point in the Middle Ages without speaking of Augustine, however, would have been utterly unthinkable, so in the brief remarks that follow I will begin with Augustine, then move on to consider some aspects of the reception of the other three major Latin doctors – Jerome, Ambrose and Gregory – and along the way comment on the relevance of two other writers, Quodvultdeus of Carthage and Caesarius of Arles, to this dimension of Anglo-Saxon learning.

Because no one in Western Europe had access to a substantially complete collection of Augustine's writings before the twelfth century, it is to be expected that only a portion of Augustine's vast output was known in pre-Conquest England. At least parts of Augustine's *Confessiones* must have been available in England in the early eighth century – Bede, at any rate, quotes from the *Confessiones* in four of his works, including his commentary on Genesis, where on eight occasions he quotes from the probing analysis of time and eternity in books 12–13 (Kelly 1990) – but whether through a lapse in the book trade or through the destruction of libraries wrought by the Vikings, there is no evidence for this work's circulation from the mid-ninth to the late eleventh century, and the earliest surviving English copies are in post-Conquest manuscripts based on exemplars imported from Flanders (Webber 1996, 1997: 201). Similarly, although the *De doctrina christiana* was known to Bede, who draws on it for the opening chapter of his *De schematibus et tropis* and who incorporates a passage from the end of book 3 into the introduction to his commentary on the Apocalypse, this work all but disappeared from English libraries and scriptoria for a full two centuries before it came to light again at the end of the eleventh century (Gorman 1985: 19; Parkes 1997: 12–13). The *Soliloquia* is another Augustinian work that must have been known fairly early on, since King Alfred translated it into Old English, but the earliest surviving English manuscript of the Latin original was written on the continent after Alfred's time and was not certainly in England until the eleventh century (Rella 1980: 15). Ælfric was of course an avid student of Augustine and had thoroughly digested a significant cross-section of the corpus of Augustine's sermons and scriptural commentaries. In a late homily on 'The Servant's Failure to Forgive' based largely on Augustine's *Sermo* 83, Ælfric even makes a point of acknowledging his debt when he writes that 'Her is mucel andgit eow monnum to witenne, and we nimæð herto to ðissere trahtnunge Augustinum ðone wisæ, ðe we wæl truwiæð' ('There is much knowledge for you men to know here, and we rely for this commentary on Augustine the wise, whom we greatly trust') (Irvine 1993: 38, lines 48–50).

Today there is a great temptation to think of Augustine fundamentally as a philosopher and theologian, a profound thinker whose most lasting contributions to intellectual history are his treatises on free will, grace, the Trinity and the nature of the human soul, but it is worth recalling that during the Middle Ages he was also an important source for knowledge about medicine and natural science. In one of his Gospel homilies, for instance, Bede looks to Augustine's *De diversis quaestionibus* for an allegorical interpretation of the number forty-six (the number of years it took to build the temple), which Augustine explains in terms of the developmental stages of the human embryo:

> This number of years [forty-six] is also most apt for the perfecting of our Lord's [physical] body. Writers on natural history tell us that the form of the human body is completed within this number of days. During the first six days after conception it has a likeness to milk; during the following nine days it is changed to blood; next, in twelve [days] it becomes solid; during the remaining eighteen [days] it is formed into the perfect features of all its members; and after this, during the time remaining until birth, it increases in size. Six plus nine plus twelve plus eighteen make forty-five. If to this we add one, that is the day on which the body, divided into its separate members, begins to grow, we find the same number of days in the building up of our Lord's body as there were [years] in the construction of the temple. (Martin and Hurst 1991: 8).

This may not be the passage that leaps to our minds as a specimen of quintessentially Augustinian thought, but it is nevertheless indicative of Augustine's importance as a transmitter of ancient Greek medical knowledge, and in fact a closely analogous statement on the development of the embryo, once again within the context of an exposition of the symbolism of the number forty-six, is found in the *Laterculus Malalianus* attributable to Archbishop Theodore, who modelled his account on the very same passage in Augustine's *De diversis quaestionibus* (Stevenson 1995: 138–9, 196–7).

One of the difficulties in accounting for the reception of Augustine in Anglo-Saxon England is that he was such a dominant figure in the early Christian church that many works by lesser-known authors eventually came to circulate spuriously under his name, which in most cases meant that the true author's identity lapsed into obscurity. One writer who fell into this trap is Augustine's late contemporary Quodvultdeus of Carthage, who during the 430s composed thirteen catechetical sermons that are almost never properly attributed to him in manuscript. Bede and Ælfric were both familiar with a long sermon by Quodvultdeus entitled *Adversus quinque haereses*, a polemical attack against the five enemies of the Christian church (the pagans, Jews, Manicheans, Sabellians and Arians), but both thought this sermon was by Augustine, and it was not until the twentieth century that Quodvultdeus' name once more became reattached to his own work. Another victim of this habit of misattribution was Caesarius of Arles, whose sermons are often transmitted in early English manuscripts anonymously or under Augustine's name. A typical example is the copy of Caesarius's *Sermo* 220 in Dublin, Trinity College Library 174 (Salisbury, this part s. xi$^{4/4}$), fols 98v–99r, where it is introduced by the erroneous rubric 'Item sermo sancti Augustini de sancto Stephano' ('Another sermon by St Augustine on St Stephen'). Likewise, an unprinted sermon in Worcester, Cathedral Library, F. 92 (Worcester, s. xi^2), fols 63r–64r, beginning 'Legimus primum parentem nostrum Adam' ('We read that our first parent Adam'), based in part on Caesarius's *Sermo* 171, is falsely labelled 'Item sermo sancti Augustini episcopi' ('Another sermon by St Augustine the bishop'). These examples are late but are representative of a long tradition of misrepresentation which among Anglo-Saxon writers goes back at least to Boniface, who twice quotes from Caesarius in his correspondence, although in both cases he claims to be taking his information from Augustine (Levison 1946: 140, n. 7). The lesson here is simply that medieval readers who thought they were reading Augustine were not always accurately informed, and of course this same problem extends to an enormous number of works that came to be wrongly ascribed to Bede, Ambrose, Isidore and other established authorities who had widely recognizable names.

Even if their author's true identity was not always known, however, Caesarius' sermons were routinely plundered by Anglo-Saxon homilists, and there is good reason to count him among the *patres* who profoundly influenced English preaching and sermon-writing in the tenth and eleventh centuries. Over twenty-five Old English homilies, including ten by Ælfric, are partly based on sermons by Caesarius, who furnished Anglo-Saxon homilists with vivid descriptions of Doomsday, stern warnings against the evils of drunkenness and stirring admonitions to repent (Trahern 1976, 1986). Whereas English readers were more liable to turn to Augustine, Ambrose or Gregory for weighty expositions of doctrinal matters, they tended to look to Caesarius for colourful stories and simple moralizing lessons such as those he had originally addressed to the peasants living in his own diocese in south-east Gaul during the early sixth century. Thus Blickling Homily 10, for Rogationtide Wednesday, borrows a chilling exemplum from Caesarius's *Sermo* 31, *De elemosinis*, to drive home the theme that we must abandon our love of worldly things, especially now that the end of time is near. Here the homilist's teaching that it is folly to value earthly possessions leads to a macabre anecdote about a prosperous and worldly man who comes to realize the error of his misplaced devotion only too late, at the moment when his grieving kinsman, now returning to the grave, is confronted by the accusing voice of the decaying body:

> Then the bones of the dead man called to him and thus said, 'Why have you come here to see us? Now you can see here a bit of dust and the residue of worms where previously you saw a purple garment interwoven with gold. Behold there now dust and dry bones where before you saw limbs after flesh's kind, fair to look upon. O my friend and kinsman, be mindful of this, and convince yourself that you are now what I once was, and after a time you shall be what I am now. Remember this, and know that my riches that I once had are all vanished and come to nought, and my dwellings are decayed and perished. But turn to yourself and incline your heart to counsel, and merit that your prayers be acceptable to God almighty'. (Morris 1967: 112)

This haunting theme, known as 'the dry bones speak', is adapted for use in two other Old English homilies (Vercelli 13 and Irvine 7; see Cross 1957 and Irvine 1993: 183–6), and can ultimately be traced to an ancient Roman *memento mori* distich that happens to be preserved in the Latin epitaph which Alcuin fashioned for himself shortly before his death in 804, a portion of which reads 'Quod nunc es fueram, famosus in orbe, viator, / Et quod nunc ego sum, tuque futuris eris' ('What thou art now, famous in the world, I have been, traveller, / And what I am now, thou wilt be in the future') (Wallach 1959: 256, 264). The original Roman distich, which adopts the rhetorical stance of an address by an entombed body to a passing wayfarer who pauses at its sepulchre to read the inscription, has simply been drawn out into a moralizing exemplum by Caesarius and then refigured by the Old English homilist as an address from a body to its kinsman.

Of the church Fathers read by the Anglo-Saxons, Jerome stands out as the one whose exegetical methods most persistently call into question problems concerning language and individual word meanings (today Jerome would be classed as a staunch philologist), and a branch of learning which he was largely responsible for bequeathing to the Anglo-Saxons is the science of etymology. The interpretations of names which Jerome first systematically codified in his *Liber interpretationis hebraicorum nominum* and *Quaestiones hebraicae in Genesim et in libros Regum* are frequently echoed in Anglo-Saxon literature, as in Ælfric's statement that the name Peter means *oncnawende* 'acknowledging' (Jerome's term is *agnoscens*) or in the characterization of Seth in *Genesis A* 1145 as *sædberend*, from the Hieronymian etymology of Seth as *semen* 'seed' (Robinson 1993: 187, 196–8). Jerome's preoccupation with language fuelled his reputation as an exegete interested primarily in the literal or historical sense of scripture. Among the works Bede claims to have authored is a compilation of excerpts from Isaiah, Daniel, the twelve prophets and a portion of Jeremiah, with chapter divisions taken *ex tractatu beati Hieronimi* (*HE* V.24). Bede was apparently acquainted with nearly the entire corpus of Jerome's Biblical commentaries, as well as his treatise against Rufinus, and a substantial number of Jerome's letters are quoted by Bede and Aldhelm (Laistner 1952: 242, 246, 251). The glosses collected in the Leiden Glossary also reveal that Jerome's commentary on Matthew and his *De viris inlustribus* were among the books studied at the Canterbury school of Theodore and Hadrian (Lapidge 1996b: 150–2), and the Canterbury commentaries on the Pentateuch and Gospels draw repeatedly on Jerome for information regarding literal and textual matters such as the sevenfold punishment of Cain, the age of Ishmael at the time he was cast out with his mother Agar, and the tripartite division of the soul (Bischoff and Lapidge 1994: 203–4). Many of Jerome's works appear to have been unknown in England during the early period, but by the early twelfth century the libraries at Christ Church and St Augustine's, Canterbury, together could claim a virtually complete set of his writings (James 1903: 38–40, 219–21).

Of the four great Latin doctors, Ambrose was evidently least well known to the Anglo-Saxons. Some twenty-nine of his compositions (not counting individual hymns or epistles) survive in English manuscripts prior to the twelfth century, although predictably the majority of these date towards the end of the period. Disregarding hymns and extracts from *In Lucam* that circulated in versions of Paul the Deacon's Homiliary, only six Ambrose manuscripts survive that were either owned or produced in England before the eleventh century. Another twenty-two date between s. xi[in] and s. xi/xii, of which seventeen are post-Conquest (Bankert et al. 1997). These compositions include a range of works on exegetical, dogmatic, moral and ascetic topics, including the influential *Hexameron*, a serial commentary on the six days of creation which employs the allegorical methods of Philo and Origen. The concept of *mens absentia cogitans* in *The Wanderer* has been thought to derive from Ambrose's theory of the flight of the soul as set forth in the *Hexameron* (Clemoes 1969), and the *Hexameron* has also been identified as a plausible source for the allegorical description of the nest in *The Phoenix* (Gaebler 1880; Trahern 1963: 51–7). Ambrose's *Hexameron* and commentary on Luke were both important sources for Bede's commentaries on Genesis and Luke (Laistner 1957: 128). His numerous works on virginity are especially well represented in late Anglo-Saxon and early Anglo-Norman manuscripts; his earliest treatise on this topic, *De virginibus ad Marcellinam*, was an important model for Aldhelm's prose *De virginitate* (Lapidge and Herren 1979: 56–7). As the originator of the great tradition of 'Ambrosian' hymnody, Ambrose also made a profound contribution to early English liturgical practice as embodied in the several Anglo-Saxon witnesses to the 'Old' and 'New Hymnal'. Bede wrote a modest corpus of hymns on various feasts of the liturgical year and on the six days of creation, all in the Ambrosian metre of iambic dimetre and all demonstrably in imitation of Ambrose's compact style (Lapidge 1996a: 328–30); and both the *Regularis concordia* and Ælfric's *Letter to the Monks of Eynsham* call for Ambrose's hymns to be sung on particular occasions (Milfull 1996: 24–5; Jones 1998: 114–15, 160–3).

As sponsor of the Augustinian mission of 597 and apostle of the English church, Gregory the Great was by far the most intensively studied church Father in Anglo-Saxon England and the only one whose entire literary and exegetical oeuvre (save perhaps for the fragmentary homilies on the Canticle of Canticles) could be located in English libraries, though not necessarily all in the same library at once. Bede, who devoted one of the longest chapters of his *Historia ecclesiastica* to an appraisal of Gregory's life and work (*HE* II, 1), knew all of Gregory's works except his *Epistolae*, and even these must have been available in England by the mid-eighth century, since Boniface sent a set which he had himself transcribed in Rome to Archbishop Egbert of York (Laistner 1957: 129; Gneuss 1996a: 664). Two of Gregory's works, the *Cura pastoralis* and *Dialogi*, were selected by King Alfred to serve as foundational docu-ments for his ninth-century educational reform, and the fact that Alfred translated the first of these himself suggests he had a personal interest in Gregory's writings, in this case a manual on the moral, educational and social responsibilities of the ideal Christian administrator, a category that includes kings as well as bishops. The *Cura pastoralis* in particular has a strong claim for being known in England since the advent of Roman literacy, as the Metrical Preface to Alfred's Old English translation of the *Cura pastoralis* informs us that Augustine brought a copy of this book with him when he arrived in England:

> þis ærendgewrit   Agustinus
> ofer sealtne sæ   suðan brohte
> iegbuendum,   swa hit ær fore
> adihtode   dryhtnes cempa
> Rome papa.
> (Dobbie 1942: 110)

Augustine brought this work from the south over the salt sea to the island-dwellers, exactly as the Lord's champion, the pope of Rome, had previously set it out. (Keynes and Lapidge 1983: 126)

Gregory's forty *Homiliae in Evangelia*, which circulated both as an independent collection and as individual readings in many medieval homiliaries (thirty-two of the forty were included in Paul the Deacon's Homiliary, for instance), were quite possi-bly the most influential of all Gregory's works in Anglo-Saxon England. Ælfric mod-elled portions of his own homilies on thirty-three of Gregory's Gospel homilies (Förster 1894: 1–17; Smetana 1959: 182, 186–98, 201–2; Pope 1967–8: 1.168; Oetgen 1982; Godden 2000: liii). Four of Gregory's Gospel homilies also provided material for entries in the *Old English Martyrology* on Saints Emiliana (5 January), Cassius (29 June), Processus and Martinianus (2 July) and Felicitas (23 November) (Cross 1985a: 232–3, 1985b: 107), while a passage from Gregory's *Dialogi* lies behind the entry for Benedict of Nursia (21 March) (Cross 1985a: 245–6), and the *Moralia in Iob* is at least the ultimate source for a portion of the entry on the Decollation of John the Baptist (29 August) (Cross 1975: 156–7, 1985a: 246). The early English devotion to Gregory is nowhere more emphatically expressed than the eighth-century Whitby *Life*, which asserts that Gregory's ties to the English are so intimate that on Doomsday, when all the races of the world assemble for judgement and each race is presented to God by its own apostolic sponsor, the English will be brought forward by Gregory himself, whom the Whitby biographer reverently calls *apostolicum nostrum sanctum Gregorium* (Colgrave 1968: 82–3).

Assessments of Anglo-Saxon learning tend to vacillate between pessimistic claims for near-universal illiteracy on the one hand and exaggerated praise for the intellectual achievements of pioneering scholars such as Theodore and Aldhelm on the other. Clearly a balanced view of the whole picture lies somewhere between these two extremes. Many patristic works now deemed milestones of Biblical interpretation or Christian theology were absent from Anglo-Saxon libraries, yet there are several authentic sermons by Augustine that are today known only from copies in early English manuscripts (Lambot 1954). For much of the period English clerics could claim no great proficiency in Latin and were relatively ignorant of patristic literature, yet Bede's commentaries and Ælfric's homilies are by any standard remarkable feats of erudition that had a lasting impact. Most Anglo-Saxons surely never owned or read a Bible, yet no history of the medieval Bible would be complete without serious attention to the Codex Amiatinus, the Lindisfarne Gospels and the Canterbury commentaries on the Pentateuch and the Gospels. The terrain of early English Biblical and pastristic learning, in other words, was marked by an erratic and complex arrangement of soaring peaks and hollow valleys, some of which are by now well charted, while others are in dire need of a fresh survey.

REFERENCES

Primary sources

Bischoff, Bernhard and Michael Lapidge 1994. *Biblical Commentaries from the Canterbury School of Theodore and Hadrian.* Cambridge Studies in Anglo-Saxon England 10. Cambridge.

Clayton, Mary 1998. *The Apocryphal Gospels of Mary in Anglo-Saxon England.* Cambridge Studies in Anglo-Saxon England 26. Cambridge.

Colgrave, Bertram 1927. *The Life of Bishop Wilfrid by Eddius Stephanus.* Cambridge.

—— 1968. *The Earliest Life of Gregory the Great by an Anonymous Monk of Whitby.* Cambridge.

—— and R. A. B. Mynors, eds 1969. *Bede's Ecclesiastical History of the English People.* Oxford Medieval Texts. Oxford.

Crawford, S. J. 1969. *The Old English Version of the Heptateuch, Ælfric's Treatise on the Old and New Testament and his Preface to Genesis.* Early English Text Society, o.s. 160. London, 1922. Repr. with the text of two additional manuscripts transcribed by N. R. Ker, 1969.

Cross, James E. and Thomas D. Hill 1982. *The Prose Solomon and Saturn and Adrian and Ritheus.*

McMaster Old English Studies and Texts 1. Toronto, Buffalo and London.

Dobbie, Elliott Van Kirk 1942. *The Anglo-Saxon Minor Poems.* Anglo-Saxon Poetic Records 6. New York.

Godden, Malcolm 2000. *Ælfric's Catholic Homilies. Introduction, Commentary and Glossary.* EETS, s.s. 18. Oxford.

Healey, Antonette DiPaolo 1978. *The Old English Vision of St Paul.* Speculum Anniversary Monographs 2. Cambridge, MA.

Hurst, D. 1960. *Bedae expositio in Lucae evangelium.* Corpus Christianorum Series Latina 120. Turnhout.

Irvine, Susan 1993. *Old English Homilies from MS Bodley 343.* Early English Text Society, o.s. 302. Oxford.

Jones, Christopher A. 1998. *Ælfric's Letter to the Monks of Eynsham.* Cambridge Studies in Anglo-Saxon England 24. Cambridge.

Keynes, Simon and Michael Lapidge 1983. *Alfred the Great: Asser's Life of King Alfred and Other Contemporary Sources.* Harmondsworth.

Lapidge, Michael and Michael Herren 1979. *Aldhelm: The Prose Works.* Cambridge and Totowa, NJ.

Liuzza, R. M. 2000. *The Old English Version of the Gospels. Vol. II: Notes and Glossary*. EETS, o.s. 314. Oxford.

Martin, Lawrence T. and David Hurst 1991. *Bede the Venerable. Homilies on the Gospels. Book Two. Lent to the Dedication of the Church*. Cistercian Studies Series 111. Kalamazoo.

Morris, R[ichard] 1967. *The Blickling Homilies of the Tenth Century*. Early English Text Society, o.s. 58, 63, 73. London, 1874–80; repr. 1967.

Plummer, Charles 1896. *Venerabilis Baedae Opera Historica*. 2 vols. Oxford.

Pope, John 1967–8. *Homilies of Ælfric. A Supplementary Collection*. 2 vols. Early English Text Society, o.s. 259–60. London.

Stevenson, Jane 1995. *The 'Laterculus Malalianus' and the School of Archbishop Theodore*. Cambridge Studies in Anglo-Saxon England 14. Cambridge.

Stokes, Whitley 1905. 'The Evernew Tongue'. *Ériu* 2, 96–162.

Symons, Thomas, Sigrid Spath, Maria Wegener and Kassius Hallinger 1984. *Regularis Concordia Anglicae Nationis*. Corpus Consuetudinum Monasticarum VIII.3: Consuetudinum Saeculi X/XI/XII. Monumenta Non-Cluniacensia. Siegburg.

Secondary sources

Bankert, Dabney Anderson, Jessica Wegmann and Charles D. Wright 1997. *Ambrose in Anglo-Saxon England with Pseudo-Ambrose and Ambrosiaster*. Old English Newsletter Subsidia 25. Kalamazoo.

Bately, Janet M. 1982. 'Lexical Evidence for the Authorship of the Prose Psalms in the Paris Psalter'. *Anglo-Saxon England* 10: 69–95.

Biggs, Frederick M. 1991. 'Biblical Glosses in Ælfric's Translation of Genesis'. *Notes & Queries* 236: 286–92.

Brown, George Hardin 1987. *Bede the Venerable*. Boston.

Bruce, F. F. 1983. 'Tradition and the Canon of Scripture'. *The Authoritative Word: Essays on the Nature of Scripture*, pp. 59–84. Ed. Donald K. McKim. Grand Rapids.

Butler, Cuthbert 1924. *Benedictine Monachism: Studies in Benedictine Life and Rule*. 2nd edn. Cambridge and New York.

Clemoes, Peter 1969. '*Mens absentia cogitans* in *The Seafarer* and *The Wanderer*'. *Medieval Literature and Civilization: Studies in Memory of G. N. Garmonsway*, pp. 62–77. Eds Derek Pearsall and Ronald A. Waldron. London.

—— 1974. 'The Composition of the Old English Text'. *The Old English Illustrated Hexateuch: British Museum Cotton Claudius B. IV*, pp. 42–53. Eds C. R. Dodwell and Peter Clemoes. Early English Manuscripts in Facsimile 18. Copenhagen.

Cross, J. E. 1957. 'The Dry Bones Speak – A Theme in Some Old English Homilies'. *Journal of English and Germanic Philology* 56: 434–9.

—— 1975. 'Blickling Homily XIV and the Old English Martyrology on John the Baptist'. *Anglia* 93: 145–60.

—— 1985a. 'On the Library of the Old English Martyrologist'. *Learning and Literature in Anglo-Saxon England: Studies Presented to Peter Clemoes on the Occasion of his Sixty-fifth Birthday*, pp. 227–49. Eds Michael Lapidge and Helmut Gneuss. Cambridge.

—— 1985b. 'The Use of Patristic Homilies in the Old English Martyrology'. *Anglo-Saxon England* 14: 107–28.

Discenza, Nicole Guenther 1998. '"Wise Wealhstodas": The Prologue to Sirach as a Model for Alfred's Preface to the *Pastoral Care*'. *Journal of English and Germanic Philology* 97: 488–99.

Duchet-Suchaux, Monique and Yves Lefèvre 1984. 'Les noms de la Bible'. *Le Moyen Age et la Bible*, pp. 13–23. Eds Pierre Riché and Guy Lobrichon. Bible de tous les temps 4. Paris.

Fischer, Bonifatius 1985. *Lateinische Bibelhandschriften im frühen Mittelater*. Vetus Latina: Aus der Geschichte der lateinischen Bible 11. Freiburg.

Förster, Max 1894. 'Über die Quellen von Ælfrics exegetischen Homiliae Catholicae'. *Anglia* 16: 1–61.

Gaebler, H. 1880. 'Über die Autorschaft des angelsächsischen Gedichtes vom "Phönix"'. *Anglia* 3: 488–526.

Gneuss, Helmut 1996a. 'Anglo-Saxon Libraries from the Conversion to the Benedictine Reform'. *Angli e Sassoni al di qua e al di là del mare. 26 aprile–1° maggio 1984*, vol. 2, pp. 643–88. Settimane di studio de centro italiano di studi sull'alto medioevo XXXII. Spoleto, 1986. Repr. in Gneuss, *Books and Libraries in*

Early England, no. 2. Variorum Collected Studies Series 558.

——1996b. 'Liturgical Books in Anglo-Saxon England and their Old English Terminology'. *Learning and Literature in Anglo-Saxon England: Studies Presented to Peter Clemoes on the Occasion of his Sixty-fifth Birthday*, pp. 91–141. Eds Michael Lapidge and Helmut Gneuss. Cambridge, 1985, Repr. in Gneuss, *Books and Libraries in Early England*, no. 5. Variorum Collected Studies Series 558.

Gorman, M. M. 1985. 'The Diffusion of the Manuscripts of Saint Augustine's "De Doctrina Christiana" in the Early Middle Ages'. *Revue Bénédictine* 95: 11–24.

Hall, Thomas N. 1990. 'Gospel of Pseudo-Matthew'. *Sources of Anglo-Saxon Literary Culture: A Trial Version*, pp. 43–5. Eds Frederick M. Biggs, Thomas D. Hill and Paul E. Szarmach. Medieval and Renaissance Texts and Studies 74. Binghamton, NY.

——1996. 'The *Euangelium Nichodemi* and *Vindicta Saluatoris* in Anglo-Saxon England'. *Two Old English Apocrypha and their Manuscript Source: The Gospel of Nichodemus and The Avenging of the Saviour*, pp. 36–81. Ed. J. E. Cross. Cambridge Studies in Anglo-Saxon England 19. Cambridge.

Hill, Joyce 1992. 'Ælfric and Smaragdus'. *Anglo-Saxon England* 21: 203–37.

James, M. R. 1903. *The Ancient Libraries of Canterbury and Dover*. Cambridge.

Jost, Karl 1927. 'Unechte Ælfrictexte'. *Anglia* 51: 82–103, 177–219.

Kelly, Joseph F. 1990. 'Augustine, *Confessiones*'. *Sources of Anglo-Saxon Literary Culture: A Trial Version*, p. 71. Eds Frederick M. Biggs, Thomas D. Hill and Paul E. Szarmach. Binghamton, NY.

Ker, N. R. 1960. *English Manuscripts in the Century after the Norman Conquest*. Oxford.

Laistner, M. L. W. 1952. 'The Study of St Jerome in the Early Middle Ages'. *A Monument to Saint Jerome: Essays on Some Aspects of his Life, Works and Influence*, pp. 235–56. Ed. Francis X. Murphy. New York.

——1957. 'The Library of the Venerable Bede', *Bede: His Life, Times, and Writings*, pp. 237–66. Ed. A. H. Thompson. Oxford, 1935, Repr. *The Intellectual Heritage of the Early Middle Ages: Selected Essays*, pp. 117–49. Ed. Chester G. Starr. Ithaca, NY, 1957.

Lambot, C. 1954. 'La tradition manuscrite anglo-saxonne des sermons de saint Augustin'. *Revue Bénédictine* 64: 3–8.

Lapidge, Michael 1994. 'Surviving Booklists from Anglo-Saxon England'. *Learning and Literature in Anglo-Saxon England: Studies Presented to Peter Clemoes on the Occasion of his Sixty-fifth Birthday*, pp. 33–89. Eds Michael Lapidge and Helmut Gneuss. Cambridge, 1985. Repr. with revisions *Anglo-Saxon Manuscripts: Basic Readings*, pp. 87–167. Ed. Mary P. Richards. Basic Readings in Anglo-Saxon England 2; Garland Reference Library of the Humanities 1434. New York and London.

——1996a. *Bede the Poet*. The Jarrow Lecture 1993. Jarrow, 1994. Repr. Lapidge, *Anglo-Latin Literature 600–899*, pp. 313–38. London and Rio Grande.

——1996b. 'The School of Theodore and Hadrian'. *Anglo-Saxon England* 15 (1986): 45–72. Repr. Lapidge, *Anglo-Latin Literature 600–899*, pp. 141–68. London and Rio Grande.

Levison, Wilhelm 1946. *England and the Continent in the Eighth Century*. Oxford.

Liuzza, Roy Michael 1998. 'Who Read the Gospels in Old English?'. *Words and Works: Studies in Medieval English Language and Literature in Honour of Fred C. Robinson*, pp. 3–24. Eds Peter S. Baker and Nicholas Howe. Toronto, Buffalo and London.

Marsden, Richard 1991. 'Ælfric as Translator: The Old English Prose *Genesis*'. *Anglia* 109: 319–58.

——1994a. 'The Old Testament in Late Anglo-Saxon England: Preliminary Observations on the Textual Evidence'. *The Early Medieval Bible: Its Production, Decoration and Use*, pp. 101–24. Ed. Richard Gameson. Cambridge Studies in Palaeography and Codicology. Cambridge.

——1994b. 'Old Latin Intervention in the Old English *Heptateuch*'. *Anglo-Saxon England* 23: 229–64.

——1995a. *The Text of the Old Testament in Anglo-Saxon England*. Cambridge Studies in Anglo-Saxon England 15. Cambridge.

——1995b. 'Theodore's Bible: The Pentateuch'. *Archbishop Theodore: Commemorative Studies on His Life and Influence*, pp. 236–54. Ed. Michael Lapidge. Cambridge Studies in Anglo-Saxon England 11. Cambridge.

——1998. '"Ask What I Am Called": The Anglo-Saxons and their Bibles'. *The Bible as Book: The*

Manuscript Tradition, pp. 145–76. Eds John L. Sharpe III and Kimberly Van Kampen. London.

—— 2000. 'Translation by Committee? The "Anonymous" Text of the Old English *Hexateuch*'. *The Old English Hexateuch: Aspects and Approaches*, pp. 41–89. Eds Rebecca Barnhouse and Benjamin C. Withers. Kalamazoo.

McGurk, Patrick 1961. *Latin Gospel Books from AD 400 to AD 800*. Publications de Scriptorium 5. Paris and Brussels.

Milfull, Inge B. 1996. *The Hymns of the Anglo-Saxon Church: A Study and Edition of the 'Durham Hymnal'*. Cambridge Studies in Anglo-Saxon England 17. Cambridge.

Mundó, A. 1950. 'Bibliotheca, Bible et lecture de carême d'après S. Benôit'. *Revue Bénédictine* 60: 65–92.

Oetgen, Jerome 1982. 'Another Source for Ælfric's Second Epiphany Homily (CH II, 3)'. *Notes & Queries* 227 [n.s. 29]: 198–9.

Parkes, M. B. 1997. '*Rædan, areccan, smeagan*: How the Anglo-Saxons Read'. *Anglo-Saxon England* 26: 1–22.

Pulsiano, Phillip 1995. 'Psalters'. *The Liturgical Books of Anglo-Saxon England*, pp. 61–85. Ed. Richard W. Pfaff. Old English Newsletter Subsidia 23. Kalamazoo.

Raith, J. 1952. 'Ælfric's Share in the Old English Pentateuch'. *Review of English Studies* n.s. 3: 305–14.

Ray, Roger 1982. 'What Do We Know about Bede's Commentaries?'. *Recherches de théologie ancienne et médiévale* 49: 5–20.

Rella, F. A. 1980. 'Continental Manuscripts Acquired for English Centres in the Tenth and Early Eleventh Centuries: A Preliminary Check-list'. *Anglia* 98: 107–16.

Robinson, Fred C. 1968 (1993). 'The Significance of Names in Old English Literature'. *Anglia* 86 (1968): 14–58. Repr. in Robinson (1993), *The Tomb of Beowulf and Other Essays on Old English*, pp. 185–218. Cambridge, MA, and Oxford.

Smetana, Cyril 1959. 'Ælfric and the Early Medieval Homiliary'. *Traditio* 15: 163–204.

Trahern, Joseph B., Jr 1963. '"The Phoenix": A Critical Edition'. PhD diss. Princeton, NJ.

—— 1976. 'Caesarius of Arles and Old English Literature: Some Contributions and a Recapitulation'. *Anglo-Saxon England* 5: 105–19.

—— 1986. 'Ælfric: More Sources for Two Homilies'. *American Notes & Queries* 24: 110–11.

Wallach, Luitpold 1959. *Alcuin and Charlemagne: Studies in Carolingian History and Literature*. Ithaca, NY.

Webber, Teresa 1996. 'The Diffusion of Augustine's Confessions in England during the Eleventh and Twelfth Centuries'. *The Cloister and the World: Essays in Medieval History in Honour of Barbara Harvey*, pp. 29–45. Eds John Blair and Brain Golding. Oxford.

—— 1997. 'The Patristic Content of English Book Collections in the Eleventh Century: Towards a Continental Perspective'. *Of the Making of Books: Medieval Manuscripts, their Scribes and Readers: Essays Presented to M. B. Parkes*, pp. 191–205. Eds P. R. Robinson and Rivkah Zim. Aldershot.

19

The Irish Tradition

Charles D. Wright

In 597, the same year Pope Gregory the Great's envoy Augustine arrived in Kent to evangelize the Anglo-Saxons, the Irish saint Columba (Colum Cille) died in Iona, an island monastery off the western coast of Scotland. Although the impetus for Columba's settlement in Iona had been spiritual (or political?) exile rather than missionary zeal, the Irish became deeply involved in the conversion of the Anglo-Saxons in 635, when Aidan was sent from Iona to minister to the fledgling Northumbrian church at the request of King Oswald, who had been baptized and instructed by the Irish while in exile during the reign of Edwin (Bede, *Historia ecclesiastica* [*HE*] III.3–5). Aidan was consecrated as bishop and given a site for a new monastery at the island of Lindisfarne, near Oswald's stronghold at Bamburgh on the Bernician coast. For the next three decades, as the successors of Augustine laboured in the south of England (Paulinus having abandoned York in 633), the conversion of much of the north and the early cultural formation of the English church in Northumbria and Mercia were dominated by Iona and its daughter house at Lindisfarne, where many of the first generation of northern English monks, priests and bishops were trained and educated (Campbell 1971; Bullough 1982; Mayr-Harting 1991; sporadic penetration of Irish monks and missionaries further south is documented by Campbell 1987 and Sims-Williams 1990: 105–8). Lindisfarne was governed by Irish abbots until 664, when Colmán retired to Iona and thence to Inishbofin after the Synod of Whitby, taking with him those of his countrymen who were unwilling to accept the synod's decision in favour of the Roman Easter, as well as a group of English monks who were eventually given their own foundation in Ireland at Mag Éo ('Mayo of the Saxons') (*HE* III.25–6, IV.4; Chadwick 1963).

The coincidence of events in 597 is, of course, just that; and while it is tempting to see it as symbolic of the contrast between the Irish and Roman missions and the ultimate eclipse of the former by the latter, we should be cautious in evaluating the sources which give the impression that the early English church was starkly polarized between them. Bede, whose *Historia ecclesiastica* is our primary documentary witness to the period of the missions, was an apologist for the Romanist party that had prevailed at the Synod of Whitby. Bede's dramatic account of the synod (*HE* III.25) has memorably epitomized the opposition between the 'Roman' and 'Irish' missions; yet on Bede's own showing, the opposing parties at Whitby were not drawn up along strict ethnic or geographical lines. The southern Irish had already accepted the Roman calculation of Easter by about 632/3, and one of the Irish 'Romani' (as those who had conformed to Roman observance were called) named Rónán helped precipitate the controversy in Northumbria by disputing with Aidan's successor Fínán. Again, one of the most prominent Whitby Romanists was the Frankish bishop Agilbert, who, as Bede informs us (*HE* III.7), had for many years studied the Bible in Ireland. Oswiu's decision in favour of the Roman Easter would not, in any case, have expunged the formative spiritual and intellectual influences which some three decades of intensive Irish missionary activity and pastoral care had already fostered in the Northumbrian church. At Lindisfarne itself, the continuity of Irish traditions was assured through Oswiu's appointment (at Colmán's request) of Eata, who had been one of twelve English boys originally recruited by Aidan (*HE* III.26). By the time Bede published his history in 731, the remaining Irish churches had all adopted Roman practice; Iona, the last holdout, conformed in 716 through the efforts of Egbert, who had come from another Anglo-Saxon foundation in Ireland, Rath Melsigi (*HE* V.22).

In almost all respects apart from the Easter question, Bede's attitude towards the Irish was profoundly sympathetic, indeed grateful and admiring (cf. Pepperdene 1958; Goffart 1988: 309–13, 326–7). Two things above all impressed Bede about the Irish: their personal austerity and their scriptural learning. In the *Historia ecclesiastica* Bede reserved the term *continentia* (sometimes *magna continentia*) almost exclusively for Irish ascetics (Columba, Fursa, Aidan and Adamnán of Coldingham) or for their English followers (Chad and Cuthbert, as well as the Anglo-Saxon monks at Mayo). Rigorous ascetic and penitential practices were a hallmark of Irish spirituality (Gougaud 1927). The Irish presence in England and on the continent was due in no small measure to their conception of spiritual pilgrimage as a voluntary and permanent exile from one's homeland (Charles-Edwards 1976; Angenendt 1982). Fursa had come to East Anglia (*c*.630) on such a pilgrimage, founding a monastery at *Cnobheresburg* before moving on to Gaul (*HE* III.19). By the ninth century such impulses had been tempered by a new emphasis on monastic stability (Hughes 1987a), but as late as 891, according to the *Anglo-Saxon Chronicle*, three Irishmen arrived in Cornwall in a coracle without any oars, having set out from Ireland 'for the love of God' and caring not where they put to shore. The Old English poem *The Seafarer* has been plausibly interpreted as an Anglo-Saxon reflex of the ideal of spiritual pilgrimage (Whitelock 1950; Henry 1966; Ireland 1991).

Wherever Irish *peregrini* settled, they drew attention to themselves with their robust mortifications and regimens of prayer. A particularly bracing exercise involved immersion in cold rivers, which various Irish saints are said to have endured for long periods with their hands extended in the gesture of prayer known as the 'cross-vigil' (Ireland

1997). Both Cuthbert – that most 'Celtic' of Anglo-Saxon bishops (cf. Stancliffe 1989) – and the English visionary Dryhthelm (*HE* V.12) adopted this practice. The emphasis on individual ascesis and devotional expression in Irish spirituality manifested itself also in special forms of private prayer such as the breviate psalter (Bishop 1918: 195–6; Dumville 1972: 384–5, 396) and the 'lorica', an invocation of the Trinity against spiritual and physical dangers, characteristically expressed in litanic form with elaborate anatomical lists intended to assure that no limb or organ was left unnamed and thus potentially unprotected (Gougaud 1911–12). Anglo-Saxon prayer-books of the so-called Tiberius group (The Book of Cerne, The Book of Nunnaminster, and the Harley and Royal prayer-books) contain various prayers of Irish origin or inspiration (Hughes 1987b; Bestul 1986: 104–10; Mayr-Harting 1991: 181–6; Sims-Williams 1990: 273–327; Brown 1996: 137–8), including a breviate psalter and several prayers of the lorica type, such as the Lorica of Laidcenn (on which see Herren 1973). Loricas are also found among the marginalia of Cambridge, Corpus Christi College 41 (s. xi[1]), together with stanzas from the hymn of pseudo-Secundinus in praise of Patrick (headed by an invocation naming both Patrick and Brigit) for use as a charm (Grant 1979: 1–26). The Old English poem *A Journey Charm* in the same manuscript is arguably a lorica, and influence of the lorica tradition has been traced elsewhere in Old English poetry (Hill 1981).

The Anglo-Saxons also adopted the Irish custom of private penance with its attendant genre, the confessor's handbook or penitential (see Frantzen 1983; Bieler 1963). The Irish system of commutations was endorsed by Theodore of Canterbury, and a penitential which transmits his teachings, compiled by the self-styled *Discipulus Umbrensium*, refers to a *libellus Scottorum* which has been identified as the Penitential of Cummian. Theodore's teachings on penance were, in turn, rapidly transmitted to Ireland (Hughes 1987c: 61–3; Charles-Edwards 1995). Bede has an amusing story of one Irishman (Adamnán of Coldingham) who maintained a strict fast until the end of his life after his confessor (the Irish term was *anmcharae* 'soul-friend') had returned to Ireland and died without having told him he could stop (*HE* IV.25). The spiritual benefit of private confession found dramatic literary expression in a motif occurring in more than a dozen Old English confessional and homiletic texts and in the poem *Christ III* (lines 1301–11): it is better to confess one's sins before one man in this life, warns this 'penitential motif', than before God and the assembled hosts of angels, devils and men at the Last Judgement (see Godden 1973). The allusion to the three companies at Judgement is an unmistakable sign of Irish influence (Wright 1993: 85–8; Breeze 1994). Latin parallels for the motif as a whole have been found in a letter of Alcuin (no. 280, addressed to the monks of Ireland) and a sermon doubtfully attributed to Boniface (where the term *familiae* reflects a distinctively Irish formulation), to which may be added the following from the Hiberno-Latin *Catechesis Cracoviensis* 84: 'Inde devet unusquisque dare confessionem ad alterum qui potest discernere inter bonos et malos, aut sapientem, quam coram familie celi et terre in die judicii' ('On that account everyone ought to make confession to another who can discriminate among good persons and bad, or to a wise man, [rather] than before the hosts of heaven and earth on the Day of Judgement'; on this collection, see Amos 1990; Wright 1990b: 118–19).

The *magna continentia* of Irish saints such as Columba and Fursa opened a window to the next world. Adomnán devoted an entire book of his *Vita Columbae* to the angelic apparitions enjoyed by the saint, including visions of departing souls being conducted into heaven. Although this work was apparently unknown to Bede, he was familiar with a continental *Vita prima Sancti Fursei*, from which he excerpted part of Fursa's vision of heaven and hell (*HE* III.19). The author of the *Old English Martyrology* and Ælfric (*Catholic Homilies*, Second Series, Feria III in Letania Maiore) both related Fursa's vision (see Cross 1981: 178–80; Szarmach 1987). A more elaborate tour of the next world was that accorded the Anglo-Saxon layman Dryhthelm, which occurs in a context that is strongly suggestive of Irish influence (*HE* V.12). Dryhthelm recounted his vision to Hæmgisl, a monk of Melrose who later retired to Ireland to live a solitary life, and to the learned King Aldfrith, who had been instructed by the Irish (Ireland 1996). By then a monk inhabiting a cell near Melrose, Dryhthelm took up the Irish practice of penitential immersion. In both Fursa's and Dryhthelm's visions, devils are said to have recorded in a book their sinful 'thoughts, words, and deeds', a triad ubiquitous in Irish sources (Sims-Williams 1995a: 109–10). The same motif occurs in the vision of the thegn of Cenred, which Bede relates immediately after that of Dryhthelm, and here the devils claim the soul with the words *noster est iste*, closely similar to an account of the going-out of souls in the 'Three Utterances' sermon (*noster est ille uir*) (Colgrave and Mynors 1969: 500, n. 1; Sims-Williams 1990: 255). Rudolf Willard (1937: 160) believed that this sermon had been transmitted through 'the Celtic culture of the British Isles', and R. E. McNally (1979: 134–6) concluded independently that it was of Irish origin; the discovery of many additional Latin manuscripts has confirmed that it was especially popular in insular circles in the eighth and ninth centuries (Wright 1987a: 135–6), ultimately generating an Old Irish version and no fewer than four independent Old English versions (for these see especially Willard 1935; Bazire and Cross 1990: 116–23; Wack and Wright 1990).

Bede tells us (*HE* III.27) that English students flocked to Ireland not only to seek 'a more austere life' (*continentior uita*), but also to pursue Biblical studies (*diuina lectio*). The roll-call of Anglo-Saxon exchange students there includes Æthelhun and Æthelwine (*HE* III.27), Chad and Egbert (III.27, IV.3, V.9), Wihtberht (V.9), the two Hewalds (V.10) and Willibrord (V.10). We have little direct testimony as to the nature of Irish Biblical studies during this period. Aldhelm, who was in a position to know, refers in his letter to Heahfrith (who had spent six years in Ireland 'sucking the teat of wisdom') to instruction in 'the fourfold honeyed oracles of allegorical or rather tropological disputation of opaque problems in aetherial mysteries' (*Epistola ad Heahfridum*; trans. Lapidge and Herren 1979: 161–2), suggesting an emphasis on 'Alexandrian' methods; yet surviving Hiberno-Latin Biblical commentaries also show a remarkable interest in the literal, 'Antiochene' approach. If anything is typical of Irish exegetical methods, however, it is the complacent juxtaposition of alternative interpretations of passages from scripture and of explications *historialiter* with those *moraliter* and *spiritualiter* (Bischoff 1966–81a: 221–2). Hiberno-Latin psalm commentaries indebted to the Antiochene exegete Theodore of Mopsuestia (Ramsay 1912a, 1912b) are the most programatically literal, distinguishing two historical levels (the first referring to the time of David, the second to later Jewish history), but these also add moral and mystical senses (Ó Néill 1979; McNamara 1973, 1984, 1998; De Coninck 1999). This Irish fourfold scheme appears in the eighth-century *Glossa in Psalmos* in Vatican, Biblioteca Apostolica Pal. lat. 68, which preserves the colophon of a Northumbrian scribe named Edilbericht, and (with some modification) in the Alfredian prose Introductions to Psalms 1–50 in the *Paris Psalter* (Ó Néill 1981). Another somewhat surprising source of authority for early Irish exegesis was the British heresiarch Pelagius (Zimmer 1901; Frede 1961; Kelly 1978), whose commentary on the Pauline Epistles supplied the majority of Latin glosses in the Irish/Northumbrian manuscript Cambridge, Trinity College B. 10. 5 + London, British Library, Cotton Vitellius C. viii, dating from the first half of the eighth century (Lowe 1972: no. 133; Bishop 1964–8; Brown 1993a: 218); two Old English glosses in this manuscript show close similarities to the Irish Würzburg glosses (Ní Chatháin 1987: 192–6).

The Irish interest in historical explication of scripture was driven not so much by an avowed preference for 'Antiochene' exegesis (the use of Theodore of Mopsuestia's commentary on the Psalms, via an epitome of Julian of Eclanum's Latin translation, being a special case) as by an encyclopaedic *curiositas* that manifested itself in a fascination with literal details concerning Biblical persons, places and events (Bischoff 1966–81a: 222). Irish scholars mined the works of Jerome and Isidore of Seville for information regarding the meaning of Hebrew names and for synonyms in the 'three sacred languages' of Hebrew, Greek and Latin (McNally 1958). A regular feature of early Irish Gospel-books is the inclusion of glossaries of Hebrew names, a practice followed by the Anglo-Saxons (McGurk 1998; Szerwiniack 1994: 194). Isidore's *Etymologiae* became available in Ireland at a remarkably early date (see Bischoff 1966–81b; Herren 1996a; for a fragment of Glastonbury provenance in Irish script of *c*.680 × 700, see Carley and Dooley 1991). Known in Ireland as the 'Culmen', it was said in one legend to have been acquired in a trade for the Irish epic *Táin Bó Cualnge* (see Ó Máille 1921–3)!

Patristic authority was, moreover, freely supplemented by information gleaned from apocryphal writings for such literal details as the names of nameless Biblical figures (Bischoff 1966–81a: 215–17). The Irish were active in disseminating dialogues of the *Joca monachorum* type, which incorporated this kind of apocryphal lore and related literal-historical trivia such as Biblical 'firsts' (Wright 1987a: 137–9; Bayless 1998; Irish parallels for various items in the Old English *Prose Solomon and Saturn* and *Adrian and Ritheus* dialogues are noted by Cross and Hill 1982: 9–11 and Cross 1986: 79–80). The names of the wives of Noah and his sons listed in the *Prose Solomon and Saturn* and in *Genesis A* (lines 1543–8), for example, can be traced to Irish sources (Cross and Hill 1982: 86–7). Major gaps in the Biblical narrative (e.g. the fall of the rebel angels, the post-lapsarian lives of Adam and Eve and the infancy of Jesus) were made good from apocryphal sources such as the *Vita Adae* and Gospel of Thomas (see generally Dumville 1973; McNamara 1975; McNamara and Herbert 1989).

The Irish also had access to two apocryphal apocalypses that mapped the journey of souls after death and foretold the signs of the Last Judgement. The Seven Heavens apocryphon, the first of these, survives in a Latin epitome among Hiberno-Latin homiletic texts in Karlsruhe, Badische Landesbibliothek Aug. perg. 254 fols 153–213 (s. viii[ex]), the so-called *Apocrypha Priscillianistica* (see Wright 1990a, 1993: 64–6), but both Irish and Old English versions also exist, and the text was probably transmitted to Anglo-Saxon England by the Irish, whether directly or through contacts in insular missionary centres on the continent (Willard 1935; McNamara 1975: 141–3; Stevenson 1983; Bauckham 1993). Another item in the *Apocrypha Priscillianistica* cites the Apocalypse of Thomas, the source of the seven signs of Doomsday that appear in the Middle Irish *Saltair na Rann* ('Psalter of the Quatrains') and *Tenga Bithnua* ('The Evernew Tongue') (Bihlmeyer 1911: 555–6; Heist 1952; McNamara 1975: 128–33) and in four Old English sermons (Förster 1955; Biggs 1990a; Swan 1998). There is no evidence that any of these Old English sermons depends directly on an Irish or Hiberno-Latin version of Thomas, though one of the earliest manuscripts of the interpolated version (Vatican, Pal. lat. 220, s. ix[1]), written on the continent by an Anglo-Saxon scribe, contains Hiberno-Latin sermons (including the Three Utterances) and a probably Irish redaction of the *Visio Pauli* (Wright 1990c, 1993: 111–12).

Manuscript evidence for transmission of apocryphal material to England in conjunction with Hiberno-Latin writings is afforded by London, British Library, Royal 5 E. xiii, a mid-ninth-century Breton manuscript that was in England by the tenth century. This composite manuscript contains in its first part a variant text of yet another item from the *Apocrypha Priscillianistica*, and in the second part extracts from the *Collectio canonum Hibernensis*, a narrative concerning the siege of Jerusalem (introduced by further extracts from the *Hibernensis*), a Latin fragment closely related to the Book of Enoch ch. 106, and, in a slightly later hand, the Gospel of Nicodemus (Dumville 1973: 331; Biggs 1990b; Petitmengin 1993; Cross 1999: 72–4). In the tenth century Brittany was one major channel of transmission to Anglo-Saxon England of Hiberno-Latin texts, particularly penitentials (Frantzen 1983: 128–30; Dumville 1992a: 112–16, 1994; McKee 1999: 286–8). But at least one version of another apocryphal text, the 'Sunday Letter of Christ', was transmitted to England directly from Ireland (cf. Priebsch 1899; McNamara 1975: 60–3). This occurs in the Old English homilies Pseudo-Wulfstan XLIII and XLIV in association with reports of the post-mortem visions of an Irish deacon named Niall. We know from a letter of *c*.835 by Ecgred, bishop of Lindisfarne, that the Sunday Letter, along with other 'mendacious ravings concerning the Old and New Testaments' and accounts of Niall's visions, was being spread in Mercia in the early ninth century through a book belonging to an Anglo-Saxon priest named Pehtred (see Whitelock 1982; Lees 1985, 1990; Wright 1993: 221–4).

Aldhelm's letter concerning Heahfrith's studies in Ireland also mentions the grammatical and geometrical arts, as well as the 'twice-three scaffolds of the art of physics'

(Lapidge and Herren 1979: 161), a somewhat unusual categorization that was, however, common in Irish tradition (Bischoff 1966–81c). It seems unlikely that this abstract scheme was ever fully implemented in the Irish curriculum (see, however, Charles-Edwards 1998: 66–7 on Columbanus' early education); but other sources suggest that grammar and computus, at least, were intensively cultivated along with Biblical studies. Grammar was, of course, the foundation of *diuina lectio* (Irvine 1994: 286–7), and the Irish – for whom Latin was the 'white language of the scriptures' – were instrumental in the development of elementary Latin grammars based on Donatus but supplied with citations from Christian authors and paradigms of Christian words (see Holtz 1981, 1983; Law 1982a, 1982b; these authorities disagree, however, on the relative significance of Irish and Anglo-Saxon contributions to the tradition of 'insular' grammars). Irish scholars also employed a system of 'construe marks' to assist in parsing Latin texts (Draak 1957, 1967; for their possible relation to syntactical glosses found in Anglo-Saxon manuscripts, see Robinson 1973: 468; Korhammer 1980: 46). Several computistical works of Irish origin were known in Anglo-Saxon England (Jones 1943: 105–13); indeed, Bede's own computistical collection has been shown to derive from one compiled in south-east Ireland in 658 (Ó Cróinín 1983).

Computus, in turn, required and was aligned with investigations *de naturis rerum*: according to an Irish maxim, the five things known by the ecclesiastical scholar are the courses of the sun, moon, and sea, the days of the week and the feasts of the saints (Wright 1993: 57, n. 45). The Irish consulted patristic hexameral treatises and Isidore's *De natura rerum* for 'creation science', and their preoccupation with cosmology and sacred geography is reflected in a number of early Hiberno-Latin works, including Columba's (?) *Altus prosator* and Adomnán's *De locis sanctis*. Adomnán presented King Aldfrith with a copy of his work (*HE* V.15), and Bede incorporated substantial extracts from it in his history (*HE* V.16–17). Bede was also familiar with the Hiberno-Latin cosmological treatise *Liber de ordine creaturarum*, and indirectly through this work with parts of the Irish Augustine's *De mirabilibus sacrae scripturae*, which attempted to rationalize Biblical miracles as extensions of God's continuing 'governance' of physical nature (on these and other seventh-century Hiberno-Latin cosmological writings, see Smyth 1996). Alcuin was to cite from the *De mirabilibus* directly in his *Interrogationes et responsiones in Genesin* (MacGinty 1987: 79). Later Irish writings often embellish 'scientific' lore with apocryphal cosmology, as when Hiberno-Latin Genesis commentaries invariably state that God commanded the waters to congregate in the 'seventh part' of the earth – a detail drawn from 4 Ezra and echoed in the Old English 'Devil's Account of Hell' exemplum in Vercelli Homily IX (Wright 1993: 25–7, 185–7).

To what extent formal studies beyond elementary Latin grammar and *diuina lectio* (focused particularly on the Psalms) would have been cultivated in a missionary context in England itself is uncertain. According to Bede, the pupils of Aidan were expected to occupy themselves 'either with reading the scriptures or learning the psalms' (*HE* III.5), a modest enough requirement, and Pádraig P. Ó Néill (1991) has argued that Irish missionaries concentrated on pastoral care rather than scholarship. This is presumably why so many Anglo-Saxon students who, like Heahfrith, desired more advanced instruction sought it in Ireland itself (though Aldhelm himself had been taught by an Irish master at Malmesbury). The arrival of Theodore and Hadrian and the establishment of the school of Canterbury, however, offered a powerful domestic alternative to such monastic sabbaticals abroad, and Aldhelm loudly championed the superior instruction to be had at Canterbury, which was conspicuously strong in certain areas where the Irish were conspicuously weak (e.g. the study of Greek and quantitative metre: see Lapidge 1996a; Orchard 1994: 26). Aldhelm was thus a transitional figure, whose writings show traces (sometimes in parodic form) of his early education in the Irish tradition (Gwara 1989; Orchard 1994: 39–42, 58–60, 70–1, 96–7; Howlett 1994), but whose intellectual outlook was fundamentally reshaped by his access to the learning and culture of the Mediterranean world at the school of Canterbury. Benedict Biscop's travels to Rome (*HE* IV.18; *Historia abbatum* 1–13) were instrumental in effecting a similar intellectual reorientation in Northumbria. If the Synod of Whitby marked a formal break from the Northumbrian church's institutional alignment with Ireland, Biscop's foundation of Benedictine monasteries at Wearmouth and Jarrow with a well-stocked library acquired abroad (and augmented by his successor Ceolfrith) ultimately did more to enable it to emerge from the cultural fosterage of Iona and Lindisfarne (cf. Brown 1993b).

That the Irish element in Anglo-Saxon learning and literacy had been crucially formative until at least the third quarter of the seventh century is evident already at the material level of textual production. The several grades of 'insular' script which Anglo-Saxon scribes chiefly employed up until the general adoption of Caroline minuscule in the tenth and eleventh centuries were based originally upon Irish scripts, although English scribes contributed much to their subsequent refinement (Bischoff 1990: 83–94; Brown 1989; Brown 1993a, 1993c). Along with Irish scripts came certain distinctive abbreviations (Lindsay 1915: 498–500; Boyle 1996: 3–5) and characteristic forms of punctuation (Parkes 1993: 23–9), as well as features of presentation and layout – what Malcolm Parkes (1987) has termed a 'grammar of legibility' – such as *litterae notabiliores* (enlarged letters), diminuendo (a graduated decrease in letter size following a large initial), and word-separation (Saenger 1997: 83–99). Even the writing material and its methods of preparation were distinctive in comparison to continental practice: 'insular' membrane has a suede-like finish, with hair and flesh sides virtually indistinguishable; the sheets were generally pricked and ruled after folding (thus requiring prickings in both margins to guide the rulings); and gatherings of ten (made by sewing together five folded and nested sheets) were sometimes preferred to gatherings of eight (Brown 1993d; cp. Irish *cíne* 'gathering of five', 'booklet', with OE *cine* 'sheet of parchment folded twice', 'quaternio'). Indeed, it can be extremely difficult or impossible to tell the difference between Irish and Anglo-Saxon manuscripts on palaeographical grounds alone, and so great a palaeographer as E. A. Lowe was reduced to citing 'temperamental differences' between the Irish and English as the decisive criterion in attributing the 'sobriety' and 'orderliness' of the Book of Durrow to English workmanship (1972: xvi–xviii; cf. Parkes 1982: 16–17).

It is possible, of course, to acknowledge the existence of distinctive and culturally specific features of style without essentializing them as racial characteristics. Yet such features can also be freely transferred between adjacent cultures and freely amalgamated with indigenous traditions and with techniques borrowed from more distant cultures, as happened in Northumbrian scriptoria where Irish forms of script and decoration – themselves adapted from late antique Roman and Romano-British models (Brown 1993e) – were taken over and transformed through influences emanating from Italy. Decorative motifs derived from native Anglo-Saxon metalwork, notably animal ornament (Campbell and Lane 1993; Whitfield 1995), were in turn assimilated by Irish artists, resulting in a 'Hiberno-Saxon' style that culminated in the great illuminated Gospel-books of Durrow, Lindisfarne and Kells (see Henderson 1987). The artistic synthesis achieved in these manuscripts is such that we may never be certain as to their precise dates, origins and interrelationships, or be able to disentangle fully the respective contributions of Irish and Anglo-Saxon craftsmanship. The peripatetic and reciprocal nature of the 'cultural interplay' (Netzer 1994) during this period is typified by the movement of Willibrord from Rath Melsigi to Echternach, where the Augsburg Gospel-book was produced (see Ó Cróinín 1984, 1989), and by the presence of an accomplished Irish calligrapher named Ultán at a dependancy of Lindisfarne (Aediluulf, *De abbatibus*, lines 208–13; but see Nees 1993 for a sceptical reading of the passage).

The direction of literary influences can be equally difficult to determine with confidence in many cases. Initially, of course, circumstances favoured the transmission of literary forms and motifs from Ireland to England, for the simple reason that the Irish had the advantage of more than a century's accumulated experience of Christian culture and Latin literary tradition when they began to evangelize and instruct the Anglo-Saxons. Various Hiberno-Latin writings are known to have circulated in Anglo-Saxon England, ranging from scientific treatises to Biblical commentaries, penitentials and canonical compilations, moral-didactic tracts, prayers and poems. The influence of some of these writings on specific Anglo-Latin or Old English texts has been documented (a general survey is provided by Cross 1999; for Hiberno-Latin Biblical commentaries, florilegia and homily collections, see Wright 1990b, 1992). I have already noted Bede's familiarity with certain Irish scientific and computistical works. One of these, the *Liber de ordine creaturarum*, was also used by the author of the *Old English Martyrology* in the ninth century and by Ælfric and an anonymous Old English homilist in the tenth and eleventh (Cross 1971: 570; 1972). Bede's exegesis shows only sporadic contacts with Hiberno-Latin Biblical commentaries (Kelly 1982, 1986), but Bede was careful to base interpretation of scripture on the authoritative works of the Fathers, and in any case he would probably have regarded as trivial some of the characteristic methods and preoccupations of Irish exegesis. It is telling that Bede singled out for ridicule an unfortunate comparison (which he had encountered in a Hiberno-Latin commentary on the Catholic Epistles) between the Holy Spirit and a pipe (comparisons of the type *more fistulae* were much employed in Irish Biblical scholarship; see Bischoff 1966–81a: 219).

Both Aldhelm and Bede were familiar with works of the eccentric grammarian Virgilius Maro, whose most likely home was Ireland (Herren 1995, 1996b, 1996d). Aldhelm's 'hermeneutic' style was not modelled on the *Hisperica Famina*, as once believed (Winterbottom 1977), but he was familiar with these almost certainly Hiberno-Latin works (Grosjean 1956: 65–7) and made sparing use of 'Hisperic' words (Winterbottom 1977: 48; Pheifer 1987: 29, n. 40; Harvey and Power 1997). Hisperic words such as *idama* 'hand' (Howlett 1995, 1997: 123–5) and sense neologisms such as *c(h)araxare* meaning 'to write' (Herren 1996c) and *dodrans* meaning 'floodtide' (Brown 1975) are found in certain Anglo-Latin writers and charters (see also Bullough 1991: 303–8; Lapidge 1993a: 138, n. 2, 1996b: 292–3), while lemmata from Hisperic texts (including *Rubisca* and the Breton-Latin *Adelphus adelpha mater*) are included in the Corpus, Épinal-Erfurt and Harley glossaries (Herren 1987: 53, 1996e). Hiberno-Latin writings (including Adomnán's *De locis sanctis* and the pseudo-Isidorian *De ordine creaturarum* and *De ortu et obitu patriarcharum*) were available to the Old English Martyrologist (Cross 1981).

Two Hiberno-Latin compilations helped shape the literary representation of ideal kingship in Anglo-Saxon England. Kingship is among the most prominent themes of the seventh-century *Proverbia Grecorum*. Although there are no Anglo-Saxon manuscripts of the *Proverbia* as a whole, a twelfth-century book-list from Lincoln mentions a 'Librum prouerbiorum grecorum inutilem' (Simpson 1987: 2–3; Thomson 1989: xiv). Moreover, five of the *Proverbia* are cited in Anglo-Saxon manuscripts of the B-recension of the *Collectio canonum Hibernensis*, and ten (under the heading *De nomine regni*) in the tract on kingship by the Norman Anonymous in Cambridge, Corpus Christi College 415 (s. xi/xii or xii[in]; Gneuss 1981: no. 107; see Simpson 1987: 16–18). The Anglo-Saxon Cathuulf's admonitory letter to Charlemagne of *c*.775 incorporates several of the *Proverbia* on kingship, including an enumeration of the 'eight columns that support the kingdom of a just king'. Wulfstan used the same motif (by way of Sedulius Scottus' *De rectoribus christianis*) in his *Institutes of Polity* (Jost 1959: 52; cf. Sauer 1980: 354). Anton Scharer (1996: 197–8) has recently shown that Asser drew several laudatory images from the *Proverbia* in his Life of Alfred.

Even more influential was the Hiberno-Latin tract *De duodecim abusiuis saeculi*, composed probably *c*.630 × 650, which circulated widely under the names of Cyprian, Augustine and Patrick (Anton 1982; Breen 1987). Pseudo-Cyprian's description of the unjust king (*rex iniquus*), the ninth 'abuse', draws on the native Irish genre of *tecosca* ('counsels') and related gnomic traditions dealing with the duties and prerogatives of kings (Smith 1927), which embody (often in Christianized form) the native Irish concept of *fír flathemon* 'the prince's truth' (Dillon 1947: 250–1; Binchy 1970: 9–10; Byrne 1973: 24–6; Anton 1982: 593–5). Central to this concept is the belief that the justice or iniquity of the king will manifest itself not only in the martial and material fortunes of his kingdom, but also in the sympathetic responses of the natural world, affecting the climate as well as the fertility of beasts and crops. Pseudo-Cyprian imported this concept within a Biblical framework (cf. Jaski 1998; Meens 1998).

De duodecim abusiuis contributed significantly to the ideology of Christian kingship on the continent (Anton 1968, 1982, 1989), and was cited (either directly or from a closely parallel extract attributed to Patrick in the *Collectio canonum Hibernensis*) by Anglo-Saxon writers from Bede to Ælfric. The tract's list of royal virtues informed Bede's description of Oswald (*HE* III.9; see Folz 1980: 50–) and Boniface's exhortation (*Ep.* 73: 147) to Æthelbald of Mercia (Anton 1968: 74). In the tenth century, it was popular with the leaders of the Benedictine Reform movement: Æthelwold donated a manuscript containing it to Peterborough (Lapidge 1994: 54, 1993b: 197, 204), and it was translated into Old English by his pupil Ælfric, who also made use of it in his Homily for the Sunday after Ascension Day (cf. Lawson 1994: 148–9). Abbo of Fleury incorporated passages (taken from the decisions of the Council of Paris of 829) in his *Collectio canonum* for Hugh Capet and Robert the Pious (477–8; see Lawson 1994: 143), and Dunstan also made use of *De duodecim abusiuis* in his coronation admonition to Edgar (Wormald 1986: 161–2). The reformers generally ignored or attenuated its cosmological dimension, as was generally the case in the continental reception of the work. But the passage associating the king's justice with the fecundity of nature was quoted by Cathuulf, and recalled by Alcuin (who seems to have known Cathuulf's letter as well) in his letter (18: 51) of 793 to King Æthelred concerning the sack of Lindisfarne: 'Legimus quoque, quod regis bonitas totius est gentis prosperitas, victoria exercitus, aeris temperies, terrae habundantia, filiorum benedictio, sanitas plebis' ('We also read that the goodness of the king is the prosperity of the nation, victory of the army, calmness of the atmosphere, abundance of the earth, blessing of sons, and health of the people').

The numerological structure and litanic style of *De duodecim abusiuis* are characteristic of much Irish Christian literature in both Latin and the vernacular. Numerical motifs were assiduously collected, freely invented, and extensively employed by Irish writers in virtually all genres. The Hiberno-Latin *Liber de numeris* represents the logical extreme of this 'enumerative style': a tract made up entirely of enumerations grouped in numerical order. Enumerations drawn from Hiberno-Latin florilegia and commentaries appear in various Old English works, but especially in anonymous homilies (Wright 1993: 40–105). Irish authors, particularly homilists, also frequently employed lengthy runs of short parallel or antithetical clauses linked by homoeoteleuton (McNally 1965: 172–3; Wright 1993: 32, 243–7). Sequences of this kind, an inheritance of Late Latin *Kunstprosa*, were much favoured by Christian writers for their effectiveness as a paraenetic strategy (Norden 1909: 1.616–23; Augustine, *De ciuitate Dei* XI.18, specially recommended antithesis). What is distinctive about their use by Irish writers, besides their mere frequency, is their often unrestrained extension. The pseudo-Isidorian *Liber de ortu et obitu patriarcharum*, for example, extends a Gregorian formula describing Christ as 'caelo excelsior, inferno profundior, terra longior, mari latior' ('higher than heaven, deeper than hell, longer than the earth, broader than the sea') into a string of fifteen parallel items (p. 52, lines 158–64; cf. Wright 1993: 246–7, n. 124).

An example of the litanic style in Old English which can confidently be ascribed to Irish influence is a sequence contrasting the teachings of God and of the devil in the soul-and-body homily in Oxford, Bodleian Library, Junius 85/86, which is modelled directly on a Hiberno-Latin sermon (Wright 1987b). Again, there is an Irish (vernacular) parallel for the litanic form and part of the contents of an Old English homily in praise of the archangel Michael among the marginalia of Cambridge, Corpus Christ College 41, whose Irish associations have been noted above (Wright 1993: 262, n. 167; Johnson 1998: 85–90). Such concrete if somewhat isolated examples participate in a broader stylistic tradition whose origins can be traced to the Fathers and the Christian rhetoricians of late antique Gaul, and which was inherited and transmitted by Irish authors such as Columbanus (see Tristram 1985: 335–6, 1995, who stresses indirect transmission of stylistic influences to Anglo-Saxon homilists through continental compilations drawing on Hiberno-Latin and other sources). A more distinctive stylistic feature is the numerical *gradatio*, a favourite device of Irish vernacular rhetoric (e.g. Cú Chulainn has 'seven dimples, and seven rays of light shining from each dimple') but one whose use in Old English is limited to texts and motifs influenced by Irish sources, notably Vercelli Homily IX and the prose *Solomon and Saturn* 'Pater Noster Dialogue' (Wright 1993: 165–74, 249–52).

Because texts in the common literary language of Latin were much more likely to pass between Ireland and England than those in either vernacular tongue, there is a strong presumption that Irish literary influences, both stylistic and thematic, were transmitted primarily through the medium of Hiberno-Latin writings (whether composed in Ireland itself or by Irish *peregrini* on the continent). There are, to be sure, no *a priori* grounds for excluding the possibility that some Anglo-Saxon authors could have known Irish vernacular writings, or even have had access to Irish oral traditions through direct personal contacts. We know of several persons during the period of the Irish mission who were bilingual in Irish and Old English and who sometimes acted as interpreters. The royal brothers Oswald and Oswiu, both of whom had been baptized and instructed at Iona, spoke Irish fluently (*HE* III.3; III.25), and Oswald served as interpreter for Aidan, whose knowledge of Old English was imperfect. King Aldfrith, son of Oswiu by an Irish princess, also spoke Irish and even enjoyed considerable posthumous fame as a sage and poet in Ireland, though none of the surviving works attributed to him (under his Irish name Flann Fína) appears to be genuine (Ireland 1999). Chad's brother Cedd served as interpreter at Whitby. Given the regular exchanges between the two countries, and the existence of Anglo-Saxon foundations within Ireland such as Mayo and Rath Melsigi, we can safely assume that functional bilingualism was not a rare phenomenon (cf. Dumville 1981: 111–15). Direct literary evidence of contacts between Irish and Anglo-Saxon vernaculars is, however, disappointingly slight. Setting aside occasional borrowings of Irish words into Old English (see Förster 1921), the most significant attestation of vernacular diglossia is the smattering of Irish words and phrases in a small number of Old English charms.

Some of the 'Irish' is indecipherable, having been garbled in the transmission, if indeed it was ever much more than hocus-pocus; but enough is intelligible to have led Howard Meroney (whose 1945 study, made on the basis of printed texts alone, is still the most comprehensive) to postulate 'professional contact' between Anglo-Saxon and Irish leeches, and Hildegard Tristram (1993: 167, n. 47) has pointed out that the orthography of some of these Irish words indicates oral transmission. A remarkable instance of the Irish ogham script used in an Anglo-Saxon context has recently been uncovered by Patrick Sims-Williams (1995b) in the cosmological diagram accompanying Byrhtferth's *Enchiridion*.

Other lexical evidence is invariably mediated through the common learned language of Latin. The early Latin–Anglo-Saxon Épinal-Erfurt and second Erfurt glossaries contain a few Old Irish words (Pheifer 1987: 29). The Psalter gloss in Vatican, Pal. lat. 68, mentioned above as an example of the Irish scheme of Psalm exegesis, also contains glosses in both vernaculars (McNamara 1986: 19–26). Irish glosses in Anglo-Saxon manuscripts may, of course, have merely been copied from an exemplar without necessarily being comprehended, reflecting separate diachronic layers rather than an active synchronic diglossia. Indirect evidence for the semantic influence of an Irish word in a literary context appears in the Old English prose *Solomon and Saturn* 'Pater Noster Dialogue'. Among various motifs and stylistic features in this text suggestive of Irish influence is an allusion to 'victories' (*sigefæstnisse*) of the wind, based on an enumerative motif found in the *Collectanea Bedae* and *Hisperica Famina*, where the Latin equivalents (respectively *victoriae* and *trophea*) reflect the semantic influence of Old Irish *búaid*, which means 'distinguishing characteristic' or 'special virtue' as well as 'victory'. There is a well-attested tradition in Irish literature of enumerating the *búada* of persons and things, but no vernacular enumeration of the *búada* of the wind seems to have survived, so we must again reckon with the mediation of Hiberno-Latin sources (Wright 1990e, 1993: 252–5; further Latin examples are cited by Wright in Bayless and Lapidge 1998: 219). A case of sense-borrowing from Hiberno-Latin is afforded by the Old English word *egor*, whose meaning in glosses and poems such as *Genesis A* has been affected by the 'Hisperic' use of the word *dodrans* in the sense 'tidal wave' (Brown 1975). A different kind of example, in this case an Anglo-Latin calque on a vernacular Irish term, is the expression *castra beorum* in Aediluulf's *De abbatibus* 577, evidently a Latinization of the Irish Otherworld term *tír na mbéo* 'land of the living' (Sims-Williams 1982: 247–8).

That formulations grounded in vernacular Irish literary traditions such as lists of *búada* and designations of the Otherworld could be so unobtrusively woven into Anglo-Saxon texts (having first been transferred into a Christianized Hiberno-Latin form) leads one to ask whether native mythological motifs or larger narrative multiforms might have been similarly transmitted. Scholars have, indeed, made various attempts to trace the influence of Irish secular literature in *Beowulf*. The most radical was James Carney's (1955) theory that *Beowulf* was directly modelled upon the Old Irish *Táin Bó Fraích*, but Carney's argument was based on exceedingly tenuous parallels, and seems never to have been taken seriously by Anglo-Saxonists (cf. Reichl 1982:

147–51; Tristram 1997: 76–8). Nor have the Celtic mythological parallels advanced by Martin Puhvel (1979) been found compelling. Much attention has been paid to an Irish folktale oicotype (a geographically restricted variant of an international folktale type) known as 'The Hand and the Child' since Kittredge (1903: 222–45) and von Sydow (1914) compared Beowulf's fight with Grendel to this folktale, whose hero tears off the monstrous hand of a creature that has been seizing children through the window or chimney of a king's hall, and then pursues it to an Otherworldly lair, where the creature dwells with a hag. The 'Irish hypothesis' has been defended by some more recent scholars (notably Carney, Puhvel, Murphy 1953: 184–8 and Scowcroft 1999), and criticized by others (Reichl 1982: 140–4; Liberman 1986: 383; Stitt 1992: 203–4; Tristram 1997: 76–9; Fjalldal 1998: 82–4). The fundamental stumbling-block is the existence of analogues far afield for nearly every folklore motif that has been claimed as distinctively Celtic, justifying David Dumville's sceptical assessment that 'the common ethos and the inevitably common folk-tale elements of this kind of literature ensure that any investigations must be pursued at the fruitless level of comparative folklore studies' (1981: 120; cf. Liberman 1986: 362).

More promising leads have turned up in the investigation of what might be called ecclesiastical folklore. Charles Donahue (1949–51) argued that the *Beowulf*-poet's sympathetic portrayal of pagan heroes who worshipped a single God was indebted to the Irish conception of a 'natural good' exemplified by pre-Christian figures such as Conchobar. Donahue (1950) and Carney (1955: 102–14) compared the poet's description of the descent of monsters from the line of Cain with closely similar passages in Irish sources, where one also finds parallels for the apparent confusion of Cain and Cham (see now Mellinkoff 1979, 1981: 194; Orchard 1995: 68–79). J. E. Cross (1986: 82–3, 92–100) has drawn attention to an elaborate discussion of the monstrous races descended from Cain/Cham in the Hiberno-Latin exegetical compendium known as the *Reference Bible*. Possible common sources such as Isidore and Cassian make it impossible to presume direct influence, but the Irish were apparently instrumental in the dissemination of this kind of monster-lore (for a judicious assessment of the 'fertile blend of traditions' reflected in insular sources, see Orchard 1995: 58–85).

Carney (1955: 113–14) also suggested that an apocryphal legend may have inspired the *Beowulf*-poet's description of the runes inscribed on the hilt of the giant-sword retrieved by Beowulf from Grendel's mere, which record the story of the Flood and the feud between God and the giants (lines 1687–98). According to this legend, columns (or plates) of different materials were inscribed with secret knowledge by antediluvian men so that at least one column would survive if a flood or fire ravaged the earth (Lutz 1956: 42–5; Cross 1986: 82, 88; Orchard 1995: 67–8; Myrick 1995). In some versions, the inscriptions are made by Seth or his descendants (often specifically Enoch) and relate either to the story of Adam and Eve (in the *Vita Adae et Euae* 49.3–50.3) or to astronomy or letters and the liberal arts in general (as in Josephus' *Antiquitates Iudaei* and Remigius of Auxerre's commentary on Donatus; for these see Lutz 1956). In others, the inscriptions are made by Cham and relate to secret knowledge or 'wicked arts' (as in Cassian's *Conlationes* VIII. xxi. 7–8). Hiberno-Latin texts, including the *Liber de numeris*, *Reference Bible* and several grammatical treatises, transmit sometimes conflated or awkwardly harmonized versions of these legends, variously identifying Enoch, Cham or descendants of Cain as the makers of the inscribed plates or columns. But two later Irish vernacular texts, *Dúan in choícat ceist* ('Poem of the Fifty Questions') and one version of *Lebor Gabála Érenn* ('Book of the Taking of Ireland'), afford still closer parallels with *Beowulf* in that both state that descendants of Cain (as specified in the gloss to *Dúan in choícat ceist* in Dublin, National Library of Ireland, G 3; Carney 1955: 114, n. 1), or specifically Cam (*Lebor Gabála* I. 160), inscribed 'stories' (*scéla*) associated with their race, rather than letters or secret arts (cf. Myrick 1995: 22, n. 13).

Finally, the scenery of Grendel's mere shares elements with 'stock descriptions of hell' (Tristram 1978) in various Old English homilies, but particularly in Blickling Homily XVI. This homily and *Beowulf* are mutually dependent upon a lost (possibly Old English) version of the *Visio Pauli*, which can be partially reconstructed from surviving Latin redactions, one of the most important being the probably Irish Redaction XI in Vatican, Pal. lat. 220, which uniquely combines the trees from the 'Hanging Sinners' scene with the beast-filled river from the 'Bridge of Hell', which are separate in all other surviving redactions (Wright 1990c, 1993: 106–36).

Eschatological material is particularly conspicuous in Old English poems and anonymous homilies influenced by Irish texts and traditions. Two major legends dealing with the fates of souls after death, the Seven Heavens apocryphon and Three Utterances sermon, have already been mentioned. The compilation which preserves the unique Latin text of the Seven Heavens apocryphon, the *Apocrypha Priscillianistica*, also preserves a text which is the ultimate source of a Doomsday motif in an Old English Rogationtide homily and in the epilogue to Cynewulf's *Elene*, according to which Christ will demand a 'pledge' (Latin *arrha*, OE *wed*) for the sinful thoughts, words and deeds of each person, who will have nothing to pledge but the soul itself (Wright 1990d). Characteristically enumerative motifs based on Irish models include the 'three companies' of angles, men and devils (noted above in connection with the 'penitential motif') and the 'Seven Joys of Heaven', variations of which occur in some eight OE homilies (Hill 1969a; Wright 1993: 102–5). Both motifs occur in *Christ III*, whose author incorporated a variety of apocryphal Doomsday images from Irish tradition (Hill 1969b, 1986) and adopted a fourfold division of souls at Judgement that was common in insular eschatology (Biggs 1989–90). Rhetorical and descriptive topoi derived from the short redactions of the *Visio Pauli*, the 'Men with Tongues of Iron' and the multi-appendaged 'Monster of Hell' contributed significantly to the common stock of motifs in insular descriptions of Heaven and Hell (Wright 1993: 145–74). Irish accounts of the Christian Heaven and Hell also absorbed native images associated with the Otherworld. I have argued elsewhere that 'The Devil's Account of the Next World' exemplum from Vercelli Homily IX incorporates a 'demonized version' of a popular Celtic narrative motif known as the 'Iron House' and sensual imagery associated with the benevolent Otherworld in Irish tradition (Wright 1993: 189–214). Any reconstruction of the mode of transmission is inevitably speculative, but it is likely that the homilist's immediate source was a Hiberno-Latin tract or homily that had already assimilated native Otherworld motifs within a framework of Christian-Latin eschatological and visionary traditions.

Irish Christian texts and traditions thus remained fertile sources for English authors throughout the Anglo-Saxon period. As Denis Bethell has remarked, 'up to 1066 we can still say that English and Irish monks shared a common cultural world in which the Irish could still be teachers' (1971: 125). Although there is no primary witness comparable to Bede for the four centuries following Whitby, there is ample evidence of continuing cultural contacts between Ireland and England in contemporary historical documents, often in incidental references (Bethell 1971; Hughes 1987c; Kelly 1975). Contacts are better documented in the ninth and tenth centuries, especially during the culturally expansive reigns of Alfred and Æthelstan. The three Irishmen whose spiritual pilgrimage took them to Cornwall in 891 were received at the court of King Alfred. The same entry in the *Anglo-Saxon Chronicle* records the death of Suibne mac Maele Umai, 'the greatest teacher among the Irish'. Asser (*Vita Ælfredi regis c.*102) informs us that Alfred gave alms to Irish churches, and as we have seen, Alfred's own prose Introductions to the first fifty Psalms in the Paris Psalter adapt an Irish model of psalm exegesis. The Metrical Calendar of Hampson, with obits for Alfred and his wife, was composed shortly after his reign either by an Irishman residing in England or by an Englishman using Irish sources (McGurk 1986: 89). Irish and Breton scholars were among the visitors to the cosmopolitan court of Alfred's grandson Æthelstan (Wood 1983; Dumville 1992b: 154–8), whose library contained Irish texts and manuscripts, including a copy of the Metrical Calendar of Hampson and the Mac Durnan Gospels (Keynes 1985: 153–9, 193–6).

I have suggested elsewhere that the reign of Æthelstan (927–39) provides a plausible milieu for certain Irish-influenced anonymous homilies and perhaps also for *Solomon and Saturn I* and the prose *Solomon and Saturn* 'Pater Noster Dialogue', in both of which Solomon expounds the fantastic powers of the elaborately personified Pater Noster (Wright 1993: 267–70). The *Solomon and Saturn* dialogues, however, could be somewhat earlier, perhaps from Alfred's time. A possible clue to their provenance occurs in a Middle Irish poem ('Mac at-cuala is domain tair') on the origins of the various parts of the mass liturgy, recently edited by Brian Ó Cuív (1993: 267). One stanza refers tantalizingly to Dunstan and the 'high king of the noble English' (*ardríg Saxan saerdha*), attributing to them respectively the composition of the Agnus Dei and the 'Septinair'. Ó Cuív was unable to identify a *Septenarius* in the mass, but the key to its meaning in the poem lies in its placement between the Sanctus and the Agnus Dei, the slot occupied in the Roman liturgy by the Pater Noster, a prayer comprising seven petitions (Jungmann 1959: 463–70). Now the poem attributes this 'Septinair' not only to an unnamed English king apparently associated with Dunstan, but also to Solomon. Moreover, an earlier stanza uses the terms *organ* and *cantairecht* to refer generally to liturgical chant, reminiscent of the unusual application of the words *organ* and *cantic* to the Pater Noster in both *Solomon and Saturn* texts (cf. Ó Néill 1997, who assumes a reference to the use of the Pater Noster as a canticle in the monastic Office). The poem's cryptic allusion to Dunstan and an *ardrí Saxan* who, with Solomon, is supposed to have 'composed' the 'Septinair' (the verb *ro-cum* in this context has perhaps the sense 'determined, appointed', that is introduced it into the mass) may therefore provide independent confirmation of a literary association between Solomon and the Pater Noster at an Anglo-Saxon court in contact with Ireland. We know that during the 930s Dunstan resided at the court of Æthelstan, whom the Annals of Ulster (as Ó Cuív notes, without pressing the identification) style *rex Saxonum* and *rí Saxan*. According to his anonymous biographer 'B', Dunstan had 'applied himself attentively' to the books of Irish *peregrini* at Glastonbury, and Hiberno-Latin materials, including liturgical texts, are included in the portion of Dunstan's 'Classbook' known as the *Liber Commonei* (Lapidge 1986: 92–4; Walsh and Ó Cróinín 1988: 89, 177–8; Breen 1992). The sole surviving manuscript which contains both *Solomon and Saturn I* and the 'Pater Noster Dialogue', Cambridge, Corpus Christi College 422, Part 1 (s. x[1]) may well have been written during Æthelstan's reign; but even if they were composed earlier and we dissociate Dunstan and the 'high king of the English' by identifying the latter with Alfred (whom Asser, ch. 76, compared to Solomon), well-documented contacts with Irish churches, scholars and exegetical traditions during his reign would provide an equally hospitable milieu for these texts.

Officially sponsored cultural exchanges at Anglo-Saxon royal courts were not, of course, the only possible means of transmission, even if they are inevitably the best documented. (In any case, the manuscript transmission of Hiberno-Latin texts, once introduced, was not dependent on further direct personal exchanges.) There must also have been various unauthorized back-channels of which we can have only rare glimpses. In 816 the council of *Celchyth* forbade wandering clerics *de genere Scottorum* from exercising ecclesiastical functions, a sanction which, as Kathleen Hughes observed (1987b: 61), 'proves conclusively that Irish clerics had been ministering, and presumably in sufficient numbers, to provoke opposition'. We know of the Anglo-Saxon priest Pehtred's book, with its account of Niall's visions and the Sunday Letter, only because it elicited the condemnation of a bishop of Lindisfarne. By a similar chance we learn of the presence in Northumbria in the early eleventh century of an Irish poetaster and 'grammarian' named Moriuht, whose misadventures and intellectual pretensions were satirized by Warner of Rouen (Pelteret 1989: 108–9). Captured by Danes, Moriuht was sold at a slave-market in Corbridge to a nunnery, where his sexual predations caused an uproar – or so Warner claims. One hastens to add that Pehtred and Moriuht are hardly typical examples of 'Irish influence' in Anglo-Saxon England! Yet their case histories remind us that the movement of persons and ideas was not restricted to the more visible comings and goings of the ecclesiastical elite.

Future research may enable us to correlate literary influences with particular historical moments (and to clarify their direction) more precisely than has been possible hitherto. We await publication of still unedited or inadequately edited Irish and Hiberno-Latin texts to support continuing work integrating textual and source studies with close investigation of manuscript transmission and specific historical contexts. Again, despite its frequently remarked continuity, 'the Irish tradition' was by no means static and unchanging from the time of the missions to England and the continent through the disturbances of the Viking Age and the reforms of the Céli Dé. In many respects, the nature of that tradition and its influence in Anglo-Saxon literature and culture still remain to be defined.

REFERENCES

Primary sources

A Journey Charm. Ed. Elliott van Kirk Dobbie 1942. *The Anglo-Saxon Minor Poems*, pp. 126–8. Anglo-Saxon Poetic Records 8. New York.

Abbo of Fleury. *Collectio canonum*. Patrologia Latina 139: 473–508.

Adelphus adelpha mater. Ed. and trans. Michael W. Herren 1987. *The Hisperica Famina II: Related Poems*, pp. 105–11. Studies and Texts 85. Toronto.

Adomnán. *De locis sanctis*. Ed. and trans. Ludwig Bieler and Denis Meehan 1958. *Adamnan's De Locis Sanctis*. Scriptores Latini Hiberniae 3. Dublin.

——*Vita Columbae*. Ed. and trans. Alan Orr Anderson and Majorie Ogilvie Anderson 1991. *Adomnan's Life of Columba*. 2nd edn. Oxford. Also trans. Richard Sharpe 1995. *Adomnán of Iona: Life of St Columba*. New York.

Aediluulf. *De abbatibus*. Ed. Alastair Campbell 1967. *Æthelwulf: De abbatibus*. Oxford.

Ælfric. *Catholic Homilies*. Second Series. Ed. Malcolm Godden 1979. *Ælfric's Catholic Homilies: The Second Series*. Early English Text Society, s.s. 5. Oxford.

——*De duodecim abusivis*. Ed. Ruby D.-N. Warner 1917. *Early English Homilies from the Twelfth Century Ms Vespasian D.XIV*, pp. 11–19. Early English Text Society, o.s. 152. London. Another version ed. Richard Morris 1867–8. *Old English Homilies of the Twelfth and Thirteenth Centuries*, pp. 296–304. Early English Text Society, o.s. 29, 34. London. Repr. 1988.

——*Dominica Post Ascensionem Domini*. Ed. John C. Pope 1966. *Homilies of Ælfric: A Supplementary Collection*. 2 vols, 1.378–95. Early English Text Society, o.s. 259–60. London.

Alcuin. *Epistolae*. Ed. Ernst Dümmler 1895. *Alcuini Epistolae*, pp. 1–493. Monumenta Germaniae Historica, Epistolae, 4. Berlin.

——*Interrogationes et responsiones in Genesin*. Patrologia Latina 100: 516–66.

Aldhelm. *Epistola ad Heahfridum*. Ed. Rudolf Ehwald 1919. *Aldhelmi Opera*, pp. 488–94. Monumenta Germaniae Historica, Auctores Antiquissimi, 15. Berlin.

Alfred. Prose Introductions to Psalms 1–50. Eds James W. Bright and Robert L. Ramsay 1907. *Liber Psalmorum: The West-Saxon Psalms, Being the Prose Portion, or the 'First Fifty', of the so-called Paris Psalter*, pp. 1–22. Boston.

Altus Prosator. Eds J. H. Bernard and R. Atkinson 1898. *The Irish Liber Hymnorum*. 2 vols, 1.62–83. Henry Bradshaw Society 13–14. London.

The Anglo-Saxon Chronicle. Eds J. Earle and Charles Plummer. Repr. with bibliographical note by Dorothy Whitelock 1952. *Two of the Saxon Chronicles Parallel*. Oxford.

Apocalypse of Thomas. Ed. D. P. Bihlmeyer 1911. 'Un texte non interpolé de l'Apocalypse de Thomas'. *Revue Bénédictine* 28: 270—82. Irish versions: *see Saltair na Rann* and *Tenga Bithnua*. Old English versions: *see* Förster 1955.

Apocrypha Priscillianistica. Ed. Donatien de Bruyne 1907. 'Fragments retrouvés d'apocryphes priscillianistes'. *Revue Bénédictine* 24: 318–35.

Asser. *Vita Ælfredi regis*. Ed. W. H. Stevenson 1904, rev. Dorothy Whitelock 1959. *Asser's Life of King Alfred*. Oxford. Trans. Simon Keynes and Michael Lapidge 1983. *Alfred the Great*. Harmondsworth.

Augustine of Hippo. *De ciuitate Dei*. Eds B. Dombart and A. Kalb 1955. 2 vols. Corpus Christianorum, Series Latina, 47–8. Turnhout.

Augustinus Hibernicus. *De mirabilibus sacrae scripturae*. Patrologia Latina 35: 2149–2020.

'B'. *Vita S. Dunstani*. Ed. William Stubbs 1874. *Memorials of Saint Dunstan*, pp. 3–52. Roll Series 63. London.

Bede. *Historia abbatum*. Ed. Charles Plummer 1896. *Venerabilis Bedae Opera Historica*. 2 vols, 1.364–87. Oxford.

——*Historia ecclesiastica gentis Anglorum*. Eds and trans. Bertram Colgrave and R. A. B. Mynors 1969. Oxford Medieval Texts. Oxford.

Beowulf. Ed. Frederick Klaeber 1950. *Beowulf and the Fight at Finnsburg*. 3rd edn with 1st and 2nd supplements. Boston.

Blickling Homily XVI. Ed. (as Homily XVII) Richard Morris 1874–8, repr. in 1 vol. 1967. *The Blickling Homilies of the Tenth Century*, pp. 196–227. Early English Text Society, o.s. 58, 63, 73. London.

Boniface. Letter to Æthelbald of Mercia. Ed. M. Tangl 1916. *Sancti Bonifacii et Lulli epistolae*, pp. 146–55. Monumenta Germaniae Histroica, Epistolae Selectae, 1. Berlin.

Byrhtferth. *Enchiridion*. Eds and trans. Peter S. Baker and Michael Lapidge 1995. *Byrhtferth of Ramsey: Enchiridion*. Early English Text Society, s.s. 15. Oxford.

Cassian. *Conlationes*. Ed. M. Petschenig. *Corpus Scriptorum Ecclesiasticorum Latinorum* 13/2. Vienna.

Catechesis Cracoviensis. Partial edn. Pierre David 1937. 'Un receuil de conférences monastiques irlandaises du VIIIe siècle'. *Revue Bénédictine* 49: 62–89.

Cathuulf. *Letter to Charlemagne*. Ed. Ernst Dümmler 1895. Monumenta Germaniae Historica, Epistolae 4, pp. 501–4. Berlin.

Christ III. Eds Geoge Philip Krapp and Elliott van Kirk Dobbie 1936. *The Exeter Book*, pp. 27–49. Anglo-Saxon Poetic Records 3. New York.

Collectanea Pseudo-Bedae. Eds Matha Bayless and Michael Lapidge 1998. Scriptores Latini Hiberniae 14. Dublin.

Collectio Canonum Hibernensis. Ed. F. W. H. Wasserschleben 1885. *Die irische Kanonensammlung*. 2nd edn. Leipzig.

Columba (attrib.). *See Altus Prosator*.

Council of *Celchyth* (816). Eds A. W. Haddan and W. Stubbs 1869–71. *Councils and Ecclesiastical Documents Relating to Great Britain and Ireland*, 3 vols, 3.79–84. Oxford.

Cummian. *Paenitentiale*. Ed. and trans. Ludwig Bieler 1963. *The Irish Penitentials*, pp. 108–35. Scriptores Latini Hiberniae 5. Dublin.

Cynewulf. *Elene*. Ed. George Philip Krapp 1932. *The Vercelli Book*, pp. 66–102. Anglo-Saxon Poetic Records 2. New York.

De mirabilibus sacrae scripturae. *See* Augustinus Hibernicus.

'Discipulus Umbrensium'. Recension U of the *Iudicia Theodori*. Ed. P. Finsterwalder 1929. *Die Canones Theodori Cantuariensis und ihre Überlieferungsformen*, pp. 239–334. Weimar.

Dúan in choícat ceist. Ed. Kuno Meyer 1903. 'Mitteilungen aus irischen Handschriften'. *Zeitschrift für celtische Philologie* 4: 234–7. Ed. and trans. Hildegard L. C. Tristram 1986. *Sex aetates mundi: Die Weltzeitalter bei den Angelsachsen und den Iren*, pp. 285–93. Anglistische Forschungen 65. Heidelberg.

Dunstan. *Promissio Regis*. Ed. William Stubbs 1874. *Memorials of St Dunstan*, pp. 355–7. Rolls Series 63. London.

Ecgred, bishop of Lindisfarne. Letter to Wulfsige. Ed. Dorothy Whitelock 1982. 'Bishop Ecgred, Pehtred and Niall'. *Ireland in Early Mediaeval Europe: Studies in Memory of Kathleen Hughes*, pp. 48–9. Eds Dorothy Whitelock, Rosamund McKilterick and David Dumville. Cambridge. Trans. Dorothy Whitelock 1979. *English Historical Documents I*, pp. 875–6. 2nd edn. London.

Épinal-Erfurt Glossary. Ed. J. D. Pheifer 1974. *Old English Glosses in the Épinal-Erfurt Glossary*. Oxford.

Genesis A. Ed. George Philip Krapp 1931. *The Junius Manuscript*, pp. 1–87. Anglo-Saxon Poetic Records 1. New York.

Glossa in Psalmos. Ed. Martin McNamara 1986. *Glossa in Psalmos: The Hiberno-Latin Gloss on the Psalms of Codex Palatinus Latinus 58 (Psalms 39.11–151.7)* Studi e Testi 310. Vatican City.

Gospel of Thomas. Irish version: ed. and trans. James Carney 1964. *The Poems of Blathmac*, pp. 90–105. Irish Texts Society 47. Dublin.

Hisperica Famina. Ed. F. J. H. Jenkinson 1908. *The Hisperica Famina*. Cambridge. Partial edn Michael W. Herren 1974. *Hisperica Famina I: The A-Text*. Studies and Texts 31. Toronto.

Isidore of Seville. *Etymologiae*. Ed. W. M. Lindsay 1911. *Isidori Hispalensis Episcopi Etymologiarum sive Originum Libri XX*. 2 vols. Oxford.

——*De natura rerum*. Ed. and trans. Jacques Fontaine 1960. *Isidore de Séville. Traité de la nature*. Bordeaux. Also in Patrologia Latina 83: 963–1018.

Laidcenn mac Baith. *Lorica* ('Suffragare Trinitatis unitas'). Ed. and trans. Michael W. Herren 1987. *The Hisperica Famina II: Related Poems*, pp. 76–89. Studies and Texts 85. Toronto.

Lebor Gabála Érenn. Ed. and trans. R. A. S. Macalister 1938–56. 5 vols. Irish Texts Society 34, 35, 39, 41, 44. Dublin.

Liber de numeris. Partial edn R. E. McNally 1957. *Der irische Liber de numeris: Eine Quellenanalyse des pseudo-isidorischen Liber de numeris*. Inaugural-Dissertation. Munich. Also partial edn Patrologia Latina 83: 1293–1302.

Liber de ordine creaturarum. Ed. and trans. Manuel C. Díaz y Díaz 1972. *Liber de ordine creaturarum: Un anónimo irlandés del siglo VII*. Santiago de Compostela. Also in Patrologia Latina 83: 913–54.

Liber de ortu et obitu patriarcharum. Ed. J. Carracedo Fraga 1996. Corpus Christianorum, Series Latina, 108E. Turnhout.

'Mac at-cuala is domain tair'. *See* Ó Cuív 1993.

Metrical Calendar of Hampson. Ed. Patrick McGurk 1986. 'The Metrical Calendar of Hampson: A New Edition'. *Analecta Bollandiana* 104: 79–125.

Old English Homily *In laudem Sancti Michaelis*. Ed. and trans. Raymond J. S. Grant 1982. *Three Homilies from Cambridge, Corpus Christi College 41*, pp. 56–64. Ottawa.

Old English Homily *In letania maiore*. Eds Joyce Bazire and J. E. Cross 1990. 2nd edn. *Eleven Old English Rogationtide Homilies*, pp. 47–54 (no. 3). King's College London Medieval Studies 4. London.

Old English Martyrology. Ed. Günter Kotzor 1981. *Das altenglische Martyrologium*. Bayerische Akademie der Wissenschaften, Phil-hist. Klasse, Abhandlungen, n.f. 88/1–2. Munich.

Paris Psalter. *See* Alfred.

The Prose Solomon and Saturn and Adrian and Ritheus. Eds and trans. Thomas D. Hill and J. E. Cross 1982. Toronto.

The Prose *Solomon and Saturn* 'Pater Noster Dialogue'. Ed. Robert Menner 1941. *The Poetical Dialogues of Solomon and Saturn*, pp. 168–71. New York.

Proverbia Grecorum. Ed. Dean Simon 1987. 'The "Proverbia Grecorum"'. *Traditio* 43: 1–22.

Pseudo-Cyprian. *De duodecim abusivis saeculi*. Ed. Siegmund Hellmann 1909. *Pseudo-Cyprianus de xii abusivis saeculi*, pp. 32–60. Texte und Untersuchungen zur Geschichte der altchristlichen Literatur 3/4. Leipzig.

Pseudo-Wulfstan. Homilies XLIII and XLIV. Ed. Arthur S. Napier 1888; repr. with suppl. Klaus Ostheeren 1967. *Wulfstan: Sammlung der ihm zugeschriebenen Homilien nebst Untersuchungen über ihre Echtheit*, pp. 205–26. Dublin.

Reference Bible. Ed. Gerard McGinty 2000. *Pauca problesmata de enigmatibus ex tomis canonicis*. Corpus Christianorum, Continuatio Mediaevalis, 17. Turnhout. Partial edn J. E. Cross 1986. 'Towards the Identification of Old English Literary Ideas – Old Workings and New Seams'. *Sources of Anglo-Saxon Culture*, pp. 92–100. Ed. Paul E. Szarmach. Kalamazoo.

Rubisca. Ed. and trans. Michael W. Herren 1987. *The Hisperica Famina II: Related Poems*, pp. 94–103. Studies and Texts 85. Toronto.

Saltair na Rann. Ed. Whitley Stokes 1883. Anecdota Oxoniensia, Mediaeval and Modern Series, 1/3. Oxford. Partial edn and trans. David Greene and Fergus Kelly 1976. *The Irish Adam and Eve Story from Saltair na Rann, I: Text and Translation*. Dublin.

The Seafarer. Eds George Philip Krapp and Elliott van Kirk Dobbie 1936. *The Exeter Book*, pp. 143–7. Anglo-Saxon Poetic Records 3. New York.

Seven Heavens apocryphon. Irish versions: *Tenga Bithnua*, ed. and trans. Georges Dottin 1907. 'Une rédaction moderne du *Teanga Bithnua*'. *Revue Celtique* 28: 295–7; *Fís Adamnáin*, ed. Ernst Windisch 1880. *Irische Texte* 1.165–96. Leipzig; trans. John Carey 1998. *King of Mysteries: Early Irish Religious Writings*, pp. 267–9. Dublin. Old English version: ed. Rudolf Willard 1935. *Two Apocrypha in Old English Homilies*, pp. 4–6. Beiträge zur englischen Philologie, 30. Leipzig. Latin version: ed. Donatien De Bruyne 1911. 'Fragments retrouvés d'apocryphes priscillianistes'. *Revue Bénédictine* 24: 323–4.

Solomon and Saturn I and II. Ed. Robert Menner 1941. *The Poetical Dialogues of Solomon and Saturn*, pp. 80–104. New York.

The Sunday Letter. Irish versions: ed. J. G. O'Keeffe 1905. 'Cáin Domnaig'. *Ériu* 2: 189–211; J. G. O'Keeffe 1907. 'Poem on the Observance of Sunday'. *Ériu* 3: 143–7. Old English versions: *see* Pseudo-Wulfstan.

Tenga Bithnua. Ed. and trans. Whitley Stokes 1905. 'The Evernew Tongue'. *Ériu* 2: 96–162.

Three Utterances sermon. Latin versions: ed. Rudolf Willard 1937. 'The Latin Texts of *The Three Utterances of the Soul*'. *Speculum* 12: 147–66; Mary F. Wack and Charles D. Wright 1990. 'A New Latin Source for the Old English "Three Utterances" Exemplum'. *Anglo-Saxon England* 20: 187–202. Old English versions: ed. Rudolf Willard 1935. *Two Apocrypha in Old English Homilies*, pp. 38–57. Beiträge zur englischen Philologie 30. Leipzig. Old Irish version: ed. Carl Marstrander 1911. 'The Two Deaths'. *Ériu* 5: 120–5.

Vercelli Homily IX. Ed. Donald G. Scragg 1992. *The Vercelli Homilies and Related Texts*, pp. 158–84. Early English Text Society, o.s. 300. Oxford.

Visio Pauli. Ed. Theodore Silverstein 1935. *Visio Sancti Pauli: The History of the Apocalypse in Latin together with Nine Texts*. Studies and Documents 4. London.

——Redaction XI. Ed. M. E. Dwyer 1988. 'An Unstudied Redaction of the *Visio Pauli*'. *Manuscripta* 32: 121–38.

Vita Adae et Evae. Ed. W. Meyer 1878. *Abhandlungen der Königlichen Bayerischen Akademie der Wissenschaften*, philos.-philol. klasse 14/3, pp. 185–250. Munich. Irish version: *see Saltair na Rann*.

Vita prima Sancti Fursei. Ed. (omitting the visions) Bruno Krusch 1920. *Vita Virtutesque Fursei Abbatis Latiniacensis et de Fuilano Additamentum Nivialense*. Monumenta Germaniae Historica, Scriptores Rerum Merovingicarum, 4, pp. 423–51, 779–80. Hanover. Ed. (of the visions) M. P. Ciccarese 1984–5. 'Le visioni di S. Fursa'. *Romanobarbarica* 8: 231–303.

Warner of Rouen. *Moriuht*. Ed. Christopher J. McDonough 1995. *Warner of Rouen. Moriuht: A Norman Latin Poem from the Early Eleventh Century*. Studies and Texts 121. Toronto.

Wulfstan. *Institutes of Polity*. Ed. Karl Jost 1959. *Die 'Institutes of Polity, Civil and Ecclesiastical'*:

Ein Werk Erzbischof Wulfstans von York. Schweizer anglistische Arbeiten 47. Bern.

Secondary sources

Amos, Thomas L. 1990. 'The *Catechesis Cracoviensis* and Hiberno-Latin Exegesis on the *Pater Noster*'. *Proceedings of the Irish Biblical Association* 13: 77–107.

Angenendt, Arnold 1982. 'Die irische Peregrinatio und ihre Auswirkungen aus dem Kontinent vor dem Jahre 800'. *Die Iren und Europa im früheren Mittelalter*. 2 vols, 1.52–79. Ed. Heinz Löwe. Stuttgart.

Anton, Hans Hubert 1968. *Fürstenspiegel und Herrscherethos in der Karolingerzeit*. Bonner Historische Forschungen, 32. Bonn.

——1982. 'Pseudo-Cyprian De duodecim abusivis saeculi und sein Einfluß auf den Kontinent, insbesondere auf die karolingischen Fürstenspiegel'. *Die Iren und Europa im früheren Mittelalter*. 2 vols, 1.568–617. Ed. Heinz Löwe. Stuttgart.

——1989. 'Zu neuerer Wertung Pseudo-Cyprians ("De duodecim abusivis saeculi") und zu seinem Vorkommen in Bibliothekskatalogen des Mittelalters'. *Würzburger Diözesangeschichtsblätter* 51: 463–74.

Bauckham, Richard 1993. 'The *Apocalypse of the Seven Heavens*'. *Apocrypha* 4: 141–75.

Bayless, Martha 1998. 'The *Collectanea* and Medieval Dialogues and Riddles'. *Collectanea Pseudo-Bedae*, pp. 13–24. Scriptores Latini Hiberniae 14. Eds Martha Bayless and Michael Lapidge. Dublin.

——and Michael Lapidge, eds 1998. *Collectanea Pseudo-Bedae*. Scriptores Latini Hiberniae 14. Dublin.

Bazire, Joyce and J. E. Cross, eds 1990. *Eleven Old English Rogationtide Homilies*. 2nd edn. King's College London Medieval Studies 4. London.

Bestul, Thomas H. 1986. 'Continental Sources of Anglo-Saxon Devotional Writing'. *Sources of Anglo-Saxon Culture*, pp. 103–26. Ed. Paul E. Szarmach. Kalamazoo.

Bethell, Denis 1971. 'English Monks and Irish Reform in the Eleventh and Twelfth Centuries'. *Historical Studies VIII*, pp. 111–35. Ed. T. D. Williams. Dublin.

Bieler, Ludwig, ed. and trans. 1963. _The Irish Penitentials_. Scriptores Latini Hiberniae 5. Dublin.

Biggs, Frederick M. 1989–90. 'The Fourfold Division of Souls: The Old English "Christ III" and the Insular Homiletic Tradition'. _Traditio_ 45: 36–51.

—— 1990a. 'Apocrypha. IV. Apocryphal Apocalypses. Apocalypse of Thomas'. _Sources of Anglo-Saxon Literary Culture: A Trial Version_, pp. 68–9. Eds Frederick M. Biggs, Thomas D. Hill and Paul E. Szarmach. Binghamton, NY.

—— 1990b. 'Apocrypha. I. Old Testament Apocrypha. I Enoch'. _Sources of Anglo-Saxon Literary Culture: A Trial Version_, pp. 25–7. Eds Frederick M. Biggs, Thomas D. Hill and Paul E. Szarmach. Binghamton, NY.

Bihlmeyer, D. P. 1911. 'Un texte non interpolé de l'Apocrypse de Thomas'. _Revue Bénédictine_ 28: 270–82.

Binchy, D. A. 1970. _Celtic and Anglo-Saxon Kingship_. Oxford.

Bischoff, Bernhard 1966–81a. 'Wendepunkte in der Geschichte der lateinischen Exegese im Frühmittelalter'. _Mittelalterliche Studien: Ausgewählte Aufsätze zur Schriftkunde und Literaturgeschichte_. 3 vols, 1.205–73. Stuttgart.

—— 1966–81b. 'Die europäische Verbreitung der Werke Isidors von Sevilla'. _Mittelalterliche Studien: Ausgewählte Aufsätze zur Schriftkunde und Literaturgeschichte_. 3 vols, 1.171–94. Stuttgart.

—— 1966–81c. 'Eine verschollene Einteilung der Wissenschaften'. _Mittelalterliche Studien: Ausgewählte Aufsätze zur Schriftkunde und Literaturgeschichte_. 3 vols, 1.273–88. Stuttgart.

—— 1990. _Latin Palaeography: Antiquity and the Middle Ages_. Trans. Dáibhí Ó Cróinín and David Ganz. Cambridge.

Bishop, Edmund 1918. _Liturgica Historica: Papers on the Liturgy and Religious Life of the Western Church_. Oxford.

Bishop, T. A. M. 1964–8. 'Notes on Cambridge Manuscripts. Part VII: Pelagius in Trinity College B. 10. 5'. _Transactions of the Cambridge Bibliographical Society_ 4: 70–7.

Boyle, Leonard 1996. 'Opening Address'. _Irland und Europa im früheren Mittelalter: Bildung und Literatur_, pp. 1–6. Eds Próinséas Ní Chatháin and Michael Richter. Stuttgart.

Breen, Aidan 1987. 'Pseudo-Cyprian _De Duodecim Abusivis Saeculi_ and the Bible'. _Irland und die Christenheit: Bibelstudien und Mission_, pp. 230–45.

Eds Próinséas Ní Chatháin and Michael Richter. Stuttgart.

—— 1992. 'The Liturgical Materials in MS Oxford, Bodleian Library, Auct. F.4/32'. _Archiv für Liturgiewissenschaft_ 34: 121–53.

Breeze, Andrew 1994. 'The Three Hosts of Doomsday in Celtic and Old English'. _Miscelánea_ 15: 71–9.

Brown, Alan K. 1975. 'Bede, a Hisperic Etymology, and Early Sea Poetry'. _Mediaeval Studies_ 37: 419–32.

Brown, Julian 1993a. 'The Irish Element in the Insular System of Scripts to c. AD 850'. _Die Iren und Europa im früheren Mittelalter_. 2 vols, 1.101–19. Ed. Heinz Löwe. Stuttgart, 1982. Repr. _A Palaeographer's View: The Selected Writings of Julian Brown_, pp. 201–20, 284–7. Eds Janet Bately, Michelle Brown and Jane Roberts. London.

—— 1993b. 'An Historical Introduction to the Use of Classical Latin Authors in the British Isles from the 5th to the 11th Century'. _La cultura antica nell'occidente Latino dal VII all'XI secoto_, Settimane di studi del centro italiano di studi sull'alto medioevo 22, pp. 237–99. Spoleto, 1975. Repr. _A Palaeographer's View: The Selected Writings of Julian Brown_, pp. 141–77, 276–84. Eds Janet Bately, Michelle Brown and Jane Roberts. London.

—— 1993c. 'Tradition, Imitation and Invention in Insular Handwriting of the Seventh and Eighth Centuries'. R. W. Chambers Memorial Lecture, University College, London, 1978. _A Palaeographer's View: The Selected Writings of Julian Brown_, pp. 179–200, 284. Eds Janet Bately, Michelle Brown and Jane Roberts. London.

—— 1993d. 'The Distribution and Significance of Membrane Prepared in the Insular Manner'. _La Paléographie Hébraïque médiévale_, pp. 127–35. Paris, 1974. Repr. _A Palaeographer's View: The Selected Writings of Julian Brown_, pp. 125–40, 276. Eds Janet Bately, Michelle Brown and Jane Roberts. London.

—— 1993e. 'The Oldest Irish Manuscripts and their Late Antique Background'. _Irland und Europa: die Kirche im Frühmittelalter_, pp. 311–27. Eds Próinséas Ní Chatháin and Michael Richter. Stuttgart, 1984. Repr. _A Palaeographer's View: The Selected Writings of Julian Brown_, pp. 221–41, 287. Eds Janet Bately, Michelle Brown and Jane Roberts. London.

Brown, Michelle P. 1989. 'The Lindisfarne Scriptorium from the Late Seventh to the Early Ninth Century'. *St Cuthbert, his Cult and his Community to A.D. 1200*, pp. 151–63. Eds Gerald Bonner, David Rollason and Clare Stancliffe. Woodbrige.

—— 1996. *The Book of Cerne: Prayer, Patronage and Power in Ninth-Century England*. London.

Bullough, Donald A. 1982. 'The Missions to the English and Picts and their Heritage (to *c.*800)'. *Die Iren und Europa im früheren Mittelalter*. 2 vols, 2.80–98. Ed. Heinz Löwe. Stuttgart.

—— 1991. 'The Educational Tradition in England from Alfred to Ælfric: Teaching *utriusque linguae*'. *La scuola nell'occidente latino dell'alto medioevo*, Settimane di studio del centro italiano di studi sull'alto medioevo 19 (Spoleto, 1972), pp. 453–94. Repr. in Bullough, *Carolingian Renewal: Sources and Heritage*, pp. 297–34. Manchester.

Byrne, Francis John 1973. *Irish Kings and High-Kings*. London.

Campbell, Ewan and Alan Lane 1993. 'Celtic and Germanic Interaction in Dalriada: The 7th-century Metalworking Site at Dunadd'. *The Age of Migrating Ideas: Early Medieval Art in Northern Britain and Ireland*, pp. 52–63. Eds R. Michael Spearman and John Higgitt. Edinburgh.

Campbell, James 1971. 'The First Century of Christianity in England'. *Ampleforth Journal* 76: 12–29.

—— 1987. 'The Debt of the Early English Church to Ireland'. *Irland und die Christenheit: Bibelstudien und Mission*, pp. 332–46. Eds Próinséas Ní Chatháin and Michael Richter. Stuttgart.

Carley, James P. and Ann Dooley 1991. 'An Early Irish Fragment of Isidore of Seville's *Etymologiae*'. *The Archaeology and History of Glastonbury Abbey: Essays in Honour of the Ninetieth Birthday of C. A. Ralegh Radford*, pp. 135–53. Eds Lesley Abrams and James P. Carley. Woodbridge.

Carney, James 1955. *Studies in Irish Literature and History*. Dublin.

Chadwick, Nora K. 1963. 'Bede, St Colmán and the Irish Abbey of Mayo'. *Celt and Saxon: Studies in the Early British Border*, pp. 186–205. Ed. Nora K. Chadwick. Cambridge.

Charles-Edwards, Thomas 1976. 'The Social Background to Irish *Peregrinatio*'. *Celtica* 11: 43–59.

—— 1995. 'The Penitential of Theodore and the *Iudicia Theodori*'. *Archbishop Theodore: Commemorative Studies on his Life and Influence*, pp. 141–74. Ed. Michael Lapidge. Cambridge Studies in Anglo-Saxon England 11. Cambridge.

—— 1998. 'The Context and Uses of Literacy in Early Christian Ireland'. *Literacy in Medieval Celtic Societies*, pp. 62–82. Ed. Huw Pryce. Cambridge.

Cross, James E. 1971. Review of *Homilies of Ælfric: A Supplementary Collection*, ed. J. C. Pope. *Studia Neophilologica* 43: 569–71.

—— 1972. '*De ordine creaturarum liber* in Old English Prose'. *Anglia* 90: 132–40.

—— 1981. 'The Influence of Irish Texts and Traditions on the *Old English Martyrology*'. *Proceedings of the Royal Irish Academy* 81C: 173–92.

—— 1986. 'Towards the Identification of Old English Literary Ideas – Old Workings and New Seams'. *Sources of Anglo-Saxon Culture*, pp. 77–101. Ed. Paul E. Szarmach. Kalamazoo.

—— 1999. 'On Hiberno-Latin Texts and Anglo-Saxon Writings'. *The Scriptures and Early Medieval Ireland*, pp. 69–79. Ed. Thomas O'Loughlin. Instrumenta Patristica 31. Turnhout.

—— and Thomas D. Hill, ed. 1982. *The Prose Solomon and Saturn and Adrian and Ritheus*. Toronto.

De Coninck, Lucas 1999. 'The Composite Literal Gloss of the Double Psalter of St.-Ouen and the Contents of MS Vat. Pal. Lat. 68'. *The Scriptures and Early Medieval Ireland*, pp. 81–93. Ed. Thomas O'Loughlin. Instrumenta Patristica 31. Turnhout.

Dillon, Myles 1947. 'The Archaism of the Irish Tradition'. *Proceedings of the British Academy* 33: 245–64.

Donahue, Charles 1949–51. '*Beowulf*, Ireland and the Natural Good'. *Traditio* 7: 263–77.

—— 1950. 'Grendel and the *Clanna Cain*'. *Journal of Celtic Studies* 1: 167–75.

Draak, Martje 1957. 'Construe Marks in Hiberno-Latin Manuscripts'. *Mededelingen van de koninklijke Nederlandse Akademie van Wetenschappen, Afdeling Letterkunde* 20: 261–82. Amsterdam.

—— 1967. 'The Higher Teaching of Latin Grammar in Ireland during the Ninth Century'. *Mededelingen der koninklijke Nederlandse Akademie van Wetenschappen, Afdeling Letterkunde* 30: 107–44. Amsterdam.

Dumville, David N. 1972. 'Liturgical Drama and Panegyric Responsory from the Eighth Century? A Re-examination of the Origin and Contents of the Ninth-century Section of the Book of Cerne'. *Journal of Theological Studies* n.s. 23: 374–406.

—— 1973. 'Biblical Apocrypha and the Early Irish: A Preliminary Investigation'. *Proceedings of the Royal Irish Academy* 73C: 299–338.

—— 1981. '"Beowulf" and the Celtic World: The Uses of Evidence'. *Traditio* 37: 109–60.

—— 1992a. *Liturgy and the Ecclesiastical History of Late Anglo-Saxon England*. Woodbridge.

—— 1992b. *Wessex and England from Alfred to Edgar*. Woodbridge.

—— 1994. 'Ireland, Brittany and England: Transmission and Use of the *Collectio canonum Hibernensis*'. *Irlande et Bretagne, vingt siècles d'histoire: actes du colloque de Rennes (29–31 mars 1993)*, pp. 85–95. Eds Catherine Laurent and Helen Davis. Rennes.

Fjalldal, Magnús 1998. *The Long Arm of Coincidence: The Frustrated Connection between Beowulf and Grettis saga*. Toronto.

Folz, R. 1980. 'Saint Oswald roi de Northumbrie, étude d'hagiographie royale'. *Analecta Bollandiana* 98: 49–74.

Förster, Max 1921. 'Keltisches Wortgut im Englischen: eine sprachliche Untersuchungen'. *Texte und Forschungen zur englischen Kulturgeschichte: Festgabe für Felix Liebermann*, pp. 119–242. Eds M. Förster and K. Wildhagen. Halle.

—— 1955. 'A New Version of the Apocalypse of Thomas in Old English'. *Anglia* 73: 6–36.

Frantzen, Allen J. 1983. *The Literature of Penance in Anglo-Saxon England*. New Brunswick, NJ.

Frede, Hermann Josef 1961. *Pelagius, der irische Paulustext, Sedulius Scottus Vetus Latina*. Aus der Geschichte der lateinischen Bibel 3. Freiburg im Breisgau.

Gneuss, Helmut 1981. 'A Preliminary List of Manuscripts Written or Owned in England up to 1100'. *Anglo-Saxon England* 9: 1–60.

Godden, Malcolm R. 1973. 'An Old English Penitential Motif'. *Anglo-Saxon England* 2: 221–39.

Goffart, Walter 1988. *The Narrators of Barbarian History (AD 550–800)*. Princeton, NJ.

Gougaud, Louis 1911–12. 'Étude sur les *loricae* celtiques et sur les prières qui s'en rapproachent'.

Bulletin d'ancienne littérature et de'archéologie chrétiennes 1: 265–81; 2: 33–41, 101–27.

—— 1927. *Devotional and Ascetic Practices in the Middle Ages*. London.

Grant, Raymond J. S. 1979. *Cambridge, Corpus Christi College 41: The Loricas and the Missal*. Costerus, n.s. 17. Amsterdam.

Grosjean, Paul 1956. 'Confusa caligo: Remarques sur les *Hisperica Famina*'. *Celtica* 3: 35–85.

Gwara, Scott 1989. 'Aldhelm's *Ps* and *Qs* in the *Epistola ad Ehfridum*'. *Notes & Queries* 234: 290–3.

Harvey, Anthony and Jane Power 1997. 'Hiberno-Latin *scaltae*'. *Ériu* 48: 277–9.

Heist, William W. 1952. *The Fifteen Signs before Doomsday*. East Lansing, MI.

Henderson, George 1987. *From Durrow to Kells: The Insular Gospel-books 650–800*. London.

Henry, P. L. 1966. *The Early English and Celtic Lyric*. London.

Herren, Michael W. 1973. 'The Authorship, Date of Composition and Provenance of the So-called *Lorica Gildae*'. *Ériu* 24: 35–51.

——, ed. 1987. *The Hisperica Famina II. Related Poems*. Studies and Texts 85. Toronto.

—— 1995. 'Virgilius Maro Grammaticus: A Spanish Jew in Ireland?'. *Peritia* 9: 51–71.

—— 1996a. 'On the Earliest Irish Acquaintance with Isidore of Seville'. *Visigothic Spain: New Approaches*, pp. 243–50. Ed. Edward James. Oxford, 1980. Repr. (with original pagination) in Herren, *Latin Letters in Early Christian Ireland*. Aldershot.

—— 1996b. 'Some New Light on the Life of Virgilius Maro Grammaticus'. *Proceedings of the Royal Irish Academy* 79C: 27–71. Repr. (with original pagination) in Herren, *Latin Letters in Early Christian Ireland*. Aldershot.

—— 1996c. 'Insular Latin *c(h)araxare (craxare)* and its Derivatives'. *Peritia* 1 (1982): 273–80. Repr. (with original pagination) in Herren, *Latin Letters in Early Christian Ireland*. Aldershot.

—— 1996d. 'The Hiberno-Latin Poems in Virgil the Grammarian'. *De Tertullien aux Mozarabes. Mélanges offerts à Jacques Fontaine*, pp. 141–55. Ed. Louis Holtz. Paris, 1992. Repr. (with original pagination) in Herren, *Latin Letters in Early Christian Ireland*. Aldershot.

—— 1996e. 'Hiberno-Latin Lexical Sources of Harley 3376, a Latin–Old English Glossary'.

Words, Texts and Manuscripts: Studies in Anglo-Saxon Culture Presented to Helmut Gneuss, pp. 371–9. Ed. Michael Korhammer. Woodbridge, 1992. Repr. (with original pagination) in Herren, *Latin Letters in Early Christian Ireland*. Aldershot.

Hill, Thomas D. 1969a. 'The Seven Joys of Heaven in "Christ III" and Old English Homiletic Texts'. *Notes & Queries* 214: 165–6.

—— 1969b. 'Notes on the Eschatology of the Old English *Christ III*'. *Neuphilologische Mitteilungen* 70: 672–9.

—— 1981. 'Invocation of the Trinity and the Tradition of the *Lorica* in Old English Poetry'. *Speculum* 56: 259–67.

—— 1986. 'Literary History and Old English Poetry: The Case of *Christ I, II*, and *III*'. *Sources of Anglo-Saxon Culture*, pp. 3–22. Ed. Paul E. Szarmach. Kalamazoo.

Holtz, Louis 1981. *Donat et la tradition de l'enseignement grammatical: Etude sur l'Ars Donati et sa diffusion (IVe–IXe siècle) et édition critique*. Paris.

—— 1983. 'Les grammariens hiberno-latins étaient-ils des anglo-saxons?'. *Peritia* 2: 170–84.

Howlett, D. R. 1994. 'Aldhelm and Irish Learning'. *Archivum Latinitatis Medii Aevi* 52: 37–75.

—— 1995. 'Insular Latin *idama, iduma*'. *Peritia* 9: 72–80.

—— 1997. 'Israelite Learning in Insular Latin'. *Peritia* 11: 117–52.

Hughes, Kathleen 1987a. 'The Changing Theory and Practice of Irish Pilgrimage'. *Journal of Ecclesiastical History* 11 (1960): 143–51. Repr. (with original pagination) *Kathleen Hughes. Church and Society in Ireland, AD 400–1200*. Ed. David Dumville. London, 1987.

—— 1987b. 'Some Aspects of Irish Influence on Early English Private Prayer'. *Studia Celtica* 5 (1970): 48–61. Repr. (with original pagination) *Kathleen Hughes. Church and Society in Ireland, AD 400–1200*. Ed. David Dumville. London, 1987.

—— 1987c. 'Evidence for Contacts between the Churches of the Irish and English from the Synod of Whitby to the Viking Age'. *England before the Conquest: Studies in Primary Sources Presented to Dorothy Whitelock*, pp. 49–67. Eds Peter Clemoes and Kathleen Hughes. Cambridge, 1971. Repr. (with original pagination) *Kathleen Hughes. Church and Society in Ireland, AD 400–1200*. Ed. David Dumville. London, 1987.

Ireland, Colin 1991. 'Some Analogues of the O. E. *Seafarer* from Hiberno-Latin Sources'. *Neuphilologische Mitteilungen* 92: 1–14.

—— 1996. 'Aldfrith of Northumbria and the Learning of a *Sapiens*'. *A Celtic Florilegium: Studies in Memory of Brendan O Hehir*, pp. 63–77. Eds Kathryn A. Klar, Eve Sweetser and Claire Thomas. Lawrence, MA.

—— 1997. 'Penance and Prayer in Water: An Irish Practice in Northumbrian Hagiography'. *Cambrian Medieval Celtic Studies* 34: 51–66.

——, ed. 1999. *Old Irish Wisdom attributed to Aldfrith of Northumbria: An Edition of Bríathra Flainn Fhína Maic Ossu*. Medieval and Renaissance Texts and Studies 20. Tempe, AZ.

Irvine, Martin 1994. *The Making of Textual Culture: 'Grammatica' and Literary Theory, 350–1100*. Cambridge.

Jaski, Bart 1998. 'Early Medieval Irish Kingship and the Old Testament'. *Early Medieval Europe* 7: 329–44.

Johnson, Richard F. 1998. 'Archangel in the Margins: St Michael in the Homilies of Cambridge, Corpus Christi College 41'. *Traditio* 53: 63–91.

Jones, Charles W. 1943. *Bedae Opera de Temporibus*. Cambridge, MA.

Jost, Karl 1959. *Die 'Institutes of Polity, Civil and Ecclesiastical': Ein Werk Erzbischof Wulfstans von York*. Schweizer anglistische Arbeiten 47. Bern.

Jungmann, Josef 1959. *The Mass of the Roman Rite: Its Origins and Development (Missarum solemnia)*. Trans. Francis A. Brunner. Rev. edn in 1 vol. Charles K. Riepe. New York.

Kelly, Joseph F. 1975. 'Irish Influence in England after the Synod of Whitby: Some New Literary Evidence'. *Éire/Ireland* 10: 35–47.

—— 1978. 'Pelagius, Pelagianism and the Early Christian Irish'. *Mediaevalia* 4: 99–124.

—— 1982. 'The Venerable Bede and the Irish Exegetical Tradition on the Apocalypse'. *Revue Bénédictine* 92: 393–406.

—— 1986. 'Bede and Hiberno-Latin Exegesis'. *Sources of Anglo-Saxon Culture*, pp. 65–76. Ed. Paul E. Szarmach. Kalamazoo.

Keynes, Simon 1985. 'King Athelstan's Books'. *Learning and Literature in Anglo-Saxon England: Studies Presented to Peter Clemoes*, pp. 143–201. Eds Michael Lapidge and Helmut Gneuss. Cambridge.

Kittredge, George Lyman 1903. 'Arthur and Gorlagon'. *Harvard Studies and Notes in Philology and Literature* 8: 149–275.

Korhammer, Michael 1980. 'Mittelalterliche Konstruktionshilfen und altenglische Wortstellung'. *Scriptorium* 34: 18–58.

Laistner, M. L. W. 1957. *Thought and Letters in Western Europe AD 500 to 900*. Rev. edn Ithaca, NY.

Lapidge, Michael 1986. 'Latin Learning in Dark Age Wales: Some Prolegomena'. *Proceedings of the Seventh International Congress of Celtic Studies*, pp. 91–107. Eds D. E. Evans, John G. Griffith and E. M. Hope. Oxford.

—— 1993a. 'The Hermeneutic Style in Tenth-Century Anglo-Latin Literature'. *Anglo-Saxon England* 4 (1975): 67–111. Repr. in Lapidge, *Anglo-Latin Literature 900–1066*, pp. 105–49. London.

—— 1993b. 'Æthelwold as Scholar and Teacher'. *Bishop Æthelwold: His Career and Influence*, pp. 89–117. Ed. Barbara Yorke. Ipswich, 1988. Repr. in Lapidge, *Anglo-Latin Literature 900–1066*, pp. 183–211. London.

—— 1994. 'Surviving Booklists from Anglo-Saxon England'. *Learning and Literature in Anglo-Saxon England: Studies Presented to Peter Clemoes*, pp. 33–89. Eds M. Lapidge and Helmut Gneuss. Cambridge, 1985. Repr. with revisions *Anglo-Saxon Manuscripts: Basic Readings*, pp. 87–167. Ed. Mary P. Richards. Garland Reference Library of the Humanities 1434; Basic Readings in Anglo-Saxon England 2. New York and London.

—— 1996a. 'The Study of Greek at the School of Canterbury in the Seventh Century'. *The Sacred Nectar of the Greeks: The Study of Greek in the West in the Early Middle Ages*. Ed. M. W. Herren. King's College London Medieval Studies 2, pp. 169–94. London, 1992. Repr. in Lapidge, *Anglo-Latin Literature 600–899*, pp. 123–39. London.

—— 1996b. '*Beowulf*, Aldhelm, the *Liber Monstrorum* and Wessex'. *Studi Medievali*, 3rd ser. 23 (1982): 151–92. Repr. in Lapidge, *Anglo-Latin Literature 600–899*, pp. 271–312. London.

—— and Michael W. Herren, trans. 1979. *Aldhelm: The Prose Works*. Cambridge.

Law, Vivien 1982a. *The Insular Latin Grammarians*. Woodbridge.

—— 1982b. 'Notes on the Dating and Attribution of Anonymous Latin Grammars of the Early Middle Ages'. *Peritia* 1: 250–67.

Lawson, M. K. 1994. 'Archbishop Wulfstan and the Homiletic Element in the Laws of Æthelred II and Cnut'. *The Reign of Cnut: King of England, Denmark and Norway*, pp. 141–64. Ed. Alexander R. Rumble. London.

Lees, Clare 1985. 'The "Sunday Letter" and the "Sunday Lists"'. *Anglo-Saxon England* 14: 129–51.

—— 1990. 'Apocrypha. II. Apocryphal Gospels. Sunday Letter'. *Sources of Anglo-Saxon Literary Culture: A Trial Version*, pp. 38–40. Eds Frederick M. Biggs, Thomas D. Hill and Paul E. Szarmach. Binghamton, NY.

Liberman, Anatoly 1986. '*Beowulf – Grettir*'. *Germanic Dialects: Linguistic and Philological Investigations*, pp. 353–401. Eds Bela Brogyanyi and Thomas Krömmelbein. Amsterdam Studies in the Theory and History of Linguistic Science, ser. IV: Current Issues in Linguistic Theory 38. Amsterdam.

Lindsay, W. M. 1915. *Notae Latinae: An Account of Abbreviations in Latin Manuscripts of the Early Minuscule Period (ca. 700–850)*. Cambridge.

Lowe, E. A. 1972. *Codices Latini Antiquiores*, vol. 2: *Great Britain*. 2nd edn. Oxford.

Lutz, Cora E. 1956. 'Remigius' Ideas on the Origin of the Seven Liberal Arts'. *Medievalia et Humanistica* 10: 32–49.

MacGinty, Gerard 1987. 'The Irish Augustine: *De Mirabilibus Sacrae Scripturae*'. *Irland und die Christenheit: Bibelstudien und Mission*, pp. 70–83. Eds Próinséas Ní Chatháin and Michael Richter. Stuttgart.

Mayr-Harting, Henry 1991. *The Coming of Christianity to Anglo-Saxon England*. 3rd edn. University Park, PA.

McGurk, Patrick 1986. 'The Metrical Calendar of Hampson: A New Edition'. *Analecta Bollandiana* 104: 79–125.

—— 1998. 'An Edition of the Abbreviated and Selective Set of Hebrew Names Found in the Book of Kells'. *The Book of Kells: Proceedings of a Conference at Trinity College, Dublin 6–9 September 1992*, pp. 102–32. Ed. Felicity O'Mahoney. Aldershot, 1994. Repr. in McGurk, *Gospel Books and Early Latin Manuscripts*. Aldershot.

McKee, Helen Simpson 1999. 'Breton Manuscripts of Biblical and Hiberno-Latin Texts'. *The*

Scriptures and Early Medieval Ireland, pp. 275–90. Ed. Thomas O'Loughlin. Instrumenta Patristica 31. Turnhout.

McNally, R. E. 1958. 'The "Tres Linguae Sacrae" in Early Irish Bible Exegesis'. *Theological Studies* 19: 395–403.

——1965. '"Christus" in the Pseudo-Isidorian "Liber de ortu et obitu patriarcharum"'. *Traditio* 21: 167–83.

——1979. '"In Nomine Dei Summi": Seven Hiberno-Latin Sermons'. *Traditio* 35: 121–43.

McNamara, Martin 1973. 'Psalter Text and Psalter Study in the Early Irish Church (AD 600–1200)'. *Proceedings of the Royal Irish Academy* 73C: 201–98.

——1975. *The Apocrypha in the Irish Church*. Dublin.

——1984. 'Tradition and Creativity in Early Irish Psalter Study'. *Irland und Europa: Die Kirche im Frühmittelalter*, pp. 338–89. Eds Próinséas Ní Chatháin and Michael Richter. Stuttgart.

——, ed. 1986. *Glossa in Psalmos: The Hiberno-Latin Gloss on the Psalms of Codex Palatinus Latinus 58 (Psalms 39.11–151.7)*. Studi e Testi 310. Vatican City.

——1998. 'The Psalms in the Irish Church. The Most Recent Research on Text, Commentary, and Decoration – with Emphasis on the So-called Psalter of Charlemagne'. *The Bible as Book: The Manuscript Tradition*, pp. 89–103. Eds John L. Sharpe III and Kimberly van Kampen. London.

——and Máire Herbert, trans. 1989. *Irish Biblical Apocrypha: Selected Texts in Translation*. Edinburgh.

Meens, Rob 1998. 'Politics, Mirrors of Princes and the Bible: Sins, Kings and the Well-being of the Realm'. *Early Medieval Europe* 7: 345–57.

Mellinkoff, Ruth 1979. 'Cain's Monstrous Progeny in "Beowulf": Part I, Noachic Tradition'. *Anglo-Saxon England* 8: 143–62.

——1981. 'Cain's Monstrous Progeny in Beowulf: Part II, Post-Diluvian Survival'. *Anglo-Saxon England* 9: 183–97.

Meroney, Howard 1945. 'Irish in the Old English Charms'. *Speculum* 20: 172–82.

Murphy, Gerard 1953. *Duanaire Finn*, vol. III. Early Irish Text Society 43. Dublin.

Myrick, Leslie Diane 1995. 'The Stelographic Transmission of Prediluvian Scéla: An Apoc-

ryphal Reference in the Irish Lebor Gabála'. *Zeitschrift für celtische Philologie* 47: 18–31.

Nees, Lawrence 1993. 'Ultán the Scribe'. *Anglo-Saxon England* 22: 127–46.

Netzer, Nancy 1994. *Cultural Interplay in the Eighth Century: The Trier Gospels and the Making of a Scriptorium at Echternach*. Cambridge.

Ní Chatháin, Próinséas 1987. 'Notes on the Würzburg Glosses'. *Irland und die Christenheit: Bibelstudien und Mission*, pp. 190–9. Eds Próinséas Ní Chatháin and Michael Richter. Stuttgart.

Norden, Eduard 1909. *Die antike Kunstprosa vom VI. Jahrhundert v. Chr. bis in die Zeit der Renaissance*. 2 vols. 2nd edn. Leipzig.

Ó Cróinín, Dáibhí 1983. 'The Irish Provenance of Bede's Computus'. *Peritia* 2: 229–47.

——1984. 'Rath Melsigi, Willibrord, and the Earliest Echternach Manuscripts'. *Peritia* 3: 17–49.

——1989. 'Is the Augsburg Gospel Codex a Northumbrian Manuscript?'. *St Cuthbert, his Cult and his Community to AD 1200*, pp. 189–201. Eds Gerald Bonner, David Rollason and Clare Stancliffe. Woodbridge.

Ó Cuív, Brian 1993. 'St Gregory and St Dunstan in a Middle-Irish Poem on the Origins of the Liturgical Chant'. *St Dunstan: His Life, Times and Cult*, pp. 273–97. Eds Nigel Ramsay, Margaret Sparks and Tim Talton-Brown. Woodbridge.

Ó Máille, Tomás 1921–3. 'The Authorship of the Culmen'. *Ériu* 9: 71–6.

Ó Néill, Pádraig P. [Patrick P. O'Neill] 1979. 'The Old-Irish Treatise on the Psalter and its Hiberno-Latin Background'. *Ériu* 30: 148–64.

——1981. 'The Old English Introductions to the Prose Psalms of the Paris Psalter: Sources, Structure, and Composition'. *Studies in Philology* 78: 20–38.

——1991. 'Irish Cultural Influence on Northumbria: The First Thirty Years, AD 635–664'. *Crossed Paths: Methodological Approaches to the Celtic Aspect of the European Middle Ages*, pp. 11–23. Eds Benjamin T. Hudson and Vickie Ziegler. Lanham, MD.

——1997. 'On the Date, Provenance and Relationship of the "Solomon and Saturn" Dialogues'. *Anglo-Saxon England* 26: 139–65.

Orchard, Andy 1994. *The Poetic Art of Aldhelm*. Cambridge studies in Anglo-Saxon England 8. Cambridge.

——1995. *Pride and Prodigies: Studies in the Monsters of the Beowulf-Manuscript*. Cambridge.

Parkes, Malcolm B. 1982. *The Scriptorium of Wearmouth–Jarrow*. Jarrow Lecture 1982. Jarrow.

——1987. 'The Contribution of Insular Scribes of the Seventh and Eighth Centuries to the "Grammar of Legibility"'. *Grafia e interpunzione del Latino nel medioevo: Seminario internazionale Roma, 27–29 settembre 1984*, pp. 15–30. Ed. Alfonso Maierù. Rome. Repr. in Parkes, *Scribes, Scripts and Readers: Studies in the Communication, Presentation and Dissemination of Medieval Texts*, pp. 1–18. London.

——1993. *Pause and Effect: An Introduction to the History of Punctuation in the West*. Berkeley.

Pelteret, David A. E. 1989. 'Slave Raiding and Slave Trading in Early England'. *Anglo-Saxon England* 9: 99–114.

Pepperdene, Margaret W. 1958. 'Bede's *Historia Ecclesiastica*: A New Perspective'. *Celtica* 4: 253–62.

Petitmengin, Pierre 1993. 'La compilation "De vindictis magnis magnorum peccatorum": Exemples d'anthropogaphie tirés des sièges de Jérusalem et de Samarie'. *Philologia Sacra: Biblische und patristische Studien für Hermann T. Frede und Walter Thiele zu ihrem siebzigsten Geburtstag*. Vetus Latina, 24. 2 vols, 2.622–38. Ed. Roger Gryson. Freiburg.

Pheifer, J. D. 1987. 'Early Anglo-Saxon Glossaries and the School of Canterbury'. *Anglo-Saxon England* 16: 17–44.

Priebsch, R. 1899. 'The Chief Sources of some Anglo-Saxon Homilies'. *Otia Merseiana* 1: 129–47.

Puhvel, Martin 1979. *Beowulf and Celtic Tradition*. Waterloo, Ontario.

Ramsay, R. L. 1912a. 'Theodore of Mopsuestia and St Columban on the Psalms'. *Zeitschrift für celtische Philologie* 8: 421–51.

——1912b. 'Theodore of Mopsuestia in England and Ireland'. *Zeitschrift für celtische Philologie* 8: 452–97.

Reichl, Karl 1982. 'Zur Frage des irischen Einflusses auf die altenglische weltliche Dichtung'. *Die Iren und Europa im früheren Mittelalter*. 2 vols, 1.138–70. Ed. Heinz Löwe. Stuttgart.

Robinson, Fred C. 1973. 'Syntactical Glosses in Latin Manuscripts of Anglo-Saxon Provenance'. *Speculum* 48: 443–75.

Saenger, Paul 1997. *Space Between Words: The Origins of Silent Reading*. Stanford.

Sauer, Hans 1980. 'Zur Überlieferung und Anlage von Erzbischof Wulfstans "Handbuch"'. *Deutsches Archiv für Erforschung des Mittelalters* 36: 341–84.

Scharer, Anton 1996. 'The Writing of History at King Alfred's Court'. *Early Medieval Europe* 5: 177–206.

Scowcroft, Mark R. 1999. 'The Irish Analogues to *Beowulf*'. *Speculum* 74: 22–64.

Simpson, Dean 1987. 'The Proverbia Grecorum'. *Traditio* 43: 1–22.

Sims-Williams, Patrick 1982. 'The Evidence for Vernacular Irish Literary Influence on Early Medieval Welsh Literature'. *Ireland in Early Medieval Europe: Studies in Memory of Kathleen Hughes*, pp. 235–57. Eds Dorothy Whitelock, Rosamund McKitterick and David Dumville. Cambridge.

——1990. *Religion and Literature in Western England 600–800*. Cambridge Studies in Anglo-Saxon England 3. Cambridge.

——1995a. 'Thought, Word and Deed: An Irish Triad'. *Ériu* 29 (1978): 78–111. Repr. (with original pagination) in Sims-Williams, *Britain and Early Christian Europe: Studies in Early Medieval History and Culture*. Aldershot.

——1995b. 'Byrhtferth's Ogam Signature'. *Essays and Poems Presented to Daniel Huws*, pp. 283–91. Eds Tegwyn Jones and E. B. Fryde. Aberystwyth, 1994. Repr. (with original pagination) in Sims-Williams, *Britain and Early Christian Europe: Studies in Early Medieval History and Culture*. Aldershot.

Smith, Roland 1927. 'The *speculum principum* in Early Irish Literature'. *Speculum* 2: 411–45.

Smyth, Marina 1996. *Understanding the Universe in Seventh-Century Ireland*. Woodbridge.

Stancliffe, Clare 1989. 'Cuthbert and the Polarity between Pastor and Solitary'. *St Cuthbert, his Cult and his Community to AD 1200*, pp. 21–44. Eds Gerald Bonner, David Rollason and Clare Stancliffe. Woodbridge.

Stevenson, Jane 1983. 'Ascent through the Heavens, from Egypt to Ireland'. *Cambridge Medieval Celtic Studies* 5: 21–35.

Stitt, Michael J. 1992. *Beowulf and the Bear's Son: Epic, Saga, and Fairytale in Northern Germanic Tradition*. New York.

Swan, Mary 1998. 'The *Apocalypse of Thomas* in Old English'. *Leeds Studies in English* n.s. 29: 333–46.

Szarmach, Paul E. 1987. 'Ælfric, the Prose Vision, and the *Dream of the Rood*'. *Studies in Honour of René Derolez*, pp. 592–602. Ed. A. M. Simon-Vandenbergen. Ghent.

Szerwiniack, Olivier 1994. 'Des receuils d'inter-prétations de noms hébreux chez les Irlandais et le Wisigoth Théodulf'. *Scriptorium* 48: 187–258.

Tristram, Hildegard L. C. 1978. 'Stock Descriptions of Heaven and Hell in Old English Literature'. *Neuphilologische Mitteilungen* 79: 102–13.

——1985. *Sex aetates mundi: die Weltzeitalter bei den Angelsachsen und den Iren*. Anglistische Forschungen 165. Heidelberg.

——1993. 'Vom Abschaben irischer Hand-schriften im alten England'. *Schriftlichkeit im frühen Mittelalter*, pp. 155–77. Ed. Ursula Schaefer. ScriptOralia 53. Tübingen.

——1995. *Early Insular Preaching: Verbal Artistry and Method of Composition*. Österreichische Akademie der Wissenshaften, Philosophisch-historische Klasse, Sitzungsberichte, 623; Veröffentlichungen der Keltischen Kommis-sion, 11. Vienna.

——1997. 'What's the Point of Dating "Beowulf"?'. *Medieval Insular Literature between the Oral and the Written II: Continuity of Trans-mission*, pp. 65–80. Ed. H. L. C. Tristram. Tübingen.

von Sydow, Carl W. 1914. 'Irisches in Beowulf'. *Verhandlungen der 52. Versammlung deutscher Philologen und Schulmänner in Marburg von 29. September bis 3. Oktober 1913*, pp. 177–9. Leipzig.

Wack, Mary F. and Charles D. Wright 1990. 'A New Latin Source for the Old English "Three Utterances" Exemplum'. *Anglo-Saxon England* 20: 187–202.

Walsh, Maura and Dáibhí Ó Cróinín, eds. 1988. *Cummian's Letter De Controversa Paschali and the De ratione conputandi*. Studies and Texts 86. Toronto.

Whitelock, Dorothy 1950. 'The Interpretation of *The Seafarer*'. *The Early Cultures of North-west Europe*, pp. 259–72. Eds Cyril Fox and Bruce Dickins. Cambridge.

——1982. 'Bishop Ecgred, Pehtred and Niall'. *Ireland in Early Mediaeval Europe: Studies in Memory of Kathleen Hughes*, pp. 47–68. Eds Dorothy Whitelock, Rosamund McKittenick and David Dumville. Cambridge.

Whitfield, Niamh 1995. 'Formal Conventions in the Depiction of Animals on Celtic Metalwork'. *From the Isles of the North: Early Medieval Art in Ireland and Britain*, pp. 89–104. Ed. Cormac Bourke. Belfast.

Willard, Rudolf 1935. *Two Apocrypha in Old English Homilies*. Beiträge zur englischen Philologie, 30. Leipzig.

——1937. 'The Latin Texts of *The Three Utterances of the Soul*'. *Speculum* 12: 147–66.

Winterbottom, Michael 1977. 'Aldhelm's Prose Style and its Origins'. *Anglo-Saxon England* 6: 39–76.

Wood, Michael 1983. 'The Making of King Aethelstan's Empire: An English Charle-magne?'. *Ideal and Reality in Frankish and Anglo-Saxon Society: Studies Presented to J. M. Wallace-Hadrill*, pp. 250–72. Ed. Patrick Wormald with Donald Bullongh and Roger Collins. Oxford.

Wormald, Patrick 1986. 'Celtic and Anglo-Saxon Kingship: Some Further Thoughts'. *Sources of Anglo-Saxon Culture*, pp. 151–83. Ed. Paul E. Szarmach. Kalamazoo.

Wright, Charles D. 1987a. 'Apocryphal Lore and Insular Tradition in St Gall, Stiftsbibliothek MS 908'. *Irland und die Christenheit: Bibelstudien und Mission*, pp. 124–45. Eds Próinséas Ní Chatháin and Michael Richter. Stuttgart.

——1987b. '*Docet Deus, Docet Diabolus*: A Hiberno-Latin Theme in an Old English Body-and-Soul Homily'. *Notes & Queries* 232: 451–3.

——1990a. 'Apocrypha. IV. Apocryphal Apoca-lypses. Apocrypha Priscillianistica'. *Sources of Anglo-Saxon Literary Culture: A Trial Version*, pp. 69–70. Eds Frederick M. Biggs, Thomas D. Hill and Paul E. Szarmach. Binghamton, NY.

——1990b. 'Hiberno-Latin and Irish-influenced Biblical Commentaries, Florilegia, and Homily Collections'. *Sources of Anglo-Saxon Literary Culture: A Trial Version*, pp. 87–123. Eds Fred-erick M. Biggs, Thomas D. Hill and Paul E. Szarmach. Binghamton, NY.

——1990c. 'Some Evidence for an Irish Origin of Redaction XI of the *Visio Pauli*'. *Manuscripta* 34: 34–44.

——1990d. 'The Pledge of the Soul: A Judgment Theme in Old English Homiletic Literature and

Cynewulf's *Elene*. *Neuphilologische Mitteilungen* 91: 23–30.

——1990e. 'The Three "Victories" of the Wind: A Hibernicism in the *Hisperica Famina*, *Collectanea Bedae*, and the Old English *Prose Solomon and Saturn* Pater Noster Dialogue'. *Ériu* 41: 13–25.

——1992. 'Hiberno-Latin Writings in *Sources* of Anglo-Saxon Literary Culture'. *Old English Newsletter*, 25, 3: 21–3.

——1993. *The Irish Tradition in Old English Literature*. Cambridge Studies in Anglo-Saxon England 6. Cambridge.

Zimmer, Heinrich 1901. *Pelagius in Irland. Texte und Untersuchungen zur patristischen Literatur*. Berlin.

20
Continental Germanic Influences
Rolf Bremmer

'Britain is an island' is how the Venerable Bede significantly opens the first chapter of his *Historia ecclesiastica* (*HE* I.1). Bede's lively and sympathetic description of the geographical situation and natural resources of this island also includes a passage on the languages spoken in Britain at the time of his writing (*c.*730):

> At the present time, there are five languages in Britain, just as the divine law is written in five books, all devoted to seeking out and setting forth one and the same kind of wisdom, namely the knowledge of sublime truth and of true sublimity. These are the English, British, Irish, Pictish, as well as the Latin languages; through the study of the scriptures, Latin is in general use among them all.

With this observation, Bede drives home both the reality of the Babylonian confusion of tongues and its redeeming factor: the Christian faith which through the medium of Latin has enabled the various peoples of Britain to surmount their vast linguistic differences. At the same time, Bede's remark is also an indication of the limitations of the intertribal cultural communication in Britain at the time, in that the subjects of intellectual traffic would be predominantly confined to matters theological, and that the participants in this exchange were trained clergy. Theirs was a literate world, united around the Latin version of the Bible and the quickly growing corpus of liturgical, exegetical, didactic and canonical Latin literature that accompanied it. Being literate was being Latinate, and this privilege was reserved for the happy few who had devoted their lives to the service of God. This raises the interesting question of how laypeople coped with the reality of a multilingual community in Britain, and beyond, on the continent. In this chapter, therefore, several topics need to be addressed before we can tackle its main problem, the influence of continental Germanic on Old English literature. They are: the continental Germanic roots of the Anglo-Saxons, multilingualism in Anglo-Saxon England and Western Europe, and cultural relations between Anglo-Saxon England and the West European continent.

When the Anglo-Saxon tribes set sail to Britain in the fifth century AD – sometimes directly, sometimes in stages along the coast of northern Germany and Frisia down to the Rhine estuary – they spoke a language that differed only marginally from that of their neighbours. The branching of Germanic into its various sub-groupings, with the exception of Gothic and other, minor East Germanic dialects, still had to take place, and was probably accelerated by their departure. After the middle of the fifth century, Scandinavian (or North Germanic) adopted its own peculiar shape. On the continent, though, West Germanic for some time remained more or less the same until, in the southernmost regions of Germany (the Alemanni and the Bavarians) and in northern Italy (the Lombards), a shift in the consonants – stops or plosives became fricatives – in the sixth century marked an important distinction that led to the development of Old High German. This change did not affect the variety spoken in northern Germany and the Low Countries. However, in the coastal areas of these regions, from northern France to Jutland (Denmark), the dialect had developed certain characteristics which set it apart from the dialects further inland, whilst at the same time it retained great similarities to the Old English dialects, which together are variously called Ingvaeonic or North Sea Germanic. Because of Frankish expansionist politics in the seventh century (the Franks spoke an inland variety), this large coastal dialect continuum gradually lost its foothold, but was retained in Frisia, where it acquired a shape of its own, Old Frisian. For this reason, Old English and Old Frisian became the most closely related languages within West Germanic during the Anglo-Saxon period. Also closely related, if to a lesser degree, were Old Saxon, a group of dialects spoken in the northern half of Germany, and Old Dutch (or Old Low Franconian), spoken away from the coast in the Netherlands south of the Rhine down to present-day northern France. Below that line (see map 2) the majority of the population spoke an early form of French, but the Frankish secular and religious aristocracy remained bilingual for a long time.

It should be borne in mind that these continental West Germanic languages were taking shape only gradually during the early Anglo-Saxon period (up to about AD 800), and that their mutual differences were growing slowly but steadily, as did those of the Old English dialects (Anglian, Mercian, West Saxon and Kentish) in England. When the migration period had come to an end around AD 600, interregional mobility also decreased. The mainly agricultural way of life did not allow for much travelling, and hence advanced the growth of dialects that were increasingly less mutually intelligible. Again, this situation applies as much to Anglo-Saxon England as it does to the Germanic-speaking continent.

We have all had some experience in talking to someone who speaks the same language but hails from an area different from our own. With some adjustments of the ear, Americans, for example, can converse with Scots without having to accommodate their pronunciation, and the other way around. Something similar will have been the case in those early days, especially among the mobile members of society like traders, nobles and the clergy (Moulton 1988; Hellgardt 1996). When St Augustine – himself

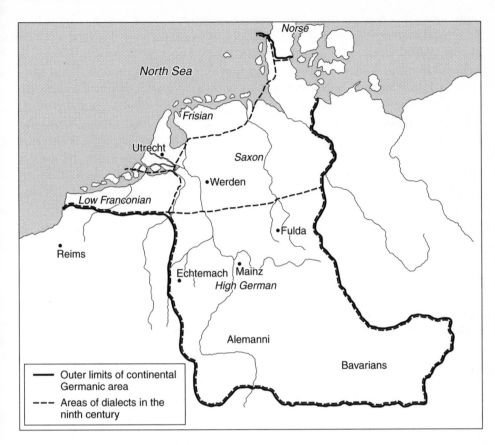

Map 2 The continental German dialects

an Italian – set out from Rome in 596 on his missionary expedition to England, he stopped in France to recruit some Frankish interpreters (*HE* I.25) to enable a fruitful conversation with the still pagan King Æthelbert of Kent. Æthelbert was used to hearing Frankish: trading and cultural links between his kingdom and the lands immediately across the narrowest part of the Channel were close and intense. Small wonder that his wife Bertha was a Frankish royal princess and, moreover, a Christian who had been allowed, as part of the marriage contract, to bring along to Kent a Frankish bishop in her following. The Frankish lilt that may have sounded so attractive to Æthelbert proved appalling to Anglo-Saxons who lived more remote from Francia. Bede (*HE* III.7) reports how the Frankish missionary Agilberht preached at the court of the West Saxon King Coenwealh some sixty years after Augustine had landed in Kent, but was fairly soon commanded to leave because the king, only famil-iar with the *lingua Saxonum*, 'was fed up with [his] barbarous speech' (*pertaesus bar-*

barae loquellae). The same Agilberht, having meanwhile become bishop of Paris, also attended the famous Synod of Whitby in 663/4, at which occasion the Northumbrian Bishop Wilfrid acted as his interpreter (*HE* III.25; Hines 1995: 56–7). Wilfrid, as we know from his near-contemporary biography (Farmer and Webb 1983), had travelled to Rome when he was about sixteen or seventeen years old, and must have become familiar with Frankish when he stayed in Lyons for a longer period of time, if not long enough to betray by his speech that he was an Englishman, something which was to save his life (chs 3–6). Also, later in his life his linguistic skills came to stand him in good stead: in 686, driven ashore in Frisia by a storm, he spent a winter at the court of King Aldgisl, and preached the Gospel with much success to the Frisians, baptizing most of the chieftains (*principes*) and some thousands of commoners (ch. 26).

Bede also relates the presence of a different category of continentals in England. A striking instance is his account of Imma, a Northumbrian thane, who had been taken captive by the Mercians, but was sold later on to a Frisian slave-trader based in London (*HE* IV.22). Nowhere does Bede indicate that the Frisian and Imma had any difficulties in understanding each other. Slightly later, around 770, we know of a sizeable community of Frisian traders in York who had their own quarter in the town. One of their community was Liudger, who was rounding off his training for the priesthood at Alcuin's cathedral school. With his fellow tribesmen, he was forced to repatriate by the Northumbrians in a bout of ethnic cleansing, as a result of a Frisian having killed a native of York (Altfrid, *Vita Liudgari* I.10–11).

The pattern of continental Germans of various dialects present in Anglo-Saxon England as we can discern it from Bede's *Historia* is confirmed throughout the centuries after him. When staging his programme for educational reform, King Alfred invited some prominent continental clergymen: John from Old Saxony, Grimbold from Francia. Even in the intimate circle of his family, Alfred had become accustomed to the Frankish tongue. When still a boy, he was taken by his father Æthelwulf, an old widower by then, on a twelve-month journey to Rome. On their way home, the royal company sojourned at the court of Charles the Bald in Francia, who gave his 12-year-old daughter Judith in marriage to the ageing Æthelwulf. The newly weds were received with great joy in Wessex, according to the *Anglo-Saxon Chronicle* (for the year 855, A and C versions). The marriage did not last long, however; within two years the old king had died, whereupon his son, Alfred's older brother, Æthelwulf, much to the abhorrence of the clergy, married his father's widow (Bremmer 1995: 63–4). Besides such royal and ecclesiastical continental VIPs, other foreigners frequented Alfred's court, attracted by his kindness and generosity. 'Many Franks, Frisians, Gauls, Danes, Welshmen, Irishmen and Bretons subjected willingly to his lordship, nobles and commoners alike' (Asser, *Vita Ælfredi* ch. 76; Keynes and Lapidge 1983). Surely, cacophony must have ruled in the king's hall at times! Amongst the Frisians, there will have been traders and sailors (Bremmer 1981). Their reputation as masters of the sea also induced Alfred to enrol them as commanders of his fleet in a naval encounter with the Vikings. The *Anglo-Saxon Chronicle* reports for the year 896 the death of several of these naval experts by name, along with a number of unnamed Frisians.

Also after Alfred's time, continental clergymen kept coming to England. One of these was Frithegod of Canterbury, a Frankish monk who served in the household of Archbishop Oda. Skilled in handling a quill, Frithegod made a name for himself among posterity by composing poetry, but in Latin and that interspersed with Greek – 'damnably difficult' even according to the experts (Lapidge 1988). Another learned Frank, Abbo of Fleury, spent two years at the abbey of Ramsey in the late tenth century. His *Passio S. Edmundi* has become famous through Ælfric's translation. Continental presence in English monasteries and chapter houses culminated in the eleventh century, especially through the influx of Flemish monks, as a result of the Benedictine Reform (for a survey see Lapidge 1986; on placenames see Dietz 1993).

Naturally, documentation focuses on the activities of the upper crust of society. The West Saxon kings were keen on tying up their dynasty with continental aristocrats. One of Alfred's daughters, Ælfthryth, was joined in matrimony to Count Baldwin II of Flanders, while four daughters of Alfred's son Edward the Elder saw their future across the North Sea: Edith married Otto I of Saxony (and emperor of Germany); Eadgifu was taken in marriage by Charles the Simple, king of the Franks; Ealhhild became wife of Hugh, an influential Frankish duke; while Ælfgifu spent her life as a Bavarian duchess in the northern Alps (Smyth 1995: 108). During an uprising against Charles the Simple, Eadgifu returned to England with their son Louis, who then received his education at the court of King Athelstan. When, as a young adult, he returned to France to assume the kingship there, he was nicknamed 'd'Outremer' ('from across the sea'), a hint that he spoke English rather than French.

Most of the males just mentioned played an important part in a meeting at Visé on the Meuse, just north of Liège (Belgium) near the present-day Dutch border, in 942. The occasion of the meeting was an attempt to reconfirm the friendly relations between Louis and Otto as well as to reconcile Louis with Duke Hugh. Otto had been found willing to assume the role of intermediary. Also present were Duke William of Normandy, a supporter of Louis, as well as some Saxon dukes. From a detailed account of these negotiations, it becomes clear that most negotiators were bilingual, and some even trilingual, the languages used being French, Saxon, Anglo-Saxon and Danish (Christophersen 1992).

King Alfred's four granddaughters followed well-beaten paths. As early as the late seventh century, Anglo-Saxon missionaries had found their way to the continent. Wilfrid, Willibrord and Boniface – to mention just the most important ones – had preached the Gospel to Frisians, Franks and Saxons, and in their company numerous Anglo-Saxon monks had followed. Their concerted efforts to convert their next of kin and tongue (Bede calls them *gens nostra* 'our people') resulted not only in firmly establishing the church in what is now the Low Countries and large parts of Germany, but also in the foundation of monastic centres that maintained strong ties with England for a long time, amongst which Utrecht, Echternach, Fulda and Werden figured most prominently. Unquestionably their efforts were successful also because of the great similarity in language. New converts were often sent to England for further education. We have already seen the case of the Frisian Liudger, but other instances are known, too.

It is important to establish these links between Anglo-Saxons and continental Germans, for the question must be raised of what effect they had on the cultural exchange between them. No doubt the Christian Anglo-Saxons were above all anxious to convey the Christian faith and the literary baggage that came with it. Many Anglo-Saxon Latin manuscripts found their way to the newly founded monasteries, and were copied there in the insular script. Their contents were all religious, especially Gospel-books, Psalters and exegetical works, but also included textbooks intended for learning Latin. Boniface, for example, wrote a Latin grammar for his Frankish pupils at Fulda. Occasionally, such manuscripts contained Old English interlinear glosses or even entire glossaries, which were duly copied by continental scribes. At first such copying was executed intelligently, but later on, when first-hand acquaintance with Old English had disappeared, the result is sometimes incomprehensible (see Ker, _Catalogue_: 475–84). To the former category belongs, for example, the _Leiden Riddle_, a Northumbrian translation of Aldhelm's _De lorica_ riddle copied in Reims in northern France on the verso of the last leaf of the manuscript, now preserved in Leiden – hence its name – containing a collection of Latin riddles composed by Aldhelm and Symphosius. Judging by the script (Caroline minuscule), the scribe was not an Anglo-Saxon. The latter category is exemplified by a version of _Caedmon's Hymn_, as preserved in a copy of Bede's _Historia ecclesiastica_, made in Brabant (Belgium) in the fifteenth century (O'Donnell 1996).

The point of this survey, of course, is to establish that speakers of continental Germanic languages were comprehensible to at least a limited number of Anglo-Saxons, especially those who had travelled on the continent or were familiar with the various dialects through commercial, political or religious intercourse. The next thing to ask, then, is what possibilities there may have been for conveying narratives from continental speakers to Anglo-Saxons. The question is not so hypothetical as it may seem. Taking Anglo-Saxon heroic literature into consideration, it soon becomes obvious that its content is Germanic in a wider sense, rather than English. The scene of _Beowulf_ is set for the major part in Scandinavia; _Waldere_ deals with a Burgundian prince at the court of Attila the Hun; the _Finnsburg Fragment_ with Frisia; _Deor_ and especially _Widsith_ – whose very name suggests his international experience – with a whole range of continental and Scandinavian peoples and heroes. How did the subject matter of these poems end up in England? However much generations of scholars have tried to settle this problem, their answers have not helped a great deal to elucidate this issue. Basically, two options are open: either the stories were taken along with the Anglo-Saxons when they invaded Britain in the fifth and sixth centuries, or they arrived at a later, indeterminate time by way of international contacts (see Frank 1991: 93–5). In the latter case it cannot be established whether they were brought to England by continental Germans or picked up by Anglo-Saxons on the continent.

None of these poems reveals any trace of being a translation of a continental song, made at some monk's or nun's desk. Since secular narrative in particular was an oral affair, we shall never know by what way, or when, they came to England. What we do know, however, is that there were plenty of festive occasions at which an international company was present and which offered an excellent opportunity to exchange and learn new stories.

In *Beowulf*, for example, celebrating the hero's victory over Grendel, King Hrothgar's *scop* sings extensively before a mixed Danish-Geatish audience the adventures of Hengest in the hall of King Finn of the Frisians. Any member in Beowulf's following with a creative ear could have grasped the gist of the story and reperformed it back home in Geatland. Deor, for instance, laments how his position as his lord's favourite singer had been taken by Heorrenda, a name unique in Anglo-Saxon England, but familiar in the Middle High German epic *Kudrun* as that of a famous singer, Hôrant. Apparently for an Anglo-Saxon audience, a foreign singer at an English court was not remarkable. Closer to home, the *Gesta Herewardi*, admittedly a late source (twelfth century) but dealing with events taking place in the mid-eleventh century, gives a vivid account of a wedding party at the court of a Cornish nobleman where guests of various nationalities were present, including the protagonist, the Anglo-Saxon Hereward himself, who is given the harp, and plays and sings to the great admiration of the multilingual guests (Anderson 1977).

Though stories could be transferred from one speech community to another in this way, it does not say much about the form in which they were received. This is not the place to dwell on the problem of oral formulaic composition, but it should be noted that besides a number of shared oral themes, the Germanic peoples also had a number of stock formulas in common, which would certainly have supported a better understanding of a narrative performed in a related language. In the 1960s, at the height of the first thrill of the discovery of the oral formulaic nature of Old English poetry, Robert Kellogg (1965) made an important first exploration within the framework of the oral formulaic theory of the stock of formulas shared between Old Saxon and Old High German alliterative poetry on the one hand, and Old English on the other. No one has taken up Kellogg's initiative in further establishing such parallels. Old Frisian, too, has such formulas in common with Old English. Unlike Old Saxon and Old High German, Old Frisian cannot boast of alliterative poetry, but its large corpus of legal texts contains many passages drafted in rhythmic, alliterative prose of the kind that we also know from Old English literature (Stanley 1984). Many alliterative collocations are understandably peculiar to Old Frisian, but at least some fifty of these are also found in other Old Germanic languages, an indication that the Frisians too participated in the Germanic poetic heritage. Remarkably, of these fifty, Old Frisian has at least two dozen formulas uniquely in common with Old English, testifying to the close relationship between these two languages (Bremmer 1982: 83–5).

So far, several scenarios have been presented in which it was possible for Anglo-Saxons to receive narratives from continental Germans, but it has also become clear that it is impossible to pinpoint any actual vernacular continental sources for a given secular text. Not quite surprisingly, as we shall see, the only piece of evidence we have for a direct continental source lies within the realm of religious literature.

On the continent, as mentioned, alliterative poetry was also practised, though what remains of it is not half as much in quantity and by far not as variegated in genre as the Old English corpus. For Old High German, there is the *Hildebrandslied*, a fragmentary poem preserved on a single manuscript leaf. The poem deals with a violent encounter between father and son fighting on different sides. The father, Hiltibrant, had long been in exile with Theotrich (OE Theoderic) fleeing from the hatred of the rival King Otacher (OE Eadwacer). The son thinks his father had long since died, and in the dialogue that develops between them he will not be convinced that the old man he is facing is really his father. In the ensuing hand-to-hand fight, the father kills his son. Although ostensibly conceived in Old High German, there are various indications that the text as we have it was the work of an Old Saxon scribe who made an attempt to substitute the most obvious Old High German features for forms that were more congenial to his own dialect. As such, intriguingly, the *Hildebrandslied* is a vivid example of the multilingual milieu in which such texts circulated. Interesting, too, is the presence of some features of (Anglo-Saxon) insular script, suggesting that the text of this song was written down at one of the Anglo-Saxon missionary centres in Germany. *Muspilli* is another, much longer Old High German alliterative poem, a fascinating account of the end of the world, and hence religious in nature, just as is the *Wessobrunn Prayer*. The latter poem likewise shows Anglo-Saxon traces in its script, such as the Tironian abbreviation '7' for *enti* 'and' and the runic symbol used as an abbreviation for the prefix *ga-* (cf. OE *ge-*). These remarkable scribal features have led scholars to think Fulda, or another Anglo-Saxon monastic foundation, to be the place of origin of the *Wessobrunn Prayer*, even though the dialect is clearly Bavarian, and hence a long distance to the south-east of Fulda. Minor specimens of poetry are constituted by alliterative charms, not unlike those known from the Old English corpus. All the other Old High German poetry is rhymed (for a convenient survey see Bostock 1976).

The Old Saxon poetic corpus is basically restricted to the *Heliand*, a long account in about 6,000 lines of Christ's life, which is based on Tatian's *Diatesseron*, a conflation of the four Gospels into a coherent narrative. After its first edition in 1830 (Schmeller), the poem attracted increasing attention in Germany, and more than once it was linked with Anglo-Saxon Biblical poetry, not just because of the similarity in subject matter but also on account of two Latin prefaces published in the sixteenth century from a *Heliand* manuscript owned by the reformer Martin Luther, now lost. These prefaces, one in verse and one in prose – known as *Versus in poeta* and *Praefatio*, respectively – relate how a poet through divine intervention was enabled to compose the contents of the Old and New Testament in verse. These accounts showed great resemblance to Bede's story of Caedmon (*HE* IV.24) and gave rise to all kinds of conjectures about the authorship of the *Heliand*, some even suggesting that the poet of the so-called Caedmonian poems must also have written the *Heliand*. All such speculations were brushed aside when, in 1875, Eduard Sievers – only 25 years old and a rising star in the firmament of Germanic studies – surprised the scholarly world with a slim publication of less than fifty pages in which he boldly claimed on detailed linguistic and stylistic grounds that lines 235–851 of the Old English *Genesis*, preserved in Oxford, Bodleian Library, Junius 11, were a translation from Old Saxon (Sievers 1875). This part of the poem, dealing with the Fall of the Angels and the subsequent Fall of Adam and Eve, which had already been suspected by previous scholars of being some kind of interpolation, Sievers dubbed *Genesis B*, while the remaining portions enveloping it – the original Anglo-Saxon poem – he named *Genesis A*, which is still the familiar terminology. Not long afterwards, Sievers' hypothesis was triumphantly proved to be true, when in 1894 the librarian of Heidelberg University and professor of classical languages, Karl Zangemeister, during a two-month visit to the Vatican Library, discovered a manuscript which contained not only a fragment of the *Heliand* of sixty-one lines (lines 1297–1358), but also four long fragments of an Old Saxon paraphrase of Genesis in verse, amounting to 337 lines. The crown on Sievers' hypothesis was that thirty lines of the Old Saxon *Genesis* overlapped with the Old English version (lines 790–820). The thrill of this discovery was tremendous. Within months Zangemeister, together with his colleague Wilhelm Braune, professor of German, published a fine edition of these fragments, including facsimile photostats (Zangemeister and Braune 1894).

The unexpected discovery solved old problems, but at the same time presented new ones. Stylistic features, for example, made clear that the *Heliand* and the Old Saxon *Genesis* were not the work of one and the same poet, as Sievers had surmised. Two important questions remained: how (and when) did the Old Saxon *Genesis* end up in England and who had been its translator, an Anglo-Saxon or an Old Saxon?

On palaeographical and linguistic grounds and further circumstantial evidence, it is generally assumed that the *Heliand* and *Genesis* were composed around 850, at either Fulda, Corvey or Werden – in any case, in a monastery with strong Anglo-Saxon roots. From there, one or more copies were sent round to other important religious centres to be transcribed, as well as to royal courts. One of these – and here we enter the realm of speculation – was presented to Charles the Bald, who had ordered it to be turned into an illustrated de luxe copy. This copy may have been given to King Æthelwulf on the occasion of his marriage to Charles's daughter Judith, and brought with his young queen to England. Soon afterwards it must have been donated to Canterbury. However its arrival in England can be accounted for, it is a fact that a copy of the *Heliand* and *Genesis* was present there around 900. Two indications support this assumption.

First, British Library, MS Cotton Caligula A. vii, contains a complete text of the Old Saxon *Heliand* painstakingly copied in the second part of the tenth century by an Anglo-Saxon scribe in an (imitation) Caroline minuscule so as to preserve the appearance of his exemplar. This exemplar may well have included the Old Saxon *Genesis*, although the scribe did not copy this text. Apparently there was no need for it, since an Old English *Genesis* was already known to be available, but this text did not include the Fall of the Angels, and only briefly dealt with the Fall of Man. These episodes, then, after they had been translated, were presumably inserted into the proto-Old English *Genesis*, when someone realized that precisely this crucial event in the history of salvation was found wanting.

The current opinion, summarized by its most recent editor A. N. Doane (1991: 55–64), is that it was an Old Saxon who quite slavishly made a morpheme-by-morpheme translation of the Old Saxon text, occasionally finding recourse to words or phrases that betray some familiarity with the Old English poetic diction, but still pedestrian enough for Sievers to have recognized the underlying Old Saxon. After-wards, this expanded version, after having been copied one or more times, found its way to Junius MS 11. With each turn in the copying process, the translated passage will have received some further retouching – for instance by reducing the longer lines of verse to make them resemble the shorter Old English ones, or by adapting early West Saxon forms to a later variety of that dialect – causing it to lose some of its Old Saxon garb, but nevertheless leaving the seams conspicuously intact.

Second, the illustrations in Junius MS 11, which make it unique amongst the four major Anglo-Saxon poetic manuscripts, appear to have been copied from the illustrated Old Saxon *Genesis*. This observation, first made by Barbara Raw (1976), is borne out by several illustrations which do not fit the Old English narrative but clearly belong to episodes known to us only from the Old Saxon version.

In conclusion, then, the harvest of immediately tangible influence of continental Germanic on Old English literature is restricted to *Genesis B*. Other efforts have been made to posit Old Saxon influence on Old English religious poems, notably on Cynewulf's *Christ II*, the most cogently argued attempt being that of Dietrich Hofmann (1959), who constructs a scenario to accommodate such influence. In Hofmann's view Old English Biblical poetry owes more to Old Saxon than the other way around. However, the purely linguistic evidence on which his argument is based is so slender that it can easily be argued away (Stanley 1988). It should be noted that the genre represented by *Genesis B* is religious and hence learned. But perhaps this should not be surprising after all. Religious vernacular literature could flourish only in monastic surroundings. It belonged to the literate world. The respect for the written word explains why the Old Saxon passage was translated almost verbatim. Secular literature, whether foreign or native, lived a life of its own, in an oral environment that allowed for much more room for adaptation and recreation than the forbidding text on the faces of a manuscript. Even though there were occasions when these two worlds met and must have intersected (Frank 1991: 97), the result of such encounters has been such that we shall never be able to isolate pieces of secular Old English literature that can be identified as having continental Germanic origins.

APPENDIX: SPECIMENS OF CONTINENTAL GERMANIC

A The Wachtendonck Psalter, *Old Dutch (Old Low Franconian) interlinear Psalter glosses following the Latin word order, end of tenth century*

The Modern English translation follows the word order and word division of the original glosses, to convey the 'unnaturalness' of such glossing translations.

Psalm 65, 5–7 (Vulgate; = 66 Authorized Version).

5. Cumit in gesiet uuerk Godis, egislikis an radon ouir kint manno.

6. Thie kierit seo an thurrithon, an fluode ouirlithon solun mit fuoti, tha sulun uuir blithan an imo.

7. Thie uualdonde ist an crefte sinro teuuon, ougun sina ouir thiadi scauuuont, thia uuitherstridunt ne uuerthint irhauan an sig seluan.

[Come and see (the) work of God, terrible in (his) doing towards children of men. (He) who turns (the) sea into dry (land), through (the) flood transgress (they) will on foot, there shall we rejoice in Him. (He) who is ruling in power his forever, eyes his over peoples behold, the rebellious (should) not become exalted in them selves.]

B The Hilderbrandslied, *Old High German with a sprinkling of Old Saxon, middle of ninth century*

Ik gihorta ðat seggen,
ðat sih urhetton ænon muotin,
Hiltibrant enti Haðubrant, untar heriun tuem.
Sunufatarungo, iro saro rihtun,
garatun se iro guðhamun, gurtun sih iro suert ana,
helidos, ubar hringa, do sie to dero hiltiu ritun.
(lines 1–6)

[I have heard this say, that champions met singly, Hildebrand and Hadubrand, between two (different) armies. Son-and-father adjusted their armour, prepared their battledresses, girded their swords on, heroes, over (their) ring-mail, when they rode to the battle.]

C Adam's Creation, *Old Frisian, c.1300*

Old Frisian survives mainly in manuscripts from 1300 onwards, but is so conservative in form that it can be compared to, for example, Old English and Old Saxon.

God scop thene eresta meneska – thet was Adam – fon achta wendem:

> thet benete fon tha stene,
> thet flask fon there erthe,
> thet blod fon tha wetere,
> tha herta fon tha winde,
> thene thogta fon tha wolkem,
> thet swet fon tha dawe,
> tha lokkar fon tha gerse,
> tha agene fon there sunna,

and tha ble'r'em on thene helga om. And tha scop'er Eva fon sine ribbe, Adames liava.

[God created the first human – that was Adam – out of eight substances: the bones out of stone, the flesh out of earth, the blood out of water, the heart out of wind, the thoughts out of clouds, the sweat out of dew, the locks out of grass, the eyes out of the sun, and then He inspired him with the holy breath. And then He created Eve out of his rib, Adam's beloved.]

D The Old Saxon Genesis, *middle of ninth century*

'Uuela, that thu nu, Eua, habas', quað Adam,
'ubilo gimarakot
unkara selbaro sið. Nu maht thu sean thia
suarton hell
ginon gradaga; nu thu sia grimman maht
hinana gihorean, nis hebanriki
gelihc sulicaro lognun: thit uuas alloro lando
sconiust,
that uuit hier thuruh unkas herran thank
hebbian muostun,
thar thu them ni hordis thie unk thesan haram
giried,
that uuit Uualdandas uuord farbrakun,
hebankuningas.'
(lines 1–9a)

['Ah, that you, Eve, now', said Adam, 'have marked the destiny of the two of us by evil. Now you can see the black hell gape greedily; now you can hear it roar from here, the kingdom of heaven

is not like such flames: this was the brightest of
all lands, that we two were allowed to have here
thanks to the Lord of the two of us, if you had
not listened to him who advised us two to this
offence, that we two would break the command
of the Ruler, the King of heaven.']

E   Genesis B, *Old English translation of
passage in (D) above, c.1000*

Adam gemælde and to Euan spræc:
'Hwæt, þu Eue, hæfst yfele gemearcod
uncer sylfra sið. Gesyhst þu nu þa sweartan
  helle,
grædige and gifre? Nu þu hie grimman meaht
heonane gehyran. Nis heofonrice
gelic þam lige, ac þis is landa betst,

þæt wit þurh uncres hearran þanc habban
  moston,
þær þu þam ne hierde þe uncþisne hearm
  geræd,
þæt wit Waldenes word forbræcon,
heofoncyninges.'

(lines 790–9a)

[Adam spoke and said to Eve: 'Listen, Eve, you
have marked the destiny of our two selves by
(your) evil. Do you now see the black hell, greedy
and eager? Now you can hear it roar from here.
The kingdom of heaven is not like that flame, but
this is the best of lands that we two were allowed
to have thanks to the Lord of the two of us, if you
had not listened to him who advised us two to
this offence, that we two broke the command of
the Ruler, the King of heaven.']

REFERENCES

Primary sources

Altfrid, *Vita Liudgari. Die Vitae Sancti Liudgari*. Ed.
W. Diekamp 1881. Münster.
Colgrave, Bertram and R. A. B. Mynors, eds 1969.
Bede's Ecclesiastical History of the English People.
Oxford Medieval Texts. Oxford.
Doane, A. N., ed. 1991. *The Saxon Genesis: An
Edition of the West Saxon Genesis B and the Old
Saxon Vatican Genesis*. Madison and London.
Farmer, D. H. and J. B. Webb, trans. 1983. *The
Age of Bede*. Harmondsworth.
Keynes, Simon and Michael Lapidge 1983. *The Age
of Alfred*. Harmondsworth.
Schmeller, Johan Andreas, ed. 1830. *Heliand: Poema
Saxonicum seculi noni, accurate expressum ad exemplar
Monacense insertis e Cottoniano Londinense supple-
mentis nec non adjecta lectionum varietate*. Munich.
Sievers, Eduard 1875. *Der Heliand und die angel-
sächsische Genesis*. Halle.

Secondary sources

Anderson, Earl R. 1977. 'Passing the Harp in
Bede's Story of Cædmon: A Twelfth-century
Analogue'. *English Language Notes* 15: 1–4.
Bostock, J. Knight 1976. *A Handbook of Old High
German Literature*. 2nd rev edn K. C. King and
D. R. McLintock. Oxford.

Bremmer, Rolf H., Jr 1981. 'Frisians in Anglo-
Saxon England: A Historical and Toponymical
Investigation'. *Fryske Nammen* 3: 45–94.
——— 1982. 'Old English – Old Frisian: The Rela-
tionship Reviewed'. *Philologia Frisica Anno 1981*
(Ljouwert [Leeuwarden], 1982), pp. 79–88.
——— 1995. 'Widows in Anglo-Saxon England'.
*Between Poverty and the Pyre: Moments in the
History of Widowhood*, pp. 55–88. Eds Jan
Bremmer and Lourens van den Bosch. London
and New York.
Christophersen, Paul 1992. 'The Spoken Word in
International Contacts in Carolingian Europe'.
NOWELE 20: 53–64.
Dietz, Klaus 1993. 'Die kontinentale Örtlichkeit-
snamen der altenglischen Annalen'. *Anglo-
Saxonica: Beiträge zur Vor- und Frühgeschichte der
englischen Sprache und zur altenglischen Literatur*,
pp. 483–514. Eds Klaus R. Grinda and Claus-
Dieter Wetzel. Munich.
Frank, Roberta 1991. 'Germanic Legend in Old
English Literature'. *The Cambridge Companion to
Old English Literature*, pp. 88–106. Eds Malcolm
Godden and Michael Lapidge. Cambridge.
Hellgardt, Ernst 1996. 'Mehrsprachigkeit im
Karolingerreich'. *Beiträge zur Geschichte der
deutschen Sprache und Literatur* 118: 1–48.
Hines, John 1995. 'Focus and Boundary in Lin-
guistic Varieties in the North-West Germanic

Continuum'. *Friesische Studien II*, pp. 35–62. Eds Volkert F. Faltings, Alastair G. H. Walker and Ommo Wilts. NOWELE Suppl. 12. Odense.

Hofmann, Dietrich 1959. 'Die altsächsische Bibelepik ein Ableger der angelsächsischen geistlichen Epik?'. *Zeitschrift für deutsches Altertum* 89: 173–90. Repr. with postscript *Der Heliand*, pp. 315–43. Eds Jürgen Eichhoff and Irmengard Rauch 1972. Wege der Forschung 321. Darmstadt.

Kellogg, Robert L. 1965. 'The South Germanic Oral Tradition'. *Medieval Linguistic Studies in Honor of Francis Peabody Magoun, Jr.*, pp. 66–74. Eds Jess B. Bessinger Jr and Robert P. Creed. London.

Lapidge, Michael 1986. 'The Anglo-Latin Background'. *A New Critical History of Old English Literature*, pp. 5–37. Eds Stanley B. Greenfield and Daniel G. Calder. New York and London.

——1988. 'A Frankish Scholar in Tenth-century England: Frithegod of Canterbury/Fredegaud of Brioude'. *Anglo-Saxon England* 17: 45–65.

Moulton, William G. 1988. 'Mutual Intelligibility among Speakers of Early Germanic Dialects'. *Germania: Comparative Studies in the Old Germanic Languages and Literatures*, pp. 9–28. Eds Daniel G. Calder and T. Craig Christy. Wolfeboro and Cambridge.

O'Donnell, Daniel 1996. 'A Northumbrian Version of *Cædmon's Hymn* (*Eordu* Recension) in Brussels, Bibliothèque Royale, MS 8245-57, ff. 62r²–v¹: Identification, Edition and Filiation'. *Beda Venerabilis: Historian, Monk and Northumbrian*, pp. 139–65. Eds L. A. J. R. Houwen and A. A. MacDonald. Mediaevalia Groningana 19. Groningen.

Raw, Barbara 1976. 'The Probable Derivation of Most of the Illustrations in Junius 11 from an Illustrated Old Saxon *Genesis*'. *Anglo-Saxon England* 5: 133–44.

Smyth, Alfred P. 1995. *King Alfred the Great*. Oxford.

Stanley, E. G. 1984. 'Alliterative Ornament and Alliterative Rhythmical Discourse in Old High German and Old Frisian Compared with Similar Manifestations in Old English'. *Beiträge zur Geschichte der deutschen Sprache und Literatur* 106: 184–217.

——1988. 'The Difficulty of Establishing Borrowings between Old English and the Continental West Germanic Languages'. *An Historic Tongue: Studies in English Linguistics in Memory of Barbara Strang*, pp. 3–16. Eds Graham Nixon and John Honey. London and New York.

Zangemeister, Karl and Wilhelm Braune 1894. 'Bruchstücke der altsächsischen Bibeldichtung aus der Bibleotheca Palatina'. *Neue Heidelberger Jahrbücher* 4: 205–94.

21

Scandinavian Relations

Robert E. Bjork

Anglo-Saxon literary relations with Scandinavia could be much simpler in the nineteenth and early twentieth centuries than they are now. A Dane such as Frederik Hammerich, for example, might proclaim the filiations firm and obvious and the English merely resentfully blind to them (1873: 3). An Englishman such as Sir William Craigie could pronounce the connections slender and tenuous, Scandinavian impact on English literature not manifesting itself 'until quite recent times' (1931: 7). Other early works on the subject seem implicitly to reinforce Craigie's view, dealing as they do with Scandinavian influences from the seventeenth century on (Nordby 1901; Seaton 1935), but not all early scholars share the opinion. Frederick Metcalfe is a prime example. Pondering the similitude between Old English and Old Norse literature, he exclaims, 'If this is Pygmalion's statue in all its pale inanimate beauty, that is the statue warmed into flesh and blood, with the breath of life and motion breathed into its nostrils' (1880: 175). Less metaphorical and less effusive, scholars at the beginning of the twenty-first century take a more moderate yet still positive view.

But what do we actually know about Anglo-Scandinavian literary (i.e. poetic) relations before 1066? We have some fairly indisputable historical facts, first of all, that point towards the probability of such relations. The violent clashing of Viking and Anglo-Saxon cultures on the east and west coasts of England that began in *c.*786 resulted in Danish and Norwegian settlements from Northumbria to Essex and in the reign of the Dane Cnut the Great as king of England from 1016 to 1035. It had a raft of other results as well. Hundreds of distinctively Scandinavian stone monuments, for instance, indicate the melding of two cultures (Bailey 1980) as do hundreds of English place- and personal names containing Scandinavian elements (Fellows-Jensen 1975). The English language, too, bears a Scandinavian stamp. The lexicon is replete with Scandinavian terms from the Viking age (such as 'die', 'window', 'law', 'theft'), and even a central feature of the language – the pronominal system – was transmuted by contact with Old Norse. The ambiguous Old English 'hie', for example, could mean 'they', 'them' or 'her'; and 'him' could as perplexingly mean 'them', 'to him' or 'to it'. Replacing the native pronouns with the Old Norse 'they', 'them' and 'she/her' clarified matters.

Scholarship on Old Norse literature lends further credence to the probability of Anglo-Scandinavian literary relations. It is conceivable, for example, that the Helgi poems in the *Edda* may have been composed in the Danelaw and that the Old Norse *Vǫluspá* ('Prophecy of the Seeress'; see Calder et al. 1983: 114–19) could have been directly influenced by the sermons of Bishop Wulfstan of York and the Old English poem *Judgement Day II* (Butt 1969: 82–103; but see the strong objections in Lindow 1987: 308–24). It is likewise conceivable that the Old Norse *Vǫlundarkviða* ('The Lay of Vǫlundr [Weyland]'; see Calder et al. 1983: 65–9) may have taken shape in Scandinavian Yorkshire (McKinnell 1990) and that King Æthelred II (978–1016) patronized the Old Norse court poet Gunnlaugr ormstunga (Lawson 1993: 6). And it seems that there was a strong English influence on skaldic poetry, revealed in English borrowings and Anglicisms, for most of the Viking age. Indeed, during the reign of Cnut, London may well have been skaldic poetry's centre of production and distribution in the North (Frank 1985: 179).

It is less certain, however, that Anglo-Scandinavian literary influence went both ways, despite the probability that it did. At least four problems compound the uncertainty: (1) no direct and demonstrable quotations or translations establish an Old Norse text as the source of an Old English one; (2) the random nature and limited number of surviving texts in both languages restricts our ability to find points of contact, which therefore could have been either more or less numerous than we might think; (3) the relatively late date of Old Norse texts (post-twelfth-century) severely complicates any attempt to demonstrate their influence on earlier Old English texts (pre-twelfth-century); and (4) our inability to fix the dates and relative chronology of texts in either language adds further complexity to our search for a literary give-and-take. Such problems seem insurmountable: and they may well be.

What can be done? Under the circumstances, I think, the best thing is simply to dwell in possibility. A verbal echo, the resonance of a theme or genre, the seeming replication of a scene or narrative construct – if heeded – can lead to a broader understanding of an entire cultural milieu and open the way to later, unanticipated demonstrations of influence or connection that we might otherwise have missed. Dwelling in impossibility, in the rigid belief that an absence of proof is the proof of absence, surrounds us and our conception of Old English poetry in silence.

Take *Beowulf* for a start. In 1815, Grímur Jónsson Thorkelin asserted in his preface to the first edition of the poem not that *Beowulf* shows Scandinavian influence, but that it is Scandinavian (indeed pure Danish) through and through. Someone, probably Alfred the Great, who was keen on collecting masterpieces and translating them into Old English brought the poem to England (Bjork 1996: 303–5). Thorkelin's contention almost completely vanished under a wave of scholarly abuse, of course. 'One scholar proposes, another disposes', as Roberta Frank wryly observes (1990: 75), and in this case, many disposed. But the wildness of his view apart, Thorkelin began the discussion of how the poem relates to Scandinavia, a discussion that continues unabated. The German scholar Gregor Sarrazin carried on the cause of a lost Scandinavian original for *Beowulf* until the end of the nineteenth century, when an Icelander, Guðbrandur Vigfússon, noted the similarity of the poem to the Old Norse *Grettis saga*. Since then the debate, with occasional detours into other Old Norse literature (see Garmonsway and Simpson 1968; Dronke 1969b; Fulk 1989; Tolley 1996), has centred on the nature of the relationship between the two texts. While some scholars have felt that relationship to be literary, one work reflecting itself in the other, most seem now to feel that both texts derive from a North European folktale type (Andersson 1997: 129–34; see also Orchard 1995: 140–68; Fjalldal 1998). Concentrating less on specific texts has had a salutary, broadening effect.

Part of the effect has been a turn towards genre criticism, which has proven fruitful in studies of *Beowulf* and the poem's possible literary relationship to Scandinavia. Theodore M. Andersson, for example, begins with the genre of the traditional Germanic heroic lay and views *Beowulf* against that backdrop, specifically against 'the correspondence of scenic inventory' (1980: 220) in a group of poems. Common to the Old English *Fight at Finnsburg*, the Old High German *Hildebrandslied* ('The Lay of Hildebrand'; see Calder et al. 1983: 147–9), and the Old Norse poems *Atlakviða* ('The Lay of Atli [Attila the Hun]'), *Atlamál* ('The Lay of Atli'), *Hamðismál* ('The Lay of Hamðir'; see Calder et al. 1983: 138–41) and *Hlǫðskviða* ('The Lay of Hlǫðr') are ten components. Each poem contains '(1) battle scenes (throughout), (2) hall scenes of (ominous) conviviality, (3) hall battles, (4) journeys in quest of heroic confrontation, (5) sentinel scenes, (6) welcoming scenes, (7) the use of intermediaries, (8) the consultation of heroes with kings or queens, (9) incitations or flytings, (10) leave-taking scenes' (Andersson 1980: 221; see also Magennis 1996: 48–51 on hall scenes of feasting in *Atlakviða*). *Beowulf* contains precisely the same inventory as well as a possible verbal echo from the three Eddic lays, indicating that the poet probably exploited a defined body of conventional material in creating the epic.

Similarly, Joseph Harris (1982: 236) views *Beowulf* against the backdrop of convention and regards the poem as a *summa litterarum*, a unique compilation of the oral genres of the Germanic early Middle Ages (see also Harris 1994). Of the eleven or so genres he discerns in the poem, he examines two, the genealogy in lines 4–64 and the praise poem in lines 867b–915. The opening of *Beowulf*, he finds, shares an 'emphasis on the death and burial of the rulers' with Old Norse genealogical poems such as *Ynglingatal* ('List of the Ynglingar') and the poem praising Beowulf after his fight with Grendel shares a praise-plus-exempla structure with Old Norse poems such as *Eiríksmál* ('The Lay of Eiríkr')' (1982: 237, 240). In other articles, Harris (1979, 1992) looks at two more genres, the flyting or verbal duel between Beowulf and Unferth in the context of the Old Norse *senna* (see also Russom 1978: 10–13; Clover 1980) and Beowulf's last words (lines 2724ff) in the context of the death-song tradition in Old Norse (see also Lönnroth 1971: 13–16). Roberta Frank (1979) explores yet another genre, the *erfidrápa* or memorial eulogy, and its possible influence on the laments at the end of the poem. Most recently, Susan E. Deskis examines the maxim in the context of the medieval proverb tradition. The similar use of sententious material in the Old Norse *Hávamál* ('The Speech of Hávi [Óðinn]'; see Calder et al. 1983: 71–83), *Sigrdrífumál* ('The Lay of Sigrdrífa'; see Calder et al. 1983: 88–92), and *Beowulf* point to 'a well-established and widely practiced appreciation for the uses of *sententiae* in poetic expression' (1996: 142; see also Harris 1994: 54–7). In such traditional forms as the folktale, the heroic and memorial lays and the proverb, then, we find more of the Scandinavian in *Beowulf*.

More resides in possible traditional Nordic locutions in the poem as well. Roberta Frank calls our attention, for example, to line 2439 of *Beowulf* (*miste mercelses* 'missed the target'), where the verb *missan* plus a genitive object reflects common Old Norse, not Old English, usage; to line 316, where the coastguard's *Mæl is me to feran* ('time for me to go') echoes the Old Norse hero Helgi's remark as he leaves for Valhǫll in *Helgakviða Hundingsbana II*: *Mál er mér at ríða* (1979: 11–12); and to some syntactic peculiarities in the poem that can be explained by reference to Old Norse, such as the six atypical occurrences of a demonstrative pronoun following the accusative form of a compound noun (1981: 133–4). Even the flyting between Beowulf and Unferth may boast of skaldic technique. Unferth's duplicitous, manipulative wordplay and deliberate misinterpretations – essentially skaldic strategies for fooling the uninitiated – are penetrated easily by Beowulf, who deftly solves the riddle of Unferth's speech and uses a recognizable Old Norse half-line twice as he does so. *On sund reon* ('to row on the sea', lines 512, 539) closely matches *á vág róa* or *á sió róa* ('to row to sea'; Frank 1987: 346–7).

The hunt for the Nordic connection for other Old English poems has not occurred on such a grand scale as it has for *Beowulf*, and it has tended to focus either on localized effects within individual poems or on generic similarities across languages. Some of the localized effects seem present merely to accommodate the needs and expectations of a secular Anglo-Scandinavian audience. It is remotely possible, for example, that expanded references to splendid landscape in *Genesis A* and specifically the use of the adjective *ælgrene* ('completely green'; cf. Old Norse *algrœn*) in lines 197, 1517, 1751 and 1787 serve to make the material in the poem more familiar to a vernacular audience steeped in the Germanic secular tradition (Magennis 1996: 148). It is possible, too, that the same audience heard with pleasure the Old Norse system ringing behind 'hafaþ under heofonum heahfæstne dom' ('will keep his lofty and secure renown here below the heavens'; Bradley 1982: 340) at the end of *Widsith* (Harris 1985a: 125) and was more affected than it might have been by *Cædmon's Hymn* had the poem not contained language reminiscent of the opening of *Vǫluspá*. There the Old Norse poet, like Cædmon, announces his intention to recite things from the beginning (North 1991: 17–18). Similarly, *Wulf and Eadwacer* lines 16–19, possibly representing a rare instance in Old English of Old Norse *ljóðaháttr* metre (see, e.g. Lawrence 1902: 253; North 1991: 45), may have struck a familiar chord just as a line in *The Dream of the Rood* may have. All creation's weeping at Christ's death in line 55 is replicated in all creation's weeping for the death of Baldr in the Old Norse *Snorra Edda* (Swanton 1987: 123). It is perhaps even more likely that a potential, chilling echo of Old Norse in *Soul and Body II* may have intensified audience response to that poem. There the soul, having to return to its mortal coil every seven days for 300 years, reviles the rotting corpse *caldan reorde* (Krapp and Dobbie 1936: 175; 'with a cold voice', line 15). The same phrase occurs in the Old Norse *Atlakviða* when Atli's messenger arrives in court with an ominous invitation: '[v]reiþi sáz ðeir Húna. / Kallaþi ðá Knéfrøþr kaldri rǫddo' (Dronke 1969a: 3; 'they feared the wrath of the Huns; then Knéfrǫþr called out with a cold voice'; Calder et al. 1983: 130). As an epithet for speech, cold 'has the connotations "sinister", "hostile", "fate-bringing"' in Old Norse (Dronke 1969a: 47), and it has the same connotations in the Old English poem.

Echoes can have larger implications as well, with perhaps more specific connections to Scandinavian tradition. The Scandinavianisms in the Viking's speech in *The Battle of Maldon*, for instance, may represent 'the first literary use of dialect in English' and are a 'vivid element' in the dramatic presentation of the Norseman (Robinson 1976: 123–4). Likewise, *The Wanderer* contains at least three words probably influenced by or borrowed from Old Norse (*gliwstafum* 'joyfully', from *glý*; *hrimceald* 'ice-cold', from *hrímkaldr*; *hriþ* 'snowstorm', from *hríþ*; Dunning and Bliss 1969: 58, 60–1). At the close of the Wanderer's ruminations on transience, the poem also includes a gnomic utterance that is Old English or Old Norse to the core: 'her bið feoh læne her bið freond læne / her bið mon læne her bið mæg læne', lines 108–9 (Dunning and Bliss 1969; 'here wealth is ephemeral; here a friend is ephemeral; here man is ephemeral; here a kinsman is ephemeral'; Bradley 1982: 325). These lines seem to echo or be echoed either by stanza 76 of *Hávamál* ('Deyr fé, deyia frœndr, / deyr siálfr it sama'; Dunning and Bliss 1969: 122; 'Cattle die, kinsmen die, you yourself will likewise die'; Calder et al. 1983: 76) or by Eyvindr Finnsson skaldaspillir in 966 ('Deyr fé, deyia frændr, / eyþisk land ok láþ', 'Cattle die, kinsmen die, land and realm are emptied'; Frank 1979: 5, 1990: 76). Given the uncertainties of dating *The Wanderer* and *Hávamál*, we cannot tell which text may have influenced which. Given the meaning of 'skaldaspillir' ('plagiarist'), we *can* tell that Eyvindr may not be the best bet as originator of the insight. Whatever the source, however, the Anglo-Saxons and Vikings clearly shared a taste for the sentiment of transience heard in both *The Wanderer* and *Hávamál* and ringing faintly, too, in *Elene* ('[feoh] æghwam biþ / læne under lyfte', lines 1269–70; Gradon 1996; 'Wealth is ephemeral for everyone below heaven'; Bradley 1982: 196) and more strongly in *The Rhyming Poem*: 'Dreamas swa her gedreosaþ, dryhtscype gehreosaþ, / lif her men forleosaþ, leahtras oft geceosaþ' (lines 54–5; Krapp and Dobbie 1936: 168; 'thus joys here perish, lordship goes to ruin, men lose their lives here, they often choose vices').

A shared literary taste can account for some peculiarities of other Old English poems as well, a taste partially explained by the presence of Old Norse skalds such as Eyvindr Finnsson skaldaspillir and Gunnlaugr ormstunga in Anglo-Saxon England. Egill Skallagrímsson helpfully boasts, in fact, that he bore 'Óþins mjǫþ á Engla bjǫþ' (Nordal 1933: 186; 'Óðinn's mead [poetry] to the fields of England'), and one draught of that mead, Egill-borne or not, represents a new or resuscitated kind of Old English poetry. The royal eulogy seems to have begun during the reign of Æthelstan (925–39) and 'can plausibly be held to emerge as the result of skaldic influence' (Opland 1980: 172; see also Lapidge 1981; Harris 1985b: 248–54). *The Battle of Brunanburh, The Capture of the Five Buroughs, The Coronation of Edgar, The Death of Edgar, The Death of Alfred* and *The Death of Edward* from *The Anglo-Saxon Chronicle* are all panegyrics in the Scandinavian, not Anglo-Saxon, mode: they celebrate an event elliptically rather than just narrate it chronologically (Opland 1980: 172). Closer scrutiny of one of these poems, *The Battle of Brunanburh*, makes the case more striking. Possible Old Norse influence appears in such lexical items as *cnear* ('warship', line 35a) and *guþhafoc* ('battle-hawk' or 'eagle', line 64a; Hofmann 1955: 165–7; see also Kuhn 1969, 1977), but other resonances seem specifically skaldic. John D. Niles notes three kennings (*garmitting* 'spear-meeting', line 50a; *gumena gemot* 'assembly of men', line 50b; *wæpengewrixl* 'weapon-exchange', line 51a) that smack of the skald in designating battle 'ironically in terms of peaceful social interchange' (1987: 360). He also discusses two other possible skaldic conceits. 'Feld dænnede / secga swate' ('the field resounded with the sweat [blood] of men', lines 12b–13a) contains, not synaesthesia, but skaldic ellipsis, in which the poet leaps from a literal field on which weapons resound and draw blood to a contracted metaphor in which the blood itself resounds (1987: 362; see also Harris 1986: 61–8). And 'ðær læg secg mænig / garum ageted' ('there lay many a man poured out [bled to death] with spears', lines 17b–18a) seems equally indebted to the elliptical techniques of the skalds (1987: 363).

Old English religious poems as well, coloured perhaps by a pagan brush, may be seasoned, too, with a pinch or two of the skaldic. The exuberant stylization of the *Andreas* and *Exodus* poets, for example, revealed in such bold metaphors as *sæbeorg* ('sea-mountain') and *beorhhliðu* ('mountain-slopes') for huge waves, may actually be appreciative appropriation (Hall 1984, 1989). The *Exodus* poet in particular appears to flatter the Viking poets through imitation. In two important and persuasive articles, Roberta Frank shows that the infamous and perplexing pillar of cloud in *Exodus* that God creates as a shield against the sun for the Israelites (lines 71b–85) makes perfect sense when read against skaldic descriptions. The five epithets for shield in the passage (*bælc* 'board'; *nett* 'net'; *wolcen* 'cloud'; *segl* 'sail'; *feldhus* 'tent') have exact counterparts in Old Norse, where they constitute a traditional part of skaldic vocabulary (Frank 1987: 340–1, 1988: 193–5), and the metaphoric density of the passage seems likewise traditionally Norse (1988: 196). The poem's beasts of battle passage, too, contains four unusual Old English words, 'each of which seems to allude to a familiar skaldic motif'. *Wælceasega* ('chooser of the slain', line 164a), for instance, recalls Old Norse *valkyria* and *valkjósandi* (1987: 349–50). Lastly, the idiosyncratic structure of *Exodus* – together with its rambunctious language and imagery – are reminiscent of the late tenth-century *þórsdrápa* of Eilífr Goðrúnarson. Both poems relate a journey, the crossing of a body of water, the harrowing or destruction of the enemy, and a final triumph, and both 'have many of the same stylistic mannerisms and twitches, reflexes perhaps of similar rhetors attempting to produce a similar sense of salvation' (1988: 197). A number of the poem's oddities thus 'may mark the spots where [the poet] is exploiting his audience's familiarity with a kind of poetry now forgotten' (1988: 196).

Lending evidentiary weight to such things as the verbal echo or reverberation of kenning or skaldic conceit for the Scandinavian literary influence on the Anglo-Saxons are generic similarities between Old English and Old Norse poems. The twelve extant Old English metrical charms appear to be both our oldest Germanic literary relics (Greenfield and Calder 1986: 255) and our earliest evidence of a literary connection to Scandinavia. As some of them relate to *Skírnismál* ('The Lay of Skírnir'; see especially stanzas 25–36 in Calder et al. 1983: 175–6) as analogues, for instance, they suggest a time of origin for the Old Norse poem 'when the Norse and insular races were on familiar speaking terms and enjoyed enriching their stories of entertainment from each other' (Dronke 1997: 402; see also Harris 1975). The Old Norse *Vǫluspá* and one of the Old English Judgement Day poems, as we have seen, also suggest a time of mutual enrichment as do, perhaps, various wisdom and elegiac poems.

Wisdom literature and elegy are the most widely represented genres in both Old English and Old Norse and so have attracted a good deal of scholarly attention. Of the several possible examples of Old English poems of wisdom and learning, four have been especially discussed in regard to their Scandinavian relations. *Gifts of Men* and *Fortunes of Men* bear analogic relationships to stanza 3 of the Old Norse *Hyndluljóð* ('The Lay of Hyndla'; see Calder et al. 1983: 70), stanza 69 of *Hávamál* and *Sigrdrífumál*. The diversity of gifts in *Gifts* is matched in *Hyndluljóð* and *Hávamál*, and many items, such as riches, wisdom and courage, appear in both the Old English and the Old Norse (Russom 1978: 2–3). Furthermore, lines 8–17 of *Gifts* is an expanded version of the notion expressed in the first line of *Hávamál*: 'Erat maðr allz vesall, þótt hann sé illa heill' ('No man is entirely wretched, though he be feeble'; Russom 1978: 3). The Old English begins, 'Ne biþ ænig ðæs earfoþsælig | mon on moldan . . .' (Krapp and Dobbie 1936: 137; 'There is no one on earth so poorly off . . .'; Bradley 1982: 326). *Sigrdrífumál*, on the other hand, contains both a list of talents and a catalogue of misfortunes and thereby bears a marked resemblance to the Old English *Fortunes of Men*; both poems also warn in similar terms of the perils of strong drink (Russom 1978: 4). The points of similarity between the Old English and Old Norse examples suggest 'a tradition of poetic organization that might well have been the common inheritance of England and Scandinavia' (Russom 1978: 4).

Other poems of wisdom equally suggest commonality. The similarities among gnomes in *Hávamál*, *Sigrdrífumál* and the Old English *Maxims I* and *Maxims II* give us insight into the shared culture of the Scandinavians and Anglo-Saxons, for instance, and the poems in Old English and Old Norse that contain lists also contain strong evidence of mutually inherited poetic techniques. The list in stanzas 40–1 of *Grímnismál* ('The Lay of Grímnir'; see Calder et al. 1983: 83–8) detailing what parts of the universe come from what parts of Ymir's body, for example, shares its basic structure with the list of living things in *Solomon and Saturn*, lines 419–25 (Jackson 1998: 362–6). In addition, the whole of *Solomon and Saturn* turns on the dialogue form, as does its Old Norse analogue, *Vafþrúðnismál* ('The Lay of Vafþrúðnir'; see Calder et al.

1983: 169–72), and *Vafþrúðnismál* itself introduces each of Oðinn's twelve questions with a number formula, thus sharing a relatively unusual structural device with the Old English *Precepts*, where a father's ten admonishments to his son are likewise prefaced by numbers (Hansen 1988: 45). The Old English *Rune Poem* and riddles, too, which have their affinities with wisdom literature (Halsall 1981: 38–42), have Old Norse analogues that point to a shared cultural heritage if not to direct literary influence (see Calder et al. 1983: 166–7 [*Rune Poem*]; 106–12 [riddles]). Both the mnemonic Old English and Old Norwegian runic poems, for instance, tie gnomic assertions to each letter of the alphabet.

While wisdom literature offers some possible points of contact and many more of commonality between the Old English and Old Norse poetic traditions, the elegy seems to offer yet more. The genre itself, first of all, seems to derive from Common Germanic ritual lament in which a known heroic figure contrasts the joys and griefs of his or her life in the first person (Harris 1983: 47–8). The genre develops from that ur-genre in slightly different ways in the two languages. In Old English, it moves from *Wulf and Eadwacer*, 'still close to a specific heroic legend and offering little or no generalizing philosophy', to *The Wife's Lament*, which contains no proper names but an increase in gnomic wisdom, to *The Wanderer*, which generalizes the individual autobiography to all humans, and then to *The Seafarer*, where autobiography is reduced even further and subordinated to a symbolic end (Harris 1983: 49). In Old Norse, there seem to be just three stages. The genre begins in *Guðrúnarkviða II* ('The Second Lay of Guðrún'; see Calder et al. 1983: 26–9) with more narrative complexity than its Old English analogues can claim, moves to such poems as *Guðrúnarhvǫt* ('Guðrún's Chain of Woes'; see Calder et al. 1983: 35–6) with narrative frames for the monologues, and then to *Guðrúnarkviða III* (see Calder et al. 1983: 29–30), where the narrative-dramatic context dominates the elegiac monologue almost entirely (Harris 1983: 50). But even as the two traditions seem to grow in different ways, we find shared local effects, such as instances of exaggerated grief, that point to a shared Germanic heritage (Harris 1983: 52–4). And we also find that some Old English elegies actually show signs of possibly having crossed paths with Old Norse.

We have already seen some Scandinavianisms in *The Wanderer*, and we can discern some, too, in at least four other Old English elegies. *The Wife's Lament*, which bears a generic likeness to the Old Norse *grátr* ('weeping, lament') genre exemplified in *Oddrúnargrátr* ('The Lament of Oddrún'; see Calder et al. 1983: 32–5), offers a possible parallel to two Old Norse compositions. In stanza 6 of *Helreið Brynhildar* ('Brynhildr's Ride to Hel'), we read that 'Lét hami vára hugfullr konungr / . . . undir eic borit' (Neckel 1962: 220; 'The bold king had our skins . . . borne under an oak'; Calder et al. 1983: 31); and in *Hervararljóð* ('The Waking of Angantýr'), we hear Hervǫr cry out in line 43, 'vekk yðr alla und viðar rótum' (Gordon 1957: 144; 'wake up all of you, under the roots of trees'). The wife in the Old English poem also dwells *under actreo* (Krapp and Dobbie 1936: 211; 'under an oak tree', lines 27a, 36a). Similarly, the *anfloga* ('lone-flyer'), the rapacious bird of thought in lines 58–64 of *The Seafarer*, may also have its Old Norse antecedent. Stanza 20 of *Grímnismál* ('The Lay of Grímnir'), for instance, concerns Huginn and Munninn, Óðinn's birds of prey and wisdom, and contains two verbal correspondences with the lines of *The Seafarer*. *Hyge* ('thought') in the Old English poem, which the speaker says 'cymeþ eft to me' (Krapp and Dobbie 1936: 145; 'comes again to me', line 61b), is comparable to *Huginn*, a name derived from 'thought', whom the Old Norse speaker fears 'aptr né komiþ' (Neckel 1962: 61; 'will not come back') (North 1991: 105). And for *Deor*, too, there are provocative echoes from Old Norse. First, the strophic form of the poem and the use of a refrain typify Old Norse, not Old English, practice (Taylor 1998: 6). And second, the correspondence between the Old English poem and *Vǫlundarkviða* 'in two identical situations, (*a*) *nede* and *nauþir* used of the bonds placed on Weland and on Vǫlundr, and (*b*) *eacen* and *barni aukin* used of Beadohild's and Bǫþvildr's pregnancy . . . , suggests a definite relationship between the two poems' (Dronke 1997: 276).

Finally among the elegies, the slightly bizarre *Rhyming Poem*, unique in Old English poetry in being composed entirely in end-rhyme, may be viewed in at least two ways as influencing or being influenced by Old Norse literature. Generally, the poem is analogous in structure to two-part, Christian–pagan compositions such as *Njáls saga*, which extol the virtues of the Christian way of life by juxtaposing them to the vagaries and woes of the heroic world. The speaker of the *Rhyming Poem* actually seems to share heroic attributes, such as munificence, with Egill's uncle in *Egils saga Skalla-Grímssonar* (Olsen 1979: 51–2). Specifically, however, in its use of end-rhyme the poem could either have occasioned or have been occasioned by Egill's *Hǫfuðlausn* ('Head Ransom'), written in 936 and included in ch. 60 of his saga (Krapp and Dobbie 1936: xlviii–xlix; Opland 1980: 170). Both poems, like many others we have seen, seem to offer good evidence that in England, 'Anglo-Saxon and Norse poets could meet and hear each other perform' (Opland 1980: 170), and both poems bounce along, springing on the buoyant rhymes at the end of each of their half-lines. Listen to a few words from each and my attempt to imitate them. Egill writes:

> Vestr fórk of ver, en ek Viþris ber
> munstrandar mar, svá's mitt of far.
> (lines 1–2; Nordal 1933: 185)

Across the waves I travelled west, carrying the sea of Óðinn's breast [poetry], such was my bequest.

And the Anglo-Saxon poet intones:

> Me lifes onlah   se ðis leoht onwrah,
> ond ðæt torhte geteoh,   tillice onwrah.
> (lines 1–2)

To me He granted life, He who showed this light, and furnished all that's bright, uncovered as is right.

Clearly, the remarkably close similarities in rhyming and rhythmic technique in these poems can be well explained by one poet having imitated the other (or by both poets having been independently influenced by Latin hymns [Macrae-Gibson 1983: 14]). But if imitation is present, we do not know whether the techniques were mixed in Óðinn's mead that Egill brought to England or whether Egill discovered them in England and carried them back home. Whichever way the influence may have gone, however, *The Rhyming Poem* is the only one of its kind in Old English, stopped in its tracks perhaps by an Anglo-Saxon Harry Bailey, exasperated by its relentless Sir Thopas lilt and begging for no more. 'For pleynly at a word', as Harry perhaps might have put it in this circumstance, 'Thy drasty rymyng is nat worth a toord.' (For a complete translation and sympathetic reading of the poem, see Macrae-Gibson 1983.)

The realm of possibility we have just visited is manifestly larger and more variegated from within than it appears to be from without. And our brief foray into it demonstrates that little more accompanies us when trying to ascertain Scandinavian influence on Old English poetry than a feeling similar to Metcalfe's. It is probable that the influence was mutual, that the Anglo-Saxons were as much swayed by the poems of the Vikings as the Vikings were by theirs, but proving that influence definitively is at this moment beyond our capabilities. The situation may not change. Nevertheless, we would be wise to persevere, to continue venturing outside the confines of the Old English corpus seeking its larger north European or Indo-European context. As we do so, stanza 5 of the *Hávamál* provides both some guidance on our journey and a modest justification for it: 'Vitz er þorf, þeim er víða ratar, / dælt er heima hvat' (Neckel 1962: 17; 'Wit he needs, he who roams widely; everything is easy at home'; Calder et al. 1983: 72).

REFERENCES

Primary sources

Bradley, S. A. J., trans. 1982. *Anglo-Saxon Poetry*. London and Melbourne.

Calder, Daniel G., Robert E. Bjork, Patrick K. Ford and Daniel F. Melia, trans. 1983. *Sources and Analogues of Old English Poetry II: The Major Germanic and Celtic Texts in Translation*. Cambridge and Totowa.

Dronke, Ursula, ed. and trans. 1969a. *The Poetic Edda*. Vol. 1: *Heroic Poems*. Oxford.

——1997. *The Poetic Edda*. Vol. 2: *Mythological Poems*. Oxford.

Dunning, T. P. and Alan J. Bliss, eds 1969. *The Wanderer*. London.

Garmonsway, G. N. and Jacqueline Simpson, trans. 1968. *Beowulf and its Analogues*. Including 'Archaeology and *Beowulf*'. Rev. 1980 Hilda Ellis Davidson. London.

Gordon, E. V. 1957. *An Introduction to Old Norse*. 2nd edn. Oxford.

Gradon, P. O. E., ed. 1996. *Cynewulf's Elene*. Rev. edn. Exeter.

Halsall, Maureen, ed. 1981. *The Old English Rune Poem: A Critical Edition*. McMaster Old English Studies and Texts 2. Toronto, Buffalo and London.

Krapp, George Philip and Elliott van Kirk Dobbie, eds 1936. *The Exeter Book*. Anglo-Saxon Poetic Records 3. New York and London.

Macrae-Gibson, O. D., ed. 1983. *The Old English Riming Poem*. Cambridge.

Neckel, Gustav, ed. 1962. *Edda. Die Lieder des*

Codex Regius nebst verwandten Denkmälern, 1: *Text*. 4th edn rev. Hans Kuhn. Heidelberg.

Nordal, Sigurþur, ed. 1933. *Egils saga Skalla-Grímssonar*. Íslenzk Fornit 2. Reykjavik.

Swanton, Michael, ed. 1987. *The Dream of the Rood*. Rev. edn Exeter.

Secondary sources

Andersson, Theodore M. 1980. 'Tradition and Design in *Beowulf*'. *Old English Literature in Context: Ten Essays*, pp. 90–106, 171–2. Ed. John D. Niles. Cambridge. Repr. *Interpretations of Beowulf: A Critical Anthology*, pp. 219–34. Ed. R. D. Fulk. Bloomington, 1991.

—— 1997. 'Sources and Analogues'. *A Beowulf Handbook*, pp. 125–48. Eds Robert E. Bjork and John D. Niles. Lincoln, London and Exeter.

Bailey, Richard N. 1980. *Viking Age Sculpture in Northern England*. London.

Bjork, Robert E. 1996. 'Grímur Jónsson Thorkelin's Preface to the First Edition of *Beowulf*, 1815'. *Scandinavian Studies* 68: 290–320.

Butt, Wolfgang 1969. 'Zur Herkunft der Vǫlospá'. *Beiträge zur Geschichte der deutschen Sprache und Literatur* 91: 82–103.

Clover, Carol. J. 1980. 'The Germanic Context of the Unferð Episode'. *Speculum* 55: 444–68. Repr. *Beowulf: Basic Readings*, pp. 127–54. Ed. Peter S. Baker. Basic Readings in Anglo-Saxon England 1. New York and London, 1995.

Craigie, William 1931. *The Northern Element in English Literature*. Toronto.

Deskis, Susan E. 1996. *Beowulf and the Medieval Proverb Tradition*. Medieval and Renaissance Texts and Studies 155. Tempe, AZ.

Dronke, Ursula 1969b. 'Beowulf and Ragnarǫk'. *Saga-Book of the Viking Society* 17: 302–25.

Fellows-Jensen, Gillian 1975. 'The Vikings in England: A Review'. *Anglo-Saxon England* 4: 181–206.

Fjalldal, Magnús 1998. *The Long Arm of Coincidence: The Frustrated Connection Between Beowulf and Grettis saga*. Toronto, Buffalo and London.

Frank, Roberta 1979. 'Old Norse Memorial Eulogies and the Date of *Beowulf*'. *The Early Middle Ages, Acta* 6: 1–19.

—— 1981. 'Skaldic Verse and the Date of *Beowulf*'. *The Dating of Beowulf*, pp. 123–39. Ed. Colin Chase. Toronto, Buffalo and London.

—— 1985. 'Skaldic Poetry'. *Old Norse-Icelandic Literature: A Critical Guide*, pp. 157–96. Eds Carol J. Clover and John Lindow. Islandica 45. Ithaca, NY, and London.

—— 1987. 'Did Anglo-Saxon Audiences have a Skaldic Tooth?' *Scandinavian Studies* 59: 338–55.

—— 1988. 'What Kind of Poetry is *Exodus*?'. *Germania: Comparative Studies in the Old Germanic Languages and Literatures*, pp. 191–205. Eds Daniel G. Calder and T. Craig Christy. Cambridge and Wolfeboro.

—— 1990. 'Anglo-Scandinavian Poetic Relations'. *American Notes & Queries* n.s. 3: 74–9.

Fulk, R. D. 1989. 'An Eddic Analogue to the Scyld Scefing Story'. *Review of English Studies* n.s. 40: 313–22.

Greenfield, Stanley B. and Daniel G. Calder 1986. *A New Critical History of Old English Literature*. New York.

Hall, J. R. 1984. 'Exodus 449a: *beorhhliðu*'. *American Notes & Queries* 22: 95–6.

—— 1989. 'Old English *sæbeorg*: Exodus 442a, Andreas 308a'. *Papers on Language and Literature* 25: 127–34.

Hammerich, Frederik 1873. *De episk-kristelige oldkvad hos de gotiske folk*. Copenhagen.

Hansen, Elaine Tuttle 1988. *The Solomon Complex: Reading Wisdom in Old English Poetry*. McMaster Old English Studies and Texts 5. Toronto, Buffalo and London.

Harris, Joseph 1975. 'Cursing with the Thistle: *Skírnismál* 31, 6–8, and OE Metrical Charm 9, 16–17'. *Neuphilologische Mitteilungen* 76: 26–33.

—— 1979. 'The *Senna*: From Description to Literary Theory'. *Michigan Germanic Studies* 5: 65–74.

—— 1982. 'Beowulf in Literary History'. *Pacific Coast Philology* 17: 16–23. Repr. *Interpretations of Beowulf: A Critical Anthology*, pp. 235–41. Ed. R. D. Fulk. Bloomington, 1991.

—— 1983. 'Elegy in Old English and Old Norse'. *The Old English Elegies*, pp. 46–56. Ed. Martin Green. London and Toronto.

—— 1985a. 'Eddic Poetry'. *Old Norse-Icelandic Literature: A Critical Guide*, pp. 68–156. Eds Carol J. Clover and John Lindow. Islandica 45. Ithaca, NY, and London.

—— 1985b. 'Die altenglische Heldendichtung'. *Europäisches Frühmittelalter*, pp. 237–76. Ed.

Klaus von See. Neues Handbuch der Literatur-wissenschaft 6. Wiesbaden.

——1986. '*Brunanburh* 12b–13a and Some Skaldic Passages'. *Magister Regis: Studies in Honor of Robert Earl Kaske*, pp. 61–8. Eds Arthur Groos et al. New York.

——1992. 'Beowulf's Last Words'. *Speculum* 67: 1–32.

——1994. 'A Nativist Approach to *Beowulf*: The Case of the Germanic Elegy'. *Companion to Old English Poetry*, pp. 45–62. Eds Henk Aertsen and Rolf H. Bremmer Jr. Amsterdam.

Hofmann, Dietrich 1955. *Nordisch–englische Lehn-beziehungen der Wikingerzeit*. Biblioteca Arnam-agnæana 14. Copenhagen.

Jackson, Elizabeth 1998. '"Not Simply Lists": An Eddic Perspective on Short-item Lists in Old English Poems'. *Speculum* 73: 338–71.

Kuhn, Hans 1969. 'Die Dróttkvættverse des Typs "bestr erfiði Austra"'. *Afmælisrit Jóns Helgas-onar: 30 júní 1969*, pp. 403–17. Eds Jakob Benediktsson et al. Reykjavik. Repr. Kuhn, *Kleine Schriften* 6: 105–16. Ed. Dietrich Hofmann in collaboration with Wolfgang Lange and Klaus von See. Berlin, 1969–78.

——1977. 'Uns ist Fahrwind gegeben wider den Tod: Aus einer grossen Zeit des Nordens'. *Zeitschrift für deutsches Altertum und deutsche Literatur* 106: 147–62.

Lapidge, Michael 1981. 'Some Latin Poems as Evidence for the Reign of Athelstan'. *Anglo-Saxon England* 9: 61–98.

Lawrence, W. W. 1902. 'The First Riddle of Cynewulf'. *Publications of the Modern Language Association* 17: 247–61.

Lawson, M. K. 1993. *Cnut: The Danes in England in the Early Eleventh Century*. London and New York.

Lindow, John 1987. 'Norse Mythology and Northumbria: Methodological Notes'. *Anglo-Scandinavian England*, pp. 308–24. Eds John Niles and Mark Amodio. *Scandinavian Studies* 59.3.

Lönnroth, Lars 1971. 'Hjálmar's Death Song and the Delivery of Eddic Poetry'. *Speculum* 46: 1–20.

Magennis, Hugh 1996. *Images of Community in Old English Poetry*. Cambridge Studies in Anglo-Saxon England 18. Cambridge.

McKinnell, John 1990. 'The Context of *Vǫlun-darkviða*'. *Saga-Book of the Viking Society* 23: 1–27.

Metcalfe, Frederick 1880. *The Englishman and the Scandinavian; or, A Comparison of Anglo-Saxon and Old Norse Literature*. Boston.

Niles, John D. 1987. 'Skaldic Technique in *Brunanburh*'. *Anglo-Scandinavian England*, pp. 356–66. Eds John D. Niles and Mark Amodio. *Scandinavian Studies* 59.3.

Nordby, Conrad Hjalmar 1901. *The Influence of Old Norse upon English Literature*. New York.

North, Richard 1991. *Pagan Words and Christian Meanings*. Costerus, n.s. 81. Amsterdam and Atlanta.

Olsen, Alexandra Hennessey 1979. 'The Heroic World: Icelandic Sagas and the Old-English *Riming Poem*'. *Pacific Coast Philology* 14: 51–8.

Opland, Jeff 1980. *Anglo-Saxon Oral Poetry: A Study of the Traditions*. New Haven, CT, and London.

Orchard, Andy 1995. *Pride and Prodigies: Studies in the Monsters of the Beowulf-manuscript*. Cambridge.

Robinson, Fred C. 1976. 'Some Aspects of the *Maldon* Poet's Artistry'. *Journal of English and Germanic Philology* 75: 25–40. Repr. Robinson, *The Tomb of Beowulf and other Essays on Old English*, pp. 122–37. Oxford and Cambridge, MA, 1993.

Russom, Geoffrey R. 1978. 'A Germanic Concept of Nobility in *The Gifts of Men* and *Beowulf*'. *Speculum* 53: 1–15.

Seaton, Ethel 1935. *Literary Relations of England and Scandinavia in the Seventeenth Century*. Oxford.

Taylor, Paul Beekman 1998. *Sharing Story: Medieval Norse–English Literary Relationships*. New York.

Tolley, Clive 1996. 'Beowulf's Scyld Scefing Episode: Some Norse and Finnish Analogues'. *Arv* 52: 7–48.

PART V
Debates and Issues

22
English in the Post-Conquest Period
Elaine Treharne

On 14 October 1066, William, duke of Normandy, defeated Harold, the Anglo-Saxon king, at the battle of Hastings, thereby precipitating arguably the most significant political and governmental upheaval of the medieval period. William's reign saw the consolidation of the Anglo-Norman kingdom and the virtual wholesale replacement of the Anglo-Saxon aristocratic and ecclesiastical personnel by Norman successors. This imposition of a new ruling class was to have serious consequences, not only for the English people themselves, but also for the production and survival of their native literature. While the pre-Conquest period witnessed the parallel use of English and Latin for the recording of texts – both literary and documentary, secular and religious – the post-Conquest period introduced a third language into the equation: French or Anglo-Norman (Kibbee 1991). Latin was the language of the church and its courts, of a substantial proportion of the government's documentation, and of scholarship. French was used, increasingly throughout the twelfth and thirteenth centuries, as the language of law, administration, and secular aristocratic and religious literature (Clanchy 1993). English, displaced to a degree by the dominant modes of expression of French and Latin, was confined to religious and educational materials, to chronicling by some native writers, to a scattering of legal materials, and to some other more individualistic productions until the end of the twelfth century. It should be remembered, however, that in spite of the relegation of English to the minor written language, it was still the spoken language of the vast majority of the population.

Even though English became the minority written language from *c.*1060–*c.*1200 and beyond, there is a notable body of texts that survives from this period. Manuscripts extant from the mid-eleventh century to the beginning of the thirteenth that contain Old English, or works derived from earlier, pre-Conquest exemplars, number over fifty. To this substantial collection can be added the manuscripts from pre-1100 that contain the English annotations and glosses of twelfth- and thirteenth-century users; there are over one hundred surviving examples. It is the case, therefore, as these manuscript witnesses evince, that English was demonstrably an important and utilitarian literary language throughout this period. Numerous scholars to date have tended to underestimate the amount and significance of surviving vernacular texts in the two centuries following the Norman Conquest. In a very recent volume, for example, Thomas Hahn suggests that what was produced in this period represents a 'sporadic reproduction of an obsolete literary standard' (1999: 72), and that the intelligibility of Old English or late West Saxon is to be doubted. Similarly, Clanchy (1993: 212) writes that:

> Although Anglo-Saxon was not used after the 1070s by the king's government or by the clergy as a whole, it found defenders in the monastic antiquarian reaction which maintained English ways in the face of the Norman conquerors. Those monastic houses like Worcester and Rochester which produced the first cartularies were also among those which were most concerned to preserve a knowledge of Anglo-Saxon. Anglo-Saxon texts continued to be copied for a century after the Conquest and some works survive only in copies made in the twelfth century.

The key issue here is the insistence by these and other scholars that what survives after the Conquest until the emergence of new works in English in the last part of the twelfth century and early thirteenth, such as Laȝamon's *Brut* and the Katherine Group (Hahn 1999), is simply the product of the antiquarian endeavours of a few, usually monastic, writers. Not only is the material written in English often derogated by critics to an attempt to reproduce the past, or to cling on to a defunct national literary heritage, but it is also dismissed as an archaic and useless body of texts. The result of comments such as these, and preceding ones, has been the neglect of most of the manuscripts and their contents written in English in the post-Conquest period.

The neglect occasioned by this misrepresentation of what survives needs to be rectified, for there is much of interest in the texts that are extant. Not only are the various scribes' conscious and unconscious emendations to the language of the original texts crucial for an understanding of the evolution of literary English in this period (Liuzza 2000), but it is also possible to deduce some of the intellectual, political and theological concerns of the copyists or manuscript compilers. Sustained study of the texts written in English, then, allows us an insight into the vitality of the native vernacular literature. From an examination of the material written in English in the later eleventh and twelfth centuries it is possible to infer the ostensible motives of those compiling manuscripts, the potential audience of vernacular literature, the resources given over in (usually) monastic institutions to the production of these manuscripts, and the contemporary relevance of the works produced for their writers and users. Such a reappraisal permits the categorical assertion that late West Saxon, the literary dialect of the later Anglo-Saxon era, as it developed into early Middle English, was still a living form of standard written English, and that its uses were essential in the propagation of religious and didactic, legal and historical learning.

In terms of the language issues involved in studying this material, a single example will suffice to demonstrate that the scribes at work copying Old English texts were not simply mechanically reconstituting the original. A deliberate attempt was often made by scribes to update the texts lexically, grammatically and phonologically. In the mid-twelfth-century manuscript Cambridge, Corpus Christi College 303, for example, one of the scribes, the senior one responsible for the correction of many of the mistakes made by his colleagues throughout the manuscript, imposed his own forms of language onto the exemplar he was copying. One can compare the following extract from an early copy of Ælfric's Homily for the second Sunday after Pentecost (Clemoes 1977: 369), which is the first excerpt, with that from the much later Corpus 303, page 251, which is the second:

> Nu cwyð se halga gregorius þæt sum arwurþe munuc wæs on ðam earde. licaonia swiðe eawfæst his nama wæs martirius; se ferde be his abbodes hæse to sumum oþrum mynstre on his ærende. þa gemette he be wege sumne licþrowere licgende eall tocinen. 7 nahte his feþes geweald. cwæð ðæt he wolde genealæcan his hulce gif he mihte; ða ofhreow þam munuce þæs hreoflian mægenleaste. 7 bewand hine mid his cæppan. 7 bær to mynstre weard; Ða wearð his abbude geswutelod hwæne he bær; 7 hrymde mid micelre stemne 7 cwæð; Yrnað earma 7 undoþ þæs mynstres geat ardlice; for þan ðe ure broþor martirius berð ðone hælend on his bæce;

> Nu cweð se halige Gregorius þæt sum arwurðe munec wes on þan earde þe is gehaten licaonia swiðe eawfest. his nama wes martyrius. Se ferde be his abbotes hese to sume oðre mynstre on his erende. þa gemette he be wegge sumne licþrowere liggende al tocinen 7 nahte his fotes gewald; Cweð þet he wolde genehlecen his hulcan gyf he mihte. þa ofreaw þan munece þes hreoflian megenlest. 7 bewand hine mid his cappan; 7 ber to mynstre ward. þa werð his abbote geswutoled hwane he bere 7 clupode mid mucelre stemne 7 cweð. Yrnad swiðe 7 undoð þes mynstres gate raðe for ðan ðe ure broðer martirius berð þone helende uppen his rugge.

> Now the saintly Gregory relates that a certain pious and very devout monk was in the country of Licaonia, and his name was Martirius. He journeyed at his abbot's request to another monastery on his errand. Then he met on the way a leper lying all twisted, who had lost control of his ability to walk. He said that he wanted to get back to his hut if he could. Then the monk took pity on the leper's weakness, and enveloped him with his cope, and carried him towards the monastery. Then it was revealed to his abbot whom he carried, and he called out with a loud voice and said: 'Run, servant, and unlock the gates of the monastery quickly, because our brother Martirius carries the Saviour on his back!'

The linguistic alterations made by the scribe in Corpus 303 to his source text, represented here by the late tenth- or early eleventh-century version contained in Cambridge, University Library, Gg. 3. 28, range from spelling emendations (*cweð* ('said') for *cwyð* or *ber* ('carried') for *bær*, for instance), which may represent the scribe's own dialectal forms, to lexical replacement (*clupode* ('called') for *hrymde*, *raðe* ('quickly') for *ardlice*, *rugge* ('back') for *bæce*), which may well be the scribe's own efforts at updating the language of the original. There are also alterations to the morphology of the earlier text that again suggest a conscious attempt to make the language more contemporary. For example, the dative singular *-um* ending of *sumum oþrum* in the first extract has become modified to the levelled *sume oðre* of the second extract. If these methods of copying were isolated incidents, an idiosyncratic scribe perhaps, then it would not necessarily amount to significant linguistic data, but this type of scribal editing of an earlier text is very common in the twelfth century, and shows that these texts were meant to be used and useful to an audience whose main language was English. Moreover, and perhaps more importantly, the emendations to the text clearly demonstrate that the scribe was able to comprehend the earlier forms of English, thus illustrating that this literary dialect of Ælfric – late West Saxon – was still understood in the mid-twelfth century.

The fifty or so manuscripts written from *c*.1060 to *c*.1200 include a wide range of texts, many of them copied or adapted from earlier exemplars, as is the case with the above example. To this category one can assign many of the religious prose works of the period: the homilies in manuscripts such as Cambridge, Corpus Christi College, 302, and London, British Library, Cotton Faustina A. ix, for example, both probably produced in the south-east in the first quarter of the twelfth century; or the homilies in Oxford, Bodleian Library, Bodley 343, copied in the West Midlands in the second half of the twelfth century. The hagiographic texts contained in Cambridge, University Library, Ii. 1. 33, a manuscript possibly of south-eastern origin, datable to the second half of the twelfth century (Schipper 1983; Treharne 1998), are also, for the most part, copies of earlier Old English works. The English legal texts copied into the Rochester codex, the *Textus Roffensis*, or the early twelfth-century manuscript Cambridge, Corpus Christi College, 383, produced at St Paul's Cathedral, London, bear witness to the importance placed by twelfth-century manuscript compilers on vernacular law-codes dating from the pre-Conquest period (Wormald 1999).

Some of the surviving texts are, in contrast to these copies, original compositions or themselves post-Conquest English translations from Latin sources. Original compositions in English, by which I mean texts that are not based on earlier works in that language, are rare until the second half of the twelfth century. Two poetic texts, discussed in detail recently by Seth Lerer (1999: 7–34), belong to this category. *The Rime of King William* and *Durham* are the only surviving poems composed in English between *c*.1060 and *c*.1170, and, rare as they are, they do illustrate that there is no lacuna (as many scholars imply) in verse production in the post-Conquest period. The latter, and later, poem, *Durham*, provides a poetic narrative of that city's history, one that 'seeks to catalogue the scope of human and divine creation' (Lerer 1999: 21). *The Rime of King William*, contained in Oxford, Bodleian Library, Laud Misc. 636 (*The Peterborough Chronicle*), for the year 1087, is 'An elegy for an age as much as for a king . . . [that] . . . constitutes a powerfully literary, and literate, response to the legacies of pre-Conquest English writing' (Lerer 1999: 12). Indeed, *The Rime of King William* is contained in a manuscript that is in its entirety probably the most famous twelfth-century work in English. *The Peterborough Chronicle* is the latest of the historical manuscripts collectively known as *The Anglo-Saxon Chronicle*, the earliest manuscript of which dates from the late ninth century (Swanton 1998). *The Peterborough Chronicle* contains annals, or year entries, that extend the Anglo-Saxon text used as a source up to the year 1121, to cover the following years, 1122–54. This period includes part of the reign of Henry I, the civil war between Stephen and Matilda (Clanchy 1998), and the entire reign of King Stephen (1135–54). These continuations to the source text were made by two scribes, the first copying the annals for the years 1122–31, and the second retrospectively adding the years 1132–54. What makes these continuations remarkable is the language employed by the scribes, which is more comprehensively contemporary than that preserved in other, copied texts (Burrow and Turville-Petre 1992: 73–8). Also very significant is the way in which events occurring in England at that time are recorded with a distinctly English bias. Most anthologies of Middle English texts use *The Peterborough Chronicle* as the earliest example of Middle English, and cite the annals copied by the later scribe (Bennett and Smithers 1982: 201–12) for the fascinating account he gives of the miseries that had befallen the country during the reign of Stephen. The reader is told during the annal for 1137 (Treharne 2000: 258–9):

> I ne can ne I ne mai tellen alle þe wunder ne alle þe pines ðat hi diden wrecce men on þis land; and ðat lastede þa xix wintre wile Stephne was king, and ævre it was uuerse and uuerse. Hi læiden gæildes on the tunes ævre umwile, and clepeden it 'tenserie'. þa þe uurecce men ne hadden nammore to gyven, þa ræveden hi and brendon alle the tunes ðat wel þu myhtes faren al a dæis fare, sculdest thu nevre finden man in tune sittende, ne land tiled. þa was corn dære, and flec and cæse and butere, for nan ne wæs o þe land. Wrecce men sturven of hungær. Sume ieden on ælmes þe waren sum wile rice men; sume flugen ut of lande. Wes nævre gæt mare wreccehed on land, ne nævre hethen men werse ne diden þan hi diden.

> I cannot, nor will I, tell of all the horrors nor all the tortures that they performed on the wretched people of this land; and that lasted nineteen years while Stephen was king, and it always became worse and worse. They laid taxes on the villages all the while, and called it 'tenserie'. Then when the wretched people had no more to give, they robbed them and burned all the villages so that you might journey all of a day's journey, but you would never find a person living in a village, nor land tilled. Then corn was expensive, and meat and cheese and butter, because there was none in the land. Wretched people starved of hunger. Some lived by alms of those who were at one time powerful men; some fled from the land. There was never a more wretched time in the land, nor did the heathen men do any worse things than they did.

In this extract, the horror felt by the monastic writer when he witnessed the hardships imposed upon the native people by the Norman overlords as they fought the civil war is explicit. The comparative description of the Norman overlordship with the earlier Viking attacks ('the heathen men') provides an English, and historically contextual, perspective on current events. This personal narrative is not the propaganda of the twelfth-century Latin historiographer, nor is it the putative objective, and official, chronicling of the writers of the earlier versions of *The Anglo-Saxon Chronicle*. It is, instead, a moving and heartfelt account of the social and religious ills witnessed by the author. That it is written in English reminds the reader of its non-official status, and its survival as a unique opinion of the contemporary state of the nation is all the more notable precisely because it is a voice of the individual in an age of the monolithic institution.

A similar contemporary world-view is echoed in another prose work, somewhat surprisingly perhaps, because it is an adaptation of an earlier Old English text, the *Dicts of Cato* (Cox 1972). This didactic and pedagogic text, used in its Latin form for teaching young monks the rudiments of Latin grammar (Lapidge 1982), was translated into Old English at least three times. The three surviving versions are contained in London, British Library, Cotton Julius A. ii, Cotton Vespasian D. xiv, and Cambridge, Trinity College, R. 9. 17. Each of these manuscripts dates from the post-Conquest period, and appears to have originated in the south of England. None of the versions is identical to the other, and it seems that each was copied independently from a common Old English source, and adapted to fit its respective manuscript context. The version of the text in Cotton Vespasian D. xiv is found among numerous religious and educative prose pieces. It illustrates very many spelling and grammatical variations in comparison with the other two versions of the *Dicts*, but, more significantly, it also has seven additional admonitory apophthegms. The reader is told, for example, of the hardship that will come to a nation ruled by a foreign king (Cox 1972: 15, E):

> Wa þære þeode þe hæfð ælðeodigne cyng – ungemetfæstne, feoh georne, and unmild-heortne – for on þære þeode byð his gitsung, and his modes gnornung on his earde.

> It will be miserable for the nation that has a foreign king – immoderate, eager for money, and merciless – for his avarice will be on the people, and his mind's discontent on his land.

This political sentiment is obviously similar to that voiced by the second scribe of *The Peterborough Chronicle* Continuations. Its appearance in the *Dicts*, whether by design because of the manuscript's compiler, or by accident because of its inclusion in the direct source, is suggestive of topical concerns in the copying of material in Old English in this period. This topicality, in turn, indicates that the vernacular had an immediacy and utility that have only rarely been recognized and noted by modern medievalists.

Reinforcing this aspect of the native vernacular text copied in the twelfth century are other works that demonstrate an integral concern with contemporary intellectual and theological issues. The *Life of Saint Nicholas* and *Life of St Giles*, for example, copied into Cambridge, Corpus Christi College, 303, a Rochester manuscript of *c*.1140, are both products of one author, who translated and adapted Latin lives of these saints at some point in the post-Conquest period (Treharne 1997: 72–8). The translator of these texts frequently makes reference to his saints as *Godes deorling* ('God's darling'), *Godes þeowe* ('God's servant'), *Godes freond* ('God's friend'), and consistently ensures that his saints are seen to be working their numerous miracles only through the grace of God, and without any inherent miraculous powers. This feature of the English texts, a predominant concern with theocentricity and orthodoxy, is much more emphatic than in the surviving Latin analogues. The author also omits Biblical and historical material evident in the Latin lives to focus essentially on the words and deeds of the saints, thereby making the saint the complete focus of the text, and clarifying the texts' didactic message. The same orthodoxy, clarity and emphasis of the personal relationship between the saint and God that are exemplified in the English *Lives* of Giles and Nicholas are also apparent in the *Life of St Margaret*, copied into the same manuscript (Clayton and Magennis 1994; Magennis 1996). In the *Life of Margaret* the English translator is responsible for adapting his source so that the text's orthodoxy is maintained, and the close relationship between the virgin saint and God is emphasized. Thus, the vernacular *Life* in Corpus 303 differs both substantially and accidentally from all other Latin and English versions, including that copied in Old English into the mid-eleventh-century Canterbury manuscript, British Library, Cotton Tiberius A. iii. In the latter *Life*, as in most Latin versions, Margaret is swallowed by a demonic dragon, which attacks her while she is imprisoned. Upon making the sign of the cross, Margaret bursts unharmed from the dragon, which subsequently disappears (Clayton and Magennis 1994: 122–3). This particular episode, declared apocryphal in the late fifth-century decrees of Pope Gelasius, is altered in the twelfth-century *Life* in Corpus 303. In this version, Margaret makes the sign of the cross as the dragon approaches to swallow her; the dragon disintegrates and disappears from the prison cell (Clayton and Magennis 1994: 162–3). With this small but important alteration, the adaptor of the Corpus text eliminates the more apocryphal elements of the text, and creates a less sensationalist, and potentially more orthodox, scene. This adaptor also attempts to contemporize the text, casting Margaret very much in the role of the Bride of Christ. The personal relationship, one of love and trust that is fostered by the careful and repeated prayers of Margaret, represents a new direction in spirituality in the post-Conquest period. This is best exemplified by Anselm of Canterbury's writings emphasizing the individual Christian's ability to have a meaningful and loving connection with God through the power of prayer and self-awareness (Magennis 1996; Chenu 1997; Morris 1972). What is significant, then, about the elements of the three texts discussed here is that they reflect post-Conquest theological and hagiographical trends: the *Lives* are made contemporary by the adaptor in a way that suggests the English texts were formulated with a specifically twelfth-century audience in mind. The theory that Old English was copied merely for antiquarian purposes is once more undermined, and it becomes apparent that the texts written and copied after the Conquest were created to be used and useful.

Perhaps the most striking example of a manuscript created for a specifically twelfth-century audience, partially out of existing literature and partially using new material, is London, British Library, Cotton Vespasian D. xiv (Warner 1917; Irvine 2000). This is arguably the most perplexing codex to survive from this century, for it is difficult to discern a thematic unity or purpose behind its compilation. Its complexity foregrounds the central questions asked by scholars working with all extant post-Conquest Old English prose: for whom, in particular, was this manuscript created?

Where, and with what resources, was it written? Why is there such a diversity of types of texts?

Cotton Vespasian D. xiv contains a range of material: from moralistic texts, such as the *Dicts of Cato*; to straightforward educative texts, such as excerpts from the *Elucidarius* of Honorius Augustodunensis; to prognosticatory and prophetic texts; to snippets of texts containing central Christian doctrine. The abbreviated *Elucidarius* is one of only two prose texts that we know was definitely translated into English after 1100. The author of the lengthy Latin original, Honorius Augustodunensis, composed his work in *c*.1100 to address and resolve the problems of reforming the English church (Flint 1975). The work is comprised of questions and answers concerning knowledge of God, the nature of evil, and eschatalogical issues. It is a dialogue between a pupil and a master that seeks to provide a thorough Christian education. The excerpts in Vespasian D. xiv are carefully selected to give important information concerning fundamental tenets of Christianity; for example, the nature of sin and the concept of free will are discussed (Warner 1917: 140–5). This type of material illustrates a format known as *quaestiones et responses* ('question and answer') long used by teachers and patristic writers, but particularly developed in the twelfth century (Chenu 1997: 292–300). The *Elucidarius* is one of three such dialogic texts surviving in English from this period, the other two being *Solomon and Saturn* and *Adrian and Ritheus*, which are extant respectively only in the two mid-twelfth-century manuscripts, London, British Library, Cotton Julius A. ii, and Cotton Vitellius A. xv (Hollis and Wright 1992; Cross and Hill 1982).

From analysing the nature of these texts it is clear that in the post-Conquest period, English was used as a literary medium to educate, utilizing the most current textual methods. These texts show the need in the twelfth century for straightforward material detailing answers to fundamental questions that might be asked by the Christian while learning, or encountered by one whose duties included that of pastoral care. Furthermore, the basic encyclopaedic Christian and ethical knowledge imparted by these texts is certainly illustrative of the general, but more learned, tendencies by scholars in the twelfth century to provide material in similar formats in Latin for educating the literate. What twenty-first century scholars still need to resolve is the issue of who the audience for these vernacular texts might have been.

Cotton Vespasian D. xiv has been described as 'a preacher's commonplace book' with an 'overall plan [which] is moral and instructive' (Handley 1974: 244). It is conceivable that this manuscript was copied at a monastic scriptorium, perhaps Christ Church, Canterbury, or, less likely, Rochester (Richards 1988; Treharne 1998) for use by preachers whose parishes were within the originating monastery's ownership. But the manuscript itself does not show obvious signs of having been used in this way, and its actual intended audience may also have been novice monks or nuns (Irvine 2000). It seems unlikely that novice religious would have been educated using English if they were able to undertake a more official, Latin-based training, but it is less unlikely that older novices, adult learners, might have been the intended recipients of such English texts. Whatever the specific audience, it is clear that some of the hom-

ilies by Ælfric that are contained in Cotton Vespasian D. xiv, and in many other manuscripts from the twelfth and early thirteenth centuries also (Swan 1996, 1997, 2000),
have been curtailed or adapted specifically to excise material that the compiler appears
to have deemed extraneous or potentially confusing for any user; this does suggest a
relatively unlearned audience, more familiar with English than Latin learning. The
Homily for the Assumption of the Virgin Mary from Ælfric's Second Series of *Catholic
Homilies* (Warner 1917: 47–50), for example, is inserted between the two halves of
Ælfric's First Series *Catholic Homily* for the Assumption, and is shorter by some eleven
lines than Ælfric's original (Godden 1979: 255–9). The omitted passage follows
Ælfric's repudiation of the apocryphal legend of the Assumption and, from other surviving manuscript copies, it is apparent that it deals with the dangers of listening to
heretical lies, urging instead an adherence to orthodox interpretations. Joyce Hill comments that Ælfric, within this passage, highlights the 'dangerous accessibility [of
apocryphal material] to the unlearned' (Hill 1993: 26–7), yet this important authorial statement is partially, and perhaps deliberately, excised by the compiler of Cotton
Vespasian D. xiv. This may be due to no more than the constraints of space within
the manuscript itself, but the omission might very well point to the compiler's desire
not to enter into a debate on non-orthodox versus orthodox teaching. Such a concern
suggests that the potential user(s) of the manuscript were deemed by the compiler to
be relative beginners in the sphere of Christian theology.

While Ælfric's works undoubtedly form the majority of the contents of many
English religious compilations in the late eleventh, twelfth and early thirteenth centuries, it is evident that numerous alterations to the texts were being made in the
process of manuscript production. What becomes clear, with regard both to Ælfric's
works and to those of anonymous authors, is that these manuscripts do not illustrate
merely mechanical copying, or, to put it another way, do not represent attempts to
preserve intact the Anglo-Saxon religious literary heritage by antiquarian-minded
manuscript producers. Instead, there is a deliberate selection process in operation at
compilation level, one which can be used to demonstrate the contemporary nature
of the manuscripts themselves: they were designed not for instant committal to the
monastic library's shelves, but for the benefit of a real audience, perhaps essentially
unlearned, who only had access to the vernacular.

Whether or not this audience might have received this information and education
through the mediation of a teacher, perhaps a monk or nun, perhaps a parish priest, is
a vexed question. There are numerous glossators and annotators at work on pre-
Conquest and post-Conquest English manuscripts in the twelfth, thirteenth and fourteenth centuries (Ker, *Catalogue*). It is difficult, at first glance, to discern who these
manuscript users are, and whether they were scouring the manuscripts for material of
use to them personally or in a pastoral, public capacity. A survey of the glosses and
notes, however, shows that, in almost all cases, while such markings are sporadic they
are nevertheless clustered within specific texts. In the late tenth-century manuscript,
London, British Library, Royal 7 C. xii (Clemoes and Eliason 1966), twelfth-century
annotations and glosses occur in groups located at specific homilies for major feasts in

the church year. Similarly, thirteenth-century glossing in the twelfth-century manuscript, Cotton Faustina A. ix, is at its most sustained level in the texts for major occasions such as Palm Sunday. The work of the notators is also of a remarkably similar kind: the annotator, by supplying a name, or updating a word, or changing a spelling or the syntax seeks to explicate the text, in terms of both its lexical intelligibility and its semantic clarity. One is able to detect that the level of expansion suggests the text is being modified in minor ways to suit an audience less educated than the annotator; in other words, the modifications suggest that the text is being prepared for reading to, or use by, people other than the annotator himself or herself.

Easily the best-known example of a religiously motivated user and author of English texts is a person labelled the 'Tremulous Hand' of Worcester. Christine Franzen (1991) has given a thorough account of the work of this late twelfth-, early thirteenth-century scholar who worked with some of the Latin and English medieval manuscripts probably belonging to Worcester Cathedral Priory. The Tremulous Hand extensively glossed, provided annotations for, and made word-lists from a variety of volumes containing mostly religious and educative works. Not only did this scribe cull material from books he perceived to be useful in the collection, but he also copied out English verse, now collectively known as *The Worcester Fragments* (Moffat 1987). In this series of loosely related poetic works, he bemoans the loss of English learning, demonstrating explicitly the allegiance to 'Englishness' that his manuscript work implicitly reveals (Hahn 1999: 74–5; Collier 1995, 1998). Current religiosity is captured in the fragment known as *The Debate of the Body and Soul*, in which the theme of the transience of human life links the world of the Old English elegies to the world of the Middle English lyric. Like the twelfth-century scribes that preceded him, this is no mechanical or antiquarian scribe, but one whose work utilized the resources around him to be reworked and recontextualized for a new audience.

Precisely what the agenda of this scholar might have been is not known, but it seems likely that he was engaged in some kind of teaching or pastoral role that, at times, specifically involved the use of English, and not Latin. The fact that he was able to spend some years working on the manuscripts in the collection (Franzen 1991) also suggests that this material was not itself being frequently used by others. The gradual decline in intelligibility of the pre-Conquest form of written English, together with the creation of new didactic and historical texts written wholly in contemporary twelfth- or thirteenth-century English (such as the *Brut*, *Ancrene Wisse* and *Poema Morale*), may indicate why the Tremulous Hand and the other glossators, annotators and scribes appear as relatively isolated scholars in a wider world of substantial Latin and Anglo-Norman manuscript production. But there are over one hundred and fifty manuscripts that survive from *c*.1060–*c*.1200 that prove that English remained a viable and relevant mode of written communication. As I have briefly demonstrated, if it were not for the compilers and copyists of the post-Conquest period, working with the pre-Conquest Old English textual resources available to them, we would obviously not have a record of the continued and topical interest in these texts; moreover, in the case of the many unique Old English texts that survive from the late eleventh and twelfth centuries, without these scribes' careful and selective copying we would not have copies of these works at all.

REFERENCES

Primary sources

Bennett, J. A. W. and G. V. Smithers, eds 1982. *Early Middle English Verse and Prose*, with a glossary by N. Davis. 2nd edn. Oxford, 1968.

Burrow, J. A. and Thorlac Turville-Petre, eds 1992. *A Book of Middle English*. Oxford.

Clayton, Mary and Hugh Magennis, eds 1994. *The Old English Lives of St Margaret*. Cambridge Studies in Anglo-Saxon England 9. Cambridge.

Clemoes, Peter, ed. 1977. *Ælfric's Catholic Homilies: The First Series: Text*. Early English Text Society, s.s. 17. Oxford.

——and Norman Eliason, intro. 1966. *Ælfric's First Series of Catholic Homilies: British Museum Royal 7 c. xii, fols. 4–218*. Early English Manuscripts in Facsimile 13. Copenhagen.

Cox, R. S. 1972. 'The Old English Dicts of Cato'. *Anglia* 90: 1–42.

Cross, James E. and Thomas D. Hill, eds 1982. *The Prose Solomon and Saturn and Adrian and Ritheus, edited from the British Library Manuscripts with Commentary*. McMaster Old English Studies and Texts 1. Toronto.

Godden, Malcolm, ed. 1979. *Ælfric's Catholic Homilies: The Second Series*. Early English Text Society, s.s. 5. Oxford.

Irvine, S., ed. 1993. *Old English Homilies from Bodley 343*. Early English Text Society, o.s. 302. London.

Moffat, D., ed. 1987. *The Soul's Address to the Body: The Worcester Fragments*. East Lansing.

Swanton, M., ed. 1998. *The Anglo-Saxon Chronicle*. London.

Treharne, E. M., ed. 1997. *The Old English Life of St Nicholas with the Old English Life of St Giles*. Leeds Texts and Monographs 15. Leeds.

——, ed. 2000. *Old and Middle English: An Anthology*. Oxford.

Warner, R. D.-N., ed. 1917. *Early English Homilies from the Twelfth Century MS. Vesp. D. XIV*. Early English Text Society, o.s. 152. Woodbridge.

Secondary sources

Chenu, M.-D. 1997. *Nature, Man, and Society in the Twelfth Century*. Medieval Academy Reprints for Teaching 37. Toronto.

Clanchy, Michael 1993. *From Memory to Written Record: England 1066–1307*. 2nd edn. Oxford.

——1998. *England and its Rulers: 1066–1272*. 2nd edn. Oxford.

Collier, W. E. J. 1995. '"Englishness" and the Worcester Tremulous Hand'. *Leeds Studies in English* n.s. 26: 37–8.

——1998. 'A Thirteenth-Century Anglo-Saxonist'. *Anglo-Saxon Texts and Contexts*, pp. 149–66. Ed. G. Owen-Crocker. *Bulletin of the John Rylands University Library of Manchester* 79, 3.

Flint, V. 1975. 'The "Elucidarius" of Honorius Augustodunensis and Reform in Late Eleventh-Century England'. *Revue Bénédictine* 85: 178–98.

Franzen, Christine 1991. *The Tremulous Hand of Worcester: A Study of Old English in the Thirteenth Century*. Oxford.

Hahn, Thomas 1999. 'Early Middle English'. *The Cambridge History of Medieval English Literature*, pp. 61–91. Ed. David Wallace. Cambridge.

Handley, Rima 1974. 'British Museum MS. Cotton Vespasian D. xiv'. *Notes & Queries* 21: 243–50.

Hill, Joyce 1993. 'Reform and Resistance: Preaching Styles in Late Anglo-Saxon England'. *De l'Homélie au Sermon: Histoire de la Prédication Médiévale*, pp. 15–46. Eds Jacqueline Hamesse and Xavier Hermand. Louvain-la-Neuve.

Hollis, Stephanie and Michael Wright, eds 1992. *English Prose of Secular Learning*. Annotated Bibliographies of Old and Middle English Literature IV. Cambridge.

Irvine, Susan 2000. 'The Compilation and Use of Manuscripts Containing Old English in the Twelfth Century'. *Rewriting Old English in the Twelfth Century*, pp. 41–61. Eds M. Swan and E.

M. Treharne. Cambridge Studies in Anglo-Saxon England 30. Cambridge.

Kibbee, Douglas 1991. *For to Speke Frenche Trewely: The French Language in England, 1000–1600: Its Status, Description and Instruction*. Amsterdam Studies in the Theory and History of Linguistic Science 60. Amsterdam.

Lapidge, M. 1982. 'The Study of Latin Texts in late Anglo-Saxon England: (1) The Evidence of Latin Glosses'. *Latin and the Vernacular Languages in Early Medieval Britain*, pp. 99–140. Ed. Nicholas Brooks. Leicester.

Lerer, Seth 1999. 'Old English and its Afterlife'. *The Cambridge History of Medieval Literature*, pp. 7–34. Ed. David Wallace. Cambridge.

Liuzza, R. M. 2000. 'Scribal Habit: The Evidence of the Old English Gospels'. *Rewriting Old English in the Twelfth Century*, pp. 146–65. Eds Mary Swan and Elaine M. Treharne. CSASE 30. Cambridge.

Magennis, Hugh 1996. '"Listen Now All and Understand": Adaptation of Hagiographical Material for Vernacular Audiences in the Old English Lives of St Margaret'. *Speculum* 71: 27–42.

Morris, Colin 1972. *The Discovery of the Individual 1050–1200*. Church History Outlines 5. London.

Pulsiano, Phillip and Elaine M. Treharne, eds 1998. *Anglo-Saxon Manuscripts and their Heritage*. Aldershot.

Richards, M. P. 1988. *Texts and their Traditions in the Medieval Library of Rochester Cathedral Priory*. Transactions of the American Philosophical Association 78.3. Philadelphia.

Schipper, W. 1983. 'A Composite Old English Homiliary from Ely: Cambr. Univ. MS Ii. 1. 33'. *Transactions of the Cambridge Bibliographical Society* 8: 285–98.

Swan, M. 1996. 'Holiness Remodelled: Theme and Technique in Old English Composite Homilies'. *Models of Holiness in Medieval Sermons*, pp. 35–46. Ed. Beverly Mayne Kienzle. Louvain-la-Neuve.

—— 1997. 'Old English Made New: One *Catholic Homily* and its Reuses'. *Leeds Studies in English* n.s. 28: 1–18.

—— 1998. 'Memorialised Readings: Manuscript Evidence for Old English Homily Composition'. *Anglo-Saxon Manuscripts and their Heritage*, pp. 205–17. Eds P. Pulsiano and E. Treharne. Aldershot.

—— 2000. 'Ælfric's Catholic Homilies in the Twelfth Century'. *Rewriting Old English in the Twelfth Century*, pp. 62–82. Eds Mary Swan and Elaine M. Treharne. CSASE 30. Cambridge.

—— and Elaine M. Treharne, eds 2000. *Rewriting Old English in the Twelfth Century*. Cambridge Studies in Anglo-Saxon England 30. Cambridge.

Teresi, L. 1998. 'An Electronic Investigation of the Language in MSS London, British Library, Cotton Faustina A. ix and Cambridge, Corpus Christi College, 302'. *Anglo-Saxon Texts and Contexts: Bulletin of the John Rylands University Library of Manchester* 79, 3: 133–48. Ed. G. Owen-Crocker.

Treharne, Elaine M. 1998. 'The Dates and Origins of Three Twelfth-Century Old English Manuscripts'. *Anglo-Saxon Manuscripts and their Heritage*, pp. 185–211. Eds Phillip Pulsiano and Elaine Treharne. Aldershot.

Wormald, P. 1999. *The Making of English Law: King Alfred to the Twelfth Century*. Oxford.

23

Anglo-Saxon Studies: Sixteenth to Eighteenth Centuries

Timothy Graham

By the late Middle Ages, the language of the Anglo-Saxons was a dead language, presenting insuperable difficulties of comprehension and scorned in centres that owned copies of Old English texts. That Old English is a subject of study today is the fruit of the pioneering labours of generations of scholars who, beginning in the second quarter of the sixteenth century, undertook the task of recovering the knowledge of the language and bringing into the public domain texts written in it. The achievements of the first generations were substantial: they rescued from loss or destruction the Anglo-Saxon manuscripts upon which all subsequent study has ultimately depended; their transcriptions have in some cases preserved for posterity texts whose originals subsequently perished; they issued the earliest editions of Old English texts, and furnished the tools on which scientific study of the language could be based; and their efforts led to the eventual inclusion of Old English within the university curriculum. The purposes that impelled these early Anglo-Saxonists varied in character from antiquarian-historical to religio-political to, eventually, the more purely philological. This chapter will assess the nature and describe the progress of their work from the sixteenth-century beginnings up until the eighteenth century.

First Steps: Leland, Talbot and Recorde

It was primarily antiquarian interests that motivated the first three scholars known to have applied themselves to Old English studies: John Leland (*c.*1502–52), Robert Talbot (*c.*1505–58) and Robert Recorde (*c.*1510–58). Leland, the leading antiquarian of his generation, was chaplain and librarian to Henry VIII. In 1533, just three years before the Dissolution of the Monasteries, which was to have so profound an impact on the fate of medieval libraries, he received Henry's commission, as he himself later put it, 'to peruse and dylygentlye to searche all the lybraryes of Monasteryes and collegies of thys your noble realme, to the entent that the monumentes of auncyent wryters, as wel of other nacyons as of your owne prouynce, myghte be brought out of deadly darkenesse to lyuelye lyght' (Bale 1549: sig. B.viii^r). Leland's travels led him to conceive the major, and finally unfulfilled, project of his late years, a large-scale topographical description of Britain. According to his contemporary John Bale (1495–1563), Leland's antiquarian researches led him to master the historical vernaculars of the British Isles, including Old English ('Saxonyshe'): 'he not onlye applyed hym selfe to the knowledge of the Greke and Latyne tongues, wherin he was (I myghte saye) excellentlye lerned. But also to the stodye of the Bryttyshe, Saxonyshe, and Walshe tongues, and so muche profyted therin, that he most perfitelye vnderstode them' (Bale 1549: sig. B.iiii^v).

In reality, however, Leland's efforts with Old English were less full, and less expert, than Bale's comments suggest. No annotations by him have been recognized in any surviving Old English manuscript. There are a few Old English jottings in his *Collectanea*, and these reveal the limited scope of his interest in the language. One major set is a list of Old English placenames that he excerpted from MS C of the *Anglo-Saxon Chronicle* (British Library, Cotton Tiberius B. i), which he borrowed from Robert Talbot (Leland 1770: IV.122–5). The list indicates that Leland was interested in Old English texts primarily in so far as they might assist his researches in historical topography and toponymy. The *Collectanea* also contain an Old English word-list of some 181 entries that he excerpted from Ælfric's *Glossary* – apparently from a copy that no longer survives and that he may have found at Glastonbury Abbey (Leland 1770: IV.134–6; Buckalew 1978). While the list suggests that Leland made some attempt to build up a vocabulary of Old English, there is no hard evidence to show that he undertook anything approaching a methodical study of the language.

Much more impressive were the endeavours of Robert Talbot, a churchman who, after obtaining benefices in several counties, was made a prebendary of Norwich Cathedral in 1547, and became cathedral treasurer. He published nothing, but his surviving notebook (Cambridge, Corpus Christi College 379), and his annotations in vernacular and Latin manuscripts of the Anglo-Saxon period and later, reveal keen antiquarian interests. Some ten manuscripts containing Old English passed through his hands, including copies of the Old English Hexateuch and Gospels, Bede and Orosius, the *Anglo-Saxon Chronicle*, homilies, miscellaneous ecclesiastical and legal texts, and Ælfric's *Grammar* and *Glossary*. Their varying provenances (including Abingdon, Canterbury, Exeter and Worcester) suggest a concerted attempt on Talbot's part to track down Old English materials. Transcriptions in his hand include some from originals that have subsequently disappeared: Cambridge, Corpus Christi College 111, contains his copies of a set of Abingdon charters that then belonged to Dr George Owen (d. 1558) but that subsequently disappeared, while CCCC 379, his notebook, has his transcription of most of the now missing first leaf of the illustrated manuscript of the Hexateuch (British Library, Cotton Claudius B. iv), which carried the opening of Ælfric's *Preface to Genesis*. Talbot's notebook also includes his transcription of annal 893 of the F-text of the *Anglo-Saxon Chronicle*, which, because of its reference to the Lympne estuary in Kent, he quotes in full within the longest item in the notebook, his annotations on the British portion of the third-century Roman road-book known as the *Itinerarium Antonini*. Talbot's extensive notes on the *Itinerarium* reveal that, like Leland's, his antiquarian studies focused on British historical topography and toponymy. This overarching interest explains why many of his entries in Anglo-Saxon manuscripts simply record in the margin those placenames that are mentioned in the text. Other notes of his, though (for example, in British Library, Cotton Nero A. i), comment on religious issues, and foreshadow the kinds of preoccupations that were to characterize the studies of the Parker circle a few years later.

The method by which Talbot taught himself Old English is hinted at by the scattering of Latin glosses that he entered in his copy of the Old English Gospels (Oxford, Bodleian Library, Bodley 441), and by the Latin definitions that he included in an Old English word-list (derived from the Old English translations of Genesis and of Orosius' *Historiarum contra paganos libri septem*) that he compiled in his notebook. The glosses and definitions match the wording found in the Latin versions of the texts, and suggest that Talbot studied the vernacular versions side by side with copies of the Latin on which they were based (see Graham 1996: 5–6). The Old English translations had of course originally been made to assist Anglo-Saxons who had difficulty with Latin, but now the function was reversed, with the Latin serving as the key to the meaning of the Old English. This technique was to be used by others in the generations following Talbot.

The Welshman Robert Recorde, a physician by training, is chiefly known as the author of textbooks on mathematics and astronomy, including *The Grounde of Artes* (1540) and *The Castle of Knowledge* (1551). However, he was also an antiquarian of wide-ranging interests that led him to collect manuscripts and to dabble in Old English. The principal evidence for his Anglo-Saxon endeavours is to be found in one of his manuscripts, which contains an abridged version of the *Chronica maiora* of Matthew Paris (Cambridge, Corpus Christi College 138). Recorde supplemented the account of the years 449–871 in this chronicle by adding in its margins some twenty-five extracts from two Old English texts: the C-version of the *Anglo-Saxon Chronicle* (British Library, Cotton Tiberius B. i) and the copy of the so-called West Saxon genealogy that prefaces the Old English translation of Bede's *Historia ecclesiastica* in Cambridge University Library, Kk.3.18. As both manuscripts on which he drew are known to have passed through Talbot's hands, it seems likely that Recorde, like Leland, was able to borrow from Talbot, evidently the doyen of Old English studies during this period.

Nor did Recorde confine his study of Tiberius B. i to its copy of the *Chronicle*. The manuscript also contains a copy of the Old English version of Paulus Orosius' *Historiarum contra paganos*, which supplements Orosius' text with an account of the visit to King Alfred's court by the Scandinavian trader Ohthere, who regaled the king with his description of his travels in the northern seas. Recorde had read this account, for in the 'Epistle Dedicatorie' of his algebraical treatise *The Whetstone of Witte* (1557), addressed to the governors and members of the Muscovy Company, he compliments the Company on its success in charting the north-eastern waters and notes that

'Nother euer any before . . . had passed that voiage, excepte onely Ohthere, that dwelte in Halgoland: whoe reported that iorney to the noble Kyng Alurede: As it doeth yet remaine in aunciente recorde of the olde Saxon tongue' (Recorde 1557: sig. a.iii^{rv}; Brewer 1952–3: 202–5). This passing reference provides the only evidence that Recorde had read at least part of the Old English Orosius: there are no notes by him in the manuscript itself to indicate his study of the text. This circumstance not only serves as a reminder that the earliest Anglo-Saxonists may have read more widely than surviving evidence allows us to know; it also alerts us to the possibility that during this early period, others too may have studied Old English manuscripts, but left no record of their work.

Nowell, Lambarde, and the Work of the Parker Circle

There seems to be no direct line of continuity between the first three known Anglo-Saxonists, all of whom died during the 1550s, and the next phase of activity, which began in the 1560s and in which the central figures were Laurence Nowell (1530–69 or soon after), William Lambarde (1536–1601), Archbishop Matthew Parker (1504–75) and his assistant John Joscelyn (1529–1603). None of this 'second generation' seems to have been personally acquainted with Leland, Talbot or Recorde, although Nowell and Lambarde used, and Parker succeeded in acquiring, some of the manuscripts that had passed through the earlier scholars' hands. Major themes of this second phase of activity are the focused study of legal texts and the *Anglo-Saxon Chronicle*, the examination and exploitation of manuscripts for the evidence that they could contribute to contemporary religious debates, and the appearance of the first printed editions of Old English texts.

The career of Nowell, who was long confused with his namesake the dean of Lichfield, has now been established as accurately as is possible from available evidence (Flower 1935; Berkhout 1998). He appears to have developed an interest in Old English only *c*.1562, when, following a period of travel on the continent, he joined the household of Sir William Cecil, Queen Elizabeth's secretary of state, where he served as tutor to Cecil's ward, the young Edward de Vere. Although Nowell published nothing, during the following years, until he left for the continent again in 1567 (a journey from which he was not to return), he studied and made transcriptions from several Anglo-Saxon manuscripts, as well as compiling his own *Vocabularium Saxonicum*, a dictionary of some 6,000 entries that is the first major contribution to Old English lexicography (Marckwardt 1952). Nowell seems to have been the only sixteenth-century Anglo-Saxonist to take any noticeable interest in Old English poetry. His signature and the date 1563 are entered – apparently as an ownership inscription – in the *Beowulf*-manuscript, while his hand can also be found in the Exeter Book, where he has glossed a few lines of *Christ* and added titles to two sections of that poem and two of *Guthlac*. His complete transcription of the manuscript now British Library, Cotton Otho B. xi, includes what is now our primary witness to the poetic text *The Seasons for Fasting*, as the original was lost when the manuscript suffered grave damage in the fire that devastated the Cotton library in 1731.

Nowell's principal work as an Anglo-Saxonist, however, centred on historical and legal texts. He knew five of the seven surviving manuscripts of the *Anglo-Saxon Chronicle* (MSS B, C, D, E and G), and in the various transcripts that he prepared from them (discussed in Lutz 1982: 310–38) he attempted to compile for himself as full a set of Anglo-Saxon annals as he could. Having prepared his first transcript, British Library, Additional 43703, from MS G in 1562, he concentrated in subsequent work on transcribing those portions of the other manuscripts that differed from or added to the text of G. Both Add. 43703 and its companion volume, Add. 43704 – which contains his transcriptions of portions of E (dated 1565), C and D – reveal that like his predecessors in the field, Nowell was keenly interested in historical toponymy, for he has written out neatly in the margins those placenames mentioned in the text. Nowell himself was an accomplished cartographer – it was as a mapmaker as well as a tutor that he had originally been recommended to Cecil – and his toponymical interests manifest themselves again in his set of maps of the British Isles contained in British Library, Cotton Domitian A. xviii, where he has entered the placenames in Old English forms in script imitating Anglo-Saxon minuscule. While he obtained many of the names from his reading of the *Chronicle* and other historical sources, others are apparently his own invented back-formations from the sixteenth-century forms of the names.

The texts of Otho B. xi that Nowell transcribed into Add. 43703 in 1562 included the laws of Kings Alfred and Ine. Nowell later added to his transcription variant readings that he found in two or three other manuscripts, and finally produced a handwritten fair copy of the laws of Alfred, now British Library, Dept of Printed Books, Henry Davis Collection 59 (M 30). This stands as the first effort at a critical edition (accompanied by a facing-page English translation) of an Old English text (Berkhout 1998: 11–12). Apparently the first to realize the potential importance that knowledge of the Anglo-Saxon laws could hold in the context of a legal system based on precedent, Nowell initiated a tradition that was to bear fruit in the work of the great legal historians of the seventeenth century, Edward Coke (1552–1634), John Selden (1584–1654) and Henry Spelman (*c.*1564–1641), who all exploited Anglo-Saxon sources.

Nowell's closest friend and associate during the years he devoted to Old English was William Lambarde, who had received legal training at Lincoln's Inn. Lambarde was later to initiate what was to develop into a long and distinguished tradition when he published the first history of an English county; his *A Perambulation of Kent*, which included his discussion of the Old English forms of Kentish placenames, appeared in 1576. When Nowell left England in 1567, he entrusted all his papers, including his Old English transcripts, to Lambarde, who annotated and expanded the materials, for example by adding entries to Nowell's *Vocabularium Saxonicum*. Lambarde's most important contribution was to bring Nowell's legal materials to completion and to publish them in 1568 as *Archaionomia, sive de priscis Anglorum legibus libri*, an edition with accompanying Latin translation of some dozen Old English law-codes. The book was printed by John Day of Aldersgate, and used the special Anglo-Saxon font that Day had created in 1566 for the first ever printing of an Old English text, *A Testimonie of Antiquitie, Shewing the Ancient Fayth in the Church of England Touching the Sacrament of the Body and Bloude of the Lord*, a publication undertaken under the inspirational impulse of Matthew Parker, archbishop of Canterbury (1559–75).

It is the work of Parker and those associated with him that stands as the most vigorous achievement of Anglo-Saxon studies in the sixteenth century. In addition to *A Testimonie*, Parker was also responsible for *The Gospels of the Fower Euangelistes* (1571), an edition of the Old English Gospels ostensibly edited by John Foxe; and *Ælfredi regis res gestæ* (1574), which included, as well as the Latin text of Asser's *Life of King Alfred*, the first printing of Alfred's Old English *Preface* to his translation of Pope Gregory's *Cura pastoralis*. Less immediately visible than these publications, but equally impressive, is the vast amount of close study of Latin and Old English texts of the Anglo-Saxon period carried out by the Parker circle and attested by evidence surviving in the manuscripts that they used.

From current perspectives, Parker's most important accomplishment was to assemble and pass on to posterity the first major collection of Anglo-Saxon manuscripts to be formed in the wake of the Dissolution of the Monasteries. Parker's manuscript-gathering activities appear to have become intense in the mid-1560s; from 1566 he enlisted the help of several of his bishops, who searched their cathedral libraries for Anglo-Saxon and other medieval materials that they then despatched to him (Wright 1951: 221–3). At his death, he entrusted the bulk of his collection to Corpus Christi College, Cambridge, of which he had been Master from 1544 until 1553, and which retains the books to this day.

Parker's ownership has materially affected the state in which his manuscripts have come down to us and now present themselves for study. He had most of the manuscripts rebound, and in the process he would occasionally combine together items of different provenances, as happened with Cambridge, Corpus Christi College 201, in which he brought together a miscellaneous collection of ecclesiastical and other texts perhaps from Winchester and a Latin and Old English copy, from Exeter, of the *Capitula* of Theodulf of Orléans. Alternatively, he might remove a group of leaves from one manuscript to insert them into another, as he did in the case of the leaves carrying the text of Ælfric's Old English translation of Alcuin's *Interrogationes Sigewulfi in Genesin*, formerly in CCCC 178 but now in CCCC 162. If manuscripts reached him in an incomplete state, with leaves missing at the front or back, so that their first text began acephalously or their last text lacked its end, he might attempt to 'neaten' the appearance of the manuscript by erasing the surviving portion of the incomplete text; this he did with a section of the Old English translation of the *Regularis concordia* at the beginning of CCCC 201 and the opening of a homily on virginity at the end of CCCC 198. By contrast, on occasion he made good a defect by inserting fresh leaves with a specially prepared transcript of the missing text written by one of his scribes in a calligraphic hand imitating Anglo-Saxon minuscule, as has happened at the beginning of CCCC 449, a copy of Ælfric's *Grammar* and *Glossary*. There is also evidence that Parker may on occasion have passed over to his binders, for them to use as they would, leaves of incomplete text that he believed to be of no use: CCCC 557, which was put together in its present form only in the 1950s, consists of two small fragments of a leaf of a unique Old English homily on the Legend of the True Cross, rescued from two of Parker's printed books in which they had been used as binding reinforcements (see Page et al. 1995). Apparently Parker, lacking the full text of the homily, was prepared to jettison the portion that had survived.

The extent to which Parker was prepared to 'tamper' with his Anglo-Saxon manuscripts must not, however, be allowed to obscure the degree of close attention that he and those associated with him – primarily his Latin secretary, John Joscelyn – directed to the texts of the manuscripts. The nature and scope of this attention have been fully recognized and analysed only in recent years (see Page 1993; Graham 1997). Primate of a church that had broken with Rome and was still establishing its own identity, Parker believed that the manuscripts offered proof that the stance of the Church of England on key doctrinal matters was justified by history. Three issues in particular preoccupied him, elicited his marginal comments in the manuscripts, and guided his choice of what should be the first Old English texts to be published. These issues were the true nature of the bread and wine consecrated at the Eucharist; the legitimacy of the use of the vernacular within the ecclesiastical context; and the question of whether it was lawful for clergy to marry (Parker himself was a married cleric).

All these were issues on which Parker's church disagreed fundamentally with Rome, and all are articulated in *A Testimonie of Antiquitie*, Parker's first Old English publication. The principal item in the book is one of Ælfric's Easter homilies, in which Ælfric discusses the Eucharist in terms that led Parker to conclude that the Anglo-Saxon church did not believe in transubstantiation (Leinbaugh 1982: 52). The homily is followed in *A Testimonie* by two Old English extracts, and one in Latin, from Ælfric's pastoral letters for Bishops Wulfsine and Wulfstan: extracts in which Ælfric again discusses the Eucharistic bread and wine. The final set of texts in *A Testimonie* consists of Old English versions of the Lord's Prayer, the Creed and the Ten Commandments, included expressly to demonstrate that 'it is no new thyng to teache the people of God the Lordes prayer, and the articles of their beliefe in the Englishe tounge wherby they mought the better serue their God, and holde faste their profession of Christianitie' (Parker 1566: sig. K.v^v). Clerical marriage is discussed in the Introduction, which quotes evidence that many Anglo-Saxon priests were married and notes that only from the time of Archbishop Lanfranc (1070–89) was the priestly vow of chastity incorporated into the rite of ordination. Parker exploited the evidence for clerical marriage at greater length in his *A Defence of Priestes Mariages*, issued probably in 1566 or 1567, in which he makes extensive use of Anglo-Saxon and later sources.

The 1571 edition of the Old English Gospels addressed the issue of the legitimacy of vernacular translations of the scriptures. It is no accident that the sixteenth-century English translation that is printed in the outer margins of the pages, to help readers to understand the Old English, is that of the Bishops' Bible of 1568, a translation which Parker had inspired and co-ordinated (and which, in the same year as the Old English Gospels were published, all churchwardens were ordered to obtain for their churches). The Old English text, by demonstrating the longstanding pedigree of vernacular translations, provided the legitimation for Parker's own version. As Foxe's preface, addressed to Queen Elizabeth, expressed it: 'we haue published thys treatise . . . especially to this end, that the said boke imprinted thus in the Saxons letters, may remaine in the Church as a profitable example, & president of olde antiquitie, to the more confirmation of your gratious procedinges now in the Church agreable to the same.'

The 'polemical' nature of the work of the Parker group can, however, be overemphasized. Parker was also responsible for a series of historical publications which included, as well as editions of Matthew Paris and 'Matthew of Westminster', the *Ælfredi regis res gestæ*. As the manuscript on which the edition was based was largely destroyed by fire in 1731 (see Prescott 1998: 265–74), the edition has assumed added importance as a key witness to Asser's text – and has prompted vigorous scholarly disagreements about the extent and nature of Parker's editorial interventions. The preface demonstrates that Parkerian interest in Old English extended well beyond the exploitation of vernacular sources for contemporary religious debates, for Parker there comments on how study of documents written in Old English is vital for all who wish to learn the history of English institutions in general. Parker's chief lieutenant, John Joscelyn, indeed, ranged widely in his consultation of Anglo-Saxon manuscripts, and made a significant contribution to the development of the study of the language. Annotations in Joscelyn's easily recognizable, somewhat cramped, informal italic hand occur plentifully in the margins and interlines not only of manuscripts at Corpus Christi College, but also of others that passed through Parker's hands or belonged to Joscelyn himself and that are now in the British and Bodleian Libraries; his (now damaged) notebook, British Library, Cotton Vitellius D. vii, contains his transcriptions of passages of particular interest to him.

Like Nowell, Joscelyn made a close study of the different copies of the *Anglo-Saxon Chronicle*; but whereas Nowell had been reticent about annotating the manuscripts themselves, many entries in Joscelyn's hand, noting variants in one or more of the other manuscripts, are to be found in MSS A, B and D (Lutz 1982: 339–56). Much of the historical material that Joscelyn studied, both Anglo-Saxon and later, was incorporated into Parker's *De antiquitate Britannicæ ecclesiæ & priuilegiis ecclesiæ Cantuariensis* of 1572; Joscelyn was responsible for a large portion of the text, which includes biographies of the archbishops of Canterbury and accounts of the main events of their times.

For the generations of Anglo-Saxonists who followed him, however, Joscelyn's most valuable work lay in his unpublished materials for the study of the Old English language. Already in the 1560s he had begun to compile Old English word-lists (now London, Lambeth Palace Library 692) based upon his study of individual manuscripts, lists in which most entries include Joscelyn's Latin definitions of the Old English headwords. With the assistance of Matthew Parker's son John (1548–1619), Joscelyn went on to produce a two-volume manuscript dictionary of more than 20,000 entries (British Library, Titus A. xv + xvi), in which most entries are illustrated by at least one quotation, of which the source is noted (see Graham 2000). Significantly larger than Nowell's *Vocabularium Saxonicum*, Joscelyn's dictionary, after it had passed into the library of Sir Robert Cotton, was to be of service to several of the seventeenth-century lexicographers, notably Sir Simonds D'Ewes, who made a complete transcript (British Library, Harley 8 + 9) to which he then added his own further entries. Joscelyn was, in addition, the first to write an Old English grammar, again assisted by John Parker (whose index to it is now Bodleian Library, Bodley 33). The grammar too was exploited by others, but it has not survived; nothing is known of its fate after Cotton lent it to his former schoolteacher, the historian William Camden, in 1612. Joscelyn, then, provided his fellow Anglo-Saxonists with the two fundamental tools for the study of the Old English language, a dictionary and a grammar. The publication of such tools was to be a major theme of Anglo-Saxon studies in the seventeenth century.

From the Death of Parker to Wheelock's Edition of Bede

Although Joscelyn continued his work on Old English after Parker's death, the removal of archiepiscopal patronage and impetus made it much more difficult to bring projects through to publication. There was no significant new edition of an Old English text until 1623; the intervening period saw little more than the recycling of excerpts from the Parkerian publications by William Camden and others, and the issue of an Old English glossary of some 900 entries at the end of the Dutchman Richard Verstegan's *A Restitution of Decayed Intelligence* (1605). None the less, manuscripts continued to be collected and studied – not least by members of the Society of Antiquaries, which, following its foundation *c.*1586, maintained its existence for some twenty years until James I, concerned at the increasingly political bent of its meetings, closed it down. The membership included Lambarde and the young Henry Spelman, and Anglo-Saxon manuscripts were among the records exploited by members as they prepared for their weekly meetings, at each of which two subjects were discussed on which each member was expected to present the fruit of his investigations (Wright 1958).

It was also during this period that Sir Robert Cotton (1571–1631), another member of the Society, formed the second great collection of Anglo-Saxon manuscripts: Cotton acquired his first manuscripts in 1588 (Tite 1994: 5), and during the next three decades or so he gathered in the Lindisfarne Gospels, the *Beowulf*-manuscript, the illustrated copy of the Old English Hexateuch, five of the seven copies of the *Anglo-Saxon Chronicle*, and numerous other manuscripts containing Old English verse and prose. During the 1610s and 1620s, his library (housed first at Blackfriars and from 1622 at Cotton House within the Palace of Westminster, at the very nerve-centre of London) became the most important collection in the country, not least because of the liberality with which Cotton allowed scholars access and his willingness to lend volumes. Old English manuscripts were consulted and borrowed by, among others, John Selden (1584–1654) and James Ussher (1581–1656), who referred to the manuscripts in their legal and ecclesiastical writings, while Cotton's librarian, Richard James (1592–1638), provided many of the manuscripts with contents lists and made occasional transcriptions from them in his notebooks, now in the Bodleian Library.

Among those to borrow from the Cotton library was a significant, and undervalued, figure in the history of Anglo-Saxon studies. William L'Isle (*c.*1569–1637) resigned a fellowship at King's College, Cambridge, some time after 1608, to settle on the estate he had inherited at nearby Wilbraham. He devoted himself largely to making translations from Latin, French and Old English, and in 1623 published *A Saxon Treatise Concerning the Old and New Testament*, an edition, with accompanying English translation, of Ælfric's *Letter to Sigeweard* enumerating and briefly discussing the content of the various books of the Bible. L'Isle's preface is of especial interest for his description therein of the steps he took to teach himself Old English (see Murphy 1968: 346–7). It also emerges from the preface that the book was, like Parker's *A Testimonie of Antiquitie* – of which, indeed, L'Isle included a full reprint at the end of *A Saxon Treatise* – principally directed against adherents of the Roman Catholic church. Ælfric notes in the course of the *Letter to Sigeweard* which Biblical books he himself has translated, and thereby offers proof that vernacular translations of the scriptures have a long pedigree stretching back to Anglo-Saxon times. L'Isle describes his own purpose as being 'to dash . . . [the daughter of Babel's] children against the stones: Such I meane as maintaine against the truth, weake and childish opinions, and such as are easie to bee refuted; for so they doe that allow no Scripture at all in vulgar tongues, or hold it but a new come doctrine; whom this Treatise doth manifestly conuince' (L'Isle 1623: sig. b2ʳ).

L'Isle entertained ambitious plans, hinted at in his preface, for a major edition of the Old English scriptures, plans evidenced by his two surviving workbooks in the Bodleian Library, Laud Misc. 201 and 381. These contain his transcriptions and/or translations of as much of the Old Testament as he could find in Old English. Nor did he confine himself to the books for which full translations existed: the Hexateuch, the Psalms, and Ælfric's homilies on Judges, Job and Esther (homilies in which Ælfric paraphrases the content of those books). He also systematically studied some ten homiliaries in Cambridge libraries, excerpting from them any vernacular quotations from the Old Testament that the homilist might happen to make (see the table in Lee 2000: 232–42). Among the manuscripts that he studied was one containing the Middle English *Ancrene Wisse* (Cambridge, Corpus Christi College 402). His transcriptions of the Biblical quotations in this text archaized the spellings and the vocabulary in order to make the Middle English appear to be Old English (Lee 2000: 225–31; Pulsiano 2000: 187–91). L'Isle has been criticized for this 'doctoring' of his source, although he may have worked from the belief that the quotations had themselves ultimately been adapted from a full text of the Old English Bible that had not survived, and that he was therefore 'restoring' the passages to something approaching their original form (cf. L'Isle 1623: sig. e2ʳ). L'Isle's ultimate, never fulfilled aim was to piece together all the Old English Biblical material that he was able to find, and to publish it as 'Remaines of the Saxon English Bible'. Had he succeeded, this would have been the largest Old English publication hitherto accomplished. As it was, he still managed to rescue one significant item of Old English prose from permanent loss, for his transcription, in Laud Misc. 381, of Ælfric's homily on Esther (published in Assmann 1886) was made from an original that subsequently perished.

L'Isle's correspondence with Cotton (for which see Graham 2002) establishes that he also planned an edition of the *Anglo-Saxon Chronicle*. L'Isle himself owned MS E, the Peterborough copy, but his work towards an edition progressed no further than his entering, on paper leaves that he inserted into that manuscript, variant readings that he encountered in MSS A and G. It fell to another, Abraham Wheelock (1593–1653), to publish the first edition of the *Chronicle*, appended to his monumental edition of the Latin and Old English versions of Bede's *Historia ecclesiastica*, which appeared at Cambridge in 1643.

Wheelock was also the first person to hold an official university post in Anglo-Saxon studies, for in 1639 he was appointed to a newly created Cambridge lectureship in 'British and Saxon Antiquities'. The lectureship was the brainchild of the antiquary Sir Henry Spelman (*c.*1564–1641), a vigorous promoter of Anglo-Saxon studies. Spelman himself drew extensively on Old English materials for his *Archæologus* and *Concilia*, published in 1626 and 1639 respectively; his son John (1594–1643) published an edition of the Latin and Old English Psalters in 1640 – the first published Old English edition to include variants obtained from the collation of different manuscripts – and wrote a *Life of King Alfred* which appeared posthumously in 1678. Henry Spelman also sought to encourage the publication of an Old English grammar and dictionary, projects that brought him into contact – not always harmonious – with Sir Simonds D'Ewes (1602–50) and the Dutchman Johannes de Laet (1581–1649), who were working on their own dictionary projects in the late 1630s (Bekkers 1970: XVIII–XXV; Hetherington 1975). Plans for the Cambridge lectureship grew out of a visit that Spelman paid to Cambridge to seek out Old English materials that he could use in his *Concilia*. Finding much more than he expected, he decided that he needed an on-the-spot amanuensis to copy materials on his behalf. His choice fell on Wheelock, at the time university librarian and lecturer in Arabic, and their collaboration over the following years, recorded in their correspondence preserved in Cambridge University Library, Dd.3.12, and London, British Library, Add. 34600 + 34601, was sufficiently fruitful to impel Spelman to endow the Anglo-Saxon lectureship (see Oates 1986: 185–8). The university authorities accepted his proposal in 1639–40. Wheelock was to deliver two lectures a term, and was to make himself available on two afternoons a week to those who wished to learn Old English. None of his lectures has survived, so we cannot know their content, but they were apparently historical rather than linguistic in nature, and based on extensive researches, for Wheelock notes in one of his letters to Spelman that to prepare 'one Lecture in these

Antiquities' required more time than twenty lectures of a grammatical nature, such
as he delivered to his Arabic students (Add. 34601, fol. 21v).

The principal achievement of Wheelock's tenure of the lectureship was the publication in 1643 of his edition of Bede and the *Chronicle*. It was reissued in 1644 along
with a reprint of Lambarde's *Archaionomia* into which Wheelock incorporated some
Old English legal texts (notably the *Canons of Edgar*) not known to Lambarde in 1568.
Wheelock's publication, like those of Parker and L'Isle, had an overt religio-political
aim. In his preface to the reader, he commented on how manuscript materials that
bore witness to the practices and beliefs of the Anglo-Saxon church could help to
settle controversies that were dividing the church of his own time. In this connection, it has been insufficiently appreciated that his Bede edition includes a substantial amount of supplementary material appended to the individual chapters and
intended to provide further illustrative evidence for points discussed by Bede. Most
of this material Wheelock excerpted from Anglo-Saxon homiliaries in Cambridge
libraries (principally Cambridge University Library, Gg.3.28, Ii.1.33 and Ii.4.6, and
Trinity College, B.15.34). His intensive study of these and several other manuscripts
is revealed by the marginal annotations and copious index notes that he entered in
them. For Wheelock as for other early Anglo-Saxonists, manuscript evidence provides
the means for a much fuller assessment of his achievement than is possible on his published work alone; the scope and thoroughness of his investigation of the manuscripts
encourage respect for this first holder of an Anglo-Saxon lectureship, who was able to
fulfil his duties while occupying two other significant university posts.

Somner's *Dictionarium*, Junius, and the Oxford Saxonists

Following Wheelock's death in 1653, no successor was appointed to the Cambridge
lectureship. Instead, thanks to Ussher's intervention, half the stipend was assigned to
assist the publication of the Old English dictionary on which the antiquary William
Somner (1606–69), registrar to the ecclesiastical court of Canterbury, had been
working for some years. In the late 1640s Somner collaborated with Simonds D'Ewes
as the latter strove to complete his own dictionary project. Somner's *Dictionarium
Saxonico-Latino-Anglicum* is based on the manuscript dictionaries of Nowell and
D'Ewes (the latter being a transcript of Joscelyn's with additions), on published Old
English texts, and on his own transcripts of Anglo-Saxon manuscripts (see Lutz 1988).
The *Dictionarium* was published at Oxford in 1659; Somner incorporated into it an
edition of Ælfric's *Grammar*. Thus, nearly a century after Nowell had begun compil-
ing his *Vocabularium Saxonicum*, the two indispensable tools for the scientific study of
Old English – a dictionary and a grammar – were at last available in print.

For the latter part of the seventeenth century and on into the eighteenth, Oxford
was to be the focus for Anglo-Saxon studies (cf. Fairer 1986; Lutz 2000: 48–64).
Already Gerard Langbaine (1609–58), Provost of Queen's College, had attempted
an edition of the *Anglo-Saxon Chronicle*, but had been pre-empted by Wheelock. Of

fundamental importance for the later seventeenth-century efflorescence of Anglo-Saxon studies at Oxford was the work of Francis Junius (1591–1677), who bequeathed his manuscripts, and the Anglo-Saxon types that had been cut for him, to the University of Oxford. Junius was, by far, the greatest philologist of the early Anglo-Saxonists. After studying theology and mathematics at Leiden, in 1621 he took up a post in the household of Thomas Howard, earl of Arundel, whose family he served for the next thirty years. His interest in comparative Germanic philology developed *c*.1645 (Breuker 1998: 140). In 1648–9 he was helping Simonds D'Ewes with his dictionary (Hetherington 1980: 102, 107–9), and it was probably around this time that Junius began to make his own transcripts of Old English texts, principally from manuscripts in the Cotton library (Stanley 1998). These transcripts, all executed in Junius' small, neat version of Anglo-Saxon minuscule, are a monument of accuracy and careful industry; many include Junius' listings of variants derived from his collations against other manuscripts. The most important of the transcripts include Bodleian Library, Junius 12, which contains his copy of the metrical passages of Cotton Otho A. vi, the unique, and now badly damaged, manuscript of the metrical version of King Alfred's translation of Boethius' *De consolatione philosophiae* (Robinson and Stanley 1991: no. 5). Junius, indeed, was apparently the first to recognize the metrical structure of Old English poetry (Wheelock had failed to recognize the poetic nature of *The Battle of Brunanburh* and the other *Chronicle* poems). His edition of the Old English *Genesis*, issued at Amsterdam in 1655, was the first publication of a major poetic text. For the edition, Junius used a 'prose' layout, but made the metrical structure clear by placing a point at the end of each poetic half-line (a practice in which he was encouraged by the generous pointing of his source manuscript, Bodleian Library, Junius 11).

Junius' links with Oxford developed from several visits paid during his employment by the Howards and afterwards, and were strengthened by his collaboration with Thomas Marshall (1621–85), the future Rector of Lincoln College, on an annotated edition of the Gothic and Anglo-Saxon Gospels, published at Dordrecht in 1665 while the two were resident in the Netherlands. Junius returned to England in 1675, settling in Oxford. The forty years following his death and his bequest to the university were to be the most fruitful yet for Anglo-Saxon studies. In 1679 an Anglo-Saxon lectureship was established at Queen's College, which produced a crop of young Anglo-Saxonists in the ensuing years. The first holder of the lectureship, William Nicolson (1655–1727), was to leave Oxford in order to take up an ecclesiastical appointment in the north only two years later, but he continued to support Old English publication projects even after he became bishop of Carlisle in 1702. Nicolson's successor Edward Thwaites (1667–1711), appointed to the lectureship in 1698, quickly developed a reputation as a humane and inspiring teacher, and in 1699 had fifteen students studying under him.

The arrival of Junius' Anglo-Saxon types at Oxford coincided with the efforts of John Fell (1625–86), Dean of Christ Church, to revitalize the University Press. The projects favoured by Fell included the production of an Anglo-Saxon grammar, a task eventually assigned to George Hickes (1642–1715), Marshall's protégé at Lincoln

College. Appointed dean of Worcester in 1683, Hickes was to spend his later life in hiding, for following the Revolution of 1688 he refused to swear the oath of allegiance to William and Mary. His politically awkward status as a non-juror did not, however, prevent his energetic masterminding of important projects. His *Institutiones grammaticæ Anglo-Saxonicæ, et Moeso-Gothicæ* of 1689 was the first major publication to use the Junian types, and included the first (admittedly cursory) printed catalogue of Anglo-Saxon manuscripts (Gneuss 1993). The next years witnessed three major Old English editions, all the work of Queensmen: Edmund Gibson's *Chronicon Saxonicum* (1692), a conflated edition of the *Chronicle* based on five of its versions; Thwaites's *Heptateuchus, liber Job, et evangelium Nicodemi* (1698), which also included the *Judith* fragment contained in the *Beowulf*-manuscript; and Christopher Rawlinson's edition of the Old English Boethius (1698), in which, for the first time, Old English verse was laid out half-line by half-line. All these books used the Junian types, and were based in part on Junius' transcripts.

By 1698 Hickes had already been at work for some five years on a revised edition of his *Institutiones grammaticæ*. The project grew beyond expectation, and was finally published in 1703–5 as the massive *Linguarum veterum septentrionalium thesaurus grammatico-criticus et archæologicus* which, with its companion volume, Humfrey Wanley's *Librorum veterum septentrionalium . . . catalogus historico-criticus* (1705), furnished a monumental compendium to Anglo-Saxon studies, the largest and most impressive contribution to the field that had yet appeared. As a consequence of Hickes's difficult personal circumstances and absence from Oxford, many of the logistical tasks connected with getting the books through the press were assumed by Thwaites; and, as the *Thesaurus* incorporates extensive materials supplied by others, it stands as a monument to the spirit of collaboration that existed among the Oxford Saxonists (Bennett 1948; Harris 1992). The original grammatical chapters of the *Institutiones* were expanded by six major new chapters on Anglo-Saxon dialects and poetry and their later development (for which Thwaites provided quotations from the *Ormulum* and Thomas Tanner a transcript of *The Land of Cockayne*), and among the entirely new sections of the book was Hickes's *De linguarum veterum septentrionalium usu dissertatio epistolaris*, a 159-page tour de force on the uses of medieval Germanic material for historical research, in which, for the first time, charters were treated as a fundamental source for Anglo-Saxon history.

It was in 1699 that Hickes handed over the task of expanding his catalogue of Anglo-Saxon manuscripts to Humfrey Wanley (1673–1726), a draper's apprentice from Coventry whose remarkable skill in manuscript studies, developed in his spare time, caused his local bishop to secure him a place at Oxford. Wanley worked as an assistant at the Bodleian Library from 1696 until 1700 (finding time to visit the manuscript collections of Cambridge in 1699; see Gneuss 2001), and then moved to London to take up an appointment as assistant secretary to the newly founded Society for the Promotion of Christian Knowledge. So impressive did Hickes find Wanley's abilities that in 1701 he wrote that 'Mr. Wanley . . . has the best skill in ancient hands and MSS. of any man not only of this, but, I believe, of any former age' (Harris 1992:

349). That skill is seen at its most remarkable in the immaculate facsimiles of manuscript pages that Wanley compiled in his recently rediscovered 'Book of Specimens' (Longleat House 345; see Keynes 1996: 126–35). His *Catalogus* is outstanding for the fullness of his manuscript descriptions and for the uncanny accuracy of his palaeographical judgements. Wanley was the first to articulate the fundamental palaeographical principle that dated materials (notably charters) provide the touchstone for the assessment of hands in undated manuscripts. For more than two centuries, the *Catalogus* was to furnish the essential tool for researchers and editors seeking information on the surviving copies of Old English texts; it was finally superseded only with the publication in 1957 of N. R. Ker's immaculate *Catalogue of Manuscripts Containing Anglo-Saxon*.

One other associate of Hickes's circle, while she played no part in the production of the *Thesaurus*, has the distinction of being the first woman known to have studied Old English. Elizabeth Elstob (1683–1756), who, having been orphaned at an early age, opted to live with her brother William after he went up to Queen's College in 1696, conceived an enthusiasm for Anglo-Saxon studies on seeing his transcript of the Old English Orosius. Accompanying William to London on his appointment as vicar of St Swithun's in 1702, she devoted the next years to developing expertise in the northern languages, and in 1709 published – using Anglo-Saxon types made to her own specifications – *An English-Saxon Homily on the Birth-Day of St Gregory*, an edition, with accompanying translation, of Ælfric's homily for St Gregory's day in which Ælfric provides an account of the conversion of the Anglo-Saxons (see Sutherland 1994). Over the next years Elstob worked on a complete edition, including collations, of Ælfric's *Catholic Homilies*, and so impressed Hickes by her work that he described her transcript as 'the most correct that ever I saw' and observed that the edition 'would be of great advantage to the Church of England against the papists'. Sadly, lack of funds caused Elstob to abandon the project. In 1715, however, she succeeded in publishing *The Rudiments of Grammar for the English-Saxon Tongue*. Undertaken in response to the request of a female enthusiast, and drawing heavily on Hickes's grammar while modifying and in certain respects sharpening his presentation (see Hughes 1982), Elstob's was the first grammar of Old English to be written in Modern English and thus to appeal to an audience wider than the traditionally academic.

The same year, 1715, witnessed the death of Hickes, the inspirational leader of the Saxonists, and thereby marked the end of an era. Thwaites, his chief collaborator, had died four years earlier, while others had gone on to prominent ecclesiastical careers (Nicolson and Gibson both became bishops), or had otherwise had their interests redirected. Elizabeth Elstob, whose brother William died a few months before Hickes, was obliged by debt to leave London; she was to surface years later as a schoolteacher in Worcestershire, but she published no more. Although 1722 saw the publication of John Smith's great Bede edition, and Thomas Hearne's *Johannis confratris et monachi Glastoniensis chronica* (1726) included the first printing of *The Battle of Maldon* (the only manuscript of which perished in the Cotton fire just five years later), the remainder of the eighteenth century was largely barren for Anglo-Saxon studies. The few significant publications to appear depended on materials compiled by the late seventeenth-century scholars: Edward Lye's *Dictionarium Saxonico et Gothico-Latinum* (1772) drew heavily on lexicographical materials assembled by Junius (Dekker 2000: 340), and Daines Barrington's edition of the Old English Orosius (1773) was based on William Elstob's transcript. Towards the end of the century, however, there were glimmerings of future developments. In 1786, the Danish scholar G. J. Thorkelin, visiting England in search of texts illustrative of Danish antiquities, accidentally chanced upon *Beowulf*, which until then had attracted no significant interest; and within a generation, major advances in the science of philology were to make Old English texts the focus of fresh and sustained attention in England and on the continent alike.

REFERENCES

Primary sources

Bale, John 1549. *The Laboryouse Journey and Serche of Johan Leylande, for Englandes Antiquitees, Geuen of Hym as a Newe Yeares Gyfte to Kynge Henry the VIII. in the .XXVII. Yeare of his Reygne, with Declaracyons Enlarged: by Johan Bale*. London. Facsimile repr. Amsterdam, 1975.

Barrington, Daines, ed. 1773. *The Anglo-Saxon Version, from the Historian Orosius. By Ælfred the Great. Together with an English Translation from the Anglo-Saxon*. London.

Elstob, Elizabeth, ed. 1709. *An English-Saxon Homily on the Birth-Day of St Gregory: Anciently Used in the English-Saxon Church. Giving an Account of the Conversion of the English from Paganism to Christianity*. London.

——1715. *The Rudiments of Grammar for the English-Saxon Tongue, First Given in English: with an Apology for the Study of Northern Antiquities*. London. Facsimile repr. Menston, 1968.

Foxe, John, ed. 1571. *The Gospels of the Fower Euangelistes Translated in the Olde Saxons Tyme out of Latin into the Vulgare Toung of the Saxons, Newly Collected out of Auncient Monumentes of the Sayd Saxons, and Now Published for Testimonie of the Same*. London.

Gibson, Edmund, ed. 1692. *Chronicon Saxonicum*. Oxford.

Hearne, Thomas, ed. 1726. *Johannis, confratris et monachi Glastoniensis, chronica sive historia de rebus Glastoniensibus*. Oxford. 2 vols.

Hickes, George 1689. *Institutiones grammaticæ*

Anglo-Saxonicæ, et Moeso-Gothicæ. Oxford, Facsimile repr. Menston, 1971.

——1703–5. *Linguarum vett. septentrionalium thesaurus grammatico-criticus et archæologicus*. Oxford. Facsimile repr. Menston, 1970.

Junius, Francis, ed. 1655. *Cædmonis monachi paraphrasis poetica Genesios ac præcipuarum sacræ paginæ historiarum, abhinc annos M.LXX. Anglo-Saxonice conscripta*. Amsterdam. Facsimile repr., ed. Peter J. Lucas. Early Studies in Germanic Philology 3. Amsterdam and Atlanta, 2000.

——and Marshall, Thomas, eds 1665. *Quatuor D. N. Jesu Christi euangeliorum versiones perantiquæ duæ, Gothica scil. et Anglo-Saxonica*. Dordrecht.

Lambarde, William 1568. *Archaionomia, sive de priscis Anglorum legibus libri, sermone Anglico, vetustate antiquissimo, aliquot abhinc seculis conscripti, atque nunc demum, magno iurisperitorum, & amantium antiquitatis omnium commodo, e tenebris in lucem vocati*. London.

Leland, John 1770. *Joannis Lelandi antiquarii de rebus Britannicis collectanea*. Ed. Thomas Hearne. 2nd edn. London. 6 vols.

L'Isle, William, ed. 1623. *A Saxon Treatise Concerning the Old and New Testament*. London.

Lye, Edward 1772. *Dictionarium Saxonico et Gothico-Latinum*. London.

Marckwardt, Albert H., ed. 1952. *Laurence Nowell's 'Vocabularium Saxonicum'*. University of Michigan Publications, Language and Literature, 25. Ann Arbor. Repr. New York, 1971.

Parker, Matthew, ed. 1566. *A Testimonie of Antiquitie, Shewing the Ancient Fayth in the Church of*

England Touching the Sacrament of the Body and Bloude of the Lord here Publikely Preached, and also Receaued in the Saxons Tyme, aboue 600. Yeares Agoe. London. Facsimile repr. Amsterdam and New York, 1970.

———, ed. 1566/7? *A Defence of Priestes Mariages.* London.

———1572. *De antiquitate Britannicæ ecclesiæ & priuilegiis ecclesiæ Cantuariensis, cum archiepiscopis eiusdem 70.* London.

———, ed. 1574. *Ælfredi regis res gestæ.* London.

Rawlinson, Christopher, ed. 1698. *An. Manl. Sever. Boethii consolationis philosophiæ libri V. Anglo-Saxonice redditi ab Alfredo, inclyto Anglo-Saxonum rege.* Oxford.

Recorde, Robert 1557. *The Whetstone of Witte, whiche is the Seconde Parte of Arithmetike: Containyng Thextraction of Rootes: the Cossike Practice, with the Rule of Equation: and the Woorkes of Surde Nombers.* London.

Smith, John, ed. 1722. *Historiae ecclesiasticae gentis Anglorum libri quinque, auctore sancto & venerabili Baeda, presbytero Anglo-Saxone, una cum reliquis ejus operibus historicis in unum volumen collectis.* Cambridge.

Somner, William 1659. *Dictionarium Saxonico-Latino-Anglicum voces, phrasesque præcipuas Anglo-Saxonicas, e libris, sive manuscriptis, sive typis excusis, aliisque monumentis tum publicis tum privatis, magna diligentia collectas; cum Latina et Anglica vocum interpretatione complectens.* Oxford. Facsimile repr. Menston, 1970.

Spelman, Henry 1626. *Archæologus, in modum glossarii ad rem antiquam posteriorem.* London.

———1639. *Concilia, decreta, leges, constitutiones, in re ecclesiarum orbis Britannici.* London.

Spelman, John 1640. *Psalterium Davidis Latino-Saxonicum vetus.* London.

———1678. *Ælfredi magni Anglorum regis invictissimi vita tribus libris comprehensa.* Ed. Obadiah Walker. Oxford.

Thwaites, Edward, ed. 1698. *Heptateuchus, liber Job, et evangelium Nicodemi; Anglo-Saxonice. Historiæ Judith fragmentum; Dano-Saxonice.* Oxford.

Verstegan, Richard 1605. *A Restitution of Decayed Intelligence: in Antiquities. Concerning the Most Noble and Renovvmed English Nation.* Antwerp. Facsimile repr. Ilkley, 1976.

Wanley, Humfrey 1705. *Librorum vett. septentrionalium . . . catalogus historico-criticus.* Oxford. Facsimile repr. Menston, 1970.

Wheelock, Abraham, ed. 1643. *Historiæ ecclesiasticæ gentis Anglorum libri V. a venerabili Beda presbytero scripti . . . quibus in calce operis Saxonicam chronologiam . . . contexuimus.* Cambridge.

Secondary sources

Assmann, Bruno 1886. 'Abt Ælfrics angelsächsische Bearbeitung des Buches Esther'. *Anglia* 9: 25–38.

Bekkers, Johannes Antonius Frederik 1970. *Correspondence of John Morris with Johannes de Laet (1634–1649).* Nijmegen.

Bennett, J. A. W. 1948. 'Hickes's "Thesaurus": A Study in Oxford Book-Production'. *English Studies*, n.s. 1: 28–45. Repr. *The Humane Medievalist and Other Essays in English Literature and Learning, from Chaucer to Eliot*, pp. 225–46. Ed. Piero Boitani. Rome, 1982.

Berkhout, Carl T. 1998. 'Laurence Nowell'. *Medieval Scholarship: Biographical Studies on the Formation of a Discipline*, vol. 2: *Literature and Philology*, pp. 3–17. Ed. Helen Damico. Garland Reference Library of the Humanities 2071. New York and London.

Breuker, Ph. H. 1998. 'On the Course of Franciscus Junius's Germanic Studies, with Special Reference to Frisian'. *Aspects of Old Frisian Philology*, pp. 42–68. Eds Rolf H. Bremmer Jr, Geart van der Meer and Oebele Vries. Amsterdamer Beiträge zur älteren Germanistik 31/32. Amsterdam and Atlanta. 1990. Repr. with corrections *Franciscus Junius F.F. and his Circle*, pp. 129–57. Ed. Rolf H. Bremmer Jr. Studies in Literature 21. Amsterdam and Atlanta.

Brewer, D. S. 1952–3. 'Sixteenth, Seventeenth and Eighteenth Century References to the Voyage of Ohthere (Ohtheriana IV)'. *Anglia* 71: 202–11.

Buckalew, Ronald E. 1978. 'Leland's Transcript of Ælfric's *Glossary*'. *Anglo-Saxon England* 7: 149–64.

Dekker, Kees 2000. ' "That Most Elaborate One of Fr. Junius": An Investigation of Francis Junius's Manuscript Old English Dictionary'. *The Recovery of Old English: Anglo-Saxon Studies in the Sixteenth and Seventeenth Centuries*, pp. 301–43. Ed. Timothy Graham. Publications of the Richard Rawlinson Center. Kalamazoo.

Fairer, David 1986. 'Anglo-Saxon Studies'. *The History of the University of Oxford*, vol. 5: *The*

Eighteenth Century, pp. 807–29. Eds L. S. Sutherland and L. G. Mitchell. Oxford.

Flower, Robin 1935. 'Laurence Nowell and the Discovery of England in Tudor Times'. *Proceedings of the British Academy* 21: 47–73. Repr. *British Academy Papers on Anglo-Saxon England*, pp. 1–27. Ed. E. G. Stanley. Oxford, 1990.

Gneuss, Helmut 1993. 'Der älteste Katalog der angelsächsischen Handschriften und seine Nachfolger'. *Anglo-Saxonica: Beiträge zur Vor- und Frühgeschichte der englischen Sprache und zur altenglischen Literatur. Festschrift für Hans Schabram zum 65. Geburtstag*, pp. 91–106. Eds Klaus R. Grinda and Claus-Dieter Wetzel. Munich. Repr. Helmut Gneuss, *Books and Libraries in Early England*. Variorum Collected Studies Series, CS 558. Aldershot, 1996.

—— 2001. 'Humfrey Wanley Borrows Books in Cambridge'. *Transactions of the Cambridge Bibliographical Society* 12: 2.

Graham, Timothy 1996. 'The Earliest Old English Word-list from Tudor England'. *Medieval English Studies Newsletter* 35: 4–7.

—— 1997. 'The Beginnings of Old English Studies: Evidence from the Manuscripts of Matthew Parker'. *Back to the Manuscripts: Papers from the Symposium 'The Integrated Approach to Manuscript Studies: A New Horizon' Held at the Eighth General Meeting of the Japan Society for Medieval English Studies, Tokyo, December 1992*, pp. 29–50. Ed. Shuji Sato. Occasional Papers of the Centre for Medieval English Studies 1. Tokyo.

—— 2000. 'John Joscelyn, Pioneer of Old English Lexicography'. *The Recovery of Old English: Anglo-Saxon Studies in the Sixteenth and Seventeenth Centuries*, pp. 83–140. Ed. Timothy Graham. Publications of the Richard Rawlinson Center. Kalamazoo.

—— 2002. 'William L'Isle's Letters to Sir Robert Cotton'. *Early Medieval Texts and Interpretations*. Eds Elaine M. Treharne and Susan Rosser. Tempe, AZ.

Harris, Richard L., ed. 1992. *A Chorus of Grammars: The Correspondence of George Hickes and his Collaborators on the 'Thesaurus Linguarum Septentrionalium'*. Publications of the Dictionary of Old English 4. Toronto.

Hetherington, M. S. 1975. 'Sir Simonds D'Ewes and Method in Old English Lexicography'.

Texas Studies in Literature and Language 17: 75–92.

—— 1980. *The Beginnings of Old English Lexicography*. Spicewood (privately printed).

Hughes, Shaun F. D. 1982. 'The Anglo-Saxon Grammars of George Hickes and Elizabeth Elstob'. *Anglo-Saxon Scholarship: The First Three Centuries*, pp. 119–47. Eds Carl T. Berkhout and Milton McC. Gatch. Boston.

Keynes, Simon 1996. 'The Reconstruction of a Burnt Cottonian Manuscript: The Case of Cotton MS. Otho A. I'. *British Library Journal* 22: 113–60.

Lee, Stuart 2000. 'Oxford, Bodleian Library, MS Laud Misc. 381: William L'Isle, Ælfric, and the *Ancrene Wisse*'. *The Recovery of Old English: Anglo-Saxon Studies in the Sixteenth and Seventeenth Centuries*, pp. 207–42. Ed. Timothy Graham. Publications of the Richard Rawlinson Center. Kalamazoo.

Leinbaugh, Theodore H. 1982. 'Ælfric's *Sermo de Sacrificio in Die Pascae*: Anglican Polemic in the Sixteenth and Seventeenth Centuries'. *Anglo-Saxon Scholarship: The First Three Centuries*, pp. 51–68. Eds Carl T. Berkhout and Milton McC. Gatch. Boston.

Lutz, Angelika 1982. 'Das Studium der angelsächsischen Chronik im 16. Jahrhundert: Nowell und Joscelyn'. *Anglia* 100: 301–56.

—— 1988. 'Zur Entstehungsgeschichte von William Somners *Dictionarium Saxonico-Latino-Anglicum*'. *Anglia* 106: 1–25.

—— 2000. 'The Study of the Anglo-Saxon Chronicle in the Seventeenth Century and the Establishment of Old English Studies in the Universities'. *The Recovery of Old English: Anglo-Saxon Studies in the Sixteenth and Seventeenth Centuries*, pp. 1–82. Ed. Timothy Graham. Publications of the Richard Rawlinson Center. Kalamazoo.

Murphy, Michael 1968. 'Methods in the Study of Old English in the Sixteenth and Seventeenth Centuries'. *Mediaeval Studies* 30: 345–50.

Oates, J. C. T. 1986. *Cambridge University Library: A History*, vol. 1: *From the Beginnings to the Copyright Act of Queen Anne*. Cambridge.

Page, R. I. 1993. *Matthew Parker and his Books*. Sandars Lectures in Bibliography, 1990. Kalamazoo.

——, Mildred Budny and Nicholas Hadgraft

1995. 'Two Fragments of an Old English Manuscript in the Library of Corpus Christi College, Cambridge'. *Speculum* 70: 502–29.

Prescott, Andrew 1998. 'The Ghost of Asser'. *Anglo-Saxon Manuscripts and their Heritage*, pp. 255–91. Eds Phillip Pulsiano and Elaine M. Treharne. Aldershot.

Pulsiano, Phillip 2000. 'William L'Isle and the Editing of Old English'. *The Recovery of Old English: Anglo-Saxon Studies in the Sixteenth and Seventeenth Centuries*, pp. 173–206. Ed. Timothy Graham. Publications of the Richard Rawlinson Center. Kalamazoo.

Robinson, Fred C. and Stanley, E. G., eds 1991. *Old English Verse Texts from Many Sources: A Comprehensive Collection*. Early English Manuscripts in Facsimile 23. Copenhagen.

Stanley, E. G. 1998. 'The Sources of Junius's Learning as Revealed in the Junius Manuscripts in the Bodleian Library'. *Franciscus Junius F.F. and his Circle*, pp. 129–57. Ed. Rolf H. Bremmer Jr.

Studies in Literature 21. Amsterdam and Atlanta.

Sutherland, Kathryn 1994. 'Editing for a New Century: Elizabeth Elstob's Anglo-Saxon Manifesto and Ælfric's St Gregory Homily'. *The Editing of Old English: Papers from the 1990 Manchester Conference*, pp. 213–37. Eds D. G. Scragg and Paul E. Szarmach. Cambridge.

Tite, Colin G. C. 1994. *The Manuscript Library of Sir Robert Cotton*. The Panizzi Lectures, 1993. London.

Wright, C. E. 1951. 'The Dispersal of the Monastic Libraries and the Beginnings of Anglo-Saxon Studies. Matthew Parker and his Circle: A Preliminary Study'. *Transactions of the Cambridge Bibliographical Society* 1.3: 208–37.

——1958. 'The Elizabethan Society of Antiquaries and the Formation of the Cottonian Library'. *The English Library before 1700*, pp. 176–212. Eds Francis Wormald and C. E. Wright. London.

24

Anglo-Saxon Studies in the Nineteenth Century: England, Denmark, America

J. R. Hall

Late June 1824, London. Two men, unacquainted with one another, recorded references to Anglo-Saxon that help define the state of the discipline in the early nineteenth century. One of them, an Englishman, entered an observation in his diary; the other, a German, wrote a letter to Thomas Jefferson.

The diarist was Frederic Madden, age 23, employed by the record office of the Tower of London to copy documents at the British Museum (Ackerman 1972: 5–7). Six months earlier Madden had been befriended by John J. Conybeare, formerly professor of Anglo-Saxon at Oxford. Through Conybeare, who had collated Grímur Johnson Thorkelin's 1815 edition of *Beowulf* with the *Beowulf*-manuscript in the British Museum, Madden learned that the edition teemed with textual error and resolved to undertake his own collation. On 15 June Madden called on Conybeare – only to learn, to his grief, of Conybeare's sudden death three days earlier. On 21 June Madden began collating Thorkelin's text of the poem against the manuscript. Two days later he confided to his diary his ambition to edit *Beowulf*.

> I occupied myself in tak[in]g facsimiles fr[o]m t[he] MS. of Beowulf, & in continuing the collation of it. Now Conybeare is dead, I am at perfect liberty to publish it in any way I please; & if I am not prevented by Bosworth, certainly will do it some day or other, with copious illustrations. It is a reproach to our Saxon scholars, that only one edition of this poem sh[oul]d ever have been published, & that by a *foreigner* – & still more, in so *faulty a manner*, that neither the text nor the translation are correct for six lines together! (diary, 23 June 1824: 146.34; Kiernan 1998: 121)

The German who wrote to Thomas Jefferson was Georg Blaettermann, to whom Jefferson, seeking professors for the newly founded University of Virginia, offered the professorship of modern languages, provided that Blaettermann include Anglo-Saxon among his course offerings. On 26 June – three days after Madden dreamed in his diary of editing *Beowulf* – Blaettermann, then teaching in London, wrote Jefferson a three-page letter of acceptance in French, in the final paragraph of which he refers to preparing himself to teach Anglo-Saxon:

> Quant à l'Anglo-Saxon, je l'ai fait l'objet de mes études depuis le moment que je me sais mis au rang des candidats pour la chaire des langues modernes de votre College et je tacherai en continuant d'étudier d'en saisir si bien l'esprit que je pourrai le faire étudier avantageusement à mes élèves. (1824: [3])

> As for Anglo-Saxon, I made it the object of my studies from the moment I placed myself among the candidates for the chair of modern languages at your college, and I shall try, while continuing to study, to capture its spirit so well that I will be able to have my students study it to advantage.

What do these excerpts from Madden and Blaettermann help to show about the state of Anglo-Saxon studies at the time? First, that they had an international dimension; second, that they had a nationalist aspect; and third, that they lacked professional standing.

The international dimension of Anglo-Saxon studies is most obviously seen in the fact that Jefferson hired Blaettermann, a German, to teach Anglo-Saxon, along with other modern languages, in America. It is also seen in the fact that Madden refers to Thorkelin, the first editor of *Beowulf*, as a *'foreigner'*. Although *Beowulf* was first mentioned in print more than a century earlier by an Englishman, Humfrey Wanley, in his great catalogue of Anglo-Saxon manuscripts (1705: 218–19), was discussed in print a decade before Thorkelin's edition by another Englishman, Sharon Turner, in his monumental *The History of the Anglo-Saxons* (1805: 4.398–408, 414–16), and was mentioned again in print a few years later by Conybeare (Hall 1987: 380–1), the poem lay in obscurity until Grímur Johnson Thorkelin, an Icelander employed as an archivist by the king of Denmark, published his edition in 1815. In 1817, prompted largely by Thorkelin's work, Rasmus Rask, a Dane, published in Stockholm *Angel-saksisk Sproglære*, the first scientific grammar of Anglo-Saxon (Aarsleff 1983: 182–5), which included a well-edited passage from *Beowulf* (pp. 163–6).

A second point emerging from the excerpt from Madden is that the international interest in Anglo-Saxon studies elicited nationalist sentiments. When Madden refers to the fact that a foreigner was the first person to edit *Beowulf*, he does so with disapproval, the implication being that *Beowulf* belongs to the English (similarly Turner 1820: 3.326). Thorkelin thought differently. He entitled his edition *De Danorum Rebus Gestis Secul. III & IV. Poëma danicum dialecto anglosaxonica*, 'On the Danes' Exploits in the Third and Fourth Centuries: A Danish Poem in Anglo-Saxon Dialect'. One of the reviewers of Thorkelin's edition, Nicholaus Outzen, argued vigorously, however, that the poem is not Danish but German, composed by a native of Schleswig (Shippey and Haarder 1998: 16–20, 123–31).

Although the excerpt from Blaettermann's letter exhibits no evidence of nationalism, it is notable that he wishes to teach students not simply the literal sense of Anglo-Saxon but *l'esprit*. What Blaettermann means is clarified in an earlier passage in the letter, in which he states the pedagogic doctrine that language should not be studied apart from its historical context: 'il faut nécessairement qu'il fasse voir l'influence que l'histoire religieuse et politique a exerceé sur elle et sur le Caractère et le destin du peuple' (p. [2]), 'it is necessary that [the teacher] make clear the influence that religious and political history has exerted on [literature] and on the character and destiny of the people'. The doctrine must have pleased Jefferson, who had taught himself Anglo-Saxon and wanted students at his university to learn it as well, believing that the Anglo-Saxons were the forerunners of freedom-loving Americans (Horsman 1981: 18–24).

The third point suggested by the excerpts from Madden and Blaettermann is the lack of professional standing of Anglo-Saxon studies. Although Blaettermann, who would become the first academic to teach Anglo-Saxon in America, held a doctorate from the University of Leipzig, he tells Jefferson that he has made the language the object of his study since expressing interest in the position at the new university. The study of Anglo-Saxon had begun in earnest in nineteenth-century Germany with the publication of Jacob Grimm's German grammar (1819–37), but one could not then specialize in the language at a university.

The situation was but little better in England. Although there was strong interest and some expertise in Anglo-Saxon in the last decade of the seventeenth century and first few decades of the eighteenth, the rest of the eighteenth century saw a decline in both (Adams 1917: 85–113). As the nineteenth century dawned, only Turner, an English attorney turned historian, whose four-volume *History of the Anglo-Saxons* (1799–1805) broke new ground, was productively pursuing Anglo-Saxon studies. Richard Rawlinson had established a chair of Anglo-Saxon at Oxford, the first holder assuming the position in 1795, but 'Anglo-Saxon professors at that time were sometimes defined as "persons willing to learn Anglo-Saxon"' (Carlyle 1900). Those who did learn it were necessarily self-taught and not necessarily well taught. Of the first seven holders of the chair, only James Ingram (1803–8), Conybeare (1808–12) and Thomas Silver (1817–22) published any Anglo-Saxon scholarship (Tashjian et al. 1990b: 99–100), and their work displays the shortcomings of gentleman scholars. Madden knew little Anglo-Saxon, but his bold plan to edit *Beowulf*, given the scholarly landscape of the time, was less outlandish than it sounds.

In considering the excerpts from Madden's diary and Blaettermann's letter, I have focused on three points to show the state of the study in 1824: international interest, nationalist sentiment and the lack of professional standing of Anglo-Saxon as a discipline. In the rest of the century, international interest remained strong, nationalist sentiment varied in intensity and focus, and the knowledge of Anglo-Saxon gradually grew more professional.

Although Madden never published an edition of *Beowulf* – instead becoming a great Middle English scholar (Ackerman 1972) – in the next ten years the poem evoked much attention. In 1826 John Conybeare's *Illustrations of Anglo-Saxon Poetry*, edited by his brother, William D. Conybeare, was published, containing many passages from the poem in Anglo-Saxon and in translation, along with John Conybeare's collation of Thorkelin's edited text with the manuscript. In 1829, N. F. S. Grundtvig, who had subjected Thorkelin's edition to a devastating review soon after its appearance in 1815 (Cooley 1940: 54–67) and, self-taught in Anglo-Saxon, had published a translation of the poem in Danish in 1820, travelled to London from Copenhagen to collate his handwritten text of the poem with the manuscript in the British Museum (Kelly 1979: 90–110). The next summer he returned to transcribe the Exeter Book (Bradley 1998: 8–9) and, at the invitation of the firm of Black, Young and Young, published a prospectus for a series of Anglo-Saxon editions, *Bibliotheca Anglo-Saxonica* (1830). The first two of ten volumes were to be an edition and English translation of *Beowulf*. In that same summer another prospective editor of the poem arrived in England, Benjamin Thorpe. Thorpe, an Irish businessman working on the continent (Toldberg 1947: 289–91), developed an intense interest in Northern literature and began studying in Denmark in 1826 with Rask (who had, with Grundtvig, begun an edition of *Beowulf* in 1816, since abandoned). Thorpe did what Conybeare and Madden had done before him – collated Thorkelin's text of 1815 with the manuscript – finishing the task on 13 August 1830 (Hall 1987: 395). Thorpe's edition did not appear, however, until 1855, Grundtvig's (in Danish) not until 1861, both pre-empted by John M. Kemble, whose edition of *Beowulf* was published in 1833.

Kemble, a graduate of Trinity College, Cambridge, became an enthusiast for the new philology, as practised by Jacob Grimm, while visiting Germany in 1829. In fact, he tells Grimm in a letter that he originally made a transcript of *Beowulf* in summer 1832 to send him but that, at the urging of friends, he decided to bring out an edition on his own. Kemble's edition marks an immense improvement over Thorkelin's in situating the poem historically, in providing a much more accurate text, in indicating emendations and in dividing the verse into half-lines. Yet unlike Thorkelin, who furnished a Latin translation parallel to the Anglo-Saxon, Kemble offered no rendering, and his glossary, treating twenty-three words, was decidedly meagre. Fortunately, the hundred copies printed of the first edition were soon sold out, affording Kemble the opportunity to publish a second edition in 1835–7, in which he supplies a lucid prose translation, sophisticated philological notes and a detailed glossary of 128 pages (Hall 1994: 246–9). Kemble's glossary, focusing on a single poem, is more precisely executed than Bosworth's comprehensive *A Dictionary of the Anglo-Saxon Language*, published in 1838, more than seven years in the making.

The publication of Bosworth's dictionary serves to show that *Beowulf* was far from the sole concern of Anglo-Saxon scholars during those years. Grundtvig in his prospectus projected ten volumes for *Bibliotheca Anglo-Saxonica*, of which *Beowulf* was to occupy only the first two. Another scholar with sweeping ambitions was Thorpe, who edited the poems of the Junius Manuscript in 1832, an anthology of prose and verse, *Analecta Anglo-Saxonica*, in 1834, and another ten editions before he died in 1870 (Pulsiano 1998: 90–1), making him the most prolific editor in the history of Anglo-Saxon studies – this for a man whose first edition appeared when he was 50 years old. The key to Thorpe's stunning productivity is that he was content with journeyman work, always producing, never polishing, always publishing, never perfecting.

Although Thorpe is often linked with Kemble, his friend, as one of the two great Anglo-Saxonists of the period, in Germanic philology Kemble far outshone Thorpe and everyone else in England. The light he cast was not always kind. In reviewing Thorpe's *Analecta Anglo-Saxonica* for the *Gentleman's Magazine* in 1834, Kemble did not content himself with praising the work but went out of his way to impugn the English tradition of Anglo-Saxon scholarship, especially holders of the Anglo-Saxon chair at Oxford. Oxford scholars responded in the same vein, decrying the importation of alien German philology, and so was born the 'Anglo-Saxon Controversy' (Aarsleff 1983: 195–205). Kemble's final word in the quarrel, entitled by the *Gentleman's Magazine* 'Mr. Kemble on Anglo-Saxon Accents' (1835), is a minor masterpiece of comparative philology, in which he discusses short and long vowels in Germanic languages, taking occasion to correct not only Thorpe but Thorpe's teacher, Rask. Before long Kemble undertook to correct his own master, Grimm (1837: 45–9).

Although during the three successive summers he spent in England, 1829–31, Grundtvig was politely received, English scholars resented his ambitions with their literature and promoted their own programme through the Society of Antiquaries (Pulsiano 1998: 79–80). Grundtvig republished his prospectus in 1831 but soon realized that he could not compete with English scholars on their own ground and reluctantly stepped aside, later describing his *Bibliotheca Anglo-Saxonica* as 'kvalt i Födselen' – 'strangled at birth' (1840: 10). Grundtvig's Anglo-Saxon efforts, however, were far from fruitless.

In 1835 a protégé of his, Ludvig Christian Müller, published a small anthology of Anglo-Saxon verse and prose, *Collectanea Anglo-Saxonica*, in which he draws on Grundtvig's expertise and transcription of the Exeter Book to edit for the first time two riddles and the opening twenty-nine lines of *Christ I* (1835: 63–6; Bradley 1998: 6, 25). Grundtvig himself in 1840 published *Phenix-Fuglen et Angelsachsisk Kvad*, an edition of *The Phoenix*, the first major poem from the Exeter Book edited in its entirety. Grundtvig went on to publish learned Anglo-Saxon essays during the 1840s, but Frederik Schaldemose's translation of *Beowulf* in 1847 was probably better known to the public and went into a second printing in 1851. Basing his work on Kemble's edition and translation, he conveniently supplies the Anglo-Saxon and Danish in parallel columns after the manner of Thorkelin, who parallels the Anglo-Saxon text with a Latin translation. Unlike Müller, Schaldemose – whose literal translation is so different from Grundtvig's fanciful rendering of 1820 – was no follower of Grundtvig and upbraids him in the preface for harshly faulting Thorkelin more than a quarter of a century earlier, adding that he fully expects Grundtvig to vilify him as well (Shippey and Haarder 1998: 20). Grundtvig did not respond, however, and a Danish version of the English Anglo-Saxon Controversy was averted.

Danish scholars pursued Anglo-Saxon studies with no less nationalist interest than did the English. In the dedicatory letter to Johan Bülow in his grammar of 1817 – a letter Thorpe tactfully omitted from his translation in 1830 – Rask declares that the main purpose of studying Anglo-Saxon is the light it can shed on Danish language and history, a view also shared by Müller and earlier scholars in the tradition of 'Scandinavian Anglo-Saxonism' (Bjork 1997: 115–22). Grundtvig's ambitions for promoting Anglo-Saxonism were more daring. S. A. J. Bradley observes:

> Back home in Denmark in 1838 Grundtvig could confide to his Danish audience the view that England was a prodigal son and Denmark the venerable father praying for his return and rediscovery of his true life-of-the-heart which resided of course in the ancient Northern culture: his main aim in his visits to England, he said 'was to get into contact with the Englishman and win him for the Anglo-Saxon and so for Scandinavia'. (1994: 48)

Grundtvig's aim was never realized. German Anglo-Saxonism, as earlier preached and promoted by Kemble, exerted much more influence on nineteenth-century English and American scholars than did Scandinavian Anglo-Saxonism.

Scandinavian Anglo-Saxonism had, however, an early American adherent, Henry Wheaton, United States chargé d'affaires in Denmark, who in the late 1820s became acquainted with Rask and other Danish scholars (Baker 1937: 87–93). In one essay, ostensibly a review of Conybeare's *Illustrations* and of Thorpe's translation of Rask's Anglo-Saxon grammar, Wheaton spends more than half the space on Scandinavian literature, which he sees as superior to Anglo-Saxon (1831). Later, in a review of Bosworth's dictionary, Wheaton puts aside his Scandinavian predilection as he knowledgeably surveys Germanic language families, Anglo-Saxon history and Anglo-Saxon scholarship and laments that 'so little has yet been done to advance the study of the Anglo-Saxon in this country. The university of Virginia is the only institution in which a provision has been expressly made for instruction in it' (1838: 377). Despite Wheaton's encouragement, Anglo-Saxon did not readily take hold on college campuses, and the first Anglo-Saxon reader published in the United States did not appear for more than a decade.

The reader, entitled, like Thorpe's, *Analecta Anglo-Saxonica* (1849), was edited by Louis F. Klipstein, a third generation German-American, his paternal grandfather having come to the country as a surgeon with Hessian soldiers during the Revolution (Genzmer 1933). After he graduated from Hampden-Sydney College in 1832, Klipstein taught at a school in 1833–4 in Charlottesville, where, presumably, he made the acquaintance of Blaettermann and so of Anglo-Saxon. In the 1840s he married a wealthy South Carolina woman, who financed (with progressively dwindling funds and enthusiasm) the publication of three Anglo-Saxon books as well as the *Analecta*, on the promise of which Klipstein had received a PhD *in absentia* from the University of Giessen (Fischer 1927). Although the texts rely heavily on earlier editions, especially Thorpe's, Klipstein often departs from them in marking long vowels and in his textual and explanatory notes and demonstrates intelligent engagement with sense and grammar. What today's scholars find more remarkable, however, is Klipstein's commitment to political Anglo-Saxonism, as sometimes seen in the ninety-page ethnological essay in *Analecta*, in which he envisions America as the avatar of the Anglo-Saxon race and destined to expand and command (Mora and Gómez-Calderón 1998: 329–36).

Anglo-Saxonism was in the American air. Henry Wadsworth Longfellow composed a long essay on Anglo-Saxon literature, Ralph Waldo Emerson lectured on it, Henry David Thoreau ventured to capture its spirit in verse, James Russell Lowell praised its 'homespun' diction, and Walt Whitman celebrated it – along with himself (Bernbrock 1961: 66–121 *passim*). In the 1840s an American businessman, William G. Medlicott, set about teaching himself Anglo-Saxon and began a book collection with special focus on Anglo-Saxon titles, of which he managed to amass some 440 by 1878 (Hall 1990: 40–4). In 1850 John Seely Hart, principal of Central High School, Philadelphia, introduced the teaching of Anglo-Saxon to his students, an experiment lasting four years. Hart himself was an erudite philologist and lectured before the American Association for the Advancement of Education in December 1854, in which he extolled Anglo-Saxon as the bone and flesh and ornament of English, urging his listeners to staunch the infusion of loan words, called 'intruders', into the language (1856: 52–6; Hall 1997a: 142–7). Finally, George P. Marsh, a lawyer, politician, American minister to Italy and self-taught philologist, exalted the 'Gothic' race and culture (Kliger 1946) even as in *Lectures on the English Language* (1859) and in *The Origin and History of the English Language, and of the Early Literature it Embodies* (1862) he evinces far-flung linguistic learning.

Anglo-Saxonism was in the American air, but in American colleges the air was thin. As Wheaton noted in 1838, the language was regularly available only at the University of Virginia. In 1839 Edward D. Sims, after studying in Germany at the University of Halle in 1836–8, introduced Anglo-Saxon to Randolph-Macon College, teaching it there until 1842, when he relocated to the University of Alabama (Kern 1903; Callaway 1925: 12–13). With Sims' death in 1845, instruction in Anglo-Saxon at Alabama died as well. In 1840 the self-taught William C. Fowler – son-in-law of Noah Webster, who years earlier had also learned some of the language on his own (Laird 1946) – introduced Anglo-Saxon to Amherst College, but again the study ended there in 1843 when Fowler resigned (Bright 1914: cxix). Meanwhile at Virginia, Blaettermann was fired in 1840 for maltreating his wife and was replaced by Charles Kraitsir, a Hungarian polyglot, who, however, won little more favour than Blaettermann and was let go in 1843 (Bruce 1920: 157–62). Virginia's next Anglo-Saxonist, Maximilian Schele De Vere, proved endearingly, enduringly successful, teaching there for half a century. Educated in Germany (PhD and JUD), Schele taught not only French, Spanish, Italian and German as well as Anglo-Saxon, but 'offered successful courses in comparative philology, at a period when few American colleges had recognized the value of the comparative method' (Gordon 1935). His *Outlines of Comparative Philology*, containing seventy-five chapters in 434 pages, is a sweeping survey of the field displaying such enthusiasm for Grimm's Law that the author felt compelled to present it twice (1853: 218–19, 356–7).

In his provocatively entitled tome, *Glossology: Being a Treatise on the Nature of Language and on the Language of Nature*, Kraitsir asks, 'Pray, how do we stand as to Anglo-Saxonism? Which of the many universities (say UNIVERSITIES) in this fair land *converts* its attention to this *unique* language of the patriarchs of England?' (1852: 18).

The answer to Kraitsir's question is only two at the time: Schele taught Anglo-Saxon at Virginia, and Francis James Child, fresh from study in Germany in 1849–51, taught it at Harvard (Thompson 1936: 250). By the end of the decade the language was available at only two more places of learning: at Lafayette College, under the virtually self-taught Francis A. March, and at the University of Mississippi, under the self-taught William D. Moore (Hall 1997b: 60). Things did not improve much during the next decade. In *A Manual of Anglo-Saxon for Beginners*, Samuel M. Shute, another self-taught Anglo-Saxonist, laments, 'The study of the Anglo-Saxon language in this country, is limited to a very small number of students. Instruction in it is given, probably, in six or eight of our colleges, and but little time is allotted to it' (1867: iii). Shute's assessment is accurate: in addition to Virginia, Harvard, Lafayette, Mississippi and Shute's own Columbian College (later renamed George Washington University), the language was offered only at Haverford College, where it was introduced in 1867 by Thomas Chase, who, like Child, had studied in Germany and elsewhere in Europe in 1853–5 (Hall 1997b: 46, 61). Anglo-Saxonism was much touted; Anglo-Saxon was little taught.

The case was similar in England, where Anglo-Saxon was little taught by publishing Anglo-Saxonists in colleges until the last two decades of the nineteenth century. Beginning in the 1830s, however, much scholarship was published by non-academics. Thorpe and Kemble reinvigorated Anglo-Saxon scholarship, but neither enjoyed an academic appointment, nor did Thomas Wright, Kemble's quondam disciple, who wrote widely on medieval literature and published *An Essay on the State of Literature and Learning under the Anglo-Saxons* (1839), 'the first survey of the field of Old English literature by a man with training and knowledge sufficient for the purpose' (Savage 1935: 246–7). A friend of Wright's and a prolific French medievalist, Francisque Michel, published an annotated bibliography, *Bibliothèque anglo-saxonne* (1837), but held no position in England. Edwin Guest was a barrister when he wrote *A History of English Rhythms* (1838), which deals extensively with Anglo-Saxon literature (2: 4–102, 397–405, 430–1; Savage 1935: 219–29). John Petheram, who wrote the admirable *An Historical Sketch of the Progress and Present State of Anglo-Saxon Literature in England* (1840), was a bookseller (Hall 1997b: 44).

Churchmen also contributed to Anglo-Saxon scholarship. Bosworth was British chaplain at Rotterdam when he published his dictionary (1838). Joseph Stevenson, who edited *Rituale Ecclesiæ Dunelmensis* (1840), and Daniel H. Haigh, who wrote *The Anglo-Saxon Sagas* (1861), were ministers in the Church of England before becoming Catholic priests (Cooper 1898, Sutton 1890). T. O. Cockayne, whose *Leechdoms, Wortcunning, and Starcraft of Early England* (1864–6) and *The Shrine* (1864–70) manifest immense learning, was another minister of the Church of England. For all his erudition, Cockayne never taught Anglo-Saxon at a university (Brodribb 1887).

Did not any qualified Anglo-Saxonists teach Anglo-Saxon in English universities? Reviewing Thorpe's *Analecta Anglo-Saxonica*, Kemble recommended the work as 'an excellent class book for the London University and King's College' (1834: 393) – expecting that the two new schools would teach Anglo-Saxon 'in honourable contradistinction to the antiquated methods of Oxford' (Chambers 1939: 347) – yet for years R. G. Latham was the only trained philologist teaching at either place. After graduating in 1832 from Cambridge, Latham studied for a year in Germany, Denmark and Norway, and in 1839, at the age of 27, was chosen as professor of English language and literature at University College, London (Battany 1892; Bellot 1929: 114). In 1841 he published *The English Language*, with ample attention to Anglo-Saxon. The first such work of its kind in England (Müller 1858: 263), the book went through five editions, its length increasing from some 400 pages to more than 700 (Quirk 1961: 12–14). Although Latham resigned his professorship at University College in 1845 – too soon to establish a philological tradition at the school – he maintained an active interest in language and literature for the rest of his life but devoted himself to other pursuits as well: especially medicine, in which he earned an MD; ethnology, on which he lectured; and dissipation, of which he was both a wilful master and willing servant (Bellot 1929: 114–15). In 1842, with Edwin Guest and others, Latham helped transform the Philological Society from a student club at University College to a national organization (Quirk 1961: 9–10). Meanwhile, at Oxford the Rawlinson chair was occupied continuously, but only two holders since 1822 – Robert Meadows White (1834–9) and John Earle (1849–54) – managed publications on Anglo-Saxon (Tashjian et al. 1990b: 101).

Richard Wülker observed in 1885 that the study of Anglo-Saxon in England was vibrant in the 1830s and 1840s but that it reached a standstill in the 1850s and in the 1860s actually declined, giving way to Middle English studies with the advent of the Early English Text Society (Wülker 1885: 64). None the less, the 1850s witnessed a critical turning point in Anglo-Saxon as an academic discipline. After Earle's term expired in 1854, the Rawlinson chair was left unfilled for four years, and the period of tenure was redefined into a lifetime appointment (Tashjian 1990: 87, 93; Palmer 1965: 71–2). The inaugural holder of the new chair in 1858 was Bosworth: for the first time in its history the professorship went to a well-established Anglo-Saxon scholar. After Bosworth's death in 1876, Earle was again elected to the chair, his rival being Thomas Arnold, of University College, Oxford, who in 1876 had published an edition and translation of *Beowulf* and some twenty years later a critical study, *Notes on Beowulf* (1898). Earle held the professorship until 1903, publishing diverse kinds of scholarship (Plummer 1912).

The reconstitution of the Rawlinson chair to carry a lifetime appointment meant that for the last four decades of the nineteenth century Anglo-Saxon was taught at Oxford not by persons simply willing to learn the language or by gifted amateurs but by professionals. Bosworth did more than fill the Rawlinson chair at Oxford. He gave £10,000, better than half the earnings from his dictionary, to his alma mater, Trinity College, Cambridge, for establishing an Anglo-Saxon chair there after his death (Bradley 1886; Keynes 1992: 54). In 1878 Walter W. Skeat was unanimously elected the first holder of the professorship (Brewer 1998). Although Skeat's primary field was Middle English, he published a solid body of Anglo-Saxon scholarship as well.

In 1885 Oxford established the Merton Professorship of English Language and Literature (Palmer 1965: 79). The position need not have gone to an Anglo-Saxonist, but did. Appointed was a former student of Earle's at Oxford, A. S. Napier, who had gone to Germany for graduate work, receiving a PhD from Göttingen in 1882 (Ker 1970: 153–5). With the acquisition of Napier, Oxford enjoyed the services of a second German-trained Germanic philologist, the first being Max Müller, who served as professor of modern European languages in 1854–68 and professor of comparative philology in 1868–1901 and whose lectures Napier had attended along with Earle's as a student at Oxford (Ker 1970: 153). A few years later Oxford hired another comparative philologist with a PhD from Germany, Joseph Wright, whom Müller had brought to Oxford to lecture on Germanic languages, including Anglo-Saxon, for the Association for the Higher Education of Women. In 1891 Wright became Müller's assistant, a decade later succeeding him to the professorship (Boyd 1937; Palmer 1965: 124–6).

Wright was not the only Oxford academic, apart from those responsible for directly teaching Anglo-Saxon, who knew the language professionally. Charles Plummer, fellow and chaplain of Corpus Christi College (*Who Was Who* 1929: 842–3), brought out a revised and much improved edition of Earle's *Two of the Saxon Chronicles Parallel* (1892–9), notable for its attention to manuscript relations (Hall 1995: 155–6), and W. H. Stevenson, associated successively with Merton, Exeter and St John's Colleges (Poole 1937), was a master of Anglo-Saxon palaeography (Sisam 1953: 276).

Cambridge also had its share of scholars who knew Anglo-Saxon. Years before Skeat assumed the Anglo-Saxon chair, Guest served as master of Caius College from 1852 almost until his death in 1880 (Marshall 1890). In 1876 J. Rawson Lumby, a divine and a Biblical scholar of St Catharine's College, published an excellent edition of *Be Domes Dæge* and other Anglo-Saxon poems (Lupton 1901; Hall 1995: 156–7). In 1892 Israel Gollancz, of Christ's College, published an edition of *Cynewulf's Christ*, dedicating it to Skeat, 'Magistro Discipulus' ('disciple to master'). Three years later Gollancz published *The Exeter Book, Part I*, in some ways a model of editing (Stanley 1985: 240–1; Hall 1995: 172–3). In 1896 he was named the first lecturer in English literature at Cambridge (Hyamson 1937). In 1894, A. J. Wyatt, an MA candidate at Christ's College, published the first edition of *Beowulf* in England since Arnold's in 1876. All earlier English editions being long out of print, Wyatt's filled an immediate need, and he brought out a second edition in 1898. For forty-seven years, until his death in 1935, Wyatt served as a tutor in English for the University Correspondence College, Burlington House, Cambridge (*Times* 1935).

Some scholars at schools other than Oxford and Cambridge also knew Anglo-Saxon. In 1865 Henry Morley, who had worked with Charles Dickens on his periodicals, was appointed professor of English language and literature at University College, London, holding the post until 1889 (Gairdner 1894; Bellot 1929: 335–9; Chambers 1939: 354–7). W. P. Ker, educated at Glasgow and Oxford, succeeded Morley to the professorship and taught there for thirty-three years (Chambers 1937). Morley and Ker were essentially literary critics. T. Northcote Toller, however, was a pure philologist.

Equipped with an MA from Christ's College, Cambridge, he was appointed assistant lecturer in English language and literature at Owens College (later the Victoria University of Manchester) in 1870 and named Smith Professor in 1880. Toller devoted some forty years to revising and supplementing Bosworth's Anglo-Saxon dictionary, the first two fascicles appearing in 1882, the revised dictionary as a whole in 1898, and the supplement as a whole in 1921.

In the last three decades of the century, as in earlier decades, Anglo-Saxon scholarship in England enjoyed the benefit of scholars not attached to universities. F. J. Furnivall was less important as a scholar than as a promoter of scholarship. After graduating from Cambridge in 1847, he studied law, but his passion for social and educational reform and for literature soon absorbed most of his attention (Lee 1912: 61–2). At Furnivall's urging, the Philological Society in 1858 undertook the *New English Dictionary on Historical Principles* – today known as the *Oxford English Dictionary* – and three years later he was appointed editor, serving until 1878 (Pearsall 1998: 126–30). In 1864, to supply edited material for the dictionary, Furnivall founded the Early English Text Society. It is true that, as Wülker notes (1885: 64), the society led to the eclipse of Anglo-Saxon literature by Middle English; it is also true, however, that the society published a dozen Anglo-Saxon editions in the nineteenth century alone. One of Furnivall's best friends and supporters, Richard Morris, a minister and schoolmaster, contributed many editions to the society (Cotton 1901). Morris's edition of *The Blickling Homilies* (1874–80) has not been superseded. Another minister contributing to Anglo-Saxon studies was Stopford A. Brooke (Jacks 1927). After prolonged study of German and English scholarship, he wrote a well-received work of literary criticism, *The History of Early English Literature, Being the History of English Poetry from its Beginnings to the Accession of King Ælfred* (1892).

Not a literary critic in the least was Walter de Gray Birch, for many years senior assistant in the Department of Manuscripts, British Museum, and a passionate student of diplomatics (*Who Was Who* 1929: 93). In his greatest Anglo-Saxon work, *Cartularium Saxonicum: A Collection of Charters Relating to Anglo-Saxon History* (1885–93), Birch insisted on presenting the texts 'as they actually stand in their manuscripts, with whatever errors the scribes of these manuscripts have perpetuated; thereby inviting emendations from [readers], rather than attempting myself to emend what appears faulty or incorrect' (1893: 3.vi). Henry Bradley, another notable scholar, had no formal training beyond grammar school; while employed for more than twenty years as an office clerk, he taught himself classical and modern European languages. After moving from Sheffield to London, Bradley came to the attention of James Murray, who hired him as an editor of the *New English Dictionary* in 1889 (Craigie 1937). Bradley published articles and reviews on Anglo-Saxon literature, but his greatest contribution to the field was submerged and diffuse – in thousands of entries for the dictionary. Another scholar devoted to lexicography was John R. Clark Hall, who, after earning an MA and PhD, went on to become a barrister (*Who Was Who in Literature* 1979). In his spare time he worked hard and long on *A Concise Anglo-Saxon Dictionary for the Use of Students* (1894), by which he hoped to make available a comprehensive single-

Wealhtheow as anxious that Hrothulf, Hrothgar's nephew, will attempt to seize the throne from her son, Hrethric, after Hrothgar dies, and he understands Unferth (Hunferth) as someone who will incite Hrothulf to rebellion (Chambers 1959: 426–30; Shippey and Haarder 1998: 63–5, 497–9).

Finally, the Danish scholar Hermann Möller stands somewhat apart from the Grundtvigian tradition. Living in North Frisia after its conquest by German forces in 1864, Möller was trained in German universities, wrote in German and taught Germanic philology at the University of Copenhagen for more than thirty-five years, beginning in 1883 (Bach 1982). In *Das altenglische Volksepos in der ursprünglichen strophischen Form*, he draws on a North Frisian folktale to try to elucidate the relationship between the *Finnsburg Fragment* and the Finnsburg episode in *Beowulf* (1883: 1.46–102; Chambers 1959: 254–7; Shippey and Haarder 1998: 400–6) and, more radically, reconstructs *Beowulf* and the *Finnsburg Fragment* into quatrains in an effort to reconstruct the putative original poems before later poets contaminated them (1883: 1.103–60, 2.vii–lxxv; Shippey and Haarder 1998: 406–10).

Denmark developed its own tradition of Anglo-Saxon studies and felt menaced by nearby German states: Möller was the only nineteenth-century Danish Anglo-Saxonist to attend a German university. England had its own tradition of Anglo-Saxon studies and felt a sharp sense of rivalry with German scholarship: only a handful of English Anglo-Saxonists – Kemble, Latham, Sweet, Napier and Joseph Wright – studied at German universities. America, however, had little independent tradition of Anglo-Saxon studies, was too remote to feel threatened by Germany and felt more awe than rivalry for German scholarship (Thompson 1936: 251): twenty American scholars travelled to Germany to study Anglo-Saxon and related subjects. Earlier I mentioned the first three: Sims in 1836–8, Child in 1849–51 and Chase in 1853–5. The others studied in Germany between 1859 and 1892. (For supporting references to the Americans mentioned in the following paragraphs, see Hall 1997b: 46–51. On Henry Wood and Henry Johnson, not included in Hall 1997b, see *NCAB* 1906 [Wood] and *NCAB* 1933 and Sills 1933 [Johnson].)

Nine of the seventeen were Southerners, five of them Schele's students at the University of Virginia: Thomas R. Price, James A. Harrison, James M. Garnett, J. Douglas Bruce and Charles W. Kent. After Price returned to America, he taught at Randolph-Macon College, where he reintroduced the study of Anglo-Saxon (not offered there since Sims' time), then at the University of Virginia and at Columbia. Two students Price taught at Randolph-Macon, Robert Sharp and William M. Baskerville, also pursued graduate education abroad. Back at home, Baskerville taught at Wofford College and at Vanderbilt. One of his Wofford students, James Kirkland, also studied in Germany, as did one of his students at Vanderbilt, C. C. Ferrell.

The remaining eight Americans who sought philological training in Germany were Northerners. Two had undergraduate degrees from the College of New Jersey (later renamed Princeton), Theodore W. Hunt and James M. Hart; two others were graduates of Haverford College, Henry Wood and Francis B. Gummere. The remaining four held undergraduate degrees from various places: Francis A. Blackburn, University of Michigan; Henry Johnson, Bowdoin College; Albert S. Cook, Rutgers; and James W. Bright, Lafayette College.

Studying in Germany may have been the most professional means for Americans to learn Anglo-Saxon, but it was not the only one. Many learned the language on their own or, as the discipline became established in the latter decades of the century, at American colleges. Earlier I touched on a dozen Americans who taught themselves at least some Anglo-Saxon: Jefferson, Wheaton, Longfellow, Marsh, Klipstein, Thoreau, Medlicott, John S. Hart, Webster, Fowler, Moore and Shute. Three of them – Fowler, Moore and Shute – were the first to teach a regular course in Anglo-Saxon at their colleges. Five other self-taught men also introduced the subject at various schools: Hiram Corson, St John's College (Annapolis), 1868, and Cornell, 1871; Thomas Raynesford Lounsbury, Yale, 1870; Stephen H. Carpenter, University of Wisconsin, 1871; Morgan Callaway (Sr), Emory College, 1876; and Melville Best Anderson, Knox College, 1881, and Stanford, 1891.

It would not be strictly correct to say that Francis A. March learned Anglo-Saxon without a teacher, because he had been introduced to the language at Amherst College by Fowler in 1841. Fowler's knowledge of Anglo-Saxon seems to have been rudimentary, however, and for practical purposes March may be said to have learned the language on his own. March learned it by mastering German scholarship. In 1870, fifteen years after he introduced the study to Lafayette College, he published *A Comparative Grammar of the Anglo-Saxon Language*, in which he illustrates Anglo-Saxon by reference to Sanskrit, Greek, Latin and five early Germanic languages. The book received triumphant acclaim in Germany, demonstrating that an American could not only make himself wholly at home in Germanic philology but integrate it into a system greater than the sum of its parts (Bright 1914: cxxviii–xii; Malone 1933).

Thanks to men like March, to the many Americans who studied Anglo-Saxon in Germany and to two native Germans with doctorates who came to the United States to teach in 1892 – Ewald Flügel, of Stanford, and Frederick Klaeber, of the University of Minnesota – by the end of the nineteenth century America had developed a strong tradition of Anglo-Saxon scholarship. The scholar most responsible was Bright, who, after graduating from Lafayette, earned a PhD from Johns Hopkins before going to Germany for post-doctoral work. Not long after his return, he was back at Johns Hopkins, where for four decades he laboured indefatigably promoting philological studies on the German model. No fewer than seventeen Anglo-Saxon doctoral dissertations written in America before 1900 were done at Johns Hopkins under his direction. Some of his students became well-known scholars in their own right: for example, Morgan Callaway Jr, Frederick Tupper, Clarence G. Child and George P. Krapp (Malone 1927: 124–6).

Altogether, Johns Hopkins awarded nineteen PhDs in Anglo-Saxon before the year 1900, nearly half of the thirty-nine Anglo-Saxon doctorates granted by American universities in the last two decades of the century. The remaining twenty doctorates were granted by various places of learning – Harvard, Columbia, Tulane, Bryn Mawr, New

York University, Stanford, Yale and Cornell (Hall 1997b: 54–5). But these eight places represent less than a quarter of those teaching Anglo-Saxon in America in the late nineteenth century. By 1899 the subject could be studied in every part of the country.

Gustav Körting lists thirty-six scholars who taught English philology at twenty-two German universities in the late 1880s (1888: xix, 25–30). About two dozen of the scholars were Anglo-Saxonists, including such luminaries as Julius Zupitza, Eduard Sievers, Friedrich Kluge and Richard Paul Wülker. In the 1890s America had at least as many Anglo-Saxonists as Germany, among them men comparable to the leading German scholars: March, Cook, Bright and Klaeber. England did not have as many Anglo-Saxonists as Germany or America but did have its share and could boast of such scholars as Sweet, Napier, Toller and Gollancz. The state of the study in Denmark was not nearly as vigorous. Yet even after Stephens died in 1895, three scholars – Rønning, Olrik and Möller – carried on Danish Anglo-Saxon scholarship as inaugurated by Thorkelin, Rask and Grundtvig.

Earlier, after quoting Madden's journal entry and Blaettermann's letter to Jefferson, I remarked that the state of Anglo-Saxon studies in 1824 may be characterized as possessing an international dimension, as eliciting nationalist sentiment and as lacking professionalism. By the end of the nineteenth century the international aspect was dynamic, and nationalist sentiment remained strong. Germany claimed Anglo-Saxon as a Germanic language, England and America claimed it as their mother-tongue, and Denmark claimed the central Anglo-Saxon poem, *Beowulf*, as based on Danish sources and largely about Danes. A sea change had come about, however, in academic standing. In 1824 Anglo-Saxon could not be studied anywhere rigorously. Seventy-five years later it could be studied at more than four dozen universities on two continents under trained professionals.

REFERENCES

Primary sources

Arnold, Thomas, ed. and trans. 1876. *Beowulf: A Heroic Poem of the Eighth Century.* London.
——1898. *Notes on Beowulf.* London.
Birch, Walter de Gray, ed. 1885–93. *Cartularium Saxonicum: A Collection of Charters Relating to Anglo-Saxon History.* 3 vols. London.
Blaettermann, Georg 1824. Letter to Thomas Jefferson dated 26 June. Huntington Library. HM 9228. 3 pp.
Bosworth, J[oseph] 1838. *A Dictionary of the Anglo-Saxon Language.* Revised edn 1898. Ed. T. Northcote Toller. London.
Brooke, Stopford A. 1892. *The History of Early English Literature, Being the History of English Poetry from its Beginnings to the Accession of King Ælfred.* London.
Cockayne, [Thomas] Oswald, ed. 1864–6. *Leechdoms, Wortcunning, and Starcraft of Early England.* London.
——1864–70. *The Shrine. A Collection of Papers on Dry Subjects.* London.
Conybeare, John Josias 1826. *Illustrations of Anglo-Saxon Poetry.* Ed. William Daniel Conybeare. London.
Gollancz, Israel, ed. and trans. 1892. *Cynewulf's Christ: An Eighth Century English Epic.* London.
——, ed. and trans. 1895. *The Exeter Book, Part I: Poems I–VIII.* EETS o.s. 104. London.
Grimm, Jacob 1819–37. *Deutsche Grammatik.* 4 vols. Göttingen.

Grundtvig, N. F. S. 1830. *Bibliotheca Anglo-Saxonica. Prospectus, and Proposals of a Subscription, for the Publication of the Most Valuable Anglo-Saxon Manuscripts, Illustrative of the Early Poetry and Literature of Our Language. Most of Which Have Never Yet Been Printed.* 2nd edn 1831. London.

——, ed. 1840. *Phenix-Fuglen et Angelsachsisk Kvad.* Copenhagen.

——, ed. 1861. *Beowulfes Beorh eller Bjovulfs-Drapen, det Old-Angelske Heltedigt, paa Grund-Sproget.* Copenhagen and London.

Guest, Edwin 1838. *A History of English Rhythms.* 2 vols. London.

Haigh, Daniel H. 1861. *The Anglo-Saxon Sagas; An Examination of their Value as Aids to History.* London.

Hall, John R. Clark 1894. *A Concise Anglo-Saxon Dictionary for the Use of Students.* London and New York. 2nd edn 1916. Cambridge. 3rd edn 1931. 4th edn 1960. With suppl. Herbert D. Meritt.

Hammerich, Fr[ederik] 1873. *De episk-kristelige oldkvad hos de gotiske folk.* Copenhagen.

Hart, John S. 1856. 'On the Study of the Anglo-Saxon Language; or, the Relations of the English Language to the Teutonic and Classic Branches of the Indo-European Family of Languages'. *American Journal of Education* 1: 33–66.

Kemble, John M. 1833. *The Anglo-Saxon Poems of Beowulf, The Travellers Song and The Battle of Finnes-burh.* 2nd edn, with trans. 2 vols. 1835–7. London.

[——] 1834. Review of *Analecta Anglo-Saxonica*, by Benjamin Thorpe. *Gentleman's Magazine* n.s. 1 (April): 391–3.

——1835. 'Mr. Kemble on Anglo-Saxon Accents'. *Gentleman's Magazine* n.s. 4 (July): 26–30.

——1837 'Letter to M. Francisque Michel'. Michel 1837: 1–63.

Klipstein, Louis F. 1849. *Analecta Anglo-Saxonica. Selections, in Prose and Verse, from the Anglo-Saxon Literature: with an Introductory Ethnological Essay, and Notes, Critical and Explanatory.* 2 vols. New York and London.

Kraitsir, Charles 1852. *Glossology: Being a Treatise on the Nature of Language and on the Language of Nature.* New York.

Latham, R. G. 1841. *The English Language.* 2nd

edn 1848. 3rd edn 1850. 4th edn 1855. 5th edn 1862. London.

Lumby, J. Rawson, ed. 1876. *Be Domes Dæge, De Die Judicii, An Old English Version of the Latin Poem Ascribed to Bede.* EETS o.s. 65. London.

Madden, Frederic 1819–72. Diary. Oxford, Bodleian Library. 43 vols. MSS. Eng. hist. C. 140–82.

March, Francis A. 1870. *A Comparative Grammar of the Anglo-Saxon Language; in which its Forms are Illustrated by those of the Sanskrit, Greek, Latin, Gothic, Old Saxon, Old Friesic, Old Norse, and Old High-German.* New York.

Marsh, George P. 1859. *Lectures on the English Language.* Rev. edn 1862. New York and London.

——1862. *The Origin and History of the English Language, and of the Early Literature it Embodies.* New York and London.

Michel, Francisque 1837. *Bibliothèque anglo-saxonne.* Vol. 2. *Anglo-Saxonica.* Eds P. de Larenaudière and Francisque Michel. Paris and London.

Möller, Hermann 1883. *Das altenglische Volksepos in der ursprünglichen strophischen Form.* 2 vols. Kiel.

Morris, R[ichard], ed. and trans. 1874–80. *The Blickling Homilies.* EETS o.s. 58 (1874), 63 (1876), 73 (1880).

Müller, Ludvig Christian 1835. *Collectanea Anglo-Saxonica maximam partem nunc primum edita et vocabulario illustrata.* Copenhagen.

Olrik, Axel 1903–10. *Danmarks Heltedigtning: En Oltidsstudie.* 2 vols. *Förste Del, Rolf Krake og den Ældre Skjoldungrække.* 1903. *Anden del, Starkad den Gamle og den yngre Skjoldungrække.* 1910. Copenhagen.

Petheram, John 1840. *An Historical Sketch of the Progress and Present State of Anglo-Saxon Literature in England.* London.

Plummer, Charles, ed. 1892–9. *Two of the Saxon Chronicles Parallel.* 2 vols. Oxford.

Rask, R[asmus] K. 1817. *Angelsaksisk Sproglære tilligemed en kort Læsebog.* Stockholm. Rev. edn trans. as *A Grammar of the Anglo-Saxon Tongue, with a Praxis,* by B. Thorpe. Copenhagen. 1830. 3rd edn 1879. London.

Rönning [Rønning], F[rederik] 1883. *Beovulfs-Kvadet. En Literær-historisk Undersølgelse.* Copenhagen.

Schaldemose, Frederik, ed. and trans. 1847. *Beowulf og Scopes Widsið, to angelsaxiske Digte, med*

Oversættelse og oplysende Anmærkninger. Rpt 1851. Copenhagen.

Schele De Vere, M[aximilian] 1853. *Outlines of Comparative Philology.* New York.

Schrøder, Ludvig 1875. *Om Bjovulfs-drapen. Efter en række foredrag på folkehöjskolen i Askov.* Copenhagen.

Shute, Samuel M. 1867. *A Manual of Anglo-Saxon for Beginners; Comprising a Grammar, Reader, and Glossary, with Explanatory Notes.* New York.

Stephens, George 1866–1901. *The Old-Northern Runic Monuments of Scandinavia and England, Now First Collected and Deciphered.* Vols 1–2. 1866–7. Vol. 3. 1884. London, Edinburgh and Copenhagen. Vol. 4. Ed. Sven Otto Magnus Söderberg. 1901. London, Edinburgh and Lund.

Stevenson, Joseph, ed. 1840. *Rituale Ecclesiæ Dunelmensis.* Surtees Society 10. London and Edinburgh.

Sweet, Henry, ed. and trans. 1871. *King Alfred's West-Saxon Version of Gregory's Pastoral Care.* 2 vols. EETS o.s. 45, 50. London.

Thorkelin, Grím[ur] Johnson, ed. 1815. *De Danorum Rebus Gestis Secul. III & IV. Poëma danicum dialecto anglosaxonica.* Copenhagen.

Thorpe, Benjamin, ed. 1834. *Analecta Anglo-Saxonica. A Selection in Prose and Verse, from Anglo-Saxon Authors of Various Ages; with a Glossary. Designed Chiefly as a First Book for Students.* 2nd edn 1846. London.

Toller, T. Northcote 1921. *An Anglo-Saxon Dictionary Based on the Manuscript Collections of Joseph Bosworth. Supplement.* Oxford.

Turner, Sharon 1799–1805. *The History of the Anglo-Saxons.* 4 vols. 2nd edn 2 vols. 1807. 3rd edn 3 vols. 1820. London.

Wanley, Humphrey [Humfrey] 1705. *Librorum vett. septentrionalium . . . catalogus historico-criticus.* Oxford.

Wheaton, Henry 1831. 'Anglo-Saxon Language and Literature'. *North American Review* 33: 325–50.

——1838. 'The Anglo-Saxon Language'. *New York Review* 3: 362–77.

Wright, Thomas 1839. *An Essay on the State of Literature and Learning under the Anglo-Saxons.* London.

Wyatt, A. J., ed. 1894. *Beowulf. Edited with Textual Foot-notes, Index of Proper Names, and Alphabetical Glossary.* 2nd edn 1898. Cambridge.

Secondary sources

Aarsleff, Hans 1983. *The Study of Language in England, 1780–1860.* 2nd edn. Minneapolis and London.

Ackerman, Robert W. 1972. 'Sir Frederic Madden and Medieval Scholarship'. *Neuphilologische Mitteilungen* 73: 1–14.

Adams, Eleanor N. 1917. *Old English Scholarship in England from 1566–1800.* New Haven, CT.

Bach, H. 1982. 'Møller (Moeller), Martin Thomas Herman(n), 1850–1923'. *DBL* 10: 235–6.

Baker, Elizabeth Feaster 1937. *Henry Wheaton, 1785–1848.* Philadelphia.

Battany, George Thomas 1892. 'Latham, Robert Gordon, M.D. (1812–88)'. *DNB* 32: 168–9. Rpt 11: 609–10.

Bellot, H. Hale 1929. *University College, London, 1826–1926.* London.

Bernbrock, John E. 1961. 'Walt Whitman and "Anglo-Saxonism"'. Diss., University of North Carolina at Chapel Hill.

Bjork, Robert E. 1997. 'Nineteenth-century Scandinavia and the Birth of Anglo-Saxon Studies'. Frantzen and Niles 1997: 111–32.

Boyd, James 1937. 'Wright, Joseph (1855–1930)'. *DNB 1922–1930*: 923–5.

Bradley, Henry 1886. 'Bosworth, Joseph, D.D. (1789–1876)'. *DNB* 5: 440–2. Rpt 2: 902–4.

Bradley, S. A. J. 1994. ' "The First New-European Literature": N. F. S. Grundtvig's Reception of Anglo-Saxon Literature'. *Heritage and Prophecy: Grundtvig and the English Speaking World*, pp. 45–72. Eds A. M. Allchin, D. Jasper, J. H. Schjørring and K. Stevenson. Norwich.

——1998. *N. F. S. Grundtvig's Transcriptions of the Exeter Book.* Skrifter Udgivet af Grundtvig Selskabet 28. Copenhagen.

Brewer, Charlotte 1998. 'Walter William Skeat (1835–1912)'. Damico 1998: 139–49.

Bright, James Wilson 1914. 'An Address in Commemoration of Francis Andrew March, 1825–1911'. *Publications of the Modern Language Association* 29: cxvii–cxxxvii.

Brodribb, Arthur Aikin 1887. 'Cockayne, Thomas Oswald (1807–1873)'. *DNB* 11: 176. Rpt 4: 632.

Bruce, Philip Alexander 1920. *History of the University of Virginia 1819–1919.* Vol. 2. New York.

Callaway, Morgan, Jr 1925. 'The Historic Study of the Mother-tongue in the United States: A Survey of the Past'. University of Texas *Studies in English* 5: 5–38.

Carlyle, E. Irving 1900. 'White, Robert Meadows (1798–1865)'. *DNB* 61: 74–5. Rpt 21: 74–5.

Chambers, R. W. 1937. 'Ker, William Paton (1855–1923)'. *DNB 1922–1930*: 467–9.

—— 1939. *Man's Unconquerable Mind: Studies of English Writers, from Bede to A. E. Housman and W. P. Ker.* London.

—— 1959. *Beowulf: An Introduction to the Study of the Poem with a Discussion of the Stories of Offa and Finn.* 3rd edn. With suppl. C. L. Wrenn. Cambridge.

Cooley, Franklin 1940. 'Early Danish Criticism of *Beowulf*'. *English Literary History* 7: 45–67.

Cooper, Thompson 1898. 'Stevenson, Joseph (1806–1895)'. *DNB* 54: 240–2. Rpt 18: 1127–9.

Cotton, J. S. 1901. 'Morris, Richard (1833–1894)'. *DNB* 66: 196. Rpt 22: 1068.

Craigie, W. A. 1937. 'Bradley, Henry (1845–1923)'. *DNB 1922–1930*: 103–4.

DAB: Dictionary of American Biography. Eds Allen Johnson and Dumas Malone. 20 vols. 1928–36. Rpt 1946. 10 vols. Same pagination. New York.

Damico, Helen, ed. 1998. *Medieval Scholarship: Biographical Studies on the Formation of a Discipline.* Vol. 2. New York and London.

DBL: Dansk Biografisk Leksikon. Ed. Svend Cedergreen Bech. 16 vols. 1979–84. Copenhagen.

DNB: Dictionary of National Biography. 66 vols. Eds Leslie Stephen and Sidney Lee. 1885–1901. Rpt 1921–68. London.

DNB Sec. Supp.: Dictionary of National Biography. Second Supplement. Ed. Sidney Lee. 3 vols. 1912. London.

DNB 1912–1921: Dictionary of National Biography 1912–1921. Eds H. W. C. Davis and J. R. H. Weaver. 1927. London.

DNB 1922–1930: Dictionary of National Biography 1922–1930. Ed. J. R. H. Weaver. 1937. London.

Fischer, Walther 1927. 'Aus der Frühzeit der amerikanischen Anglistik: Louis F. Klipstein (1813–79)'. *Englische Studien* 62: 250–64.

Frantzen, Allen J., and John D. Niles, eds 1997. *Anglo-Saxonism and the Construction of Social Identity.* Gainesville.

Gairdner, James 1894. 'Morley, Henry (1822–1894)'. *DNB* 39: 78–9. Rpt 13: 975–6.

Genzmer, George Harvey 1933. 'Klipstein, Louis Frederick'. *DAB* 10: 446–7. Rpt 5.2.

Gordon, Armistead Churchill Jr 1935. 'Schele De Vere, Maximilian'. *DAB* 16: 423–4. Rpt 8.2.

Hall, J. R. 1987. 'The Conybeare "Cædmon": A Turning Point in the History of Old English Scholarship'. *Harvard Library Bulletin* 33 (1987 for 1985): 378–403.

—— 1990. 'William G. Medlicott (1816–1883): An American Book Collector and his Collection'. *Harvard Library Bulletin* n.s. 1.1: 13–46.

—— 1994. 'The First Two Editions of *Beowulf*: Thorkelin's (1815) and Kemble's (1833)'. *The Editing of Old English: Papers from the 1990 Manchester Conference*, pp. 239–50. Eds D. G. Scragg and Paul E. Szarmach. Cambridge.

—— 1995. 'Old English Literature'. *Scholarly Editing: A Guide to Research*, pp. 149–83. Ed. D. C. Greetham. New York.

—— 1997a. 'Mid-Nineteenth-century American Anglo-Saxonism: The Question of Language'. Frantzen and Niles 1997: 133–56.

—— 1997b. 'Nineteenth-century America and the Study of the Anglo-Saxon Language: An Introduction'. *The Preservation and Transmission of Anglo-Saxon Culture*, pp. 37–71. Eds Paul E. Szarmach and Joel T. Rosenthal. Kalamazoo.

—— 1998. 'F. J. Furnivall's Letter to the Royal Library, Copenhagen, Asking that the Thorkelin Transcripts of *Beowulf* Be Sent to London for the Use of Julius Zupitza'. *Notes & Queries* 45: 267–72.

Hemmingsen, Lars 1998. 'Axel Olrik (1864–1917)'. Damico 1998: 267–81.

Horsman, Reginald 1981. *Race and Manifest Destiny: The Origins of American Racial Anglo-Saxonism.* Cambridge, MA.

Hyamson, A. M. 1937. 'Gollancz, Sir Israel (1864–1930)'. *DNB 1922–1930*: 351–2.

Jacks, Graham Vernon 1927. 'Brooke, Stopford Augustus (1832–1916)'. *DNB 1912–1921*: 68–9.

Kelly, Birte 1979. 'The Formative Stages of Modern *Beowulf* Scholarship, Textual, Historical and Literary, Seen in the Work of Scholars of the Earlier Nineteenth Century'. PhD Thesis, University of London.

Ker, Neil 1970. 'A. S. Napier, 1853–1916'. *Philological Essays: Studies in Old and Middle English*

Language and Literature in Honour of Herbert Dean Meritt, pp. 152–81. Ed. James L. Rosier. The Hague and Paris.

Kern, A. A. 1903. 'A Pioneer in Anglo-Saxon'. *Sewanee Review* 11: 337–44.

Keynes, Simon 1992. *Anglo-Saxon Manuscripts and Other Items of Related Interest in the Library of Trinity College, Cambridge. Old English Newsletter*, Subsidia 18. Binghamton, NY.

Kiernan, Kevin S. 1998. 'The Conybeare–Madden Collation of Thorkelin's Beowulf'. *Anglo-Saxon Manuscripts and their Heritage*, pp. 117–36. Eds Phillip Pulsiano and Elaine M. Treharne. Aldershot.

Kliger, Samuel 1946. 'George Perkins Marsh and the Gothic Tradition in America'. *New England Quarterly* 19: 524–31.

Körting, Gustav 1888. *Encyklopaedie und Methodologie der englischen Philologie*. Heilbronn.

Laird, Charlton 1946. 'Etymology, Anglo-Saxon, and Noah Webster'. *American Speech* 21.1: 3–15.

Lee, Sidney 1912. 'Furnivall, Frederick James (1825–1910)'. *DNB Sec. Supp.* 2: 61–6.

Lupton, Joseph Hirst 1901. 'Lumby, Joseph Rawson (1831–1895)'. *DNB* 66: 111–12. Rpt 22: 983–4.

MacMahon, Michael K. C. 1998. 'Henry Sweet (1845–1912)'. Damico 1998: 167–75.

Malone, Kemp 1927. 'Historical Sketch of the English Department of the Johns Hopkins University'. *Johns Hopkins Alumni Magazine* 15: 116–28.

——1933. 'March, Francis Andrew'. *DAB* 12: 268–70. Rpt 6.2.

Marshall, Edward Henry 1890. 'Guest, Edwin (1800–1880)'. *DNB* 23: 318–19. Rpt 8: 761–2.

Mora, María José and María José Gómez-Calderón 1998. 'The Study of Old English in America (1776–1850): National Uses of the Saxon Past'. *Journal of English and Germanic Philology* 97.3: 322–36.

Müller, E. 1858. 'Das Studium angelsächsischer Sprache und Literatur in Deutschland'. *Archiv für das Studium der neueren Sprachen und Literaturen* 24: 249–66.

NCAB: National Cyclopædia of American Biography. 63 vols. Eds George Derby, James Terry White, Raymond D. McGill and H. A. Harvey. 1893–1984. New York.

NCAB 1906. 'Wood, Henry'. 13: 585.

NCAB 1933. 'Johnson, Henry'. 23: 263.

Onions, C. T. 1927. 'Sweet, Henry (1845–1912)'. *DNB 1912–1921*: 519–20.

Palmer, D. J. 1965. *The Rise of English Studies: An Account of the Study of English Language and Literature from its Origins to the Making of the Oxford English School*. London, New York and Toronto.

Pearsall, Derek 1998. 'Frederick James Furnivall (1825–1910)'. Damico 1998: 125–38.

Plummer, Charles 1912. 'Earle, John (1824–1903)'. *DNB Sec. Supp.* 1: 540–1.

Poole, A. L. 1937. 'Stevenson, William Henry (1858–1924)'. *DNB 1922–1930*: 811–12.

Pulsiano, Phillip 1998. 'Benjamin Thorpe (1782–1870)'. Damico 1998: 75–92.

Quirk, Randolph 1961. *The Study of the Mother-tongue. An Inaugural Lecture Delivered at University College London 21 February 1961*. London.

Savage, David J. 1935. 'Old English Scholarship in England 1800–1840'. Diss., Johns Hopkins University.

Shippey, T. A. and Andreas Haarder, eds 1998. *Beowulf: The Critical Heritage*. London and New York.

Sills, Kenneth C. M. 1933. 'Johnson, Henry'. *DAB* 10: 101–2. Rpt 1946. 5.2.

Sisam, Kenneth 1953. *Studies in the History of Old English Literature*. Oxford.

Skovmand, Roar 1983. 'Schrøder, Ludvig Peter, 1836–1908'. *DBL* 13: 218–21.

Stanley, E. G. 1985. 'Unideal Principles of Editing Old English Verse'. *Proceedings of the British Academy* 70 (1985 for 1984): 231–73.

Sutton, C. W. 1890. 'Haigh, Daniel Henry (1819–1879)'. *DNB* 23: 440–1. Rpt 8: 883–4.

Tashjian, Georgian R. 1990. 'Richard Rawlinson and the Anglo-Saxon Professorship at Oxford: The Endowment and its Supervision'. Tashjian et al. 1990a: 83–98.

——, David R. Tashjian and Brian J. Enright, eds 1990a. *Richard Rawlinson: A Tercentenary Memorial*. Kalamazoo.

——, David R. Tashjian and Brian J. Enright 1990b. 'Publications on Anglo-Saxon Studies by Rawlinsonian and Rawlinson–Bosworth Professors.' Tashjian et al. 1990a: 99–111.

Thompson, C. R. 1936. 'The Study of Anglo-Saxon in America'. *English Studies* 18: 241–53.

Times, The (London) 1935. 'Mr. A. J. Wyatt' (obituary). Friday, 26 July. 16.

Toldberg, Helge 1947. 'Grundtvig og de engelske antikvarer'. *Orbis Litterarum* 5: 258–311.

Wawn, Andrew 1995. 'George Stephens, Cheapinghaven, and Old Northern Antiquity'. *Studies in Medievalism* 7: 63–104.

Who Was Who: A Companion to "Who's Who" Containing the Biographies of Those Who Died During the Period 1916–1928 1929. London.

Who Was Who in Literature, 1906–1934 1979. 'Hall, John Richard Clark'. 1: 483–4. Detroit.

Wrenn, C. L. 1946. 'Henry Sweet'. *Transactions of the Philological Society*: 177–201.

Wülker, Richard 1885. *Grundriss zur Geschichte der angelsächsischen Litteratur.* Leipzig.

25

Anglo-Saxon Studies in the Nineteenth Century: Germany, Austria, Switzerland

Hans Sauer

Introduction

The flood of publications on Old English we witness today is not an entirely new phenomenon. Even in nineteenth-century Germany, Old English studies were vigorous, and scholars and philologists published quite a number of books, doctoral dissertations and articles. In the following survey, I can therefore only single out some of the major scholars and some of the groundbreaking work among the contributions of the German-speaking countries (Germany, Austria, Switzerland) to Old English studies in the nineteenth century. I shall first deal with the study of language, and then with the study of literature, in the order poetry, prose, glossaries and glosses, followed by a few remarks on textual criticism, on the relation of pagan and Christian elements, as well as on the relation of historical and mythical elements, and on literary histories, and histories. The study of language and literature can, of course, not always be strictly separated, and a discipline such as metrics embraces both language and literature. Important journals and series of books are also mentioned, as well as the relation of people and institutions; these sections are followed by a brief conclusion and a list of references.

I do not stop at 1899 sharp; some important work published after 1900 and enterprises which began in the nineteenth century but continued into the twentieth are also included. After all, some of the concepts that were first developed in the nineteenth century are still used today and some of the books written or edited in the nineteenth century have not yet been replaced and were re-edited or reprinted in the twentieth. Several of the studies and editions mentioned are not confined to Old English, but treat it in a larger context, in particular in the framework of Indo-European or of Germanic. Further information can be found in the works listed in the references; see especially Wülker (1885) for a bibliographical survey compiled in the late nineteenth century, and McNamee (1968) for the early dissertations.

Language

Following the lead given by the English scholar Sir William Jones (1746–94), the nineteenth century saw the rise of historical-comparative philology. Its main achievement was to show that languages such as English, German, Latin, Greek, Sanskrit and many others ultimately go back to a common mother-tongue, which has been called Indo-European (IE; in German: *Indogermanisch*), and which can be reconstructed at least partly by comparing the languages which developed from it. This discovery also made a better description of Old English possible and helped to place it more precisely among related languages. Together with Old High German, Old Norse, Gothic and others, Old English goes back to Germanic (Gmc), which occupies an intermediate stage between Indo-European on the one hand and Old English, Old High German etc. on the other.

German scholars played a leading role in the development of historical-comparative philology. One of its founders as well as one of its most important proponents was Jakob Grimm (1785–1863). Grimm, for example, first formulated what was later called Grimm's Law in his honour (in German: Erste germanische Lautverschiebung); he coined terms like ablaut (gradation) and umlaut (mutation), strong and weak verbs, strong and weak adjectival declensions, and so forth. Grimm also was the first scholar to distinguish clearly between inflexion (creating different forms of the same word) and word-formation (creating new words). The title of Grimm's monumental *Deutsche Grammatik* in four volumes (1819–37, and later editions) is today perhaps a little misleading, but it reflects Grimm's pan-Germanic ideas: it is not just a grammar of German, but a comparative grammar of all the Germanic languages, including Old English – *deutsch*, for Grimm embraced all the Germanic peoples and languages. It has sections dealing with phonology (in the first edition, the section actually claimed to deal with letters, not with sounds!), inflectional morphology, word-formation (*c*.1000 pages), and syntax. Grimm was very prolific; in addition to the *Deutsche Grammatik* he also also wrote a *Deutsche Mythologie* in three volumes (1835; 4th edn 1875–8; English translation: *Teutonic Mythology*), which, once more, is not just a German mythology, but a Germanic mythology, and *Deutsche Rechtsalterthümer* [*Ancient German Law*] in two volumes (1828; 2nd edn 1854). As all these books show, Grimm was not confined to the study of language. His interests were much broader, and he dealt with the culture and history of the Germanic peoples as well as with their literature. In England, Grimm's ideas were mainly spread by John Mitchell Kemble (1807–57). The literature on Grimm is quite extensive. For details see, for example, Wiley (1971); Antonsen (1990); Stanley (1994: 5ff); Busse (in Fürbeth et al. 1999: 269–76); as well as subsequent sections here.

Jakob's brother, Wilhelm Grimm (1786–1859), was also a scholar, and wrote, for example, *Über deutsche Runen* (1821). Other important scholars of the period were Franz Bopp (1791–1867) and August Schleicher (1821–68). Schleicher first devised the family tree of the IE languages which in a modified form is still used today. With their discoveries and theories, these and other scholars also put the study of Old English on a sounder basis.

The first generation of historical linguists was followed by the Neogrammarians (*Junggrammatiker*; Leipzig school), who tried to achieve even more rigorous scholarly standards; well known is their hypothesis that sound-changes work without exception. This proved not to be the exact case, but it gave rise to important discoveries such as Verner's law. On the Neogrammarians, critics such as Jankowsky (1972) and Einhauser (1989) are useful.

The second half of the nineteenth century also saw the publication of large handbooks that summarized the state of the art and included new research as well. Karl Brugmann (1849–1919) and Berthold Delbrück (1842–1922) published their *Grundriß der vergleichenden Grammatik der indogermanischen Sprachen* in five volumes, some of which were divided into two parts (1897–1900).

Hermann Paul (1846–1921) edited the *Grundriss der germanischen Philologie* (1891–1893; 2nd edn 1901–9). Volume I of Paul's *Grundriss* contains a chapter on the history of the English language by Friedrich Kluge, with the collaboration of Dietrich Behrens and Eugen Einenkel; this was also printed as a separate book in 1899 under the title *Geschichte der englischen Sprache*. Volume II of Paul's *Grundriss* has chapters on Old English literature and on metrics. The section on Old English literature was written by Bernhard ten Brink for the first edition (1893) and by Alois Brandl for the second edition; the section on metrics was written by Eduard Sievers – in a modified form, Sievers' chapter was also published as a separate book (Sievers 1893; see 'Metrics' below).

The first large-scale historical grammars of English were published in the second half of the nineteenth century, too. They usually include sections on sounds (what would be called phonology today), forms (that is, inflexional morphology), word-formation and syntax. Karl Friedrich Koch wrote a *Historische Grammatik der englischen Sprache* in three volumes (1863–9; 2nd edn 1878–91) and Eduard Mätzner compiled an *Englische Grammatik*, also in three volumes and on historical principles (1859–65; 3rd edn 1880–5). They were followed by Max Kaluza's *Historische Grammatik der englischen Sprache*, three volumes (1900–1; 2nd edn 1906), and Karl Luick's *Historische Grammatik der englischen Sprache* (1914–40). The latter deals only with the history of sounds, but treats this topic very thoroughly and is still basic today (cf. Kastovsky and Bauer 1988).

A study of Germanic word-formation, concentrating on suffixation, was written by Friedrich Kluge, *Nominale Stammbildungslehre der altgermanischen Dialekte* (1887; 3rd edn 1926). This is still useful for Old English, too, especially since there is as yet no comprehensive treatment of Old English word-formation (I am working on one).

The most important scholar for Anglo-Saxon studies among the Neogrammarians was Eduard Sievers (1850–1932). He wrote a grammar of Old English which, in the revision by Karl Brunner, is still one of the most comprehensive today, at least as far as phonology and morphology are concerned; there are no chapters on syntax and vocabulary (E. Sievers, *Angelsächsische Grammatik*, 1882; 3rd edn 1898; trans. as *An*

Old English Grammar, A. S. Cook, 1885, 3rd edn 1903; Karl Brunner, *Altenglische Grammatik. Nach der angelsächsischen Grammatik von Eduard Sievers*, 3rd edn 1965, usually cited as Sievers–Brunner.) For Sievers' discovery of the principles of Germanic verse, and for his postulation of an Old Saxon source for the Old English *Genesis B* poem, see 'Metrics' and 'The Junius manuscript' below.

Dictionaries

Dictionaries and glossaries are important tools for the understanding and interpretation of Old English texts as well as for philological and linguistic studies. Among the German contributions to Old English lexicography, the following are important.

After the completion of his collective edition of Old English poetry (see below), Christian W. M. Grein compiled a comprehensive dictionary of the vocabulary of Old English poetry, his *Sprachschatz der angelsächsischen Dichter* (1861–4, originally published as vols 3–4 of his *Bibliothek der angelsächsischen Poesie*); this proved to be so successful that there was a second edition in 1912, edited by J. J. Köhler and F. Holthausen, and a reprint in 1974. Grein usually gives the lemmata in context (with line numbers) and the definitions of the meaning partly in German and partly in Latin.

The only etymological dictionary of Old English was published by Ferdinand Holthausen, *Altenglisches etymologisches Wörterbuch* (1934; 2nd edn with a bibliographical supplement by H. C. Matthes, 1963; repr. 1974). Holthausen's etymological dictionary has its weaknesses; for example, it rarely gives reconstructed earlier forms (e.g. hypothetical Germanic forms), but mostly lists only related forms from other languages or dialects, without indicating the precise nature of the relationship. Nevertheless it has not been replaced so far, because writing an etymological dictionary which meets modern standards is a huge task; the new *Dictionary of Old English* (DOE), which has been in progress since 1986 (planning began in 1969), excludes etymologies on principle. Alfred Bammesberger is working on a new etymological dictionary of Old English.

The oldest and best-known etymological dictionary of German, Friedrich Kluge's (1856–1926) *Etymologisches Wörterbuch der deutschen Sprache*, was first published in 1883; its most recent edition is the twenty-third by Elmar Seebold (1995). Kluge also provides important information on those OE words which have cognates in German.

Metrics

Several scholars wrote studies of Germanic and Old English verse (see Wülker 1885: 108f). A comprehensive history of English metre, beginning with Old English, was published by Jakob Schipper, *Englische Metrik*, three volumes (1881–8). The principles governing Germanic, and thus also Old English, alliterative verse were, however, first clearly stated by Eduard Sievers in a number of articles and then in his *Altgermanische Metrik* (1893). Sievers established the five possible types of the alliterative half-line (A, B, C, D, E) and their sub-types, and dealt with apparent or real exceptions, such as hypermetrical verses (*Schwellverse*). His scheme has been widely accepted as well as refined by later scholars and teachers, such as Max Kaluza in his *Englische Metrik in historischer Entwicklung* (1909) and by A. J. Bliss in the 1950s and 1960s. Even those who disagree with Sievers usually acknowledge the merits of his theory and take him as a point of departure.

One of the early opponents of Sievers' theory was Andreas Heusler (1865–1940). Whereas Sievers and his followers assume that only the number of stressed syllables is fixed in the half-line, while the number of unstressed syllables can vary, thus yielding an irregular duration, Heusler believed in regular, measurable duration and steady rhythms; for example, in his *Über germanischen Versbau* (1894) and in his *Deutsche Versgeschichte mit Einschluß des altenglischen und altnordischen Stabreimverses* (3 vols, 1925–9). On Sievers and Heusler see, for example, the articles in Damico et al. (1998).

Poetry

Comprehensive editions

After a number of readers and partial editions (such as those by Ludwig Chr. Müller 1835; Heinrich Leo 1838; Friedrich Ebeling 1847; Ludwig Ettmüller 1950; Max Rieger 1861), the first collective edition of all the Old English poetic texts known at the time, including the poems in the four manuscripts mentioned below, was printed by Christian W. M. Grein (1825–77) as *Bibliothek der angelsächsischen Poesie* (*Library of Anglo-Saxon Poetry*), two volumes (1857–8; 2nd rev. edn Richard P. Wülker [also spelled Wülcker, 1845–1910] in 3 vols, 1881–98); Grein also translated most of OE poetry into German in his *Dichtungen der Angelsachsen* (1857–9). In his edition, Grein 'established the layout and presentation of Old English editions as they persist to this day' (Doane 1991: 6). As a collection, it was only superseded by the Anglo-Saxon Poetic Records, edited by G. P. Krapp and E. van Kirk Dobbie (1931–53), which now in its turn is in need of revision. Stanley (1994: 23) quotes John Earle's evaluation of Grein in 1892: 'Grein's output was of such eminence as to dwarf all other labours, before or since, upon Anglo-Saxon poetry in general, and upon the *Beowulf* in particular'; see further below.

Beowulf *and the* Beowulf-*manuscript*
(London, British Library, Cotton Vitellius A. xv)

The most successful separate German edition of *Beowulf* was first published in 1863 by Moritz Heyne (1837–1906); it was used, revised and republished for a hundred years and went into seventeen editions: Heyne–Schücking's *Beowulf*, ed. Else von Schaubert, seventeenth edition, three volumes (1958–61; vol. 1: text; vol. 2: commentary; vol. 3: glossary; usually called Heyne–Schücking–Schaubert's *Beowulf*). Another important edition was undertaken by Ferdinand Holthausen (1905–6; 8th edn 1948); this edition is noted for its many emendations. A successor to Holthausen's edition was published by Gerhard Nickel and others in three volumes (1976–82; vol. 1: text and translation; vol. 2: commentary; vol. 3: glossary). The first facsimile of *Beowulf* together with a transliteration was edited by Julius Zupitza (1844–95) for the Early English Text Society (EETS) (o.s. 77, 1882); a second edition, with new photographs, but with Zupitza's transliteration retained, was published as EETS, o.s. 245 (1959). The first detailed description of the *Beowulf*-manuscript was written by Max Förster (1869–1954) in 1919 (*Die Beowulf-Handschrift*). Förster was criticized by Kiernan (1981), but Kiernan's arguments have not met with general approval. An influential critic of *Beowulf* was Karl Müllenhoff (1818–84), who, among other things, regarded *Beowulf* as a kind of allegory of the elements and of the seasons, with, for example, Grendel representing fire and water (cf. Stanley 1994: 16ff, and see below). One of the great *Beowulf* scholars of the twentieth century, Friedrich (Frederick) Klaeber (1863–1954), was born in Germany and died in Germany, but he spent most of his active academic life in the USA. Klaeber's edition of *Beowulf* is still regarded as one of the best. For early critical opinions on *Beowulf*, see Shippey and Haarder (1998).

The Junius manuscript (Oxford, Bodleian Library, Junius 11)

One of the early comprehensive editions of the four (or five) Biblical poems contained in this manuscript is K. W. Bouterwek's *Caedmon's des Angelsachsen biblische Dichtungen* (1847–51). His title still reflects the older belief that the poems were by Cædmon, which is, however, not the case. Bouterwek also did not yet clearly distinguish between the separate poems in Junius 11; he printed them continuously, and without headings. The first and longest poem in the Junius manuscript is the Old English *Genesis*. In a monograph of 1875, *Der Heliand und die angelsächsische Genesis*, Eduard Sievers claimed that a part of it must be a translation or transliteration of an Old Saxon poem on Genesis, namely lines 235–851, now usually called *Genesis B*. Following Sievers' suggestion, these lines were inserted into *Genesis A*, an originally Old English poem which comprises lines 1–234 and 852–2936. This theory was confirmed beyond doubt when in 1894 parts of the Old Saxon poem posited by Sievers were actually discovered by Karl Zangemeister in a Vatican manuscript (Palatinus Latinus 1447). A. N. Doane, the most recent editor of *Genesis B*, calls Sievers' theory (postulated when Sievers was only 25 years old) 'one of the most amazing feats of nineteenth-century Germanic philology' (1991: 7) and 'perhaps the most famous romance of Germanic philology' (1991: ix).

The Vercelli Book (Vercelli, Biblioteca Capitolare, CXVII)

This manuscript containing OE poetry and prose was taken to Vercelli in northern Italy probably in the eleventh or twelfth century. It was seen at Vercelli by Friedrich

Blume (and briefly described in his *Iter Italicum*, 1824, I. 99), and transcribed in 1834 by C. Maier of Tübingen (see Ker 1957: no. 394). Jacob Grimm (see above) published one of the first editions of the poems *Andreas* and *Elene* contained in the Vercelli Book (*Andreas und Elene*, 1840), and he also mentions Cynewulf as the poet of *Elene* (1). A reduced facsimile edition of the verse was published by R. Wülker, *Codex Vercellensis*, 1894. Max Förster then became the principal authority on the Vercelli Book in the early twentieth century (on Förster, see the article in Damico et al. 1998). He printed a facsimile edition in 1913 (*Il Codice Vercellese*), the first complete facsimile of an Anglo-Saxon codex, which was only superseded by Celia Sisam's facsimile in 1976; also in 1913 Förster published a description of the manuscript together with an edition of some of the homilies (*Der Vercelli-Codex CXVII nebst Abdruck einiger altenglischer Homilien der Handschrift*), and twenty years later, he edited homilies I–VIII (*Die Vercelli-Homilien. I. Hälfte*, 1932 – the second part unfortunately never appeared). The work begun by Förster was only completed by P. Szarmach's partial edition of 1981, *Vercelli Homilies IX–XXIII*, and by D. G. Scragg's comprehensive Early English Text Society edition of 1992, *The Vercelli Homilies*.

The Exeter Book (Exeter, Exeter Cathedral 3501)

This is a miscellany of Old English poetry containing many different poems. The first comprehensive study (including an edition) of the group of poems now known as the Old English elegies was done by Ernst Sieper, *Die altenglische Elegie* (1915); an important edition of the Old English riddles was published by Moritz Trautmann in the same year: *Die altenglischen Rätsel* (1915). A complete facsimile of the manuscript together with a thorough introduction was printed in 1933 with the collaboration of Max Förster: *The Exeter Book of Old English Poetry*, with introductory chapters by R. W. Chambers, Max Förster and Robin Flower.

Prose

Alfred (848–99) and his circle

The works of King Alfred the Great were mainly edited by English scholars (on his laws, however, see below), but some of the translations which were certainly or possibly made by his helpers were edited by German-speaking scholars. Particularly important among these is *Bischof Waerferths von Worcester Übersetzung der Dialoge Gregors des Grossen*, ed. Hans Hecht (1900–7), and *König Alfreds Übersetzung von Bedas Kirchengeschichte*, ed. Jacob Schipper (1897–9). Later research established that the OE translation of Bede's *Historia Ecclesiastica* was made not by Alfred, but perhaps by one of his helpers. An important historical study was Reinhold Pauli's *König Alfred und seine Stelle in der Geschichte Englands* (1851); an extensive analysis of King Alfred's syntax was written by Ernst Wülfing, *Die Syntax in den Werken Alfreds des Großen*, two volumes (1894–1901).

Æthelwold (c. 910–84)

Bishop Æthelwold of Winchester, one of the leaders of the monastic revival and Ælfric's teacher, translated the *Rule of St Benedict* into Old English; this text, which still survives in several manuscripts, was first edited by Arnold Schröer, *Die angelsächsischen Prosabearbeitungen der Benediktinerregel* (1885–8; reprinted with a supplement by Helmut Gneuss, 1964).

Ælfric (c. 955–c. 1025)

Ælfric's identity was not clearly recognized at first, and he was sometimes confused with an archbishop of the same name; for example in Wright–Wülcker (see below). The 'fundamental study of Ælfric's life and writing' (Pope 1967: I, 1) was Eduard Dietrich's 'Abt Aelfric: Zur Literaturgeschichte der angelsächsischen Kirche' (*Zeitschrift für historische Theologie*, 25 [1855]: 487–594, 26 [1856]: 163–256). Dietrich established Ælfric's identity and, among other things, first identified some of Ælfric's homilies and tracts that were not included in his *Catholic Homilies* and *Lives of Saints*. Some of those were then published by Bruno Assmann in his *Angelsächsische Homilien und Heiligenleben* (1889), together with several anonymous homilies. Ælfric's Old English and Latin pastoral letters were printed by Bernhard Fehr in his *Die Hirtenbriefe Ælfrics* (1914). Ælfric's Grammar and Glossary had been printed critically on the basis of all extant manuscripts by Julius Zupitza, *Ælfrics Grammatik und Glossar* (1880). All of these three editions (Assmann 1889; Fehr 1914; Zupitza 1880) were reprinted with additional material in the 1960s (Assmann in 1964 and Fehr in 1966, both with supplements by Peter Clemoes, and Zupitza in 1966 with a supplement by Helmut Gneuss), and neither Fehr nor Zupitza has been superseded by new editions as yet. The pioneering study of Ælfric's Latin sources for his *Catholic Homilies* was Max Förster's dissertation *Über die Quellen von Aelfric's Homiliae Catholicae* (1892) and its sequel, 'Über die Quellen von Ælfrics exegetischen *Homiliae Catholicae*', *Anglia* 16 (1894), 1–61. Once more, Förster's study has not really been superseded – what later research revealed is that Ælfric probably did not use a different manuscript for each source, but for a large part the Latin homiliary by Paulus Diaconus, where most of his sources had already been collected.

Wulfstan (c. 950–1023)

The canon of the writings of Archbishop Wulfstan, Ælfric's contemporary, was established only gradually. Arthur S. Napier, an Englishman who studied in Germany and later became professor in Oxford, wrote his dissertation *Über die Werke des altenglischen Erzbischofs Wulfstan* (1882) in German, and he also published his edition *Wulfstan: Sammlung der ihm zugeschriebenen Homilien . . .* (1883) in Germany (reprinted with a supplement by Klaus Ostheeren, 1967). Apart from Wulfstan's genuine homilies, this edition contains also a number of homilies wrongly attributed to Wulfstan, but it is still valuable precisely because of this, since it remains the only edition of some of them. A decisive advance in separating Wulfstan's genuine homilies from spurious ones was made by Karl Jost in a number of articles and then in his *Wulfstanstudien* (1950).

Anonymous Homilies

On Max Förster and his work on the Vercelli Homilies, see above.

Laws

A collective edition of the Old English laws was published by Reinhold Schmid, *Die Gesetze der Angelsachsen* (1832; 2nd edn 1858). His work was superseded by the monumental edition of Felix Liebermann, *Die Gesetze der Angelsachsen*, three volumes (1903–16; repr. 1960). Vol. 1 contains the texts (often in parallel columns to show the different versions in several manuscripts) together with a German translation; vol. 2 a glossary of Old English words as well as of legal terms; and vol. 3 a commentary. Scholarly advances have been made in a number of details since Liebermann. For example, some of the laws of Æthelred and of Cnut have been identified as the work of Archbishop Wulfstan; see above. Furthermore, Liebermann prints a selection of excommunication formulae, which belong to the rites of the church rather than to secular legislation (see Sauer 1996), but they also show the close cooperation between church and state. Liebermann's edition remains unsurpassed as a whole, however.

Glossaries and Glosses

The Épinal Glossary (Épinal, Bibliothèque Municipale 72(2), written around 700) is one of the earliest records of the English language, and certainly the longest of the early witnesses. It was discovered in the library in Épinal in 1835 by Franz Joseph Mone (1796–1871); Mone also printed a number of glossaries and glosses (see Wülker 1885: 77f). A facsimile of Épinal was published by Otto Schlutter in 1912; Schlutter furthermore wrote a number of articles on OE glosses and glossaries.

A substantial number of the Old English glossaries were printed in collective volumes. Richard Wülker revised T. Wright's edition of Old and Middle English glossaries: T. Wright, *Anglo-Saxon and Old English Vocabularies*, second edition by R. Wülker, two volumes (1884; repr. 1968, usually cited as Wright–Wülker). Old English here, as often in the nineteenth century, refers to what is now called Middle English. Although Wright–Wülker is in need of revision, it is still a handy collection. The large collection by Elias Steinmeyer and Eduard Sievers, *Die althochdeutschen Glossen*, five volumes (1879–1922), contains not only Old High German glosses and glossaries, but also Old English ones (cf. Cameron 1973: secn D).

Among the Latin texts with OE glosses, the Psalter plays a prominent role; approximately thirteen Psalter manuscripts with OE glosses still survive. Some of these were printed by German scholars around the turn of the century, such as *Der altenglische Regius-Psalter*, ed. Fritz Roeder (1904), *Der Cambridger Psalter*, ed. Karl Wildhagen (1910; repr. 1964), and others; see Cameron (1973: secn C 7).

Critical Concerns

Textual criticism

One of the concerns of philology was, and still is, the presentation of a correct text. This involves, among other things, the emendation of scribal mistakes or of mechanical loss of text in the manuscripts, such as the *Beowulf*-manuscript. A more ambitious aim is the restoration of the original text (assuming that many manuscripts are just later copies of earlier but lost originals), but this is often impossible to achieve, and even its theoretical justification is doubted by some scholars. Textual criticism is, however, not confined to the correction of mistakes and the filling in of gaps. Since Old English scribes had different practices from what we are accustomed to today, editors of poems also have to decide about line division, and all editors have to decide about word-division, punctuation, capitalization (which is connected with the identification of proper names) and so forth; this involves knowledge of Old English metrics, syntax, morphology, word-formation, historical background and so on.

Among the nineteenth-century German philologists, Grein was the most important editor as far as Old English poetry is concerned. Kelly (1983: 248) evaluates his work with respect to *Beowulf*:

> Grein . . . sums up much of the achievement of early textual scholarship by including most of the best emendations proposed by his predecessors, always with due acknowledgment, and by adding many important readings of his own. In presentation and other aspects of editing, such as word and line division and punctuation, his was the first modern edition of *Beowulf*.

The discussion about editorial policies continues to this day (see, for example, Scragg and Szarmach 1994).

A much more drastic approach, which tried to get beyond the extant written versions, was the attempt to distinguish several original parts in some poems, especially in *Beowulf*. This took up the *Liedertheorie*, first developed by Karl Lachmann, which claimed that longer poems, especially epics, were made up of shorter poems of different origins. Karl Müllenhoff, *Die innere Geschichte des Beowulf* (1869), for example, applied this theory to *Beowulf*; he believed that *Beowulf* was made up of at least six originally distinct lays, composed by different poets, which in his opinion could still be clearly recognized. This type of view is no longer accepted today; it has, however, affinities to the dissection of *Beowulf* and other poems into Christian and pagan elements, to be discussed in the next section.

Pagan and Christian elements

Another concern of nineteenth-century philology, which also continued into the twentieth century, is the search for the remains of poetry in the ancient Germanic tradition and of features of Anglo-Saxon paganism which lie half-buried beneath the later Christian layer. This preoccupation, too, started with Jakob Grimm, who expressed his ideas, for example, in the introduction to his 1840 edition of *Andreas* and *Elene*, two obviously Christian poems. For Grimm, Anglo-Saxon poetry was rooted in paganism, but then the pagan element died due to the influence of Christianity (e.g. 1840: lviii). For a long time, scholars were often biased in favour of the supposedly old, mythical, pagan Germanic features, dating back to an indefinite past, and many regarded the Christian elements as later, monkish additions and even corruptions, which had weakened and eventually destroyed the Germanic spirit and its poetry. A practical consequence of this attitude was that poems like *Beowulf* or the elegies *The Wanderer* and *The Seafarer* were often dissected into an original part or original parts, which allegedly represented the pagan Germanic core, and later Christian additions and interpolations.

This view, which was attacked, for example, by F. Klaeber, is no longer accepted today. Most scholars nowadays assume that the Christian elements are integral parts of the poems; they point to the fact that most of the poetry as we have it is preserved in manuscripts written around 1000, probably by monks or clerics, and that much of the poetry, such as *Beowulf* and the elegies, was probably also composed by Christian poets, who, however, looked back at their past and who also used the inherited poetic conventions, even introducing them into Biblical poetry and saints' lives. For details, see Stanley (1975); Busse in Fürbeth et al. (1999: 272ff).

It cannot, of course, be denied that some Old English texts actually contain pagan elements. This is in particular true of several of the metrical charms and of the prose charms, but often the relation between pagan and Christian elements in the charms is quite complex (Cameron 1973: nos. A 43 & B 23; see, for example, Storms 1948).

Pagan reminiscences were detected not only in entire texts, but even in single words. An extensive discussion evolved, for example, about the word *wyrd* 'fate, fortune, destiny, providence etc.', which was often interpreted as a pagan term, but most scholars are much more cautious about its meaning today and also admit a Christian interpretation (see, for example, Weber 1969; Stanley 1975).

Historical and mythical elements

A great deal of research, much of it speculative, was devoted to the historical and especially to the mythical elements in Germanic, including Old English, literature, and in *Beowulf* in particular. Jacob Grimm's *Deutsche Mythologie* (1835) was mentioned above; another early study was Franz Joseph Mone, *Untersuchungen zur Geschichte der teutschen Heldensage* (1836), which was intended to complement Wilhelm Grimm's *Die deutsche Heldensage* (1829). A little later followed Karl Simrock's successful *Handbuch der deutschen Mythologie* (1853, 1878).

Literary Histories and Histories

The first German literary history that included a chapter on Old English (Anglo-Saxon) literature was Ludwig Ettmüller's *Handbuch der deutschen Literaturgeschichte* (1847). A successful survey of medieval English literature, including the Old English period, was then written by Bernhard ten Brink, *Geschichte der englischen Literatur* (1877, 1899, 1893); ten Brink also contributed the chapter on Old English literature to the first edition of Paul's *Grundriss* (see above). A kind of literary history combined with a thorough bibliographical survey and review of research is Wülker (1885), which is therefore also still a basic source of information for the German contribution to Old English studies in the nineteenth century (but, of course, not confined to German scholarship).

An important history of the Anglo-Saxon period was J. M. Lappenberg, *Geschichte von England*, vol. 1: *Angelsächsische Zeit* (1834). This was translated into English by Benjamin Thorpe, *History of England under the Anglo-Saxon Kings*, two volumes (1845).

New literary histories were published in the 1920s by Andreas Heusler and Levin L. Schücking within Oskar Walzel's large collection *Handbuch der Literaturwissenschaft*. The division of labour between the two authors mirrors the distinction between Old English literature which counts as 'Germanic' and Old English literature which counts as 'Christian'. Andreas Heusler, in his volume *Die altgermanische Dichtung* (1926), describes Old English poetry in the context of Old German and Old Norse literature, and he deals mainly with the secular poetry. His principal subdivision within this area is into 'lower' genres (such as charms, didactic verse [*Spruchdichtung*], mnemonic and catalogue verse [*Merkdichtung*] etc.) and 'higher' genres (for example, *Preislied*, elegies, narrative-heroic poetry etc.). Hans Hecht and Levin L. Schücking collaborated on the volume *Die englische Literatur im Mittelalter* (1927), where Schücking wrote the section on Old English and early Middle English literature, and Hecht wrote the section on later Middle English literature. In his section on Old English literature, Schücking deals mainly with the religious poetry.

Journals and Series of Books

A number of German journals devoted to modern languages in general or to English philology in particular were founded in the nineteenth century; they often contained articles devoted to Old English and editions of Old English texts. Some of the leading journals, as far as Old English is concerned, were: *Archiv für das Studium der neueren Sprachen und Literaturen*, founded by Ludwig Herrig (vol. 1: 1845; still in progress [vol. 238: 2001]); *Anglia. Zeitschrift für englische Philologie*, founded by R. P. Wülker and Moritz Trautmann (vol. 1: 1878; also still in progress [vol. 119: 2001]); *Englische Studien*, founded by Eugen Kölbing (vol. 1: 1877; vol. 76: 1944).

Among the series of editions and monographs, the Bibliothek der angelsächsischen Prosa (BASP, Library of Anglo-Saxon Prose) should be mentioned first. It was founded by C. W. M. Grein as a supplement to his series Bibliothek der angelsächsischen Poesie; later, R. Wülker acted as general editor. Some of the editions of Old English prose texts and glosses mentioned above (Schröer 1885–8; Assmann 1889; Schipper 1897–9; Hecht 1900–7; Wildhagen 1910; Fehr 1914; Förster 1932) were published in this series. Altogether, this series comprises thirteen volumes, the first of which appeared in 1872 and the last in 1932 (Josef Raith's edition of the *Old English Penitential of Pseudo-Ecgbert* [Halitgar]). Many of these editions have not yet been superseded, and a number of them were reprinted in the 1960s, partly with new introductions or supplements.

Another important series was and still is the Sammlung kurzer Grammatiken germanischer Dialekte (Collection of Short Grammars of Germanic Dialects). E. Sievers' Old English grammar was published there, as well as Sievers' study of Germanic metrics, and F. Kluge's study of Germanic word-formation. 'Short' is a relative term here: Sievers' *Grammar* in the revision by Brunner comprises more than 400 pages.

Other series of monographs include the Studien zur Englischen Philologie (StEPh) and the Anglistische Forschungen (AF). In the StEPh, ninety-six volumes were published between 1897 and 1939. The AF began in 1901; they are also still in progress: vol. 287 was published in 2001. In both series, many volumes were devoted to Old English topics and texts and in the AF, many still are.

People and Institutions

In the first half of the nineteenth century, English did not yet exist as a university subject. It was dealt with partly in the context of German or Germanic philology and partly in the context of modern languages (see J. R. Hall's chapter in this book; furthermore, Finkenstaedt 1983; Haenicke and Finkenstaedt 1992; Mayer and Finkenstaedt 1992); that is, Old English scholars were often professors of Germanic, or they were simultaneously professors of French (or Romance languages) and English. Professors of Germanic or German philology who also wrote on Old English were, for example, Jakob Grimm (who thought that Old English literature was part of the heritage of German literature; see his preface to *Andreas und Elene*), Ludwig Ettmüller, Moritz Heyne (the editor of *Beowulf*), Friedrich Kluge, Hermann Paul and Eduard Sievers. Friedrich Blume, who discovered the Vercelli Book, was a professor of law.

The further rise of the study of Old English language and literature and of the history of English was connected with the establishment of English as a university subject. The first professorships and especially the first chairs (full professorships) specifically for English philology were established in German universities in the

1870s, and many of them were occupied by eminent Old English scholars, most of whom have been mentioned in the preceding sections (cf. Gneuss 1990: 54; see further the somewhat divergent table in Finkenstaedt 1983: 214f, and, in more detail, Haenicke 1979). At many of these universities, quite a number of doctoral dissertations dealing with Old English were produced. Some of the leading English and American scholars of Old English had also studied in Germany; for example, John M. Kemble, Henry Sweet, Arthur S. Napier and A. S. Cook.

But not all Old English scholars were university professors. C. W. M. Grein, the leading editor of Old English poetry in his time, was mainly a librarian; much to his regret, he was never able to go to England and see the manuscripts. Carl Friedrich Koch and Eduard Mätzner, the authors of voluminous historical grammars, were schoolmasters, and Felix Liebermann, the leading authority on the Anglo-Saxon laws, was a private scholar who got an honorary professor's title in addition to many other honours (he was the brother of the painter Max Liebermann). Otto Schlutter also seems to have been a private scholar.

Women played only a minor role among the Old English scholars. The only woman mentioned here, Else von Schaubert (1886–1977), was also the first woman who completed an habilitation (a second dissertation as a prerequisite for becoming a professor) in English philology (1922 in Breslau); she taught at the university, but in spite of her qualification never got tenure as a professor.

Conclusion

On the whole, the contribution of German scholars and philologists to Old English studies was certainly very important and laid the foundations for much on which we still rely today in the areas of Old English language and literature, including editions of texts. Among the scholars that can be singled out, in approximate chronological order, are: Jacob Grimm as one of the founding fathers of historical-comparative philology; Christian W. M. Grein as the leading editor and commentator of Old English poetry; Eduard Sievers as the discoverer of the principles governing Germanic verse as well as of the source of the Old English *Genesis B*, and as a writer of an Old English grammar; Richard Wülker as an editor of texts as well as of a series of books and as an historian of Old English studies; Julius Zupitza as an editor of texts and facsimiles; and, with much of his activity extending into the twentieth century, Max Förster as an identifier of sources, a describer of manuscripts, and also as a critical editor of texts.

Acknowledgements

For helpful advice, I am indebted to Helmut Gneuss and Thomas Finkenstaedt.

References

Primary sources

Assmann, Bruno, ed. 1889. *Angelsächsische Homilien und Heiligenleben*. Bibliothek der angelsächsischen Prosa 3. Cassel. Repr. 1964.

Behrens, Dietrich and Eugen Einenkel. 1889. *Geschichte der englischen Sprache*. Strassburg.

Bouterwerk, K. W., ed. 1847–50. *Cædmon's des Angelsachsen biblische Dichtungen*. Elberfeld.

Brandl, Alois 1908. *Geschichte der altenglischen Literatur*. Strassburg.

Brink, Bernhard ten 1877, 1893. *Geschichte der englischen Literatur*. 2 vols. Strassburg (vol. 2 by Brandl).

Brugmann, Karl and Berhold Delbrück. 1897–1900. *Grundriss der vergleichenden Grammatik der indogermanischen Sprachen*. 5 vols. Strassburg.

Brunner, Karl 1965. *Altenglische Grammatik. Nach der angelsächsischen Grammatik con Eduard Sievers*. 3rd edn. Tübingen.

Chambers, R. W., Max Förster and Robin Flower, eds 1933. *The Exeter Book of Old English Poetry*. London.

Dietrich, Eduard 1855–6. 'Abt, Aelfric: Zur Literaturgeschichte der angelsächsischen Kirche'. *Zeitschrift für historische Theologie* 25 (1855): 487–594; 26 (1856): 163–256.

Doane, A. N., ed. 1991. *The Saxon Genesis: An Edition of the West Saxon Genesis B and the Old Saxon Vatican Genesis*. Madison, WI.

Ettmüller, Ludwig 1847. *Handbuch der deutschen Litteraturgeschichte*. Leipzig.

Fehr, Bernhard, ed. 1914. *Die Hirtenbriefe Aelfrics in altenglischen und lateinischer Fassung*. Hamburg. Repr. Darmstadt 1966.

Förster, Max 1892. *Über die Quellen von Aelfrics Homiliae Catholicae*. Berlin.

——1894. 'Über die Quellen von Aelfrics exegetischen *Homiliae Catholicae*'. *Anglia* 16: 1–61.

——1913a. *Il Codice Vercellese*. Rome.

——1913b. *Der Vercelli-Codex CXVII nebst Abdruck einiger altenglischer Homilien der Handschrift*. Hallen an der Saale.

——1919. *Die Beowulf-Handschrift*. Munich.

——, ed. 1932. *Die Vercelli-Homilien zum ersten Male*. Hamburg. Repr. Darmstadt 1964.

——1943. *Der Flussname Themse und Sippe*. Studien zur Anglisierung Keltischer Eigennamen und Lautchronologie der Altbritschen. Munich.

Grein, Christian W. M. 1857–8. *Bibliothek der angelsächsischen Poesie*. 2 vols. 2nd rev. edn Richard Wülker. 3 vols.

——1857–9. *Dichtungen der Angelsachsen*. Göttingen.

——1861–4. *Sprachschatz der angelsächsischen Dichter*. Cassel, Göttingen, 2nd edn Heildelberg 1912, eds J. J. Köhler and F. Holthausen. Repr. Heidelberg 1974.

Grimm, Jacob 1819–37. *Deutsche Grammatik*. 4 vols. Göttingen.

——1828. *Deutsche Rechtsalterthumer*. Göttingen. 2nd edn 1854.

——1835. *Deutsche Mythologie*. 3 vols. Berlin. 4th edn 1875–8.

——, ed. 1840. *Andreas und Elene*. Cassel.

Grimm, Wilhelm 1821. *Über deutsche Runen*. Göttingen.

Hecht, Hans 1990–7. *Bischof Waerferths von Worcester Übersetzung der Dialoge Gregors des Grossen*. Leipzig.

——and Levin L. Schücking 1927. *Die englische Literatur im Mittelalter*. Wildpark-Potsdam.

Heusler, Andreas 1894. *Über germanischen Versbau*. Berlin.

——1925–9. *Deutsche Versgeschichte mit Einschluss des altenglischen und altnordischen Stabreimverses*. 3 vols. Berlin.

——1926. *Die altgermanische Dichtung*. Berlin.

Heyne, Moritz, ed. 1863. *Beowulf: angelsächsisches Heidengedicht*. Paderborn.

Holthausen, Ferdinand, ed. 1905–6. *Beowulf, nebst dem Finnsburg-bruchstück*. Heidelberg and New York.

——1934. *Altenglisches etymologisches Wörterbuch*. Heidelberg. 2nd edn with bibliographical suppl. by H. C. Matthes, 1963. Repr. Heidelberg 1974.

Jost, Karl 1950. *Wulfstanstudien*. Bern.

Kaluza, Max 1990–1. *Historische Grammatik der englischen Sprache*. 3 vols. Berlin. 2nd edn 1906.

——1909. *Englische Metrik in historischer Entwicklung*. Berlin.

Kluge, Friedrich 1883. *Etymologisches Wörterbuch der deutschen Sprache*. Strassburg.

——1887. *Nominale Stammbildungslehre der altgermanischen Dialekte*. Halle. 3rd edn 1926.

Kock, Karl F. 1863–9. *Historische Grammatik der englischen Sprache*. 3 vols. 2nd edn 1878–91.

Lappenberg, J. M. 1834. *Geschichte von England*, vol. 1: *Angelsächsische Zeit*. Göttingen.

Luik, Karl 1914–40. *Historische Grammatik der englischen Sprache*. Leipzig.

Mätzner, Eduard 1859–65. *Englische Grammatik*. 3 vols.

Mone, Franz Joseph 1836. *Untersuchungen zur Geschichte der deutschen Heldensage*. Göttingen.

Müllenhoff, Karl 1869. *Die innere Geschichte des Beowulf*.

Napier, Arthur S. 1882. *Über die Werke des altenglischen Erzbischofs Wulfstan*. Berlin.

——, ed. 1883. *Wulfstan: Sammulung der ihm zugeschrieben Homilien*. Berlin. Repr. with suppl. by Klaus Ostheeren 1967.

Paul, Hermann 1891–3. *Grundriss der germanischen Philologie*.

Pauli, Reinhold 1851. *König Alfred und seine Stelle in der Geschichte Englands*. Göttingen.

Pope, John C., ed. 1967. *Homilies of Ælfric. A Supplementary Collection*. Early English Text Society, o.s. 259. London.

Roeder, Frit, 1904. *Der altenglische Regius-Psalter*.

Schipper, Jacob 1881–8. *Englische Metrik*. 3 vols. Vienna and Leipzig.

——1887–9. *König Alfreds Übersetzung von Bedas Kirchengeschichte*. Cassel. Schröer, Arnold, ed. 1885–8. *Die angelsächsischen Prosabearbeitungen der Benediktinerregel*. Cassel. Repr. with suppl. by Helmut Gneuss 1964.

——, ed. 1888. *Die Winteney-Version der Regula S. Benedicti*. Cassel. Repr. with suppl. by Mechthild Gretsch 1978.

Sieper, Ernst, ed. 1915. *Die altenglische Elegie*. Strassburg.

Sievers, Eduard 1882a. *Angelsächsische Grammatik*. 3rd edn 1898 [transl. A. S. Cook, *Old English Grammar*, 1885; 3rd edn 1903].

——1882b. *Der Heliand und die angelsächsische Genesis*.

——1893. *Altgermanische Metrik*. Halle.

Simrock, Karl 1853. *Handbuch der deutschen Mythologie*. 5th edn 1878.

Steinmeyer, Elias and Eduard Sievers, eds 1879–1922. *Die althochdeutschen Glossen*.

Thorpe, Benjamin, trans. *History of England under the Anglo-Saxon Kings*. London.

Trautmann, Moritz, ed. 1915. *Die altenglischen Rätsel*. Heidelberg.

Wildhagen, Karl, ed. 1910. *Der Cambridger Psalter*. Halle.

Wright, T., ed. 1884. *Anglo-Saxon and Old English Vocabularies*. London. 2nd rev. edn Richard Wülker, 1884. Repr. 1968.

Wülfing, Ernst 1894–1901. *Die Syntax in den Werken Alfreds des Grossen*. 2 vols.

Wülker, Richard 1885. *Grundriss zur Geschichte der angelsächsischen Literatur*. Leipzig.

——1894. *Codex Vercellensis*. Halle.

Zupitza, Julius, ed. 1880. *Aelfrics Grammatik und Glossar*. Cassel.

Secondary sources

Antonsen, Elmer H., ed. 1990, *The Grimm Brothers and the Germanic Past*. Amsterdam.

Cameron, Angus, 1973. 'A List of Old English Texts'. *A Plan for the Dictionary of Old English*, pp. 25–36. Eds Roberta Frank and Angus Cameron. Toronto.

Damico, Helen, with Donald Fennema and Karmen Lenz, eds. 1998. *Medieval Scholarship: Biographical Studies on the Formation of a Discipline. Vol. 2: Literature and Philology*. New York.

Einhauser, Eveline 1989. *Die Junggrammatiker*. Trier.

Finkenstaedt, Thomas 1983. *Kleine Geschichte der Anglistik in Deutschland*. Darmstadt.

Fürbeth, Frank, et al., eds 1999. *Zur Geschichte und Problematik der Nationalphilologien in Europa*. Tübingen.

Gneuss, Helmut 1990. *Die Wissenschaft von der englischen Sprache: Ihre Entwicklung bis zum Ausgang des 19. Jahrhunderts*. Munich. English version Helmut Gneuss 1996. *English Language Scholarship: A Survey and Bibliography from the Beginnings to the End of the Nineteenth Century*. Binghamton, NY.

Haenicke, Gunta 1979. *Zur Geschichte der Anglistik an deutschsprachigen Universitäten 1850–1925*. Augsburger I-&I-Schriften 8. Augsburg.

Haenicke, Gunta and Thomas Finkenstaedt 1992. *Anglistenlexikon 1825–1990: Biographische und bibliographische Angaben zu 318 Anglisten*. Augsburger I-&I-Schriften 64. Augsburg.

Jankowsky, Kurt R. 1972. *The Neogrammarians*. The Hague.

Kastovsky, Dieter and Gero Bauer, eds 1988. *Luick Revisited*. Tübingen.

Kelly, Birte 1983. 'The Formative Stages of *Beowulf* Textual Scholarship'. Part I: *Anglo-Saxon England* 11: 247–74; Part II: *Anglo-Saxon England* 12: 239–75.

Ker, N. R. 1957. *Catalogue of Manuscripts Containing Anglo-Saxon*. Oxford. Repr. with suppl. 1990.

Kiernan, Kevin S. 1981. *Beowulf and the Beowulf Manuscript*. Ann Arbor. 2nd edn 1996.

Mayer, Alois and Thomas Finkenstaedt 1992. *Anglistenregister 1825–1990*. Augsburg.

McNamee, Lawrence 1968. *Dissertations in English and American Literature*. New York.

Sauer, Hans 1996. 'Die Exkommunicationsriten aus Wulfstans Handbuch and Liebermanns Gesetze'. *Bright is the Ring of Words: Festschrift für Horst Weinstock, zum 65. Geburtstag*. Eds C. Pollner et al. Bonn.

Scragg, D. G. and Paul E. Szarmach, eds 1994. *The Editing of Old English*. Cambridge.

Shippey, T. A. and Andreas Haarder, eds 1998. *Beowulf: The Critical Heritage*. London and New York.

Stanley, Eric G. 1975. *The Search for Anglo-Saxon Paganism*. Cambridge.

——1994. *In the Foreground: Beowulf*. Cambridge.

Storms, Godefrid 1948. *Anglo-Saxon Magic*. Den Haag.

Weber, Gerd Wolfgang 1969. *Wyrd: Studien zum Schicksalsbegriff der altenglischen und altnordischen Literatur*. Bad Homburg.

Wülker, Richard 1885. *Grundriss zur Geschichte der angelsächsischen Litteratur*. Leipzig.

26

By the Numbers: Anglo-Saxon Scholarship at the Century's End

Allen Frantzen

Tradition takes what has come down to us and delivers it over to self-evidence; it blocks our access to those primordial 'sources' from which the categories and concepts handed down to us have been in part quite genuinely drawn. Indeed it makes us forget that they have had such an origin, and makes us suppose that the necessity of going back to these sources is something which we need not even understand.

Martin Heidegger, 'The Task of Destroying the History of Ontology'

Most reflections on Anglo-Saxon scholarship published in the twentieth century were characterized by optimism, and justly so: for most of the century Anglo-Saxon studies was an expanding field. To judge from the heft of the *Old English Newsletter* and the annual programme of the International Medieval Congress at Western Michigan University, one might think that the subject still thrives. But at the century's end the amount of scholarship Anglo-Saxonists produce can no longer be read as a sign of institutional health. Anglo-Saxon studies are pursued more widely and vigorously than ever, but the optimism has evaporated. Three decades of steadily declining academic positions in Old English ensure that fewer Anglo-Saxonists will hold the secure academic positions that, for most of the twentieth century, supported careers in the field. One hundred years ago research universities were just beginning to incorporate English studies into the curriculum. Anglocentric thinking drove academic life, and Anglo-Saxon studies formed the first stage, if not the very foundation, of the English curriculum. But Anglo-Saxon studies no longer play a major role in English education. As if to cement this fact, the new *Cambridge History of Medieval Literature* appeared in 1999. It contains thirty-one essays in over 1,000 pages but only one entry, 'Old English and its Afterlife', comments on the pre-Conquest period, dealing chiefly with the survival of Old English poetry. As this highly influential volume presents it, Old English language and literature have been effectively eliminated from 'the history of medieval English literature' (Wallace 1999).

Anglo-Saxon studies at the end of the twentieth century manifested two diverging trends: a shrinking pedagogical base (few departments require or even offer work in

Anglo-Saxon; Frantzen 1992; compare Bessinger 1966) and a rapidly expanding bibliography. A single explanation suffices for these contradictory data. In order to justify
its existence, the discipline of Anglo-Saxon studies is being forced to expand into areas
beyond the philological and literary critical work that the discipline traditionally
comprised. This dispersal finds Anglo-Saxonists working in (to name a few outside
fields) linguistics; women's studies; gay, lesbian and queer studies; postcolonial
studies; and hypermedia and other technologies. When even 'medieval' is defined, as
it is by Wallace (1999), as ranging from the Norman Conquest to 1547(!), their presence in non-medieval fields forces Anglo-Saxonists to articulate what it is that they
do. Clarity about the ends of Anglo-Saxon studies was once routine, as I showed in
Desire for Origins (1990; see also Frantzen and Venegoni 1986). But such clarity, formerly part of a political agenda that scholars find objectionable, and now intimately
associated with theoretical explicitness that still alienates many, is not characteristic
of current practices of Anglo-Saxon studies. This is especially true of Anglo-Saxon
studies as constituted by the sources projects (SASLC, FONTES), the largest institutional endeavours in the field apart from the *Dictionary of Old English* (itself a model
of methodological rigour). The survival of their projects will continue to require
Anglo-Saxonists to address the ideological and theoretical issues that link them to
other disciplines.

My objective is to examine the shifting ideologies of Anglo-Saxon studies by historicizing the discipline in terms of its productivity, as measured in books and articles about Old English topics. In this chapter, I relate twentieth-century Anglo-Saxon
scholarship to work in Old and Middle English in the previous century, and then
examine some publications that help us measure how, in twentieth-century England
and America, Anglo-Saxon scholarship fared both on its own and in the wider realm
of medieval studies.

The Chivalric Contexts of Nineteenth-century Anglo-Saxonism

Anglo-Saxon studies proliferated in Germany in the nineteenth century, as Hans Sauer
shows in his chapter in this book. But in England the professional study of Old
English emerged in the shadow of Middle English studies, a subject whose early phases
were dominated by romance. Middle English itself was liberated from the classification of 'ancient' only in the mid-nineteenth century. Frederick Madden published the
first edition of *Sir Gawain and the Green Knight* in 1839 in a volume called *Syr Gawayne:
A Collection of Ancient Romance Poems by Scottish and English Authors*. Madden's work
seems to be little more than an archaizing curiosity, not a proper originary point for
medieval studies. Writing for the Bannatyne Club of Edinburgh, Madden (who duti-
fully claimed the poem's author was Scots) presented the poem in a theme-based collection about Gawain, a supposedly historical figure of national significance described
by the editor as 'our hero'. Yet, as David Matthews (1999) has shown, the edition
reveals a great deal about Madden's expectations of his readers and his vision of the

cultural significance of this and other poems. Madden's text, marvellously uncompromising in its conservatism, made no concessions to the Club's audience. There was no glossary or other critical apparatus; abbreviations were not expanded, compounding the difficulties of the poem's dialect. This conservatism had its advantages, lost though they have been on subsequent editors of the poem. The so-called 'bob', the first of five short rhymed lines ending each stanza, was printed where the manuscript puts it, at the side of the line before it (Tolkien and Gordon 1967: 152). No other edition observes this placement of the 'bob', which, when read in its original position, subtly alters the implications of almost every stanza of the poem. (A forthcoming electronic edition of the poem will demonstrate the importance of this remarkable fact; see Arthur 1998.)

Madden collected stories about Gawain and represented them in what Matthews calls a 'type facsimile' of the manuscript. Madden sought to reproduce a manuscript as an icon – old, authentic, part of the past (Edwards 1987: 41–2; Matthews 1999: 128). When *Sir Gawain* was re-edited by Richard Morris for the Early English Text Society in 1864, the poem looked very different. Glosses appeared on the page, the text was emended, and the 'bob' was put in the place it has occupied since (see Matthews 1999: 129 for a facsimile of the opening page). Morris, like modern editors, sought to frame the text in apparatus that modernized it. Editors after Madden added and expanded that apparatus, and, using their new philological training, explored the relationship between texts, sources and analogues. Morris' edition had introduced the poem to the future of editing.

The Early English Text Society (EETS) was part of a mid-nineteenth-century general education movement propelled by such reforming figures as Frederick Furnivall, who founded EETS, the Chaucer Society, the Ballad Society, the New Shakespeare Society, the Wyclif Society, the Browning Society and the Shelley Society (Murray 1977: 89). EETS was an alternative to the gentlemen's clubs that had sponsored earlier editions. Matthews has compared the usefulness of *Sir Gawain* and other Middle English texts to these two groups, arguing that gentlemen-antiquarians used medieval texts to mark and preserve class differences while liberals used the texts to try to reconcile class differences (1999: 115–16). Class standing was certainly on Madden's mind. One of a number of ambitious young scholars who benefited from the patronage of wealthy clubs formed to memorialize English history and culture, he was knighted in 1833. Matthews argues that Madden sought to rehabilitate the dubious reputation Gawain had acquired in the works of Malory and to present him in the French tradition instead, as a hero and – ironically – a model English gentleman (Matthews 1999: 132–3). Chivalry was not merely an idealized representation of the past, then, but a code of conduct that spoke to the needs of the modern world.

This idea seems implicit in the selection of texts that appeared first in the EETS series. According to Richard Morris' account in the first volume, EETS was formed 'with the object of publishing a series of Early English Texts – especially those related to KING ARTHUR' (1864b: 1). Morris' edition of *Sir Gawayne and the Green Knight* was published in 1864. Seven of the first ten volumes were romances; the third text in the extra series was *Caxton's Book of Curtesye* (Furnival 1868). The choice of subject matter was determined by a long-standing belief in the broad appeal, supposed historical realism and cultural value of romances: stories about nobles and gentles were desirable for everybody and were especially suitable for 'gentling' the lower classes.

EETS editions were intended to supply the texts needed for the *New English Dictionary* (later the *Oxford English Dictionary*; Murray 1977: 139), just as a call for new editions has been part of the work of the current *Dictionary of Old English* (Frank and Cameron 1983). Not surprisingly, the exacting nature of the philological project worked against the populist aims of EETS. In a classic comment, Henry Sweet admitted that he had only reluctantly provided a Modern English translation to the EETS edition of the *Pastoral Care*. The text was 'of exclusively philological interest', he wrote, implying that anybody interested in studying it should know Old English already. Significantly, he would have replaced the translation with Latin parallels and 'full critical commentary' (1871: ix). Sweet was not alone in his views. Of the Early English *Genesis and Exodus* Morris wrote that 'the philological value of the poem, fully compensates . . . for the absence of great literary merit', an early juxtaposition of terms (philological value, literary merit) that was to become something of a refrain in later editions and criticism (quoted in Matthews 1999: 154). These comments indicate how far from popular the aims of EETS actually were. Romances were chosen for their popular appeal and cultural currency, but the approach to editing them was driven by new technologies of language study that required precise differentiation of stages of the language's development.

Before the advent of EETS, *Sir Gawain* and other poems were called 'ancient', not 'medieval' or 'Middle English'. The most significant difference between Madden's and Morris' editions of *Sir Gawain* is the way in which each edition names the history into which it places the text. Madden referred to the poem as one of several 'ancient' tales. Morris, by contrast, saw the poem as an 'early English' text ('Early English' is, of course, still used by EETS and by Early English Manuscripts in Facsimile). 'Middle English' did not appear as a classification until 1879, when it was used by Walter Skeat in his introduction to the Wycliffite New Testament, first edited in 1850 by Forshall and Madden (Matthews 1999: xxxi). The recognition of these stages of the historiography of English, itself a mark of professionalization, reveals the emergence of scholarly discipline as a distinct, increasingly refined and specialized form of cultural production that continues today.

The place of 'Old English' in the developing medievalism of the late nineteenth century was, compared to 'Middle English', a small one. The words 'Old English' as opposed to 'Early English' appeared for the first time in an EETS title in Morris' *Old English Homilies of the Twelfth and Thirteenth Centuries* (1867, 1868). There and in Morris' *An Old English Miscellany* (1872) 'Old English' merely indicates post-Conquest texts and language both English and old. For texts written before the Norman Conquest, 'Old English' was preferred to 'Anglo-Saxon'. In *King Alfred's West-Saxon Version of Gregory's Pastoral Care*, Henry Sweet wrote, 'I use "Old English" throughout this work to denote the unmixed, inflectional stage of the English lan-

guage, commonly known by the barbarous and unmeaning title of "Anglo-Saxon"'
(1871: v). In his *Anglo-Saxon Primer*, Sweet declared that 'the oldest stage of English
. . . is now generally called "Old English", though the name "Anglo-Saxon" is still
often used' (1876: 1), a view promptly enshrined in the *New English Dictionary* (q.v.).
The first Old English text published by EETS, Morris' edition of *The Blickling Homilies*, appeared in 1874. Morris bears out Sweet's earlier perspective in his comment
that 'The Blickling Homilies, though now for the first time published, have not been
altogether unknown to old [sic] English scholars' (v). The words 'Old English' were
not attached to a pre-Conquest text until the appearance of Thomas Miller's edition
of *The Old English Version of Bede's Ecclesiastical History* (1890–8).

The interchangeableness of 'Anglo-Saxon' and 'Old English' as we now use them
was only grudgingly granted by Sweet in 1876 (neither term is to be confused with
'semi-Saxon'; on the EETS distinction among forms of early English, and on its plans
to publish texts in all of them, see 'Sixth Report' 1870: 3, and Matthews 1999: 200,
n. 25). Countering the 'ignorance and literary intolerance' that 'may sneer at "Anglo-
Saxon"', Sweet wrote that 'even if Old English were totally destitute of intrinsic merit,
it would still form a necessary link in the history of our language' (1876: xi). In 1967
C. L. Wrenn observed that by the middle of the nineteenth century 'Old English' was
used 'for language and literature up to about AD 1100', so that continuity from Old
to Middle to Modern English could be suggested (ix). But nineteenth-century practice was far from uniform. As we have seen, 'Old English' was applied to what we
would consider both Old and Early Middle English texts, and when the *OED* definition of 'Anglo-Saxon' was written, the term referred both to English language and
to English culture. In 1929 Kemp Malone showed that the term 'Old English' served
both inclusionary and exclusionary functions as a means of relating Anglo-Saxon
culture to the rest of English history (see also Stanley 1994). For some the term
marked the first phase of a history that continued up to the present. But for those
who believed that the history of the English nation (or the history of its literature)
began with the Conquest or after, 'Old English' referred to a civilization 'before'
English, or what Malone calls 'pre-English' (1929: 181) – i.e. not 'English' at all. In
a paper for the first Modern Language Association meeting (1883), James Morgan
Hart maintained that everything before the Conquest was as 'foreign to our way of
thinking as if it had been expressed in a foreign tongue' (Hart 1884–5: 85–6). When
'Old English' and 'Anglo-Saxon' became interchangeable, the inclusionary force of
'Old English' finally won out over such views as Hart's. To judge from *The Cambridge
History of Medieval Literature*, either term now operates as exclusionary.

The exclusionary force of 'Old English' was directed at the primitivism of
Germanic or 'pre-English' culture. Tensions between England and Germany were a
shaping factor in nineteenth-century Anglo-Saxon studies, and, thanks to two world
wars, helped to shape the subject in the twentieth century as well. Sweet's preface to
The Oldest English Texts is an extraordinarily bitter commentary on the influence of
German scholarship in England by someone who studied in Germany himself before
he went to Oxford. A difficult man, Sweet sought a post there for years without success

(he was often 'splendidly right', a colleague said, 'but nobody could be more deplorably and pigheadedly wrong'; Murray 1977: 77). In Sweet's view textual editing and language study had become entirely too Germanic. Sweet lamented that he and other English scholars were reduced 'to the humble role of purveyors to the swarms of young program-mongers turned out every year by the German universities' and that an English scholar could not compete with them except by 'Germanizing himself and losing all his nationality' (Sweet 1885: v). Germany's system of national education, grasp of technology and manufacturing capacity had made it the most economically advanced country in Europe, and German had become an indispensable scholarly language. British historian John Seeley summed up English admiration of German research by saying, 'Good books are in German' (quoted in Eksteins 1989: 71; Dockhorn 1950: 217). American research universities were planned according to the German model, and in America the German professor was presented as a hero of intellectual freedom whose life had the sole aim of scholarly distinction accompanied by a freedom that Hart called 'inexpressibly fascinating' (1874: 267); Sweet's reaction was not exactly paranoid. By the end of the nineteenth century, there were thirty-five Anglo-Saxonists in Germany at work in twenty-one universities. Hans Aarsleff could produce the names of only five English scholars working in Old English at this time, a number easily exceeded by a rough count of Anglo-Saxon philologists in America (Aarsleff 1967: 181–2; Frantzen 1990: 72).

That there were few skilled hands for the work of EETS is clear from a survey of editors involved in the first 101 editions (1864 to 1893). Morris edited 19 of these volumes, Furnivall 14 and Skeat 13 of them, these three men together producing 46 editions, nearly half the total. Five other scholars produced four or more editions each (H. B. Wheatley [7], F. Horstmann [6], J. Small and F. Hall [Hall 1 alone, 4 with Small], J. R. Lumby [4] and T. Wright [4]). Significantly, only two volumes of the first fifty – Sweet's *Pastoral Care* (nos. 45 and 50) – contained an Old English text; ten more Old English volumes followed of the next fifty published: *The Blickling Homilies* (nos. 58, 63, 73); *Be Domes Dæge* (no. 65); Ælfric's *Lives of Saints* (nos. 76, 82, 94); *Beowulf* in autotype (no. 77); *Orosius* (no. 79); and Sweet's *Oldest English Texts* (no. 83). (Horstmann is the first German contributor, I think, and his editions do not begin to appear until 1886.)

Sweet's exasperated comments hint at German domination of medieval scholarship. *Sir Gawain and the Green Knight* is a case in point. Non-editorial scholarship on the poem began in 1876 with Trautman's essay on versification and vocabulary; from 1876 to 1882, five articles appeared, all in German. In 1883, a Zurich dissertation in English was published; five more articles appeared before 1886, again all in German (Blanch 1983). It might have been Madden's aim to fashion Gawain into a model suitable for English gentlemen – an ambition reflected in D. S. Brewer's admiring comment on Malory's reshaping of Arthurian tales ('This is the style of Malory: the style of a gentleman' [1968: 19]) – but the hands in charge of scholarship on the poem were German. The hands in charge of Anglo-Saxon scholarship were also German. Usually, when nationalism is mentioned in the context of Anglo-Saxon history, the implied context is the Norman Conquest (Simmons 1990). But, as Sweet's comments indicate, that was not the only international context to have shaped the field. World War I remade the world, disrupting Anglo-Saxon studies but not altering them in a significant way. World War II might have reshaped the world less dramatically, but it helped to give Anglo-Saxon studies a prominence the subject has only recently surrendered.

Mid-twentieth-century Perspectives

A view of Anglo-Saxon studies as they appeared after the Great War is found in *The Study of Anglo-Saxon*, published by H. M. Chadwick in 1941. Looking back on twenty-eight years as professor of Anglo-Saxon at Cambridge University, Chadwick linked conflicts within the discipline in the first half of the twentieth century to those of the century before. He congratulated himself and his students on rescuing the subject from the 'narrowly linguistic point of view' from within which the study of Anglo-Saxon had been conducted in the first decades of the century. Chadwick traced the isolation of Anglo-Saxon as he found it at Cambridge in 1917, 'cut off from all its historical and cultural connections' (1941: xv), to the mid-nineteenth-century split between language and history. Subsequent to that split, Chadwick claimed, historians used Anglo-Saxon sources in translation, 'without reference to the original texts', while scholars who knew the language began 'to regard the historical and legal works as lying outside their province' (1941: 45). Chadwick pointed out that ancient history had always belonged to scholars of the classics and that no one would have presumed to study ancient history without knowing Greek and Latin. Had Anglo-Saxon been attached to history instead of literature, the isolation of Anglo-Saxon language from historical and cultural contexts might have been prevented, although poetry might then have been regarded as out of place (1941: 50).

Chadwick admitted that the connection with (later) English studies 'has led to a very great increase in the number of people who have at least some knowledge of Anglo-Saxon', since English literature was a popular topic and Anglo-Saxon was compulsory within it. But he disapproved of the requirement to study Anglo-Saxon, 'since to force it upon a larger number of students is, in my experience, a mere waste of time for both student and teacher' (1941: 48). This is, of course, a considerable irony, since it was chiefly as a requirement in departments of English that Anglo-Saxon studies thrived in the twentieth century. Successful efforts have been mounted in recent years to retain Anglo-Saxon as a 'compulsory subject' at Oxford University (Jackson 1993; Lee 1998; 'Oxford Dons' 1998). The logic of the position Chadwick criticized as outdated sixty years ago is still the profession's strongest defence.

Under Chadwick's leadership Cambridge's celebrated 'Department of Anglo-Saxon and Kindred Subjects' took shape. In 1958, Dorothy Whitelock succeeded Chadwick as Elrington and Bosworth Professor of Anglo-Saxon Studies at Cambridge. In her inaugural lecture, *Changing Currents in Anglo-Saxon Studies*, Whitelock traced the creation of the chair she held to the will of the Rev. Dr. Joseph Bosworth (1878), then Rawlinson Professor of Anglo-Saxon at Oxford. Bosworth intended to found a chair 'of Anglo-Saxon civilisation', she argued, and it was this mission that Chadwick had so successfully realized. Whitelock countered the disparaging views of Anglo-Saxon culture taken by earlier writers, including E. Wingfield-Stratford, who in 1930 remarked that 'Saxon civilisation . . . deserved and was bound to fall' (Whitelock 1958: 3). Reviewing her lecture, F. M. Stenton commented that Whitelock promoted 'the enlarged conception of Anglo-Saxon history now prevalent' (1959: 519) and added that 'the vitality of a rapidly expanding subject is the impression most likely to remain with those who have followed [Whitelock's] survey of the Anglo-Saxon scene'. He specifically endorsed Whitelock's view of the importance of Anglo-Saxon history and acknowledged that Anglo-Saxon studies was 'a rapidly expanding subject' (520). Chadwick's vision of Anglo-Saxon studies as historically based, expanding and multi-disciplinary was regarded as a reality by both Whitelock and Stenton.

The expansion of Anglo-Saxon studies celebrated in these works depends in part on what, from a North American perspective, might be called the local, even provincial, character of the subject. In the 1955 reissue of *The Study of Anglo-Saxon*, Nora K. Chadwick contributed her own perspective to 'reviewing the position of Anglo-Saxon studies as a whole' (x). 'Modern facilities have brought out [our; *sic*] country's past within the present knowledge of the poorest and least educated', she wrote. 'The development of buses and youth hostels has brought the more remote, and often, therefore, the better preserved of our ancient sites within easy reach' (xi). Presumably she was arguing that more people than university students were able to travel to such sites inexpensively. Both Chadwicks believed in the appeal of Anglo-Saxon studies to the 'non-academic student of history' addressed by H. M. Chadwick (1941: 57). Outside the universities 'there is a wide-spread impression that Anglo-Saxon and kindred studies are unattractive and impracticable for the home student', he wrote, but he believed that such a view was deeply misguided. 'Indeed, I doubt whether there is any other subject which the home reader will find easier to take up in his spare time, and from which he is likely to obtain more interest and intellectual satisfaction' (1941: xvi). *A Guide to Old English*, by Bruce Mitchell and Fred Robinson (1996), still presents Old English grammar as a subject suitable for independent learners to master on their own, although most undergraduates find the textbook a challenge even in the classroom.

Chadwick assumed that Anglo-Saxon studies appealed to a wide reading audience; he noted work in Anglo-Saxon by bankers as well as librarians, 'leisured students', local government officials, and 'home students' who could learn Old English 'in a small fraction of the time' that universities required (1941: 56–9). Such students needed guidance, he realized, but he did not advocate 'any kind of elaborate organisation' and its attendant expenses (1941: 59). Many organizations designed to promote popular knowledge of medieval texts had been formed in the nineteenth century, obviously, among them the EETS. Chadwick's vision of Anglo-Saxon studies as a subject to be pursued informally is indebted to these organizations and to the tradition of amateur scholars whose enthusiasms created Anglo-Saxon studies (Adams 1917; Berkhout and Gatch 1982; Frantzen 1990).

H. M. Chadwick's book was written 'in the early days of the Second World War', Nora Chadwick noted, 'at a time when anxiety for the present and the future was too intense to allow most of us to spare much reflection for the past. Only those who, like the author of this book, were no longer of an age to fulfil the more active demands of the time were in a position to reflect more or less at leisure on the continuity of history, and the origin and formative elements in the civilisation which we were struggling to maintain' (1955: ix). In other words, Chadwick was able to write *The Study of Anglo-Saxon* because he was not able to go to war. Nora Chadwick's remark, an epitome of the political context of Anglo-Saxon studies, directly connects the war effort to reflection on 'the continuity of history' and the 'origins and formative elements of the civilisation' over which the war was being fought. She described the medieval period as 'the first great period of the predominance of the international, as against the national ideal' and warned that '[w]e must not allow our sense of the value and interest of the Anglo-Saxon nation to betray us into a narrow nationalism' (1955: xii). At the turn of the last century, an unembarrassed like between scholarship and politics was characteristic of academic discourse. At the Modern Language Association meeting of 1902, James Wilson Bright, author of *Bright's Anglo-Saxon Reader*, a book now known as *Bright's Old English Grammar and Reader* (Cassidy and Ringler 1971), declared that the philologist should take part in 'the work of guiding the destinies of the country', since 'the philological strength and sanity of a nation is the measure of its intellectual and spiritual vitality' (lxii).

In retirement in 1945, H. M. Chadwick took up the subject of nationalism in a study that argued against isolationism and ignorance of foreign peoples. Commenting on the ascendancy of Germany in modern Europe, he acknowledged 'the apparent invincibility of [the Germans'] army' and stressed their 'intellectual achievements'. 'In particular through their discovery of the value of a University', Chadwick wrote, 'they have actually succeeded in establishing a world domination.' Chadwick noted that Germans contributed far more state support to education and added: 'Among Germans of to-day it is a commonplace that all that they value most in their national characteristics and ideology is inherited from their heathen ancestors of long ago' (1945: 138–9; Frantzen 1990: 95). After World War II, as Anglo-Saxon studies became institutionalized and professionalized, ideological candour became less apparent. Instead, as the subject responded to the tenor and methods of literary criticism in departments of English, the analysis of texts as literature became more important than their situation in historical and political contexts.

Late Twentieth-century Anglo-Saxon Studies by the Numbers

I discuss this shift in *Desire for Origins*. My aim here is to set against it statistics that measure the output of Anglo-Saxonists in various fields in both nineteenth- and twentieth-century Anglo-Saxon studies. Using *A Bibliography of Publications on Old*

Table 1 Greenfield and Robinson entries for 'General Works'

Subject area (GR 3–872)	1800s	1900s
Bibliographies (3–51)	3 (1879)	47
Dictionaries (52–82)	14 (1832)	7
Concordances, etc. (83–107)	7 (1891)	18
Manuscript studies (108–258)	41 (1802)	104
Modern collections in OE or translation, including grammars (259–411)	50 (1861)	95
Collections of essays (412–51)	2 (1846)	38
Historical and linguistic studies (452–529)	21 (1806)	51
Histories and surveys (530–611)	29 (1805)	50
Studies of themes and topics (612–94)	7 (1807)	78
Special vocabulary and semantic studies (695–757)	5 (1880)	59
Textual criticism (758–72)	2 (1854)	12
Studies of style and language (773–801)	2 (1873)	29
Studies of scholars and scholarship (801a–72)	17 (1821)	60
Total	200	648

English Literature to the End of 1972 by Stanley B. Greenfield and Fred C. Robinson, I counted books and articles published in selected areas to generate a background for more specific data. I have measured the output in various areas of six annual bibliographies in *Anglo-Saxon England* spread over twenty-seven years (1971–98). I also counted articles and book reviews concerning Old English in this period in *Speculum*, the journal of the Medieval Academy of America and arguably the most important interdisciplinary journal for medieval studies. Finally I tracked sessions on Old and Middle English topics at meetings of the Modern Language Association of America during these decades, MLA being the largest and most important international organization to which both Anglo-Saxonists and scholars in other fields belong.

My attempt to portray Anglo-Saxon scholarship by the numbers, so to speak, does not produce an objective representation of the field. The numbers depend on the categories of scholarship as these sources have defined them, and such definitions are often ambiguous. But together these bibliographies, journals and programmes offer a useful and, I believe, a consistent, overview. (Acts of classification are never simple, as the many cross-references in Greenfield and Robinson attest. Many works could be counted under more than one category, but I counted works only in their primary [i.e. numbered] listing. A small margin for error should be factored into these figures, for which no statistical significance is claimed.)

In 'General Works on Old English Literature', the first section of their *Bibliography of Publications on Old English to the End of 1972*, Greenfield and Robinson include bibliographies, dictionaries, concordances, manuscript catalogues and studies, collections of texts and essay collections, as well as other kinds of inquiry. Table 1 lists

Table 2   Greenfield and Robinson entries for general prose and
for Ælfric

Subject area (GR 5139 ~ 5368)	1800s	1900s
Surveys and topic studies (5139–55)	3	16
Studies in style and language (5156–80)	1	24
Ælfric		
General studies of Ælfric (5185–216)	8	23
Editions of homilies (5281–97)	8	8
Studies of homilies (5298–339)	5	39
Editions of *Lives of Saints* (5340–5)	4	2
Studies of *Lives of Saints* (5346–68)	6	15
Total	35	127

subject areas and entries for the 1800s and 1900s. I include the earliest date for an entry in each category in the 1800s (in some categories the first entry dates from the 1700s). Each subject area is followed by the Greenfield and Robinson (GR) entry numbers it includes. All numbers and percentages are rounded to the nearest whole number.

The nineteenth century was more productive than the twentieth century in one area only, dictionaries. But nineteenth-century production of concordances, manuscript studies, modern collections (including grammars), historical and linguistic studies, and histories and surveys constitutes a sizeable portion of this section of the Greenfield and Robinson entries, ranging from 28 per cent to 37 per cent. This is especially impressive given that in six of thirteen fields the entries for the 1800s do not begin until the mid-nineteenth-century or after. Fifty collections, including translations of Anglo-Saxon sources and grammars, were produced in thirty-nine years; seven concordances were produced in the last nine years of the century. English scholars were responsible for the first nineteenth-century entries in all fields except studies of style and language. But among the newest and most rapidly developing areas – special vocabulary and semantic studies and studies of style and language – work by German scholars predominated.

I also examined selected areas of prose studies, including general surveys, studies of style and language, general studies of Ælfric, and editions of his homilies and *Lives of Saints* (table 2). In all these areas there were 162 entries between 1800 and 1972, thirty-five of them, or 22 per cent, from the 1800s.

The distribution of studies in poetry is reasonably comparable. In all the areas surveyed in table 3, there were 2,389 entries between 1800 and 1972, 411 of them, or 17 per cent, from the 1800s.

I also examined the entries for 'General Works', prose and various poems by decade in the twentieth century (table 4).

Table 3   Greenfield and Robinson entries for poetry, including *Beowulf*

Subject area (GR 874 ~ 4326)	1800s	1900s
General poetry		
Comprehensive studies (874–914)	16	26
Thematic studies (915–1075)	23	136
Textual criticism (1076–1133)	13	45
Studies of style (1134–1254)	12	111
Prosody (1256–1388)	44	89
Battle of Maldon		
Editions (1555–60)	1	5
Translations (1561–8)	4	4
Studies (1569–1612)	4	41
Beowulf		
Editions (1632–56)	15	10
Translations (1657–1766)	40	71
Studies of history, culture and authorship (1767–2357)	111	478
Textual criticism (2358–708)	34	316
Literary interpretations (2709–3031)	16	306
Style and language (3032–144)	14	99
Studies of scholars (3175–96a)	3	20
Christ		
Editions (3263–6)	2	2
Translations (3267–8)	0	2
Studies (3269–43)	12	62
The Dream of the Rood		
Editions (3482–7)	1	5
Translations (3488–96)	3	7
Studies (3497–527)	2	29
Genesis A and B		
Editions (3686a–95)	6	4
Translations (3696–701)	4	3
Studies (3703–89)	25	62
The Seafarer		
Editions (4276)	0	1
Translations (4277–82)	1	5
Studies (4283–326)	5	39
Total	411	1978

In the category of 'General Works', the total number of entries from 1900 to 1969 is 651, with an average per decade of eighty-four entries. Both the 1930s and the 1950s are above that average, but no marked increase appears until the 1960s, when there were 141 publications, 21 per cent of the total output from 1900–72. Although

Table 4   Greenfield and Robinson entries by decade, 1900–72

Decade	1900–9	1910–19	1920–9	1930–9	1940–9	1950–9	1960–9	1970–2	Total	Seven-decade average, 1900–69
General works	75	68	68	91	48	97	141	63	651	84
Prose	17	13	10	13	9	16	33	16	127	16
Beowulf	123	144	177	184	106	185	305	79	1303	175
Christ	17	8	2	5	4	4	13	9	62	8
Rood	4	3	1	2	2	5	15	9	41	5
Genesis	4	11	7	3	5	6	19	10	65	87
Maldon	3	2	6	7	2	3	21	6	50	6
Seafarer	0	3	1	5	4	6	16	5	40	5
Total	243	252	272	310	180	322	563	197	2339	306

only three years of the 1970s are included, entries for those years total sixty-three, or 10 per cent of the total for the whole century.

Prose studies fluctuated within a narrow range in the first half of the twentieth century but increased rapidly in the 1960s, when thirty-three publications in these areas appeared, compared to an average of sixteen per decade for the century. *Beowulf* studies, the most active area of Old English scholarship surveyed here, averaged 175 entries per decade. They dropped to a low of 106 in the 1940s, a figure almost tripled in the 1960s. Figures for other Old English poems also show a sudden increase in the 1960s. From 1900–59 the bibliography lists eight studies of *The Dream of the Rood* (excluding editions and translations). Fourteen were published in the 1960s; seven more appeared 1970–2. The decades from 1900 to 1959 averaged six entries for *Genesis A* and *B*, while nineteen appeared in the 1960s. Of a total of fifty-nine works concerning *The Battle of Maldon* (see table 3), nine were published in the 1800s and fifty in the 1900s, twenty-one of them in the 1960s alone.

These data offer an opportunity for at least rough co-ordination between the production of Anglo-Saxon studies and their national and international contexts, the world wars in particular. The Greenfield and Robinson entries do not immediately show the effect of World War I on Anglo-Saxon scholarship. The number of entries in 'General Works' in the decade of the war declined about 10 per cent from the decade before. But the war's impact on some areas is more evident. In vocabulary studies (Greenfield and Robinson nos. 695–757), for example, an area of unquestioned German domination, all nine entries between 1910 and 1919 are in German (including five Kiel dissertations) and all appeared between 1910 and 1912. Of fourteen studies of theme in this decade, ten appeared in or before 1914 (four in German), four in 1916 or 1917 (only one in German). *Beowulf* studies also slowed in Germany during the war; of some thirty German entries under the heading 'cultural and historical/authorship and date' in Greenfield and Robinson (the largest category for work on the poem), nineteen appeared before 1915.

However, entries for the poem itself actually increased during this decade, and even in Germany scholarly production continued. Max Förster's *Il Codice Vercellese con Omelie e Poesie in Lingua Anglosassone* (Rome, 1913) was reviewed in two German periodicals in 1915 and in another in 1919; Förster's edition of the Vercelli homilies, published in Halle in 1913, was reviewed in German in 1915. When all fields are included, table 4 shows the decade of the war to have been slightly more productive than the decade before. If work in Germany slowed, Old English scholarship in the United States and England was not clearly affected, even though American and British universities were then rife with anti-German sentiment (Graff 1987: 128–9, 135; Eagleton 1983: 29).

World War II, on the other hand, had a dramatic impact on Anglo-Saxon scholarship. Table 4 shows fewer entries for the 1940s than for any other in the century, followed by sharp increases in subsequent decades. When the generation that fought World War II left colleges and graduate schools and joined the tenure stream of the academy, publications in all areas of Anglo-Saxon scholarship recorded in table 4 increased sharply. American universities had grown steadily since the turn of the century. Between 1900 and 1940 the percentage of the eligible population attending college rose from 4 to 14 per cent; enrolments shot up 40 per cent between 1940 and 1964. To be sure, war veterans made up only one group involved in this dramatic increase, which reflects the widespread belief that a college education had become necessary for economic well-being (Graff 1987: 155).

But veterans took distinctive views of the cultural transformation in which they participated. In *Doing Battle*, his memoir of the post-war period, Paul Fussell offers a jaundiced account of the veteran's role in post-war education. At Harvard, students on the GI Bill (such as Fussell, with a BA from Pomona College) discovered 'faculty snottiness toward entering graduate students, very like the snottiness with which senior officers in the army habitually treated their juniors'. Bartlett Jere Whiting, the medievalist who directed the graduate programmes when Fussell arrived, 'laughed cruelly' when Fussell admitted that he had studied French by correspondence course. If Harvard's requirement of three languages for the PhD did not discourage such students, 'the requirement of philology – two terms of Old English, one of Middle English – probably would' (1996: 194). Later, having found the seemingly formidable language requirements farcically easy to meet, Fussell earned his PhD and went on to achieve tenure at Rutgers. Fussell contrasts the heavy teaching load of assistant professors of English at Rutgers University in the 1950s to 'the new[,] easy, expansive, academic era of the sixties and seventies', with their 'more generous research handouts' (1996: 225, 257). The Greenfield and Robinson bibliography clearly demonstrates the effects of the new emphasis on research in American universities during the 1960s.

The Greenfield and Robinson bibliography stops with publications in 1972. The bibliography in the annual publication *Anglo-Saxon England* begins in 1971 and provides a good starting point for an analysis of productivity in the following three decades. Table 5 shows the number of articles in selected categories.

Table 5   Entries by field in *Anglo-Saxon England* biographies

Subject	1971 v. 1[a]	1972 v. 2	1982 v. 12	1983 v. 13	1996 v. 25	1997 v. 26	% increase from v. 1 to v. 26
General	16	22	56	44	66	70	338
OE language	75	46	78	116	79	132	76
OE lit., general	7	6	9	10	12	21	200
Poetry, general	10	10	16	18	24	23	130
Beowulf	20	17	54	51	53	42	110
Other poetry	35	44	64	71	53	55	57
Prose	14	17	32	32	19	34	143
Anglo-Latin	15	13	49	56	48[b]	63	320
Archaeology	93	87	244	212	171	169	82
Palaeography	11	14	29	56	73	23	109
History	49	32	89	93	128	102	108
Reviews	131	155	161	160	150	164	25

[a] Entries for vol. 1 include entries in vol. 2 marked as omitted from vol. 1.
[b] Does not include *Fontes* (the 1997 bibliography included ninety-four entries for the *Fontes Anglo-Saxonici*, a field not listed in the earlier years).

These figures reveal a remarkable increase across the disciplines in Anglo-Saxon studies, although the growth was not steady. The bibliography in vol. 13 was the largest of the six surveyed (919 entries, compared to 476 for vol. 1). When compared to the entries in vol. 1 (1971), entries for vol. 26 (1997) show increases ranging from 25 per cent (reviews) to 338 per cent (general studies). Areas showing the most growth are Anglo-Latin and 'general studies'; well behind in rate of increase are 'general studies of Old English literature', prose and general studies of poetry. *Beowulf* criticism and work in history and palaeography increased less markedly (but still impressively, somewhat over 100 per cent). Areas showing the smallest increase are reviews, 'other poetry', 'language', and archaeology. However, every area showed increased output.

Late Twentieth-century Anglo-Saxon Studies in Context

To understand how the increased production of Anglo-Saxon studies correlates with the status of medieval studies more generally, I look to venues in which Old English scholarship has traditionally appeared, *Speculum* and the Modern Language Association.

In 1998, responding to a challenge by women who believed their work was under-represented in *Speculum*, the Medieval Academy *Newsletter* published figures on authors of book reviews and on authors of reviews (Wenger 1998: 3). The data show a sharp increase in the number of books submitted for review in the journal (table 6).

Table 6   Number of authors of books reviewed and noticed

Number/%	1978	1988	1998
No. of authors of books received	546	892	1108
No. of authors of books reviewed	229	350	362
% reviewed of total received	42%	39%	33%
No. of authors of books noticed	47	137	248
% noticed of total received	9%	15%	22%
Total no. of authors of reviewed and noticed books	276	487	610
% reviewed and noticed of total received	50%	55%	55%

Table 7   Number of articles, reviews and notices

Number/%	1978	1988	1998
No. of articles	23	17	19
No. of articles on OE	3	1	4
% OE articles	13%	6%	21%
No. of reviews	236	361	474
Reviews of OE	11	6	21
% OE reviews	5%	2%	4%

The total number of authors of books reviewed and noticed jumped 121 per cent, but the number of authors whose books were reviewed increased just 58 per cent; the number of authors of books noticed (their contents described but not analysed) increased fivefold.

The articles, reviews and brief notices in *Speculum* represent a broad view of medieval studies. How well is the increase in Anglo-Saxon scholarship registered in *Speculum*? Much depends, of course, on what counts as work in 'Old English' or 'Anglo-Saxon'. I included work addressing any topic in Anglo-Saxon language, literature and culture, but included work concerning Latin authors only if they were part of the Anglo-Saxon world (hence I included work about Theodore of Canterbury, Bede, Aldhelm and Alcuin). I did not include work dealing with the continent or Celtic and Irish studies.

Tables 7 and 8 compare productivity between 1978 and 1998 as measured by articles, reviews and brief notices published in *Speculum*. Table 7 gives numbers for three years at the beginning, middle and end of these decades; table 8 gives averages of all volumes in this period. (Percentages are rounded up to the nearest whole number.)

The distribution of articles dealing with Anglo-Saxon subjects ranges from a high of 21 per cent in 1996 to a low of 0 per cent in 1986, 1989, 1991 and 1997 (in five

Table 8   Average articles, reviews and notices 1978–87, 1988–97, 1978–97

Number/%	1978–87	1988–97	1978–97
Average no. articles	22	18	20
Average no. OE articles	3	1	2
% OE articles	12%	7%	10%
Average no. reviews	283	399	341
Average no. OE reviews	14	11	13
% OE reviews	5%	3%	4%

other years there was only one article in the field published in *Speculum*). These figures compare favourably with an earlier decade which I selected at random, 1927–36,
during which an average of thirty-nine articles per year was published, with just over
two per year, on average, in Old English subjects, or about 5 per cent. The total of
articles published in *Speculum* 1927–36 was almost twice the total number for
1978–97. While the number of articles has decreased, the number of articles in Old
English has remained the same and hence has doubled in proportion to the total.

Comparison of reviews published in these two periods indicates that books concerning Anglo-Saxon are receiving less attention in *Speculum* now than formerly. From
1927–36 there was an average of forty-four reviews per year, with an average of just
over two reviews per year concerning work in Old English, or 5 per cent of the total
number of books reviewed. This percentage is equal to that for 1978–87, when the
average number of books reviewed or noticed was 283 and the average number of
Anglo-Saxon books was fourteen, or 5 per cent. In 1988–97, however, the average
number of books reviewed or noticed grew to 399, but the average number of reviewed
books concerning Anglo-Saxon declined to eleven, or 2.7 per cent, just over half
the percentage of the previous decade. When measured in these terms, Anglo-Saxon
studies are receiving proportionately less attention as medieval studies expand and
diversify. At the same time, the Medieval Academy has expanded the ratio of reviews
to articles in each volume. The journal of the Medieval Academy of America continues to be a valuable and friendly forum for outstanding work in Anglo-Saxon scholarship. But the shrinking representation of Anglo-Saxon books that are reviewed or
given brief notice is disturbing. When it comes to notice of their work in *Speculum*,
Anglo-Saxonists must be prepared to settle for a smaller piece of a larger pie.

Even less encouraging than the data from *Speculum* is the representation of Anglo-
Saxon studies at the annual meeting of the Modern Language Association. It was
through the Modern Language Association of America that Old English was most
successfully institutionalized in the United States. Early issues of *PMLA* (*Publications
of the Modern Language Association*), the journal of the MLA, contained a smattering of
papers on Old English from conventions at which only a few papers had been read.
MLA ceased to be a small organization in 1920 as the result of a membership drive

designed to enlarge the group to at least 500 members ('Calling all Members' 1921: iii). Up to 1921, MLA was organized into general divisions: an English section, a Romance section (where Old English papers were read) and others. In 1921 MLA reorganized itself into a more complex structure. Two large divisions were formed, English I and English II, the former going up to 1650; English I meetings sometimes contained papers on Old English topics. A second structure was also formed, dividing English into twelve sections, Old English naturally falling into English I. MLA adhered to this format for its annual meeting until 1976, when the current divisional structure emerged. Since 1976 MLA has included an Old English Division, which now sponsors three sessions at each convention. In 1976, however, there was only one session sponsored by the Old English Division and another seminar on teaching *Beowulf* – only two sessions on Old English out of some nearly 666, compared to eight sessions in Middle English. Old English sessions soon improved on these modest beginnings but continued to be outpaced by Middle English in the next two decades.

Using the Subject Index to MLA programmes from 1978–97, I surveyed those sessions classified by the MLA programme as belonging to Old and/or Middle English categories (only one case concerned both Old and Middle English; I categorized it as Old English; Chicago, 1990, no. 121). The divisions were nearly evenly matched in 1978–80, with Middle English offering five sessions each year and Old English either three or four. But after 1980 Middle English offerings began to expand, climbing to seven sessions in 1981 and thereafter falling into single digits in only three of the next sixteen years (the last time in 1997). Middle English sessions reached a high of fifteen in 1982 (there were thirteen in 1994, twelve in 1988, and eleven in 1983, 1990, 1991, 1995 and 1996). Old English, by comparison, offered more than three or four sessions (including the division meetings) only four times in twenty years (six in 1983, five in 1982, 1986 and 1988). In twelve of twenty years only division-sponsored sessions and no special sessions took place in the area of Old English. Special sessions are meant to address topics 'not adequately accommodated through convention programs arranged by the divisions and discussion groups' ('About the MLA Convention' 1998: 1253); it is clear that Anglo-Saxonists are content to let division-sponsored sessions represent their interests and are either uninterested in proposing special sessions for MLA or unsuccessful at getting their proposals approved by the MLA programme committee.

Between 1978 and 1997 the MLA convention itself grew. Setting aside 1980, when an apparently catastrophic meeting at Houston drew only 524 sessions (down 134 from the previous year), MLA meetings in the 1980s averaged 708 sessions; in the 1990s they averaged 754 (reaching an all-time high of 888 sessions in San Francisco in 1998; at Chicago in 1999 there were 793 sessions). Middle English offerings seem to have grown slightly during this time, averaging 9.8 sessions for the 1980s and 10.6 for the 1990s. But during these decades Old English lost ground, averaging 4.0 sessions for the 1980s and only 3.2 for the 1990s, when special sessions were offered in Old English only twice in nine years (in 1990 and 1994).

This glimpse of Anglo-Saxon at the Modern Language Association suggests that Anglo-Saxonists find little that connects them to their colleagues in other areas of the MLA. Yet many Old English scholars teach Middle as well as Old English, and the main venue for Anglo-Saxon studies in North America is the English department; likewise, in Great Britain Anglo-Saxon is conducted mainly within departments of English language and literature. Even though most Anglo-Saxonists in North America work in English departments, Anglo-Saxonists do not seem strongly identified with the MLA. If for no other reason than to ensure a continuing connection to the MLA for Anglo-Saxonists in the future, it would behove Anglo-Saxonists to organize special sessions for the MLA meeting, including those that explore links between Old English and other areas, among them early Middle English, and those that bridge English and other Germanic and also Scandinavian languages.

Conclusion

MLA confronts Anglo-Saxonists with the most aggressively theoretical aspects of contemporary language, literary and cultural study. A discussion of critical theory seems an appropriate way to conclude a review of Anglo-Saxon studies in the twentieth century. Although Anglo-Saxonists have done well in integrating new critical methodologies into their subject, the discipline as a whole has managed to absorb theoretical innovation without experiencing a transformation. Bibliographies include work on sex and gender or theory under 'general and miscellaneous', for example, consigning work that is concentrated on a cultural problem rather than on a text or major figure to the bibliographies' least distinctive categories. This process makes it difficult to recognize that such work belongs to traditional disciplinary categories even as it challenges them (Frantzen 1994: 35–8). Helen Bennett's (1989) analysis of the treatment of feminist scholarship in Anglo-Saxon studies, which shows how that work was seen as supplementary, remains timely.

Anglo-Saxonists rarely confront revisionist views of scholarly disciplines and seem averse to reflecting on the relation of their own disciplinary practices to the political worlds in which Anglo-Saxon studies have played a part. Suggestions that Anglo-Saxon studies are connected to such traditions have been flatly denied. Daniel G. Calder's important study of surveys and histories of Old English literature concludes with a confident comment about the objectivity of scientific methods:

> We are in a better position than our predecessors have ever been to analyze the literature, both poetry and prose, without preconceptions. To our inherited philological base we have added a much improved technical understanding, encompassing advances in palaeography and in the study of sources and cultural backgrounds. (1982: 244)

At a 1988 meeting of the Old English Division of the Modern Language Association, Calder said that the author of these remarks was Peter Clemoes, editor of *Anglo-Saxon*

England, the journal in which his article appeared. The tenor of this comment is very different from both Calder's essay and his MLA paper, and no doubt it is Clemoes, not Calder, who claims that Anglo-Saxonists today can 'analyze the literature, both poetry and prose, without preconceptions' (Calder 1989).

Most Anglo-Saxonists would admit by now that there is no analysis, scholarly or otherwise, 'without preconceptions', only work that acknowledges its preconceptions and work that does not. In *Desire for Origins* I suggested that the search for origins so prominent in nineteenth-century Anglo-Saxon scholarship affected current Anglo-Saxon studies, including the source study projects, *Fontes Anglo-Saxonici* and the Sources of Anglo-Saxon Literary Culture, too. Joyce Hill (1993; Frantzen 1994) and Katherine O'Brien O'Keeffe (1994) challenged my criticisms, both seeking to exculpate these projects from any politics whatsoever. O'Keeffe argues that I conflate the terms 'source' and 'origin' in order to 'charge that source work is at base positivist' (70). 'Positivism' is a mistaken label for source study, she claims, and, depending on how the term is defined (the terms 'needs no introduction', she writes [54]), that might be true. On this issue, however, O'Keeffe has confused my criticism of the sources projects with that of Martin Irvine, who believes the sources projects are positivist (Irvine 1991: 278, n. 16; O'Keeffe 1994: 54). (This is a worrying error for a defender of source study!) I registered several criticisms of the sources projects, but positivism was not one of them. I did argue, as had Ruth Waterhouse before (1987: 18–19), and as Clare A. Lees has since (1991: 161), that these projects did not clearly articulate their objectives and that they were, to say the least, undertheorized. Elsewhere, O'Keeffe merely mentions the extensive discussion by Lees that, from a different perspective, confirms many of my criticisms about the sources projects (O'Keeffe 1994: 57, n. 26; Lees 1991: 160–2). O'Keeffe herself faults the explication of these projects offered by Thomas D. Hill in the same year in which my book appeared (Hill 1990: xv–xxix; O'Keeffe 1994: 58). In order to counter my claim that such projects were undertheorized, she cites essays by Janet Bately, James E. Cross and Hill (O'Keeffe 1994: 69). But despite their merits, these essays contain no theorizing of the sources projects beyond the vocabulary and methods traditional to them. Certainly they offer nothing to compare to the eclectic mix of ideas from Heidegger, Derrida and Lyotard that O'Keeffe herself employs (each figure cited once, I believe).

As the quotation at the beginning of this chapter suggests, Heidegger's thoughts on origins are relevant to Anglo-Saxon studies. He identified the ease with which tradition becomes self-evident, blocking access 'to those primordial "sources" from which the categories and concepts handed down to us have been in part quite genuinely drawn', an ease that 'makes us forget that they have had such an origin', tempting us to suppose 'that the necessity of going back to these sources is something which we need not even understand' (1962: 42). For Heidegger the 'sources' from which categories and concepts are drawn constitute 'an origin' so self-evident that we do not feel the need to go back to it. Seeking to sidestep the ideological implications of the word 'source', O'Keeffe follows Robert Menner in claiming that a 'source' is tangible while origins are 'remote' (1994: 64): a source is supposedly specific, while an origin is an ideological construct. O'Keeffe argues that I 'invest in a definition of "source" which the word (given its use within the Old English community) simply cannot sustain' (65). Thus the Sources of Anglo-Saxon Literary Culture, which deal with *sources*, do not need to take up the problem of *origins*.

This manoeuvre, it seems to me, is tradition at work, an attempt to use what Heidegger calls 'categories and concepts handed down to us' and to 'deliver [them] . . . over to self-evidence'. A search for origins, it would seem, cannot be carried out according to the traditions of our discipline: 'the Old English community' uses 'source' in a way that isolates it from the worrisome ideological implications of the word, that is, the function of a 'source' as an origin. But the possibility remains that the traditional use of the word 'source' might be a way of evading an awkward political history. For surely no consensus about the meaning or use of the 'source' has been sought, much less reached, by Anglo-Saxonists. If any part of the community should undertake to reach such a consensus, it is surely the sources projects, and this, by O'Keeffe's own admission, they have failed to do. O'Keeffe herself entertains a more vital concept of Anglo-Saxon studies. She positions Old English scholarship between 'history and theory, object and subject, fact and interpretation, reason and desire': 'I would suggest that the work in Old English is actually produced in the space between two such discourses: the one seeking objectivity, the other grounding itself in the frank admission of subjective desire' (1994: 72). She poses a challenge to the sources projects that I gladly endorse: a challenge not only to articulate a theory of sources, but to explain why these origins are desired.

Desire has not figured prominently in my review of twentieth-century Anglo-Saxon studies 'by the numbers', which might seem to be an attempt at objectivity that neglects the grounding of Anglo-Saxon studies in the desires of those who practise them. But it is worth asking if the discourses of desire and objectivity allow for the space imagined by O'Keeffe. One could argue that the numbers speak to desire, even as they remain silent about it, and that they reveal two conflicting wishes. The sharply increasing productivity within Anglo-Saxon studies speaks to the life of the field and to the dedication of scholars, new and old. But there is no denying that work within the field, from outside the field, meets with a tepid reception from scholars who see their interests lying elsewhere. Anglo-Saxonists want to turn inward to measure their well-being, for from that perspective our discipline seems to thrive. At the same time, scholars of Middle English, our nearest neighbours, are turning away from Anglo-Saxon studies and seem increasingly invested in identifying their work with early modern studies. The new *Cambridge History of Medieval Literature* includes developments in English literature up to 1547 but discusses only the 'afterlife' – not the 'shelf life' – of Anglo-Saxon literature.

Challenging such dismissals of Anglo-Saxon culture – and Wallace's is not the first; in 1992 Anne Middleton also wrote about medieval studies comprehensively and omitted Anglo-Saxon studies – is necessary, but it is not an end in itself (Richardson 1994). I have argued for the need to create a new audience for Anglo-Saxon studies by articulating connections between our subjects and the subject matter of other disciplines and periods (Frantzen 1990: 212–14). Critical theory is an effective means of bridging these divisions. Theoretically minded Anglo-Saxonists have done their part to establish links between Anglo-Saxon studies and the modern world. If our colleagues remain unpersuaded by our efforts, we must persevere in them none the less, for most Anglo-Saxonists of the future will pursue research and teaching in contexts we now regard as untraditional. As they continue to make Old English texts part of gender studies and cultural studies, for example, they will unavoidably teach less grammar and more Old English in translation. By refusing to take origins for granted, they can strengthen their ties to the rest of the academy as it too is transformed. One benefit of talking about origins is that Anglo-Saxon studies themselves are a point of origin for the modern academy, just as Anglo-Saxon culture is a point of origin to which later English cultures frequently returned. Anglo-Saxonists who read later materials are conscious of links between those materials and Anglo-Saxon texts, ideas and traditions. Scholars who have not read Anglo-Saxon sources, however, often do not see even the possibility of such connections.

Those connections constitute the past of Anglo-Saxon studies, which only in the last century acquired their disciplinary isolationism; articulating those connections is the future of Anglo-Saxon studies. To begin, we must unmask the role of tradition both in delivering our subject over to self-evident stereotypes and in enabling our colleagues to forget the origins of their subject in our own. The need to go back to Anglo-Saxon sources is not lost on any Anglo-Saxonist, but, to paraphrase Heidegger, the necessity of going back to the Anglo-Saxons is something too many scholars do not think they need even to attempt. Only Anglo-Saxonists can intervene in this delusion; by doing so, we can ensure the future of our work.

Acknowledgements

My thanks to Andrew W. Cole, Mary Dockray-Miller, Christina Heckman, Stephen J. Harris, David Matthews, Julie Towell and Fiona Sewell for their assistance with this chapter.

References

Aarsleff, Hans 1967. *The Study of Language in England 1780–1860*. Minnesota.

'About the MLA Convention Program' 1998. *Publications of the Modern Language Association* 113: 1252–9.

Adams, Eleanor N. 1917. *Old English Scholarship in England from 1566 to 1800*. New Haven, CT.

Arthur, Karen 1998. 'Playing the Editing Game with an Electronic Sir Gawain and the Green Knight'. *Exemplaria* 10: 69–96.

Bennett, Helen 1989. 'From Peace Weaver to Text Weaver: Feminist Approaches to Old English Literature'. *Old English Newsletter* Subsidia 15: 23–42.

Berkhout, Carl T. and Milton McC. Gatch, eds 1982. *Anglo-Saxon Scholarship: The First Three Centuries*. Boston.

Bessinger Jr, Jess B. 1966. 'The Status of Old English in America Today: A Survey of Old English Teaching in America'. *Old English Newsletter* 1: 1.

Blanch, Robert J. 1983. *Sir Gawain and the Green Knight: A Reference Guide*. Troy.

Brewer, D. S., ed. 1968. *Malory: The Morte Darthur*. London.

Bright, James Wilson 1903. 'Concerning the Unwritten History of the Modern Language Association of America'. *Publications of the Modern Language Association* 18: 62.

Calder, Daniel G. 1982. 'Histories and Surveys of Old English Literature: A Chronological Review'. *Anglo-Saxon England* 10: 201–44.

—— 1989. 'The Canons of Old English Criticism Revisited'. *Old English Newsletter* Subsidia 15: 11–21.

'Calling All Members' 1921. *Publications of the Modern Language Association* 36: iii.

Cassidy, F. G. and Richard N. Ringler, eds 1971. *Bright's Old English Grammar and Reader*. New York.

Chadwick, H. Munro 1941. *The Study of Anglo-Saxon*. 2nd edn, rev. and enlarged Nora K. Chadwick. Cambridge, 1955.

—— 1945. *The Nationalities of Europe*. Cambridge. Repr. New York, 1973.

Dockhorn, Klaus 1950. *Der deutsche Historismus in England*. Göttingen.

Douglas, Wallace 1985. 'Accidental Institution: On the Origin of Modern Language Study'. *Criticism in the University*, pp. 35–61. Eds Gerald Graff and Reginald Gibbons. Evanston.

Eagleton, Terry 1983. *Literary Theory: An Introduction*. Minnesota.

Edwards, A. S. G. 1987. 'Observations on the History of Middle English Editing'. *Manuscripts and Texts: Editorial Problems in Later Middle English*, pp. 34–48. Ed. Derek Pearsall. Cambridge.

Eksteins, Modris 1989. *Rites of Spring: The Great War and the Birth of the Modern Age*. New York: Doubleday.

Förster, Max 1913a. *Il Codice Vercellese con Omelie e Poesie in Lingua Anglosassone*. Rome.

—— 1913b. *Der Vercelli-Codex CXVII nebst Abdruck einiger ae Homilien der Handschrift*. Halle.

Frank, Roberta and Angus Cameron 1983. *A Plan for the Dictionary of Old English*. Toronto.

Frantzen, Allen J. 1990. *Desire for Origins: New Language, Old English, and Teaching the Tradition*. New Brunswick, NJ.

—— 1992. 'A Recent Survey of Teaching Old English and its Implications for Anglo-Saxon Studies'. *Old English Newsletter* 26: 34–45.

—— 1994. 'Who Do these Anglo-Saxonists Think They Are, Anyway?'. *Æstel* 2: 1–43.

—— and Charles L. Venegoni 1986. 'The Desire for Origins: An Archaeological Analysis of Anglo-Saxon Studies'. *Style* 20: 142–56.

Furnival, Frederick J., ed. 1868. *Caxton's Book of Curtesye*. Early English Text Society, e.s. 3. London.

Fussell, Paul 1996. *Doing Battle: The Making of A Skeptic*. New York.

Graff, Gerald 1987. *Professing Literature: An Institutional History*. Chicago.

Greenfield, Stanley B. and Fred C. Robinson 1972. *A Bibliography of Publications on Old English Literature to the End of 1972*. Toronto.

Hart, James Morgan 1874. *German Universities: A Narrative of Personal Experience*. New York.

—— 1884–5. 'The College Course in English Literature, How it May Be Improved'. *Publications of the Modern Language Association* 1: 85–6.

Heidegger, Martin 1962. *Being and Time*. Trans. John Macquarrie and Edward Robinson. New York.

Hill, Joyce 1993. Review of Allen J. Frantzen, *Desire for Origins*. *Anglia* 111: 161–4.

Hill, Thomas D. 1990. 'Introduction'. *Sources of Anglo-Saxon Literary Culture: A Trial Version*, pp. xv–xxix. Eds Frederick M. Biggs, Thomas D. Hill and Paul E. Szarmach. Binghamton, NY.

Irvine, Martin 1991. 'Medieval Textuality and the Archaeology of Textual Culture'. *Speaking Two Languages*, pp. 181–210. Ed. Allen J. Frantzen. Albany, NY.

Jackson, Peter 1993. 'The Future of Old English'. *SELIM* 3: 158.

Lee, Stuart D. 1998. 'Ælfric and War'. University of Oxford, unpublished paper.

Lees, Clare A. 1991. 'Working with Patristic Sources: Language and Contexts in Old English Homilies'. *Speaking Two Languages*, pp. 157–80. Ed. Allen J. Frantzen. Albany, NY.

Madden, Sir Frederic, ed. 1839. *Sir Gawayne: A Collection of Ancient Romance-Poems, by Scotish and English Authors, Relating to that Celebrated*

Knight of the Round Table. Bannatyne Club. Edinburgh.

Malone, Kemp 1929. 'Anglo-Saxon: A Semantic Study'. *Review of English Studies* 5: 173–85.

Matthews, David 1999. *The Making of Middle English, 1765–1910*. Minnesota.

Middleton, Anne 1992. 'Medieval Studies'. *Redrawing the Boundaries*, pp. 12–40. Eds Stephen Greenblatt and Giles Gunn. New York.

Miller, Thomas, ed. 1890–8. *The Old English Version of Bede's Ecclesiastical History of the English People*. Early English Text Society, O.S. 95, 96, 110, 111. London. Repr. 1959–63.

Mitchell, Bruce and Fred Robinson 1996. *An Introduction to Old English*. Oxford.

Morris, Richard, ed. 1864. *Sir Gawayne and the Green Knight*. Early English Text Society, o.s. 4. London.

——, ed. 1867, 1868. *Old English Homilies and Homiletic Treatises*. Early English Text Society, o.s. 29, 34. London.

——1872. *An Old English Miscellany*. Early English Text Society, o.s. 49. London.

——, ed. 1874. *The Blickling Homilies of the Tenth Century*. Early English Text Society, o.s. 58, 63, 73. London.

Murray, K. M. Elisabeth 1977. *Caught in the Web of Words: James Murray and the Oxford English Dictionary*. New Haven, CT.

O'Keeffe, Katherine O'Brien 1994. 'Source, Method, Theory, Practice: On Reading Two Old English Verse Texts'. *Bulletin of the John Rylands University Library of Manchester* 76: 51–73.

'Oxford Dons Try to Slay Beowulf' 1998. *The Times*, 21 June.

Richardson, Peter 1994. 'The Consolation of Philology'. *Modern Philology* 93: 1–13.

Simmons, Clare A. 1990. *Reversing the Conquest: History and Myth in Nineteenth-Century British Literature*. New Brunswick, NY.

'Sixth Report to the Committee' (of EETS) 1870. *William Lauder: The Minor Poems*. Ed. F. J. Furnivall. London.

Skeat, Walter W., ed. 1890. *Ælfric's Lives of Saints*. Early English Text Society, o.s. 94, 114. London. Repr. 1966.

Stanley, E. G. 1994. 'Old English = Anglo-Saxon'. *Notes & Queries* 1995, 240 (n.s. 42.2): 168–73.

Stenton, F. M. 1959. Review of Dorothy Whitelock, *Changing Currents in Anglo-Saxon Studies*. *English Historical Review* 74: 519–20.

Sweet, Henry, ed. 1871. *King Alfred's West-Saxon Version of Gregory's Pastoral Care*. Early English Text Society, o.s. 45, 50. London.

——1876. *Sweet's Old English Primer*. 9th edn, rev. Norman Davis. Oxford, 1970.

——ed. 1885. *The Oldest English Texts*. Early English Text Society, o.s. 83. London.

Tolkien, J. R. R. and E. V. Gordon, eds 1967. *Sir Gawain and the Green Knight*. Rev. edn Norman Davis. Oxford.

Wallace, David, ed. 1999. *The Cambridge History of Medieval English Literature*. Cambridge.

Waterhouse, Ruth 1987. '"Wæter æddre asprang": How Cuthbert's Miracle Pours Cold Water on Source Study'. *Parergon* 5: 1–27.

Wenger, Luke 1998. 'Selected Data on Women in Medieval Studies'. *Medieval Academy News* 131 (September): 3, 6.

Whitelock, Dorothy 1958. *Changing Currents in Anglo-Saxon Studies*. Inaugural Lecture. Cambridge.

Wrenn, C. L. 1967. *A Study of Old English Literature*. New York.

27

The New Millennium

Nicholas Howe

What does it mean to be a poet of an abandoned culture? It means that I have to be aware of Auden but Auden need never have heard of me.

Jacob Glatstein

Horoscope, projection of earnings, dirge, crystal-ball reading, elegy, oracular pro-nouncement – all are guesses about the future. As such, they are the province of seers or charlatans, not scholars. For scholars, even those who do not specialize in histori-cal fields, tend to look backwards to justify their work through a Santayana-like faith that knowing the past might help us live otherwise in the future. When one con-siders all that happened to Anglo-Saxon England in the first century of the last new millennium, however, imagining Old English studies into the new millennium seems at times like tempting fate. While the discipline need not follow the same course as did the culture it studies, one notes that both have been transformed by things French.

Yet scholars in minor fields, that is to say, currently unfashionable ones, must worry about the future and make guesses about it, as if predicting the pay-out of their pension plan or their chances with a stranger they dream of romancing. Scholars in such fields are also likely to admit that elegy is a claim on the future, a gamble that there will be someone waiting then to hear the lament of the maker. To be told that one has no future is the cruellest put-down in any vocabulary – political, scholarly, personal – because it relegates one to a past that cannot be salvaged even for decora-tion, like the historical allusions affixed to postmodern buildings.

When we Anglo-Saxonists talk among ourselves about the future, one can often hear a gloomy undercurrent to even measured statements of optimism (see Whitelock 1958; Robinson 1975; Healey 1987; Howe 1990; Frank 1997). This tone conveys our anxieties about how changes within the academic world since the mid-1970s or so have left our discipline diminished, marginal, imperilled or, as I propose in this chapter, freed from a position of privilege that in the end did it more harm than good. For now, though, I want to speculate that our sometimes gloomy tone may be attributed as well to a lifetime spent reading a literature marked by an elegiac melody: its one long poem ends with the death of the hero and the certain doom of his people; its most compelling lyrics lament a lost home and time of prosperity; its most memorable evocation of place celebrates the crumbling masonry of a city built in the distant past by giants; its most stirring sermon reads the presence of outsiders as presaging destruction for the native English. While the corpus of Old English is larger and more varied than these examples, they do play a prominent and persistent role in our teaching of the language and its literature. In our courses, both introductory and advanced, these are the texts we teach year in and year out: *Beowulf*, *The Seafarer*, *The Wanderer*, *The Ruin*, *Sermo Lupi ad Anglos*. No wonder our ear is so finely attuned to the blue note.

Whether Anglo-Saxonists come to this literature with a predisposition for the transience of things and thus for elegiac lament, or whether the frequent teaching of these texts creates that disposition in us, is probably an unanswerable question. What matters is that our disciplinary gloom sometimes takes a self-dramatizing form: our canonical texts portray the end of things, and we who read them can feel that we are also at an end of things. The predictable irony is that the turn of the first Christian millennium was not an especially pressing theme for Anglo-Saxons living and writing around the year 1000. Perhaps they had no need to settle their end-of-time sentiments on any one year; perhaps they knew that a certain residual gloom about one's life and work was prudent self-protection against an inevitable fall in worldly fortune.

Thinking about the future of any discipline should make its members uneasy and impatient – uneasy with claims either triumphalist or apocalyptic, impatient with the whole business of introspection. This kind of meta-discussion will probably have far less effect on the future than will some study, quietly being written at the same moment, that will recast our basic working assumptions. Moreover, thinking within the category of the millennium has an imposed quality about it: it is 1999 as I write and it will be 2001 when this piece appears, but will that make any great difference? The millennial turn matters, in the end, only as it gives licence for us to ask questions that might otherwise be left unasked from professional courtesy or disciplinary loyalty. Has Old English had its moment as a scholarly field? Should we let it settle into a decent scholarly obscurity of a sort that one associates with an honorable field like Egyptology? Would it really matter if Old English shed its claims to disciplinary prestige and found a small, if somewhat precarious, niche in some universities throughout the English-speaking world? Should we not admit that this process is well advanced and cannot be reversed, though perhaps it can be slowed?

If there are useful answers to these questions, they are most likely to begin with the discipline's history and politics. As it rose to pre-eminence in academic English studies during the first quarter of the twentieth century, Old English rested on two premises that seemed, when both were widely accepted, to be irrevocably intertwined. In retrospect, they have come to seem very different in historical and theoretical validity. Yet we could only see how different these premises were as they came untwined. Both were models of tradition, claims of an unbroken historical continuity from past to present: Old English was the earliest definable stage in the flow of the English language; and Old English was the earliest stage in the grand procession of English literature. As long as English studies, and the departments that institutionalized the field, held to a philological model of the discipline or to a philologically inspired vision of English literature, these two claims could hold together. English literature moved in a series of consecutive and related stages because the language in which it was composed moved in a series of consecutive and related stages. These premises were neatly phrased in the tagline for the basic literature survey: 'From *Beowulf* to Virginia Woolf'. When that line was updated to the cooler 'From *Beowulf* to Tom Wolfe', it was already too late because *Beowulf* was slipping out of the canon; or, depending on your perspective, being pushed out. And Tom Wolfe never really made it into the canon.

Starting with the classic New Criticism of the 1940s and 1950s, and then gaining far greater force with the advent of the Higher Theory we now call poststructuralism in the 1970s and 1980s, something happened that put paid to this model of the discipline and to the place of Old English within it. To shrink the argument of entire books into a neat formulation, English literary studies jettisoned the historical model of language as its foundation, and in doing so radically attenuated the claims Old English could make on the larger discipline (see further Graff 1987; Frantzen 1990). If one no longer subscribed to a paradigm in which English language and literature proceeded in tandem, then the originary moment of the language – Old English – could no longer exert a claim of precedence on the larger discipline. With the loss of that claim came, inevitably if slowly, a pronounced decline in prestige for those who worked in Old English.

The loss of this linguistic-historical rationale for studying Old English need not in itself have been damaging to the place of Old English within the larger field. That is, it would have been far less consequential if there had been another literary-historical argument to reattach Old English to the discipline. But even the most partisan and engaged Anglo-Saxonists had to draw up short when challenged to demonstrate a purely literary continuity from Old English to Middle English and thus, by necessary extension, to all later English literature. Much as they might snicker at the cliché which labels Chaucer the 'father of English poetry', scholars in Middle English are savvy enough to know that it has its political uses for connecting their field to all that follows in ways that even a basic undergraduate-level anthology of English literature can make palpable. One might cite in this regard the new *Cambridge History of Medieval English Literature*, which opens with a chapter entitled 'Old English and its Afterlife' and then devotes the remainder of its 1,000-plus pages to the Middle English period and beyond. This fine chapter, by Seth Lerer, argues for the persistent relation of late eleventh- and twelfth-century texts to the Anglo-Saxon period, but its conclusions are overwhelmed by the relentlessly forward-looking claims of the volume as a whole. Quite tellingly its editor, David Wallace, spends far more time in his 'General Preface' arguing his grounds for pushing 'medieval' to 1547 than he does suggesting his reasons for beginning in 1066, and thus effectively excluding Old

English from the category of 'medieval'. Is it too alarmist to wonder if Anglo-Saxonists have more to fear from the exclusions practised against their field by later medievalists than by postmodern or postcolonial theorists?

Unlike their colleagues in Middle English, those working in Old English could make only a few pale claims about the relation of that literature to later periods in the canon. Anglo-Saxonists of a more sceptical mind were likely to admit that the argument was tenuous at best, but they also knew that it could hold as long as the philological paradigm survived. And Anglo-Saxonists concerned with the relations between England and continental Germania, whether linguistic or cultural or historical, had never much cared about the place of Old English in English departments anyway because their interests lay elsewhere in the university.

One can see in retrospect that these shifts in disciplinary thinking happened slowly, gradually and perhaps inexorably. What made the process difficult for Anglo-Saxonists to observe, let alone to act on, was that they occupied through the 1960s and at least into the early 1970s a position of privilege in many English departments in English-speaking universities. The most visible sign of this status was that Old English was very frequently the only period-course required of all doctoral students, that is, the only requirement that was historical rather than methodological (as was, for example, the usual bibliography course). For Anglo-Saxonists in many universities, this state of affairs meant that their courses were scheduled regularly and were fully enrolled. When all seems well with your place in the department, it is easy to assume that the rationale for your position is self-evidently persuasive to your colleagues and will pass unchallenged by them (for a report on the teaching of Old English in 1966, see Bessinger 1967).

The consequences of Old English as a required course in American doctoral programmes – and here I write from anecdote and personal observation – were not good for the field. Too many graduate students in English who would later go on to become eminent in the field and/or powerful in English departments (these not always being one and the same) took Old English without being convinced of its value or beauty. At the very least, they did their Old English and concluded there was no compelling reason why it should have been required of them as scholars working in other areas and periods any more than some other field should uniquely (or arbitrarily) have been required of Anglo-Saxonists. When the demand for curricular change came in departments, as it must come with generational regularity, those students who had done time in Old English were now professors and knew from their own experience that one could be a first-rate scholar of the early novel or of Victorian poetry without remembering a word of Old English. One could even be a distinguished Chaucerian with just a few rudiments of Old English, as more than one such scholar has ruefully admitted to me over the years.

I sometimes wonder how many of our colleagues closed their Klaeber for good on the day of their *Beowulf* exam; the number can never be known but it may well have been more than a few; or so one can deduce from the gradual marginalization of Old English in English departments. For would that process have altered the scene for

Anglo-Saxonists as fundamentally as it has if generations of students who sat through required Old English had been convinced of its uniquely originary status and thus of its claims on the discipline as a whole? The required Old English course gave Anglo-Saxonists an unmatched opportunity to win the hearts and minds of graduate students, if not necessarily convincing them to become Anglo-Saxonists, then at least persuading them of the value of the field. Had that happened, Anglo-Saxon would arguably be as widely taught in the late 1990s as it once was.

It may seem a heretical or self-punishing position for an Anglo-Saxonist, but let me suggest as a useful hyperbole that nothing has been as damaging to the state of Old English in American universities, that nothing can better explain the fall of the field from its departmental eminence, than that the subject was taught in required courses by professors who failed to convince students and colleagues that it was an intellectually valid requirement. I doubt that most students objected to Old English *per se*, and I believe that many were willing to be persuaded of the subject's value. But I am also willing to argue that many walked away from the required Old English course with a healthy distrust for any claim that a given field should be privileged as a required course of study. This reaction against Old English coincided with a sweeping, often intoxicating change in critical and theoretical models that called into question all structures of hierarchy, all myths of originary status and all claims to fixed authority in interpretation. In the face of such a revolution, what chance did Old English stand?

In 1962, Kemp Malone, eminent Anglo-Saxonist, redoubtable philologist and textual editor, served as president of the Modern Language Association. That honour may seem dubious to some but it tends sociologically to signal which fields within the larger discipline are honoured by members of the profession. No Anglo-Saxonist has followed Malone in the position, and it seems unlikely another will as long as the current paradigms in the discipline hold. The timing of Malone's presidency of the MLA seems almost too precise within the terms of my argument: that the privileged position of Old English within the larger discipline of English studies was giving way (as we can see in retrospect) at about the same moment when one of its leading scholars enjoyed high institutional honour. There is historical precedent for this seeming paradox that prestige can be at its greatest just when it is about to be lost. In his classic study of privilege and its power, *The Old Regime and the Revolution*, Alexis de Tocqueville entitles a chapter with two claims: 'That the Reign of Louis XVI was the Most Prosperous Period of the Old Monarchy, and How this Very Prosperity Hastened the Revolution' (1998: 217).

As Tocqueville demonstrates in *The Old Regime*, the lines of cultural continuity between pre- and post-Revolutionary France were more persistent than the old revolutionaries would have cared to admit or the yet-older aristocrats would have dared to hope in the years immediately following 1789. Something similar might be said of the culture wars that recently ran through English studies. An Anglo-Saxonist assessing the situation in 1999 can see that the field has survived in a diminished form, though arguably for that same reason in a rejuvenated one. Ten years ago one might have been much gloomier, when the MLA Job Information List had few announcements for Old English and many for specialities such as the 'Late Frankfurt School'. (The field listed in this announcement is no my invention, for who could be that parodically clever?) Perhaps paradoxically, the 1980s and 1990s can now be seen as marking a major development in Old English studies, the emergence of what I have elsewhere called teasingly 'Big Anglo-Saxonism', by analogy with the phenomenon in North American universities known as 'Big Science' (Howe 1997). For it was during these two decades that the planning for, and first fruits appeared from, a variety of large-scale collaborative projects: most centrally, the *Dictionary of Old English* being written at the University of Toronto, but also the *Sources of Anglo-Saxon Literary Culture*, the *Fontes Anglo-Saxonici*, *Anglo-Saxon Manuscripts in Facsimile*, *A Thesaurus of Old English* and *Seenet: Society for Early English and Norse Electronic Texts*.

These projects entail considerable human and institutional resources; they are models of collaborative work on a scale never before seen in the field; and they will, when done, provide scholars with an extraordinary body of material about Anglo-Saxon England. Calling them databases underestimates the quality of thought and originality of research that have gone into their preparation. The challenge facing us as Anglo-Saxonists will be *not* to treat them as databases, as more complete or user-friendly or accurate versions of older resources in the field, such as Joseph Bosworth and T. Northcote Toller's *An Anglo-Saxon Dictionary*, or N. R. Ker's *Catalogue of Manuscripts Containing Anglo-Saxon* or J. D. A. Ogilvy's *Books Known to the English, 597–1066*. As the quantity of our knowledge increases in more codified and ordered forms, we will have to learn ways of using this knowledge so that it does not paralyse or bury us. Whatever feelings of financial envy we humanists might have towards 'Big Science', we can learn from it that the scale of research affects the making of knowledge. Or, to put it in other terms, the quantity of data available to address a specific problem can have radical implications for the quality of thinking that circulates within a discipline.

I suspect that the first effect these large projects will have on the field, when they become available in final form, will be to collapse some of our long-standing linguistic and historical models: for instance, that denotation is fixed across a range of texts (especially when they are datable in close proximity to each other) and is also consistent within a given text; or that tradition works in explicit, linear ways as manifested through direct and acknowledged citations. As more and more evidence is gathered meticulously and presented imaginatively, Anglo-Saxonists will need to recognize that they will be faced with a set of complex theoretical questions they had not foreseen. After the *DOE*, *Fontes*, *SASLC* and company arrive, we will not do business as usual because their findings will teach us that our usual ways of working were often simply matters of convenience. For all that we struggled to justify our assumptions about fixed denotation or direct influence, we should also recognize that they are much easier to work with than are the obvious alternatives: that the meaning of a given word can shift, even within a few lines of the same lyric poem; or that influence is often at its most profound in subterranean, oblique and even duplicitous ways.

As the field absorbs the findings of large collaborative projects, certain opportunities for revisionist scholarship will emerge. For instance, we will no longer be as confident as we are now that cataloguing every appearance of a set of Old English words is the same thing intellectually as comprehending the ways these words functioned as a semantic field or cultural text in Anglo-Saxon England. We will move away from studies that schematize a field of words to studies that recognize that shifts in types of usage or context played – then as now – a significant role in how words are used, in how speakers do things with words. We will wrestle more specifically with the ways social and ethnic variation affected language. Nor will we feel so certain that tracking every reference in an Old English writer to his Latin sources is the same thing intellectually as knowing how they shaped his thinking, or how he knowingly drew from them to further his exegetical and interpretative ends – and in doing so read for partisan rather than purely scholarly purposes. More radically, we will move away from ideas of influence that see tradition as the generational inheritance of *auctoritas*, or that trace its workings only at the level of explicit quotation or allusion (either verbal or visual), and instead see tradition as more provisional, shiftable and fragmented than we would like or sometimes find convenient. This latter shift in thinking about tradition within Old English studies might also, and more vitally, suggest how we can relate Old English to the rest of English literature and culture in ways that avoid the simplifying pieties of the great sweep of 'Eng. Lit.' contained in 'From *Beowulf* to . . .'.

As Anglo-Saxonists shape the future of their field by working interpretatively with the findings produced by these research projects, we must also remember the sardonic caution sounded by the medieval historian Sylvia Thrupp in speaking of developments in her discipline a generation ago: 'so far, knowing more about medieval society has not produced any radically new ways of thinking about it' (quoted in Freedman and Spiegel 1998: 689). Thrupp's words are a necessary reminder that dictionaries, source studies and the like are not inherently transformative of the discipline that produced them. In some instances, they grow from a different scholarly impulse: to reassert traditional working practices against new theoretical developments by amassing, on a scale previously unknown, the body of established knowledge. That the amassing of knowledge can ever be ideologically neutral seems unlikely, as medievalists know from reading such works as Isidore of Seville's *Etymologiae* or Vincent of Beauvais' *Speculum mundi*.

The large projects under way in Old English studies can, however, enable transformative work if their users do not regard them as fixed or final in form, as *summae* of the discipline, but instead respect them as progress reports or provisional gatherings. There is something in the boundedness of Anglo-Saxon materials, I sometimes think, that encourages fantasies of total knowledge within the discipline. That reading all of Old English poetry is not simply possible (as seems hardly true of Middle English) but quite easy; that we have a concordance that can list not only all of the words in Old English but also all of their individual appearances – such facts of our daily working existence can tempt us into dreams of total knowledge. Or yet more dangerous, they can tempt us into postponing our historical and interpretative work until all the databases have been complied, collated, corrected, supplemented and the like, by which time, of course, another generation will suggest that these resources need to be redone. The limited nature of materials available to Anglo-Saxonists can lead us in a different and more engaging direction, though, towards developing interpretative moves that will make our words and works reveal more than they have in the past. For if all we do is repackage what we know, then we have little hope as a discipline.

Whatever thoughts James Murray and his fellow editors of the *Oxford English Dictionary* might have had about the uses of their work, one can see today that it did change in far-reaching and unexpected ways the critical practice of reading English-language poetry. After the *OED*, it was not business as usual, albeit with a better filing system for English words. From the *OED* came ways of reading that were attuned to the historically shifting and variable denotations of words. The classic, though by no means sole, work to articulate these new possibilities of reading was William Empson's *Seven Types of Ambiguity*, which appeared in 1930, just three years after the final fascicle of the original *OED*.

This example of how the *OED* changed the ways people read and think about language and its use in texts can open the door to imagining what might be done by the first generation of Anglo-Saxonists to grow up using the complete *DOE*, *SASLC*, *Fontes* and other resources yet to be imagined. About this prospect, there is something heartening and liberating. There is also something utopian about it, at least for those of us already in the middle of our careers: not only is it set a generation or so into the future but it also ignores the institutional realities confronting the discipline. And this brings us to the dilemma facing Old English studies today: never has there been so rich a production of scholarship in the field, and never has there been so anxious a time about its place in the world, especially about faculty positions for newly trained scholars. A surplus of scholarship and a shortage of employment are not unique to Old English studies. What may be more particular to the field is a sense that this flourishing of scholarship is unlikely to improve the institutional position of the discipline and thus, among other possibilities, yield more jobs for new scholars.

As a first step towards thinking through this dilemma, we Anglo-Saxonists would do well to assume (if only for tactical purposes) that the field will not be likely to enjoy the prestige and centrality it had from, say, the 1920s to the 1960s or even 1970s, from the time English studies established itself in British and North American universities by supplanting classics as the prestigious literary field, to the time when English studies redefined itself with structuralist and poststructuralist theory. The narcissism of the present, especially of a postmodern present that stylizes rather than engages the past, is a major source of our disciplinary predicament. Walter Benjamin, one of the great reluctant critics of modernity in the 1930s, anticipated this predicament when he wrote: 'For every image of the past that is not recognized by the present as one of its own concerns threatens to disappear irretrievably' (1968: 255). To which one might add, except of course to scholars, for their social value is to intervene (as it were) between the elements of Benjamin's final phrase: things from the past disappear into the void of the present, and scholars must retrieve them for the future. Trained as he was in Germanic philology, Benjamin would certainly have known not to expect honour or reward for doing this salvage work. But he would also have known that this work cannot proceed without a vivid sense of the present, an understanding of why at certain moments the present will engage one image from the past to the exclusion of others.

This chapter about the new millennium opens with a quotation from Jacob Glatstein, a Yiddish poet who was born in Lublin, Poland, in 1896 and who died in New York City in 1971 (Howe 1976: 452). His words have haunted the writing of this chapter, partly as a reminder that its subject is finally an issue of local concern, and partly as a matter of injustice because Glatstein was arguably a better poet than Auden. He had the bad luck, or the moral obstinacy, to write in a dying language. For those who read him in Yiddish through the grim years of the twentieth century, he was the great poet who did not court celebrity but remained within his 'abandoned culture' (for his great lament for the Yiddish makers, 'Yiddishkayt', see Howe et al. 1987: 462–6). His adjective is ironic and instructive, for abandonment in this case had to do not with intrinsic value but with the larger events of the world. If, on the edge of 2000, Anglo-Saxonists translate in some quietly modest way the terms of Glatstein's remark, we would have to say that we must know postmodernism and its discontents and they need not know Old English.

And yet, one last qualification: Anglo-Saxonists have much to say to these discontents. The questions that run through postmodern thought have analogues and historical precedents that we can identify and explore. We can provide a kind of historical dimension and density to the larger conversation that surrounds us if we reimagine the terms of our expertise slightly. Anglo-Saxon England both before and after the Norman Conquest might thus be read as a shifting setting for the postcolonial moment. Its complex linguistic populations offer virtually unparalleled opportunities for historicizing the workings of creolization. Its movement towards some commonality called *Engla lond* challenges theories of nationalism that predicate its rise on the post-religious secularism of early modern Europe. The same historical discontinuity that has recently led to the isolation of Old English studies might in future serve to reconnect it to the larger discipline of English studies. The absence of explicit cultural continuity between Anglo-Saxon England and beyond is only part of the story, for the tradition was complicated by a persistent return to things Anglo-Saxon by later readers and writers. This state of affairs speaks vividly to the current sense of tradition as fragmentary, malleable, contradictory, interrupted rather than unified, fixed, harmonious, flowing.

In the new millennium, I suspect, we will have the future we create today by writing studies that deepen and complicate our sense of the period, its culture, its persistent value; and by teaching students who will have the wit and intellectual freedom to do work then that we cannot imagine now.

REFERENCES

Benjamin, Walter 1968. *Illuminations: Essays and Reflections.* Ed. and intro. Hannah Arendt. New York.

Bessinger Jr, J. B. 1967. 'A Survey of Old English Teaching in America in 1966'. 'The Status of Old English in America Today'. 'A Selection from Correspondents' Personal Comments on the Status and Value of Old English Studies in America Today'. *Old English Newsletter* 1.1: 1–13.

Empson, William 1966. *Seven Types of Ambiguity.* New York. Rev. of 1930 edn.

Frank, Roberta 1997. 'The Unbearable Lightness of Being a Philologist'. *Journal of English and Germanic Philology* 96: 486–513.

Frantzen, Allen J. 1990. *Desire for Origins: New Language, Old English, and Teaching the Tradition.* New Brunswick, NJ.

Freedman, Paul and Gabrielle Spiegel 1998. 'Medievalisms Old and New: The Rediscovery of Alterity in North American Medieval Studies'. *American Historical Review* 103: 677–704.

Graff, Gerald 1987. *Professing Literature: An Institutional History.* Chicago.

Healey, Antonette di Paolo 1987. 'Old English Language Studies: Present State and Future Prospects'. *Old English Newsletter* 20.2: 34–45.

Howe, Irving 1976. *World of Our Fathers.* New York.

——, Ruth Wisse and Khone Shmeruk, eds 1987. *The Penguin Book of Modern Yiddish Verse.* New York.

Howe, Nicholas, ed. 1990. 'Old English Studies'. Special issue of *American Notes & Queries* n.s. 3.2: 43–85.

—— 1997. 'Anglo-Saxon Studies in the Twenty-First Century'. Round table discussion. International Society of Anglo-Saxonists, Palermo.

Lerer, Seth 1999. 'Old English and its Afterlife'. *Cambridge History of Medieval English Literature*, pp. 7–34. Ed. David Wallace. Cambridge.

Robinson, Fred C. 1975. 'Anglo-Saxon Studies: Present State and Future Prospects'. *Mediaevalia* 1: 63–77.

Tocqueville, Alexis de 1998. *The Old Regime and the Revolution.* Vol. 1. Eds François Furet and Françoise Mélonio. Trans. Alan S. Kahan. Chicago.

Wallace, David 1999. 'General Preface'. *Cambridge History of Medieval English Literature*, pp. xi–xxiii. Ed. David Wallace. Cambridge.

Whitelock, Dorothy 1958. *Changing Currents in Anglo-Saxon Studies: An Inaugural Lecture.* Cambridge.

Selected Further Reading

This section is arranged under the following headings: audience and literacy; bibliographies, encyclopaedias and Old English scholarship; books and manuscripts; cultural context; linguistic context; literature: general; periodicals; poetry; prose; websites.

AUDIENCE AND LITERACY

Brown, George 1995. 'The Dynamics of Literacy in Anglo-Saxon England'. *Bulletin of the John Rylands University Library of Manchester* 77: 109–42.

Clanchy, M. T. 1992. *From Memory to Written Record: England 1066–1307*. Oxford.

Cross, J. E. 1972. 'The Literate Anglo-Saxons – On Sources and Disseminations'. *Proceedings of the British Academy* 58: 3–36.

Howe, Nicholas 1993. 'The Cultural Construction of Reading in Anglo-Saxon England'. *The Ethnography of Reading*, pp. 58–79. Ed. Jonathan Boyarin. Berkeley, CA.

Lerer, Seth 1991. *Literacy and Power in Anglo-Saxon Literature*. Lincoln, NE.

Liuzza, R. M. 1998. 'Who Read the Gospels in Old English?'. *Words and Works: Studies in Medieval English Language and Literature in Honour of Fred C. Robinson*, pp. 3–24. Eds Peter S. Baker and Nicholas Howe. Toronto.

McKitterick, R. 1989. *The Carolingians and the Written Word*. Cambridge.

——, ed. 1990. *The Uses of Literacy in Early Medieval Europe*. Cambridge.

Ong, Walter J. 1984. 'Orality, Literacy, and Medieval Textualization'. *New Literary History* 16: 1–12.

Wormald, P. 1977. 'The Uses of Literacy in Anglo-Saxon England and its Neighbours'. *Transactions of the Royal Historical Society* 5th ser., 27: 95–114.

BIBLIOGRAPHIES, ENCYCLOPAEDIAS AND OLD ENGLISH SCHOLARSHIP

Adams, Eleanor N. 1917. *Old English Scholarship in England from 1566–1800. Yale Studies in English*. New Haven, CT. Repr. Hamden, CT, 1970.

Bately, Janet 1993. *Anonymous Old English Homilies: A Preliminary Bibliography of Source-studies*. Binghamton, NY.

Berkhout, Carl T. and Milton McC. Gatch, eds 1982. *Anglo-Saxon Scholarship: The First Three Centuries*. Boston.

Greenfield, S. B. and F. C. Robinson 1980. *A Bibliography of Publications on Old English Literature to the End of 1972*. Toronto.

Hasenfratz, R. 1993. *Beowulf Scholarship: An Annotated Bibliography 1979–1990*. New York. For additions to Hasenfratz's *Beowulf* bibliography, see also *http://spirit.lib.uconn.edu/Medieval/beowulf.html*

Healey, A. diP. and R. L. Venezky 1980. *A Microfiche Concordance to Old English*. Toronto.

Keynes, S. 1993. *Anglo-Saxon History: A Select Bibliography*. 2nd edn. Old English Newsletter Subsidia 13. Binghamton, NY.

Lapidge, M. and R. Sharpe 1985. *A Bibliography of Celtic–Latin Literature 400–1200*. Dublin.

Lapidge, M., J. Blair, S. Keynes and D. Scragg 1999. *Blackwell Encyclopaedia of Anglo-Saxon England*. Oxford.

Reinsma, Luke 1987. *Ælfric: An Annotated Bibliography*. New York.

Venezky, R. L. and S. Butler 1985. *A Microfiche Concordance to Old English: The High Frequency Words*. Toronto.

Books and manuscripts

Reproductions of Old English manuscripts can be found in the Early English Manuscripts in Facsimile series (Copenhagen). Microfiche facsimiles of Old English manuscripts are produced in the series Anglo-Saxon Manuscripts in Microfiche Facsimile (MRTS, Arizona). Numerous digitized images of manuscripts are also available at the British Library, Bodleian Library and Cambridge University Library websites.

Gameson, Richard, ed. 1994. *The Early Medieval Bible: Its Production, Decoration and Use*. Cambridge Studies in Palaeography and Codicology. Cambridge.

Gneuss, H. 1981. 'A Preliminary List of Manuscripts Written or Owned in England up to 1100'. *Anglo-Saxon England* 9: 1–60.

Ker, N. R. 1957. *Catalogue of Manuscripts Containing Anglo-Saxon*. Oxford. Repr. with suppl. 1990.

Ogilvy, J. D. A. 1967. *Books Known to the English, 597–1066*. Cambridge, MA.

—— 1981. 'Addenda et Corrigenda' (to *Books Known to the English*). *Mediaevalia* 7: 281–325.

Parkes, M. B. 1993. *Pause and Effect: An Introduction to the History of Punctuation in the West*. Berkeley, CA.

Pulsiano, P. and E. M. Treharne, eds 1998. *Anglo-Saxon Manuscripts and their Heritage*. Aldershot.

Richards, M. P., ed. 1994. *Old English Manuscripts: Basic Readings*. New York.

Robinson, F. C. 1994. *The Editing of Old English*. Oxford.

Scragg, D. G. and P. Szarmach, eds 1994. *The Editing of Old English: Papers from the 1990 Manchester Conference*. Cambridge.

Temple, E. 1976. *Anglo-Saxon Manuscripts 900–1066*. London.

Cultural context

Bischoff, B. and M. Lapidge 1994. *Biblical Commentaries from the Canterbury School of Theodore and Hadrian*. CSASE 10. Cambridge.

Blair, John and Richard Sharpe 1992. *Pastoral Care before the Parish*. Leicester.

Campbell, J. 1986. *Essays in Anglo-Saxon History*. London.

Burton, J. 1994. *Monastic and Religious Orders in Britain, 1000–1300*. Cambridge.

Clayton, M. 'Homiliaries and Preaching in Anglo-Saxon England'. *Peritia* 4: 207–42.

Conner, P. W. 1993. *Anglo-Saxon Exeter: A Tenth-century Cultural History*. Woodbridge.

Conrad O'Briain, H., A. M. D'Arcy and J. V.

Scattergood, eds 1999. *Text and Gloss: Studies in Secular Learning and Literature Presented to Joseph Donovan Pheifer*. Dublin.

Cubitt, Catherine 1995. *Anglo-Saxon Church Councils c.650–850*. London.

Dumville, D. N. 1992. *Wessex and England from Alfred to Edgar*. Woodbridge.

Frantzen, A. J. 1983. *The Literature of Penance in Anglo-Saxon England*. New Brunswick, NJ.

Gretsch, Mechthild 1999. *The Intellectual Foundations of the English Benedictine Reform*. CSASE 25. Cambridge.

Hill, D. 1981. *An Atlas of Anglo-Saxon England*. Oxford.

Hollis, S. 1992. *Anglo-Saxon Women and the Church*. Woodbridge.

Howe, Nicholas P. 1989. *Migration and Mythmaking in Anglo-Saxon England*. New Haven, CT.

Irvine, M. 1994. *The Making of Textual Culture: 'Grammatica' and Literary Theory, 350–1100*. Cambridge.

Lapidge, M. 1993. *Anglo-Latin Literature 900–1066*. London.

—— 1996. *Anglo-Latin Literature 600–899*. London.

Loyn, Henry 1994. *The Vikings in Britain*. Oxford.

Morrell, M. C. 1965. *A Manual of Old English Biblical Materials*. Knoxville.

Nelson, J. L. 1986. *Politics and Ritual in Early Medieval Europe*. London.

North, Richard 1997. *Heathen Gods in Old English Literature*. CSASE 22. Cambridge.

Parsons, David, ed. 1975. *Tenth-century Studies: Essays in Commemoration of the Millennium of the Council of Winchester and Regularis Concordia*. Chichester.

Stafford, Pauline 1989. *Unification and Conquest: A Political and Social History of England in the Tenth and Eleventh Centuries*. London.

Stenton, F. M. 1971. *Anglo-Saxon England*. 3rd edn. Oxford.

Whitelock, D., M. Brett and C. N. L. Brooke, eds 1981. *Councils and Synods with other Documents relating to the English Church I. AD 871–1204*. 2 vols. Oxford.

Wright, C. E. 1939. *The Cultivation of Saga in Anglo-Saxon England*. Edinburgh.

Yorke, Barbara, ed. 1988. *Bishop Æthelwold: His Career and Influence*. Woodbridge.

LINGUISTIC CONTEXT

Brooks, Nicholas, ed. 1982. *Latin and the Vernacular Languages in Early Medieval Britain*. Leicester.

Cameron, Angus 1974. 'Middle English in Old English Manuscripts'. *Chaucer and Middle English Studies in Honour of Rossel Hope Robbins*, pp. 218–29. Ed. Beryl Rowlands. London.

Hogg, R. M., ed. 1990. *The Cambridge History of the English Language. Vol. I: The Beginnings to 1066*. Cambridge.

Laing, Margaret 1993. *Catalogue of Sources for a Linguistic Atlas of Early Medieval English*. Woodbridge.

Mitchell, B. 1985. *Old English Syntax*. 2 vols. Oxford.

—— and F. C. Robinson, eds 2001. *A Guide to Old English*. 6th edn. Oxford.

Roberts, J. and C. Kay, with Lynne Grundy 1995. *A Thesaurus of Old English*. King's College London Medieval Studies 11. 2 vols. London.

Sauer, Hans 1997. 'Knowledge of Old English in the Middle English Period'. *Language History and Linguistic Modelling: A Festschrift for Jacek Fisiak on his 60th Birthday*, pp. 791–814. Eds Raymond Hickey and Stanislaw Puppel. Trends in Linguistics, Studies and Monographs 101. Berlin.

LITERATURE: GENERAL

Biggs, F. M., T. D. Hill and P. E. Szarmach, with K. Hammond, eds 1990. *Sources of Anglo-Saxon Literary Culture: A Trial Version*. Binghamton, NY.

Clemoes, P., ed. 1959. *The Anglo-Saxons: Studies in Some Aspects of their History and Culture*. London.

Crossley-Holland, K., ed. 1984. *The Anglo-Saxon World: An Anthology*. Oxford.

Damico, H. and A. Hennessey Olsen, eds 1990. *New Readings on Women in Old English Literature*. Bloomington, IN.

Frantzen, A. J., ed. 1990. *Desire for Origins: New Language, Old English, and Teaching the Tradition*. New Brunswick, NJ.

——, ed. 1991. *Speaking Two Languages: Traditional Disciplines and Contemporary Theory in Medieval Studies*. Albany, NY.

Godden, M. and M. Lapidge, eds 1991. *The Cambridge Companion to Old English Literature*. Cambridge.

Greenfield, Stanley B., ed. 1963. *Studies in Old English Literature in Honor of Arthur G. Brodeur*. Eugene, OR.

——and D. G. Calder 1986. *A New Critical History of Old English Literature*. New York.

Grundy, Lynne 1991. *Books and Grace: Ælfric's Theology*. King's College London Medieval Studies 6. London.

Hicks, C., ed. 1992. *England in the Eleventh Century*. Harlaxton Medieval Studies 2. Stamford.

Korhammer, M., ed. 1992. *Words, Texts and Manuscripts: Studies in Anglo-Saxon Culture Presented to Helmut Gneuss*. Cambridge.

Lapidge, M. and H. Gneuss, eds 1985. *Learning and Literature in Anglo-Saxon England: Studies Presented to Peter Clemoes*. Cambridge.

Roberts, Jane and Janet L. Nelson, eds 1997. *Alfred the Wise: Studies in Honour of Janet Bately*. Cambridge.

——, eds 2000. *Essays on Anglo-Saxon and Related Themes in Memory of Lynne Grundy*. King's College London Medieval Studies 17. London.

Rosier, J. L., ed. 1970. *Studies in Old and Middle English Language and Literature in Honor of Herbert Dean Meritt*. The Hague.

Sisam, Kenneth 1953. *Studies in the History of Old English Literature*. Oxford.

Stanley, E. G., ed. 1966. *Continuations and Beginnings: Studies in Old English Literature*. London.

Szarmach, P. E. with V. D. Oggins, eds 1986. *Sources of Anglo-Saxon Culture*. Kalamazoo.

PERIODICALS

Anglia

Anglo-Saxon England

British Library Journal

Bulletin of the John Rylands University Library of Manchester

Early Medieval Europe

English Historical Review

English Language Notes

English Studies

Journal of Ecclesiastical History

Journal of English and Germanic Philology

Journal of Medieval History

Leeds Studies in English

Medium Ævum

Modern Language Notes

Modern Philology

Neuphilologische Mitteilungen

Neophilologus

Old English Newsletter

Papers on Language and Literature

Proceedings of the British Academy

Review of English Studies

Revue Bénédictine

Speculum

Studia Neophilologica

Studies in Philology

Traditio

Transactions of the Cambridge Bibliographical Society

Year's Work in English Studies

POETRY

Aertsen, Henk and Rolf H. Bremmer Jr, eds 1994. *Companion to Old English Poetry*. Amsterdam.

Allen, M. J. B. and D. G. Calder 1976. *Sources and Analogues of Old English Poetry: The Major Latin Texts in Translation*. Cambridge.

Baker, Peter S., ed. 1995. *Beowulf: Basic Readings*. New York and London.

Bessinger, J. B. and P. H. Smith 1969. *A Concordance to Beowulf*. Ithaca, NY.

——1978. *A Concordance to the Anglo-Saxon Poetic*

Records. Ithaca, NY.

Bjork, Robert E. and John D. Niles, eds 1997. *A Beowulf Handbook*. Lincoln.

Calder, Daniel G., ed. 1979. *Old English Poetry: Essays on Style*. Berkeley, CA.

Chase, Colin, ed. 1980. *The Dating of Beowulf*. Toronto.

Clemoes, P. 1995. *Interactions of Thought and Language in Old English Poetry*. CSASE 12. Cambridge.

Creed, Robert P., ed. 1967. *Old English Poetry: Fifteen Essays*. Providence, RI.

Damico, H. and J. Leyerle, eds 1993. *Heroic Poetry in the Anglo-Saxon Period: Studies in Honor of Jess B. Bessinger*. Kalamazoo.

Foley, John Miles 1988. *The Theory of Oral Composition: History and Methodology*. Bloomington, IN.

Fulk, R. D. 1992. *A History of Old English Meter*. Philadelphia, PA.

Huppé, Bernard F. 1959. *Doctrine and Poetry*. Albany, NY.

——1970. *The Web of Words*. Albany, NY.

Liuzza, Roy Michael 1999. *Beowulf: A New Verse Translation*. Peterborough, ON.

Nicholson, Lewis E., ed. 1963. *An Anthology of Beowulf Criticism*. Notre Dame, IN.

——and Dolores Warwick Frese 1975. *Anglo-Saxon Poetry: Essays in Appreciation*. Notre Dame, IN.

O'Brien O'Keeffe, Katherine 1990. *Visible Song: Transitional Literacy in Old English Verse*. CSASE 4. Cambridge.

——, ed. 1994. *Old English Shorter Poems: Basic Readings*. New York.

Pasternack, C. B. 1995. *The Textuality of Old English Verse*. CSASE 15. Cambridge.

Russom, G. 1987. *Old English Poetic Metre*. Cambridge.

Shippey, Tom 1976. *Poems of Wisdom and Learning in Old English*. Cambridge.

PROSE

Bately, Janet 1980. 'Old English Prose Before and During the Reign of Alfred'. *Anglo-Saxon England* 17: 93–138.

——, ed. 1986. *The Anglo-Saxon Chronicle: A Collaborative Edition 3: MS A*. Cambridge.

DiNapoli, R. 1995. *An Index of Theme and Image to the Homilies of the Anglo-Saxon Church*. Hockwold cum Wilton, Norfolk.

Gatch, M. McC. 1977. *Preaching and Theology in Anglo-Saxon England: Ælfric and Wulfstan*. Toronto.

Lees, Clare 1999. *Tradition and Belief: Religious Writing in Late Anglo-Saxon England*. Minneapolis, MN.

Swanton, M., ed. 1997. *The Anglo-Saxon Chronicle*. London.

Szarmach, Paul E., ed. 1996. *Holy Men and Holy Women: Old English Prose Saints' Lives and their Contexts*. Albany, NY.

——, ed. 1999. *Old English Prose: Shorter Readings*. New York.

——and Bernard Huppé, eds 1978. *The Old English Homily and its Backgrounds*. Albany, NY.

Wilcox, J., ed. 1994. *Ælfric's Prefaces*. Durham Medieval Texts 9. Durham.

Zettel, P. H. 1982. 'Saints' Lives in Old English: Latin Manuscripts and Vernacular Accounts'. *Peritia* 1: 17–37.

WEBSITES

The major electronic resource, Labyrinth, is a dedicated medieval site, with links to all other relevant sites. It is located at: *http://www.georgetown.edu/labyrinth/labyrinthhome.html*

Index